REDEEMING THE LAND

A Bible Study on Dislodging Evil Spirits, Breaking the Curse and Restoring God's Blessing Upon the Land

by Gwen Shaw

D1289606

Engeltal Press
P. O. Box 447
Jasper, Arkansas 72641
U.S.A.

Copyright © Gwen R. Shaw 1987
End-Time Handmaidens, Inc.
P. O. Box 447
Jasper, Arkansas 72641

Printed in the United States of America

TABLE OF CONTENTS

INTRODUCTION

The powerful message contained in this Bible Study is one that I believe will change your world.

For too long, we, God's people, have sat back and waited for some "chosen few" to do something about the wickedness around us. We have blamed our politicians, our educational institutions and our churches for the moral decay and the increase in crime, abortions, satanism, poverty and plagues that have become a part of our society.

The time has come for each one of us to stand up and be counted. We can all do something positive. In fact, we must! And we must do it now! Time is running out! Either we will fulfil our destiny in the Kingdom; or Satan will fulfil his intended destiny for us—total destruction of the planet and its inhabitants.

I pray that God will stir your heart with this challenging message as He stirred mine when these end-time truths were put in my hands from one of God's front-line soldiers, Pastor Richard Langworthy of Bulawayo, Zimbabwe.

In November of 1986, my husband, Col. Jim Shaw, and I had the privilege of ministering in his lively church, Bulawayo Christian Centre. Sunday evening, after the service, Pastor Langworthy shared these truths and experiences with us at the supper table. Later, we heard him speak at a meeting in the capital, Harare. I owe much of the contents of this book to this fine soldier of the Cross.

There is one more special servant of God who has a great share in the message of this Bible Study, although I have never met him; he is Pastor Colin Wilkinson of England. God raised him up to call out the saints of Great Britain to combat the increased demonic control Satan was getting over the British Isles. One of God's saints had, in a vision, seen the British Isles totally in darkness, caused by demonic forces. As a result of that vision, God's people there have become involved in prayer cells they call "Action Stations"; and now they are redeeming the land by the method described in this Bible Study.

For too long the church of Christ has sat by the "Rivers of Babylon," weeping dejectedly with our harps hanging from the willows. Now, it is time for the "daughters of Zion" to deliver ourselves by calling upon the Lord to break our chains of bondage, slothfulness, and apathy, and to fulfil our destiny.

May we all soon be able to say with Israel of old, *"When the Lord turned again the captivity of Zion, we were like them that dream. Then was our mouth filled with laughter, and our tongue with singing: then said they among the heathen, The Lord hath done great things for them. The Lord **hath** done great things for us; whereof we are glad"* (Psalm 126:1−3).

—Gwen R. Shaw

CHAPTER ONE

GOD'S ORIGINAL CREATED WORK WAS PERFECT

I. God Created the World

This fact is the foundation of all truth and knowledge. To deny this truth will cause great tragedy and ruin because it is the groundwork upon which all truth, knowledge, science, wisdom and spiritual revelation is built. When man denies this fundamental fact he builds on a false, erroneous and perverse foundation that ultimately results in total destruction.

1. The Bible, the Word of God to man, begins with this vital truth. Genesis 1:1, *"In the beginning God created the heaven and the earth."*

2. The Apostle John, the writer of the fourth Gospel, begins his account of the life of Jesus Christ with this same fundamental truth. John 1:1-4, *"In the beginning was the Word, and the Word was with God, and the Word was God. The same was in the beginning with God. All things were made by him; and without him was not any thing made that was made."*

3. Paul, the great Apostle, in his letter to the Colossians builds upon this important truth in Colossians 1:16-17, *"For by him were all things created, that are in heaven, and that are in earth, visible and invisible, whether they be thrones, or dominions, or principalities, or powers: all things were created by him, and for him. And he is before all things, and by him all things consist."*

II. This Great Truth Can Only Be Accepted Through Faith

The writer of Hebrews in Hebrews 11:3 gives us a clue as to why the truth of creation is not accepted by many when he says, *"**Through faith** we understand that the worlds were framed*

1

by the word of God, so that things which are seen were not made of things which do appear.'' It takes **faith** to believe this truth. Man's heart is so filled with unbelief that he cannot easily accept this great truth. It is only as we learn to know God and love Him and understand how truly great He is, that we find it easy to believe the true account of creation as it is revealed to us in God's Word.

III. Everything Was Created Out of Nothing

The magnitude of the great creative work of God is beyond our powers of perception. It is only as the Holy Spirit reveals it to us that we can truly understand how great was the work of creation. Hebrews 11:3 says that the worlds were framed by the Word of God and that *"things which are seen were not **made** of things which do appear."* This word "made" is *ginomai* in the original Greek (No. 1096 in the Strong's Concordance). The Strong's Concordance numerical system is used in this Bible study to help the student to identify quickly the words for further research in the original Hebrew and Greek.) It can be interpreted, "to form, to be made or created from nothing." It is the same word used by John in John 1:3, *"All things were made* (ginomai) *by him; and without him was not any thing made* (ginomai) *that was made* (ginomai).*"* God literally created the world out of **nothing**. (This is the foundation of all truth. To reject this truth is fatal.)

Is it any wonder then that the world is in such a chaotic condition? When we removed our Bibles out of our schools and taught our children the lies of the theory of evolution, we took from them the true foundation of all knowledge and understanding, and without this we can only have perversion and ruin. Even Charles Darwin, on his death bed, regretted the seeds of error he had sown. The following is a true story told

2

in *Voices from the Edge of Eternity* compiled by John Myers, published by Voice Publications.

Lady Hope's Visit With Charles Darwin

It may surprise many students of evolution to learn that in the closing days of his life, Charles Darwin returned to his faith in the Bible. The following account is told by Lady Hope, of Northfield, England, a wonderful Christian woman who was often at his bedside before he died:

It was one of those glorious autumn afternoons that we sometimes enjoy in England when I was asked to go in and sit with Charles Darwin. I used to feel, when I saw him, that his fine presence would make a grand picture for our Royal Academy, but never did I think so more strongly than on this particular occasion.

He was sitting up in bed, propped up by pillows, gazing out on a far-stretching scene of woods and corn fields which glowed in the light of a marvelous sunset.

His features lit up with pleasure as I entered the room. He waved his hand toward the window as he pointed out the beautiful sunset scene beyond. In his other hand he held an open Bible, which he was always studying.

"What are you reading now?" I asked.

"Hebrews," he answered. " 'The Royal Book' I call it." Then as he placed his fingers on certain passages, he commented on them.

I made some allusion to the strong opinions expressed by many on the history of the Creation, and then their treatment of the earlier chapters of the book of Genesis. He seemed distressed, his fingers twitched nervously and a look of agony came over his face as he said, "I was a young man with unformed ideas. I threw out queries, suggestions, wondering

3

all the time about everything. To my astonishment the ideas took like wildfire. People made a religion of them.''

Then he paused, and after a few more sentences on the holiness of God and "the grandeur of this Book," looking tenderly at the Bible which he was holding all the time, he said: "I have a summer house in the garden which holds about thirty people. It is over there (pointing through the open window). I want you very much to speak there. I know you read the bible in the villages. Tomorrow afternoon I should like the servants on the place, some tenants, and a few neighbors to gather there. Will you speak to them?''

"What shall I speak about?'' I asked.

*"**Christ Jesus**," he replied in a clear, emphatic voice— adding in a lower tone, "**and His Salvation**. Is not that the best theme? Then I want you to sing some hymns with them. You lead on your small instrument, do you not?''*

The look of brightness on his face, as he said this, I shall never forget; for he added: If you make the meeting at three o'clock, this window will be open, and you will know that I am joining in with the singing." [1]

What a dramatic scene! Here we see the very soul of Darwin exposed to us in the last years of his life. What a different picture from the young Darwin! Speaking about the Bible, he uses the expression, "The grandeur of this Book," revealing his love and respect for the Holy Bible. And when he is reminded of the then newly-awakened evolutionary movement in theology and its accompanying "higher criticism," which destroyed the Biblical faith of multitudes, he responds with a look of agony which clearly expresses how he deplored the mistakes of his younger years. His statement, "I was a young man with unformed ideas" clearly reveals that he himself no longer believed in those theories of evolution...if he indeed ever had!

4

IV. The World Was Created Perfect

When God created the world it was as perfect as Heaven. The motto of everything God did was excellence. God, looking over His finished work, called it **"good."**

a. Genesis 1:4, *"And God saw the light, that it was **good** (towb in Hebrew, no. 2896)."*

b. Genesis 1:10, *"And God called the dry land Earth; and the gathering together of the waters called he Seas: and God saw that it was **good** (towb)."*

c. Genesis 1:12, *"And the earth brought forth grass, and herb yielding seed after his kind, and the tree yielding fruit, whose seed was in itself, after his kind: and God saw that it was **good** (towb)."*

d. Genesis 1:16-18, *"And God made two great lights; the greater light to rule the day, and the lesser light to rule the night; he made the stars also. And God set them in the firmament of the heaven to give light upon the earth, And to rule over the day and over the night, and to divide the light from the darkness: and God saw that it was **good** (towb)."*

e. Genesis 1:20, 21, *"And God said, Let the waters bring forth abundantly the moving creature that hath life, and fowl that may fly above the earth in the open firmament of heaven. And God created great whales and every living creature that moveth, which the waters brought forth abundantly, after their kind, and every winged fowl after his kind: and God saw that it was **good** (towb)."*

f. Genesis 1:25, *"And God made the beast of the earth after his kind, and cattle after their kind, and every thing that creepeth upon the earth after his kind: and God saw that it was **good** (towb)."*

This Hebrew word *towb* (2896) has a very full meaning. It can be interpreted "good, excellent, pleasant, lovely, delightful, convenient, joyful, fruitful, precious, sound, cheerful,

5

kind, correct, righteous, virtuous, happiness and moral goodness."

V. Man Was Created Perfect

The greatest and most perfect of all of God's created works was man. When God created Adam He said, *Let us make man in our image, after our likeness...So God created man in his own image, in the image of God created he him; male and female created he them."* (Genesis 1:26, 27).

The word "man" in our English Bible was two different words in the original Hebrew text.

1. *Adam* (120), which usually refers to mankind in the collective sense, persons, someone, a generic word for man as the image of God.

2. *Iysh* (376), which means "a man, a male."

Every reference to man from Genesis 1:1 to 2:22 was the Hebrew word *adam* (mankind). By this we realize that Eve also was made in God's image, for God really said, *"Let us make man in our image and after our likeness."* (Genesis 1:26)

The human being was the highest order of God's creative works, the crowning work of *Elohiym* (430). Not only was man created perfect in form and structure, he also was perfect, in that God breathed in man His very own Spirit-life, and man became a living soul, gifted with His eternal Spirit of life. It is this breath of God still which causes man to resemble God more than any other created being.

Genesis 2:7, *"And the Lord God formed man of the dust of the ground, and breathed into his nostrils the breath of life, and man became a living soul."*

Let us look more closely at several very important words in this verse:

1. formed—*yatsar* (3335)—"to squeeze or mould into a

6

form." God "spoke" the world and all it contains into existence, but He formed man with His own hands.

2. man—*adam* (120)—"mankind";

3. dust—*aphar* (6083)—"dust, clay, ashes, gold dust";

4. ground—*'adamah* (127)—"earth, ground, land" (Adam was taken out of *adamah*);

5. breathed—*naphach* (5301)—"to puff, to inflate, to blow hard, kindle, to expire, to snuff out";

6. nostrils—*aph* (639)—refers to the breathing part of the body, specifically the nose, nostril, face.

7. breath—*neshamah* (5397)—"a puff of air, a breath, living soul"; it seems to be synonymous with *nephesh* and is often found in connection with *ruwach*. This gives it the meaning of "spirit."

8. life—*chay* (2416)—"life, to revive." It is associated with breath, prosperity and vitality;

9. living—*chay* (2416)—same as above;

10. soul—*nephesh* (5315)—"life, spirit, soul, the inner person."

If you take time to study these words and to understand their original meaning you will discover many wonderful, hidden truths in them.

The thing that makes the creation of man so great is the touch of eternal God in his being. Even as our earthly, physical bodies contain the genes of our earthly parents, so our eternal spirit within contains the eternal likeness and essence of God who is the Father of all spirits (Hebrews 12:9).

In recapping what we have just said:

1. God created the world.

2. This truth can only be accepted through faith.

3. The world was created out of nothing.

4. God created man (mankind).

5. Man was perfect, for he was in the likeness and image

7

of God. It is impossible for man to have greater perfection than this.

VI. The World and All Creation (Including Man) Is Upheld, Sustained and Kept by God

God is the source of all life. If He, for only one second, removed His sustaining, preserving, life-giving power, everything would disintegrate like the golden carriage which brought Cinderella to the Prince's ball.

Hebrews 1:3 clearly reveals that all things are upheld by the Word of His power. In the original Greek, the word "upholding" is *phero* (5342)—"to uphold, to sustain, to bear with, to carry, to be actuated by the Holy Spirit."

God not only upholds His created works, He also will carry through His plans, for the word also means "to carry out, to lead in a certain direction."

God has an ultimate destiny for all of His created work and He will carry it through. With this confidence we can rest in His love and power, for if He had enough power to create this world, He also has enough power to restore all that Satan has destroyed and fulfil His ultimate destiny for His creation. That is what this Bible study is all about. God wants to begin a mighty work of restoration of all things. And God is going to use His overcomers to do this mighty work.

Yes, I know we are facing hard times, even tribulation days, but it is in the days of darkness that we are called to **arise and shine** with the glory of God, for He commands, *"Arise, shine; for thy light is come, and the glory of the Lord is risen upon thee. For, behold, the darkness shall cover the earth, and gross darkness the people: but the Lord shall arise upon thee, and his glory shall be seen upon thee."* (Isaiah 60:1, 2)

Even as the prophet Daniel prophesied concerning these days (Daniel 9:25), *"The street shall be built again, and the wall, even in troublous* (disturbed, afflicted) *times,"* for God shall have a people who shall be strong and do exploits because they know their God (Daniel 11:32).

The word "know" is *yada* (3045) which means "to know intimately, to discern, to understand. God will have this calibre of people in these last days of this dispensation who will go forth in mighty power and anointing to **REDEEM THE LAND**.

STUDY QUESTIONS

1. Read Genesis chapter one, John 1:1-14 and Hebrews 11:1-3.

2. What is the foundation of all truth?

3. Give three Scriptures to prove that God is the Creator of this world.

4. Out of what was the world created? Explain the Greek word *ginomai*.

5. What was the condition of the world when God created it?

6. What was God's highest and most perfect creation?

7. Give Scripture to prove that God is the Sustainer of all creation.

8. Memorize Genesis 2:7 and Hebrews 11:3.

CHAPTER TWO

SATAN—HIS TITLES, HIS WORKS AND HIS AIMS

Although the world and all that is in it was created perfect (*towb*, 2896), all have become corrupted through sin. This terrible decay and ruin did not only come because of Adam's **one** act of sin. The condition in which we find the world today is because of **many** acts of sin and evil throughout the ages.

Satan has always sought to lead both the angels and mankind astray. While he still was the anointed cherub that covered the throne of God, i.e. the special guardian angel of the throne-room (Ezekiel 28:14), his heart became filled with pride and he led one third of the angels (Revelation 12:4) in insurrection against God, which resulted in his being cast out of Heaven together with the angels who followed him (Ezekiel 28:16, 17).

I. Satan's Titles

Satan has different names in the Bible. Let us take a moment to study only a few of them, that we might better know our arch enemy.

1. Lucifer (Isaiah 14:12)—*heylel* in Hebrew (1966). It comes from the same root word as *halal* (1984) from which we get the well-known word of praise—hallelujah! (*Halal*) means "to be bright, to shine, to be splendid, to praise, to celebrate, glorify, be famous."

This indicates that Lucifer must have been the chief musician of Heaven and the leader of all praise and worship.

2. Son of the Morning—*ben* (1121) does not only mean "son, grandson, boy, child," etc.; it also means "favourite." Morning is *shachar* in Hebrew (7837)—"early, light, morning."

11

Son of the morning could just as correctly be translated "**Favourite of the Light**." Is it any wonder that he can transform himself into an angel of light (II Corinthians 11:14) when he once was the prince of light?

This word "transform"—*metaschematizo* (3345) in II Corinthians 11:14 is not to be mistaken with the Greek word *metamorphoo* (3339), which means "the miracle of transformation from an earthly form into a supernatural one which is denoted by the radiance of both the countenance and garment" as took place with Christ on the Mount of Transfiguration (Matthew 17:2, Mark 9:2, 3). It means **complete change of condition**, whereas *metaschematizo* only implies a change of appearance which can be very deceptive. At the resurrection of the dead, the bodies of the Christians will experience *metamorphoo* (I Corinthians 15:51, Romans 12:1, 2, II Corinthians 3:18).

Spiros Zodhiates explains in *The Hebrew Greek Key Study Bible* (see the advertisement in the back of the this book) that with *metamorphoo* the idea of transformation refers to an **invisible process in Christians which takes place or begins to take place already during their life in this age.**[1] Praise God! We are even now being changed from glory to glory as we look upon Him and stay close to Him.

Satan is no longer the Son of the Morning, nor is he a true angel of light. This was his former title and position of honour before his fall, but he knows how to change his outward form so that he can appear to be beautiful, good and full of light and truth. He has deceived many into following him by taking on this form.

Metamorphoo is a change of **essence**, whereas *metaschematizo* is a change of **appearance**.

3. Satan (I Chronicles 21:1, Matthew 4:10)—Hebrew *Satan* (7853). This word is actually the same in English as it is in the

12

original Hebrew. It means "attacker, adversary, resister, opposer, enemy, persecuter, accuser."

In Greek it is *satanas* (4567). In both languages it can be interpreted as "one who bears a grudge, carries animosity, seduces and then accuses (like the prosecuting attorney in the court room)."

4. Devil (John 8:44)—Greek *diabolos* (1228) which means "accuser, one who falsely accuses, one who divides people without any reason." The word "devil" is not found in the Old Testament.

There are many other names for Satan in the Bible such as:

5. Abaddon (Revelation 9:11)—"destroyer, ruiner, place of destruction, annihilation, downfall."

6. Angel of the Bottomless Pit (Revelation 9:11).

7. Apollyon (Revelation 9:11)—"Annihilator, destroyer."

8. Accuser (Revelation 12:10).

9. Adversary (I Peter 5:8).

10. Belial (II Corinthians 6:15)—"Uselessness, corruption, lawless, worthless, wicked."

11. Beelzebub (Matthew 12:24)—"Lord of the flies, Lord of the heavenly habitation." He was a pagan god. He was regarded by the Jews as the most wicked and evil of all demonic spirits.

12. God of this world (II Corinthians 4:4).

13. Murderer (John 8:44).

14. Prince of Devils (Matthew 12:24).

15. Prince of the Power of the Air (Ephesians 2:2).

16. Prince of this World (John 14:30).

17. Ruler of Darkness (Ephesians 6:12).

18. Serpent (Genesis 3:4, Revelation 12:9).

19. Tempter (Matthew 4:3).

20. Unclean spirit (Matthew 12:43).

21. Wicked one (Matthew 13:19).

13

22. *Dragon* (Revelation 12:9).
23. *Father of Lies* (John 8:44).

There are many other names which the Bible gives us.

II. The Work and Aim of Satan

Satan's Past Existence

All of Satan's work is evil because he is evil. Jesus, in describing Satan as a thief, said, *"The thief cometh not, but for to steal, and to kill, and to destroy: I am come that they might have life, and that they might have it more abundantly."* (John 10:10). This is the great comparison between Jesus and Satan. However, Satan has tried to appear in the likeness of Jesus and has deceived multitudes into following him.

Satan was cast out of Heaven and cursed by God because he tried to throw God off the throne and seize the throne. It was a real attempted coup d'état. Isaiah, describing this scene which took place in the ancient times, said, *"For thou hast said in thine heart, I will ascend into heaven, I will exalt my throne above the stars of God: I will sit also upon the mount of the congregation, in the sides of the north: I will ascend above the heights of the clouds; I will be like the Most High."* (Isaiah 14:13, 14).

He was a usurper and an insurrectionist. He divides friends, families, ministries, and nations. He causes hatred, angers, jealousies and every kind of evil. Through sin he defiles the land.

Satan's greatest aim is to cause men to transgress the laws of God, so that man will sin and bring a curse upon himself and the land. Then God will have to reject both man and the land, because both man and the land are defiled by sin.

Leviticus 18:24-25, 28, *"Defile not ye yourselves in any of these things: for in all these the nations are defiled which*

14

I cast out before you: And the land is defiled: therefore I do visit the iniquity thereof upon it, and the land itself vomiteth out her inhabitants....That the land spew not you out also, when ye defile it, as it spewed out the nations that were before you.''

Defile is *tame* (2930), "to profane, pollute, make unclean, desecrate."

Leviticus 18 lists some of the gross sins of adultery, incest, sodomy, perversion, idolatry and human sacrifice. These sins bring the wrath of God upon the land and the land is cursed by its inhabitants. Man cannot escape the judgment that results when he breaks God's moral codes and laws. The fact that the judges of our land, such as the Supreme Court, do not condemn these immoral acts as wrong does not alter God's laws of righteousness one iota, neither does it remove the curse.

III. Satan Causes A Curse To Come On the Land and the People

The word "curse" *arar* (779) means "to bind with a spell, to hem in with obstacles, to render powerless, to resist, to make infertile."

Richard Langworthy says, "A curse is the favour of God turned away from us and He removes His promise to uphold all things."

Without God's supporting hand we are lost and undone. There is no hope, no future and no help.

The last two verses of Leviticus 18 leave us a very fearful warning. *"For whosoever shall commit any of these abominations, even the souls that commit them shall be cut off from among the people. Therefore shall ye keep mine ordinance, that ye commit not any one of these abominable customs, which were committed before you, and that ye defile not yourselves therein: I am the Lord your God.''* (Leviticus 18:29-30).

15

IV. Satan Is the Author of All Perversion

There is a spirit of perversion in the land that is increasing as homosexuals gain acceptance. The original moral code of the USA prohibited sodomy. Promiscuity and multiple sex partners have brought a curse on our land. The alarming pandemic of AIDS has become public enemy number one! In addition we have other sexually-transmitted diseases for which there is no cure.

Few seem to realize that the current sodomy laws prohibit oral or anal intercourse between two people. Oral and anal sex acts are another form of sodomy. They are an abomination and bring a curse on the participant.

Incest is strictly forbidden by God. God said, *"None of you shall approach to any that is near of kin to him, to uncover their nakedness: I am the Lord."* (Leviticus 18:6).

Nakedness is *ervah* in the Hebrew (6172) which means "barrenness, the genitals, filthiness, uncleanness, excrement."

Sodomy is so very abominable and filthy because the rectum which contains excrement is used by the sodomist. He thereby defiles his body. God clearly warns that *"whosoever shall commit any of these abominations...shall be cut off from among the people."* Cut off (Hebrew *karath*, 3772) means "to castrate, to eliminate, to be exiled, to be destroyed." It seems that the punishment for this sin was the death penalty. The reason for this was that by giving his life, the perpetrator of the crime paid for his sin, and this removed the curse from the land.

Satan Pollutes the Land through the Shedding of Innocent Blood

Jesus said Satan was a murderer from the beginning (John 8:44). He instigated Cain to murder his brother Abel and in so doing he brought a curse on Cain and on the earth, so that

16

it could no longer yield unto man its original strength (Genesis 4:11, 12).

Murder is a very great evil because it interrupts the life of someone on earth so that that person can never fulfil his or her destiny. Murder is cruel and destructive. The one who commits murder allows the devil to control him and use him. In so doing he is, himself, cursed and he also brings a curse upon the land. The shedding of innocent blood is a sin against God because it is destroying the greatest gift that God can give and that **only** God can give—the gift of life, for the life is in the blood.

Numbers 35:33 clearly states that the land cannot be cleansed of murder except by the blood of the transgressor. *"So ye shall not pollute the land wherein ye are: for blood it defileth the land: and the land cannot be cleansed of the blood that is shed therein, but by the blood of him that shed it."*

By removing the death penalty for murder our lawmakers bring a curse down upon our land. Every time innocent blood is shed Satan gains more legal right to do even more wicked works through his evil spirits. By removing capital punishment we unleash powerful demonic spirits who are full of hate, murder and perversion. That is why some areas of our land where there has been more crime, seem to have been taken over almost completely by demon spirits. That is because sin has brought a curse on that area, and given Satan a legal right to rule over those places and people.

STUDY QUESTIONS

1. Read Isaiah 14:4-7 and Ezekiel 28:1-18.

2. What has happened to corrupt and destroy the original creation of God's planet?

3. Explain the following names of the devil and give their Scripture references:
   a. Lucifer
   b. Son of the Morning
   c. Satan
   d. Devil.

4. Give ten other names for him mentioned in the Bible and their scripture references.

5. What is Satan's greatest work and aim?

6. What is the definition of "curse"?

7. What happens as a result of a curse?

8. Explain how Satan instigates perversion and bloodshed.

9. Memorize Leviticus 18:24-28, Numbers 35:33.

CHAPTER THREE

THE FIVE ORIGINAL CURSES

The World Was Corrupted Through The Sins of Man

In Chapter Two we learned about Satan, God's and man's arch enemy, and his work and aims to destroy all of God's created works (including man) through sin, which brings a curse, thereby causing the favour of God to be turned away from His creation so that He will no longer protect and bless it. Now let us study the progression of the curses.

I. The First Curse—on the Serpent and the Animal Kingdom:

Genesis 3:1, *"Now the serpent was more subtle than any beast of the field which the Lord God had made. And he said unto the woman, Yea, hath God said, Ye shall not eat of every tree of the garden?"*

Subtle is *aruwm* (6175) in the Hebrew, which means "cunning, crafty, sly, subtle, prudent."

Satan often uses the gifts and the finer qualities which God has given us. He does not use our weaknesses so much as he does our virtues. Satan, who is a spirit, entered the wise and cunning serpent and by clothing himself in the form of a serpent deceived the unsuspecting Eve. (Our ignorance does not appear to be an excuse for sin, for in spite of Eve's naivety she was judged.)

By permitting Satan to use him, the serpent brought a great curse upon himself.

"And the Lord God said unto the serpent, Because thou hast done this, thou art cursed above all cattle, and above every beast of the field; upon thy belly shalt thou go, and dust shalt thou eat all the days of thy life." (Genesis 3:14)

19

Flavius Josephus, the renowned historian of the *History of the Jews*, left us a very interesting account of the Fall. He lived at the time of Christ and had access to both the Jewish libraries of Jerusalem and the Roman libraries of Rome. Although we do not accept his writings as being the inspired Word of God, there is no doubt that he had more detailed information than what is available to us today other than the Bible. It is good that he recorded his "History of the Jews," for in 70 A.D. these great books of the history of the Jews were all destroyed when Jerusalem was razed to the ground under General Titus, the Commander of the Roman army!

Josephus, in writing about The Fall, makes some very interesting claims.

1. "All the living creatures had one language." The commentator on this passage writes, "Hence it appears that Josephus thought at least several of the brute animals, particularly the serpent, could speak before the Fall." Romans 8:19-22, *"For the earnest expectation of the creature waiteth for the manifestation of the sons of God. For the creature was made subject to vanity, not willingly, but by reason of him who hath subjected the same in hope; Because the creature it self also shall be delivered from the bondage of corruption into the glorious liberty of the children of God. For we know that the whole creation groaneth and travaileth in pain together until now."*

2. Josephus adds that after the serpent caused the Fall, God "deprived the serpent of speech, out of indignation at this malicious disposition toward Adam. Besides this, he inserted poison under his tongue...and when he (God) had deprived him of the use of his feet, he made him go rolling all along, and dragging himself upon the ground." (Page 26 of *Antiquities of the Jews*, Chapter One, part four. See the advertisement in the back of this book.)

The fact that the animals could at one time speak should

not be strange to us when we remember that Balaam's ass spoke (Numbers 22:28-30).

II. The Second Curse—on Satan:

When God pronounced this curse on the serpent, it also fell on Satan, for he was in the serpent when the serpent was cursed. This means that Satan was cursed twice, once in Heaven and now on earth. God sentenced Satan to eat dust (*aphar*, 6083), the very substance out of which man's flesh is created. As long as man lives in the fleshly, carnal realm, he is "fodder" for the serpent. It is only as the spirit rules and we rise above the fleshly realm that we are no longer under Satan's belly, nor does he have any legal right to "eat" us. Instead, we have dominion over him, and by God's power we can bruise Satan under our feet. *"And the God of peace shall bruise Satan under your feet shortly."*(Romans 16:20).

God also sentenced Satan further, *"And I will put enmity* (hostility) *between thee and the woman, and between thy seed* (*zera*, 2233—"semen, offspring") *and her seed; it shall bruise thy head* (*rosh*, 7218—"head, highest rank, chief, leader"), *and thou shalt bruise his heel* (*ageb*, 6119—"heel, that which protrudes, the extreme rear of an army")." (Genesis 3:15)

Many believe that this was prophetic of Jesus' suffering and death on the cross. Yet, we know Jesus **gave** Himself as the sacrifice. He said, *"No man taketh it from me, but I lay it down of myself, I have power to lay it down, and I have power to take it again. This commandment have I received of my Father"* (John 10:18).

Could this Scripture then mean something else? Could the Lord be implying here that Satan would have power over those of the Lord's children who would straggle along in the rear—even those who would follow the Lord afar off? There certainly is no doubt about the fact that either we will be in the forefront of God's army, pulling down the strongholds of Satan and

21

bruising his chief demons, or we will be stragglers in the rear, whom Satan will constantly nip at and torment with many wiles, temptations and doubts.

III. The Third Curse—on Womanhood:

Genesis 3:16, *"And unto the woman he said, I will greatly multiply thy sorrow* (*itstsabown*, 6093—"worrisomeness, labour, toil, hard work, pain, sorrow, birth pangs, being in labour") *and thy conception; in sorrow* (*etsab*, 6089—the same as above) *thou shalt bring forth children; and thy desire* (*teshuwqah*, 8669—"to run after, to yearn for, to have a strong attraction for— as for the opposite sex") *shall be to thy husband* (*iysh*, 376—"man, a male, a mate, a husband"), *and he shall rule* (*mashal*, 4910—"to rule over, to govern, to have dominion, to manage") *over thee."*

This is one of the most controversial of the curses. Women in the past have suffered unbearably because of this curse, and today they are rebelling against it and refusing to accept this curse. Yet, outside of the redemptive atonement of Jesus Christ there is no deliverance from this two-fold curse. Let us now look at it closely:

1. First Part: Sorrow in connection with childbirth and children.

a. Just what God's original plan for the multiplication and reproduction of children was is hard for us to guess, but certainly it omitted the kind of pain, struggle, labour and even death which multitudes of women have suffered since that day.

Josephus writes that God "made Eve liable to the inconvenience of breeding and the sharp pains of bringing forth children."

If all the pain that women have ever suffered in childbirth since that day could be laid on one person, it could never be born, yet Jesus bore this pain also, when He suffered the agony

22

of childbirth in His hours of passion. So, today, the woman of faith can trust God to help her and make her time of confinement easy, because this too is included in the redemptive work of Jesus Christ (I Timothy 2:14, 15).

b. Another aspect of a woman's suffering in childbirth is the multiplication of her conception or pregnancies. God never intended women to endure multiple pregnancies. She was not created to be a "baby machine," who would often be rejected, by her husband for another more prolific woman who is capable of bearing sons to please her husband. In my life on the mission fields I have seen many wives rejected, and set aside or divorced, because they were not able to give their husbands a son.

In China one of the expressions used in congratulating the bride and groom with a toast on their wedding day was, "Yi nien yi-ke," meaning, "One year one piece," i.e. "May you have a baby every year," and girls were never even counted. Communist China has tried to alter the idea of many births by enforcing birth control on the people. In the Bible accounts of those families who lived hundreds of years it is obvious that women did not have multiple pregnancies. Eve had three sons: Cain, Abel and Seth. In Genesis 5:4 it says, *"And the days of Adam after he had begotten Seth were eight hundred years: and he begat sons and daughters."* So he did have more children, but they are not named and there is a possibility that he could have had them by another wife, as Eve is not mentioned here.

Noah's wife had only three sons, and even though some of the people lived almost a millenium they had very few children. Women could enjoy their children because they were not overburdened nor distraught with the cares of life. They did not need to "take the pill"—God was in control.

c. The grief which children often cause their mothers is also seen in this curse. *"In sorrow shalt thou bring forth children*

23

(ben, 1121).'' How true this was of Eve! Her firstborn son, Cain, gave her untold sorrow and grief by his disposition, his cruelty and finally by murdering the gentle, good Abel. When she gave birth to her third son, Seth, she said, *"For God...hath appointed* (brought) *me another seed instead of Abel, whom Cain slew''* (Genesis 4:25). So you see, she had never forgotten her great loss. Eve's sorrow was her very own children.

Every mother needs to know that when she holds that sweet little, innocent baby in her arms she must prepare her heart for more than joys. There will be many moments of anxiety, pain and grief during the years of the growing-up of that child and often even long after—when he is an adult, Simeon said to Mary, *"Yea, a sword shall pierce through thy own soul also''* (Luke 2:35). I know this may sound negative to the "positive thinkers," but facts are facts, and we only share what we have seen and have ourselves experienced.

2. Second Part: The subservience to her husband (or man).

Many women have sought to escape this curse by refusing to marry the man they live with. They want their independence. How foolish! As long as a woman's heart yearns after (runs after) and her body sexually desires her *iysh* (376—"man, mate or husband"), she still is subservient to him and he can rule over her and govern her emotions by the slightest raised eyebrow, touch or word.

It is only as the woman is redeemed from the curse through accepting the atoning work of Jesus that she can rise above these human soulish bondages and be released to be her husband's helpmate and companion and not his emotional love-slave. We are never to make any husband our "master." Jesus said, *"...one is your Master, even Christ..."* (Matthew 23:8).

The curse on the woman is broken through Christ, for those who are redeemed by His Blood.

Galatians 3:13 clearly states that there is a release from

24

all these dreadful curses through Christ: *"Christ hath redeemed us from the curse of the law, being made a curse for us: for it is written, cursed is every one that hangeth on a tree."*

Jesus not only "tasted death" for every man (Hebrews 2:9), He also drank our bitter cup of sorrows (myrrh) in Gethsemane that we might be released of the curse and that our glory might be restored to us. *"For it became him, for whom are all things, and by whom are all things, in bringing many sons unto glory, to make the captain of their salvation perfect through sufferings."* (Hebrews 2:10) Yes, Jesus suffered for man to release him from suffering. Six hundred years before Jesus came to earth Isaiah prophesied concerning this, so great a redemption, when he foretold, *"But he was wounded for our transgressions, he was bruised for our iniquities; the chastisement of our peace was upon him; and with his stripes we are healed."* (Isaiah 53:5) In that healing there is also deliverance promised in child-bearing. *"...the woman being deceived was in the transgression. Notwithstanding she shall be saved* (sozo, 4982—"saved, deliverance from danger and suffering") *in childbearing, if they continue in faith and charity and holiness with sobriety."* (I Timothy 2:14b, 15)

IV. The Fourth Curse—on Adam.

"And unto Adam he said, Because thou hast hearkened unto the voice of thy wife, and hast eaten of the tree, of which I commanded thee, saying, Thou shalt not eat of it: cursed is the ground for thy sake; in sorrow shalt thou eat of it all the days of thy life; Thorns also and thistles shall it bring forth to thee; and thou shalt eat the herb of the field: In the sweat of thy face shalt thou eat bread, till thou return unto the ground; for out of it wast thou taken: for dust (aphar, 6083) *thou art, and unto dust shalt thou return."* (Genesis 3:17-19)

Perhaps it might be said that the worst curse of all fell on Adam. God was angry and grieved with him because God,

25

Himself, had spoken personally to Adam and forbidden him to eat of that one tree in the garden, the tree of the knowledge of good and evil. God, in His generosity, had given Adam every other tree in the garden and told him he could freely eat from them all, except that one tree.

God has made all laws for our good. It is His love and wisdom alone that prohibits us from doing certain things. When we transgress these laws, we will reap the judgment that is our due. So it was that the greater judgment fell on Adam because he had hearkened (*shama*, 8085—"obeyed, given undivided attention to") his wife. We must never let the voice of man (even our dearest loved one) become more important than the voice of God to us. More Christians are led astray by those whom they love than by those who are hostile to them.

Man was sentenced to a life of toil and hard work, even a life without future and without hope. All would ultimately return to dust. In spite of all his toil and work, he would disintegrate in the end into the dust of the earth out of which he had been made. He would never be able to save, nor help himself, nor escape this judgment; his only hope, if there was one at all, was through the seed of the woman. It was the woman who had led him astray, and now only by the woman could he be released of this dreadful curse. Is it any wonder that there has been hidden, oft-unspoken hostility between the two sexes!

The fact that man was made responsible for the livelihood and support of both himself, his wife and his children only added to his great penalty and his anger towards woman. So, even as the woman has attempted to live without dependence upon man, man has, through the ages, made the woman his slave. While this has not been so evident in western lands, I have found it to be the case in many Eastern and Mid-Eastern lands and in the Third World countries, where the men "sat at the gate of the city" while the women did the planting, the weeding, the harvesting, the threshing, the winnowing, the grinding of the

26

grain, the tending of the sheep and cattle, the making of the meals for the household, the making of the family's garments, the weaving, the laundry (often on the stones down at the village pond), the shopping at the market, the carrying of the water for the household, the milking of the cows and goats and camels (often while great with child), and finally the birthing of their babies and the tending and raising of their children. All, as I said, while the man sat at the gate of the city, spending the day talking to other men and looking important. This I have seen with my own eyes for many years. Is it any wonder women are demanding their "equal rights" all over the world! The trouble, however, is this, that the ones who need relief won't get it, while those who already have it will ultimately end up playing the man's role—a thing for which they were never created. A chiropractor told me that women who demand equal rights in our western lands end up in factories doing man's work which is often so strenuous that they are continually suffering from physical ailments, some of which they will carry for the rest of their lives.

While some men in some lands have managed to escape this end of the curse, I have also seen others, like beasts of burden, carrying and pulling enormous loads, far too heavy for mortals. I have seen them grow old and die while they are still in their thirties because they were worn out with labour and toil. I have felt great compassion for the rickshaw puller whose skinny, almost-naked body had to struggle to pull the fat mandarin's wife and three well-padded children up a steep hill in the winter cold or the summer's scorching heat. It often took a whole day's hard labour just to buy one bowl of rice! And oh, how quickly he turned into dust! Yes, man too has suffered much in his lifetime.

27

V. The Fifth Curse—on the Ground and all Vegetation

The ground was cursed two times. It suffers under a double-portion curse.

1. The first curse was when Adam sinned. God said to Adam, *"...cursed is the ground for thy sake* (because of you)*; in sorrow shalt thou eat of it all the days of thy life; Thorns also and thistles shall it bring forth to thee; and thou shalt eat the herb of the field."* (Genesis 3:17, 18)

Up until then, there was order in growth. Now, the plant life became perverse in its growth. It developed thorns and thistles. Weeds grew where none had been planted. There was disorder and rebellion in the plant life of the world. This would cause never-ending problems for all time.

2. The second curse on the ground was when Cain murdered his brother Abel and spilled his blood on the ground. God said to Cain, *"What hast thou done? the voice of thy brother's blood crieth unto me from the ground. And now art thou cursed from the earth, which hath opened her mouth to receive thy brother's blood from thy hand. When thou tillest* (*abad*, 5647—"to work, to labour, to toil, to plough") *the ground, IT SHALL NOT HENCEFORTH YIELD UNTO THEE HER STRENGTH* (*kowach*, 3581—"Vigour, capacity, ability, power, substance, wealth")." (Genesis 4:10-12a)

Man has no recollection of the time when the earth yielded of its original strength and capacity. However, In Genesis 26:12 we read, *"Then Isaac sowed in that land, and received in the same year a hundredfold: and the Lord blessed him."* There is no doubt that the land in Isaac's day was more capable of producing better crops than it is today.

When I was a girl on the farm, we often only got five or six bushels per acre. This was because of the terrible drought and pestilence such as grasshoppers and hail. If any man got

28

forty bushels per acre, it was considered a bumper crop. Yet Isaac got 100-fold.

Today man uses fertilizers to restore strength to the land and chemicals to control the weeds and insects, but even so, we are more and more seeing the earth cursed because of the sins of man. Murder, human sacrifice, abortion, and the removal of capital punishment (allowing the murderer to live) is bringing a terrible curse on the earth. God does not always send His judgments at once. It takes time for the grapes of wrath to ripen.

Yet, if a righteous man walks in God's ways, he can break the curse like Isaac did and his land shall be blessed, while all around him his neighbours continue to labour under the curse.

STUDY QUESTIONS

1. Read Genesis chapters 2 and 3.

2. What does Genesis 3:16, 19 prove?

3. List the first five curses in their order.

4. Describe briefly each one.

5. Which, in your opinion, is the worst one?

6. Why did Satan use the serpent?

7. Why is there enmity between the serpent and the woman?

8. How was this prophecy fulfilled?

9. What other way is there to interpret Genesis 3:15?

10. Explain in detail Genesis 3:16.

11. Memorize Galatians 3:13.

Picture taken from *The Complete Works of Josephus*, p.30b.

CHAPTER FOUR

THE ORIGIN OF APOSTACY

I. The Flood

As the world population grew, the iniquity of men waxed worse and worse until the earth was corrupt (*shachath*, 9843—"destroyed, brought to ruin by pulling down, by wounding, by killing individuals, or entire communities, perversion, wickedness"), and the earth was filled with violence (*chamac*, 2555—"oppression, wickedness, wrong, injustice,violent dealing, unrighteous gain, ie. the spirit of greed"—Genesis 6:11).

In the midst of this sea of evil and madness God found only one righteous man, Noah. God, who is just, made a way of escape for Noah, his wife, his three sons and their wives, and when all was ready, God destroyed the wicked in a terrible deluge, which took place 1656 years after God created Adam. And so, the laws of God were fulfilled according to Numbers 35:33, *"So ye shall not pollute the land wherein ye are: for blood it defileth the land: and the land cannot be cleansed of the blood that is shed therein, but by the blood of him that shed it."*

One wonders what happened to the rest of the descendents of Seth. Students of Biblical genealogy differ a little, but it seems as if Adam had lived to see nine of his generations and that he died 57 years before godly Enoch was translated. He had seen the revival mentioned in Genesis 4:26 when men began to call on the name of the Lord. Adam died when Lamech, the father of Noah was sixty years old. Methusela, the son of Enoch (Jude 14), whose name some say means "after him it shall be" died in the year of the flood. Other translators say that his name means "man of the sword." Josephus, writing about the line of Seth says:

This posterity of Seth continued to esteem God as the Lord

31

Now this posterity of Seth continued to esteem God as the Lord of the universe, and to have an entire regard to virtue, for seven generations; but in process of time they were perverted, and forsook the practices of their forefathers, and did neither pay those honours to God, which were appointed them, nor had they any concern to do justice towards men. But for what degree of zeal they had formerly shewn for virtue, they now shewed by their actions a double degree of wickedness, whereby they made God to be their enemy; for many angels* of God accompanied with women, and begat sons that proved unjust, and despisers of all that was good, on account of the confidence they had in their own strength; for the tradition is that these men did what resembled the acts of those whom the Grecians call giants.

(*This notion, that the fallen angels were, in some sense, the fathers of the old giants, was the constant opinion of antiquity.)[1]

II. Noah's Sacrifice

When Noah stepped out of the Ark, the first thing he did was BUILD AN ALTAR (Genesis 8:20). This was the first altar mentioned in the Bible. He offered sacrifices to the Lord. In doing this, he redeemed the land. The Lord "smelled a sweet savour" and made a covenant with Noah; and the Noahic race (from which we have all descended) is an eternal reminder of this covenant. God put the "token of the rainbow" in the sky. Today when we see the rainbow, we remember God's promise and everlasting love toward us. The next time you look at the rainbow in the sky, rejoice, and remember that it is a sign that man has the power to redeem the land and restore to it the blessings of God. Noah made a new and wonderful beginning in a cleaned-up world.

32

III. The Curse on Ham's Descendents

Noah planted a vineyard. *"And he drank of the wine, and was drunken; and he was uncovered within his tent."* (Genesis 9:21)

People wonder that Noah should drink until he was intoxicated. But remember that before the flood (when God opened the windows of heaven, and all the fountains of the great deep were broken up—Genesis 7:11), the earth had a completely different climate, *"...for the Lord God had not caused it to rain upon the earth, and there was not a man to till the ground. But there went up a mist from the earth, and watered the whole face of the ground."* (Genesis 2:5, 6)

This change of climate could have affected the grape juice in such a way that it caused fermentation and Noah, not suspecting the effects it would now have upon him, drank it with dire results. More than one person has taken poison by mistake!

The tragedy lies, not so much in the fact that Noah drank the wine, as in the fact that while he was lying exposed, his son Ham, (some believe, also his grandson Canaan) committed some kind of sin that brought a curse on them.

The Bible does not say very much about it; in order to understand what really happened, one must "read between the lines."

"And Ham, the father of Canaan, saw the nakedness of his father, and told his two brethren without." (Genesis 9:22)

Let us look at this verse more closely. *"And Ham...saw* (*raah*, 7200—"to look upon with enjoyment, to experience, to feel, to inspect, to gain understanding") *the nakedness* (*ervah*, 6172—"nudity, the genitals") *of his father, and told* (*nagad*, 5046—"to declare, to announce, to make known, to betray, to reveal something which otherwise would not have been known") *his two brethren without."*

Why did he have to broadcast his father's shame to those

33

who knew nothing about it? Those who talk about their brothers' sins bring a greater curse upon themselves than their brother who has committed the sin.

The sins of the father are visited upon their children (Exodus 20:5). The gross disrespect that was evident in Ham also was soon seen in his decendants. It is possible that Canaan had also seen his grandfather's nakedness. Did he and his father make sport of Noah? Josephus says he laughed at his father. Some Bible scholars even ask the question, "could they have committed some unmentionable thing which the Bible text omits? God certainly hates both incest and sodomy, and there is a "hint" of both these gross sins in this ancient Bible story.

"And Noah awoke from his wine, and knew what his younger son had done unto him. And he said, Cursed be Canaan; the servant of servants shall he be unto his brethren." (Genesis 9:24, 25)

"A servant" is *ebed* (5650) in Hebrew which means "a labourer, a servant, a slave, a man in bonds."

IV. Noah's Descendants

Noah had three sons:

1. Shem: The father of the Shemites, e.g. Abraham, Ishmael, Esau, etc.

2. Japheth: The father of Russia, Europe, Greece, Germany, Poland, the Isles of the Gentiles, i.e. Great Britain, the U.S.A., Australia, Canada, etc.

3. Ham: The father of four sons:
  a. Mizraim
  b. Phut
  c. Canaan
  d. Cush.

a. Mizraim: Mizraim is one of the names of Upper and Lower Egypt. Not much is written about him, but Egypt is called "the land of Ham" (Psalm 106:22). Mizraim was the founder of Egypt.

b. Phut: Still less is mentioned about him (Ezekiel 27:10, Nahum 3:9). These Scriptures seem to indicate a country or people in Africa. Josephus says that Phut was the founder of Libya.

c. Canaan: The father of Sidon (his firstborn), Heth, the Jebusite, Amorite, Girgasite, Hivite, Arkite, Sinite, Arvadite, Zemarite, Hamathite, the families of the Canaanites from **Sidon** to **Sodom and Gomorrah** (the land of Canaan, Genesis 10:15-19)

If it is true that some act of sexual perversion took place between Ham and his son Canaan and the old man, Noah, while he was under the influence of alcohol, it would be easy to see that that spirit of sodomy stayed with this family line, for it was the descendants of Ham, through Canaan, who became the Sodomists and perverts of that time whom God destroyed with fire and brimstone in His visitation of wrath upon Sodom and Gomorrah.

d. Cush: He was apparently the eldest, whose descendants dwelt from Ethiopia to the Euphrates. They were the founders of Babylon, Nineveh, and many other cities. His descendants were also some of the Arab nations and Ethiopia. Cush begat six sons (Genesis 10:7): Seba, Havilah, Sabtah, Raamah (father of Sheba, Saudi Arabia and Dedan), Sabtechah and Nimrod.

V. Cush

Cush, the son of Ham, and grandson of Noah is generally represented as having been a ringleader in the great apostasy. He had a large share in leading mankind away from the worship of the true God. He was called Bel (the confounder). History records that he founded Babylon. Jeremiah in 50:2 refers to this Bel and prophesies that he is confounded, that is, "The Confounder is brought to confusion."[2] Hislop says Cush was known to pagan antiquity under the very character of Bel, "the Confounder." He is titled "the god of gods," from whom all the other gods had their origin. The ancients called him Chaos. Chaos is one of the names of Cush. He is also called Janus, and as such is pictured as a god with two faces—one representing Cush, the other Nimrod. He is pictured with a club. This is a very fitting symbol for him. The name of a club in Chaldee comes from the very word which signifies "to break in pieces or scatter abroad." He caused the confusion of tongues, broke the unity of the people (our unity is in our worship) and scattered the people.

Genesis 11:9, *"Therefore is the name of it called Babel* (*babel*, 894—"confusion")*; because the Lord did there confound* (*balal*, 1101—"overflow, mix, confound") *the language of all the earth: and from thence did the Lord scatter them abroad upon the face of all the earth."*

Cush was the ringleader of rebellion. He is also called Merodach (the great rebel) whom Jeremiah in 50:2 says is broken to pieces.

History records that Cush was not only the leader of apostasy, he was the original prophet of idolatry and the author of pagan rites. As the father of his deified son Nimrod (also

36

called Ninus), he became the "father of the gods." In Egypt he is also called Hermes (the son of Ham, i.e. the burnt one, the black one.")

As the two-headed (or two-faced) coin pictures—old Cush and young Cush (Nimrod)—are united (like the Father God and His Son Jesus) in the founding and building of a kingdom on earth. In this kingdom they would rule over the souls of men. Cush was the founder and Nimrod the builder, but he never finished it, for in the midst of his years he was suddenly cut off as he came to a violent death.

VI. Nimrod

Nimrod was the sixth and most powerful and wicked son of Cush. He is called "the mighty hunter before the Lord" (Genesis 10:9). He founded a great empire reaching from Babel, north along the Tigris, over Assyria where he built four more great cities, including Nineveh (Genesis 10:10-12). Here we must stop and look more closely into the powerful influence these two men (Cush, grandson of Noah, through Ham, and Nimrod (his son and the great-grandson of Noah) had upon the ancient world and Nimrod's wife (and mother) Semiramis. For this in-depth study we will go to *The Two Babylons* by Rev. Alexander Hislop* (see the advertisement in the back of this book).

It is evident that all pagan religions had their beginning in Babylon under the rebellious and powerful descendents of Ham, through his son Cush and grandson Nimrod. Although much of its original form of worship has seemingly "died out" or gone "underground" in Christian nations, Hinduism remains a close facsimile of the ancient worship that came out of Babylon in the days of Nimrod.

There is not one good thing to be said about Nimrod (who

*Used by permission of Loizeaux Brothers, Inc., Neptune, New Jersey.

37

is also known as Ninus). Cush was evil and he, the son of Cush, was many times more evil.

The name of Nimrod means "rebel, obstinate, indignant, conqueror of the leopard."

1. Nimrod, the Mighty Hunter

The King James version calls him "a mighty hunter before the Lord." A more correct translation might be "a mighty hunter against the Lord." The Jewish Encyclopaedia says, "Nimrod was he who made all people rebellious against God."

He compelled the people to worship him as a deity. That is why he was called by some Bible scholars "the mighty hunter of souls." He was the first antichrist type.

According to Eusibius he was a contemporary of Abraham who was born BC 1996.

Other scholars and historians disagree by a few years, however, there is no doubt that they must have lived almost at the same time.

Nimrod was the first deified mortal. His wife was Semiramis.

2. Nimrod, the Mighty Empire Builder

Genesis 10:11, 12, *"Out of that land* (Shinar, i.e. Babylon) *went forth Asshur, and builded Nineveh and Calah: the same is a great city."*

This English translation would more correctly be rendered, "Out of the land he (Nimrod) went forth when he was made strong (*asshur*) and builded Nineveh" etc.

This agrees with the ancient historian Justin who recorded, *Ninus (Nimrod) strengthened the greatness of his acquired dominion by continued possession (through his many victories in warfare). Having subdued, therefore, his neighbors, when*

38

by an occasion of forces, being still further strengthened, he went forth against other tribes, and every new victory paved the way for another, he subdued all the people of the East.

Justin also says that Nimrod was the first to invent magic arts and the motion of the stars. So we see Nimrod (Ninus) was the builder of Nineveh, for the name Nineveh means "the habitation of Ninus." To this day the name of the chief part of the ruins is "Nimroud."

History records that Nimrod was of a warlike disposition, ambitious for glory; he was the first to carry out war against his neighbours and he conquered all the nations from Assyria to Libya, "as they were unacquainted with the arts of war" (Justin). He is named the most ancient of the Assyrian kings. He armed and trained young men in warfare. It was his success in war that made him powerful when he first "began to be a mighty one in the earth." (Genesis 10:8)

3. Nimrod, the Mighty God

Not being content with his power and position as a mortal, he accepted the position of a god. No doubt, his father Cush, proud of his son's mighty conquests, helped to deify him. Many great conquerors have been looked upon by men as gods— Nebuchadnezzar, Alexander the Great, the Neros; even Napoleon and Hitler believed themselves to be invincible.

He was worshipped as a god, not only in Assyria, but this false religion spread rapidly to many other countries, (as anything false always does) and soon he was worshipped by the names that each different nation gave him.

Names of Nimrod

a. The Horned One: Kronos, the two-horned God, was one of his names. Saturn is the same person with another name.

39

The horn is the oriental symbol of power and might. Kronos, "the horned one" could be called "the mighty one" just as correctly. The name Kronos is applied to Saturn as "the Father of the gods." So we have both Cush and Nimrod called by the same title. It passed down from father to son, as titles often do.

"The Horned One" as applied to Nimrod, fully explains the origin of the remarkable symbol, so frequently found among the Nineveh sculptures, the gigantic horned man-bull, as representing the great divinities in Assyria. The same word that signifies bull also signifies ruler and prince.

This also, in a remarkable way, accounts for the origin of one of the deities worshipped by the Anglo-Saxons' ancestors under the name Zernebogus. This Zernebogus was "the black, malevolent, ill-omened divinity." As such he was the exact counterpart of man's idea of Satan (black with horns and hoofs).

The name Zer-nebo-gus is Chaldee and can be translated, "Seed of the prophet Cush," which is certainly who Nimrod was.

The name Cush means "burnt one, or dark coloured, or black one." His son Nimrod is sometimes pictured with negroid features. Especially in Egypt where his name is Osiris. Being the son of Cush, Nimrod would bear the same features. To the fair-complexioned Anglo-Saxons he became a god who was feared.

b. Nimrod, the Winged Bull: Another very similar symbol of Nimrod is the winged bull. The mighty kings of Babylon and Assyria who copied Nimrod adopted the winged bull as their symbol. These winged creatures were worshipped as some mighty ones—as were the other gods who also had wings, e.g. Cupid, the son of Venus. Semiramis held the same position as Nimrod.

40

In the summer of 1986 I visited the building in Berlin where that infamous decision, called the "Final Solution," was made one night in January 1942 by the high-ranking officials of the Nazi Party to exterminate all the Jews of Germany and the German-occupied nations of Europe. I noticed Babylonian winged beasts were a part of the decor of this house. It is also significant that Berlin is the city where the gates of Babylon are on display. When one remembers that Berlin was Hitler's headquarters for world dominion, is it any wonder that he became an end-time "hunter of souls" i.e. destroyer of souls, like Nimrod?!

c. Nimrod, the Centaur: The fabulous half-horse, half-man who is so prevalent in Greek mythology is believed to commemorate the original man who taught the world horsemanship. But he did not originate in Greece. The Greeks got the Centaur from Babylon. Ancient coins depicting the Centaur prove this. The Centaur, like the warrior Orion, is found in the Zodiac. The Greeks acknowledge that the original Centaur was the same as Kronos and Saturn, the father of the gods (i. e. Nimrod) who is always depicted on the ancient coins with a bow (but no arrow) who became the mighty conqueror of the souls of men. Is there any connection between him and the rider on the white horse of Revelation 6:2 who also has a bow and no arrow? Could the rider of Revelation be another godless "Nimrod" who will come forth as a mighty and powerful apostate leader of false religion, hunting and conquering the souls of men?

41

This huntsman Centaur can be traced to all nations, even to India. The antichrist will attempt to rule all the world. Rubens' famous painting "The Rape of Hippodameia" reveals the godless perversion and evil that will prevail upon the earth when his diabolic powers will be released after the **first seal** is broken. Only those who are trusting in the Blood of Jesus will be able to withstand his evil. Perhaps he is already riding.

When I was on the island of Aruba, Rev. Frederick Heemstadt, a well-known and well-respected evangelist, told us about a man he had met in the Dominican Republic, who had signed his soul over to the devil to gain great power. Every night at midnight his body would undergo a change and he became a horse from the waist down. In this grotesque form he would run through the villages attacking, molesting women and terrifying people.

One day the devil said to him, "I have an enemy here who hinders my powers. You have to kill her for me." This "enemy," whom Satan feared and hated and wanted destroyed was the little lady-pastor of the mission. At midnight, when the man's body changed, he ran over to the mission, but she wasn't there. So he went to her little cottage looking for her. He broke down the door and entered. She was on her knees praying.

When she looked up and saw this hideous creature, she said to him, "I've been waiting for you." Then she began to rebuke him in the Name of Jesus and command him to repent. He was struck with the fear of God. In holy terror he fled and ran like a desperate wild creature from another world around the village all night, begging the devil to turn him back into his human form. Through the hours of the night he became increasingly more frantic and as he saw dawn approaching, he knew that the townspeople would kill him when daylight came. He begged and begged the devil to release him from his centaur form, but the devil had forsaken him.

Finally he remembered what the little lady preacher had told him—that if he would call upon the Lord Jesus, he could be saved. He cried, "Jesus, help me!" Instantly he was released and changed back to his human form. Today he is a preacher of the Gospel. Praise God for the powerful Name of Jesus. It is mightier than the name of Centaur, Nimrod or any other demon spirit, including Satan himself. For at the Name of Jesus **every** knee shall bow (Philippians 2:10).

4. Nimrod, the Mason

Freemasonry: Hislop draws a parallel between Masonry and Nimrod. *It is admitted that the secret system of Free Masonry was originally founded on the Mysteries of the Egyptian Isis, the goddess mother, or wife of Osiris (also known as Nimrod). But what could have led to the union of a masonic body with these mysteries, had they not had particular reference to architecture, and had the god who was worshipped in them not been celebrated for his success in perfecting the arts of fortification and building? Now, if such were the case, considering the relation in which Egypt looked up to Babylon, who would naturally be the great patron of the Masonic art? The strong presumption is that Nimrod must have been the man. He was the first that gained fame in this way (as the builder of Babel). He was worshipped by the name of Ala Mahozim (the god of fortifications).* [3]

Few Christians know the real truth about Freemasonry. Even most of the Masons themselves do not know what it is all about. As the Bible says, "They have not known the depths of Satan." (Revelation 2:24). It is a system of "morality, veiled in allegory and illustrated by symbols." Oaths are taken by the candidate and horrible penalties are pronounced upon him if he should betray the secrets of Masonry. Yet, in spite of this, more and more people from fundamentalist churches are joining the

43

Masons. When they worship before their altar, they are told that they are kneeling to a Supreme Being and they swear upon the "Volume of Sacred Law." That sounds wonderful. But is the Supreme Being the same Lord Jehovah, whom we worship as God, when the Volume of Sacred Law is not the Bible? It can be a Bible, but it can just as readily be a Koran (to suit the Moslems) or the Vedas (for the Hindus), or any other Scripture that is acceptable to the majority of the people in that particular nation.

Albert Pike, who some say was an "evil genius of the first magnitude and an avowed worshipper of Satan who practiced necromancy and all forms of sorcery," rewrote the degree rituals of the southern jurisdiction in the late nineteenth century.

Albert Pike, in his 861-page book *Morals and Dogma of the Ancient and Accepted Scottish Rite of Freemasonry* reveals some astounding facts about the heart of Freemasonry. Just to mention three different statements:

1. Regarding the Bible: *The doctrines of the Bible are often not clothed in the language of strict truth, but in that which was fittest to convey to a rude and ignorant people the practical essentials of the doctrine* (Page 224).

2. Regarding the worship of God: *Masonry, around whose altars the Christian, the Hebrew, the Moslem, the Brahmin, the followers of Confuscious and Zoroaster can assemble as brethren and unite in prayer to the one God who is above all the Baalim, must needs leave it to each of its initiates to look for the foundation of his faith and hope to the written scriptures of his own religion* (page 226).

3. Regarding the tower of Babel: *The sacred Babylonian tower (Magdol) dedicated to the great Father Bal..."* (page 234).[4]

5. Names of Nimrod

Nimrod was worshipped in many nations under many

44

different names. We have already mentioned Bel, Belus (apparently he inherited this title from Cush), Ninus, Kronos, Saturn, Zernebogus (Anglo-Saxon), Osiris (Egypt), Cupid (Eros), the mighty prince (as the horned bull and winged bull) and the Centaur who was represented on the Babylonian coins and in the Zodiac by the same sign as Sagittarius (the Archer), as well as Orion.

Let me pause here to say that mythology (as we know it) in connection with the Zodiac, is entirely based on the pagan religion of Babylon and had its origin in Cush and Nimrod, who undoubtedly had access to the truth, but who perverted it to fit his perverted pagan religion. Today many Bible scholars, under the anointing of the Holy Spirit, are able to look beyond the pagan interpretation of the Zodiac and see the eternal truths of God in the stars. Books on the stars, which I can recommend, are *The Witness of the Stars* by E.W. Bullinger, *The Heavens Declare* by William D. Banks and *Signs in the Heavens* by Marilyn Hickey (see the advertisement in the back of the book.)

We should not be afraid of the true study of the stars for the "Heavens declare the glory of God." Josephus says that Abraham was "skillful in the celestial science" and that he communicated this knowledge to Egypt when he went there with Sarah.

Bel, Belus: He apparently inherited this title from his father, Cush.

Bacchus: Bacchus, the youth god, who is celebrated as the god of wine, appears very innocent-looking as he holds the cup in his right hand and the ivy branch in his left, but he is the god of drunken revelry and of such revelry and orgies that even lead to blood sacrifices. The name Bacchus means "son of Cush."

This innocent-looking demon that represents youthful fun is today possessing millions of our youth through alcohol, which,

45

when taken in excess, breaks down moral restraint, thus causing debauchery and every kind of sin, as well as crime and tragic and fatal car accidents.

Tammuz: Plato said that Tammuz, the god of the Phoenicians and Assyrians, was identical with Osiris. As the women of Egypt wept for Osiris, the women of Phoenicia and Assyria and backslidden Israel mourned for Tammuz, while the women of Greece and Rome wept for Bacchus. In Ezekiel 8:14 we read that Ezekiel was shown, by God, the daughters of Zion weeping for Tammuz in the holy temple, itself. This is what happens when God's people forsake the Lord.

Other names for Nimrod are:
Krishna (also spelled Crishna) of India
Deoius of Asia
Horus of Egypt
Jupiter of Rome
Wat-Yun of China
Adonis (the great huntsman for whom Venus is said to have made great lamentations)
Balder of Iceland and Scandinavia,
and undoubtedly still others which we do not have the time to research. Satan comes in many forms and ways, always modifying himself to suit the customs and culture of the people whom he wants to deceive.

6. Nimrod, the Emancipator or Deliverer

There is no doubt that Nimrod was very popular. The extent to which he gained the worship of the people is very amazing. What was it that he did to obtain the adoration and the worship

46

of the people? One does not need to be morally good to have an adoring following. We know this by what happened in Germany under Hitler. One only needs to make promises and pretend to care for the welfare of the people. In a day when there are so few qualified leaders whom people can trust, the time has come when it would be easy for an antichrist to arise in most lands and gain a following through treachery and flattery (Daniel 11:32, 34).

Nimrod came on the scene when the memory of the terrible deluge was still very vivid in the hearts of the descendants of Noah. In fact, Noah was still living. People feared and worshipped Jehovah alone. But the curse that Noah had put upon Ham's descendants angered and embittered them and separated them from their brothers, Shem and Japheth. In their rebellion against the curse, they turned against God. Satan entered their hearts and he promised them he would free them from the curse if they would covenant to serve him. In fact, he probably promised them the same thing he had promised Eve, "Ye shall be as gods."

Ham, the burnt one, the black one, was at first only black in his heart, but later, that darkness which was in his soul began to reflect in his countenance. (I have seen black-skinned people shine with the light of God on their faces and fair-complexioned people whose faces were covered with a veil of darkness and death.) Cush, the son of Ham set about to free himself and the people who followed him from the laws of God and righteousness, just like our Supreme Court does today. As such, he became the first great leader of Apostasy and his son, Nimrod, was lifted up as the "Apostate Emancipator and Liberator" of man. In the same way Mao Tze Tung "liberated" China, Fidel Castro "liberated" Cuba, Stalin "liberated" many European nations. People are easily brainwashed. Please read Genesis 11:1-9.

47

7. Nimrod, His End

Some scholars believe that the wild animals had increased at such a dreadful rate after the flood that the people lived in danger. So Nimrod became the master of the chase—god of the huntsmen, as he subdued the wild animals and brought the people out of the countryside to live in communities—called cities, where he promised them protection, but where he could also more easily control them, because he could "police their activities." They soon became a police-state. The present-day revival of Communism dates back to Nimrod.

Nimrod's apostasy climaxed in his building in Babylon, his capitol, the tower whose top would reach to the heavens (Genesis 11:4). It wasn't the height, but the motive that moved God to *"come down to see the city and the tower, which the children of men builded."* God sees all the works of man. Nothing is unknown to Him, nor hidden from His all-seeing eye.

Some Bible scholars believe that it was when God came down, that Nimrod was cut off. Although the Bible mentions nothing about his death, mythology and ancient tradition and religions reveal that he came to a violent end. It seems he probably was torn in pieces. Because Nimrod is identified with Osiris of Egypt, we have more light on his death. The violent death of Osiris was the central focus of all the idolatrous pagan religion of ancient Egypt.

The Egyptians annually mourned the death of Osiris. Some believe that the righteous Shem executed him, dismembered his body, and sent it to his cities as a warning of the consequences of such rebellion against God. For a time this demonic worship of a mortal went underground. That is why it became a mystery. It must be remembered that Noah was still living at this time.

Josephus' account of Nimrod and the tower of Babel is of great interest:

Now it was Nimrod who excited them to such an affront

48

and contempt of God. He was the grandson of Ham, the son of Noah,—a bold man, and of great strength of hand. He persuaded them not to ascribe it to God, as if it was through his means they were happy, but to believe that it was their own courage which procured that happiness. He also gradually changed the government into tyranny—seeing no other way of turning men from the fear of God, but to bring them into a constant dependence upon his power. He also said he would be revenged on God, if He should have a mind to drown the world again; for that he would build a tower too high for the waters to be able to reach! and that he would avenge himself on God for destroying their forefathers!

Now the multitude were very ready to follow the determination of Nimrod, and to esteem it a piece of cowardice to submit to God; and they built a tower, neither sparing any pains, nor being in any degree negligent about the work; and, by reason of the multitude of hands employed in it, it grew very high, sooner than any one could expect; but the thickness of it was so great, and it was so strongly built, that thereby its great height seemed, upon view, to be less than it really was. It was built of burnt brick, cemented together with mortar, made of bitumen, that it might not be liable to admit water. When God saw that they acted so madly, He did not resolve to destroy them utterly, since they were not grown wiser by the destruction of the former sinners; but he caused a tumult among them, by producing in them divers languages; and causing that, through the multitude of those languages, they should not be able to understand one another. The place wherein they built the tower is now called Babylon; because of the confusion of that language which they readily understood before; for the Hebrews mean by the word Babel, Confusion.[5]

Smith says Nimrod laid the first foundation of the Babylonian or Assyrian Monarchy in 1771 A.M. (after the creation of Adam) and that Noah still was living. He died at the age of 950 in 2006 A.M. He also states that Abraham was born two years later in 2008 A.M. So you see, scholars do not agree on Abraham's date of birth.

VII. Semiramis—Wife and Mother of Nimrod

A. Semiramis—the Wife of Nimrod

Perhaps it might be said that the most fascinating, blasphemous "god" of this pagan trinity is Semiramis, who, from an originally humble position, became the wife of Nimrod. She was soon elevated into a high position as the "wife of a god" (making her a goddess), co-builder of Babylon. When her husband, Nimrod, suddenly was killed, she had to invent a reason to keep her powerful position.

B. Semiramis—the Mother

In life, her husband had been honoured as a hero and a god. In death, she would have him worshipped as "the woman's seed (*zero-ashta:* the seed of *Ashta* or *Ashtoreth*) who was destined to bruise the serpent's head and in so doing, had his own heel bruised. The ancient world was familiar with the promise God had given Eve in the garden (Genesis 3:15).

Zero is Chaldee for "seed." Zeroaster is the name of the head of the fire worshippers (an Ethiopian and Parsi religion). The ancient belief was that the curse could only be removed from the earth by the great "deliverer" or "emancipator." The trace of God's promise to Eve can be found in many religions in many nations. Such as:

Greece: Apollo slaying the serpent, Pytho; Hercules strangling the serpent while he was yet in his cradle.

Horus of Egypt, Crishna of India, Thor of Scandinavia. Even the Mexicans believe in a certain Teotl (who crushed the

50

serpent). All were worshipped as gods who had crushed or killed the serpent to free man from his power over them. Satan always was an imitator and counterfeiter.

Semiramis became the original "mother," who was worshipped. She took upon herself the image of the mother of Nimrod, rather than his wife. This "lamented one" (Ninus or Nimrod) was exhibited and adored as a little child in his mother's arms. In order to secure her powerful position she claimed herself to be the "mother" of the "deliverer." Thus Nimrod became both the husband and the son of Semiramis, the first female goddess. Osiris, by which name he is called in Egypt, had as one of his great titles of dignity and honour, the name "husband of the mother."

It was from her "son" that she derived all her glory and her claims to deification. In time they were worshipped as the goddess mother and her son, and their images were worshipped with an enthusiasm that was incredible. They were adored in many nations as "mother" and "son." In the end, the mother eclipsed the son. Hislop says, "Now the son, even in his new incarnation,...was exhibited merely as a child, without any very particular attraction; while the mother, in whose arms he was, was set off with all the art of painting and sculpture. She was invested with extraordinary beauty which, in reality, belonged to her, for the beauty of Semiramis is said, on one occasion, to have quelled a rising rebellion among her subjects on her sudden appearance among them. A statue of her was erected in ancient Babylon. She was the very embodiment of everything attractive in female form—the perfection of beauty with golden tresses." She became the favourite object of worship. To justify this worship, she was raised to divinity, as well as her son.

51

C. Semiramis—Her Titles

Hislop, the author of *The Two Babylons* says, *The very name by which the Italians commonly designate the Virgin Mother, is just the translation of one of the titles of the Babylonian goddess (Semiramis).*

As Baal (or Belus) was the name of the great male divinity of Babylon (Nimrod), so the female divinity was called Beltis. This name has been found in Nineveh applied to the "Mother of the gods." Even as the Greek "Belus" represented the highest title of the Babylonian god, was undoubtedly "Baal," the Lord. Beltis, therefore, as the title of the female divinity, was equivalent to "Baalti" which in English is "My Lady." In Latin it is Mea Domina, and in Italian is corrupted into the well-known "Madonna."[6]

She was worshipped in the different nations by the names of Athena, Cybil (a name often chosen by witches today), Rhea, Astoreth, Isis (of Egypt), Diana (of Ephesus), Artemis, Despoina, Isi (in India), Hestia, Vesta, as **Madonna and child**. In China as Shengmu (Holy Mother), in Germany as Hertha, in Scandinavia as Disa, in Egypt her name was Isis and her son Osiris. In India, even to this day, she is worshipped as Isi and her son as Iswara. In Asia as Cybile and Deoius, in Pagan Rome as Fortuna and the boy Jupiter, in Greece as Ceres (the Great Mother with the babe at her breast) or as Irene, the goddess of peace with the boy Plutus in her arms. As co-builder of Babylon she shares with Nimrod the title of Goddess of Fortification.

Even the mermaid has been identified with Semiramis herself. She is frequently pictured sitting on the surface of the waters, combing her long, golden hair with a golden comb. In the ancient pictures she is depicted as having a halo around her head.

52

There is an interesting aspect of this whole Madonna and child worship, which has been recorded by Hislop:

The scheme, thus skillfully formed, took effect. Semiramis gained glory from her dead and deified husband; and in course of time both of them, under the names of Rhea and Nin, or "Goddess-Mother and Son," were worshipped with an enthusiasm that was incredible, and their images were everywhere set up and adored. Wherever the negro aspect of Nimrod was found an obstacle to his worship, this was very easily obviated. According to the Chaldean doctrine of transmigration of souls, all that was needful was just to teach that Ninus had reappeared in the person of a posthumous son, of a fair complexion, supernaturally borne by his widowed wife after the father had gone to glory. As the licentious and dissolute life of Semiramis gave her many children, for whom no ostensible father on earth would be alleged, a plea like this would at once sanctify sin, and enable her to meet the feelings of those who were disaffected to the true worship of Jehovah, and yet might have no fancy to bow down before a negro divinity. From the light reflected on Babylon by Egypt, as well as from the form of the extant images of the Babylonian child in the arms of the goddess-mother, we have every reason to believe that this was actually done. In Egypt the fair Horus, the son of the black Osiris, who was the favourite object of worship, in the arms of the goddess Isis, was said to have been miraculously born in consequence of a connection, on the part of that goddess, with Osiris after his death, and, in point of fact, to have been a new incarnation of that god, to avenge his death on his murderers. It is wonderful to find in what widely-severed countries, and amongst what millions of the human race at this day, who never saw a negro, a negro god is worshipped. But yet, as we shall afterwards see, among the civilised nations of antiquity, Nimrod almost everywhere fell into disrepute and was deposed from his original pre-eminence, expressly ob

53

deformitatem,*"on account of his ugliness." Even in Babylon itself, the posthumous child, as identified with his father, and inheriting all his father's glory, yet possessing more of his mother's complexion, came to be the favourite type of the Madonna's divine son.*[7]

When **Rome** became a great empire, it accepted the pagan religions of the lands over which it ruled. They were all incorporated into the religion of Rome. The spirits did not object to this because, after all, they were all the same spirits, only with different names.

Diana: In Acts 19 we read about Semiramis where she is called by the name of the great goddess Diana. The magnificent temple dedicated to her was one of the seven wonders of the world. It was 425 feet by 220 feet, and had 127 columns of marble, each 60 feet high. Diana was called the goddess of hunting, virginity, fruitfulness and love. The nodes on her chest, once thought to be breasts, represent the testes of bulls sacrificed for her. The temple services were performed by women and eunuchs. Her devotees would select the garments upon which they worshipped. After performing the rites, the temple prostitutes (to whom the garments belonged) would appear and offer their bodies as an act of sacrifice to the devotees. Thus, both female prostitutes and eunuchs, were used in perverse and sodomite rites in connection with the worship of Diana and other goddesses.

It is strange that in spite of there being many male gods, none could equal the power and influence of the female

54

goddesses. They were the ones with the greatest followers. They had the most magnificent temples dedicated to them.

Paul's most wonderful revival took place in Ephesus when the people forsook Diana and destroyed all their objects of worship and magic formulas, etc.

Madonna and Child Worship Incorporated into the Church

Yet, in spite of this great revival here, it was at this same city in 431 A.D. at the Council of Ephesus, that the church fathers condoned the worship of Mary, and it became an official doctrine of the church at this council. All this, in spite of the fact that Epiphanius in 403 A.D. had denounced certain ones out of Trace and Arabia for worshipping Mary as a goddess and offering cakes at her shrine. Less than 30 years later, she was proclaimed divine. There is no other explanation for this than the fact that the ruling spirit of Semiramis influenced the early church fathers to make this great error of doctrine, permitting the spirit of apostasy to come into the church, even the spirit of the harlot, Semiramis, who now would be worshipped under another new name, Mary, but old title, "Mother of God."

In summing up this chapter, I would like to use the following very well written historical account by Winkie Pratney in his astounding book, *Devil, Take the Youngest* (see the advertisement in the back of this book):

According to tradition, Nimrod's ambition and greed drove him further and further into the occult. He eventually became the high priest of devil-worship.

Along the way he joined forces with Semiramis, a stunningly beautiful, clever, but patently immoral woman who became queen and may have helped build the battlements of his Tower.

Then, without warning, with the whole world at his feet, Nimrod was suddenly summoned to eternity.

55

His end came swiftly, and in shrouded circumstances. But there is some evidence it was an act of judgment.

"(As to) how Nimrod died, Scripture is entirely silent," Hislop writes. "There was an ancient tradition that he came to a violent end...profane history speaks darkly and mysteriously, though one account tells of his having met with a violent death..."

One account has him judged by a tribunal, then sentenced to be TORN TO PIECES.

Apparently, his death shocked the world.

In the midst of his glorious career, Nimrod suddenly was cut off by a horrible, violent death.

When the shocking news spread abroad, the "devotees of pleasure felt as if the best benefactor of mankind was gone, and the gaiety of nations was eclipsed. Thus began those 'weepings of Tammuz' in the guilt of which the daughters of Israel allowed themselves to be implicated, and the existence of which can be traced not merely in annals of classical antiquity, but in the literature of the world from Ultima Thule to Japan," says Hislop.

And in the awful death of Nimrod there rose to new power his widow, Semiramis, "who from an originally humble position had been raised to share with him the throne of Babylon."

Apparently, she was a woman of great resolution and ambition.

What could she do to retain her place on the throne?

Her solution was clever and, indeed, inspired by the darkest forces with which she and Nimrod had aligned themselves.

"In life her husband had been honored as a hero," says Hislop. "In death she will have him worshipped as a god."

The "Seed of the Woman" Prophecy:

The ancient world was familiar with the Edenic prophecy of the promised "seed of the woman" who would "bruise the

56

serpent's head," and in so doing have his own heel bruised.

They knew this implied the death of the Deliverer was the only thing that could remove the curse from the world.

The idea of the Deliverer slaying the serpent runs through all the ancient traditions: Apollo slaying the serpent Pytho; Hercules strangling serpents while yet in his cradle; Horus piercing a snake's head with his spear; Calyia, the malignant serpent slain by Vishnu in his avatar of Krishna; and Thor bruising the head of the great serpent with his mace, to name a few.

Semiramis drew on her husband's use of magic and sorcery in Babel. She would make his death, "voluntary, self-sacrificial" and mystical—for the benefit of the world.

Nimrod's form of death would be covered up and made an act of devotion and a means of attaining great power.

For he would "rise again."

The means to manufacture such a bogus resurrection were there.

Although carefully protected and kept secret, the pagan initiation ceremonies Nimrod had instituted were fantastic, dramatic productions designed to awe and terrify, complete with the most advanced special effects.

The priests of Babylonian mystery-initiation ceremonies were the special-effects experts of their day.

After candidates had passed through the confessional and sworn the required oaths, one historian relates:

"Strange and amazing objects presented themselves. Sometimes the place they were in seemed to shake around them; sometimes it appeared bright and resplendent with light and radiant fire, and then again covered with black darkness; sometimes frightful noises and bellowings, sometimes terrible apparitions astonished the trembling spectators. Then at last the great god, the central object of their worship, Osiris, Tammuz, Nimrod or Adonis was revealed to them in a way most

57

fitted to soothe their feelings and engage their blind affections."

Hislop quotes one ancient account: "In a manifestation which one must not reveal...there is seen on a wall of the temple a mass of light, which appears at first at a very great distance. It is transformed, while unfolding itself into a visage evidently divine and supernatural of an aspect severe, but with a touch of sweetness...."

Enter: Tammuz, the god-child.

Somehow, Semiramis had to convey to the world that Nimrod had returned, that the "god" they loved had come back in a greater and more awesome display of his past glory.

The obvious path, if you were going to claim something so arrogantly significant, was to proclaim the fulfillment of the prophecy of the coming "seed of the woman" recorded in Genesis 3:15.

No doubt, with the full power of all the special effects, she could muster, the die was cast and she made her play to a waiting world:

"Rejoice!" she proclaimed: "The self-sacrificing god has risen again"—in the form of her son!

Son?

What son?

Where did she get the child? A small detail for one like Semiramis to whom immorality was power!

That Semiramis was sexually immoral was a matter of record; the child she brazenly presented to the world was fair, while Nimrod had been black, Hislop writes.

She may have become pregnant while Nimrod was away. Although he was killed before he could return, she brazenly claimed the baby as his.

Furthermore, she proclaimed herself a virgin, the object of a wondrous miracle. Even the most gullible of her kingdom

58

would not put up with an unfaithful queen, perhaps. Maybe her life was on the line. The actual circumstances are unknown.

But what she did was to lay the major occult foundations of demonic power in the world.

To sanctify her adultery and justify her bastard child, she announced a great lie. She was the Virgin of Prophecy!

The child she carried was the promised Messiah, the Godman, the Seed of Woman.

Nimrod had "visited her in a flash of light" and the child she bore as a result was the reincarnated king, elevated now to the status of a god.

If you hope to rule the world through a lie, better tell a **big** *one.*

It caught on.

It spread like wildfire!

The word went around the world:

"Nimrod is back; the ancient prophecy is fulfilled; who knows now what mankind can accomplish?"

The people worshiped the child, Tammuz, as both their reincarnated king and their god.

Semiramis moved smoothly, unobtrusively directing worship from behind the throne.

And thus the great launching of the mystery religion of Babylon: the pagan worship of a bogus virgin and child.[8]

STUDY QUESTIONS

1. Read Genesis chapters 6-10 and Acts 19.

2. What caused the great flood? How did this agree with Numbers 35:33, 34?

3. How did Noah redeem the land?

4. Why did Noah curse Ham's descendants?

5. Where did Noah's three sons and their families begin to populate the world? What nations are they the parents of?

6. Give a brief resume on Cush, Nimrod, Semiramis.

7. Where does Freemasonry originate?

8. Memorize Genesis 9:13.

CHAPTER FIVE

TRACING NIMROD AND SEMIRAMIS THROUGH THE HISTORY OF ISRAEL

Throughout the history of Israel one can see how the evil demonic spirits of Nimrod and Semiramis repeatedly were revived. It is impossible to mention every incidence, but we will take the more outstanding ones.

I. The Golden Calf (Exodus 32:1-35)

After the miraculous deliverance of the Children of Israel out of Egypt, when they were safely in the desert, far from any of the evil pagan worship of the false gods of Egypt, one would think that they would have been safe from idolatry. But, even as Satan stole into the Garden of Eden and destroyed the first righteous kingdom, he again tried to destroy this kingdom by enticing the people to create a golden calf and worship it while Moses was on the top of the mount for forty days, communing with God.

"And when the people saw that Moses delayed to come down out of the mount, the people gathered themselves together unto Aaron, and said unto him, Up, make us gods, which shall go before us; for as for this Moses, the man that brought us up out of the land of Egypt, we wot not what is become of him." (Exodus 32:1)

They did not tell him what to make. It was Aaron himself (who probably was a gifted sculptor) who made them the golden calf. Within hours their worship led to gross debauchery and orgies. The word "calf" in this instance is *egel* (5695). It means "a male, nearly-grown steer, or bullock." Hislop says that the golden calf of Egypt was the symbol of Nimrod. Remember, one of the names of Nimrod was Kronos, "the horned one."

61

Both the horned bull and the winged bull were symbols of Nimrod whom the Bible says was the first "to be mighty on the earth." So we trace the apostate religious spirit of Nimrod to the church in the wilderness, which God immediately crushed in great anger. "Who is on the Lord's side?" cried Moses (Exodus 32:26). The sons of Levi took up their swords and killed all the idolators. As a reward for their faithfulness to God, the Lord gave them the ministry of the priesthood and they became the Lord's chosen tribe for the ministry of the Tabernacle and the offering of the sacrifices. When one understands the truth about the worship of the golden calf and its connection with Nimrod, it is easy to understand God's great anger.

II. Balaam's Scheme to Cause Israel's Fall (Numbers 25)

We all know the story of Balaam and how he plotted a vicious scheme to cause Israel to fall into the sin of idolatry and adultery. (They always go together.)

When Balaam was called by the King of Moab to curse Israel, he was not able to do so. God turned his curse into a blessing. But Balaam invented another evil plan that would lead the Israelites into great sin. Josephus, writing about it, tells how Balaam advised the leaders of Moab,

Do you therefore set out the handsomest of your daughters...the most beautiful and send them to be near the Israelites' camp, and give them charge that when the young men of the Hebrews desire their company, they allow it; and when they are enamored of them, let them take their leaves; and if they entreat them to stay, let them not give their consent till they have persuaded them to leave off their obedience to their own laws and the worship of that God...and to worship the gods of the Midianites and Moabites.

This the Midianites did. They sent their most beautiful daughters, attractively dressed to flirt with and seduce the young men of Israel who soon were enamoured of them, began to fraternize with them, even going to their homes, eating at their feasts food that had been sacrificed to the dead and worshipping their idols (Psalm 106:28). When the young women attempted to break off the love affairs, the men were so passionately and madly in love with them (the demon of lust had seized hold of them) that they were ready to forsake the laws of God. Zimri, a prince from the tribe of Simeon openly defied Moses and brazenly took one of the foreign princesses into his tent. Josephus says that this transgression was prevalent in the whole army of Israel. By this time a dreadful plague had broken out among the people of Israel and people were dying.

Moses called the people together to pray, and as they wept before the Lord (many of them even weeping for their own sons), Phinehas, the grandson of Aaron, the High Priest, took a javelin in his hand, went into the tent where Zimri and the Midianite woman were and killed them both. In doing this, he redeemed Israel from the curse and spared them from further destruction; for already the deadly sexually-transmitted disease that had broken out in the camp had killed 24,000 children of Israel (Numbers 25:9).

Baal-Peor:

Who was the god that the young soldiers of Israel had worshipped at the insistence of their female lovers? His name, Baal-peor reveals who he was. This main deity of the Moabites was probably the same god who was worshipped by both the Moabites and Phoenicians under two other names, Chemosh (subduer) and Molech (king, law-giver). He was also the god of the Ammonites, who worshipped him by the same name as the Phoeniceans, Molech. Like the goddess Kali of India, in former times, he demanded human sacrifices. He was shaped like a human with hideous face and great outstretched hands. He was made of metal and hollow on the inside, so that a fire

63

could be built in his base. When he became red hot, the screaming human sacrifice was torn from his mother's arms and placed into its open arms where he slowly roasted to death in the arms of this evil, demonic idol-god (see picture, page 199). In II Kings 3:27 we read how, when his city was under siege, the king of Moab took his eldest son, the crown-prince, and offered him for a burnt offering to the god, Molech.

In Carthage of the Phoenician colonies, 200 boys were sacrificed at one time to Molech, hoping it would relieve the city from a siege.

Traces of this god by the name of Chemosh have been found at Babylon, Tyre and we know he was worshipped in Jerusalem.

Moslem Religion:

The Arabs worshipped a black stone as his emblem. Even now a black stone in the Kaaba at Mecca is still worshipped by all Moslems who make pilgrimages to it, hoping it will give them salvation. Mohammed was born in Mecca in 570, into the Durayah tribe of the Hashim clan who were not nomads, like most Arabs, but lived in a fertile valley. There was always a lot of fighting between the clan and the others. They were always feared by their neighbours for their hostility and warring spirit.

At that time all the Arabs were pagan idolators. They worshipped together at Mecca, which was the religious centre of Arabia. It was a real United Nations. All types of deities were worshipped there and 365 idols stood in this great courtyard. But one stone was more revered than all the others. It was reported to have great powers to do miracles. It was the great black stone which still is worshipped today. Mohammed called it "the god" (Allah), "the god of gods," and confirmed that it had power to take away the sins of the people for all who kiss it. Humans were no longer offered to it—just animals. He claimed that Allah was the one true god and he was Allah's prophet. Before his birth, Mohammed's father had dedicated

64

him to this black deity and put him "under the guardianship and protection" of this demon spirit, this false god.

Even before Mohammed, a heathen demon was worshipped in the Kaaba in Mecca. At a heathen sacrificial feast in that city, Mohammed stood up, pointed to the Kaaba stone, and cried, "La alla illa allahu!" ("There is no allah, except he be Allah.") This utterance of Mohammed's, changed into "La illahilla Allah" ("There is no God but Allah"), became the Islamic confession of faith.

The Kaaba was the first Islamic holy place. The actual nucleus of Islam lies in this commitment to Allah, the highest demon. Those who commit themselves to this spirit become prisoners of Satan.

Islam is therefore a religion which must always turn against Jesus Christ, the crucified, resurrected, coming Lord. It is an expressly anti-Christian religion of lies, boundless fatalism, and unimaginable fanaticism.

As pictured in the Koran, the holy book of Islam, Allah is a rigid god without a soul who shows no mercy. To him, man is simply a slave, having no power of decision. Allah demands the total submission of all creatures. He is selfishness taken to its logical extreme, a gruesome tyrant, who can only give commands. Faith in such a god can lead only to a dismal fatalism.

Allah is not a god who revealed himself, but a god who was given a unique position by Mohammed.[1] (Quoted from *The Unholy War* by Marius Baar).

III. Joshua Redeems the Land

When Moses died, God spoke to Joshua, *"Moses my servant is dead; now therefore arise, go over this Jordan, thou, and all this people, unto the land which I do give to them, even to the children of Israel"* (Joshua 1:2).

65

Together with the promise God warned Joshua, *"This book of the law shall not depart out of thy mouth; but thou shalt meditate therein day and night, that thou mayest observe to do according to all that is written therein: for then thou shalt make thy way prosperous, and then thou shalt have good success"* (Joshua 1:8).

The condition for prosperity and blessing has always been our obedience to God.

Over a hundred years ago, the Lord Jesus appeared to the king of Swaziland in southern Africa. Holding a Bible in His hand, the Lord told the king, "If you will read this book and obey it and teach your people to read and obey it, your people will always live in peace. There will never be wars in your land and your people will always have enough to eat. They will never be hungry. Your hills will always be green." The king, a pagan man, accepted the missionaries with "the Book" (the Bible), and Swaziland is perhaps the most peaceful nation in Africa. It lies between war-torn Mozambique and troubled South Africa. God keeps His Word!

When God promised Abraham that He would give his seed the land of Canaan, God said that the Amorites' cup of iniquity was not yet full (Genesis 15:16). He knew precisely how many years of grace they still had left. (God knows exactly how many particles of sand still are left in the hourglass.) He promised that Israel would come out of another land with great substance in the fourth generation.

When God raised up Joshua, He commissioned him to destroy all the Canaanites (Exodus 23:27), together with their altars, their images (Exodus 34:13) and groves to Ashtoreth (all groves were to her).

Joshua was God's sword against the idolatrous worshippers of the devil and all his demons. In obeying God, he cleansed the land because the land had been defiled through its multitude

66

of blood sacrifices to devils. Much innocent blood had been shed for Nimrod.

IV. Israel, During the Time of the Judges

As long as Joshua and the elders of Israel were alive, the children of Israel were faithful to Jehovah. But when the old godly generation who had known the works of God died out, another generation came after them who did not know God and love Him like they had.

Judges 2:10-13, *"And also all that generation were gathered unto their fathers: and there arose another generation after them, which knew not the Lord, nor yet the works which he had done for Israel. And the children of Israel did evil in the sight of the Lord, and served Baalim. And they forsook the Lord God of their fathers, which brought them out of the land of Egypt, and followed other gods, of the gods of the people that were round about them, and bowed themselves unto them, and provoked the Lord to anger. And they forsook the Lord, and served Baal and Ashtaroth."*

How sad! So soon after their great deliverance from Egypt and their entrance into the Promised Land, they were already worshipping Baal (the spirit or Nimrod) and Ashtoreth (Semiramis).

Over and over again in the Book of Judges we read the same story being repeated. God, in His anger, turns Israel over to the peoples and nations, whose gods they worshipped. They suffer great cruelty from the oppressor, repent, cry out to God; and God sends them a deliverer who successfully makes war against the oppressor and with His help delivers them by destroying the enemy. They live in peace as long as their deliverer is alive and as soon as he dies, they again fall back and worship other gods.

67

V. Gideon Redeems the Land (Judges 6)

It was during one of these times of oppression (when the Midianites ruled over them) that God heard their cries and sent an angel to call out Gideon, of the tribe of Manasseh, to deliver the children of Israel from the oppressor. Idolatry had so deeply infiltrated even the family of Gideon, that they had an altar to Baal and a grove. The word "grove" is *asherah* (842) in Hebrew. It was either a pillar or a symbol to the goddess Asherah who was a major Canaanite goddess associated with passion and the sea. She appears to have been the consort of Baal. They were worshipped together in Canaan. As we know that Baal was one of the titles of Nimrod and his consort was Semiramis, we can know then that the grove was a wooden symbol of worship to Semiramis.

The angel of the Lord commanded Gideon, *"Take thy father's young bullock, even the second bullock of seven years old, and throw down the altar of Baal that thy father hath, and cut down the grove that is by it: And build an altar unto the Lord thy God upon the top of this rock, in the ordered place, and take the second bullock, and offer a burnt sacrifice with the wood of the grove which thou shalt cut down"* (Judges 6:25, 26).

Before God could raise up Gideon and deliver the land, a sacrifice had to be made to cleanse the family and the land from the sin which had brought a curse on the land and the Children of Israel so that the blessings of God could come again upon Israel.

We know that when Gideon offered the sacrifice that the Spirit of the Lord came upon him, *"and he blew a trumpet and Abi-ezer was gathered after him"* (Judges 6:34).

VI. Samuel Redeems the Land (I Samuel 7:3-14)

Samuel, the mighty prophet and seer was raised up by the

Lord to lead Israel back to God. Because they had again reverted to worshipping Baal and Ashtoreth, Israel had again been oppressed by the Philistines when Samuel spoke to the House of Israel, *"If ye do return unto the Lord with all your hearts, then put away the strange gods and Ashtaroth from among you, and prepare your hearts unto the Lord, and serve him only: and he will deliver you out of the hand of the Philistines. Then the children of Israel did put away Baalim and Ashtaroth, and served the Lord only."* (I Samuel 7:3, 4).

They poured out a drink offering unto the Lord and fasted and repented of their sins (verse 6). When the Philistines heard about this gathering together in Mizpah, they prepared to wage war against Israel. Israel was full of fear and begged Samuel to pray for them. When the Philistine warlords were preparing to crush Israel, Samuel *"took a sucking lamb and offered it for a burnt offering wholly unto the Lord and Samuel cried unto the Lord for Israel, and the Lord heard him."* As Samuel was offering the sacrifice to the Lord, the Philistine army, with its giants were coming closer and closer, getting ready to attack Israel. Then the Lord thundered with a great thunder over their heads, terrifying them and they became confused and started fleeing away. Israel began to chase after them, killing many of them as they fled. *"So the Philistines were subdued, and they came no more into the coast of Israel: and the hand of the Lord was against the Philistines all the days of Samuel."* (I Samuel 7:13).

Samuel, by offering only one small baby lamb as a sacrifice, redeemed the land; and this turned God's favour towards them. He smote their enemy and gave them a great victory which resulted in many years of peace—even up to the time of Samuel's death. Then after his death, the Philistines came up again against Israel, and that was when David, who had been anointed by the anointed prophet Samuel, killed Goliath. David had the same

69

anointing on his life that Samuel did, and he was able to win many battles against the enemies of Israel.

VII. David Redeems the Land (II Samuel 21:1-14)

During David's reign there was a three-year famine in the land. This was undoubtedly caused by the lack of rain. David asked God to show him what the reason was for this time of suffering. God told him that it was the result of the innocent blood of the Gibeonites which King Saul, David's predecessor, had shed. The Gibeonites were the original natives of Gibeon who had tricked Joshua and the elders of Israel into making a peace agreement with them by saying they had heard how God was with Israel and they had come from a far country, when in truth, they were Canaanites. Joshua and the elders believed them, and they did not take counsel from the Lord. So they made a league of peace with them, which God honoured (Joshua 9:1-16).

Saul, in his religious and national zeal to establish Israel, slew many of the Gibeonites. Because of this shedding of innocent blood he had brought a curse on Israel and God had turned his face away from them. There was no blessing. So David, wisely asked the Gibeonites, *"What shall I do for you? and wherewith shall I make the atonement, that ye may bless the inheritance of the Lord?"* (II Samuel 21:3).

They answered, "You cannot pay for what Saul has done to us with Saul's silver and gold, nor his land nor inheritance, nor do we want you to kill any Israelite."

Then David answered, "I will do whatever you ask of me."

They replied to King David, "The man that consumed us, and that devised against us that we should be destroyed..., let seven of his sons be delivered unto us and we will hang them up before the Lord in Gibeon of Saul."

And the king did this. He handed over to the Gibeonites

70

seven of Saul's sons and grandsons and they died there in Gibeon where Saul had shed innocent blood—thus fulfilling Numbers 35:33, *"So ye shall not pollute the land wherein ye are: for blood it defileth the land: and the land cannot be cleansed of the blood that is shed therein, but by the blood of him that shed it."* Saul had died, so he could not atone for his sins, therefore his blood, which flowed in his offspring, had to be shed to redeem the land. *"And after that God was entreated for the land."* (II Samuel 21:14)

Today we do not need to shed human blood nor make this terrible kind of blood sacrifice to atone for the national sins of the land. Jesus is "the Son" who already died to atone for every man's sins. We only need to believe it, accept it and appropriate it. And we, too, will redeem the land and God will restore His favour and His blessing upon us.

VIII. Solomon's Dreadful Downfall and Its Consequences (I Kings 11:1-8)

When Solomon came to the throne, he was a humble and very wise young man who loved God with a very generous spirit (I Kings 3:3-15). His downfall began when he married an Egyptian princess, the daughter of Pharaoh (I Kings 3:1). He used the arm of flesh to create a diplomatic, peaceful relationship with Egypt.

Josephus says that it was still quite early in his reign when he became infatuated with many women. God had strictly warned the kings in Deuteronomy 17:16, 17, *"But he shall not multiply horses to himself, nor cause the people to return to Egypt, to the end that he should multiply horses: forasmuch as the Lord hath said unto you, Ye shall henceforth return no more that way. Neither shall he multiply wives to himself, that his heart turn not away: neither shall he greatly multiply to himself silver and gold."*

But Solomon disregarded both of these admonitions. Josephus says, "He grew mad in his love of women, and laid no restraint upon himself in his lusts; nor was he satisfied with the women of his country alone, but he married many wives out of foreign nations: Sidonians, Tyrians, and Ammonites and Edomites and he forsook the laws of Moses which forbade Jews to marry any but those who were of their own people. He also began to worship their gods which he did in order to gratify his wives, and out of his affection for them."

The Bible says, *"For Solomon went after Ashtoreth the goddess of the Zidonians, and after Milcom the abomination of the Ammonites. And Solomon did evil in the sight of the Lord, and went not fully after the Lord, as did David his father. Then did Solomon build a high place for Chemosh, the abomination of Moab, in the hill that is before Jerusalem, and for Molech, the abomination of the children of Ammon. And likewise did he for all his strange wives, which burnt incense and sacrificed unto their gods."* (I Kings 11:5-8)

It seems that the modest Jewish women did not give him the sexual thrills which these heathen women did. They came into his life, bringing their perversion and the spirits of lust with them. Soon he became possessed of demon spirits of lust and perversion. Demons of lust don't leave one because of old age. Neither do religious spirits leave people when the ones they possess go from one nation to another. I have seen that the Hindus are more zealous for their religion when they are away from India than they are in their own country. Their absence from their loved ones makes them more loyal to the religion of the family. This is true of all religions.

Because of this, these young girls whom Solomon married (many of them in their early teens) would be homesick for their families whom they had left behind, never to see again, to live with an old man who only used their young bodies to gratify his lustful desires, perhaps only once, before they would be

72

discarded and left to live in a harem with a lot of other lonely, jealous, fighting women. To pacify those who were his favourites, Solomon, in order to keep peace (remember he was the great peace-maker) compromised and built them "high places" or temples where they could worship their gods and goddesses. Although they came from many lands, they actually worshipped the same idols, only with different names.

Who Were These Gods?

1. Ashtoreth—The Goddess of the Zidonians:
Hislop says that Ashtoreth is just "the woman that made the encompassing wall."[2] That name and mural crown upon her head were surely very appropriate considering the glory given to her of her achievements in Babylon. It has been said that this goddess is the Semiramis, the goddess of love and lust, of the hunt and the original Jezebel spirit, even before the woman who married Ahab. Jezebel herself was the daughter of King Ethbaal of the Zidonians and her zeal for her religion when she married Ahab and left her homeland to live in Israel is well-known.

2. Milcom:
Milcom is just another name for Molech.

3. Chemosh—The Abomination of Moab:
Smith's Dictionary says that this "national deity of the Moabites also appears as the god of the Ammonites. He is also identified with Baal-peor, Baalzebub, Mars and Saturn." The Moabites were called the people of Chemosh (Numbers 21:29). The evil spirits like to have the people called after their names. In these days many nations will change their names. Some of them will be named after the demonic ruling spirit that is over that nation.

Remember, it was this god that had as his symbol a black

73

stone which was worshipped by the Arabs even before the days of Mohammed (*Smith's Bible Dictionary*, see the advertisement in the back of this book.). This idol represented Saturn.

4. Molech (or Moloch):

May day was the day that was dedicated to Bel. It is still called Beltane in some almanacs. This day was given to the worship of Bel. Both Bel and Molech are titles given to the same god. Molech was the god who demanded the sacrificing of humans, particularly innocent babes and children (preferably males). The pagans were taught by their priests that the souls were purified and their sins expiated if they "passed through the fire."

"Fire, thou doest expiate a sin against the gods; may this oblation be efficacious" is what the Hindus chant as they walk on fire.

Jeremiah 32:35 tells us that the people of Judah made their children "pass through the fire." Hislop says they believed that "all the strains produced by generations would be purged away and they would receive a 'light from divinity.' So the children would be purged from original sin, and through this 'purging' many a helpless babe became a victim to the bloody divinity." These were also the rites of Zoroaster, the god of fire, who was none other than Nimrod, for his name implies the "seed of Ashta." (Ashta was another name for Semiramis.)

I ask, is it from this pagan belief that the doctrine of purgatory (a place of purging by fire) came into the church which only became an actual dogma of the church in 1458 at the Council of Florence? Purgatory, it must be remembered is not hell. Pope Gregory, who claims to have discovered it about 600 A.D. describes it as "a third state of the soul," a place of purification of the souls before they entered Heaven.

The god Molech was the most dreaded of all gods. Milton describes the sentiments of multitudes in *Paradise Lost*,

74

"First Moloch, horrid king, besmeared with blood of human sacrifice, and parents' tears,

Though, for the noise of drums and timbrels loud,

Their children's cries unheard, that passed through fire

To his grim idol."

So powerful a hold did Molech have over Judah that two of their kings made their sons pass through the fire:

Ahaz—II Kings 16:3: *"But he walked in the way of the kings of Israel, yea, and made his son to pass through the fire, according to the abominations of the heathen, whom the Lord cast out from before the children of Israel."*

Manasseh—II Kings 21:6: *"And he made his son pass through the fire, and observed times, and used enchantments, and dealt with familar spirits and wizards: he wrought much wickedness in the sight of the Lord, to provoke him to anger."*

By this we understand that this degraded form of idolatry was also very prevalent in the ten northern tribes of Israel.

When Solomon built altars to these gods, he gave Molech and all these gods a legal right to rule over the people. **Satan can have no power over God's people unless we give him a legal right.**

IX. After Solomon

From the time of Solomon until Zedekiah, the last king of Judah, we have a history of repentance and backslidings. For every good king there were two or three bad ones who plunged the nation back into idolatry, bringing them under a curse. With idolatry came every form of sexual perversion.

Asa (I Kings 15:8-14), the good king (fourth from Solomon) took away the Sodomites and removed all the idols. He even removed his mother Maachah from her royal position as queen mother because she had made an idol to Ashtoreth which she worshipped. He destroyed her idol and burnt it (one must always

75

be sure to BURN idols). But he made one mistake. **He did not remove the high places.** By making this mistake, he gave the ruling spirits a legal right to return because their "roots" or their "base of operation" was still in the land. Sad to say, we see this story repeated over and over again in the lives of all the different kings of Judah.

X. Jehoshaphat (II Chronicles 20, I Kings 22:1-50)

This son of Asa was a good king. God gave him a great and miraculous deliverance from the enemy. But he "joined himself with Ahab." As a result of this friendship with Ahab, the royal house of Judah was joined in marriage to the wicked house of Ahab and Jezebel, for his son Jehoram married Athaliah, the daughter of Ahab and Jezebel.

XI. Jehoram (II Chronicles 21)

When he became king of Judah at his father's death, he was as much under the influence of his wife Athaliah as Ahab, king of the northern kingdom, had been under his wife (her mother) Jezebel. Athaliah incited Jehoram to commit murder. He murdered all his brethren and many of the princes of Judah (II Chronicles 21:4). The Bible says, *"And he walked in the way of the kings of Israel, like as did the house of Ahab: for he had the daughter of Ahab to wife: and he wrought that which was evil in the eyes of the Lord."* (II Chronicles 21:6). The curse of God fell upon him. He was afflicted with a grievous plague and his bowels fell out by reason of his sickness, so he died of a terrible disease. He was forty years old, having reigned only eight years. Ahaziah (also called Jehoash), his son, was made king. All his other sons had been killed by marauding bands of Arabians (II Chronicles 22:1).

76

XII. Ahaziah

Ahaziah, the son of Athaliah and Jehoram was twenty years old when he began to reign. He took his counsel from the wicked house of Ahab, to his destruction, which is no wonder when his grandmother was Jezebel. He went to war, gaining forces with his mother's brother, Jehoram (same name as his father), the king of Israel, against Syria. Jehoram of Israel was wounded in the battle. Ahaziah went to visit him and was assassinated by Jehu when he joined forces with his uncle, Jehoram, against Jehu.

XIII. Athaliah

As soon as Ahaziah's mother saw that her son was dead, she killed all the royal seed of the house of Judah (II Chronicles 22:10) She destroyed the house of God and dedicated the sacred things of the temple to Baal (II Chronicles 24:7). But there was one child she did not murder—that was the infant Joash, whom Jehoshabeath, the daughter of Jehoram, sister of Ahaziah and wife of Jehoida, the high priest, rescued and hid from Athaliah for six years in the house of God. He was crowned king at the age of seven (II Chronicles 24:1) at which time Athaliah was killed by the spiritual leaders of the land. And so, the "wicked woman," as the Bible calls her, died.

The ups and downs of Israel, the great revivals and terrible backslidings often depended on who was the ruling monarch. People in authority either give spirits the right to rule over a land, or they can rid the land of their evil dominion.

XIV. The Northern Kingdom—Ahab and Jezebel

Before concluding this chapter, I want to mention only one

77

important story in all the history of the Northern Kingdom of Israel.

Ahab, the son of Omri, was a weak and unrighteous king. His marriage to Jezebel, the idolatrous and wicked daughter of the king of Sidon, put him in complete bondage and servitude to her every whim. To please her, he built temples to her gods and worshipped them (I Kings 16:31, 33). Together, they brought such a terrible curse on the land that the heavens refused to give rain for three years. As Jezebel murdered the prophets, a reign of terror began. Elijah came forth prophesying fearlessly, even to Ahab.

The climax came when Elijah commanded Ahab to gather all the prophets of Baal to a great meeting on Mount Carmel. 950 prophets of Baal were challenged to prove that their god was the true god by sending down fire. After a day of frenzy and blood-letting, they gave up.

Elijah built an altar of twelve stones (one for each tribe of Israel), prepared his sacrifice, drenching it with twelve barrels of water, prayed one simple prayer, "Lord, God of Abraham, Isaac and of Israel, let it be known this day that thou art God in Israel, and that I am thy servant, and that I have done all these things at thy word. Hear me, O Lord, hear me, that this people may know that thou art the Lord God and that thou hast turned their heart back again."

Then the fire fell, consumed the burnt sacrifice and the wood and the stones and the dust and licked up the water that was in the trenches."

"And when all the people saw it, they fell on their faces: and they said, The Lord, he is the God; the Lord, he is the God." (I Kings 18:39)

Elijah put all the priests of Baal to death. They had to die, for they had caused much innocent blood to be shed in Israel through their sacrifices, and *"the land cannot be cleansed of*

78

the blood that is shed therein, but by the blood of him that shed it.'' (Numbers 35:33)

The land was redeemed. The rains came and God extended unto Israel another two hundred years—from B.C. 897 to B.C. 698, when they finally were carried into captivity because of their gross sins.

Today our western lands are standing at the brink of destruction. If we do not redeem the land, we will have no future. These are very serious times. May God help us to take warning and learn from the mistakes others have made in the past.

STUDY QUESTIONS

1. Read:
   Exodus 32
   Numbers 25:1-18
   Judges 6:1-35
   I Samuel 7:1-17
   II Samuel 21:1-14
   I Kings 11:1-8
   II Chronicles 20:1-23:21
   I Kings 22:1-50

2. In what way was Nimrod related
   a. to the golden calf (Exodus 32)
   b. to the sins of Israel with Baal-Peor (Numbers 25)
   c. to Israel in the time of the Judges (Judges 2:10-13)
   d. to the Manassite family of Gideon (Judges 6:25, 26)
   e. to the days of Samuel (I Samuel 7:4)?

3. How did the following redeem the land? Give Scripture references:
   a. Joshua
   b. Gideon
   c. Samuel
   d. David
   e. Elijah.

4. What was Solomon's most terrible sin?

5. Identify Ashtoreth, Milcom, Chemosh, Molech. How is Molech connected with Nimrod? How is Nimrod connected with Islam?

6. What was King Jehoshaphat's big mistake and how did it affect his descendents?

7. Make a simple chart of the family line of Ahab and Jehoshaphat.

8. Study the Chronology of Israel and Judah.

9. Memorize Joshua 24:15.

A carved cherub that decorated King Ahab's palace in Samaria, the capital of the Northern Kingdom of Israel (9th Century BC). It indicates the influence of pagan ideas on Israel at that time.

CHAPTER SIX

THINGS THAT GIVE THE EVIL SPIRITS
A LEGAL RIGHT TO SET UP A BASE OF OPERATION

The ruling spirits have no authority to move into an area without permission. Certain conditions give them authority to set up the base of their kingdom from whence they rule over the people in that area. What are those conditions?

I. Idolatry

"And God spake all these words, saying, I am the Lord thy God, which have brought thee out of the land of Egypt, out of the house of bondage. Thou shalt have no other gods before me. Thou shalt not make unto thee any graven image, or any likeness of any thing that is in heaven above, or that is in the earth beneath, or that is in the water under the earth. Thou shalt not bow down thyself to them, nor serve them: for I the Lord thy God am a jealous God, visiting the iniquity of the fathers upon the children unto the third and the fourth generation of them that hate me." (Exodus 20:1-5)

God had clearly commanded Israel that they must never have anything at all to do with any graven image. This is because idols represent evil spirits (I Corinthians 10:19, 20). Often the demon spirit is attached to a particular idol because the idol, after it is made, has been dedicated to that spirit. Therefore, it is his idol. He has a legal right to be anywhere where that idol is. That is why the idol must not be stored nor hidden away, smashed, thrown out, etc. It must be totally destroyed by fire (Deuteronomy 7:5).

On the mission field I have had the task of removing the idols from the homes of the converts. We did not take this task lightly. We knew the evil spirits whom these idols represented

81

lived in the house. When the idols would be cast out, these spirits would become very angry. Without the correct procedure there could be dire results. The Chinese knew enough stories of the activities of angry demons that they had respect for their powers. Many times these new-born Christians were afraid of these spirits. They did not know the Scriptures as well as we did, nor did they have the authority that comes with years of living an overcoming, Christian life.

When we came to a home that had to be cleansed of idols, the family was always gathered together, waiting. This was an important ceremony. It was not to be undertaken lightly. We first prayed together and claimed the protection of the blood of Jesus. The demons have more respect for it than many Christians do. Next, we sang a hymn like "There Is Power in the Blood." Then we read a Scripture such as Joshua 24:15, *"but as for me and my house, we will serve the Lord."* or Exodus 20:1-5. After that, in the Name of Jesus we would tear down the idols from their pedestals and places of pre-eminence, always saying, "In the Name of Jesus, I tear you down from your seat of authority and cast you from this household. Your spirit shall not rule over these people any more." We took the idols and all the emblems of worship connected with them outside, put them on a pile and burnt them right there if we were able to, or, in case of highrise apartments where it was impossible to burn them on the spot, they were carried off to be burnt elsewhere.

Then we invited the Lord and the angels to come into the home to protect it and bless it. Sometimes demons were seen leaving and angels coming in their place.

After that we sang and praised the Lord, dedicated the home to the Lord Jesus, and often hung a Scripture motto in the place of honour where the idol had been.

Some idols are worth fabulous amounts of money, but they should not be sold. God said they should be destroyed because the demonic ruling spirit to which they are dedicated will accompany them to the next place, bringing their evil powers and gaining a legal foothold in the area.

Our instructions for how to deal with idols are given in Deuteronomy 7:25, 26, *"The graven images of their gods shall ye burn with fire: thou shalt not desire the silver or gold that is on them, nor take it unto thee, lest thou be snared therein: for it is an abomination to the Lord thy God. Neither shalt thou bring an abomination into thine house, lest thou be a cursed thing like it: but thou shalt utterly detest it, and thou shalt utterly abhor it; for it is a cursed thing."*

II. Temples to Pagan Religions

We have been critical of King Solomon and the other Israelite kings who built high places, i.e. temples, to foreign gods, yet we have done the same thing in our Christian nations. We seem to have forgotten that our forefathers dedicated our nation to God. Now by our so-called broad-minded, liberal and humanistic attitudes which permit everyone to do whatever they please, we have accepted into our dedicated land the "abominable thing."

The Hindus build their temples and erect their gods and we make them objects of tourist attraction. We have either forgotten or have no understanding that we are giving the demon spirits of Nimrod, Semiramis, Molech, a legal base from which to operate. This has brought a curse upon our land. With the taking over of our land, there has come every kind of evil, such as debauchery, incest, illegal drugs, the worship of devils and a terrible scourge of witchcraft. The truth about Satan's advance on our western society is openly revealed in the bestseller *Gods of the New Age* by Caryl Matrisciana. (See the advertisement in the back of this book.)

God told Israel that they were responsible to enforce the laws of righteousness that He had given them and to make sure

83

that the foreigner who chose to dwell in Israel kept these same laws (Leviticus 18:26).

Afghanistan:

Afghanistan, one of the strongest Muslim nations, refused to permit a missionary to come into the country. Nevertheless there were some foreign workers there in places such as the U.S.A. Embassy. Because they wanted a place to worship on Sundays, they approached the authorities.

When President Eisenhower visited Afghanistan in 1959, he requested the permission of the Afghanistan government to allow a church to be built in Kabul. An agreement was made that if we in the U.S.A. would allow a mosque to be built in Washington, D.C., they would reciprocate by giving us the rights to build a Christian Church in Kabul. The building plans were signed by the Mayor of Kabul. I saw the building as it was going up and ministered to the congregation the last week of September 1969. The building was dedicated to God on May 17, 1970. Thousands, all over the world, had sacrificed to see this vision completed. Three years later June 15, the government deliberately destroyed it with a bulldozer. I believe that the Russian invasion into Afghanistan is a judgment of God on a nation that persecuted to death its own people who became Christians and also because they broke the covenant. Today we still have their mosque in Washington, D.C.

Muslim Revival:

Today there is a world-wide revival of Islam. Even in Japan, thousands are leaving Buddhism and becoming Moslems. England has thousands of mosques and even in Rome the Arabs are planning to build a mosque which will almost supercede St. Peters.

In the U.S.A. the United Nations has opened the door for the pagans to come and bring their religious spirits with them.

84

We are living in a time when, in the name of the ancient customs of the natives, demon spirits, which formerly were conquered and subdued, are again having a revival.

Peyotism:

For example in the U.S.A. and Canada, the ancient religion of the American Indians is being revived all over our nation.

What is Peyotism? The Encyclopedia Britannica gives a very good description of this once almost-dead but now very much alive religion of the American Indians. The peyote is a cactus plant, native to Mexico and southwestern U.S. "when eaten it produces extraordinary psychophysiological effects which vary with the local situation. Effects reported from laboratory studies differ from those observed under ritual conditions." (This is understandable because in rituals, spirits are summoned, a thing which does not take place in a scientific laboratory.) The drug in the peyote plant is classified by pharmacologists as an hallucinating agent.

The new revival of peyotism is very different to the former religion practiced by the early ancestors of our present-day Indians. The present-day peyotism is more demonic and thus more evil. Formerly peyote was used primarily as a medicine and to induce visions by those who were seeking supernatural revelations. It was also used in groups to help in tribal rites, evidently to induce a trance state. In the old days this religion extended from New Mexico to Oklahoma. By 1960 the old form of worship had almost disappeared, except for traces of it in Mexico.

The new form of peyotism sprang up about 1850. The religious rites include prayer, singing and meditation, centered on the peyote as a symbol of **spirits being worshipped and as a sacrament.** It developed as a religion about 1885 among the Kiowa and Comanche in Oklahoma. After 1891 it spread rapidly and became the most widespread indigenous Indian

85

religion, extending from the Great Lakes to the Rocky Mountains of Canada and south to the Sierra Nevada Mountains in the U.S. In 1918 it was incorporated as *The Native American Church* in Oklahoma. By 1960 it claimed 200,000 members.

Most peyotists consider themselves Christians, holding peyotism to be the Indian version of Christianity. Peyotist doctrine or religious theory consists of a belief in the existence of power, spirits and incarnation of powers. By "power" they mean "the immaterial and invisible supernatural force that produces characteristic effects and can be transferred from one thing to another under the proper ritual condition." They believe "Man needs power to be successful and healthy. Without it he becomes unsuccessful and ill.'" They worship the Indian and white spirits to obtain this power which gives them success and good health. Oklahoma seems to be the base from which these deceiving spirits operate to induce men to seek **success and good health**, the chief aim of the peyote religion and their symbol of spirituality. Apparently, the spirits of success, power (over the souls of men) and good health have a strong base established in that area. The worshipper eats peyote under the proper ritual conditions in order to obtain power to commune with God **and other spirits.** Often the individual went off into isolation and subjected himself to ordeals so that he would be pitied by the spirits "until some **spirit would appear** to him in a vision and give him **personal power.**" They believe that disease is produced, either by insufficient power, or by a foreign object, e.g. a curse.

Peyotism was considered wrong by the early Christian forefathers. The sale or use of peyote was prohibited in fifteen states. By the 1960s, the states of Oklahoma, Iowa, Montana, New Mexico, Texas and Utah had revised laws to allow peyote in relogous services. **The U.S. Congress has rejected nine bills that would have prohibited the use, sale and transport of peyote.**

86

Why is it so important for them to use peyote? Because it induces a trance-like state, and when the faculties of the senses and mind and will are not in full control, the spirits can come in and possess the worshipper. This causes demon possession and much sin and evil.

Areas given over to Peyotism become key bases for spirits to operate because they have been invited to come by the worshippers of Peyotism. For further information on this subject I recommend *Crying Wind*, a biographical novel which gives insight into American Indian culture. (See the advertisement in the back of this book.)

III. Murder, i.e. the Shedding of Innocent Blood

Exodus 20:13 clearly and emphatically says, ***"Thou shalt not kill."*** It was one of the ten commandments which God gave Moses for the whole world. The ten commandments were laws, not only for Israel, but for all nations, to live by.

Murder brings a curse. When Cain killed his brother Abel, God said, *"And now art thou cursed from the earth, which hath opened her mouth to receive thy brother's blood from thy hand"* (Genesis 4:11). It wasn't God who cursed him, it was the earth *adamah* (127), the dust of the ground out of which Cain was made. The evil deed which Cain had done, the anger and hatred that he had permitted Satan to put in his soul, had contaminated his own being so that the *adamah*, out of which he was created, cursed him. God said, "Thou art cursed from the *adamah*."

Murder is the shedding of innocent blood in a violent way. Blood does not need "to pour out" from the victim. Any kind of murder is evil and brings a curse.

In Numbers 35 God provided Cities of Refuge for the one who had innocently shed blood, to be able to flee to, for refuge. They had to stay there until the death of the high priest and then they could return home (Numbers 35:28).

After the flood God told Noah, *"Whoso sheddeth man's blood, by man shall his blood be shed: for in the image of God made he man."* (Genesis 9:6). This law was reinforced through God's command to Moses. The reason God said this, was because there is life in the blood (Leviticus 17:11): *"For the life of the flesh is in the blood: and I have given it to you upon the altar to make an atonement for your souls: for it is the blood that maketh an atonement for the soul."*

"For the life of all flesh is in the blood thereof: whosoever eateth it shall be cut off." (Leviticus 17:14b) The word "life" is *nephesh* (5315) in Hebrew, which carries the meaning of spirit, soul. When God created Adam, God breathed into him the breath of life, and man became a living soul (*nephesh*, 5315). There was a direct impartation of God-life (*nephesh*) into the blood of human beings, making man a higher creation than animals. This life of God is in our blood. Our blood keeps us alive. If blood does not reach any of our body's cells, that part dies. When we murder or kill someone, we are killing an extension of God, for man is made in the image of God. The only way that this great crime can be atoned for is by the murderer, himself, giving his life in payment for the one he killed. That was Old Testament law.

Today, Jesus has died for all men's transgressions and sins, including the sin of murder. If anyone accepts the shed Blood of Jesus in payment for his own crime of murder, that one can go free of the judgment. That is the only condition under which he can escape great punishment. He has to acknowledge that Jesus suffered in his place. The law is "a life for a life" (Deuteronomy 19:21), either the life of Christ, or the murderer's. For more information read all of Numbers 35.

Knowing this foundational truth, how dreadful is the sin of murder! It brings a curse on the doer, and on the place where the murder has been committed.

Satan wants to bring God's curse on people and nations and

the land. He knows that the shedding of innocent blood will work quickly to turn the favour of God away from us. Satan uses wars, riots, rebellion, the sacrifices of humans in satanic rites, and angers which result in murder. Satan's master stroke took place in the U.S.A. on January 22, 1973 when the US Supreme Court made a ruling which made abortion prior to the last ten weeks of birth (delivery) legal. In this way, murder was legalized by the leaders of our nation. They overruled the laws of God.

Since then, 25 million souls have been destroyed. This nation has brought a curse on itself, like no nation ever has in all history. And if shedding innocent blood causes a curse, then our doctors and nurses who commit this crime are cursed, our hospitals and clinics, where abortions take place, are cursed, the Supreme Court is cursed, the wombs of those who became the base area where the crime took place are cursed, and anyone who helps and co-operates with this evil is cursed.

We have given Satan a legal right over our nation, our cities, our government and our lives. His spirits of murder have been unleashed to destroy freely any life Satan wants to extinguish. Satan has caused murder to be so commonplace that today, because of our laws against capital punishment, the murderer is allowed to live, even though God said, *"the murderer shall surely be put to death."* (Numbers 35:17).

We have reversed the laws of God by suffering the murderer to live, and killing the innocent.

"And those which remain shall hear, and fear, and shall henceforth commit no more any such evil among you." (Deuteronomy 19:20)

Murder pollutes the land. The death of the slayer redeems the land from the curse. *"So ye shall not pollute the land wherein ye are: for blood it defileth the land; and **the land cannot be cleansed** of the blood that is shed therein, but by the blood of him that shed it."* (Numbers 35:33)

89

Crime is on the increase because we do not punish the evildoer and it will continue to increase until violence takes over our cities and the streets flow with blood.

IV. Witchcraft and Covens

Satanism and witchcraft is multiplying across our lands at such a drastic rate that it is appalling. Even the educated are enticed into it by their desire to delve into the unknown. In Great Britain alone, an estimated 40,000 people are involved in witchcraft and magic. This is more than in all Africa.

Covens are being established throughout our nations. Wherever there is a witches' coven, the spirits have a legal right to invade that territory. Every centre of witchcraft is a base for satanic operation. At first, Satan only demands the blood sacrifice of animals such as dogs, cats and the domesticated beasts of the field, but as soon as he gets control, he demands human sacrifices—preferably innocent children. The astronomical amount of abduction and disappearance of children cannot solely be blamed on runaways, divorced parents who take their children secretly; and sex perverts who steal them to abuse them. Many end up on the altars of Satan. Satanists have even taken over some of our churches to perform their satanic rites. With the slaughter of every child, the spirits gain a legal stronghold over that area (Leviticus 20:6). Witchcraft is the outright worship of Satan.

V. Psychotronic Warfare

For most of us the name is new, but the origin of it is as ancient as sorcery. It is the latest in warfare. According to David Lewis in his recent book, published by New Leaf Press, *Smashing the Gates of Hell in the Last Days*[1] (see the advertisement in the back of this book), the Soviets are trying to link the human mind with computers, tap into the ESP factor of the human mind, and with the use of powerful "psychotronic generators" use this sheer mental energy as a weapon of war. Mr. Lewis points out that there are two sources of power available to man, the power of God and the power of Satan. Christians are exhorted to have "the mind of Christ" (I Corinthians 2:16). When man was driven out of the Garden of Eden after the Fall, God took from him the right to eat from the tree of the knowledge of good and evil.

Ever since then, Satan has tempted man to accept clairvoyance and other satanic supernatural miracle-working powers that work through the mind. Now, the Russians are using this satanic power. They have laboratories where their technicians work at many kinds of warfare such as how to kill people (they can cause heart attacks artificially), changing the weather, (causing as much as nine feet of snow-fall to stop all travel in days of war), influencing the brains of people (thus making puppets out of them), and sending killers who will work like an automaton in the hands of another man who sits in Moscow and directs him to kill someone in the United States. They can change depressions into happiness and enthusiasm, create artificial joy and, from far away, impress soldiers or officers to push the button or not. They can cause massive electrical blackouts (such as have happened unexplainably in the U.S.A.), get information through astro-projection into highly-classified meetings, influence our senators and congressmen in their vote, hypnotize and control important leaders, control masses of people (thereby instigating mass riots to overthrow governments) and to disable our weapon system and space programme without physically touching anything. If they can bend a spoon by the power of the mind, they can destroy highly technical electronics.

The tragic thing is that the U.S.A. is spending large sums of money to get into this demonic war race with the Soviets.

91

Mr. Lewis' book gives amazing facts on our own government's involvement in this satanic type of warfare.

I ask you, can we fight the devil with the help of the devil? One of the most revolting facts is that, in order to protect ourselves, the U.S. Air Force seriously considered the "psychic shield" for its missile crewmen. The shields produced by a member of the United States Psychotronic Association would be activated by a drop of blood, hair or other organic matter from the subject. This is none other than powerful witchcraft. May America turn back to God!

We Christians are the only ones with the power to fight against the demonic forces of Satan. What will happen after the rapture takes place and the sinners and backsliders are left behind? Who will fight these demons then? What power will hold back the antichrist once He that restraineth him now is taken away?

Our military, by turning to Satan for help, is giving him a legal right to destroy us. In the end, our military leaders and our nation will be destroyed, just like Hitler and Germany were, for Hitler also got his guidance from demonic spirits. On this subject of Hitler, I would like to recommend *The Twisted Cross* by Joseph J. Carr (see the advertisement in the back of this book).

VI. The Removal of Prayer and Bible Reading From Our Schools

God told the Children of Israel that their children must be taught the Word of God (Exodus 12:26-28, Deuteronomy 4:9, 6:7). As long as our children had the Bible and prayer in their classrooms, there was a special spiritual covering and protection over them. From the day that prayer and Bible reading was taken out of our schools, our educational system became a vacuum for spirits to fill with their evil substitutes. Instead of Bible and

92

prayer, our children are subjected to such things as Transcendental Meditation, Yoga, pagan religions, misguided and immorally-taught sex education (which encourages sodomy and masturbation in the name of "alternative life-style"), promotes promiscuity, resulting in teen-age pregnancies (with their accompanying consequences of abortion and other tragedies). Witchcraft, satanism, and magic is a part of the educational curriculum. (There is no such thing as "white magic.") Crime has increased in the schools, to such a degree that some of our schools in our larger cites need to be policed by the law enforcement officers. The teaching of "death" classes has no doubt promoted suicides (some even taking place in front of the horrified eyes of the students in the classroom). There has been a lowering of the dress code, and even the disgusting trend of co-ed dormitories.

One of the most treacherous substitutes for the Word of God is humanism. Humanism is Satan's sugar-coated poisonous "pill" of rebellion against all good traditions and teachings. As Paul Kurtz, a confirmed humanist, said, "Secular humanists are committed to the use of reason and science to understand the world and solve social problems without 'the illusion of salvation or morality.' " When we assume God's position and take it upon ourselves to solve problems which only deity can handle, we make ourselves out to be gods. The worship of self is dangerously evil; if we continue in this way, we will destroy ourselves. Humanism has not only invaded our schools, it has gained acceptance in the church. Most Sunday morning sermons by both Protestant and Catholic clergy are totally humanistic.

VII. Adultery, Sodomy, Perversion And All Sexual Sins

1. Adultery:
There must be a sound and reasonable purpose that God commanded the adulterer to be put to death. *"And the man that*

93

committeth adultery with another man's wife, even he that committeth adultery with his neighbour's wife, the adulterer and the adulteress shall surely be put to death.'' (Leviticus 20:10)

Adultery causes angers, deep, deep griefs, terrible heartaches, despair, the break-up of homes, poverty and many other negative results. Adultery wears down the moral strength of man, church and nation. Ninety-nine percent of the time adultery is caused by the demon spirit of lust. Therefore, it gives the demon spirit a legal base from which to operate.

2. *Sodomy:*

Leviticus 18:22 says, *"Thou shalt not lie with mankind, as with womankind: it is abomination.''*

Sodomy is one of the most evil, disgusting, binding sins because it is more than an act of transgression. A spirit of perversion goes with it, a spirit so old that it dates from the days of Ham. Behind sodomy is the evil sin of rebellion, disrespect and perversion. The spirits that are of this type are the most unclean and disgusting spirits of the spirit world. They cause the breakdown of normal family life. God created Eve for Adam. Woman, God's most perfect, loving created gift, was His gift to man. When men reject women and turn to their own sex for sexual gratification, they are rejecting God's gift and become worshippers of their own bodies. They "love" their own bodies.

God says that those who commit the sin of sodomy are given over *"to uncleanness, through the lusts of their own hearts, to dishonour their own bodies between themselves; Who changed the truth of God into a lie, and worshipped and served the creature more than the Creator, who is blessed for ever. Amen. For this cause God gave them up unto vile affections: for even their women did change the natural use into that which is against nature: And likewise also the men, leaving the natural use of the woman, burned in their lust one toward another; men with*

94

men working that which is unseemly, and receiving in themselves that recompense of their error which was meet. And even as they did not like to retain God in their knowledge, God gave them over to a reprobate mind, to do those things which are not convenient.'' (Romans 1:24-28) Then follows a horrendous list of evils (some of which are evil spirits) which take over in the life of sodomites. Demon spirits always make room for other demon spirits.

God, knowing how this evil would spread, passed judgment on the lawbreakers. God said, *''There shall be no whore of the daughters of Israel, nor a sodomite of the sons of Israel.''* (Deuteronomy 23:17).

Sodomy and prostitutes are identical twins. They both "sell" or "rent" their organs of reproduction to satisfy perverted spirits of lust. Only the price varies. Leviticus 20:13, *''If a man also lie with mankind, as he lieth with a woman, both of them have committed an abomination: they shall surely be put to death; their blood shall be upon them.''* The punishment for sodomy was the same as for murder and adultery. The sexual act in marriage is a sacrament. The sexual act of sodomy is an abomination. *''Thou shalt not lie with mankind, as with womankind: it is abomination.''* (Leviticus 18:22) Abomination in Hebrew is *towebah* (8441). It is something which is morally disgusting. It comes from the root word *taab* (8581)—"to loath, detest, to morally abhor." The Revised Standard Version translates the verb as "prostitute" in Ezekiel 16:25. Sodomy and prostitution are connected with the pagan temple rites. Both received official sanction from the Canaanite religion. During the Kali Festival in India today there are seasons of sexual orgy associated with Astarte (Ashtoreth, i.e. Semiramis).

3. Incest, Bestiality:

Sexual intercourse within the family members is called incest. Leviticus 18 and 20 warns strictly against this sin and

95

decrees the death sentence as the punishment for these sins.

I have met so many women whose lives and personalities were terribly scarred, and sometimes even destroyed, by the older male members of the family who sexually abused them as children. The church needs to preach against these evils because this sin has even come into the church. Some of the most guilty are "respected" church men and priests.

Bestiality will unleash dreadful plagues that will destroy a nation because there is a breakdown of the laws of procreation that decrees that each should produce after his kind (Genesis 1:25). By transgressing these high laws we give the spirits of bestiality a legal right to possess us and have dominion over us.

I recommend *Honor Thy Father??* by Meridel Rawlings. This is a true story of a pastor who sexually abused his ten and 12-year-old daughters for a period of three years before he was found out; and even then, he refused to repent because he felt he had done no harm! How deceptive these demons of incest can be!

VIII. Alcoholism, Hypnosis, the Use of Drugs (Both Illegal and Prescription)

You may be surprised to find these three linked together. The reason I have linked them together is because all three work the same effects on a person's mind. They cause the person to enter a mental stage of illusion and unreality where they lose control of their inner moral strength. They cause people to do things that they would normally never do. It usually results in tragedy.

I would like to share with you the testimony of Dr. Ritchie, who witnessed the spirits' takeover and possession of a man who was intoxicated. This explains why people who are drunk become violent and dangerous. The evil spirit has control of them. This also explains why, even when a moral person drinks

96

too much, he can easily be influenced to commit adultery. It is, for example, dangerous to drink in bars with the world. One can easily lose control and be persuaded to do things which one would later deeply regret.

Dr. Ritchie had a life-after-death experience which he tells about in *Return from Tomorrow.* In his spirit body (after he died) he was allowed to witness strange things. This scene takes place in a bar room. God allowed him to witness this extremely sad scene.

Dr. Ritchie tells how Jesus drew him inside a dingy bar (near a large naval base). He saw that the living people were surrounded by a faint luminous glow like an electrical field over the entire surface of their bodies. His own spirit-body did not have it. Neither did the other spirits which he saw. Jesus was accompanying him in this experience.

At this point the Light drew me inside a dingy bar and grill near what looked like a large naval base. A crowd of people, many of them sailors, lined the bar three deep, while others jammed wooden booths along the wall. Though a few were drinking beer, most of them seemed to be belting whiskies as fast as the two perspiring bartenders could pour them.

Then I noticed a striking thing. A number of the men standing at the bar seemed unable to lift their drinks to their lips. Over and over I watched them clutch at their shot glasses, hands passing through the solid tumblers, through the heavy wooden countertop, through the very arms and bodies of the drinkers around them.

And these men, every one of them, lacked the aureole of light that surrounded the others.

Then I realized the cocoon of light must be a property of physical bodies only. The dead, we who had lost our solidness, had lost this ''second skin'' as well. And it was obvious that these living people, the light-surrounded ones, the ones actually drinking, talking, jostling each other, could neither see the

97

desperately thirsty disembodied beings among them, nor feel their frantic pushing to get at those glasses. (Though it was also clear to me, watching, that the non-solid people could both see and hear each other. Furious quarrels were constantly breaking out among them over glasses that none could actually get to his lips.)

I thought I had seen heavy drinking at fraternity parties in Richmond, but the way civilians and servicemen at this bar were going at it beat everything. I watched one young sailor rise unsteadily from a stool, take two or three steps, and sag heavily to the floor. Two of his buddies stooped down and started dragging him away from the crush.

But that was not what I was looking at. I was staring in amazement as the bright cocoon around the unconscious sailor simply opened up. It parted at the very crown of his head and began peeling away from his head, his shoulders. Instantly, quicker than I'd ever seen anyone move, one of the insubstantial beings who had been standing near him at the bar was on top of him. He had been hovering, like a thirsty shadow at the sailor's side, greedily following every swallow the young man made. Now he seemed to spring at him like a beast of prey.

In the next instant, to my utter mystification, the springing figure had vanished. It all happened even before the two men had dragged their unconscious load from under the feet of those at the bar. One minute I had distinctly seen two individuals; by the time they propped the sailor against the wall, there was only one.

Twice more, as I stared, stupefied, the identical scene was repeated. A man passed out, a crack swiftly opened in the aureole around him, one of the non-solid people vanished as he hurled himself at that opening, almost as if he had scrambled inside the other man.

Was that covering of light some kind of shield, then? Was it a protection against disembodied beings like myself?

Presumably these substance-less creatures had once had solid bodies, as I myself had had. Suppose that when they had been in these bodies they had developed a dependence on alcohol that went beyond the physical. That became mental. Spiritual, even. Then when they lost that body, except when they could briefly take possession of another one, they would be cut off for all eternity from the thing they could never stop craving.[2]

IX. Fighting, Angers, Quarrelsomeness, Hatred And An Unforgiving Spirit

All these strong, negative emotions give Satan a legal right to a person. A home where there is fighting and quarrelling becomes an early prey of the devil.

When I was in Malawi, Central Africa, a former wizard who had once had great demonic powers told me that when the spirits that controlled him wanted to do a work of evil upon the people, they looked for those who were quarrelling among themselves. It was from those kinds of people that the spirits selected the ones they abducted to be used as blood sacrifices to Satan, because they had no right nor power over those who lived in harmony and love.

There are many Christian families who need to have their relationships corrected. We need to make peace (where possible) with those with whom we have had disagreements. There are cases where we can do nothing to correct a painful relationship, and we have to shake the dust of the past off our feet and walk on, but we must be careful never to hold a grudge nor bitterness in our hearts.

Never go to sleep without confessing your sins. Unconfessed sins, even in the heart of Christians, can give the spirits a legal foothold. We must always "examine ourselves," as the Bible says in I Corinthians 11:28 because if we are careless about this area of purity in our lives, Satan has every right to strike us with

99

sickness or demon possession. Paul said that if we take Holy Communion with Jesus (He is always our unseen Guest at every Communion Table) in an unworthy manner, we eat and drink damnation unto ourselves and we shall be judged (I Corinthians 11:27-30). He even said this could cause untimely deaths. The burden of unconfessed sin troubles the heart much more than we can ever realize. It is a medical fact that the majority of men who die of heart attacks during sexual intercourse are with someone other than their wives. The guilt of sin is a "killer" and destroyer of true happiness.

I believe that the unconfessed and unrepented sins of the Christians give Satan a lot more authority over us than we ever realize. If we could see the consequences of our pride and love of self, we would be filled with remorse and regret. May God help us, as Christians, to never give Satan a legal right to come into our lives, families and churches!

X. Objects Used in Connection with Black Magic, Witchcraft, Satan Worship, Idolatry

We touched briefly on this subject in point I. of this chapter, but I feel we need to repeat it here under this heading. When an object is used in connection with the spirit world, it is dedicated to the devil. From that time on his spirits are commanded to stay and work with that particular thing. Temple idols, house-gods, instruments used in connection with worship, crystal balls, ouija boards, tarot cards, some works of art, and even buildings have demonic connections. The list can go on and on. I remember one time feeling an evil, demonic presence hovering near a beautiful painting of the famous and well-loved musician Ludwig von Beethoven. The man in whose house the painting hung was a high school teacher. A spirit of melancholy came on him and he hid himself in his bedroom and refused

100

to get out of bed for many weeks, except for necessary reasons. His wife finally left him. I had told them to take out the picture and destroy it. They took it out of the house, but stored it in the garage. The man could not be helped. I do not know why this particular portrait had a demonic presence, nor if it had anything to do with Beethoven himself. God did not reveal to me what the connection was, but I was not the only one who sensed that evil spirit's presence in connection with this painting.

The British Encyclopedia says, "Hélène von Breuning, who was something of a second mother to him, states that in boyhood Beethoven would be overcome by fits of rage. He was in no mood, during these seizures, to listen to reason; she had to wait until they subsided. This inner tension was not reduced with the years nor was his violent temper; they were inclined to be exacerbated by his deafness. He would fly into a rage if he felt slighted, or if he felt aspersions had been cast on his honour or responsibility, though in matters of social standing there was never any question of snobbery. He was aware of these outbursts, of course; indeed, he was sometimes ashamed of them and would try to make amends."

Could that have some connection with what we all felt that day as we looked at the portait?

XI. Satanically Inspired Toys

I call them by that name because there is no other possible reason that anyone could invent such hideous play-things for our children. Some of them look like actual demons. From the day that E.T. was released in our theatres, we have seen a plague of devils and demons on the market. Less evil-looking toys, such as Smurfs, Care-Bears, Cabbage-Patch dolls, and numerous other "toys" have become the "darlings" of our children. Parents buy them for their demanding children, not realizing what they

101

are doing, nor the danger that they are putting into the arms of their precious children.

Reports have come to us of how some of these "innocent looking" creatures have injured and even murdered the child who owns them. They are as dangerous in the home as a pagan idol that has been dedicated to Satan. Parents need to destroy them by fire. Shirley Smith, a Spirit-filled woman from Little Rock, Arkansas, has been warning Christians about these things and the video games for several years. I also would like to recommend *Turmoil in the Toy Box* by Phil Phillips (see the advertisement in the back of this book).

XII. Movies, Magazines, Music, Etc.

There is no doubt that spirits of violence and lust accompany the conception and production of some of our movies, theatrical performances, television programmes and printed materials. Pornographic magazines and films stir up spirits of lust. In the same way, pictures of luscious chocolate cake, charbroiled hamburgers and coca-cola ads give you a hunger and thirst for these things. Pictures of nudity and violence work on those who devour this type of "garbage." You become what you eat (physically and spiritually). The spirits who inspired the production of those evil things also accompany them, and seek to destroy unhappy, discontent, rebellious and frustrated souls.

Rock music with its subliminal message (which is hidden by its backward masking) has destroyed many lives. Much of that music has been dedicated to Satan. His evil spirits, therefore, have every right to accompany these recordings. I know a young lad who, when the Lord convicted him that these records were wrong, decided to destroy them. When he went into his bedroom to get his LPs, he saw a demonic spirit standing in the corner of the room beside them, and it seemed to be protecting them. However, when he destroyed them, that demon left the house.

102

Parents are responsible to supervise the music their children listen to and on which they spend their money.

XII. Relationships

The relationships we keep with others have a very definite influence on us—either for good or for bad. The Word of God discourages God's people from making intimate alliances with the ungodly or those who would be a bad influence on us. In Israel, God told His people to set the leper outside the camp. This was to protect the healthy from being infected with the deadly, then incurable, disease (Leviticus 13:5, 21, 33, 46, Numbers 5:3).

Remember what happened to Samson when he fell in love with Delilah (Judges 16:20-31)! Someone has said, "The devil has a woman for every man of God." That woman may even be a Christian woman. She may not have an evil heart. It could just take her moral weakness and his passion to make a union that would destroy him forever. Look at Abraham and Hagar. David and Bathsheba, the man in the Church of Corinth and his father's wife (I Corinthians 5:1), and others. Even today, many fine ministers of the Gospel have "played with fire" and got burned so badly that they can no longer serve God in the ministry, and their lives are ruined forever.

Satan uses our passions and naivete to lead God's people into unholy relationships. Don't make yourself available for the devil to destroy your life and maybe even your soul.

Satan has a legal right to destroy every marriage that is out of the will of God. We cannot emphasize too strongly the importance of marriage between those of like faith. *"Be ye not unequally yoked together with unbelievers: for what fellowship hath righteousness with unrighteousness? and what communion hath light with darkness? And what concord hath Christ with Belial? or what part hath he that believeth with an infidel? And*

103

what agreement hath the temple of God with idols? for ye are the temple of the living God; as God hath said, I will dwell in them, and walk in them; and I will be their God, and they shall be my people.'' (II Corinthians 6:14-16)

Inordinate Affections:

Whenever the devotion between two people is greater than their love for God, Satan has a legal right to bind them together with such strong soul-ties that both will be blinded to the truth and to purity. There can be unholy and unclean relationships even between two people of the same sex—relationships which will pull both persons down. It is better for some people to be separated from each other because of the bad influence they have on each other. For example, Simeon and Levi (Genesis 49:5-7).

XIV. Uncontrolled Emotions

It is important that we train our children in temperance when they are young. If we allow them to have temper tantrums, spoil them by giving them everything they want, and allowing them to do anything they want to do, and never correct them, we are raising wild monsters who will be so lawless and unrestrained that they will become totally demon-possessed. A small child, who is allowed to throw his dinner plate on the floor in a temper tantrum without being corrected, will pull the tablecloth with all the fine china off the table when he is a grown man. The child who is allowed to scream at his parents in a rage will curse them when he can talk.

I have heard of ministers of the Gospel who are so vulgar, when they lose their tempers, that one can hardly believe that they are Christians. God said that he who curses his parents should be put to death (Leviticus 20:9). God knows that anger and cursing allow the demon spirits to take over our emotions.

This opens our soul to demons, because our emotions are the expression of our soul.

STUDY QUESTIONS

1. Read:
   Exodus 20:1-17
   Numbers 35:1-34
   Leviticus 18:1-30
   Leviticus 20:1-27
   Joshua 1:8
   Exodus 12:26, 27;
   Deuteronomy 4:8, 6:7, 11:19
   Romans 1:18-32.

2. Can evil spirits attack just anyone at any time?

3. What are twelve things that give demon spirits a legal right to set up their base of operation?

4. Give a Scripture against idolatry. Why are idols dangerous?

5. How are pagan temples and mosques corrupting our land?

6. Give a brief description of Peyotism.

7. What is murder? Why does it defile the land? How can it be atoned for? In what way has murder brought great evil upon the land?

8. What have been the consequences of stopping prayer and Bible reading in our schools?

9. In what way are alcohol, drugs and hypnosis connected?

10. Why are idolatry and sexual perversion related?

11. Memorize Deuteronomy 11:19.

CHAPTER SEVEN

RANKS OF DEMONIC RULING SPIRITS

Demons have a caste system. A caste system is determined from birth. One can never rise above his caste. Hinduism, the oldest pagan religion, which dates back to the days of Nimrod and Semiramis, resembles the original satanic caste system. All other false religions have their roots in Hinduism (which had its origin in Nimrod's Apostate religion). Even the Babylonian (so-called Christian) church has many of the original trappings of the religion of Nimrod still in it. That is why the Holy Spirit calls her the whore (**the mother of harlots**) and commands the true believers to come out of her, lest they be defiled by her, and in the end be judged with her (Revelation 17:5, 18:4).

Each rank of spirits wants to be greater and higher and each rank holds those in the rank beneath them in contempt. There is absolutely no love, affection or any other of the fruits of the Spirit in the demonic spirit world. There isn't the smallest trace of **love, joy, peace, longsuffering, gentleness, goodness, faith, meekness, temperance** in their demonic characters. The only time they co-operate with each other is when they have orders from their master to conspire together to destroy a person or a ministry. Then the spirits of the different ranks co-operate until they get the job done or are defeated (a thing they hate to have happen because they will suffer great humiliation and punishment from their evil master). I recommend *The Screwtape Letters* by C.S. Lewis (see the advertisement in the back of this book.)

The Five Ranks

When Howard Pittman, who formerly worked in law enforcement, died because of a sudden rupture of an internal

107

artery while six doctors worked desperately to try to save his life, his spirit was lifted out of his body and taken to the second heaven. He was permitted to see into the spirit world of the demons. The angel of the Lord who accompanied him showed him the five ranks of evil spirits who will play the most prominent role in these end-times. (For further information read *Demons, An Eyewitness Account* by Howard Pittman. See the advertisement in the back of this book.)

I. First Rank—The Warring Spirit:

Howard Pittman saw him dressed in the uniform of the Roman soldier. These are great, eight-foot-tall, athletic type, beautifully constructed spirits who still retain much of their original angel shape and form. They are very powerful. They are the princes who have a seat on the ruling council of Satan's government. They have absolutely no love. Hate is the motivating factor of these spirits. Their eyes are full of hatred. They possess and control the earthly rulers of the nations. Daniel met up with one of them, the prince of Persia, when he fasted for 21 days for the release of the Jews from the Babylonian Captivity (Daniel 10:13). Because of his great hold over God's people, it took the power of a long fast by Daniel, with the divine help of a heavenly being who wrestled with the spirit prince of Persia, for the Jews to be released from the Babylonian captivity. When this mighty warring prince was bound and dislodged, Cyrus proclaimed liberty to the Jews and they were released to return to Judea. This same prince is playing a very important role in these end-times. He is a warring prince. He has made war between Iran and Iraq. If America is not careful she will shortly be involved with this warring spirit in the Persian Gulf where he has his headquarters (even at the site of the ancient city of Babylon).

John in Revelation 6:2 saw him riding on a white horse. He was the warring spirit that possessed Nimrod and caused him to become the ancient "mighty hunter." Today he is riding

108

again, and armies are following him. Unless God's saints rise up and possess the land, we will be engulfed in World War III very soon.

He is the spirit which makes wars between nations, and lesser battles between communities, tribes, church denominations, business associates and even church and family members.

II. Second Rank—The Demon Spirit of Greed:

He is the deputy commander of the warring spirits. He looks entirely different. He is dressed like today's businessman. He has the appearance of a "good, old friend"—rather corpulent. He is having his field-day "controlling and manipulating the money markets of the world. His work is to make one rich and another desperately poor. He causes great businesses and empires of wealth to collapse overnight and paupers to make a fortune in days. He is the controlling influence behind economic failures, depressions, recessions and famines. He forces mergers of companies and even makes competitors and enemies sit together at one table in order to survive. His end-time task is to destroy the economy of the world so that he can make the nations subservient to the antichrist system. His master stroke took place in 1973 when he controlled the politics of the world and even changed our traffic speed laws through the oil shortage which he manipulated. At that time he worked very closely with the warring prince of Persia because that is the major source of the world's oil supply. Today, with many of our own oil wells sealed, he again threatens to bring us to our knees.

He also works in ministries and homes, causing even God's people to become greedy so that they begin to misappropriate funds, build earthly kingdoms, and cause great shame to the ministry of Jesus Christ.

III. Third Rank—The Religious Spirit:

This rank is also known as the spirit of parapsychology. Rev. Pittman saw this rank of ruling spirits as being half human and half beast. They are the religious demons of the dark arts, magic, and even something as modern as Secular Humanism and as ancient as mythology. They use the God-given desire within man to worship a deity to focus man's worship on something less than God. They are the instigators of all pagan religions and the perverters of true religion. They twist truths and doctrines and cause splits and divisions, even among Bible-believing Christians. They can change their image from one religion to another. They can impress and mould people into such fanatical zeal that they think theirs is the only true religion on earth, and that everyone else is lost. They enforce codes of behaviour and dress on people and cause them to live all their lifetime in certain types and styles of clothing—even to the ridiculous. They make the worship of God appear to be a mystery which only they themselves can reveal to their followers. Religious spirits parade in the name of any religion—Judaism, Hinduism, Buddhism, Islam and Christianity—many different sects (all the way from Catholicism to Pentecostalism), and even in modern man's intellectual humanism. One must always guard his heart against the religious spirit, because if a person has it, he will think himself more spiritual than his brother, and may even go so far as to believe that he is one of the "two witnesses" mentioned in Revelation chapter 11. I have even heard of those who have proclaimed themselves to be "the Christ." This religious spirit is very prevalent in the world today and

110

will deceive many souls into accepting the antichrist when he appears in the Name of Jesus Christ.

IV. Fourth Rank—The Mystery Demon:

Howard Pittman found it hard to describe this strange spirit. He seemed to be wearing a dark shroud which covered him from head to toe. He is the spirit of infirmities, diseases, demonic possessions, insanity, epilepsy, mental breakdowns and every kind of plague and exotic disease (including the use of illegal drugs). He is the instigator of all plagues from the one that destroyed the first-born of Egypt (Exodus 12:23) to the present-day pandemic of Acquired Immune Deficiency Syndrome, which is gaining momentum every day. In New York City it is the Number One killer of young men between the ages of 30 and 38. This demon leaves a pathway of devastation and death. It is the only one that can attack young children. In many ways he is as powerful as the warring spirit. He is the one who strikes the organs of reproduction in men and women, causing hysterectomies, mastectomies and prostatectomies. He is the cause of much pain and suffering, crippling and mental disorders. Today, one of his latest inventions is Alzheimer's Disease. Yesterday it was cancer. While cancer will not decrease, now it is overshadowed by other diseases which are even more mysterious and dreaded.

Jesus carried all these curses and diseases on His body, and by His stripes we are healed. Not one of these diseases is more powerful than our Jesus Who redeemed us from all these diseases of the world (Exodus 15:26). He says in Psalm 103:3 that He heals **all** our diseases and redeems our life from destruction. This spirit brings death, but Jesus is the Resurrection and the Life.

V. Fifth Rank—The Demon Spirit of Lust and Perversion

Howard Pittman saw this spirit in the shape of a large green

111

frog, which was hanging on to the chest of a man, with his mouth near the man's mouth. The man was talking intimately with a young woman at some place of employment, and suddenly the frog entered the man's mouth and crawled down inside of him and the man was fully possessed. What many call harmless flirtations are demonically inspired possessions. This is the spirit which will compel a husband to betray his wife of many years, forsake his very own children, and even ruin his career for another woman. The fact that the other woman may not be as beautiful a person as his wife makes no difference. When he is controlled by the green frog, he becomes overwhelmed by passions which he mistakes for love. This was the spirit that destroyed King Solomon, so that he could not be reasonable, even though he was the wisest man who ever lived.

This is the spirit of sodomy, incest, perversion, bestiality and every kind of inordinate affection, including lesbianism. It is worshipped in India and Nepal as the goddess of love whose temples are "adorned" with grotesque pictures of two or more people performing every imaginable type of sexual act.

This spirit is the lowest of the demonic caste system. He is the untouchable of the demon world. His expertise is so horrible that he is despised by all the other ranks of demons. This demon of lust and perversion is playing a great role in the end-time. In fact, he is playing a key role in these last days by destroying the moral code of our society. He will open the door for the judgment of God upon all flesh as in the days of Sodom and Gomorrah). Today he rules in the sodomite cities of our nations, working with the mystery demon to destroy a generation of men—particularly young men.

We see this frog mentioned in Revelation 16:13. When the antichrist takes over, this repulsive demon will play a major role in the satanic trinity of the dragon, the beast and the false prophet.

Beloved child of God, never allow your heart to be enticed

112

by another, even a child of God, male or female, in any way that will make you a victim of this frog-like creature. Break off all unholy, secret relationships. The thing which thrills you today will destroy you tomorrow, for by permitting yourself to entertain unlawful thoughts of adultery, you give this horrible spirit the legal right to possess you. And when he comes in, he will soon bring other spirits with him.[3]

For more detailed information on this subject, I recommend *Demons, An Eyewitness Account* by Howard Pittman. It contains interesting illustrations of these spirits as he saw them.

STUDY QUESTIONS

1. Read Revelation 17:1-18:24.

2. In what way is Hinduism like the demonic spirit world?

3. Name and describe briefly the five leading demonic ranks in the spirit world.

4. Describe the end-time activities of each one.

5. In what ways are the trappings of the ancient pagan religion of Nimrod still in the church?

6. What role will the area of the Persian Gulf play in these last days?

7. Memorize Revelation 18:4.

CHAPTER EIGHT

HOW SATAN ESTABLISHES HIS TERRITORY

Satan is very well organized. His upper echelon of demons first come into an area and set up their thrones through all of the preceding methods. These are the devil's commissioned officers.

Satan uses both demonic spirits and humans to get control of an area. Wherever he has a legal right to operate, he sets up a base. Then he establishes another in an area to the left or the right of the first base; and finally he establishes a third base, either above or below the other two bases. He now has a triangle (such as the Bermuda triangle) in which he can begin to operate quite freely. He especially favours the high places, e.g. Denver, Colorado, the mile-high city in United States which has become the headquarters for all kinds of end-time satanic activity.

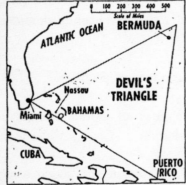

The over-all picture is something like this: he places a canopy over his triangle under which his evil spirits can operate. This canopy establishes the perimeter of the area where the spirits are free to work unhindered. That is why certain sins are more prevalent over a specific area. For example, crime, murders, sodomy, divorce, suicides, gang wars, etc. may be limited almost entirely to that one particular area that is now ruled by these spirits. We have all noticed in the news how a rapist or strangler will seem to be limited to a particular area. In Kansas City there is one area of five blocks radius, where in the space of one year, 19 rapes were reported.

114

Investigation reveals that in the days when people were migrating west, this was an area where there were a lot of saloons and all the sins of the "Wild West."

It is in the cordoned-off areas that it is very difficult to have a revival or establish a ministry. Satan puts a barrier over people's minds and causes much oppression. You will usually find a great deal of fighting and discord among the people. In the churches of that area you will find division, strife, discord, splits, discontent. Christians will have a hard time living an overcoming life. Christians lose their power to witness. Some live in fear. There are even certain satanic areas where there are repeated fatal car accidents. It is in places like this where revolutionary extremisms such as Naziism, and Communism can make great inroads. The Communists knew this. Way back in the early part of this century they laid the groundwork for their demon spirits to take over the United Sates and other democratic, free nations. They did this by satanic inspiration. The following information was captured in Düsseldorf in May 1919 by the Allied Forces. Düsseldorf is not far from Wuppertal where the Communists had one of their main headquarters. That building is now used as a Full Gospel Church.

Communist Rules for Revolution

(Captured in Düsseldorf May, 1919, by the Allied Forces)

A. Corrupt the young, get them away from religion. Get them interested in sex. Make them superficial, destroy their ruggedness.

B. Get control of all means of publicity and thereby:

1. Get the people's minds off their government by

115

focusing their attention on athletics, sexy books and plays and other trivialities.

2. Divide the people into hostile groups by constantly harping on controversial matters of no importance.

3. Destroy the people's faith in their natural leaders by holding the latter up to contempt, ridicule and obloquy.

4. Always preach true democracy but seize power as fast and as ruthlessly as possible.

5. By encouraging government extravagance, destroy its credit, produce fear of inflation with rising prices and general discontent.

6. Foment unnecessary strikes in vital industries, encourage civil disorders, and foster a lenient and soft attitude on the part of government toward such disorders.

7. By specious argument cause the breakdown of the old moral virtues: honesty, sobriety, continence, faith in the pledged word, ruggedness.

C. Cause the registration of all firearms on some pretext, with a view to confiscating them and leaving the population helpless and hopeless.

NOTE: ''The above 'Rules for Revolution' were secured by the State Attorney's office from a known member of the Communist Party, who acknowledged it to be still a part of the Communist programme for overthrowing our Government.''

George A. Brautigam
State Attorney
State of Florida

All but number C of the above (the confiscating of firearms) have almost been totally completed. May God wake His people up before it is too late!

116

So Far and No Farther!

But, praise the Lord, those demons can only go so far—and no further than their allotted area! The thing that stops them are the prayers and the holiness of God's people. Prayer cells, praying families with family altars, intercessors, all these positive things serve to keep an area clean from Satan's inroads into that region.

1. At the Kremlin

I shall never forget what the Lord showed me one day in the Kremlin. I was visiting the museum there. As I gazed upon all the different articles in the religious display I marvelled at the great love that the Russian people must have had for the Lord and the church. Tremendous sacrifices had been made by these people to the church. I asked the Lord, "Lord, how could it be that Russia, who was so religious, could have become the cradle of Communism?" The Lord answered me, "Religion and a form of worship is not enough to hold back the powers of darkness. It takes a mighty move of the Spirit of God to hold back the flood of iniquity in these last days." And then God said something more, "After Russia fell, the plan of the enemy was to take United States next. But the great outpouring of the Holy Spirit in the States stopped him. However, if America does not have another true visitation of God, and does not return to righteousness, next time when the enemy attacks, she will fall. Nothing can save her."

2. Job

God marks off the area where His children live. God knows the addresses of those who love him and, as Satan said about Job, *"Hast thou made a hedge about him and about his house,*

117

and about all that he hath on every side? thou hast blessed the work of his hands, and his substance is increased in the land.'' (Job 1:10) That's a pretty good testimony! Even Satan has to recognize that hedge of protection and blessing.

3. The Land of Goshen

When God sent the plagues to the land of Egypt, He put a hedge around the land of Goshen where His people, the Israelites lived. At least five of the ten plagues never touched the Children of Israel or their possessions.

a. The Flies (Exodus 8:22, 23):
God told Moses to tell Pharaoh, *"And I will sever in that day the land of Goshen, in which my people dwell, that no swarms of flies shall be there; to the end thou mayest know that I am the Lord in the midst of the earth. And I will put a division between my people and thy people: tomorrow shall this sign be.''*

b. The Cattle (Exodus 9:4, 6):
When a deadly disease broke out on the cattle, God again gave the promise of protection, *"And the Lord shall sever between the cattle of Israel and the cattle of Egypt: and there shall nothing die of all that is the children's of Israel....And the Lord did that thing on the morrow, and all the cattle of Egypt died: but of the cattle of the children of Israel died not one.''*

c. The Hail (Exodus 9:25, 26)
"And the hail smote throughout all the land of Egypt all that was in the field, both man and beast: and the hail smote every herb of the field, and brake every tree of the field. Only in the land of Goshen, where the children of Israel were, was there no hail.''

d. The Darkness (Exodus 10:21-23)

"And the Lord said unto Moses, Stretch out thine hand toward heaven, that there may be darkness over the land of Egypt, even darkness which may be felt. And Moses stretched forth his hand toward heaven; and there was a thick darkness in all the land of Egypt three days: They saw not one another, neither rose any from his place for three days: but all the children of Israel had light in their dwellings."

e. The Death of the Firstborn (Exodus 12:23)

"For the Lord will pass through to smite the Egyptians; and when he seeth the blood upon the lintel, and on the two side posts, the Lord will pass over the door, and will not suffer the destroyer to come in unto your houses to smite you."

God warned, *"None of you shall go out at the door of his house until the morning"* (Exodus 12:22). During the night when the destroyer passed through the land, the Lord warned His people to stay under the blood covering. We know that Satan had no legal right to smite them if they obeyed His laws of provision for their protection. This is the same law that provides the protection which we need against the demonic spirits.

4. Present-Day Miracles of Protection

I'm sure that there are many, but I can only mention a few.

a. Switzerland Spared in World War II

When the Nazi Wehrmacht (Army) was marching into one European nation after another, the little country of Switzerland looked as though it was in danger of being the next one to be invaded. Every day the Nazi soldiers marched alongside the border and mocked the Swiss soldiers, "We'll take Switzerland before breakfast," they boasted.

A godly woman who was a great intercessor received a

warning from God of the danger, and the Lord showed her she must tell it to the leaders of Switzerland. She sent the warning to them. They accepted it as from the Lord and put the largest part of their small army right there in the area that was threatened. You know the rest. God marked off Switzerland for peace. It was never invaded. It became a sea of calm in the bloody storm of Europe and a haven of refuge to many who fled the terror of Nazism.

b. Rees Howells' Mission Protected From Influenza Epidemic Plague

When the terrible influenza epidemic broke out immediately after World War I, millions died. There were more deaths from this plague than from the war.

Soon it made its way to Rees Howells' mission station in Rhodesia (now called Zimbabwe). Many were dying in the kraal nearby. The African chief sent some natives to ask Howells, "Have you had any deaths?" Mr. Howells answered, "No, have you had any?"

He replied, "Yes, many have died."

Mr. Howells asked them why their witch doctors could not help them. They replied that they had been the first to die.

Mr. Howells said, "But my God has not failed." Then he felt the Holy Spirit quicken him to add. "No one has died and no one will die on the mission station."

In the Spirit, he drew a line around the area and claimed for God to protect that whole area. Hundreds of natives came to live there. Some were sick. Even Mrs. Howells got very sick, but not one died on that mission compound. The destroyer had no power to take one single life. Howells said, "I found the Holy Spirit was stronger than the flu."

I have had the privilege of visiting that mission station. The old chapel is broken down, the roof is missing, but the walls

120

still stand. A very old man told us about the great miracles that took place there in the days of Rees Howells, God's intercessor.

c. Indonesia—Marked Off for Revival

When I first went to Indonesia in 1964 I saw how the Christians got up very early every morning to go to church to pray. It was still not fully light and yet the streets were full of God's people going to the church. After an hour of prayer we had an hour of early morning Bible study before returning home for breakfast at 7 a.m.

When the sweet savour of all those earnest prayers reached the Throne of God, He opened the windows of Heaven and poured out a great revival on the Indonesian Islands, which stretch over 2,000 miles from east to west. The amazing thing was that it was as though God had drawn an invisible line between the Islands of Indonesia and the other countries nearby. Malaysia, which is so close to Indonesia that you can see Malaysia across the Strait of Malacca on a clear day, and other nearby nations were untouched by the revival that came to Indonesia. It seemed like the Holy Spirit said, "So far and no farther!" I believe that God marked out Indonesia for revival.

If Satan can place a canopy of evil over an area because he has his servants and demons there to work, and worship and obey him, then our God certainly can put a canopy of protection and blessing, and even glory (like He did in the wilderness for the Children of Israel) and in the land of Goshen, right in the middle of Egypt. This is what will happen when the children of God pray and live a consistent holy life. Remember that God

121

put His angels with a flaming sword at the entrance of the Garden of Eden for the purpose of keeping mankind out of the garden. He still can appoint angels at any place of entrance to protect those who are under His covenant of protection (Genesis 3:24).

d. The Passion Play of Oberammergau

Fear ruled the hearts of the people of Bavaria, Germany, in the spring of 1632. King Gustav Adolf of Sweden was marching unhindered through the land, and only after he was routed by Wallenstein was Bavaria saved. As the Swedish army retreated, it burnt down villages and left behind a starving population, devoid of hope. By October, the terrible plague, the Black Death, was sweeping through the land, killing hundreds in some places and thousands in others. The people of Oberammergau tried to stop it from coming into their village by keeping out all strangers, but one man, Kaspar Schisler, who worked as a harvester in a nearby town which was infected, wanted to come home for the Feast of Dedication of the church (third Sunday in October) to be with his family in Oberammergau. He succeeded in reaching his house on the edge of the village by travelling unnoticed down steep mountain paths. He was already infected with the plague, the unmistakable swellings were on his body, and so he brought the universal epidemic to his native village. He died on the Monday after the Feast of Dedication, 1632. In the parish register of deaths, which has some gaps, there are, in the time between October 1632 and the month of the Vow, October 1633, eighty-two entries of "deaths from deadly sickness." As only the names of fathers of families are entered in the register, the number of those who died of the plague may have been much higher.

In this terrible distress, the "Six and the Twelve" (comparable with a parish council and Council of Elders) met together on the eve of the Feast of the Apostles Simon and Jude Thaddaeus (Feast: 28 October) and made a vow to perform the

"Passions-Tragedie" every ten years if their village were freed from the plague. The chronicle relates that, from the time of the vow, no one else, although infected, died of the plague.

It is a strange thing how deadly plagues often follow wars. After World War I the flu epidemic broke out, which took more lives than the entire war did. It seems that Satan has a legal right to attack with pestilence after there has been an unreasonable amount of shedding of innocent blood. Now, with the millions of aborted babies, our nation is ravished again with mysterious plagues such as AIDS.

e. Prayer Saves Harvest in Canada

When I was a young girl in Saskatchewan, Canada, my parents were farmers. We were plagued by drought, grasshoppers and all kinds of pestilence. One summer the grasshoppers attacked the farms in our area. After them came the cutworms. There were so many of them that it seemed as if the very earth was moving. They devoured everything in their path. Some of our crop was already destroyed, when my father went out into the field and knelt down and prayed, asking God to save his crop. He had a family that he had to feed that winter. God heard his prayer. The worms never ate another stalk of grain. That fall we had a crop. There is no doubt that prayer can raise up a line of demarcation which the enemy can't cross over.

STUDY QUESTIONS

1. Read Psalm 91.

2. How does Satan establish his area of operation?

3. Describe a satanic canopy and how it works.

4. Give five examples of how God did the same thing to protect and bless.

5. Name the five plagues that never touched the land of Goshen.

6. Memorize Psalm 91.

CHAPTER NINE

HOW SATAN WORKS AND WHOM HE ATTACKS

Satan will always "zero in" on an important area, or an important ministry, or a special, anointed person. I believe that every great ministry and servant of God will come under satanic attacks—some more severely than others. Didn't Satan attack Job? (Job 1) and David (I Chronicles 21:1). And Satan stood up against Israel and provoked David to number Israel. Paul was attacked by a messenger of Satan, *"And lest I should be exalted above measure through the abundance of the revelations, there was given to me a thorn in the flesh, the messenger of Satan..."*(II Corinthians 12:7). Even Jesus was tempted by Satan in the wilderness.

He has caused many great men of God to be tempted and and tried and tested. If they did not flee to God for refuge, fast and pray, they fell.

I. Satan's Attack On Our Ministry

Some years ago an angel of the Lord sent a message to me through a prophet of the Lord. He warned me that Satan was beginning to take note of the End-Time Handmaidens ministry and that it had made Satan angry; he was preparing to attack us in different ways:

a. A spirit of jealousy would come up against us through jealous Christians.

b. A spirit of slander, scandal and hideous lies would be raised up against us, but they would not succeed.

c. Some would be struck with cancer.

d. A spirit of hatred.

The angel said, "Tell Sister Gwen to tighten the reins of her being and be alert."

125

It wasn't long afterwards that all these things began to happen. We underwent an all-out attack on our ministry from the different kinds and ranks of demonic spirits. It was one of the most difficult times of my life and certainly one of the most agonizing. One of our most loved sisters got sick and died of cancer. I would wake up in the morning to see a demon spirit standing in our bedroom glaring at me out of his evil eyes. The strange thing was that he looked just like one of the persons who had come against us. We kept our peace. We battled the only way we knew how—prayer, fasting and praising the Lord. In the end, the Lord released us from their attack. Our assault had come from demon spirits who had used people. He still works the same old way.

II. Some of the Ways Satan Attacks

1. He works to damage the reputation of those in leadership.
2. He brings reproach.
3. He stirs up jealousies.
4. He sends a spirit of rebellion against leadership and causes insurrection.
5. He brings confusion through those who speak negatively and critically.
6. He causes sickness, death and accidents.
7. He lies, and causes old friends to slander one another.
8. Through theft of funds in the mails or by some of the members of the ministry he reduces finances. Satan always attacks financially.
9. Through the immoral conduct of those in leadership.
10. One of Satan's master strokes is causing false doctrine or half-truths to enter a ministry.
11. Compromise—when we compromise with evil, we let down the wall of protection.
12. Through petty nuisances such as thieves breaking in,

pipes bursting, electrical failures, loss of mailing lists, the breaking down of vital machines, fires, etc.

In January 1987 we received a letter from Jay and Meridel Rawlings, our dear friends who live in Israel. Their letter had a sad report. It told how they were under attack from the devil. I quote from their letter:

*So many times the Lord exhorted the disciples to watch and pray. Can we do any less? Certainly we who are on the **front lines of battle** desperately need your prayers and support. For example here are a few of the attacks that have tried to hinder our work lately.*

1. Our house was burglarized.

2. Fire and smoke damage in our home.

3. Repeated power failure—only in our house.

4. Broken appliances—second time in six months.

5. Broken water pipe inside a wall requiring major plumbing and plastering repair.

6. A $400.00 water bill.

7. Telephone out of order—exactly when I was waiting for an urgent call from Canada regarding my mother's health.

8. Severe back pain affecting both Bill and Jay.

*9. News that my mother has serious inoperable lung cancer requiring my presence in Canada to support her (I'm currently in Canada with my folks at this difficult time.) Please pray for my mom Sheila, 72 years young, and who is a marvelous and brave woman. We are all believing for a **miracle**!! (Here in the U.S. we just received word that the cancer has spread to the brain—Please pray).*

The latest report is that she is healed. Praise the Lord!

III. Christians Must Be Careful Not To Assist Satan in His Attack against Other Christians

The sad thing is that when Satan attacks a ministry, very

often God's people join him to help destroy that ministry. It seems as though we are too ready to see our brother fall. We take a delight that is demonically inspired. And we are often too weak and cowardly to stand by the one who is under attack. We sometimes even disassociate ourselves from him.

This is the age of BETRAYAL. We will find our dearest friends betraying us in these days. Satan will do all he can to crush God's anointed ministries. But those who are ineffectual he has not much time for. It is the ministries that are damaging his kingdom that he hates and fights.

These are the days of defamation of character, disloyalty, betrayal, greed and self-preservation. If we live a holy life, we certainly will be tested and tried, but we will come through victoriously. It is not only ministries that are targetted by Satan for destruction. Any one who is doing good (either in the political field or social work, or anything that is for the betterment of society will experience the same kind of onslaught from Satan.

Recently I have observed that well-meaning people who are attempting to organize a group to fight against alcohol have been viciously attacked by the powerful demon spirit of Bacchus. Their children have been killed by drunk drivers and in one case recently, in Michigan, a beautiful graduating student who was the president of Students Against Drunk Driving was killed by a drunk driver, together with three others. These fine people meant well in their war against alcohol, but perhaps they did not do battle in the Name of Jesus. Our only safety in our warfare against Satan is the power of the precious Blood—for we battle not with flesh and blood.

If we yield to Satan's attacks and do not withstand him, he will rule the world in the next few years. We are at the crossroads where we either hand it over to Satan or we stand against him and resist him. The Bible says that if we will resist him, he will flee from us (James 4:7). This Bible study is written

128

to help you not only defend yourself and your land against the evil forces, but to go one step further—wrest it from the devil's hands. Take back the territory which the evil one has already gained control over. The best defence is offence.

STUDY QUESTIONS

1. Read:
   Job 1:1-2:13
   I Chronicles 21:1-30
   II Chronicles 12:7-9
   Matthew 4:1-11.

2. What is the type of thing or person that Satan zeroes in on?

3. Name four persons Satan attacked and give Scripture references.

4. List six of the twelve ways Satan attacks.

5. In what way does Satan get help from Christians?

6. How has Satan attacked you? Share!

7. Memorize James 4:7.

CHAPTER TEN

WHAT HAPPENS WHEN GOD'S LAWS ARE TRANSGRESSED?

The Terrible Consequences of Transgression

It is the transgression of God's laws which gives Satan a legal right to overcome us and set up his rulership over the land, or a particular area, and even a person. The results of Satan ruling over different areas or nations are devastating and even catastrophic.

Here are just some of the things that happen when a nation breaks God's laws of righteousness and is thereby cursed.

I. The Ground Ceases To Yield Its Strength (Genesis 4:12)

Crops fail through drought, flood, pestilence, hail, storms, until the economy is ruined and the farmers lose their ability to produce and prosper. This slows down or stops the food supply of the nation. The first sign of a curse on the nation is what happens on the farms because they are the source of all the food supply. Few Americans know that every six minutes another farm closes due to bankruptcy. In Europe and Great Britain thousands of cattle and sheep, even the deer of the Laplanders, have had to be destroyed because of the fallout from Chernobyl.

II. The Land Itself "Vomits Out" Its Inhabitants (Leviticus 18:25)

There are many ways for the land to vomit out its inhabitants:

1. By famine and mass starvation, such as we are now

130

experiencing in Ethiopia, Mozambique and other nations.

2. By wars: Six million Germans of all ages, even children, died in World War II. Many believe it was punishment for the six million Jews that Hitler killed.

3. By abortion: God allows man to have the power of choice. We are free moral agents. Because we insist on murdering our very own children, God will allow it. Who is being killed and by whom? The ones who make the decision to murder their babies are as guilty as the abortionist, who holds in his hand the cruel instrument of destruction. So they both are murderers. It is therefore the murderers who are killing their offspring. They are destroying their own seed. Abortion has become a plague, a holocaust, whose numbers of victims surpass the number that Hitler murdered many times over.

4. By storms, tornadoes, hurricanes, typhoons.

5. By earthquakes (in recent years hundreds of thousands have died in earthquakes).

6. Forest fires (as I write this book, terrible fires are raging on the border of Russia and Mongolia, also in China, Alaska and California).

7. Volcanic eruptions.

8. Wars, riots, revolutions (in the 20th century we have had two World Wars and hundreds of smaller ones).

9. Instability of government—defiance and ridicule of those in high office; lack of patriotism, political problems, rulers making unwise decisions.

10. Scourge of drug addiction and alcoholism among young and old. America spent sixty billion dollars on drugs and alcohol in 1986.

11. Despotism—wicked and evil despotic rulers are placed over nations by the demonic princes of the nations, e.g. Idi Amin, Samora Machel, Hitler, Stalin, Kruschev, Mao Tze Tung and many others, (even in our time alone).

131

12. Broken marriages, fatherless children, ruined lives, family structures totally destroyed.

13. Poverty and unemployment.

14. Communism—and other forms of cruel oppression over the people.

15. By plagues or diseases, such as cancer, Alzheimer's Disease, mental disorders and sexually-transmitted diseases such as syphillis, gonorrhea, herpes simplex (which one in ten have contracted in North America, and for which there is no cure), and the deadly viral disease called AIDS (Acquired Immune Deficiency Syndrome) which was unheard of seven years ago.

It is difficult to write about AIDS because the statistics change from day to day. For example, the May 1987 edition of *Concerned Women of America* reports 30,000 Americans have been infected with the AIDS virus, and June 1987 *Reader's Digest* puts the number at 35,000 and states some 20,000 have died. One and a half million more are believed to be infected with HIV, the virus that causes AIDS. Experts believe that by the end of 1991 the total in USA alone will reach 270,000 with 179,000 deaths. As many will die in 1991 (one year alone) as in all the years of the Vietnam War. It is being compared to the Black Plague.

These estimates are very conservative since certain categories of AIDS have not been included. Cases have recently been discovered where people who have never developed "classic" AIDS have, nevertheless, died because the AIDS virus attacked their nervous system. These cases have not been included in the total number of AIDS cases reported to the public.

There is a "cover up" on the truth. But some prominent men in the field of medicine are trying to get the truth to us. The following is a quote from the *Concerned Women of America*, May 1987,

According to the British virologist Dr. Richard Tedder, "If

people who've been infected by the AIDS virus don't get killed by immunosuppression, they'll die from chronic dementia, pre-senile dementia." If his analysis is accurate, millions will die from AIDS.

Another alarming development is the recent discovery of a new strain of the AIDS virus that has gone undetected by standard blood tests. According to French Dr. Luc Montagnier of the Pasteur Institute, "This is bad news for the blood banks." An estimated 30,000 Americans have already been infected with AIDS as a result of contaminated blood transfusions. The non-detection of this new strain and the failure to include AIDS dementia in the current figures show that the situation is far worse than it appears.

Gene Antonio, author of the highly-acclaimed The AIDS Coverup?, *has listed a number of areas in which he believes the Surgeon General's report falls short. He discusses these areas in his study entitled* A Critical Evaluation of the Surgeon General's Report on AIDS.

According to Gene Antonio, that which has been totally ignored by the Surgeon General's Report, is the nature of the AIDS virus. It is a lentivirus (slow-acting virus) of which only three types are known. AIDS most closely resembles Maedi-visna lentivirus that kills sheep by causing dementia and a deadly form of lung disease, similar to lung tissue inflammation in AIDS patients. The death rate from maedi-visna is 100 percent and the infection can be spread by close contact (coughing).

The Surgeon General emphatically denies that AIDS can be spread in any other way than through sex or blood transfusions. His report states, "There is no danger of AIDS virus infection from visiting a doctor, dentist, hospital, hairdresser or beautician. AIDS cannot be transmitted non-sexually from an infected person through a health or service provider to another person."

In stark contrast, Professor William Haseltine of the

133

Harvard Medical School says that anyone "who tells you categorically that AIDS is not contracted by saliva is not telling you the truth. AIDS may in fact be transmissible by tears, saliva, bodily fluids and mosquito bites... There are sure to be cases of proven transmission through casual contact."

I am sure that you can think of other terrible consequences of man's transgression. All these and more are the result of what happens when God's laws are transgressed.

STUDY QUESTIONS

1. Read Deuteronomy 28:1-68.

2. What gives Satan a legal right?

3. Name two things that happen when a nation is cursed (from Genesis 4:11 and Leviticus 18:25).

4. Of the fifteen I listed, name ten ways that, through the judgment of God, the earth "vomited out" her inhabitants in the nations.

5. Memorize Leviticus 18:25.

CHAPTER ELEVEN

THE AUTHORITY OF THE BELIEVER OVER DEMON SPIRITS

What Is the Answer?

A better social welfare system certainly is not the answer. The power to change things does not lie in welfare. Poverty is the **result** of sin. The cure for poverty is the cure for sin. Only a great revival—only a nation turning to God can stop all this. But we can begin by one or two Spirit-filled people going to battle against the enemy of our souls. God said to Ezekiel, *"And I sought for a man among them, that should make up the hedge, and stand in the gap before me for the land, that I should not destroy it: but I found none. Therefore have I poured out mine indignation upon them; I have consumed them with the fire of my wrath: their own way have I recompensed upon their heads, saith the Lord God."* (Ezekiel 22:30, 31)

Sometimes all God needs is one revivalist, one man like:

Noah who salvaged the adamic race by his righteousness;

Abraham who was called out of Nimrod's system to begin a new race of people;

Moses who was saved to lead a nation out of a nation;

Joshua, a young slave delivered out of Egypt and trained by God and Moses to possess the land;

David, a shepherd boy, to redeem Israel from her enemies;

Elijah, to call a nation back to God;

Isaiah, Jeremiah, Ezekiel, to prophesy and sound the trumpet;

Paul, to bring the world the message of the Gospel of Regeneration;

A Deborah, a Ruth, an Esther, an Abigail, a Hannah, an Anna, a Mary. The list could go on and on. One at a time—brave souls, standing up in their day to wrest their nations from the clutches of the evil one and restore it back to God. Without

135

them, none of us would be here. We would never have had a chance to live.

II. Where Do We Begin?

God's people must be made to see the sin that is destroying us. We have become so complacent about sin that we can watch it flaunted before us on the TV or screen or in our neighbourhood without it either irking us or burdening us. The Bible says that Lot was *"vexed with the filthy conversation of the wicked"* (II Peter 2:7), i.e., he was worn down, oppressed with the filthy, unrestrained and wanton lifestyle of the wicked. It is time for us to stop hiding our heads in a hole of blind ignorance, weak, stupid indifference, and compromise with evil, and become involved with the battle for reform. Thank God for people like Phyllis Schlafly who stand against unrighteousness. They are our Deborahs of the hour.

The Ground Work

1. We must confess our sins and the sins of our nation.
2. We must seek for forgiveness.
3. Our sin must be atoned for so that the curse can be lifted.
4. A sacrifice of blood must be made.
5. Jesus made that sacrifice once and for all.
6. His sacrifice must be recognized, accepted and appropriated.
7. Satan must be rebuked and reproved and told that Jesus paid the sacrifice of His own blood, and that he (Satan) is a usurper.
8. The land is redeemed by an act of faith, which applies the Blood of Jesus to the cursed land.
9. This alone, breaks the power and authority which demons have over a land.

Romans 5:9, *"Much more then, being now justified by his blood, we shall be saved from wrath through him."*

136

I Peter 1:18, 19, *"Forasmuch as ye know that ye are not redeemed with corruptible things, as silver and gold, from your vain conversation received by tradition from your fathers; But with the precious blood of Christ, as of a lamb without blemish and without spot."*

If God recognized the blood sacrifice of Saul's sons and accepted it as atonement for the sins of Saul, how much more readily will He accept the sacrifice of His own Son for the redemption of the land. Even as the curse was lifted off Israel at that time when the perfect sacrifice was made (seven is the complete number, and seven of Saul's sons died to remove the curse caused by the shedding of innocent blood), so Jesus is the perfect Sacrifice. He is the gift of God Himself for the atonement of all cursed lands.

III. Christians Should Rule Over Demon Spirits

When God created man, He gave him authority to rule over all His creation. Demons were also originally created by God, but they were not in demonic form then. Before the fall they were angels. Angels were given to us to help us. Hebrews 1:14, *"Are they not all ministering spirits, sent forth to minister for them who shall be heirs of salvation?"*

If angels were created to serve and minister to us, then certainly, by the divine orders of God, these same created beings (though they have fallen from God's grace and glory) are subservient to us, who are heirs of salvation and they must obey us when we bind them and cast them out and dislodge them from the areas over which they rule.

It must be remembered that there is no love nor loyalty in the spirit world of the devil. Satan rules those beneath him through terror. They follow and obey him out of sheer fear.

When they joined Satan in anarchy and insurrection against God in Heaven, it wasn't because they loved Lucifer. They followed him because he promised them powerful positions in his kingdom. They were never inspired by love and loyalty but

137

by self-ambition and hunger for power. You can be sure Satan offered them the same things that he offered Jesus in the hour of His temptation in the wilderness.

Howard Pittman, who visited the spirit-world, said that the evil spirits hate and despise and are jealous of each other. Each one wants the position of the one who is above him in rank. They are ruled by fear.

You have the greatest weapon there is to rule the spirit world: the Blood of Jesus and the Name of Jesus. The demons were always cast out in the Name of Jesus. The thing that makes the Name of Jesus so powerful is His royal divine Blood which He shed. Satan fears the Blood of Jesus. And if the King of Darkness fears the Blood, how much more do his subordinates, who are weaker than he, fear the holy Blood.

We have been given authority by God and His Son to rule over all spirits of darkness.

IV. Scriptures That Give Us Authority over Demonic Powers

1. Luke 10:19, *"Behold, I give unto you power to tred on serpents and scorpions, and over all the power of the enemy; and nothing shall by any means hurt you."*

That is a carte blanche for full control of every demonic situation. It also is a command to go to war against the forces of darkness.

2. Hebrews 2:14, 15, *"Forasmuch then as the children are partakers of flesh and blood, he also himself likewise took part of the same; that through death he might destroy him that had the power of death, that is, the devil; And deliver them, who through fear of death were all their lifetime subject to bondage."*

Jesus took upon Himself our human form so that He could experience death. It was in His death (as the Sacrificed Lamb) that He destroyed Satan's full power. When we have this truth made real to us, we are free from the power of the devil to

138

intimidate us and hold us in bondage through fear. Satan's kingdom always rules through fear—never through love. When he loses his power to scare us and intimidate us, his power over us is broken.

3. I John 3:8, *"He that committeth sin is of the devil; for the devil sinneth from the beginning. For this purpose the Son of God was manifested, that he might destroy the works of the devil."*
Jesus has already destroyed the works of the devil. We only need to recognize this fact and stand on it.

4. Matthew 10:1, *"And when he had called unto him his twelve disciples, he gave them power against unclean spirits, to cast them out, and to heal all manner of sickness and all manner of disease."*
The spirits know we have the power of God to cast them out. The tragedy is that the church of Jesus Christ does not know this. For centuries these truths were not taught. So the church entered the so-called "dark age" of the medieval times, because the devil kept the Bible, that had this truth, from God's people. I am convinced that the reason the church leadership did not release the Bible to the common folk was because the leaders' lives were full of sin and corruption, and they knew that if the people knew the truth they would walk out of the church en masse. In the end, it was the Bible that set us free.

5. Luke 10:17, *"And the seventy returned again with joy, saying, Lord, even the devils are subject unto us through thy name."*
One of my greatest joys in the ministry has been to see people set free from the bondage and darkness of Satan's kingdom. No wonder they rejoiced! A compromising dead religion has no life nor power against the unseen works of darkness. But the Gospel message Jesus gave us to preach carries the authority to move Heaven and earth and hell! Hallelujah!

139

6. John 14:12, *"Verily, verily, I say unto you, He that believeth on me, the works that I do shall he do also; and greater works than these shall he do; because I go unto my Father."*

Jesus has commissioned us to continue to do His work. He has given us the same full authority which He had. The same Holy Spirit who worked through Him has been authorized by Jesus and the Father to work through us. Peter, at the house of Cornelius, said, *"God anointed Jesus of Nazareth with the Holy Ghost and with power: who went about doing good, and healing all that were oppressed of the devil; for God was with him"* (Acts 10:38).

Before Jesus was taken to Heaven, He promised us this same Holy Ghost power (Matthew 28:18-20, Mark 16:15-18, Luke 24:49, Acts 1:8).

7. II Corinthians 10:4, *"For the weapons of our warfare are not carnal, but mighty through God to the pulling down of strongholds."*

Our strength does not depend on our physical abilities nor our intelligence and not even upon our finances, but on the greatness of God within us. The most unassuming and unpretentious people in the world are sometimes giants in the Kingdom. We never heard about Caleb until he stood against the doubters and faultfinders; and then he became a giant in God. When we are giants in God, we are equal to all the demonic Goliaths. Their size will never intimidate us. We can look at the mountain that has the biggest giants in it and say with Caleb, "Give me this mountain!" (Joshua 14:12).

8. Ephesians 6:11-13, *"Put on the whole armour of God, that ye may be able to stand against the wiles of the devil. For we wrestle not against flesh and blood, but against principalities, against powers, against the rulers of the darkness of this world, against spiritual wickedness in high places. Wherefore take unto you the whole armour of God, that ye may be able to withstand in the evil day, and having done all, to stand."*

140

We have been enlisted into this holy war, whether we like it or not; so we better get our uniforms on and dedicate ourselves to the holy cause. We have many enemies out there, belonging to many ranks.

a. Ruling Spirits:

"Principalities" is *arche* (746) in Greek—"magistrates, powers, principalities, beginnings." This word comes from the root word "beginning," in reference to order or time.

"Principalities" therefore refer to the original powerful spirits who fell in the revolt against God. They would be the spirits in Satan's ruling council.

b. Authorities:

"Powers" is *exousia* (1849) in Greek, which means "authorities who allow or hinder." They have executive powers. This governing group is the authority that grants the power. The word *exousia* denotes, not so much the magistracy of a court, but the power which governs and is synonymous with *arche* (authority, thrones, dominion, or government). In I Corinthians 15:24 and Colossians 2:15 it refers to all authorities and evil powers who oppose Jesus Christ.

c. World Rulers:

"Rulers of the darkness of this world"—rulers is *kosmokrator* (2888) from *kosmos*, i.e. "world" and *krator*, i.e. "ruler"— world rulers. They are responsible for fighting the true light and leading people into darkness by blinding their eyes and sending darkness into the souls of man. When we pray for our loved ones who are blinded by Satan and who oppose us, and for those in the pagan religions, this is the arch enemy we are warring against. He rules over the nations through his power to darken the minds of men. Disobedience to God leads us into this progressive darkness because it takes us from the light.

d. Spiritual Wickedness in High Places:

"Spiritual"—this is an interesting word in Greek, *pneumatikos* (4152). It comes from the root word *pneuma* (4151)—"spirit," i.e. ethereal. Wickedness is *poneria* (4189) which means "malicious. One who not only is wicked, but his every deed and thought is wicked. All he does affects others in a negative way."

"Spiritual wickedness in high places" may not mean persons so much as the evil itself, which operates and inspires these principalities, powers and rulers of darkness. Even as peace, love and goodness motivates the good, heavenly angelic beings, so in the opposite way, this terrible spiritual wickedness motivates and controls those of Satan's spirit world. This verse describes our enemy better than any other.

9. Colossians 2:14, 15, *"Blotting out the handwriting of ordinances that was against us, which was contrary to us, and took it out of the way, nailing it to the Cross; And having spoiled principalities and powers, he made a show of them openly, triumphing over them in it."*

Verse fourteen tells how this great and final defeat took place. It was at the Cross. There and then is when our Lord spoiled, i.e. ruined, destroyed those powerful principalities (*arche*, 746) and powers (*exousia*, 1849). When He made a show of them openly (put them to shame and ridicule before all of Heaven and hell by His mighty triumph over them.

If Satan had known what master stroke against himself he had made, he would never have crucified Jesus! I Corinthians 2:8, *"Which none of the princes of the world knew: for had they known it, they would not have crucified the Lord of glory."*

Satan "self-destructed" himself when he crucified Jesus.

When Haman built the gallows on which he was going to hang Mordecai, he was "re-enacting" what happened when the devil crucified Jesus. Haman destroyed himself (Esther 7:10). This same thing happened many times over. Joseph said to his brothers, *"But as for you, ye thought evil against me; but God*

142

meant it unto good, to bring to pass, as it is this day, to save much people alive. (Genesis 50:20).

10. The Power of Forgiveness. I John 3:21, 22, *"Beloved, if our heart condemn us not, then have we confidence toward God. And whatsoever we ask, we receive of him, because we keep his commandments, and do those things that are pleasing in his sight."*

Satan can have no legal hold over any situation where God's people have forgiven and love one another. If Jesus had not forgiven those who crucified Him (including us), the world would have been damned. Jesus' death would never have had the power to set us free from our sin if Jesus had not forgiven us. When Joseph forgave his brethren, he saved them from extinction. The devil would have liked to destroy them through famine. Then all God's promises to Abraham, Isaac and Jacob would never have been fulfilled, but because Joseph forgave, God could save Israel.

You may feel you have never done any great thing for God, beloved, but if you can forgive, you not only are **doing** a great thing; you **are** great in character, for you are Christ-like.

11. John 12:31, 32, *"Now is the judgment of this world (kosmos, 2889): now shall the prince (archon, 758) of this world be cast out."* There we see Jesus use the same titles Paul used in Ephesians 6:12. The *archon* (princes, principalities, rulers) of the *kosmos* (world). Jesus goes on to say how this evil prince of the world is cast down, *"And I, if I be lifted up from the earth, will draw all men unto me."* This He said, signifying what death He would die."

12. It was through Jesus' death on the Cross alone that He could break the curse and legal right Satan had over the world, because Jesus had to become cursed for us. He took upon Himself our curse. And He could only do this by hanging because: *"Christ hath redeemed us from the curse of the law,*

143

being made a curse for us: for it is written, Cursed is every one that hangeth on a tree.'' (Galatians 3:13)

God had given Israel the Law. When they broke the Law, Satan had a legal right to prosecute them—until Jesus stepped in and accepted the punishment in their place, and thus forgave them for **all** their sins for all time, including their final sin: crucifying Him. By accepting this provision, all the Pharisees, the scribes, the Sanhedrin, the Roman authorities, the two false witnesses (Matthew 26:60) and even the one who drove the nails in His hands and feet could receive absolution of sins. They only needed to repent of their sins and accept His forgiveness

When we are forgiven, we have peace and joy, and we can serve God with a pure conscience. Satan then has no legal right to hold us back or to hinder us. Our mistakes are under the Blood of Jesus.

STUDY QUESTIONS

1. Read Matthew 10:1-42 and Luke 10:1-20.

2. How can one person turn the tide so that God can purge the land?

3. Name five men and two women whom God used to save the land?

4. How do we lay the groundwork?

5. What authority do we have over the demonic spirit world?

6. Of the thirteen Scriptures that I quoted, which give the believer authority over the demonic spirit world? Give seven.

7. Explain Ephesians 6:12, using the Greek.

8. Memorize Ephesians 6:12.

CHAPTER TWELVE

THE POWERLESS CHURCH

I. The "Called-Out Ones"

In Revelation 12:1-6 we read about a great wonder which is described as "a woman clothed with the sun and the moon under her feet and upon her head a crown of twelve stars who gave birth to a man child." This "wonder in heaven" is the eternal church.

The word "church" hardly can begin to describe its full meaning. We are so limited in our interpretation of it.

Jesus is the first One to mention the church, *"And I say also unto thee, That thou art Peter, and upon this rock I will build my church: and the gates of hell shall not prevail against it."* (Matthew 16:18)

Ekklesia (1577) comes from the word *ekkaleo* which means "to call out." It was a common term for a congregation of the *ekkletoi* (those called out or assembled in the public affairs of a free state; the body of free citizens called together by a herald, the called people. In Acts 7:38 Stephen, in speaking about the Children of Israel in the wilderness, calls them "the church in the wilderness."

II. Tracing the Church in the Bible

There is no doubt that these special called-out ones, whom we call "the church," date back many millennia of time.

1. Seth:
We see traces of "called out" ones in the line and lineage of Seth as the righteous line was separated from the wicked descendants of Cain.

146

2. Shem:

Noah had three sons. Ham's descendants became the leaders of apostasy. Japheth's became the Gentile pagans. Only Shem stayed true to God and became the godly line.

3. Terah, Abraham:

Then we see it again when God called Terah and Abraham to leave the wicked and sinful Ur of the Chaldees (the land of Nimrod) in the days of Nimrod to come out and follow the leading of the Lord. And Abraham went forth, looking for a city whose Maker and Builder was God (Hebrews 11:10). The promises God gave Abraham told of a company of people who would be very special and separated to God.

Genesis 12:1-3, *"Now the Lord had said unto Abram, Get thee out of thy country, and from thy kindred, and from thy father's house, unto a land that I will show thee: And I will make of thee a great nation, and I will bless thee, and make thy name great; and thou shalt be a blessing: And I will bless them that bless thee, and curse him that curseth thee: and in thee shall all families of the earth be blessed."*

Genesis 15:4, *"And, behold, the word of the Lord came unto him, saying, This shall not be thine heir; but he that shall come forth out of thine own bowels shall be thine heir."*

Genesis 15:18, *"In that same day the Lord made a covenant with Abram, saying, Unto thy seed have I given this land,..."*

Genesis 17:21, *"But my covenant will I establish with Isaac, which Sarah shall bear unto thee at this set time in the next year."*

4. Isaac:

Genesis 21:12b, *"in Isaac shall thy seed be called."*

Genesis 22:17, 18, *"That in blessing I will bless thee, and in multiplying I will multiply thy seed as the stars of the heaven, and as the sand which is upon the seashore; and thy seed shall possess the gate of his enemies."*

147

Genesis 24:7, *"The Lord God of heaven, which took me from my father's house, and from the land of my kindred, and which spake unto me, and that sware unto me, saying, Unto thy seed will I give this land."*

God renews the promise to Isaac, *"Sojourn in this land, and I will be with thee, and will bless thee; for unto thee,and unto thy seed, I will give all these countries, and I will perform the oath which I sware unto Abraham thy father. (Genesis 26:3).*

5. Jacob:

Isaac passed it on to Jacob.

Genesis 28:3, 4, *"And God Almighty bless thee, and make thee fruitful, and multiply thee, that thou mayest be a multitude of people; And give thee the blessing of Abraham, to thee, and to thy seed with thee; that thou mayest inherit the land wherein thou art a stranger, which God gave unto Abraham."*

God speaks it personally to Jacob in Genesis 28:13, 14, *"I am the Lord God of Abraham thy father, and the God of Isaac: the land whereon thou liest, to thee will I give it, and to thy seed; And thy seed shall be as the dust of the earth; and thou shalt spread abroad to the west, and to the east, and to the north,and to the south: and in thee and in thy seed shall all the families of the earth be blessed."*

Genesis 35:10-12, *"And God said unto him, Thy name is Jacob: thy name shall not be called any more Jacob, but Israel shall be thy name; and he called his name Israel. And God said unto him, I am God Almighty: be fruitful and multiply: a nation and a company of nations shall be of thee, and kings shall come out of thy loins; And the land which I gave Abraham and Isaac, to thee I will give it, and to thy seed after thee will I give the land."*

Long years later God speaks to Moses in the wilderness, *"And the Lord said, I have surely seen the affliction of my people which are in Egypt, and have heard their cry by reason of their*

148

taskmasters; for I know their sorrows; And I am come down to deliver them out of the hand of the Egyptians, and to bring them up out of that land unto a good land and a large, unto a land flowing with milk and honey; unto the place of the Canaanites, and the Hittites, and the Amorites, and the Perizzites, and the Hivites, and the Jebusites.'' (Exodus 3:7, 8) Compare with Genesis 15:18-21.

6. To the Church in the Wilderness God Says:

Exodus 19:4-6, *"Ye have seen what I did unto the Egyptians, and how I bare you on eagles' wings, and brought you unto myself. Now therefore, if ye will obey my voice indeed, and keep my covenant, then ye shall be a peculiar treasure unto me above all people; for all the earth is mine: And ye shall be unto me a kingdom of priests, and a holy nation. These are the words which thou shalt speak unto the children of Israel.''*

Deuteronomy 14:2, *"For thou art a holy people unto the Lord thy God, and the Lord hath chosen thee to be a peculiar people unto himself, above all the nations that are upon the earth.''*

Deuteronomy 26:18, 19, *"And the Lord hath avouched thee this day to be his peculiar people, as he hath promised thee, and that thou shouldest keep all his commandments; And to make thee high above all nations which he hath made, in praise, and in name, and in honour, and that thou mayest be a holy people unto the Lord thy God, as he hath spoken.''*

The desire of God was to have a family on the earth whom He could call His own. They would love Him, be like Him and separated from everything that would destroy them or influence them to do evil.

Deuteronomy 28:1, 2, *"And it shall come to pass, if thou shalt hearken diligently unto the voice of the Lord thy God, to observe and to do all his commandments which I command thee this day, that the Lord thy God will set thee on high above all nations of the earth. And all these blessings shall come on thee, and overtake thee, if thou shalt hearken unto the voice of the Lord thy God.''* (Continue to read up to Deuteronomy 28:14).

III. Promises of God to His Church

1. He would give them the choicest of lands, *''A land which the Lord thy God careth for: the eyes of the Lord thy God are always upon it, from the beginning of the year even unto the end of the year''* (Deuteronomy 11:12).

2. He called them His peculiar treasure who would be more precious to Him than all nations, a kingdom of priests, a holy nation (Exodus 19:4-6). A people He would *''bare upon eagles' wings.''* As priests they would commune with God. The Old Testament priests were a type of Jesus Christ. God's desire was for all his "family" to be like His perfect Son. He called His family His peculiar people (Deuteronomy 26:18). The word "peculiar" here is *cegullah* (5459) in Hebrew. It has to do with property, possession and wealth.

3. The church is the wealth of Heaven. Paul called the Philippians "his joy and his crown" (Philippians 4:1). They were His treasure in the same way that we are the Lord's treasure. God said He would open the windows of Heaven and give His people the treasure of Heaven (Deuteronomy 28:12). They would lend and never need to borrow. He also promised, *''And the Lord shall make thee the head, and not the tail''* (Deuteronomy 28:13). And He promised that all the nations of the earth would be blessed through His family (Genesis 12:3). I have counted seven times that God promised Abraham that through this chosen "family" all the nations of the world would be blessed.

IV. The Powerless Church

But what has happened? Instead of God's family or church

150

(called-out ones) being the head, we have lost our anointing, power and authority. Instead, we have become weaklings—even the tail—while the heathen have ruled over us and been thorns in our sides.

God gave Adam authority and dominion to rule His creation (Genesis 1:28). After the flood, He gave this same authority to Noah (Genesis 9:2). Later He gave it to Israel and finally to the New Testament Church.

V. How the Church Has Lost its Power

1. Babylon in the Church:

Psalm 137:1, *"By the rivers of Babylon, there we sat down, yea, we wept, when we remembered Zion."*

The church has been carried captive back to the Babylonian system. There is no joy, no victory, no power to resist our captors. It has lost its power through compromise. Nimrod, Semiramis came into the church, bringing their festive days which received, instead, saints' names, such as St. John's day, but originally were days devoted to the worship of pagan gods. The trappings of pagan Nimrodism has become such an accepted part of Christianity that if anyone speaks out against it, they are looked upon as heretics and even mercilessly killed by the church itself.

In Joshua 7 we read how Achan was put to death for stealing the Babylonian garment. It was a great sin which he committed. Because of his love for this forbidden thing, Israel lost the battle of Ai. Yet, today the church adorns herself with the Babylonian system. No wonder she has lost her power to be victorious!

2. A Flavourless Church:

In Matthew 5:13 Jesus said, *"Ye are the salt of the earth: but if the salt have lost his savour, wherewith shall it be salted? It is thenceforth good for nothing, but to be cast out, and to be trodden under foot of men.''* Because we have lost our flavour, we have lost our power to preserve. We don't even have the power to save ourselves. Instead of conquering and ruling, we are trodden under foot of men (Matthew 5:13). All over the world, the church has lost its original holy calling to witness, and therefore, it has lost its effectiveness and is put to ridicule. Through the ages the church has persecuted the church. Satan has turned us on each other and he laughs while he sits back and watches us tear each other apart. How can we fight the forces of evil when we are so busy fighting each other? The nation that is having an internal revolution can never present a united front against the enemy.

3. A Sleeping Church:

In Matthew 13:25 Jesus likens the Kingdom of Heaven unto a field which has been sown with good grain, *"But while men slept, his enemy came and sowed tares among the wheat, and went his way.'' We have been a sleeping church, unawake and unalert to the tactics of the enemy. We have lived in a state of euphoria, oblivious to the crisis we are in. A sleeping church is no better than a dead church.*

Ephesians 5:14, "Wherefore he saith, Awake thou that sleepest, and arise from the dead, and Christ shall give thee light.'' A sleeping church is as powerless against the forces of evil as a dead church. A church that is not fasting and praying is a dead church.

My heart has been deeply grieved as I have seen the church spending energy constructing massive, costly buildings for a millennium on earth, while this generation is perishing for lack of anointed missionaries. It appears to me that we have not heard the warning of the prophet, the roaring of the lion, or the growling of the bear in our streets. We are sleeping and playing, building and making merry, when all the time the devastating flood of iniquity is on the way. We could stop it if we would fast and pray. I mean REAL praying—not saying prayers. We need to travail and weep and repent and turn to God with all our hearts so that He can forgive our sins and heal our land (II Chronicles 7:14).

4. The Fatalistic, Indifferent Church:

One of the deceptive ways of thinking, which we have brought with us from the world's philosophy, is the fatalistic philosophy, "Whatever will be, will be." We lay back in our couches of ease and resign ourselves to a state of careless unconcern and apathy. We are at the stage, right now, where we will either redeem the land by fasting, prayer and casting down the strongholds of Satan, or Satan and his hordes will take dominion. There is no time left to play. Do not be deceived.

Vision of the Bear

By special permission I want to share a vision of this end-time which God gave David Lewis. I'm sure it will stir your heart as it stirred mine. For over ten years, David Lewis could not feel free to share this vision. Now, however, God has released him to tell it.

February, 1976, Chula Vista, California. This morning I had a dream of graphic, visionary quality. I was on the platform of a church in Washington, D.C. I stood in the pulpit trying to minister to the congregation. I was speaking to them about the power of prayer and fasting. I was warning the people that the world desires to rob us of our freedom to worship God and spread the Gospel.

The people were not hostile toward what I was saying, but they were not paying attention. They were distracted with inconsequential things. Some looked apathetic and bored. Some were yawning. I thought, "What is wrong. I can't get their attention." I started to make a stronger emphasis. I raised my voice. Nothing helped. I was so frustrated. The people were looking at their watches and ignoring me. They just wanted to get out of church and go home.

The pastor started making little comments that had no connection at all with what I was saying, or anything else for that matter. He addressed some irrelevant question to me, interrupting my train of thought. My level of frustration was increasing. I couldn't make any sense out of what was going on. "What in the world was I doing here?" The pastor was talking about inane things. The people were not paying attention to him either.

Finally I just quit preaching and stepped back to try and figure out what was going on. It was then that I looked out a side door that led to a room off the platform area. I was horrified to see a huge sleeping grizzly bear. I knew he could easily wake up and come out where the people were.

I slipped over to the side of the platform and quietly closed the door. It did not seem like a very strong door. I was terrified. There was no latch or lock on the door. I stood holding it shut, but knew my strength would not be enough if the sleeping bear woke up. I called to the men of the church to come and help me hold it shut. Not one, not even one person paid me any attention. I kept warning the people. I said, "If you won't help me hold the door, at least get out and save yourselves." Most of the people didn't even look my way. The few who did, chuckled tolerantly. These people were not hostile. They were just blind to the danger we faced. They were apathetic.

I was fully aware of the implication of this vision as it unfolded before me. I knew it was a warning from God that evil forces could awaken and damage the church as never before. The help I needed was not for actual physical restraint against a physical threat. The need was for intercessors to bind the powers of darkness and destruction.

154

I heard the bear stirring, awakening. He started to push the door. I could not hold it. Suddenly I was swept back as the door came crashing open. I was slammed against the wall. The bear lumbered out past me onto the platform and with one sweep of his powerful paw he killed the pastor. The animal then began savagely to ravage the people as he moved among them. No one could resist. The people screamed in terror. Their cries were so awful, I cannot even describe it. The beast attacked one after another of the people. I heard a young girl crying for help as the bear tore off her leg and then chewed on her body. People were crying pitifully. Another girl screamed, "Mama, mama, help me it's biting my head." There was a horrible crunch as her voice was silenced.

The Threat Is Real

Right now the bear has awakened. He knows we are there. He is at the door of the church.

Awaken, people of God, there is still time and there is still hope. Will you help hold the door?

Of course, I am not so foolish as to think I am the only watchman on the wall. I do not have such a grand evaluation of my own role in spreading the end-time message of warning. No one in this ministry feels that we have an exclusive on declaring both the message of warning and of potential victory. But this is the voice God is allowing you to hear right now. This is the watchman God has led to warn you at this moment. There are others crying out too.

There is a point to all of this. The beast is stirring, awakening. He has a scent of blood in his nostrils. He is hungry. He is the devourer. But he is not invincible. Will you heed the message or sleep on?

"Awake thou that sleepest, and arise from the dead, and Christ shall give thee light...Redeeming the time, because the days are evil" (Ephesians 5:14, 16).

5. *The Compromising Church:*

In our endeavour to co-exist we have become a compromising church. We have accepted humanism, not only in our schools, but also in our churches. Intellectualism has become more important to us than the pure truth of God's Word and the anointing and power of the Holy Spirit.

In our endeavour to cope with modern trends, we have tried to wed the teachings of Christ with Marxism. This is impossible! Marxism believes there is no God. It denies the creation, the miraculous, the Bible, the Deity of Christ, etc. and prepares the way for Communism. A true Marxist cannot be a Christian. In one way or another he must compromise. Yet, today we have a form of Marxist Christianity in the name of **liberal theology**.

In our endeavour to compromise, we have accepted the ancient pagan customs and religions. By encouraging their revival we have opened the door to demon worship. In the name of culture, Satan worship is again taking over in our lands with temples, Moslem mosques, Peyotism and outright Satanism. The enemy nationalizes the spirits of the aboriginal peoples in nations that had become Christian.

6. *The Ignorant Church:*

A veil of ignorance concerning spiritual warfare has taken hold of the minds of God's people. We have lost our effectiveness because of ignorance and fear. God's people don't want to hear about spiritual warfare. Our ignorance makes us an easy prey.

Binding Instead of Dislodging the Spirits

We keep on binding the devil when these demons should be rooted out and dislodged. By binding them we hinder their work but they must be cast out and dislodged completely before

156

there is deliverance. Binding is temporary—loosing is permanent.

7. *The Unforgiving Church:*

A triumphant church will be the forgiving church. Many Christians are hindered by their inability to forgive those who have offended them. Some who think themselves great in God's Kingdom are already "washed out" and they don't know it. They hate and fight their brothers. Some have conspired together to become a pack of wolves against others of God's children who have done them no harm.

I have seen Satan sow seeds of animosity in the body of Christ to such a degree that brother has ought against brother and sister against sister—and neither are able to forgive. The result is that a terrible root of bitterness has been planted in the heart, making that child of God ineffective. Satan has a legal right to set up his base of operation in any unforgiving heart. The triumphant Joel's army will never thrust one another (Joel 2:8). We can never permit ourselves to render evil for evil (I Peter 3:9).

The law of Moses demanded an eye for an eye but Jesus, when He came, gave us a new law, even the law of forgiveness, which is only able to operate through love. Matthew 5:43, 44, *"Ye have heard that it hath been said, Thou shalt love thy neighbour, and hate thine enemy. But I say unto you, Love your enemies, bless them that curse you, do good to them that hate you, and pray for them which despitefully use you, and persecute you."*

He said that if we had ought against our brother, we must go to him and try to reach a reconciliation before we bring our gift to God. He clearly told us that if we do not make peace with our brother before we reach the place of judgment, we will be severely judged.

Matthew 5:21-26 tells us that the adversary has a legal right

157

to harm us if we do not forgive. Satan knows the New Testament laws as well as he did the Old Testament laws, and he knows very well that the law Jesus gave us was the law of love and forgiveness. So if we fail to live by this law of love, Satan will "get the last farthing out of us."

Jesus could say, "The prince of the world has nothing in me" (John 14:30). Satan had no legal hold over Jesus because of His perfect life.

Sin gives Satan a legal right over a life, a family, a city, a nation and a church.

One of the reasons churches cannot grow is because there are those in leadership who have bitterness, hatred and unforgiveness. According to I Corinthians 11:27-30, if we allow unforgiveness and bitterness, we are guilty of the body and Blood of Jesus. This gives Satan a legal right to cause sickness and death.

Jesus said that if we cannot forgive others God cannot forgive us. With unforgiven sin, we are hindered from receiving answers to our prayers (Matthew 6:15).

John says, *"Beloved, if our heart condemn us not, then have we confidence toward God. And whatsoever we ask, we receive of him, because we keep his commandments, and do those things that are pleasing in his sight."* (I John 3:21, 22). Sin hinders our faith and confidence—and thereby it hinders the answers to our prayers, our relationship with God and our authority over the devil.

When Jesus forgave men their sins as He hung on the Cross, He gave us the example of what we must do. Stephen, when he was stoned, forgave those who stoned him (Acts 7:59, 60). He released his persecutors from the judgment and made it possible for them to be forgiven. Among those who had consented to the killing of Stephen was a man called Saul, who later became Paul, the mighty apostle. It was Stephen's forgiveness of Saul that released Saul to become God's man.

158

Jesus said, *"Whosoever sins ye remit, they are remitted unto them; and whosoever sins ye retain, they are retained."* (John 20:23). We have power to release people from sins against us. On the other hand, if we choose not to forgive someone's sin against us, we ourselves bear the burden of that sin through our unforgiveness, and it can become a terrible bondage to us. It allows a demonic spirit to hold us in bondage. We have the power to loose ourselves, as well as others, through forgiveness.

Sometimes pride keeps us from both forgiving and asking forgiveness. If we could see that evil spirit of pride, we would be shocked. Job 41:34 says that Leviathan is king over all the children of pride. Leviathan is the "indestructible monster-spirit" from hell who rules over many people and nations. The only way we can overcome him is by humility.

8. The Victorious Church:

Thank God, I feel that there are those who are waking up and taking their place in the Lord's end-time army. I see a church coming out of the church. Joel's army is getting ready to march. Many who study this Bible study will put on the armour of God and go forth as conquerors and make Satan's kingdom fall.

The carnal Christian will never be included in the triumphant host. *"But the natural man receiveth not the things of the Spirit of God: for they are foolishness unto him: neither can he know them, because they are spiritually discerned."* (I Corinthians 2:14) This is a spiritual warfare and it is only waged with spiritual weapons.

I Peter 2:9 says that we are God's holy nation, His royal priesthood. *"But ye are a chosen generation, a royal priesthood, a holy nation, a peculiar people; that ye should show forth the praises of him who hath called you out of darkness into his marvellous light."* When we were born again by the Holy Spirit, we were translated out of the kingdom of darkness into the Kingdom of His dear Son (Colossians 1:13). When this

159

happened, we were delivered from the powers of darkness. The evils of anger, unforgiveness and hatred do not need to hang on to us. The Prince of Darkness shall find no fault in us, whereby he has a legal right to accuse us. We are children of the light, dwelling in the light. The Prince of Darkness cannot abide in our presence. We are covered with the Blood of Jesus. The devil hates and fears the Blood and the light. Jesus said, *"...I will build my church; and the gates of hell shall not prevail against it."* (Matthew 16:18)

The eternal church is still triumphant. The same church, which in the wilderness marched under the banner of Jehovah, still marches today under the banner of His Son, Jehovah-Jesus.

For centuries the Kingdom of Heaven has suffered violence, but now, at last, His mighty ones are taking it by force. Satan shall not have dominion. *"Greater is he that is in you, than he that is in the world."* (I John 4:4)

All that we need to be able to overcome is available to us. We shall overcome in our lives, our homes, our streets, our nations. Our Captain, Jesus, is victorious. He holds in His hands the keys of death and hell (Revelation 1:18). We have nothing to fear.

By our travailing intercessory prayer we make way for the Spirit of God to be poured out on our nation. Moreover, not only does Jesus have the keys of death and hell, He has given us the keys of the Kingdom of Heaven, i.e. the keys of authority. *"And I will give unto thee the keys of the kingdom of heaven: and whatsoever thou shalt bind on earth shall be bound in heaven; and whatsoever thou shalt loose on earth shall be loosed in heaven."* (Matthew 16:19). In some parts of the world, when they want to honour a person, the mayor presents him with the key to the city. Jesus has given us the keys to the one great city that Abraham looked for all the days of his life. The city of the Kingdom of God, even spiritual Mount Zion. Hallelujah!

This is the city of victory where captive souls are set free.

160

"And in the mountain shall the Lord of hosts make unto all people a feast of fat things; a feast of wines on the lees, of fat things full of marrow, of wines on the lees well refined.

And he will destroy in this mountain the face of the covering cast over all people, and the veil that is spread over all nations.'' (Isaiah 25:6, 7)

This Mount Zion, this holy Jerusalem, is not a stationary "city"—it is a moving city, which moves whichever way and to whatever area the Holy Spirit determines. And it can be all over the world at the same time—depending on where its "citizens" are. It is a victorious city that tears the veil of covering and blindness off the minds of the people. This veil is the result of the fall; but when we, ourselves, have been redeemed and set free from the curse, we can, in turn, go out and redeem the land. We can break the power of the curse so that the veil can be removed from the minds of the people. When this happens, Satan's demonic hold will be broken and they will be free to follow Jesus. Jesus has already defeated Satan. We only have to enter in and claim the victory and remind the devil he has been defeated. He has already been judged (John 16:11). We have to remind him he is defeated and that he has to release his hold over them. Jesus said that the prince of the world is judged. This is the church against which the gates of hell can never prevail (Matthew 16:18).

9. The Exonerated Church:

Satan thrives on accusation. In Revelation 12:10 he is called "the accuser of the brethren." We know this is true because he accused Job to God Almighty. He is a powerful prosecuting lawyer. He has prepared his case against us very well when he presents it to the Eternal court of Justice. Not one of us, in our own defence, can honestly plead "not guilty" and he knows that. When all the evidence is given and the jury is ready to decide the verdict, Jesus takes the stand and swings the balance in our favour. What is He saying? Listen to His plea!

"You, being dead in sins and the uncircumcision of your flesh, I have made you alive together with Me and I have forgiven you all your trespasses, for I blotted out the laws and judgments that were against you; I have eradicated them forever by nailing them to the Cross!" (from Colossians 2:13, 14)

The prosecutor of our souls has to admit defeat. This is not a case for prosecution, when we have not committed a crime. A crime is the breaking of the law. When Jesus was crucified, Satan, in his madness, made one terrible mistake, he nailed his right to prosecute us on the Cross, together with Jesus. Hallelujah! And for all those who accept Jesus as the One who died for their sins, the One who took their place, there is no more condemnation (Romans 8:1).

Romans 5:1, 2, *"Therefore being justified by faith, we have peace with God through our Lord Jesus Christ: by whom also we have access by faith into his grace wherein we stand, and rejoice in hope of the glory of God."*

Romans 8:33, *"Who shall lay any thing to the charge of God's elect? It is God that justifieth."*

STUDY QUESTIONS

1. Read Revelation 12:1-17 and Revelation 17:1-24.

2. Explain the word "church."

3. When did the church begin?

4. Trace the church in the Old Testament.

5. In what beautiful way does God describe His church and what are His promises to it?

6. In what seven ways has the church lost its savour?

7. Describe the victorious church.

8. How is the church exonerated?

9. Memorize Romans 8:33, Colossians 2:13, 14, Matthew 16:18.

CHAPTER THIRTEEN

THE LORD'S TABLE

I. Holy Communion Is a Very Great and Holy Sacrament in the Church

This chapter is the heart of this Bible study. Before we go into the discussion of this vital subject, let us begin by reading carefully Matthew 26:26-29, *"And as they were eating, Jesus took bread, and blessed it, and brake it, and gave it to the disciples, and said, Take, eat; this is my body. And he took the cup, and gave thanks, and gave it to them, saying, Drink ye all of it; For this is my blood of the new testament, which is shed for many; for the remission of sins. But I say unto you, I will not drink henceforth this fruit of the vine, until that day when I drink it new with you in my Father's kingdom."*

Now read the revelation which the Apostle Paul received from the Lord concerning this very important sacrament of the church (I Corinthians 11:23-34).

We have read and heard these words so many times during the Holy Communion service that we don't even listen or concentrate on their very important message. These words in Corinthians are a message of life and a warning of death.

As I have already mentioned, this chapter is the heart of this book. I write it to impress upon you the great importance and significance of the Lord's Supper. It is never to be taken lightly nor in ignorance. So important is the Holy Communion that Satan counterfeits it in the black mass of the satanic rites.

Paul warned, *"For he that eateth and drinketh unworthily, eateth and drinketh damnation to himself, not discerning the Lord's body. For this cause many are weak and sickly among you, and many sleep."* (I Corinthians 11:29, 30). Then he

164

counsels us to judge ourselves so that God doesn't need to chasten nor punish us for our sins.

II. The Bread—The Body

In I Corinthians 10:16-18 we read, *"The cup of blessing which we bless, is it not the communion of the blood of Christ? The bread which we break, is it not the communion of the body of Christ? For we being many are one bread and one body: for we are all partakers of that one bread. Behold Israel after the flesh: are not they which eat of the sacrifices partakers of the altar?"*

Paul is likening the body of Christ to a loaf of bread or a levitical priesthood company who all have the same privileges of partaking of the priests' shoulder portion of meat (Leviticus 7:32-34). When we fight and devour one another with angry words, we are tearing up the body of Christ. This is what it means when He says, *"whosoever shall eat this bread, and drink this cup of the Lord, unworthily, shall be guilty of the body and blood of the Lord."* That is why Paul so strongly warns us to examine ourselves (I Corinthians 11:28) before we eat of that bread or drink of that cup.

III. More Than A Memorial

The Holy Communion is much more than a simple memorial. The Jewish Passover is a memorial (Deuteronomy 16:1-8; see verse three). For six days before the Passover, God's people were commanded to search their houses for leaven. It was symbolic of the day when we would search our hearts for sin before partaking of the Supper of the Lamb of God. If they had to be so careful then, lest, because of disregard for God's holiness they would be cut off (Exodus 12:15), how much more careful must we be now (Hebrews 2:1-3, 10:28-31)!!

165

The Passover supper was to be a perpetual remembrance throughout all generations and all places (Exodus 12:25-28). I believe God wants us to ever respect and desire the Holy Communion. The church or denomination that disregards this holy ordinance will soon become a powerless church. The Salvation Army was born in fire and blood, but the leaders never felt the need to observe the Sacrament of Holy Communion. Today in many parts of the world, it is more like a social welfare organization than the powerful army it once was.

While the Old Testament Passover supper was a memorial to Israel's great deliverance out of the land of Egypt, the Lord's supper is much more than a memorial. It is a powerful weapon against demonic spirits because it is a reminder to them of the mighty redemptive work of Jesus through His death and suffering. It is a "present day" reminder to Satan that he was defeated at the Cross and that we know it and are claiming it and therefore, he must release his stronghold over an area or a person.

IV. The Lord Is Present During Holy Communion

1. From the first, the early church observed the "breaking of bread" (Acts 2:41-43). In verse 42 this word translated "breaking of bread," (*klasis*, 2800) refers quite often to Holy Communion. The church was a powerful church—a highly respected church as it says in verse 43, *"And fear came upon every soul: and many wonders and signs were done by the apostles."* It appears as though they felt it an honour to break bread together from house to house (verse 46). The Lord's Supper became the altar of the saints, the place of high communion with the Father God. He honours us by communing with us as He promised, *"I will not drink henceforth of this fruit of the vine, until that day when I drink it new with you in my Father's kingdom."* (Matthew 26:29). His Kingdom with

166

you is not up there in Heaven. It is right here in our hearts (Luke 17:21).

2. The Lord comes and shares the Communion Table with us. Since a child I have seen the motto which says the Lord is the unseen guest at every table. How much more is He the unseen guest at our Communion table! The Jews have a tradition in which they always laid a place at the table for that unseen guest at the time of their Passover supper. That alone should tell us that the Lord is present at every Communion Service. Yet how few of us honour and respect His Divine Presence! We come to "The Table" with unwashed hearts and dare to take the holy bread from the Lord with sinful, unholy hands. Is there any wonder that there is judgment in the house of God? We are forbidden to mix sin with holiness. *"Ye cannot drink the cup of the Lord, and the cup of devils: ye cannot be partakers of the Lord's table, and of the table of devils."* (I Corinthians 10:21). We need to confess our sins and prepare our hearts before we take the Holy Communion.

V. Examine Ourselves

We must never be afraid to examine ourselves. Jesus said, *"Therefore if thou bring thy gift to the altar, and there rememberest that thy brother hath aught against thee; Leave there thy gift before the altar, and go thy way; first be reconciled to thy brother, and then come and offer thy gift."* (Matthew 5:23, 24). Unless relationships are correct, our offering of ourselves at the altar of Holy Communion is unacceptable. If we don't forgive, we cannot be forgiven. In Mark 11:25, 26 Jesus says, *"And when ye stand praying, forgive, if ye have aught against any; that your Father also which is in heaven may forgive you your trespasses. But if ye do not forgive, neither will your Father*

167

which is in heaven forgive your trespasses.'' That is the law of the New Covenant.

Jesus gave us the law of love (John 13:34). He said that if we love our brother, we live in the light and cannot stumble, but if we hate our brother, we are in darkness and have lost our way because our eyes are blind (I John 2:10, 11).

We should never go to sleep with unconfessed and unrepented sins. If we do, it gives Satan a legal right to torment us with nightmares and even worse. Neither should we take the Holy Communion without first confessing our sins. None of us is perfect. If we think we are, we could be deceived by the devil. That was one of his sins. Don't let your pride stand in the way of dealing with those hidden sins in your life.

VI. The Missionary Who Could Not Forgive

No one knows better than I the terrible things that can happen when someone takes Holy Communion without first asking forgiveness. I feel I must share two very sad things that happened in two different nations. I will only change the names.

While living in Hong Kong, I worked with a very dear missionary in the music department of the church. We often spent long moments visiting together after choir practice. Bertha shared her trials and testings with me. There was one missionary, Sally, who was from another country but worked in the same missionary organization. Sally was one of the most critical, fault-finding, provoking, contradictory people that one could meet. She seemed to take a joy out of making the lives of the other missionaries in that organization miserable by disagreeing with everything and everyone. She was the proverbial "thorn in the flesh." My friend Bertha suffered the most from her, perhaps it was because she was in a place of leadership. Bertha would pour out her heart and talk and talk about Sally to me, while I listened and sympathized. Fortunately, I did not have to have any communication with that woman myself. But I began to dislike her just by listening to Bertha's experiences.

There was another lady missionary Bertha strongly disliked. She was not of the same organization, so the two did not have much association with each other. Something had happened between them in the past which had left a root of bitterness in Bertha's heart toward this second missionary, Thelma. If Thelma ever came to the church which Bertha and her husband pastored, Bertha would avoid speaking to her or even greeting her.

Now Bertha may have had every right to be hurt and angry, but because she could not get the victory over it, Satan had a legal right to attack her. A few years went by and everything seemed to be all right.

Then one day I was asked to preach in a Sunday morning service. I often was invited to preach Sunday evening, but Sunday morning was when we had the big crowd. It was a great honour for me to have this opportunity. I fell on my knees and asked God to give me His message for the people.

The Lord gave me my first message on the power of the Blood of Jesus. He also emphasized to me the importance of taking the Holy Communion with a pure heart. (I still have those original yellow pages of notes.*) I knew God was asking me to stand in the pulpit on Sunday morning as a prophet of warning to the church—and not as a friend.

With fear and trembling, I took my place behind the pulpit, and God began to speak through my mouth. It was a very important hour in all of our lives. It was Communion Sunday. I heard the Lord warn His people through my lips that they must not take the Holy Communion without first making things right with those whom they had ought against. The warning was very

---

*These notes are the basis for Gwen Shaw's Bible study *The Power of the Precious Blood*.

169

strong. God said that if they did not heed His warning, it would be their last Communion. I knew in my heart this warning was for my friend, Bertha. With tears I pled for her to please be humble enough to heed God's warning and not take Communion without first, at least, trying to make things right. Of course, I did not point her out, but I know that the Holy Spirit had done it.

After ministering, I returned to the organ to resume my duties there. I could hardly see the notes through the tears. When the Communion emblems were passed to my friend, I prayed that she would refuse them. I knew it would be catastrophic for her if she didn't. But she was the leading woman missionary of the church and it would have been an open confession of sin before all the church, if she had refused them, and it would have taken great humility. I saw her reach out and take them and a knife went through my heart. That was the last Communion she ever took. By the next Communion Sunday she had such a severe headache that she could not leave her bed. We buried her shortly afterwards. She died of a terrible malignant brain tumour that blinded her and disabled her so completely that even if she had wanted to make things right on her deathbed, she was not able to do so. She couldn't even talk.

Her sickness and death shook me to the core of my being. Although I had preached that morning message, I did not consider myself perfect, nor was I innocent. I had listened to all that gossip about Sally and Thelma. I had even allowed my heart to become antagonistic against these two women. I knew in my heart I was guilty, too. I felt that God would smite me next. I repented, wept before God and asked for mercy. I asked Him to help me to forgive anyone that I ever had anything against. He humbled me by making me write them letters, or, if they lived in Hong Kong, by speaking to them personally. I had to write one letter that was so hard to mail, I carried it around for days before I had the courage to drop it in the mailbox.

I had to write to people who didn't even know I had anything against them—preachers, famous evangelists, etc. Each person to whom I wrote answered me very lovingly. There were ten different ones of whom I had to ask forgiveness. God didn't tell me about all these ten at once. If He had, I don't know if I would have had the courage to do it, but He only told me one at a time. And when I looked at my dear friend in a coma, who was suffering so terribly, I was afraid not to obey God. I couldn't even tell her what was happening to me. She couldn't hear any more.

But when God finished with me, He had helped me clean up the tabernacle of my heart with the candle of the convicting power of the Holy Ghost and I was a changed person.

VII. A Father's Sins Kill His Child

The second tragic incident took place in Indonesia. Again, it was a Communion Sunday and I was preaching in Semarang in a church of well over 2,000 members. The tabernacle was packed to the door. God had been moving mightily in the meetings. That morning God laid it on my heart to preach the same message I had preached in Hong Kong. I did not know the people there, like I had in Hong Kong.

Again the Holy Spirit called for the people to search their hearts, confess their sins and make things right with their brothers and sisters. With tears and trembling I warned the congregation of the terrible consequences of disobedience to the warning of the Holy Ghost. I knew God was speaking to someone very far in the back to my left. But I didn't know who it was. I begged him to please be humble enough to refuse the Bread and the Cup until he had asked forgiveness of the one he had ought against. When I sat down, I felt that someone in that audience was again disregarding the Holy Spirit's warning. The elders, who knew more than I did, wept bitterly.

171

The next morning after our 5 a.m. prayer meeting and 6-7 a.m. Bible study at the church, the elders asked me to pray for a young man. I went over to him and was going to pray for him when suddenly I felt like I would be praying for a statue. God said, "Don't pray for him. I will not answer your prayer."

I stopped and told him, "Something is terribly wrong. God will not let me pray for you. What is it?"

He broke down, weeping, "I was the one whom you warned in your sermon yesterday. There is sin and anger in my heart and God has been dealing with me for a long time, but I have rebelled against Him. I took His Holy Communion in spite of your warning—and in the night my little daughter was struck down with sickness. She is dying in the hospital. Sister Gwen, will you please, at least, come and pray for her?"

I wept with him and together with the church leaders went to the hospital. The young mother stood weeping beside her young daughter. I prayed for the child and so did they, but the angel of death took her that same day.

Two days later we all stood at the little one's grave. The father, brokenhearted, fell to his knees, sobbing and crying out, "My baby, my little girl, please forgive me. It is my sins that put you in your grave." His wife and the elders could not comfort him. But two nights later as he knelt at the altar, I went to him and laid my hands on him and prayed for him. God gave him a prophetic word of comfort and his soul was restored.

Who was this young man? What had been his problem? He had been the youth director and the minister of music in the church. Pride had entered his heart and rebellion against the leadership of the church. Because of an argument that took place, he left his ministry of music and lost his position as youth leader. In anger he had allowed Satan to plant rebellion and hate in his heart. Two times before God had dealt with him to repent. The last time, a year earlier, a prophet of God warned him that if he did not repent, God would punish him. He was told that that was his last chance.

When I preached on that fatal Sunday morning, the young man knew God had warned him many times, but he blamed others for his troubles. He refused to accept the warning of the Holy Spirit. he knew he shouldn't take the Holy Communion without going to the elders and making things right and they knew it, too. That is why they wept so much when I preached that sermon.

The price of disobedience is too high for us to pay. Let us, each one, search our hearts, and ask God to turn the candle of the Holy Spirit upon our souls. If there is any leaven of sin in our hearts, now is the time to get rid of it so that we can be free to take Holy Communion and minister it to the cursed world.

To those who might misjudge God in His dealings, I recommend the reading of the story of David and his first son by Bathsheba (II Samuel 12:1-23).

VIII. God Will Search Jerusalem With Candles

As we humble ourselves and ask God to turn His search light on our souls, God will do a deep work of sanctification in the church. God says in Zephaniah 1:12, *"And it shall come to pass at that time, that I will search Jerusalem with candles, and punish the men that are settled on their lees: that say in their heart, The Lord will not do good, neither will he do evil."*

There is a popular gospel being preached that doesn't believe in the existence of the devil, nor in the judgment for sins. It is a so-called "positive gospel" which is very pleasing to the ear and very comfortable to the unrepentant heart and the sinning "saint," but this is not the Gospel that Paul preached.

When we observe the Holy Communion, it is a very powerful and meaningful thing. We must never take it lightly.

173

IX. A Sign of Deliverance From Bondage

Passover was not only a memorial of the passover night in Egypt; it was a symbol and a reminder to themselves and the devil that they had been delivered from bondage. When we take Holy Communion, it is a sign to our enemy—the same destroyer who smote the firstborn of Egypt (Exodus 12:23)—that we have been delivered from his power and bondage and that he has no legal authority over us. Moreover, we now have authority over him. We are like the prisoner who has overpowered his cruel tormenting guard, taken his gun and is now pointing it at him and shouting, "Hands up, devil, I have got you covered with the Blood of Jesus!" The evil one can never break through that covering to harm you. That is offensive warfare at its best!

X. A Family Sacrament

The thing that kept the Jewish families together was the celebration of their feast days. They were and still are family observances. It was "a lamb for a household" (Exodus 12:3). The children, too, partook of the elements of the Passover supper. Likewise, Christians by faith can give their children Communion until the child is old enough to be instructed and taught to love and understand its meaning. As our children come to an age of accountability, they must be warned of the danger of eating and drinking unworthily. Remember that Jesus said that unless we become as little children we shall in no wise enter the Kingdom of Heaven (Luke 18:15-17, Matthew 19:14). It is a good thing for a father (or a mother in cases where there is no father) to observe Holy Communion as a family. It is especially comforting in a time of bereavement or some other family crisis. Perhaps once a week could be a time for this sacred family altar—or before a member of the family must leave to go on a journey or off to college. Many brides and grooms have chosen to

174

celebrate communion as an occasion of joy at their weddings, thereby sealing their marriage at the altar of the Lord, by honouring their covenant of marriage by linking it with the covenant God has made with them through the Blood of His Son.

Satan hates the Holy Communion. He flees from the altar of Holy Sacrament because it reminds him that he is defeated by Jesus' death (I John 3:8). The works of the devil are destroyed through the presence of Jesus. Holy Communion brings the Lord's presence to our weddings and into our homes and churches. Jesus is a happy person. He loves happy occasions, especially weddings (John 2:1-11). Jesus came to take away our sorrows and give abundant life (John 10:10). That abundant life includes joy, peace, health, prosperity, and everything good.

XI. The Power of the Broken Body of Our Lord in the Bread

All sin, misery, pain and evil was laid upon Jesus. Isaiah 53:5 says:

1. He has borne our griefs.

2. He has carried our sorrows.

3. He was wounded for our transgressions (*pesha*, 6588), that includes all our rebellions against His high and holy will.

4. He was bruised for our iniquities (*avon*, 5771—"depravity, perversion, guilt, crimes, faults, mischief").

5. The chastisement of our peace was upon Him (*muwcar*, 4148—"punishment, correction, discipline, self-control"). Where, because of our rebellion and perverseness, it might have taken centuries to correct and discipline us and mould our characters into a Christ-like nature, and thereby give us pure inner peace of mind, through Christ suffering in our stead, this great work of grace can be done in our lives in as short a time as we allow Him to work His work in us. Many have experienced

175

powerful and sudden works of sanctification in their lives with only one touch of God.

6. By His stripes we are healed. Every emotional and physical pain or wound has its source of healing in Jesus' great work of redemption. Peter identifies the messianic prophecy by Isaiah with the suffering of our Lord (I Peter 2:24).

7. Isaiah 53:8b—by the transgression of my people was He stricken (*nega*, 5061—"a blow, a stroke, a plague, such as leprosy or any other incurable disease)."

Yes, Jesus even bore our incurable diseases and plagues such as AIDS, cancer, Alzheimer's and any name that is named. That is why His Name is greater than any other name (Philippians 2:10).

As He broke the bread, Jesus said, "This is my body, which is broken for you." When we receive the bread at Holy Communion as an act of faith, we are receiving all the redemptive strength and healing that His holy Body can give us.

Jesus gave His Body to the scourgers that He might purchase healing for His creation. This healing power avails not only for us (it is the children's bread—Mark 7:27), but for the whole animal kingdom, and even for the redemption of the earth. All creation is waiting for us to set them free. *"For the earnest expectation of the creature waiteth for the manifestation of the sons of God. For the creature was made subject to vanity, not willingly, but by reason of him who hath subjected the same in hope; Because the creature itself also shall be delivered from bondage of corruption into the glorious liberty of the children of God."* (Romans 8:19-21)

XII. The Power of the Blood of Christ

While the Body of Christ gives healing, His Blood gives life, for the life is in the blood (Leviticus 17:11). As we partake of the Cup of Communion, we are receiving in faith that abundant life. The wages of sin is death (Romans 6:23. We all have sinned (Romans 6:23). So we are all under the sentence of death. But the Lord Jesus shed His Holy Blood for us and in so doing, He gave us eternal life in exchange for death. For life is in the blood and God has given it to us upon the altar to make atonement for our souls (Leviticus 17:11).

XIII. The Power of the Holy Spirit in the Anointing Oil

In Exodus 30:22-33, the Lord gave us the ingredients of the holy anointing oil for the sanctification and setting apart of the holy vessels of the sanctuary and the priesthood unto God. This oil was considered sacred and never to be used in a common way. Every vessel that was anointed with it became a consecrated vessel and was considered holy (Exodus 30:29).

All through the scriptures we can read about oil being poured out upon a person or a thing for the purpose of dedicating it to God.

1. In Genesis 28:18 Jacob poured oil on a stone and God set that place apart. It was called Bethel—the House of God.

2. The prophet Samuel poured oil on Saul, anointing him to be king of Israel (I Samuel 10:1) and on David, anointing him to be king after Saul (I Samuel 16:13).

3. Zadok, the priest, anointed Solomon to be king of Israel (I Kings 1:39).

4. God told Elijah to anoint Elisha to be the prophet who would take Elijah's place (I Kings 19:16).

5. The High Priest, Jehoida, anointed 7-year-old Jehoash to reign over Judah and thus overthrew the wicked usurper, Athaliah (II Kings 11:12).

There are many such wonderful accounts of the power and authority that is transferred or imparted upon a place or a person

177

when it is anointed with oil. God recognizes this act of faith and obedience.

6. The sick: In James 5:14-15 God gave instructions for divine healing, *"Is any sick among you? let him call for the elders of the church; and let them pray over him, anointing him with oil in the name of the Lord. And the prayer of faith shall save the sick, and the Lord shall raise him up; and if he hath committed sins, they shall be forgiven him."*

There is not only healing, but also forgiveness which takes place when the healing rays of the Lord are released upon a sick person or a sick land.

XIV. Redeeming the Land

Our lands are sick. The time has come for God's people to go forth in simple faith and obedience and redeem the land. Let us take the elements of salvation and healing from our churches into our homes and out to the nations of the world. As we partake of the broken body of Christ, we partake of His resurrection life. We impart life to ourselves. As we partake of His Body, we are renewed in strength and we can minister strength to the earth. As we partake of the cup of His Blood, we receive forgiveness and can minister redemption to the earth.

It is time to redeem the lands that have been defiled by witchcraft, abortion, murder, idolatry, etc. by holding the Lord's Supper in the areas that God shows us need redeeming. It is time to break the curse and the power the evil spirits have over an area.

We can redeem the land like Noah, Abraham, Gideon, Samuel, David and hosts of others have done. We do not need to offer a sacrifice like they did. Jesus has already shed His Blood and become the sacrifice for sin. But we need to pray over the cursed land, cast out the powers that have ruled over areas, and hold Holy Communion over those areas—reminding

178

Satan that they have been redeemed by the precious Blood of Jesus and he has to relinquish his hold over them. Satan is a usurper. He has deceived the whole world. We have authority to break his hold. We are the **only ones** who have authority over the devil. The world doesn't have it. Jesus gave it to us, *"Behold, I give you power to tread on serpents and scorpions, and over all the power of the enemy; and nothing shall by any means hurt you."* (Luke 10:19) Let us go forth in the Name of the Lord Jesus Christ. Remember, the whole creation is waiting to be delivered (Romans 8:22). May Jesus be able to say of us as He did of the seventy whom He sent out to do His mighty works, *"I beheld Satan as lightning fall from heaven."* (Luke 10:18).

And finally, we must pour oil on the redeemed land and dedicate it back to God that the whole world can become a Bethel (House of God). This is a sign that we believe that God is healing the land.

XIV. The Trinity In The Bread, Wine And Oil

The Bread—The Son: The bread is the symbol of the Lord Jesus. It portrays the body of God, the Son, who took upon Himself humanity.

The Blood—The Father: The Blood is the symbol of God, the Father of spirits. He breathed the breath of life into Adam and gave man the gift of life in his Blood, for life is in the Blood. so the Blood carries in it the presence of God—the Source and Giver of Life.

The Oil—The Holy Spirit: The oil has always been a symbol of the Holy Spirit. When Samuel anointed Saul with oil, the Spirit of the Lord came upon him and he was transformed into another man (I Samuel 10:1, 6).

Elohiym created the world (Genesis 1:1); Elohiym will redeem and restore it!

179

STUDY QUESTIONS

1. Read Matthew 26:26-29, I Corinthians 11:23-34, Isaiah 53:1-12.

2. In what way was the Passover supper like the Holy Communion?

3. Explain I Corinthians 10:16-18 and Leviticus 7:32-34.

4. Why is it so important for us to examine ourselves before taking Holy Communion?

5. Why should children partake of the Holy Communion?

6. How does the Body of Christ have power in the Holy Communion?

7. How does the Blood of Christ have power in the Holy Communion?

8. How does the oil relate to redeeming the land?

9. Why is the Holy Communion so powerful in relation to redeeming the land?

10. In what way do the bread, wine and oil represent the Holy Trinity of the Father, Son and Holy Spirit?

11. Memorize Isaiah 53:4, 5 and Matthew 5:23, 24.

CONCLUSION

WONDERFUL EXPERIENCES OF VICTORY OVER RULING SPIRITS

In conclusion I want to share with you some of the most wonderful testimonies of miraculous deliverance which took place when God's people went out to redeem the land in their areas. When this truth was first shared with me by a well-reputed man of God in Zimbabwe, Richard Langworthy, he also shared many wonderful experiences which he and other men of God, pastors, evangelists, and workers—both ordained and laymen—have had as they entered into these places of spiritual warfare in this way.

God gave them a pattern of warfare. They are not the only ones who were given this pattern. Colin Wilkinson, a humble, anointed servant of God from England has been taking this message to the British Isles. God has shown His servants the strong demonic hold which Satan has over the British Isles, but as God's people go forth in prayer-power, redeeming their land, Satan's strongholds are being broken. Jesus saw Satan fall when His disciples went out casting out demons and healing the sick (Luke 10:17-19) and the time has come for it to happen again. Already, there are thousands of prayer cells all over the world. These prayer calls are the salvation of our nations.

Here is a suggested list of steps you can take when you go forth to "redeem the land." These are more or less the steps of ministry which both Pastor Wilkinson and Pastor Langworthy use:

HOW TO BREAK THE CURSE TO REDEEM THE LAND

1. **Share your burden with others.** Get only courageous and strong intercessors who live a holy life and have

181

faith, to work with you. Unholy lives can be attacked by evil spirits. You will be coming up against strong demon princes who have ruled over their areas for centuries; and your protection is your holy life, your faith and the Blood of Jesus. Remember what happened to the seven sons of Sceva who tried to cast out demons in their own power (Acts 19:13-17).

2. **Prepare your hearts with prayer** and fasting and repentance of all sins. Cover yourself with the Blood of Jesus. You could have Holy Communion with those who stay behind. Never give way to fear!

3. **Ask God to show you the area** He wants you to go. Locate national shrines, places where murder or suicide or innumerable car accidents have taken place and where witchcraft has been practised.

4. **Go together to the area to be redeemed.**

5. **On arrival begin to praise the Lord.** Then walk around and seek God to show each one the sins that were committed there. Write them on a piece of paper and then come together and share what God has shown each one.

6. **Confess these sins to the Lord** on behalf of the transgressors. Bring everything to light. The demons don't like the light.

7. **Exalt the Lord with high praises.**
Sing in the Spirit.
Declare the victory.
Read Psalm 149:6−9 (you can also sing it!).

182

8. **Hold the Lord's Supper.** Recall how David the psalmist said, *"Thou preparest a table before me in the presence of mine enemies"* (Psalm 23:5).

   a. *Call the protecting angels of the Lord to be a canopy over you.*

   b. *Invite Jesus to come and have communion with you.* Remember, Jesus promised He would drink it with us in our Father's Kingdom. (Matthew 26:29.) He is always is with us when we take communion. He is the unseen guest at every communion "table".

   c. *Call the spirits to attention.*

   d. *Pass the bread around.*
   —Each person takes a piece and divides it in half.
   —Each person eats one half and "sows" the other half in the ground.
   The reason for this is that bread speaks of strength. (Psalm 104:15.) It speaks of the atoning and redemptive work of healing for all God's creation which was wrought through the broken, suffering body of Christ. *"And with his stripes we are healed."* (Isaiah 53:5, I Peter 2:24). Even as our bodies often experience an enduement of strength and healing through the partaking of the communion bread — so also, in faith we speak and impart strength and health to the ground which has lost its strength through the curse. (Genesis 4:12)

183

—No longer will the land be barren.

—No longer will women's wombs be barren and closed up.

—No longer will there be sickness and a curse upon the land.

You are speaking **strength, strength, strength** into the ground.

e. *Pass the cup.*

Thank God for the power of the precious Blood of Jesus. Remember together that there is redemption through the Blood. (Ephesians 1:7, Colossians 1:14.) Everyone partakes of it. Pour the rest onto the ground as a witness that the Blood of Jesus Christ has been shed to break the curse, for the release of the land from all demonic authority and that Christ forgives the land. As you pour it out say, *"The curse caused by the blood of innocent people that died here is broken once and for all! Blood is required for blood."* (Numbers 35:33, 34)

9. **Anoint the ground with oil** just as Jacob did, for its healing and dedication back to God. (Genesis 28:18, 19)

10. **Tell the spirits** that you are issuing them orders that their time of dominion is ended. The spirits are made naked by our confession. The laws that are passed in the high courts are executed by those who enforce the law. We are God's law enforcement officers and military. We are here to execute what God has already decreed.

11. **Sing in the Spirit**—rejoice and dance and praise the Lord with a glad heart. The demons can't stand praise.

12 . **Prophesy life and blessing** to the ground as God's Spirit leads.

13. **Divide Satan's Kingdom.**
Remember: Lucifer rules through fear. The spirits have no love for each other. They too, rule those beneath them through fear. Pride and jealousy, which caused him to commit insurrection, possesses the spirits of his own ranks. Those spirits all want Lucifer's position. By dividing his kingdom it is weakened. A divided kingdom cannot stand (Matthew 12:25). When you strike the shepherd, the "sheep" will scatter. When you strike the chief demon, the lesser demons will scatter (Zechariah 13:7, Matthew 26:31).

14 . **Praise God** because He has given you authority to cast down the strongholds of Satan.

"For the weapons of our warfare are not carnal, but mighty through God to the pulling down of strongholds." (II Corinthians 10:4)

"Ye are of God, little children, and have overcome them: because greater is he that is in you, than he that is in the world." (I John 4:4)

"In all these things we are more than conquerors through him that loved us." (Romans 8:37)

Satan must recognize the power of the Blood of Jesus. *"For the Lord will pass through to smite the Egyptians; and when he seeth the blood upon the lintel, and on the two side posts, the Lord will pass*

185

over the door, and will not suffer the destroyer to come in unto your houses to smite you.''

(Exodus 12:23)

TRUE TESTIMONIES

Now let Richard Langworthy tell his stories of high adventure as he shared them with us:

Curse of Drought Broken

"Let me just say, at this point in time, that we did something that was unusual in Bulawayo last year at the end of March. I took a team out, and we went and dealt with certain high places, and we dealt with certain rain gods. It was actually the first time we had gone out as a team, and we were feeling our way. We weren't quite sure what to expect. We spent the whole day out there, and that night we came back. I was lying in my bed. The sky was clear, but I was awakened at two o'clock in the morning by an electrical storm over my home and over the Bulawayo area. There were no clouds and almost no lightning. There were just the most uncanny peals of thunder and rumblings. I remember lying on my bed when I woke up, and I said, 'God, if ever I heard a war in the heavenlies between angelic beings and demons, that sounds like it.' It was such a strange noise. It was spooky!

"Sunday afternoon the first clouds came. In the past, every time the rains arrived, a cold East Wind would suddenly blow and disperse the clouds, due to a curse placed here against rain. We had taken authority over the curse. By Monday the rains came and it rained for two weeks in April in Matabeleland, saving it from the worst drought we ever had. We never, ever, in our history had so much rain in April. It went down in the records as the highest rainfall since they started recording. I believe we broke one of the curses in our area.

Ancient Places of Worship

"You can go into a community, like we have one particular suburb of Bulawayo, where a succession of murders took place. There's not a pagan shrine there, but there's a demonic oppression over that community, so we've gone in there and we've broken up the curse over that suburb. Other times we've gone to particular places of worship, where we know the people actually worship now or have worshipped there in the past. Now it may be a place of national or historical interest, and although perhaps no one has worshipped there for one or two hundred years, the ruling spirits are still there. The spirits are happy even though the people may not be going there now, and we've forgotten the fact that it was a place of worship, because they've been there for two centuries and they've established their canopies with tremendous strength.

Lifting the Demonic Canopy Through Praise

"The first afternoon when we went out, we saw a big 'dome' rock on a farm. It's about four feet high and forty feet across. It's a natural earth dome. It's got grass and thorn bushes on it, but it's hollow. You throw rocks on it and it vibrates. It goes 'Boom!' like a big bass drum. The local people won't go near it. If a cow happens to be on the dome, they throw stones at the cow—they won't go fetch it. There was a lot of other activity there: There was a resident witch on the farm, who helped control all the labourers. So we went with the farmer to this dome, and we started standing on it and praying and walking around confessing the sins as God was showing us. Then we tried to praise the Lord, and it was as though a steel plate fell

187

out of heaven upon our lips; the men found it almost impossible to say anything. When we prayed, our voices were just disappearing into the air, and it was almost as though we couldn't hear ourselves. It was the most uncanny feeling. So I called them together and I said, 'Now listen, we have got to exercise dominion. Now get your act together and declare the Lordship of Jesus! Shout until they can hear you ten kilometres away!' By faith we lifted up our voices and we started to praise, and to praise, and to praise! Then suddenly we felt that canopy lift. I could see it in their faces, all simultaneously. They looked at me and they were grinning, and it came together. Then the volume rose and the flow in the Spirit began and we started dancing in the Spirit, glorifying the name of Jesus Christ! We were binding the kings with chains through our praise, almost as with fetters of iron! We were saying, 'The army of God is in this area and we're here to bring deliverance!' Amen.

The Raintree

"We have learned that we have to literally say, 'The Blood of Christ on this ground breaks the curse forever.' I'm telling you whenever we have done that, that is when the release has come. We've stood in some places and you can literally feel the air humming with the oppression. There was one place we went seventy—eight kilometres into the bush to a raintree. It was a focal point for witch doctors and rainmakers from all of Matabeleland. They used to zoom into that place. It was a huge baobab tree with a hole in the middle into which you could put thirty to forty people. I had fourteen men with me and we decided to do a Jericho march. We marched around there seven times just to declare our authority. We fourteen men, moving around in a line, didn't get around more than one third of that tree at a time—that's how big it was. There was a swarm of killer bees in the branches which would sting anyone coming to this tree. So we marched around seven times for the inhabitants to see that we could make as much noise as we liked and the killer bees weren't moving. They just stayed in their hive as we were praying there. Finally I took the cup and threw the wine into the mouth of the 'cave' in the tree. As I did it, something snapped in the realm of the spirit. All of these men—my experienced team, local leadership and those who hadn't had much experience in this kind of warfare—spontaneously began to rejoice in the Lord out of their spirits. It had to be God! They just started to dance and to scream and to shout and to worship, because the canopy of oppression lifted instantly, and everyone, no matter how unspiritual he was, knew that he knew, that something supernatural had taken place.

Don't Waste Time

"We went out to one farm, and the men were getting a little blasé. There was a bit of a problem there, and they just weren't knitted together. They were casual, and they followed the outline, but we did not break through in the Spirit. I said to the guys afterwards, 'That was a mistake. We wasted our time coming out here. We probably did a little bit of damage, but we didn't accomplish what we were supposed to do, because it became a little bit of a routine and it mustn't be like that.'

"After we have really won a victory, I then have a group of men that are so excited that I can't contain them: They leap over thorn bushes, and over fences, and jump into trucks on the way home. It's like—I can't explain it, but something releases in your spirit, and you know that you know, the presence of God has fallen upon you. It's a wonderful feeling. I have never ever felt the check of the Holy Spirit when we have gone out.

189

With the Team from England

"When Colin Wilkinson came out from England, I took a month off to do some travelling with him around our nation. I had no cooperation from any of the leadership of the country. Earlier I had shared my vision with them and they would think I'd lost my senses, and so it was up to us to do what we believed, and to go for it. Since then, the whole situation has changed and the leaders of practically every town in Zimbabwe have gotten the vision, and they get behind teams that are now getting out there, and literally breaking up demonic strongholds in the areas.

The River God in Kariba

"We went out to Kariba to deal with the river god named 'Nyami-Nyami.' When I took one look at the church in Kariba, I knew how powerful Nyami-Nyami was. I think there were about twelve Christians and three churches. There had been division and squabbling and fighting, and it broke my heart when I saw it. So we went and bought ourselves a Nyami-Nyami, and went out to where the Sanyati meets the Zambezi River Gorge on the little island there. I took some of the Christians from that area, and the team from England (by then they had arrived) and some others, and we started praying and waiting upon God. We felt that in Kariba was one of the heads of Leviathan. The Bible says Leviathan has many heads and a body like a snake (Psalm 74:14, Isaiah 27:1). It goes down river courses, and wherever that river has been defiled, we find that

190

little places of Satanic worship and schools of witchcraft are being set up. It is one of the pinnacles of Leviathan. We prayed, and then we took Nyami-Nyami, stuck its head between two rocks, and gave it a kick. It broke clean across the neck. When that happened, the Christians from Kariba started to scream and dance and get excited, for right then the power of the evil spirit broke. Then, because it was an idol, we burned it.

Demonic United Nations

"We went to another place called the 'Tree of No Name.' Now there are actually four evergreen trees on one farm. They are scattered around there. As we were talking and praying, we discovered that there was actually no name of a ruling spirit in that area. That's why it's called the 'Tree of No Name.' The people go to pray for rain, but they don't actually go and talk to a particular demonic deity. As we were praying I just saw very clearly in my spirit a picture of a round hollow wooden ring and I saw men coming up and looping a rope around the ring and walking away from it. It was a ring with different ropes attached, going in different directions.

As I saw that, God quickened to me, out of the book of Isaiah, chapter fourteen, the fall of the devil himself, where it says he fell because of pride. I suddenly realized a pattern: the Kingdom of Heaven is based on love, but the Kindom of Darkness is based on fear; there's a rank structure of fear among demons. Also, when a third of the angels fell with the devil, it wasn't that he was full of pride and they full of love and loyalty; they fell with him, because they inherited his spirit, so he took a third of the angels with him and each one has his problem, his 'sickness.' They want to become like God, too! So every little demon wants Lucifer's job. Lucifer wants God's job—they want Lucifer's job. Pride is totally self-centered and full of self-interest. Therefore, when a ruling spirit is established over an

191

area, the other lesser spirits don't automatically fall into line. He has got to subdue them through fear. You look at any dictatorship in the world and you will see it is run by fear. You have a ruling structure and everybody's checking up on everybody else. It's based, not on loyalty, but on self-preservation. So the ruling structure is based on fear, and the ruling spirits are busy doing their best to hold on and govern the other, lesser spirits. But God said to me, 'Smite the shepherd and the sheep are scattered.' That works in a church, when the shepherd is taken out, so how much more in the realm of the demons when the ruling spirit is taken out! All his little henchmen say, 'Goody, goody'! The cat's away, the mice will play!' There's total chaos! They lose their coordination, because no spirit is going to be loyal to his brother. He says, 'The boss is gone and I don't have to do what you tell me to do! I'll do my own thing.' There is chaos in the demon-world when you strike a ruling prince.

"Furthermore, a ruling spirit is not all-knowing. Once a spirit is given charge over an area, it takes him a long time to get his rule there, to get the people in there under his dominion, and to get to know the lives of the people and get control over the families in the area. Therefore they do not like other spirits crossing their boundaries. So you get a spirit that's got one boundary zone, and another spirit that's got another boundary zone—two ruling spirits. But they don't like lateral transfers, because it takes them all their time to get full control so they can give good reports to their leader. They're very proud. But a kingdom divided against itself is going to fall, says the Bible, and so what they have is neutral zones called 'United Nations.' That's what the ruling spirits have in all countries. It's much like in the natural. For example, the Arab states will go to the United Nations and the delegates, or their ambassadors will speak to each other as though they are friends, while back at home their two armies are killing each other. But the United

Nations is designed to be a declaration to the world that 'We are brothers and there is peace in the world.' It's a neutral ground, a no-man's-land, where something can happen to bring some appearance of cohesion in our world.

That 'Tree of No Name' was a neutral area where the demons would allow the people to go and worship and pray for rain without being a threat to each other. It was a spiritual 'no-man's-land,' a token gesture of unity. When we got in there, we suddenly saw it. We spoke into the four corners of the compass; and we spoke confusion into every kingdom that had its connection with that point of land. We said, 'You shall be confused and we shall speak division, because we are standing on the focal point of your kingdoms, and we're speaking back into them.' We had the Assemblies of God leaders with us that day, and that's the first time they had ever come with us. It started to rain a little bit and drizzle, and the mothers were standing there with their children, but no one wanted to leave. Hallelujah! They were just so excited by what God was doing.

Chasing the Devils off Mount Darwin

"We left that area and climbed to Mount Darwin—all the way to the top. Before we got there, God impressed something on us. When David returned the Ark of the Covenant, he sacrificed seven times before he got home. We stood at the bottom of the mountain and held a Communion service at the base and then we had six other prayer meetings on the way up the mountain. During the final one, we redeemed the land at the very top. This mountain had caused a tremendous fear in the whole area for a long time, and we knew we were facing something of greater dimension than we had faced before. On about our fourth prayer meeting, one brother who is a hunter by profession, a good solid Christian, though not given to visions and dreams, suddenly said, 'I just don't believe what I've seen.

193

As we've been coming up the mountain, I have seen the levels of demon spirits guarding this mountain like little soldiers. As we've climbed higher, I saw them all going up over the top of the mountain and down the other side, running for their lives! Every time we moved up and prayed, they backed off, until we got to the pinnacle and they disappeared.' We took authority, and we felt that was one of the seats of Nahunda right there, and we felt to walk in and take authority and break up one of the ruling bases from which the spirit of Nahunda came out.

Breaking the Curses of a Satanist Shrine

"I've known for a while that there were Satanist shrines in a certain area. The pastor from the Assembly of God there used to be a Satanist high priest. He said to me, 'I think that I know where one of those shrines is.' So we went to the area, parked our cars and climbed to the highest point and found the place. The Satanists had painted their satanic symbols of worship on one of the round tables that were there. They had painted a big set of red lips which they would stand behind while they pronounced curses in the direction the lips faced—directly toward the city maternity hospital. Next to the lips was a picture of a human foetus, then two men fighting, with one killing the other. Finally, there was a rainbow, speaking of God's blessing, with the illuminati symbol underneath it, to signify the curse upon God's blessings. All these faced the city. As we were standing there on that rocky ledge near the table, just praying and believing God, suddenly, we all felt simultaneously that something was trying to push us over the edge of the cliff, a one hundred foot drop. It felt as though the ground was moving and my feet had no traction underneath me. I walked to the very edge and said, 'Not today, devil. You're not trying that stunt!'

"Then the pastor said, 'Richard, come here!'

"I said, 'What's the problem?'

194

"He said, 'Someone's trying to push me over the edge!'

"I said, 'We're going to have fun!' We started praying and breaking off some of the curses and the sins of the place. We also locked in on the local spirits that the Satanists were utilizing and working in conjunction with. As we started to pray and redeem the land, the demonic power was broken.

The Zimbabwe Ruins

"We went to Masvingo, the location of the Zimbabwe Ruins. I had known in my spirit that that place had been very evil in the past, and I've known it's one of the pinnacles of Zimbabwe. The first day we walked around and prayed and just believed God; and I was so disturbed in my spirit. Some of the team had gone off to see an archaeologist in the area who knew the history very well. We were going back to the remainder of the team and had a brochure about the place in the vehicle. Suddenly, I just knew that I knew what to look for, and I said to the brother, 'Give me the brochure.' I turned to the aerial view of the Ruins, an artist's view, compiled from photographs. Looking at the temple from the top, I saw what I was looking for: the inner and outer walls form almost the perfect shape of a human foetus. I said, 'I am positive that that is the centre of human sacrifice.' The team that came from the archaeologist said, 'What they used to do was skin children alive. The longer the child screamed and the more the mother cried, the happier the spirits were.' Now we started to lock in on some of the things that had happened in Zimbabwe Ruins. We went and redeemed the land on the top and at the bottom. I believe it had been literally a second Babel established here in the southern hemisphere. It was on one of the major trade routes, and it wasn't a tribe that lived there, so much as a priesthood. People came from all over southern Africa and further afield to worship and find demonic revelation. They have discovered all sorts of artifacts from India

195

and from China and places like that which are now in the local museum. One of the spirits established over that place was the spirit of Nimrod. We cast him out.

The Mountain of the Disappearing Children

"Then, after that, we climbed a certain mountain where children had been disappearing. We went with a Christian game ranger or national parks warden, who was involved in the last case where a little boy disappeared. There had been a party of school children who had gone up, and on their way down, one little guy had a fight with his brother and he had run away in broad daylight across a field on the side of the mountain, in full view of the vehicles down below. The ranger showed me where it had happened. As soon as the teacher saw the boy was missing she ran back up to look for him. You can shout at that altitude and be heard for three to five kilometres. It just echoes round and round and round, which means, if the child had shouted, they would have heard him. And you can see for miles there; but they couldn't find him. They called in the National Parks Service who came with a helicopter. Now the people in the area say that if you disturb the spirits in any way, like bringing in a helicopter, a mist will immediately fall over the mountain, obscuring visibility. The moment the helicopter came, down came the mist. The warden had radio communications with the helicopter, but the moment he hit the ground, the walkie-talkie went dead. He followed the boy's tracks into an open field where they just vanished. At that point in time the warden had a heart attack. They evacuated him to the nearest hospital where his symptoms disappeared and he was well.

"He said to me, 'I came so close to dying, I've never been so scared in all my life.

"I said, 'All right, up we go—Here's some fun!'

"We did the same thing we had done at the other mountain:

196

we prayed at the bottom, had a Communion service, prayed six times up the mountain and the seventh time at the top. While we were standing at the bottom praying, God showed me a crocodile. I thought, 'A crocodile here? I must be out of my mind.' I didn't say anything.

"About the third time we were praying, one of the other brethren said to me, 'You know, I've seen a crocodile in my spirit.'

"I said, 'That's what I saw.'

"And then one of the Black pastors said, 'The name of the people here who are the particular tribe that's supposed to guard the mountain are known as 'the people of the crocodile.' That's their name!'

"I thought, 'Hallelujah! We're beginning to zero in on what's happening around this place.'

"By the time we'd got to the top, we had started to lock in on one of the other heads of Leviathan. There was child sacrifice going on there. It wasn't a case of children just disappearing, but they were being taken by spirit to a place where three rivers originate in that valley, where Satanists sacrificed the abducted children and poured their blood into the rivers, defiling all the river valleys that came from that particular source. We redeemed the land there and as we were on the way down, the game warden said, 'I cannot believe the freedom on this mountain. I feel so free in my spirit. I'm excited about it.' There was a total change of atmosphere."

SHARE THESE TRUTHS AND REDEEM THE LAND

These wonderful experiences of great victory in Zimbabwe, Africa give us the courage and inspiration we need to join with our brothers and sisters there to catch the vision and go forth to *Redeem our Lands*. Share this Bible Study, this vision, this call of the Holy Spirit with someone of like faith and courage and vision; prepare your hearts together and go forward to do warfare in your area. Together, we shall see great victories all over the world, for the Word of God says, *"The righteous shall inherit the land, and dwell therein for ever."* (Psalm 37:29) As we seek the face of God and keep His ways, He will exalt us to inherit the land; and we shall see the wicked cut off (Psalm 37:34). The Lord will again bless our land and it shall yield its strength (Psalm 85:12) for He has given us our land for our heritage (Psalm 136:21) and the nations of the world for our inheritance (Psalm 2:8). Amen.

Molech, Moloch, Milcom from *International Bible Dictionary*, Bridge Publishing, Inc., New Jersey. Used by permission.

The Centaur, half horse and half man, appears in Greek myths as being both friendly and unfriendly to man. In general, centaurs had the characters of rude and wild mountaineers.

199

APPENDIX

THE POWER OF THE HOLY COMMUNION

When I was visiting my Coptic friends in Egypt I realized for the first time the tremendous power connected with the Holy Communion. To them it is not just a symbol of the body and blood of our Lord which they lightly partake of and then go merrily on their way. No, to them it is a renewing of their covenant relationship with God the Father through His Son Jesus Christ.

For over a thousand years Islam has been the dominant religion of Egypt. Almost the entire populace is Moslem. I asked, "How is it that you have been able to keep the faith of Jesus Christ so pure and strong for all these years when you are such a small number?"

The answer came back, "Because we gather in our churches every morning and take communion together. This is our strength. We are reminded of our covenant relationship with God through the sacrifice of His Son."

I am convinced that we in the Christian faith do not partake of the Sacred Communion as often as we should, and when we do, it is without due regard for its meaning, importance, and the power it generates in our bodies and spirits.

There is life and forgiveness in the wine when taken in faith and with the understanding that *"This is my blood of the new testament, which is shed for many for the remission of sins."* (Matthew 26:28)

And there is healing and strengthening in the bread when taken with the understanding that, *"This is my body, which is broken for you."* (I Corinthians 11:24) This truth was made real to Peter when he wrote in I Peter 2:24, *"by whose stripes ye are healed."*

Many in the Christian faith believe that the priest has the power from God to actually turn the bread and the wine into the literal body and blood of our Lord. This is called transubstantiation (the changing of one substance into another). It is a strong doctrine of the Roman Catholic church. I have met Protestants who believe it also.

201

I myself cannot accept this doctrine. Like most in the Protestant church I accept the teaching that the bread is an emblem of the body of Christ and the wine is an emblem of His Blood, in the same way that I believe that the oil, when used for anointing purposes is symbolic of the Holy Spirit and is not the actual Holy Spirit Himself.

BREAD

The definition of "bread" is "food, or sustenance; livelihood."

The curse is connected with the bread. When Adam and Eve sinned God judged them, *"In the sweat of thy face shalt thou eat bread."* (Genesis 3:19)

That meant that BREAD was to be obtained under much stress and hardship.

When Jesus called Himself the BREAD OF HEAVEN and told the people *"I am the living bread which came down from heaven: if any man eat of this bread, he shall live forever: and the bread that I shall give is my flesh, which I will give for the life of the world."* (John 6:51), *"From that time many of his disciples went back, and walked no more with him."* (John 6:66)

Jesus paid the price by suffering in His body the many wounds He bore so that man no more needs to believe that he is bound by that curse. Jesus took upon Himself every original curse God had pronounced over Adam and Eve and Creation after the fall of man.

Even as bread is made from wheat which has been bruised and crushed and sifted, so Jesus suffered the bruising, the crushing and the testings which qualified Him to become the finest of meal, ground and ready to be the loaf offering which the High Priest offered unto God as a symbol of the Bread that was to come. (Leviticus 7:12,13)

THE DUST OF THE GROUND

The curse had fallen on the ground when God pronounced, *"Cursed is the ground for thy sake; in sor-*

202

row shalt thou eat of it all the days of thy life." (Genesis 3:17)

And again, a second curse fell on the ground when Cain killed his brother Abel and his innocent blood fell on the ground. God rebuked Cain, *"What hast thou done? the voice of thy brother's blood crieth unto me from the ground. And now art thou cursed from the Earth, which hath opened her mouth to receive thy brother's blood from thy hand; When thou tillest the ground, it shall not henceforth yield unto thee her strength."*(Genesis 4:10-12)

So we see there is a curse on the ground because of:

1. Adam's disobedience. (He ate of the forbidden fruit which the ground had produced).

2. The shedding of the innocent blood of Abel. (The ground had accepted and received the blood of Abel, and thereby it too became cursed).

THE BLOOD OF ALL LIVING CREATURES IS SACRED

All blood is sacred because it has the life of God in it. *"For the life of the flesh is in the blood: and I have given it to you upon the altar to make an atonement for your souls: for it is the blood that maketh an atonement for the the soul."* (Leviticus 17:11)

Therefore the blood of man and of any living creature belongs ONLY to God. *"For the life of all flesh is the blood thereof: whosoever eateth it shall be cut off."* (Leviticus 17:14c)

When man sheds innocent blood and that blood is on his hands, his hands (i.e. his body and life) are cursed.

In the Old Testament the only way that the sin of murder could be atoned for was by the execution of the one who had killed. He had to give his life in exchange. *"Whoso sheddeth man's blood, by man shall his blood be shed: for in the image of God made he man."* (Genesis 9:6)

ABRAHAM WAS GIVEN BREAD AND WINE BY MELCHIZEDEK

When Abraham returned from rescuing Lot, he met Melchizedek (the mysterious king and priest of Salem) and was ministered to with bread and wine.

Perhaps Abraham had been forced to kill someone in order to save the life of Lot.

The High Priest, by serving Abraham bread and wine, was ministering forgiveness and healing strength to him.

After that, God made a special covenant with Abraham (Genesis 14:18-15:5). There was healing and restoration in the Bread and Wine.

BREAD IS A TYPE OF THE WORD OF GOD

In Deuteronomy 8:3 God said, *"...man doth not live by bread only, but by every word that proceedeth out of the mouth of the Lord doth man live."* Jesus used this scripture to bind and refute Satan when He was tempted in the wilderness. (Luke 4:4)

When Jesus said to the Syrophenician woman, *"For it is not meat to take the children's bread, and to cast it unto the dogs."* (Mark 7:26) he was referring to the promises of healing in the Word of God. Therefore He was speaking of the Word of God. Bread is a type of the Word of God.

When Jesus taught us to pray, "give us this day our daily bread," He was not only referring to the natural bread, but also the Word of God, the spiritual manna. In fact some daily devotionals use the title, "Daily Bread" or "Daily Manna".

The Bread is also a symbol of the Church because the Church is called the "Body of Christ." Christ is the Head (Colossians 1:18) and we are the Body.

I Corinthians 10:17 *"For we being many are one bread, and one body: for we are all partakers of that one bread."*

Thus, in the same way the Body of the Lord, the Church, is broken into fragments and scattered all over the world into every nation, tribe and culture, and is

204

silently bringing strength and healing to the world.

When the rapture takes place and the "Bread" (i.e., the Church) is taken up, there will be great spiritual hunger, weakness and death in the world.

WHY DO WE CAST THE BREAD WHEN REDEEMING THE LAND?

Because the bread is a token of:

1. The physical body of Christ.

2. The spiritual body of Christ (the Church which is scattered around the world).

3. The Word of God (i.e., the promises of God) which we claim for this sin-sick and diseased world.

Jesus said, *"I am the living bread which came down from heaven: if any man eat of this bread, he shall live for ever: and the bread that I will give is my flesh, which I will give for the life of the WORLD."* (John 6:51)

According to Spiros Zodhiates the word "world" is *kosmos* (2889). In Greek it refers to the sum total of the material universe, the beauty in it as well as the sum total of persons living in it.

Man brought the curse on this beautiful world (a gemstone among planets), and man, by "redeeming the land" (i.e., praying over it, and claiming it back to God) is working in cooperation with God's prophetic word concerning the millenium of the Kingdom of God.

According to Romans 8:22 we understand that *"the whole creation groaneth and travaileth in pain together until now."*

What a wonderful thing it will be when the curse is lifted off of this world! Jesus paid the price for its total restoration to its original form before the fall, but because Satan is the Prince of this world this truth has not been totally realized.

Our cities are filled with unsolved murders, the blood of innocents and many other terrible sins. This

205

brings a curse on our cities and nations. All who are innocent suffer from the evil, and the wrath of God that falls upon an area because of its sin affects all. The good suffer along with the bad in times of hurricanes, earthquakes, pestilence and economic crisis. Many are still lost in sin and Satan has them bound. By "redeeming" the land we break Satan's power and control over that area and the inhabitants therein, thereby releasing them out of the bondage of Satan so they can receive Jesus as their Saviour.

Just as we can claim healing for cancer, when all around us others are dying of it, and we can believe God for added years to our lives when morgues are full of bodies younger than ours, in the same way we can claim healing for our cities, our towns and our gardens.

We do not need to allow the weather to destroy our homes, nor locusts to devour our gardens. We can take authority over demonic princes, ruling over our cities and nations, the weather and plagues of insects. But we have to apply spiritual tactics of warfare (because Satan is a legalist) such as prayers, fastings, praising, marching or walking on the property (as God told Abraham to do in Genesis 13:17), and doing whatever God commands or leads us to do.

God said to Abraham *"Arise, walk through the land in the length of it and in the breadth of it; for I will give it unto thee."* (Genesis 13:17) Remember that it is yours to claim. Each case is different.

Some scatter bread as a token of redemption for the healing of the land and some pour out oil. Others sprinkle "holy water" which has been prayed over by a priest or person performing the work of cleansing.

Use whatever emblem you have faith for, and if you haven't any "leading of the Holy Spirit" to use any emblem, at least fast and pray for God to break the curse and restore His blessing in your home, your church, your city and nation.

Our object is not to promote the "scattering or planting of bread," but to break the powers of demons and to pull down the strongholds of Satan, and plead for God's mercy and forgiveness for our sins, so that the blessings of God can again be upon our nation.

206

WHY POUR OUT THE WINE?

The abortion of at least 20 million babies has brought the wrath of God upon the United States of America. Hosts of other nations are no better off than we are. We are all desperately in need of divine intervention that this slaughter of our innocents must stop, or we will be destroyed as Germany was destroyed for the slaughter of the Jews.

Some people object to letting the bread and wine fall upon the ground, since it represents the body and Blood of Jesus, but where was the broken Body of Christ laid and where did His Blood fall when He hung dying upon the Cross? If His actual body was buried in the earth and His actual Blood poured out upon the ground, how much more can the symbols of these be scattered upon the ground to represent His redemption of the land and of us who live upon it?

WHAT CAN WE DO ABOUT IT?

In Deuteronomy 21:1-9 God gave the answer and told how innocent people can be free of the guilt (and therefore the judgment of God's wrath).

God said that if someone had been killed and his blood had been shed, the elders of the city who were closely related to the slain man must sacrifice a young heifer on the spot closest to it on the ground that had not been tilled. The elders were to wash their hands over the heifer and say, *"Our hands have not shed this blood, neither have our eyes seen it. Be merciful, O Lord, unto thy people Israel, whom thou hast redeemed, and lay not innocent blood unto thy people of Israel's charge."* (Deuteronomy 21:7, 8)

God said that if they did that, the blood shed would be forgiven them. *"So shalt thou put away the guilt of innocent blood from among you, when thou shalt do that which is right in the sight of the Lord."* (Deuteronomy 21:9)

The elders (responsible citizens) of the area, who do not want sin to have dominion and therefore to bring down the curse on the land, needed to seek God's face

207

earnestly for His forgiveness for the sins of others. If by pouring out the blood, the curse that came with the shedding of innocent blood could be lifted and God's blessing of prosperity returned, then God can do the same if we will seek His face. God had promised to prosper Israel as long as they obeyed His commandments.

WHERE WAS THE BLOOD SPRINKLED?

In Old Testament times the blood was sprinkled upon:

1. The Brazen Altar—Leviticus 5:9

2. Different parts of the priest's body such as the ear, thumb, toe—Exodus 29:20.

3. Upon the priest's garments—Exodus 29:21.

4. Upon the Altar of Incense—Exodus 30:10.

5. Before the Veil—Leviticus 4:5, 6.

6. On the Mercy Seat—Leviticus 16:14.

7. On the Book of the Law—Hebrews 9:19.

8. On the people—Exodus 24:8.

9. For the cleansing from the leprosy of man—Leviticus 14:2-9.

10. For the cleansing of a house—Leviticus 14:48-53

What meaningful ceremonies these were! I especially love the meaning of the ceremony of cleansing for leprosy in the house.

As a living bird lifted its wings to fly away, after its feathers had been dipped in the blood of the sacrificed bird, it scattered the blood over the area where it flew every time it flapped its wings, until it finally dried up.

208

And so God ordained that by the sprinkling of the blood the house was cleansed. In the same act of faith we sprinkle or pour out the wine which is symbolic of the Blood which Jesus shed for the redemption of the world.

On the night of Passover God told the Children of Israel to sprinkle the blood of the lamb upon their doorposts. The destroyer could not enter the houses where the blood was.

Even as the blood on the doorposts delivered God's people, in the same way, to keep this protection, God told Israel to put the Word of God on their doorposts and gates so that they would constantly be reminded of the Promises of God. That is why the Jews still place the Mezuzah on their doors. Every house in Israel has it, and also every entrance to every hotel room.

God said that if they would do it that they would be able to live a long time in the land of their inheritance and their lives would be *"days of heaven upon the earth."* (Deutoronomy 11:21)

The bread we scatter on the "waters of humanity" will bring results, for Ecclesiastes 11:1 says, *"Cast thy bread upon the waters; for thou shalt find it after many days."*

We may not see the results of our efforts immediately, but we surely shall after many daysmaybe even after The Great Tribulation!

CHRIST IS THE REDEEMEER

What we call "redeeming the land" does not mean to imply that WE are the source or instrument for redemption. That honour goes to Christ alone. Only He could redeem the world and all of His creation! But by scattering the bread and pouring out the wine and oil we are reminding Satan of the New Covenant that was sealed with the Blood of Christ and the offering up of His body; and that through His efficacious work Satan's power was broken at the cross and resurrection. He must let go of that which has been redeemed and dedicated to the Lord, whether it be our children, our houses or our land. That is why it is proper to serve Christian children Holy Communion. It is for their protection and

209

healing. They have the right to partake, after being taught the meaning, or when the parent knows they understand.

If the angels could cast the Bread of Heaven upon the sands of the desert for the sustenance of man, what is wrong with us taking the bread from our ovens, or the bread which we purchase in the stores (special purchased wafers are not necessary) and scattering it as an act of faith for the healing of the earth?

Some who object the most strenuously to scattering the bread dump it down the disposal or into the garbage after the Communion has been served. There certainly is very little criticism about that, or about throwing the remainder of the grape juice or wine down the drain. Yet these same people object to scattering the bread as an act of faith. Isn't that unreasonable?

I am sure that when Paul started sending out aprons and handkerchiefs from his body that it was a new thing which man had never read about in the Bible before. Yet the demons recognized that act of faith, and the Bible says that *"God wrought special miracles by the hands of Paul: So that from his body were brought unto the sick handkerchiefs or aprons, and the diseases departed from them, and the evil spirits went out of them."* (Acts 19:11,12)

Nowhere in the Bible does it say that anointing oil (which is symbolic of the Holy Spirit) was poured on handkerchiefs, and given to people for the purpose of healing, yet it has been done for years and no one seems to object. Is the Holy Spirit any less of a Person of the Trinity than Jesus? Is the oil not as holy a symbol as the wine and the bread?

When the elders of Jericho met Elisha they complained that their water spring was poisoned. He told them to take a new cruse and put salt in it. He went forth to the spring of the waters and cast the salt in and said, *"Thus saith the Lord, I have healed these waters; there shall not be from thence any more death or barren land. So the waters were healed unto this day, according to the saying of Elisha which he spake."* (II Kings 2:21,22)

When the curse is lifted in its entirety the ground

210

will be no more cursed. Long lost chemicals in the soil will be restored, resulting in much healthier vegetation and therefore crops of grain, vegetables and fruit will have their original food value which they had before the Fall. The leaves of the trees will be for the healing of the nations (Revelation 22:2). Herbs will heal the sick and weakened humanity and man shall again live a thousand years. Even the cattle will rejoice in their abundant pastures (Isaiah 30:23,24).

ADAM

In closing, let us look at one more word:

ADAM: What does it mean?

In the original Hebrew it is *adam* (120). It is the same as in English.

The Hebrew words for Adam and Man are the same.

HOW WAS ADAM CREATED?

Genesis 2:7 answers that question, "And the Lord God formed man of the dust of the ground."

The word "ground" is *'adamah* (127). According to Zodhiates in Hebrew it means "'earth, ground, land, country, even the entire earth'"

The body of Adam was formed from *"adamah."* (Genesis 2:7,9)

Since we are made out of *'adamah* (i.e., earth) is it not rightful that the earth be redeemed and that the curse should be broken off of it? Otherwise how could a redeemed race continue to live on a cursed world?

Many Christians suffer because they are married to spouses who are not redeemed and are therefore under a curse. Children live in homes that are cursed. And many work for a cursed society and business world.

But in the millenium the curse will have been

broken off the entire world and its system.

Even today, God's Word promises that a righteous woman has the power to break the curse that is on her husband and family. *"For the unbelieving husband is sanctified by the wife, and the unbelieving wife is sanctified by the husband: else were your children unclean; but now are they holy."* (I Corinthians 7:14)

This is our authority in Christ. The devil cannot take our children, if the godly mother or father exerts her or his authority against the devil where they are concerned.

Let us possess our rights! Let us root out and overthrow all of Satan's divisive ways and strongholds! This is the heritage of the children of God.

CONCLUSION

WHY REDEEM WHEN THE RAPTURE IS GOING TO TAKE PLACE?

Some ask, "Why redeem the land when the rapture will take place and the Antichrist will be in control? Why not just give up and let the devil have it?" This is the question which many ask.

In reply I want you to read Jeremiah 32:6-17.

Jeremiah had prophesied the judgment of God on Judah and Jerusalem. As a result King Zedekiah was so angry he had Jeremiah put into prison.

Jeremiah knew that the people would be carried captive into Babylon, yet, God told him that his cousin was coming to see him and would offer a very valuable piece of property for sale to Jeremiah.

That is what actually happened. Hanameel visited him in prison and said, *"Buy my field, I pray thee, which is in Anathoth, which is in the country of Benjamin: for the right of inheritance is thine, and the redemption is thine; buy it for thyself."* (Jeremiah 32:8)

With the armies of Nebuchadnezzar surrounding the city it seemed a foolish thing to do. But God told Jeremiah to redeem the land even though tribulation was soon to fall on them. He paid 17 shekels of silver for it. And they sealed the deed in the presence of others and put it in an earthen vessel "that it may continue many days." (The Dead Sea Scrolls which were recently discovered are still readable after 2000 years in one such vessel). Jeremiah obeyed the Lord in spite of the economic situation. Records of this have recently been found in an archeological dig at Jerusalem.

If we do what the Lord tells us to do, it is true that time may pass, and we will go to our reward, the tribulation will come upon the earth; but a new day will come again. The battle of Armageddon will be over. The Antichrist (the Beast) and the false Prophet will be cast into the Lake of Fire (Revelation 19:20), and Satan will be bound in the pit for a thousand years. (Revelation 20:1-3) And *"houses and fields and vineyards will be possessed again in this land."* (Jeremiah 32:17)

For, as Jeremiah said, *"Ah Lord God! behold, thou hast made the heaven and the earth by thy great power and stretched out arm, and there is nothing too hard for thee:"* (Jeremiah 32:17)

Because we obey the Lord now, God will watch over the land we redeemed and when we return with the Lord as He sets up His Kingdom (Jude 14,15), we will see the final result of our act of faith.

Possess your inheritance today, dear child of God. Don't let the devil have it, *"For the right of inheritance is thine, and the redemption is thine;"* (Jeremiah 32:8)

IT WORKS!

Last of all, it works! Since we published the book *Redeeming the Land*, we have been receiving reports of testimonies from all over the world of wonderful victories gained, battles won and deliverances obtained as God's people have become involved in cosmic level spiritual warfare.

It works! And let no one say these results are obtained by some power other than God's (suggesting, as one critic has said, "Well, witchcraft works, too." Jesus himself answered that accusation, which was brought

213

against Him also: *"But when the Pharisees heard it, they said, This fellow doth not cast out devils, but by Beelzebub the prince of the devils.*

"And Jesus knew their thoughts, and said unto them, Every kingdom divided against itself is brought to desolation; and every city or house divided against itself shall not stand:

"And if Satan cast out Satan, he is divided against himself; how shall then his kingdom stand?

"And if I by Beelzebub cast out devils, by whom do your children cast them out? therefore they shall be your judges.

"But if I cast out devils by the Spirit of God, then the kingdom of God is come unto you.

"Or else how can one enter into a strong man's house, and spoil his goods, except he first bind the strong man? and then he shall spoil his house.

"He that is not with me is against me; and he that gathereth not with me scattereth abroad.

"Wherefore I say unto you, All manner of sin and blasphemy shall be forgiven unto men: but the blasphemy against the Holy Ghost shall not be forgiven unto men.

"And whosoever speaketh a word against the Son of man, it shall be forgiven him: but whosoever speaketh against the Holy Ghost, it shall not be forgiven him, neither in this world, neither in the world to come." (Matthew 12:24-32)

"Redeeming the Land" works by the finger of God. It is not by witchcraft that it works; it is by Jesus' redemption won on the Cross. It is dangerous for anyone even to suggest that deliverance is obtained by any other power, lest that one should blaspheme the Holy Spirit, *"or hath done despite unto the Spirit of grace, or count the blood of the covenant an unholy thing."* (Hebrews 10:29)

COSMIC LEVEL SPIRITUAL WARFARE

Now others are writing books on this same subject.

214

I don't usually return to a subject to address it a second time, but because of the request of many for more understanding on the subject in regard to the use of the emblems of the bread and wine, I have felt led to take time to add this appendix and sequel.

As you yourself search the scriptures with an open heart, faith will rise in your heart and you will say with Jeremiah, *"Then I knew this was the Word of the Lord."* (Jeremiah 32:8)

CHRONOLOGICAL INDEX TO THE BIBLE.

PERIOD I. FROM THE CREATION TO THE DELUGE, CONTAINING 1,656 YEARS.

A. M.	B. C.		
1	4004	The creation of the world	Gen. 1:2
"	"	Fall of our first parents, Adam and Eve, from holiness and happiness, by disobeying God. Promise of a Saviour	" 3
2	4002	Cain born	" 4:1
3	4001	Abel born	" 4:2
129	3875	Abel murdered by his brother Cain	" 4:8
130	3874	Seth born, his father, Adam, being 130 yrs. old	" 5:3
622	3382	Enoch born	" 5:18,19
687	3317	Methuselah born	" 5:21
930	3074	Adam dies, aged 930 yrs	" 5:5
987	3017	Enoch translated, aged 365 yrs	" 5:24
1042	2962	Seth dies, aged 912 yrs	" 5:8
1056	2948	Noah born	" 5:28,29
			" 6:3–22
1536	2468	The Deluge threatened, and Noah commissioned to preach repentance during 120 yrs	1 Pet. 3:20
			2 Pet. 2:5
1656	2348	Methuselah dies, aged 969 yrs	Gen. 5:27
		In the same yr. Noah enters into the ark, being 600 yrs. old	" 7:6, 7

PERIOD II. FROM THE DELUGE TO THE CALL OF ABRAHAM, CONTAINING 427 YEARS.

A. M.	B. C.		
1657	2347	Noah, with his family, leaves the ark after the deluge, and offering sacrifice, he receives the covenant of safety, of which the rainbow was the token	Gen. 8:18,19
			" 9:8, 17
1770	2234	Babel built	" 11
1770	2234	The confusion of language, and dispersion of mankind	" 11
1771	2233	Nimrod lays the first foundation of the Babylonian or Assyrian monarchy	" 10:8–11
1816	2188	Mizraim lays the foundation of the Egyptian monarchy	" 10:13
1998	2006	Noah dies, aged, 950 yrs	" 9:29
2006	1998	Abraham born	" 11:26
2008	1996	Abraham born	Gen. 11:31
2068	1936	Abraham called from Chaldean idolatry, at 60 yrs. of age	" 12:1–4
2083	1921	Abraham's second call to Canaan	" 14:1–24
2091	1913	Abraham's victory over the kings, and rescue of Lot	" 16
2094	1910	Ishmael born, Abraham being 86 yrs. old	
2107	1897	God's covenant with Abram, changing his name to Abraham; circumcision instituted; Lot delivered, and Sodom, Gomorrah, Admah and Zeboim destroyed by fire on account of their abominations	" 17–19
2108	1896	Isaac born, Abraham being 100 yrs. old	" 21

PERIOD V. FROM THE BUILDING OF SOLOMON'S TEMPLE TO THE DESTRUCTION OF JERUSALEM AND THE CAPTIVITY OF THE JEWS IN BABYLON, 412 YEARS.

B.C.	KINGS OF JUDAH BEGAN TO REIGN.	KINGS OF ISRAEL BEGAN TO REIGN.	PROPHETS.
975	Rehoboam	Jeroboam I	Ahijah, Shemaiah
958	Abijah, or Abijam	"	
955	Asa	Nadab, 954	Azariah
963	"	Baasha	Hanani
930	"	Elah	Jehu
929	"	Zimri	
"	"	Omri	
918	Jehoshaphat	Ahab	Elijah, 910–896
914	"		Micaiah
897	"	Ahaziah	Elisha, 896–838
896	"	Jehoram, or Joram	Jahaziel
892	Jehoram	"	
885	Ahaziah	"	
884	Athaliah		Jehoiada
878	Joash, or Jehoahaz	Jehu	
857	"	Jehoahaz	Jonah, 862
839	Amaziah	Jehoash	
825	"	Jeroboam II	
810	Uzziah, or Azariah	"	Joel, 800
784	"	Anarchy, 11 years	Amos, 787
773	"	Zechariah	Hos. 785–725
772	"	Shallum; Menahem	
761	"	Pekahiah	Is. 780–698
759	"	Pekah	
758	Jotham	"	Micah, 750–698
742	Ahaz	"	Obed
730	"	Hoshea	
726	Hezekiah	(Captivity, 721)	Nahum, 713
698	Manasseh	"	
643	Amon	"	Zeph. 680
641	Josiah	"	Jer. 628–586
610	Jehoahaz, or Shallum	"	Hab. 626
"	Jehoiakim	"	Dan. 606–534
599	Jehoiachin, or Coniah		
"	Zedekiah		
588	Babylonian Captivity		Obadiah, 587

217

Bible Lands in the Days of the Persians—The Earlier Kingdoms Are Also Shown

NOTES

Chapter 1
Page 4
1. John Myers, *Voices from the Edge of Eternity* (Northridge: Voice Publications, 1968), p. 239.

Chapter 2
Page 12
1. Spiros Zodhiates, ed., *The Hebrew-Greek Key Study Bible* (Chattanooga: AMG Publishers, 1984) p. 1711.

Chapter 3
Facing page 30
1. Flavius Josephus, *The Complete Works of Josephus* (Grand Rapids: Kregel Publications 1960, 1978, 1981), p. 30b.

Chapter 4
Page 32
1. Ibid, pp. 27-28.

Page 36
Rev. Alexander Hislop, *The Two Babylons* (Neptune: Loizeaux Bros., 1959), p. 27 used by permission.

Page 43
Ibid, p.

Page 44
4. Albert Pike, *Morals and Dogmas of the Ancient and Accepted Scottish Rite of Freemasonry* (Richmond: L. H. Jenkins, 1871, 1950), pp. 224, 226, 234.

Page 49
5. Flavius Josephus *The Complete Works of Josephus* (Grand Rapids: Kregel Publications, 1960, 1978, 1981), p. 30.

Page 52
6. Rev. Alexander Hislop, *The Two Babylons* (Neptune: Loizeaux Bros., 1959), p. 20.

Page 54
7. Ibid, p. 69.

Page 59
8. Winkie Pratney, *Devil Take the Youngest* (Lafayette: Huntington House, 1985), pp. 31-35.

Chapter 5
Page 65
1. Marius Baar, *The Unholy War* (Nashville: Thomas Nelson Publishers, 1980), p. 63.

Page 73
2. Rev. Alexander Hislop, *The Two Babylons* (Neptune: Loizeaux Bros., 1959), p. 308.

3. William Smith, *Smith's Bible Dictionary,* public domain.

Page 74
4. Rev. Alexander Hislop, *The Two Babylons* (Neptune: Loizeaux Bros., 1959), p. 120.

Chapter 6
Page 90
1. David Allen Lewis, *Smashing the Gates of Hell in the Last Days* (Green Forest: New Leaf Press, 1987).

Page 99
2. George G. Ritchie, M.D., *Return From Tomorrow* (Old Tappan: Fleming Revell, 1978), pp. 59-61.

Chapter 7
Page 113
1. Howard O. Pittman, *Demons, An Eyewitness Account* (Foxworth: New Philadelphian Church) Used by Permission.

INDEX

223

224

226

229

LIST OF ILLUSTRATIONS

BOOKS MENTIONED IN THIS BIBLE STUDY AND FURTHER INFORMATION ON THESE SUBJECTS

The Twisted Cross *by Joseph Carr*
This important work clearly documents the occultic and demonic influence on Adolf Hitler and the Third Reich, which led to the annihilation of six million Jews. By thorough research and documentation, it shows that Naziism was actually an occultic religion.

Devil Take the Youngest *by Winkie Pratney*
This book reveals the war on childhood being waged in America and the world today. There has been a spirit of Moloch loosed in the land; there are distinct parallels between the abduction and murder of our children and the ancient worship of Moloch—where children were placed in the idol's arms and burned alive.

The Heavens Declare *by William D. Banks*
This is a book filled with amazing, documented proof of the earliest names of the stars, and the startling messages contained in those names. This book is well documented and contains over fifty illustrations.

Backward Masking Unmasked *by Jacob Aranza*
This book exposes the backward satanic message hidden in rock and roll music, and alerts you to the dangers of the music and its mind-influencing effects .

More Rock, Country, and Backward Masking Unmasked
by Jacob Aranza
A sequel to the above book, delving further into the world of Rock music and the practice of backward masking. Includes one

chapter with guidelines for evaluating Christian music,and exposes unhealthy aspects of country music.

Child Abuse in the Classroom   *edited by Phyllis Schlafly*
A hard-hitting, factual book which explains: why the American people are dissatisfied with schools today, why we have 23 million illiterates who graduated from public schools, and why young people are experiencing such high rates of teen suicide, loneliness, premarital sex and pregnancies.

Witness of the Stars   *by E.W. Bullinger*
A classic book originally published in 1893, the author displays how the constellations witness to the accuracy of Biblical prophetic truths. Numerous celestial charts and diagrams are provided to lend vivid support to his conclusions.

Should A Christian Be a Mason?   *by E.M. Storms*
The author traces the origin of Freemasonry from its roots in Babylonian paganism to its Occult and Kabalistic connections to the present day. A revealing foreword by Rev. Jim D. Shaw, of Silver Springs, Florida, a former 33 degree Freemason

Turmoil in the Toybox   *by Phil Phillips*
A shocking exposé of the toy and cartoon industry which unmasks the New Age, Occult, violent and satanic influences that have invaded the once innocent toybox. Also explains the importance of play, and how toys will affect a child's development

War on the Saints   *by Jesse Penn-Lewis*
This is the completely unabridged version of a vital book exposing the work and tactics of the enemy. A weapon which is a must for the Christian soldier .

Smashing the Gates of Hell in the Last Days
by David Allen Lewis
Embark on a journey into new dimensions of Bible prophecy which will give you hope for end-time victory. "By our action or by our apathy we will determine the quality of life as we move through the process of time from now until the second coming.".

Signs in the Heavens *by Marilyn Hickey*
The Bible answer to Astrology and the Zodiac.

Demons: An Eyewitness Account *by Howard O. Pittman*
When the author died, God permitted him to visit the abode of demons—the Second Heaven—and return to expose them. Clearly illustrates the rank and file order of the demonic realm. A must of those engaged in spiritual warfare.

Placebo *by Howard O. Pittman*
On August 3, 1979 the author died as a result of a massive internal hemorrhage. As his spirit was lifted from his body, he was taken to the Second Heaven and stood before Jesus in the Third Heaven. He was given a message to bring back to God's latter rain soldiers in this generation.

The Day Star *by Howard O. Pittman*
An exposé of Satan and his plan to destroy America through the sin of abortion.

The Covert War *by Howard O. Pittman*
Deception is a great tool of Satan in these last days. One of the great truths put forth is that the devil is a **personal** devil. Learn of his tactics and how you can effectively expose his evil works

The Screwtape Letters *by C.S. Lewis*
This Christian classic will make you acutely aware of how Satan and his host of fallen angels work in the hearts and lives of men, especially Christians.

Josephus (Complete Works)
A classic work of the history of the Jews, written by the eminent Jewish historian Flavius Josephus. It guides from the creation of man through the time of Titus who destroyed Jerusalem during the first century, A.D.

Rees Howells Intercessor *by Norman Grubb*
This Welsh coal miner was a prince with God who truly learned the power of travailing prayer. He became the channel of a mighty revival in Africa.

Understanding the Islamic Explosion *by Bernard Palmer*
Islam is a way of life and authority, as well as a religion. This book gives valuable insights on all you should know about it

Gods of the New Age *by Caryl Matrisciana*
With her own background in drugs and Eastern mysticism, the author ably investigates the roots, progress and probable future of the New Age phenomenon.

Return From Tomorrow *by George G. Ritchie*
At the age of 20, he died in an army hospital. Nine minutes later, he returned to life. What happened to him during those nine minutes was so compelling, it changed his life forever. This book details this journey .

The Hebrew-Greek Key Study Bible
edited by Spiros Zodhiates
King James Version Bible with study system and notes by Spiros Zodhiates. Key words are identified by Strong's numbers, and treated in included lexicon and Strong's dictionaries. In bonded leather. Specify black, blue, brown, burgundy.

The Two Babylons *by Rev. Alexander Hislop*
Written in 1853, this book reveals how the Babylonian pagan religion of Nimrod has influenced the world. It traces the worship of Nimrod and Semiramis in the church

Honor Thy Father?? *by Meridel Rawlings*
A true account of how incest destroys the seemingly normal family of a small-town pastor who had hidden his darkest secret even from his wife; and an exhortation to uncover the secret world of incest, and gain victory over it by accepting God's healing.

Smith's Bible Dictionary *by William Smith*
Every subject, person, place and event mentioned in the Bible is identified and defined in this trusted Bible dictionary.

GWEN SHAW'S AUTOBIOGRAPHY!

UNCONDITIONAL SURRENDER—*Gwen Shaw*. The life story of Gwen R. Shaw, lovingly known as "Sister Gwen" to thousands of people in over one hundred nations. You will laugh and cry with her as you feel the heartbeat of a great woman of God who has given all to Him, asking only for souls in return. Your life will be challenged as you walk with her through mission field after mission field. You will never be the same when you read how God pours out His Spirit and confirms His Word. ....Hardcover #U106-82 $19.95
............................video NTSC (North American format) #GSL-99 $20.00
....video PAL (European format) #GSLP-99 $20.00

DAILY DEVOTIONALS BY GWEN SHAW

DAILY PREPARATIONS FOR PERFECTION —*Gwen Shaw*. This daily devotional comes to you exactly as the Holy Spirit spoke to the author's heart in her own private devotions. You will feel that Jesus is speaking to you every time you open it. It is loved by all; read and re-read ....Paperback #D101-32 $12.50

DAY BY DAY—*Gwen Shaw*. The author's daily devotional book based on the Psalms will give you an inspiring word directly from the Throne Room each day to fill your heart with praise to God. It was a great comfort to the author herself after the fire in 1990 that destroyed so much. (Also available in French) ....Hardcover #D101-38 $18.50

FROM THE HEART OF JESUS—*Gwen Shaw*. This devotional book is like no other. It will take you back to Bible days and you will walk and talk with Jesus and His disciples as he ministered to the people, as He suffered and died and as He rose again from the dead. These words from the heart of Jesus will go straight to your heart, bringing comfort, peace encouragement and hope! 923 pages Hardcover ....
....#F102-11 $29.95

GEMS OF WISDOM — A daily devotional based on the book of Proverbs — *Gwen Shaw*. In the Proverbs you will find instruction for upright living, honesty, justice and wisdom. Every word in the Proverbs applies to today's problems as when they were first written. If you are going through great difficulties and facing problems which seem to have no solution, you will find the answer in these Proverbs. You'll have a Proverb and an inspired writing about it for each day of the year
....Hardcover #G105-49 $25.95

IN THE BEGINNING — A daily devotional based on the book of Genesis — *Gwen Shaw*. The Book of Genesis is perhaps the most important Book in the Old Testament. It is the foundation stone of all knowledge and wisdom. Deep and wonderful truths hidden in the pages of Genesis are revealed in this devotional book. You'll be amazed at the soul-stirring writings inspired by the well-known stories of Genesis........... ....#I115-47 $27.95

CLASSIC ANOINTED BIBLE STUDIES

BEHOLD THE BRIDEGROOM COMETH!—*Gwen Shaw*. A Bible study on the soon return of Jesus Christ. With so many false teachings these days, it is important that we realize how imminent the rapture of the saints of God really is ....#B100-37 $6.50

ENDUED WITH LIGHT TO REIGN FOREVER — *Gwen Shaw*. This deeply profound Bible study reveals the characteristics of the eternal, supernatural, creative light of God as found in His Word. The "Father of Lights," created man in His image. He longs for man to step out of darkness and into His light......................................#E101-71 $6.00

GOD'S END-TIME BATTLE-PLAN—*Gwen Shaw*. This study on spiritual warfare gives you the biblical weapons for spiritual warfare such as victory through dancing, shouting, praising, uplifted hands, marching, etc. It has been a great help to many who have been bound by tradition ....#G102-35 $8.00

IT'S TIME FOR REVIVAL—*Gwen Shaw*. A Bible Study on Revival that not only gives scriptural promises of the end-time Revival, but also presents the stories of revivals in the past and the revivalists whom God used. It will stir your heart and encourage you to believe for great revival..#I103-24 $7.75

OUR MINISTERING ANGELS—*Gwen Shaw*. A scriptural Bible study on the topic of angels. Angels will be playing a more and more prominent part in these last days. We need to understand about them and their ministry......................................#O104-87 $7.50

POUR OUT YOUR HEART—*Gwen Shaw*. A wonderful Bible study on travailing prayer. The hour has come to intercede before the throne of God. The call to intercession is for everyone, and we must carry the Lord's burden and weep for the lost so that the harvest can be brought in quickly ....#P105-16 $3.75

REDEEMING THE LAND—*Gwen Shaw*. This important teaching will help you know your authority through the Blood of Jesus to dislodge evil spirits, break the curse, and restore God's blessing upon the land. A Bible study on spiritual warfare ....#R108-61 $9.50

THE FINE LINE—*Gwen Shaw*. This Bible study clearly magnifies the "fine line" difference between the soul realm and the spirit realm. Both are intangible and therefore cannot be discerned with the five senses, but must be discerned by the Holy Spirit and the Word of God. A must for the deeper Christian...............................#F101-91 $6.00

THE POWER OF THE PRECIOUS BLOOD—*Gwen Shaw*. A Bible study on the Blood of Jesus. The author shares how it was revealed to her how much Satan fears Jesus' Blood. This Bible study will help you overcome and destroy the works of Satan in your life and the lives of loved ones ....#P105-18 $4.00

THE POWER OF PRAISE—*Gwen Shaw*. When God created the heavens and earth He was surrounded by praise. Miracles happen when holy people praise a Holy God! Praise is the language of creation. If prayer can move the hand of God, how much more praise can move Him!...#P400-66 $5.00

YE SHALL RECEIVE POWER FROM ON HIGH *Gwen Shaw*. This is a much needed foundational teaching on the Baptism of the Holy Spirit. It will enable you to teach this subject, as well as to understand these truths more fully yourself...#Y107-37 $5.00

YOUR APPOINTMENT WITH GOD—*Gwen Shaw*. A Bible study on fasting. Fasting is one of the most neglected sources of power over bondages of Satan that God has given the Church. The author's experiences are shared in this Bible study in a way that will change your life ....#Y107-40 $4.50

IN-DEPTH BIBLE STUDIES

FORGIVE AND RECEIVE—An In-Depth Bible Study on Philemon for the Serious Student of God's Word—*Gwen Shaw*. This Bible Study is a lesson to the church on the much-needed truths of forgiveness and restoration. The epistle to Philemon came from the heart of Paul who had experienced great forgiveness.....#F102-01 $7.00

OTHER BOOKS BY GWEN SHAW

LOVE, THE LAW OF THE ANGELS—*Gwen Shaw*. This is undoubtedly the greatest of Gwen Shaw's writings. It carries a message of healing and life in a sad and fallen civilization. Love heals the broken-hearted and sets disarray in order. You will never be the same after reading this beautiful book about love. (Also available in French and Spanish)...Paperback #L103-97 $10.00

SONG OF LOVE—*Gwen Shaw*. She was a heart-broken missionary, far from home. She cried out to God for help. He spoke, "Turn to the Song of Solomon and read!" As she turned in obedience, the Lord took her into the "Throne Room" of Heaven and taught her about the love of Christ for His Bride, the church. She fell in love with Jesus afresh, and you will too. ....#S108-62 $7.50

THE FALSE FAST — *Gwen Shaw*. Now, from the pen of Gwen Shaw, author of *Your Appointment With God* (a Bible Study on fasting), comes an exposé on the False Fast. It will help you to examine your motives for fasting, and make your foundations sure, so that your fast will be a potent tool in the hands of God........................#F115-62 $2.50

THE LIGHT WILL COME FROM RUSSIA — *Gwen Shaw*. The thrilling testimony of Mother Barbara, Abbess of the Mount of Olives in Jerusalem. She shares prophecies which were given to her concerning the nations of the world in our time by a holy bishop of the Kremlin, ten days before his death just prior to the Russian Revolution..........#L116-24 $3.95

TO BE LIKE JESUS — *Gwen Shaw*. Based on her Throne Room experience in 1971, the author shares the Father's heart about our place as sons in His Family. Nothing is more important than *To Be Like Jesus*! ....#T116-51 $6.95

THE PARABLE OF THE GOLDEN RAIN—*Gwen Shaw*. This is the story of how revivals come and go, and a true picture, in parable language, of how the Church tries to replace the genuine move of the Spirit with man-made programs and tactics. It's amusing and convicting at the same time...#P104-94 $4.00

Prices are subject to change without notice.
You may obtain a current price list from

Engeltal Press
P.O. Box 447 • Jasper, AR 72641-0447
Phone (870) 446-2665 • Fax (870) 446-22
www.engeltalpress.com

The Bedford Handbook

The Bedford Handbook

Eighth Edition

Diana Hacker

Nancy Sommers
Harvard University

Contributing Authors
Tom Jehn
Harvard University

Jane Rosenzweig
Harvard University

Contributing ESL Specialist
Marcy Carbajal Van Horn
St. Edward's University

BEDFORD / ST. MARTIN'S

BOSTON ◆ NEW YORK

For Bedford / St. Martin's

Executive Editor: Michelle M. Clark
Senior Development Editor: Barbara G. Flanagan
Development Editor: Mara Weible
Senior Production Editor: Anne Noonan
Senior Production Supervisor: Dennis Conroy
Executive Marketing Manager: John R. Swanson
Editorial Assistant: Alicia Young
Copyeditor: Linda McLatchie
Text Design: Claire Seng-Niemoeller
Cover Design: Donna Lee Dennison
Composition: Nesbitt Graphics, Inc.
Printing and Binding: RR Donnelley and Sons

President: Joan E. Feinberg
Editorial Director: Denise B. Wydra
Editor in Chief: Karen S. Henry
Director of Marketing: Karen R. Soeltz
Director of Editing, Design, and Production: Marcia Cohen
Assistant Director of Editing, Design, and Production: Elise S. Kaiser
Managing Editor: Elizabeth M. Schaaf

Library of Congress Control Number: 2009924937

4   3

k   j   i

For information, write: Bedford / St. Martin's, 75 Arlington Street,
Boston, MA 02116   (617-399-4000)

ISBN-10:	ISBN-13:	
0-312-54430-8	978-0-312-54430-0	(Instructor's Annotated Edition)
0-312-65268-2	978-0-312-65268-5	(hardcover Student Edition)
0-312-65269-0	978-0-312-65269-2	(softcover Student Edition)

Acknowledgments

Preface for Instructors

Hacker handbooks have long been recognized as the most innovative and practical college references—the ones that respond most directly to student writers' questions and challenges. In revising *The Bedford Handbook*, our goal was to continue to respond to students by helping them make the most of their college writing experiences. Part of our revision plan—crafted with my fellow contributors and Diana Hacker's longtime editorial team—was to learn firsthand what's happening in composition classrooms and writing centers across the country.

With our plan in mind, I visited more than thirty-five colleges and universities to listen to students, teachers, and tutors talk about the challenges facing today's college writers. Throughout my travels, I heard students puzzle out the unfamiliar elements of academic writing, particularly those related to working with sources. I watched creative teachers show their students how to build arguments, synthesize sources, and strengthen their ideas through revision. I observed writing center tutors responding to students' questions about thesis statements and research assignments. And I listened, everywhere, for clues about how to develop a better, more useful reference. The eighth edition is inspired by the students, teachers, and tutors at these schools—and by the candid feedback offered by users of *The Bedford Handbook*'s earlier editions.

As you look through this new edition, you'll find many innovations—large and small—that help students make the most of their experience as college writers. For example, new boxes called *Making the most of your handbook* pull together advice from different parts of the book to help students complete any college writing assignment. To help students make the most of their teachers' feedback as they revise, we have created a new feature, *Revising with comments*, that provides concrete strategies for revision. The comments in this new feature come directly from our interviews with sixty-five students about the comments they receive most frequently.

Teachers, students, and tutors asked for more instruction on academic writing and research. In response to their requests for a more detailed treatment of thesis, we expanded the coverage: Section 1e now helps students identify problems in a draft thesis, ask relevant questions, and then revise. Students asked for more guidance in finding, evaluating, and integrating scholarly sources, so we created a case study to illustrate steps in one student's research process. Teachers asked for attention to synthesis, a key academic skill. The eighth edition features new coverage that models how students use their own language and ideas to position sources in an academic conversation. Finally, teachers and tutors asked us for grammar coverage that's more accessible and relevant, so we added new hand-edited examples that show typical grammar errors that students make when they use sources. We also completely revised our ESL material.

Diana Hacker wanted her handbooks to provide clear, straightforward guidance in response to a college student's basic question: *How do I write a good college paper?* The eighth edition of *The Bedford Handbook* continues to respond, offering even more practical advice and useful models for today's college writers. Diana taught us well, and I am not alone in saying that her method of teaching one lesson at a time helped me become a more effective composition teacher. Now as lead coauthor on her handbooks, I am honored to continue the Hacker tradition, helping students make the most of their college writing experiences as they compose their way through college and into the wider world.

Features of the Eighth Edition

What's new

Navigation help that makes sense to students

- **Making the most of your handbook.** These new boxes, running throughout the book, help students to pull together the advice they need to complete writing assignments in composition and other classes. The boxes teach students to use their handbook as a reference by prompting them to consult related advice and examples from different parts of the book as they write and revise.

REFERENCES IN THE MARGIN HELP STUDENTS FIND RELATED MATERIAL

5b View your audience as a panel of jurors

Do not assume that your audience already agre instead, envision skeptical readers who, like a pa will make up their minds a to all sides of the argumer arguing a public policy iss paper at readers who repres of opinions. In the case of th offshore drilling, for examp jury representative of those stake in the matter: envir policymakers, and consume

At times, you can deliberately narrow your you are working within a word limit, for exampl not have the space in which to address all the rounding the offshore drilling debate. Or you mig

Making the most of your handbook

You may need to consider a specific audience for your argument.

▶ Analyzing your audience: 1a

▶ Writing in a particular discipline, such as business or psychology: 7

See pages 6 and 109 for additional examples.

- **Plain-language navigation.** We have replaced traditional handbook section titles with familiar terms for quick and easy reference. Terms like *main idea*, *flow*, and *presenting the other side*, placed in the upper right-hand corners of the pages, will help students see at a glance the exact page they need. See page 47 for examples.

Concrete strategies for revising

- **Revising with comments.** Based on research with sixty-five students at colleges and universities across the country, this new boxed feature gives students targeted help with revising in response to instructors' comments on their drafts. Each box contains a sample student passage with a common instructor's comment, such as "unclear thesis," "develop more," or "cite your source." We help students understand similar comments by their instructors and give them strategies they can use to revise their own work. An example appears on page ix. ▶▶▶

- **Specific strategies for revising thesis statements.** We know that college writers often need help reworking thesis statements, no matter the discipline. A new stepped-out approach helps students identify a problem in a draft thesis, ask relevant questions, and revise based on their own responses. See page 28.

- **New coverage of portfolio keeping.** For students who are asked to maintain and submit a writing portfolio, a new section (2c) covers types of portfolios and offers tips for writing a reflective cover document. See pages 59–61.

"REVISING WITH COMMENTS" PAGES PROVIDE CONCRETE STRATEGIES

Revising with comments | Unclear thesis

Understanding the comment

When a teacher or tutor points out that your thesis is unclear, the comment often signals that readers may have a hard time identifying your essay's main point.

> Fathers are more involved in the lives of their children today than they used to be. In the past, the father's primary role was as the provider; child care was most often left to the mother or other relatives. However, today's father drives to dance lessons, coaches his child's baseball team, hosts birthday parties, and provides homework help. Do more involved fathers help or hinder the development of their children?

Unclear thesis

One student wrote this introductory paragraph in response to an assignment that asked her to analyze the changing roles of mothers or fathers.

A writer's thesis, or main point, should be phrased as a statement, not a question. To revise, the student could answer the question she has posed, or she could pose a new question and answer it. After considering her evidence, she needs to decide what position she wants to take, state this position clearly, and show readers *why* this position—her thesis—matters.

Similar comments: vague thesis • state your position • your main point?

Revising when *your* thesis is unclear

1. *Ask questions.* What is the thesis, position, or main point of the draft? Can you support it with the available evidence?

2. *Reread your entire draft.* Because ideas develop as you write, you may find that your conclusion contains a clearer statement of your main point than your current thesis does. Or you may find your thesis elsewhere in your draft.

3. *Try revising your thesis* by framing it as an answer to a question you pose, the resolution of a problem you identify, or a position you take in a debate. And put your thesis to the "So what?" test: Why would a reader be interested in this thesis?

More help with writing a clear thesis: 1c and 1e

30

See pages 33, 110, and 502 for additional examples.

Targeted content for today's students:
Academic writing and research

- **A new case study** follows one student's research and writing process, providing a detailed, illustrated model for strategizing about sources, using search tools and techniques, evaluating sources, taking notes, thinking critically about how best to use sources in a paper, and integrating a source responsibly. This self-contained section (54b) includes marginal navigation aids directing students to more detailed information throughout the book. The first page of the case study is shown on page xi. ▶ ▶ ▶

- **Synthesis, a requirement in academic writing.** More of today's college writing assignments require that students synthesize—analyze sources and work them into a conversation that helps develop an argument. New coverage of synthesis, with annotated examples in MLA and APA styles (pages 512–15 and 635–38), helps students work with sources to meet the demands of academic writing.

- **Integrating evidence in analytical papers.** New coverage in section 4, "Writing about Texts," shows students—at the sentence level—how to introduce, include, and interpret a passage in an analytical paper. See pages 94–97.

- **More help with writing assignments in other disciplines and in various genres.** For students who work with evidence in disciplines other than English, we have included annotated assignments and excerpts from model papers in psychology, business, nursing, and biology. For an example, see page 136.

- **New and up-to-date documentation models** for the sources students are using today—eighty-five new models across the three styles (MLA, APA, and *Chicago*)—with special attention to new sources such as podcasts, online videos, blogs, and DVD features. Detailed annotations for many

NEW CASE STUDY FOLLOWS ONE STUDENT'S RESEARCH AND WRITING PROCESS

Making the most of your handbook
Highlights of one student's research process (MLA style)

Anna Orlov, a student in a composition class, was assigned a research essay related to technology and the American workplace. The assignment called for her to use a variety of print and electronic sources and to follow MLA style. Orlov immediately thought of her summer internship at an insurance company and her surprise at the strict employee Internet use policy in place there. As she thought about how to turn her experience into a research project, she developed some questions and strategies to guide her research and writing.

"How do I begin a research paper?"

Before getting started, Orlov worked with a writing tutor to break her research plan into several stages. (Section numbers in blue refer to relevant discussions throughout the book.)

- Ask worthwhile questions about my topic.   1b, 46a
- Talk with a reference librarian about useful types of
  sources and where to find them.   46b
- Consider how each source can contribute
  to my paper.   47a
- Decide which search results are worth a
  closer look.   47b
- Evaluate the sources.   47d, 47e
- Take notes and keep track of the sources.   48
- Write a working thesis.   1c, 50a
- Write a draft and integrate sources.   1e–1g, 52, 53a
- Document sources.   49, 53b

Orlov began by jotting down the research question she wanted to investigate: *Is Internet surveillance in the workplace fair or unfair to employees?* She thought the practice might be unfair but knew that she needed to consider all sides of the issue. Her instructor had explained that sources uncovered in the research process would both support and challenge her ideas and ultimately help shape the paper. Orlov knew she would have to be

1b and 46a:
Posing questions for a research paper

See pages 573–82 for the entire case study.

models help students see at a glance how to format their citations. See examples on page 553. **NOTE:** The eighth edition includes up-to-date guidelines for MLA (2009) and APA (2010).

- **New MLA-style research essay** (pages 583–88)

- **New flowchart on intellectual property** (pages 486–87)

New examples, more accessible grammar coverage

- **More ESL help, presented more accessibly.** Part VI, "Challenges for ESL and Multilingual Writers," now completely revised, offers more accessible advice and more support for multilingual writers across the disciplines.

- **Grammar basics content is more straightforward than ever.** Part XI, the handbook's reference within a reference, now teaches with everyday example sentences and exercise items.

- **More academic examples** reflect the types of sentences students are expected to write in college. A new type of hand-edited example ("Writing with sources") shows typical errors students make—and how they can correct them—when they integrate sources in MLA, APA, and *Chicago* papers. See page 240 for an additional example.

▼

Writing with sources

MLA-style citation

▶ Deborah Tannen's research reveals that men and women have different ideas about communication. For example, *Tannen explains* that a woman "expects her husband to be a new and improved version of her best friend" (441).

A quotation must be part of a complete sentence. *That a woman "expects her husband to be a new and improved version of her best friend"* is a fragment—a subordinate clause. In this case, adding a signal phrase that includes a subject and a verb (*Tannen explains*) corrects the fragment and clarifies that the quotation is from Tannen.

A new collection of resources that helps instructors make the most of their handbook

- *Teaching with Hacker Handbooks,* by Marcy Carbajal Van Horn, offers practical advice on common topics such as designing a composition course, crafting writing assignments, and teaching multilingual writers. Ten lesson plans, each including strategies and materials that are ready to use or customize, support common course goals such as teaching argument, teaching paragraphs, and teaching peer review. The collection also includes a wealth of handouts, syllabi, and other materials for integrating a Hacker handbook into your course. Available in print and online (hackerhandbooks.com/teaching).

What's the same

Comprehensive coverage of grammar, academic writing, and research. A classroom tool and a reference, the handbook is designed to help students write well in any college course. This edition includes nearly one hundred exercise sets, many with answers in the back of the book.

A brief menu and a user-friendly index. Students will find help fast by consulting either the brief list of contents on the inside front cover or the user-friendly index, which works even for writers who are unsure of grammar terminology.

Citation at a glance. Annotated visuals show students where to find the publication information they need to cite common types of sources in MLA and APA styles.

Quick-access charts and an uncluttered design. The eighth edition has what instructors and students have come to expect of a Hacker handbook: a clear and navigable presentation of information, with charts that summarize key content.

What's in the Student Center

hackerhandbooks.com/bedhandbook

The handbook's companion Web site has a new name but includes many of the resources students have used before.

Grammar, writing, and research exercises with feedback for every item. More than 1,400 items offer students plenty of extra practice, and our new scorecard gives instructors flexibility in viewing students' results.

Annotated model papers in MLA, APA, *Chicago*, and CSE styles. Student writers can see formatting conventions and effective writing in traditional college essays and in other common genres: annotated bibliographies, literature reviews, lab reports, business proposals, and clinical documents.

Research and Documentation Online. This award-winning resource, written by a college librarian, gives students a jump start with research in thirty academic disciplines.

Resources for writers and tutors. Checklists, hints, tips, and helpsheets are available in downloadable format.

Resources for ESL and multilingual writers. Writers will find advice and strategies for understanding college expectations and completing writing assignments. Also included are charts, exercises, activities, and an annotated student essay in draft and final form.

Language Debates. Twenty-two brief essays provide opportunities for critical thinking about grammar and usage issues.

Access to premium content. New copies of the print handbook can be packaged with a free activation code for premium content: *The Bedford e-Handbook*, a series of online video tutorials, and a collection of resources that includes games, activities, readings, guides, and more.

Supplements for instructors

Practical

Teaching with Hacker Handbooks: Topics, Strategies, and Lesson Plans

The Bedford Handbook instructor resources (at hackerhandbooks .com/bedhandbook)

Professional

Teaching Composition: Background Readings

The Bedford Guide for Writing Tutors, Fifth Edition

The Bedford Bibliography for Teachers of Writing, Sixth Edition

Supplements for students

Print

Developmental Exercises for The Bedford Handbook

Working with Sources: Research Exercises for The Bedford Handbook

Research and Documentation in the Electronic Age, Fifth Edition

Extra Help for ESL Writers: Supplement for Hacker Handbooks

Designing Documents and Understanding Visuals: Supplement for Hacker Handbooks

Writing in the Disciplines: Advice and Models

Online

The Bedford e-Handbook

CompClass for The Bedford Handbook

Acknowledgments

I am grateful for the expertise, enthusiasm, and classroom experience that so many individuals brought to the new edition.

Contributors

My fellow coauthors wrote new content and rethought existing content to make sure that *The Bedford Handbook* reaches an ever broader range of students and meets their various needs. Jane Rosenzweig, a composition teacher and writing center director, revised the coverage of thesis statements, wrote new content for the "Writing about Texts" section, and created many new examples for our innovative "Writing with sources" grammar coverage. Tom Jehn, a composition teacher and writing in the disciplines expert, refined our research coverage and drafted the new case study in the MLA section. Marcy Carbajal Van Horn, online writing lab director, ESL specialist, and experienced composition instructor, improved the ESL coverage in the book, wrote new ESL content for the companion Web site, and is lead author of the new collection of instructor resources, *Teaching with Hacker Handbooks.*

Reviewers

For her careful review of our coverage of research and documentation, I am grateful to Barbara Fister, academic librarian at Gustavus Adolphus College. I am also thankful to a group of colleagues who helped shape our new coverage of revision by talking with us about the comments they write on their students' papers: Steve Brahlek, Palm Beach Community College; Liz Canfield, Virginia Commonwealth University; Jon Cullick, Northern Kentucky University; Tiane Donahue, Dartmouth College; Anne Fernald, Fordham University; Holly McSpadden, Missouri Southern State University; and Jennifer Whetham, Green River Community College.

For their active engagement with new manuscript and for their willingness to share teaching ideas in a Boston-based focus group, I am grateful to the following instructors: Steve Brahlek and John Ribar, Palm Beach Community College; April Childress and Joanne Messman, Greenville Technical College; Beverly Holmes and James Suderman, Northwest Florida State College; Bobbie Kilbane, Volunteer State Community College; and Chris Twiggs, Florida Community College.

Many additional reviewers either answered a detailed questionnaire about the seventh edition or reviewed new manuscript for the eighth edition: Guy Aengus, University of California, Davis; Preston Allen, Miami Dade College; Sandy Archimedes, University of California, Santa Cruz; Chris Arevalo, Austin Community College; John Avery, Green River Community College; Diane Baird, Palm Beach Community College; April Baker, Greenville Technical College; Chelle Bernstein, St. Johns River Community College; Kristin Bivens, Harold Washington College; Laura Black, Volunteer State Community College; Deborah Borchers, Pueblo Community College; Laurie Buchanan, Clark State Community College; Karen Burge, Wichita State University; Nicole Buzzetto-More, University of Maryland Eastern Shore; Andrew Cavanaugh, University of Maryland University College; Pam Clark, Frederick Community College; Victoria Cliett, Henry Ford Community College; Mark Coley, Tarrant County College Southeast; Trish Conard, Hutchinson Community College; Janet Cook, Hutchinson Community College; Brian Cooney, Gonzaga University; Michael Cripps, York College CUNY; Margot Cullen, Ohio Northern University; Bonita Dattner-Garza, St. Mary's University; Rose Day, Central New Mexico Community College; Darren DeFrain, Wichita State University; Linda Didesidero, University of Maryland University College; Africa Fine, Palm Beach Community College; Bill Fisher, Pensacola Junior College; Jane P. Gamber, Hutchinson Community College; Grace Giorgio, University of Illinois; Shon Grant, Northern Virginia Community College; Miriam Gustafson, University of New Mexico; Karen Hall, Lewiston-Auburn College; Mickey Hall, Volunteer State Community College; Elisabeth

Heard, Harold Washington College; John Jebb, University of Delaware; Laura Jeffries, Florida Community College at Jacksonville; Nikki Johnson, University of Northern Iowa; Stephanie Kamath, University of Massachusetts Boston; Kathleen Keating, Greensboro College; Jana Kinder, Florida Community College at Jacksonville; Steven Knapp, Indian River Community College; Carol Koris, Johnson & Wales University; Robert Lietz, Ohio Northern University; Michelle Lisi-D'Alauro, Lewiston-Auburn College; Keming Liu, Medgar Evers College CUNY; Barbara Lutz, University of Delaware; Paul Madachy, Prince George's Community College; John Magee, Ohio Northern University; Caroline Mains, Palo Alto College; David Marlow, University of South Carolina; Tammy Mata, Tarrant County College; Linda McCloud-Bondoc, Athabasca University; Shellie Michael, Volunteer State Community College; Gayla Mills, Randolph-Macon College; Heidi Moore, Northern Virginia Community College; Rhonda Morris, Santa Fe College; Joan Nakke, Montgomery College; Betty Nelson, Volunteer State Community College; Tom O'Neal, St. Johns River Community College; Michelle Paulsen, Victoria College; Tammy Peery, Montgomery College; Susan Perry, Greenville Technical College; Sharon Prince, Wharton City Junior College; Roberta Proctor, Palm Beach Community College; Ellen Raphaeli, Northern Virginia Community College; Kent Richmond, California State University, Long Beach; Pearl Saunders, Palm Beach Community College; Lisa Shaw, Miami Dade College; Donald Skinner, Indian River Community College; Gary Sligh, Lake-Sumter Community College; Kate Spike, Bowling Green State University; Jeniffer Strong, Central New Mexico Community College; Rebecca Sullivan, St. Johns River Community College; Tom Treffinger, Greenville Technical College; Katherine Turner, Mary Baldwin College; April Van Camp, Indian River Community College; Susan Vergnani, Santa Fe College; Lisa Wilde, Howard Community College; Dennis Williams, College of Charleston; Rita Wisdom, Tarrant County College Northeast.

Students

A number of bright and willing students helped us see which instructor comments provide the best guidance for revision. From Green River Community College: Kyle Baskin, Josué Cardona, Emily Dore, Anthony Hines, Stephanie Humphries, Joshua Kin, Jessica Llapitan, James Mitchell, Derek Pegram, Charlie Piehler, Lindsay Allison Rae Richards, Kristen Saladis, Jacob Simpson, Christina Starkey, Ariana Stone, and Joseph Vreeburg. From Northern Kentucky University: Sarah Freidhoff, Marisa Hempel, Sarah Laughlin, Sean Moran, Laren Reis, and Carissa Spencer. From Palm Beach Community College: Alexis Day, Shawn Gibbons, Zachary Jennison, Jean Lacz, Neshia Neal, Sarah Reich, Jude Rene, and Sam Smith. And from the University of Maine at Farmington: Nicole Carr, Hannah Courtright, Timothy Doyle, Janelle Gallant, Amy Hobson, Shawn Menard, Jada Molton, Jordan Nicholas, Nicole Phillips, Tessa Rockwood, Emily Rose, Nicholas Tranten, and Ashley Wyman. We also thank the students who have let us use and adapt their papers as models in the handbook: Ned Bishop, Jamal Hammond, Albert Lee, Luisa Mirano, Anna Orlov, Emilia Sanchez, and Matt Watson.

Bedford / St. Martin's

A comprehensive handbook is truly a collaborative writing project, and it is a pleasure to acknowledge and thank the enormously talented Bedford/St. Martin's editorial team, whose deep commitment to students informs each new feature of *The Bedford Handbook*. Joan Feinberg, Bedford's president and Diana Hacker's first editor, asks tough questions and offers her superb judgment on every aspect of the book. Joan's graceful and generous leadership, both within Bedford and in the national composition community, is a never-ending source of inspiration for those who are fortunate to work with her. Michelle Clark, executive editor, combines wisdom with patience, creativity with practicality, and hard work with good humor. An author could not wish for a smarter editor and collaborator than Michelle. Her voice, vision, and elegance shape each page of the eighth edition. Barbara Flanagan, senior editor, has worked on Diana Hacker's handbooks for more than twenty-five years and brings to the eighth edition her unrelenting insistence on both clarity and precision as well as her expertise in documentation. Mara Weible, editor, is a close reader extraordinaire, whose intellectual patience and persistence shaped the new case study and synthesis sections. Denise Wydra, editorial director; Karen Henry, editor in chief; John Swanson, executive marketing manager; and Jimmy Fleming, senior English marketing specialist, are treasured sources of thoughtful and innovative ideas. Their passionate commitment to *The Bedford Handbook* ensures that it will meet the needs of today's students. Anne Noonan, senior production editor, kept us on schedule and turned a complex manuscript into a superior handbook. Alicia Young, editorial assistant, expertly managed the review process, prepared documents, and edited several ancillaries. And many thanks to Linda McLatchie, copyeditor, for her thoroughness and attention to detail; to Claire Seng-Niemoeller, text designer, who always has ease of use in mind as she designs a Hacker handbook; to Donna Dennison, art director, who has given the cover a fresh new look; and to Sarah Ferguson, new media editor, who developed the book's Student Center and e-book.

And last, but never least, I offer thanks to Maxine Rodburg and Kerry Walk, friends and mentors, for sustaining conversations about teaching writing; Joshua Alper, a most demanding—and forgiving—reader; and to my daughters, Rachel and Alexandra, whose good-natured and humorous observations about the real lives of college writers are a constant source of instruction and inspiration.

—*Nancy Sommers*

How to Use This Book and Its Student Center

Though it is small enough to hold in your hand, *The Bedford Handbook* will answer most of the questions you are likely to ask as you plan, draft, and revise a piece of writing:

How do I choose and narrow a topic?

How do I know when to begin a new paragraph?

Should I write *each was* or *each were*?

When should I place a comma before *and*?

What is counterargument?

What is the difference between *accept* and *except*?

How do I cite an online newspaper article?

The book's companion Web site, the Student Center, extends the book beyond its covers. See page xxvi for details.

How to find information with an instructor's help

When you are revising an essay that your instructor has marked, tracking down information is simple. If your instructor indicates problems with a number such as *16* or a number and letter such as *12e*, you can turn directly to the appropriate section of the handbook. Just flip through the tabs at the top of the pages until you find the number in question.

If your instructor uses an abbreviation such as *w* or *dm* instead of a number, consult the list of abbreviations and revision symbols at the end of the book. There you will find the name of the problem (*wordy; dangling modifier*) and the number of the section to consult.

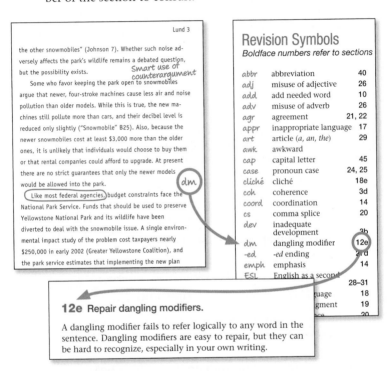

12e Repair dangling modifiers.

A dangling modifier fails to refer logically to any word in the sentence. Dangling modifiers are easy to repair, but they can be hard to recognize, especially in your own writing.

How to find information on your own

This handbook is designed to allow you to find information without an instructor's help—usually by consulting the brief menu inside the front cover. At times, you may consult the detailed menu inside the back cover, the index, the Glossary of Usage, the list of revision symbols, or one of the directories to documentation models. The tutorials on pages xxviii–xxxi give you opportunities to practice finding information in different ways.

The brief menu. The brief menu inside the front cover displays the book's contents. Let's say that you want to find out how you can write with more active verbs. Your first step is to scan the menu for the appropriate numbered topic—in this case "8 Active verbs." Then you can use the blue and green tabs at the top of the pages to find section 8.

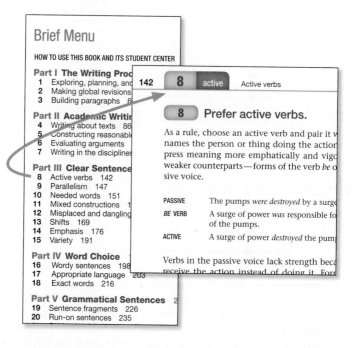

The detailed menu. The detailed menu appears inside the back cover. When the numbered section you're looking for is broken up into quite a few lettered subsections, try consulting this menu. For instance, if you have a question about the proper use of commas after introductory elements, this menu will quickly lead you to section 32b.

Once you find the right lettered subsection, you will see three kinds of advice to help you edit your writing—a rule, an explanation, and one or more hand-edited examples.

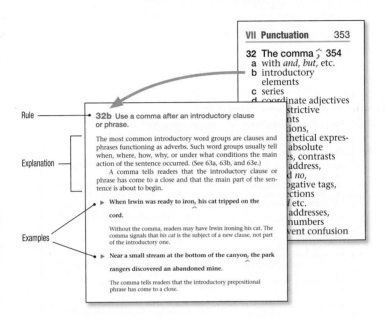

The index. If you aren't sure which topic to choose from one of the menus, consult the index at the back of the book. For example, you may not realize that the issue of whether to use *have* or *has* is a matter of subject-verb agreement (section 21). In that case, simply look up "*has* vs. *have*" in the index. You will be directed to specific pages in two sections covering subject-verb agreement.

Making the most of your handbook. You will find your way to helpful advice by using the index, the menus, or the contents. Once you get to where you need to be, you may also find references to additional related advice and models. These boxes help you pull together what you need from the handbook for each assignment.

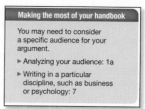

Making the most of your handbook

You may need to consider a specific audience for your argument.

▶ Analyzing your audience: 1a

▶ Writing in a particular discipline, such as business or psychology: 7

The Glossary of Usage. When in doubt about the correct use of a particular word (such as *affect* and *effect*), consult the Glossary of Usage at the back of the book. This glossary explains the difference between commonly confused words; it also includes words that are inappropriate in formal written English.

Directories to documentation models. When you are documenting a research paper with MLA, APA, or *Chicago* style, you can find documentation models by consulting the appropriate color-coded directories.

APA, page 645

Chicago, page 703

MLA, page 530

Answers to exercises. *The Bedford Handbook* has been designed so that you can learn from it on your own. By providing answers to some exercise sentences, it allows you to test your understanding of the material. Most exercise sets begin with five sentences lettered *a* through *e* and conclude with five or ten numbered sentences. Answers to lettered sentences appear in the back of the book, beginning on page 805.

Using the book's Student Center:
hackerhandbooks.com/bedhandbook

Throughout *The Bedford Handbook*, Eighth Edition, you will see references to exercises and model papers on the Student Center, the book's companion Web site. Here is a complete list of resources on the site. Your instructor may use some of this material in class; each area of the site, however, has been developed for you to use on your own whenever you need it.

- **Writing exercises** Interactive exercises, including feedback for every answer, on topics such as choosing a thesis statement and conducting a peer review

- **Grammar exercises** Interactive exercises on grammar, style, and punctuation, including feedback for every answer

- **Research exercises** Interactive exercises, including feedback for every answer, on topics such as integrating quotations and documenting sources in MLA, APA, and *Chicago* styles

- **Model papers** Annotated sample papers in MLA, APA, *Chicago*, and CSE styles

- **ESL help** Resources, strategies, model papers, and exercises to help multilingual students improve their college writing skills

- *Research and Documentation Online* Advice on finding sources in a variety of academic disciplines and up-to-date guidelines for documenting print and online sources in MLA, APA, *Chicago*, and CSE styles

- **Resources for writers and tutors** Revision checklists and helpsheets for common writing problems

- **Tutorials** Interactive resources that teach essential college skills such as integrating sources in a research paper and revising with peer comments (This area of the Web site requires an activation code.)

- **Language Debates** Mini-essays exploring controversial issues of grammar and usage, such as split infinitives

- **Additional resources** Print-format versions of the book's exercises and links to additional online resources for every part of the book

- *Re:Writing* A free collection of resources for composition and other college classes: help with preparing presentation slides, avoiding plagiarism, evaluating online sources, and more

Tutorials

The following tutorials will give you practice using the book's menus, index, Glossary of Usage, and MLA directory. Answers to the tutorials begin on page 804.

1 Using the menus

Each of the following "rules" violates the principle it expresses. Using the brief menu inside the front cover or the detailed menu inside the back cover, find the section in *The Bedford Handbook* that explains the principle. Then fix the problem. Example:

> Tutors in
> ~~In~~ the writing center/~~they~~ say that vague pronoun
> reference is unacceptable. 23

1. A verb have to agree with its subject.
2. About sentence fragments. You should avoid them.
3. Its important to use apostrophe's correctly.
4. If your sentence begins with a long introductory word group use a comma to separate the word group from the rest of the sentence.
5. When dangling, watch your modifiers.

2 Using the index

Assume that you have written the following sentences and want to know the answers to the questions in brackets. Use the index at the back of the book to locate the information you need, and edit the sentences if necessary.

1. Each of the candidates have decided to participate in tonight's debate. [Should the verb be *has* or *have* to agree with *Each*?]

2. We had intended to go surfing but spent most of our vacation lying on the beach. [Should I use *lying* or *laying*?]

3. We only looked at two houses before buying the house of our dreams. [Is *only* in the right place?]

4. In some cultures, it is considered ill mannered for you to accept a gift. [Is it okay to use *you* to mean "anyone in general"?]

5. In Canada, Joanne picked up several bottles of maple syrup for her sister and me. [Should I write *for her sister and I*?]

3 Using the menus or the index

Imagine that you are in the following situations. Using either the menus or the index, find the information you need.

1. You are a student studying health administration, and you're editing a report you've just written on the benefits of community-based urgent care clinics. You recall learning to put a comma between all items in a series except the last two. But you have noticed that most writers use a comma between all items. You're curious about the rule. Which section of *The Bedford Handbook* will you consult?

2. You are tutoring in your university's writing center. A composition student comes to you for help with her first college essay. She is revising a draft — and struggling with her use of articles (*a*, *an*, and *the*). You know how to use articles, but you aren't able to explain the complicated rules on their correct use. Which section in *The Bedford Handbook* will you and the student, a multilingual writer, consult?

3. You have been assigned to write in response to an essay you read for your composition class. Your instructor has asked that you use at least three quotations from the text in your response, which must be written in MLA style. You aren't quite sure how to integrate words from another source in your own writing. Which section in this handbook will help?

4. You supervise interns at a housing agency. Two of your interns have trouble with the -s endings on verbs. One tends to drop -s endings; the other tends to add them where they don't belong. You suspect that both problems stem from dialects spoken at home. The interns are in danger of losing their jobs because your boss thinks that anyone who writes "the tenant refuse . . ." or "the landlords insists . . ." is beyond hope. You disagree. Where can you direct your interns for help in *The Bedford Handbook*?

5. You are in a first-semester American literature course, which covers literature from the 1850s to World War II. On two different papers, your instructor has pointed out your tendency to shift between present tense and past tense as you write. When you consult your handbook, what do you discover about the rules for using verb tenses in papers about literature?

4 Using the Glossary of Usage

Consult the Glossary of Usage to see if the italicized words are used correctly. Then edit any sentences containing incorrect usage. If a sentence is correct, write "correct" after it. Example:

The pediatrician gave my daughter *a* injection for her

allergy.

1. Changing attitudes *toward* alcohol have *effected* the beer industry.

2. It is *mankind's* nature to think wisely and act foolishly.

3. This afternoon I plan to *lie* out in the sun and work on my tan.

4. Our goal this year is to *grow* our profits by 9 percent.

5. Most sleds are pulled by no *less* than two dogs and no more than ten.

5   Using the directory to MLA works cited models

Let's say that you have written a short research essay on the origins of hip-hop music. You have cited the following five sources in your essay, using MLA documentation, and you are ready to type your list of works cited. Turn to page 530 and use the MLA directory to locate the appropriate models. Then write a correct entry for each source and arrange the entries in a properly formatted list of works cited.

A book by Jeff Chang titled *Can't Stop, Won't Stop: A History of the Hip-Hop Generation.* The book was published in New York by St. Martin's Press in 2005.

An online article by Kay Randall called "Studying a Hip Hop Nation." The article appeared on the University of Texas at Austin Web site. The title of the site is *University of Texas at Austin.* You accessed the site on August 13, 2009; the last update was October 9, 2008.

A journal article by H. Samy Alim titled "360 Degreez of Black Art Comin at You: Sista Sonia Sanchez and the Dimensions of a Black Arts Continuum." The article appears in the journal *BMa: The Sonia Sanchez Literary Review.* The article appears on pages 15–33. The volume number is 6, the issue number is 1, and the year is 2000.

A sound recording entitled "Rapper's Delight" performed by the Sugarhill Gang on the CD *The Sugarhill Gang.* The CD was released in 2008 by DBK Works.

A magazine article accessed online through the database *Expanded Academic ASAP.* The article, "The Roots Redefine Hip-Hop's Past," was written by Kimberly Davis and published in *Ebony* magazine in June 2003. The article appears on pages 162–64. You found this article on April 13, 2008.

Contents

Part I
The Writing Process

1

Writing is not a matter of recording already developed thoughts but a process of figuring out what you think. Since it's not possible to think about everything all at once, most experienced writers handle a piece of writing in stages. You will generally move from planning to drafting to revising, but be prepared to return to earlier stages as your ideas develop.

1 Explore and plan; then rough out a first draft.

Before attempting a first draft, spend some time generating ideas. Mull over your subject while listening to music or driving to work, jot down inspirations, and explore your insights with a willing listener. Ask yourself questions: What do you find puzzling, striking, or interesting about your subject? What would you like to know more about? At this stage, you should be collecting information and experimenting with ways of focusing and organizing it to reach your readers.

1a Assess the writing situation.

Begin by taking a look at your writing situation. The key elements of a writing situation include the following:

- your subject
- the sources of information available to you
- your purpose
- your audience
- any constraints (length, document design, deadlines)

It is likely that you will make final decisions about all of these matters later in the writing process—after a first draft, for example. Nevertheless, you can save yourself time by thinking about as many of them as possible in advance. For a quick checklist, see the chart on page 3.

Academic English What counts as good writing varies from culture to culture and even among groups within cultures. In some situations, you will need to become familiar with the writing styles — such as direct or indirect, personal or impersonal, plain or embellished — that are valued by the culture or discipline for which you are writing.

Checklist for assessing the writing situation

Subject

- Has the subject (or a range of possible subjects) been given to you, or are you free to choose your own?
- What interests you about your subject? What questions would you like to explore?
- Why is your subject worth writing about? How might readers benefit from reading about it?
- Do you need to narrow your subject to a more specific topic (because of length restrictions, for instance)?

Sources of information

- Where will your information come from: Reading? Personal experience? Observation? Interviews? Questionnaires?
- What documentation style is required: MLA? APA? *Chicago*?

Purpose and audience

- Why are you writing: To inform readers? To persuade them? To entertain them? To call them to action? Some combination of these?
- Who are your readers? How well informed are they about the subject? What do you want them to learn?
- How interested and attentive are they likely to be? Will they resist any of your ideas?
- What is your relationship to your readers: Student to instructor? Employee to supervisor? Citizen to citizen? Expert to novice? →

Checklist for assessing the writing situation, *continued*

Length and document design

- Do you have any length specifications? If not, what length seems appropriate, given your subject, purpose, and audience?
- Is a particular document format required? If so, do you have guidelines to follow or examples to consult?

Reviewers and deadlines

- Who will be reviewing your draft in progress: Your instructor? A writing center tutor? Your classmates? A family member?
- What are your deadlines? How much time will you need to allow for the various stages of writing, including proofreading and printing the final draft?

Subject

Frequently your subject will be given to you. In a psychology class, for example, you might be asked to explain Bruno Bettelheim's Freudian analysis of fairy tales. In a composition course, assignments often ask you to respond to readings. In the business world, your assignment might be to draft a quarterly sales report.

When you are free to choose your own subject, it's a good idea to focus on something you are genuinely curious about. If you are studying television, radio, and the Internet in a communication course, for example, you might ask yourself which of these subjects interests you most. Perhaps you want to learn more about the role streaming video can play in activism and social change. Look through your readings and class notes to see if you can identify questions you'd like to explore further in an essay.

Make sure that you can reasonably investigate your subject in the space you have. If you are limited to a few pages, for

Making the most of your handbook

Effective research writers often start by asking a question.

▶ Posing questions for research: 46a

Ways to narrow a subject to a topic

Subdividing your subject

One way to subdivide a subject is to ask questions sparked by reading or talking to your classmates. If you are writing about teen pregnancy, for example, you might wonder why your city and a neighboring city have different rates of teen pregnancy. This question would give you a manageable topic for a short paper.

Restricting your purpose

Often you can restrict your purpose. For example, if your subject is preventing teen pregnancy, you might at first hope to call readers to action. Upon further reflection, you might realize that this goal is more than you could hope to accomplish, given your word limit. By adopting a more limited purpose—to show that an experimental health curriculum for sixth graders results in lower rates of teen pregnancy—you would have a manageable topic.

Restricting your audience

Consider writing for a particular audience. For example, instead of writing for a general audience on a broad subject such as teen pregnancy, you might address a group with a special interest in the subject: teens, parents, educators, or politicians.

Considering the information available to you

Look at the information you have collected. If you have gathered a great deal of information on one aspect of your subject (for example, counseling programs for pregnant teens) and less information on other aspects (such as birth control education), you may have found your topic.

example, you could not do justice to a subject as broad as "videos as agents of social change." You could, however, focus on one aspect of the subject—perhaps experts' contradictory claims about the effectiveness of "narrowcasting," or creating video content for small, specific audiences. The chart on this page suggests ways to narrow a subject to a manageable topic for a paper.

Whether or not you choose your own subject, it's important to be aware of the expectations of each writing situation. The chart on page 9 suggests ways to interpret assignments.

Sources of information

Where will your facts, details, and examples come from? Can you develop your topic from personal experience alone, or will you need to search for relevant information through reading, observation, interviews, or questionnaires?

Reading Reading is an important way to deepen your understanding of a topic and expand your perspective. Reading will be your primary source of information for many college assignments, which will generally be of two kinds: (1) analytical essays that call for a close reading of one book, essay, literary work, or visual and (2) research assignments that ask you to find and consult a variety of sources on a topic.

For an analytical essay, you will select details from the work, not to inform readers but to support an interpretation. You can often assume that your readers are familiar with the work and have a copy of it on hand, but be sure to provide enough context so that someone who doesn't know the work well can still follow your interpretation. When you quote from the work, page references are usually sufficient. When in doubt about the need for documentation, consult your instructor.

For a research paper, you cannot assume that your readers are familiar with your sources. Therefore, you must formally document all quoted, summarized, or paraphrased material.

Making the most of your handbook

Academic writing often requires that you read critically and cite your sources.

▶ Guidelines for active reading: page 87

▶ Analyzing an essay: 4d

▶ Interpreting literature: 55b

▶ Quoting, paraphrasing, and summarizing sources: 48c

Personal experience If your interest in a subject stems from your personal experience, you will want to ask what it is about your experience that would interest your audience and why. For example, if you volunteered at a homeless shelter, you might have spent some time talking to homeless children and learned about their needs. Perhaps you can use your experience to broaden your readers' understanding of the issues, to persuade an organization to fund an after-school program for homeless children, or to propose changes in legislation.

Observation   Observation is an excellent means of collecting information about a wide range of subjects, such as gender relationships on a popular television program, the clichéd language of sports announcers, or the appeal of a local art museum. For such subjects, do not rely on your memory alone; your information will be fresher and more detailed if you actively collect it, with a notebook, laptop, or tape recorder in hand.

Interviews and questionnaires   Interviews and questionnaires can supply detailed and interesting information on many subjects. A nursing student interested in the care of terminally ill patients might interview hospice nurses; a political science major might speak with a local judge about alternative sentencing for first offenders; a future teacher might conduct a survey on the use of computers in local elementary schools.

It is a good idea to record interviews to preserve any lively quotations that you might want to weave into your essay. Circulating questionnaires by e-mail or on a Web site will facilitate responses. Keep questions simple and specify a deadline to ensure that you get a reasonable number of replies. (See also 46g.)

Purpose

Your purpose will often be dictated by your writing situation. Perhaps you have been asked to draft a proposal requesting funding for a student organization, to report the results of a psychology experiment, or to write about the controversy surrounding genetically modified (GM) foods for the school newspaper. Even though your overall purpose is fairly obvious in such situations, a closer look at the assignment can help you make a variety of necessary decisions. How detailed should the proposal be? How technical does your psychology professor expect your report to be? Do you want to inform students about the GM food controversy or change their attitudes toward it?

In many writing situations, part of your challenge will be discovering a purpose. Asking yourself why readers should care about what you are saying can help you decide what your purpose might be. Perhaps your subject is magnet schools—schools that draw students from different neighborhoods because of features such as advanced science classes or a concentration on the arts. If you have discussed magnet schools in class, a description of how these schools work probably will not interest you or your readers. But maybe you have discovered that your county's magnet schools are not promoting diversity as had been planned and you want to call your readers to action. Or maybe you are interested in comparing student performance at magnet schools and traditional schools.

Although no precise guidelines will lead you to a purpose, you can begin by asking yourself which one or more of the following aims you hope to accomplish.

PURPOSES FOR WRITING

to inform	to evaluate
to persuade	to recommend
to entertain	to request
to call readers to action	to propose
to change attitudes	to provoke thought
to analyze	to express feelings
to argue	to summarize

Writers often misjudge their own purposes, summarizing when they should be analyzing, or expressing feelings about problems instead of proposing solutions. Before beginning any writing task, pause to ask, "Why am I communicating with my readers?" This question will lead you to another important question: "Just who are my readers?"

Understanding an assignment

Determining the purpose of an assignment

Usually the wording of an assignment will suggest its purpose. You might be expected to do one or more of the following in a college writing assignment:

- summarize information from textbooks, lectures, or research (See 4c.)
- analyze ideas and concepts (See 4d.)
- take a position on a topic and defend it with evidence (See 5.)
- synthesize (combine ideas from) several sources and create an original argument (See 52c and 56c.)

Understanding how to answer an assignment's question

Many assignments will ask you to answer a *how* or *why* question. Such questions cannot be answered using only facts; instead, you will need to take a position. For example, the question "*What are the survival rates for leukemia patients?*" can be answered by reporting facts. The question "*Why are the survival rates for leukemia patients in one state lower than those in a neighboring state?*" must be answered with both facts and interpretation. If a list of prompts appears in the assignment, be careful—instructors rarely expect you to answer all the questions in order. Look instead for topics, themes, or ideas that will help you ask your own questions.

Recognizing implied questions

When you are asked to *discuss*, *analyze*, *agree or disagree with*, or *consider* a topic, your instructor will often expect you to answer a *how* or *why* question.

Discuss the effects of the No Child Left Behind Act on special education programs.	=	*How* has the No Child Left Behind Act affected special education programs?
Consider the recent rise of attention deficit hyperactivity disorder diagnoses.	=	*Why* are diagnoses of attention deficit hyperactivity disorder rising?

Audience

Audience analysis can often lead you to an effective strategy for reaching your readers. A writer whose purpose was to persuade teenagers not to smoke began by making some observations about her audience (see the bottom of this page).

This analysis led the writer to focus on the social aspects of smoking rather than on the health risks. Her audience analysis also warned her against adopting a preachy tone that her readers might find offensive. Instead of lecturing, she decided to draw examples from her own experience as a smoker: burning holes in her best sweater, driving in zero-degree weather late at night to buy cigarettes, and so on. The result was an essay that reached its readers instead of alienating them.

Of course, in some writing situations the audience will not be neatly defined for you. Nevertheless, many of the choices you make as you write will tell readers who you think they are (novices or experts, for example), so it is best to be consistent.

For help with audience analysis, see the chart on page 3.

AUDIENCE ANALYSIS

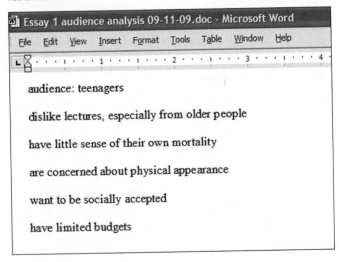

Academic audiences In the academic world, considerations of audience can be more complex than they seem at first. Your instructor will read your essay, of course, but most instructors play multiple roles while reading. Their first and most obvious roles are as coach and judge; less obvious is their role as an intelligent and objective reader, the kind of person who might reasonably be informed, convinced, entertained, or called to action by what you have to say.

Some instructors specify an audience, such as a hypothetical supervisor, readers of a local newspaper, or peers in a particular field. Other instructors expect you to imagine an audience appropriate to your purpose and your subject. Still others prefer that you write for a general audience of educated readers—nonspecialists who can be expected to read with an intelligent, critical eye.

Business audiences Writers in the business world often find themselves writing for multiple audiences. A letter to a client, for instance, might be distributed to sales representatives as well. Readers of a report might include persons with and without technical expertise or readers who want details and those who prefer a quick overview.

To satisfy the demands of multiple audiences, business writers have developed a variety of strategies: attaching cover letters to detailed reports, adding boldface headings, placing summaries in the margin, and so on.

Public audiences Writers in communities often write for a specific audience—the local school superintendent, a legislative representative, fellow members of a social group, readers of a local paper. With public writing, it is more likely that you are familiar with the views your readers hold and the assumptions they make, so you may be better able to judge how to engage those readers. If you are writing to a group of other parents to share ideas for lowering school bus transportation costs, for instance, you may have a good sense of whether to lead with a logical analysis of other school-related fees or with a fiery criticism of key decision makers.

Length and document design

Writers seldom have complete control over length. Journalists usually write within strict word limits set by their editors, businesspeople routinely aim for conciseness, and most college assignments specify an approximate length.

Your writing situation may also require certain document designs. Specific formats are used in business for letters, memos, and reports. In the academic world, you may need to learn precise conventions for lab reports, critiques, research papers, and so on. For most undergraduate essays, a standard format is acceptable (see 59).

In some writing situations, you will be free to create your own design, complete with headings, displayed lists, and perhaps visuals such as charts and graphs. For a discussion of the principles of document design, see 58.

Reviewers and deadlines

Professional and business writers rarely work alone. They work with reviewers, often called *editors*, who offer advice throughout the writing process. In college classes, too, the use of reviewers is common. Some instructors play the role of reviewer for you; others may ask you to visit your college's writing center. Still others schedule peer review sessions in class or online. Such sessions give you a chance to hear what other students think about your draft in progress—and to play the role of reviewer yourself.

Making the most of your handbook

Peer review can benefit student writers at any stage of the writing process.

▶ Guidelines for peer review: page 38

Deadlines are a key element of any writing situation. They help you plan your time and map out what you can accomplish in that time. For complex writing projects, such as research papers, you'll need to plan your time carefully. By working backward from the final deadline, you can create a schedule of target dates for completing parts of the process. (See p. 439 for an example.)

EXERCISE 1–1 Narrow five of the following subjects into topics that would be manageable for an essay of two to five pages.

1. Domestic violence and the courts
2. Performing as a musician
3. Treatments for mental illness
4. An experience with racism or sexism
5. Cell phones in the classroom
6. Images of women in video games
7. Mandatory drug testing in the workplace
8. Olympic swimmers
9. Presidential campaign funding
10. The films of the Coen brothers

EXERCISE 1–2 Suggest a purpose and an audience for five of the following subjects.

1. Graphic novels as literature
2. Genetic modification of cash crop foods
3. Government housing for military veterans
4. The future of online advertising
5. Working with special needs children
6. The challenges facing single parents
7. Obesity prevention and treatment
8. Growing up in a large family
9. The influence of African art on Picasso
10. Hybrid cars

hackerhandbooks.com/bedhandbook > Writing exercises > E-ex 1–4

1b Experiment with ways to explore your subject.

Instead of just plunging into a first draft, experiment with one or more techniques for exploring your subject, perhaps one of these:

- talking and listening
- annotating texts and taking notes
- listing
- clustering
- freewriting

- asking questions
- keeping a journal
- blogging (keeping a Weblog)

Whatever technique you turn to, the goal is the same: to generate ideas that will lead you to a question, a problem, or an issue that you want to explore further. At this early stage of the writing process, don't censor yourself. Sometimes an idea that initially seems trivial or far-fetched will actually turn out to be worthwhile.

Talking and listening

Because writing is a process of figuring out what you think about a subject, it can be useful to try out your ideas on other people. Conversation can deepen and refine your ideas before you even begin to set them down on paper. By talking and listening to others, you can also discover what they find interesting, what they are curious about, and where they disagree with you. If you are planning to advance an argument, you can try it out on listeners with other points of view.

Many writers begin a writing project by brainstorming ideas in a group, debating a point with friends, or chatting with an instructor. Others turn to themselves for company—by talking into a tape recorder. Some writers exchange ideas by sending e-mail or instant messages or by posting to discussion boards or blogs. You may be encouraged to share ideas with your classmates and instructor in an online workshop. One advantage of engaging in such discussions is that while you are "talking" you are actually writing.

Annotating texts and taking notes

When you write about a text, either a written work or a visual, one of the best ways to explore ideas is to mark up the work—on the pages of a print work (if you own a copy) or on a photocopy or printout. Annotating a text encourages you to look at it more carefully—to underline key concepts, to note contradictions in an argument, to raise questions for investigation. Here, for example, is a paragraph from an essay on medical ethics as one student annotated it.

What breakthroughs? Do all breakthroughs have the same consequences?

Breakthroughs in genetics present us with a promise and a predicament. The promise is that we may soon be able to treat and prevent a host of debilitating diseases. The predicament is that our newfound genetic knowledge may also enable us to manipulate our own nature—to enhance our muscles, memories, and moods; to choose the sex, height, and other genetic traits of our children; to make ourselves "better than well." When science moves faster than moral understanding, as it does today, men and women struggle to articulate their unease. In liberal societies they reach first for the language of autonomy, fairness, and individual rights. But this part of our moral vocabulary is ill equipped to address the hardest questions posed by genetic engineering. The genomic revolution has induced a kind of moral vertigo.

Stem cell research?

Is everyone really uneasy? Is something a breakthrough if it creates a predicament?

What does he mean by "moral understanding"?

Which questions? He doesn't seem to be taking sides.

—Michael Sandel, "The Case against Perfection"

After reading and annotating Michael Sandel's entire article, the student looked through his annotations for patterns. He noticed that several of his annotations pointed to the larger question of whether a scientific breakthrough should be viewed in terms of its moral consequences. He decided to reread the article, taking detailed notes with this question in mind.

> **Making the most of your handbook**
>
> Writing about a text or a visual is a common college assignment.
> ▸ Writing about texts: 4
> ▸ Advice on taking notes: 48c

Listing

Listing ideas—a technique sometimes known as *brainstorming*—is a good way to figure out what you know and what questions you have. Here is a list one student writer jotted down for an essay about funding for college athletics:

- Football receives the most funding of any sport.
- Funding comes from ticket sales, fundraisers, alumni contributions.
- Biggest women's sport is soccer.
- Women's soccer team is only ten years old; football team is fifty years old.
- Soccer games don't draw as many fans.
- Should funding be equal for all teams?
- Do alumni have the right to fund whatever they want?

The ideas and questions appear here in the order in which they first occurred to the writer. Later she rearranged them, grouped them under general categories, deleted some, and added others. These initial thoughts led the writer to questions that helped her narrow her topic. In other words, she treated her early list as a source of ideas and a springboard to new ideas, not as an outline.

Clustering

Unlike listing, clustering highlights relationships among ideas. To cluster ideas, write your topic in the center of a sheet of paper, draw a circle around it, and surround the circle with related ideas connected to it with lines. If some of the satellite ideas lead to more specific clusters, write them down as well. The writer of the diagram on page 17 was exploring ideas for an essay on obesity in children.

Freewriting

In its purest form, freewriting is simply nonstop writing. You set aside ten minutes or so and write whatever comes to mind, without pausing to think about word choice, spelling, or even meaning. If you get stuck, you can write about being stuck, but you should keep your fingers moving. If nothing much happens, you have lost only ten minutes. It's more likely, though, that something interesting will emerge—perhaps an eloquent sentence, an honest expression of feeling, or an idea worth further investigation. Freewriting also lets you

CLUSTER DIAGRAM

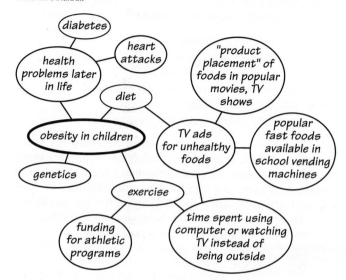

ask questions without feeling that you have to answer them. Sometimes a question that comes to mind at this stage will point you in an unexpected direction.

To explore ideas on a particular topic, consider using a technique known as *focused freewriting*. Again, you write quickly and freely, but this time you focus on a subject and pay attention to the connections among your ideas.

Asking questions

When gathering material for a story, journalists routinely ask themselves Who? What? When? Where? Why? and How? In addition to helping journalists get started, these questions ensure that they will not overlook an important fact.

Whenever you are writing about events, whether current or historical, asking questions is one way to get started. One student, whose topic was the negative reaction in 1915 to

D. W. Griffith's silent film *The Birth of a Nation*, began exploring her topic with this set of questions:

- *Who* objected to the film?
- *What* were the objections?
- *When* were protests first voiced?
- *Where* were protests most strongly expressed?
- *Why* did protesters object to the film?
- *How* did protesters make their views known?

As often happens, the answers to these questions led to another question the writer wanted to explore. After she discovered that protesters objected to the film's racist portrayal of African Americans, she wondered whether their protests had changed attitudes. This question prompted an interesting topic for a paper: Did the film's stereotypes lead to positive, if unintended, consequences?

Making the most of your handbook

Effective college writers begin by asking questions.

▶ Asking questions in academic disciplines: 7b

In the academic world, scholars often generate ideas by posing questions related to a specific discipline: one set of questions for analyzing literature, another for evaluating experiments in social psychology, still another for reporting field experiences in criminal justice. If you are writing in a particular discipline, try to find out which questions its scholars typically explore.

Keeping a journal

A journal is a collection of informal, exploratory, sometimes experimental writing. In a journal, often meant for your eyes only, you can take risks. In one entry, for example, you might freewrite. In another, you might pose questions, whether or not you have the answers. You might comment on an interesting idea from one of your classes or keep a list of questions that occur to you while reading. You might imagine a conversation between yourself and your readers or stage a debate to understand positions counter to your own. A journal is also an excellent place to play around with language for the sheer fun of it.

Keeping a journal can be an enriching experience in its own right, since it allows you to explore issues without worrying about what someone else thinks. A journal can also serve as a sourcebook of ideas to draw on in future essays.

Blogging (keeping a Weblog)

Although a blog (Weblog) is a type of journal, it is a public writing space rather than a private one. In a blog, you can express opinions, release frustrations, make observations, recap an event, have fun with language, or do some combination of these. You can work through an idea for a paper by blogging about it in different ways or from different angles. One post might be your frustrated comments about the lack of parking for commuter students at your school. Maybe the next post shares a compelling statistic about competition for parking spaces at campuses nationwide. You can continue thinking about the topic as you respond to comments from other readers about alternatives to driving to campus.

1c Draft a working thesis.

As you explore your topic and identify questions to investigate, you will begin to see possible ways to focus your material. At this point, try to settle on a tentative central idea. The more complex your topic, the more your focus will change as your drafts evolve. For many types of writing, you will be able to assert your central idea in a sentence or two. Such a statement, which ordinarily appears in the opening paragraph of your finished essay, is called a *thesis statement*.

A thesis is often one or more of the following:

- the answer to a question you have posed
- the resolution of a problem you have identified
- a statement that takes a position on a debatable topic

A tentative, or working, thesis will help you organize your draft. Don't worry about the exact wording because your main point may change as you refine your efforts. Here, for example, are one student's efforts to pose a question and draft a thesis statement for an essay in his film course.

QUESTION

In *Rebel without a Cause*, how does the filmmaker show that Jim Stark becomes alienated from his family and friends?

WORKING THESIS

In *Rebel without a Cause*, Jim Stark, the main character, is often seen literally on the edge of physical danger—walking too close to a swimming pool, leaning over an observation deck, and driving his car toward a cliff.

The working thesis offers a useful place to start writing, but it doesn't give readers a reason to continue reading. The sentence includes an observation but no indication of why that observation matters. The student's final thesis is more engaging, reflects an evolution of his ideas, and is a better response to his question.

FINAL THESIS

The scenes in which Jim Stark is on the edge of physical danger—walking too close to a swimming pool, leaning over an observation deck, and driving his car toward a cliff— suggest that he is becoming more and more agitated by the constraints of family and society.

Here, another student identifies and responds to a problem in a thesis statement for an argument paper in her composition course.

PROBLEM

Americans who earn average incomes cannot run effective national political campaigns.

WORKING THESIS

Congress should pass legislation that would make it possible for Americans who are not wealthy to be viable candidates in national political campaigns.

The student has roughed out an idea for how to solve the problem—enacting federal legislation—but her working thesis

Testing a working thesis

Once you have come up with a working thesis, you can use the following questions to refine it.

- Does the thesis require an essay's worth of development? Or will you run out of points too quickly?
- Is the thesis too obvious? If you cannot come up with interpretations that oppose your own, consider revising your thesis.
- Can you support your thesis with the evidence available?
- Can you explain why readers will want to read an essay with this thesis? Can you respond when a reader asks "So what?" or "Why does it matter?"

isn't specific enough. The student's final thesis offers a specific solution to the problem she identifies and helps her focus her draft.

FINAL THESIS

By restricting campaign spending, Congress could enable candidates without personal wealth to compete more effectively in national elections.

Keep in mind as you draft your working thesis that a successful thesis is a promise to the reader; it points both the writer and the reader in a definite direction. For a more detailed discussion of the thesis, see 1e.

1d Sketch a plan.

Once you have generated some ideas and formulated a working thesis, you might want to sketch an informal outline to see how you will support your thesis and to figure out a tentative structure for your ideas. Informal outlines can take many forms. Perhaps the most common is simply the thesis followed by a list of major ideas.

Working thesis: Television advertising should be regulated to help prevent childhood obesity.

- Children watch more television than ever.
- Snacks marketed to children are often unhealthy and fattening.
- Childhood obesity can cause diabetes and other problems.
- Dealing with these problems costs taxpayers billions of dollars.
- Therefore, these ads are actually costing the public money.
- But if advertising is free speech, do we have the right to regulate it?
- We regulate alcohol and cigarette ads on television, so why not advertisements for soda and junk food?

If you began by jotting down a list of ideas (see p. 15), you can turn the list into a rough outline by crossing out some ideas, adding others, and putting the ideas in a logical order.

Planning with headings

When writing a long college paper or a business document, consider using headings to guide your planning and to help your readers follow the organization of your final draft. While planning, you can insert your working thesis, experiment with possible headings, and type chunks of text beneath each heading. You may need to try grouping your ideas in a few different ways to suit your purpose and audience.

Making the most of your handbook

Headings can help writers plan and readers understand a document.

▶ Using headings: 58b
▶ Papers organized with headings: 56f, 57f

When to use a formal outline

Early in the writing process, rough outlines have certain advantages: They can be produced quickly, they are obviously tentative, and they can be revised easily. However, a formal outline may be useful later in the writing process, after you have written a rough draft, especially if your topic is complex.

A formal outline helps you see whether the parts of your essay work together and whether your essay's structure is logical. A formal outline will often make clear which parts of your draft should be rearranged and which parts don't fit at all.

The following formal outline brought order to the research paper in 54c, on Internet surveillance in the workplace. The student's thesis is an important part of the outline. Everything else in the outline supports it, either directly or indirectly.

Thesis: Although companies often have legitimate concerns that lead them to monitor employees' Internet usage—from expensive security breaches to reduced productivity—the benefits of electronic surveillance are outweighed by its costs to employees' privacy and autonomy.

I. Although employers have always monitored employees, electronic surveillance is more efficient.
   A. Employers can gather data in large quantities.
   B. Electronic surveillance can be continuous.
   C. Electronic surveillance can be conducted secretly, with keystroke logging programs.
II. Some experts argue that employers have legitimate reasons to monitor employees' Internet usage.
   A. Unmonitored employees could accidentally breach security.
   B. Companies are legally accountable for the online actions of employees.
III. Despite valid concerns, employers should value employee morale and autonomy and avoid creating an atmosphere of distrust.
   A. Setting the boundaries for employee autonomy is difficult in the wired workplace.
      1. Using the Internet is the most popular way of wasting time at work.
      2. Employers can't easily determine if employees are working or surfing the Web.
   B. Surveillance can create resentment among employees.
      1. Web surfing can relieve stress, and restricting it can generate tension between managers and workers.
      2. Enforcing Internet usage can seem arbitrary.

IV. Surveillance may not increase employee productivity, and trust may benefit productivity.
   A. A company shouldn't care how many hours salaried employees work as long as they get the job done.
   B. Casual Internet use can actually benefit companies.
      1. The Internet may spark business ideas.
      2. The Internet may suggest ideas about how to operate more efficiently.
V. Employees' rights to privacy are not well defined by the law.
   A. Few federal guidelines on electronic surveillance exist.
   B. Employers and employees are negotiating the boundaries without legal guidance.
   C. As technological capabilities increase, there will be an increased need to define boundaries.

Guidelines for constructing an outline

1. Put the thesis at the top.
2. Make items at the same level parallel grammatically (see section 9).
3. Use sentences unless phrases are clear.
4. Use the conventional system of numbers, letters, and indents:

I.
   A.
   B.
      1.
      2.
         a.
         b.

II.
   A.
   B.
      1.
      2.
         a.
         b.

→

5. Always use at least two subdivisions for a category, since nothing can be divided into fewer than two parts.

6. Limit the number of major sections in the outline; if the list of roman numerals (at the first level) gets too long, try clustering the items into fewer major categories with more subcategories.

7. Be flexible; be prepared to change your outline as your drafts evolve.

1e For most types of writing, draft an introduction that includes a thesis.

Generally, the introduction to a piece of writing announces the main point; the body develops it, usually in several paragraphs; the conclusion drives it home. You can begin drafting, however, at any point. If you find it difficult to introduce a paper that you have not yet written, try drafting the body first and saving the introduction for later.

Your introduction will usually be a paragraph of 50 to 150 words (in a longer paper, it may be more than one paragraph). Perhaps the most common strategy is to open with a few sentences that engage the reader and establish your purpose for writing, your main point. The sentence stating the main point is called a *thesis*. (See also 1c.) In the following examples, the thesis has been italicized.

> The debate over athletes' use of performance-enhancing substances is getting more complicated as biotechnologies such as gene therapy become a reality. The availability of these new methods of boosting performance will force us to decide what we value most in sports—displays of physical excellence developed through hard work or victory at all costs. For centuries, spectators and athletes have cherished the tradition of fairness in sports. While sports competition is, of course, largely about winning, it is also about the means by which a player or team wins. *Athletes who use any type of biotechnology give themselves an unfair advantage and disrupt the sense of fair play, and they should be banned from competition.*   —Jamal Hammond, student

As the United States industrialized in the nineteenth century, using desperate immigrant labor, social concerns took a backseat to the task of building a prosperous nation. The government did not regulate industries and did not provide an effective safety net for the poor or for those who became sick or injured on the job. However, immigrants and the poor did have a few advocates. Settlement houses such as Hull-House in Chicago provided information, services, and a place for reform-minded individuals to gather and work to improve the conditions of the urban poor. Alice Hamilton was one of these reformers. Her work at Hull-House spanned twenty-two years and later expanded throughout the nation. *Hamilton's efforts helped to improve the lives of immigrants and drew attention to problems and people that until then had been virtually ignored.*

—Laurie McDonough, student

Ideally, the sentences leading to the thesis should hook the reader, perhaps with one of the following:

a startling statistic or an unusual fact

a vivid example

a description

a paradoxical statement

a quotation or a bit of dialogue

a question

an analogy

an anecdote

Whether you are writing for a scholarly audience, a professional audience, a public audience, or a general audience, you cannot assume your readers' interest in the topic. The hook should spark curiosity and offer readers a reason to continue.

Although the thesis frequently appears at the end of the introduction, it can just as easily appear at the beginning. Much work-related writing commonly begins with the thesis.

Flextime scheduling, which has proved its effectiveness at the Library of Congress, should be introduced on a trial basis at the main branch of the Montgomery County Public Library. By offering flexible work hours, the library can boost employee morale, cut down on absenteeism, and expand its hours of operation.

—David Warren, student

For some types of writing, it may be difficult or impossible to express the central idea in a thesis sentence; or it may be unwise or unnecessary to put a thesis sentence in the essay itself. A personal narrative, for example, may have a focus too subtle to be distilled in a single sentence. Strictly informative writing, like that found in many business memos, may be difficult to summarize in a thesis. In some academic fields, such as nursing, writers may produce reports that do not require a thesis. In such instances, do not try to force the central idea into a thesis sentence. Instead, think in terms of an overriding purpose, which may or may not be stated directly.

> **Making the most of your handbook**
>
> The thesis sentence is central to many types of writing.
>
> ▶ Writing about texts: 4
> ▶ Writing arguments: 5
> ▶ Writing research papers: 50 (MLA), 56a (APA), 57a (*Chicago*)
> ▶ Writing literature papers: 55c

Academic English If you come from a culture that prefers an indirect approach in writing, you may feel that asserting a thesis early in an essay sounds unrefined and even rude. In the United States, however, readers appreciate a direct approach; when you state your point as directly as possible, you show that you value your readers' time.

Characteristics of an effective thesis

An effective thesis sentence should be a central idea that requires supporting evidence; it should be of adequate scope for an essay of the assigned length; and it should be sharply focused. (See also 1c.)

When constructing a thesis sentence, you should ask yourself whether you can successfully develop it with the sources available to you and for the purpose you've identified. Also ask if you can explain why readers should be interested in reading an essay that explores this thesis. If your thesis addresses a question or problem that intrigues you, then it will probably interest your readers as well. If your thesis would be obvious to everyone, then your readers will be less compelled to read on.

A thesis must require proof or further development through facts and details; it cannot itself be a fact or a description.

DRAFT THESIS — The first polygraph was developed by Dr. John A. Larson in 1921.

PROBLEM The thesis is *too factual*. A reader could not disagree with it or debate it; no further development of this idea is required.

STRATEGY *Enter a debate* by posing a question about your topic that has more than one possible answer. For example: Should the polygraph be used by private employers? Your thesis should be your answer to the question.

REVISED THESIS — Because the polygraph has not been proved reliable, even under controlled conditions, its use by private employers should be banned.

A thesis should be an answer to a question, not a question itself.

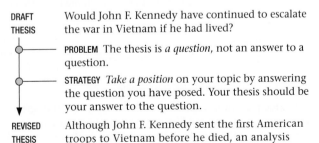

DRAFT THESIS — Would John F. Kennedy have continued to escalate the war in Vietnam if he had lived?

PROBLEM The thesis is *a question*, not an answer to a question.

STRATEGY *Take a position* on your topic by answering the question you have posed. Your thesis should be your answer to the question.

REVISED THESIS — Although John F. Kennedy sent the first American troops to Vietnam before he died, an analysis of his foreign policy suggests that he would not have escalated the war had he lived.

A thesis should be of sufficient scope for your assignment; it should not be too broad.

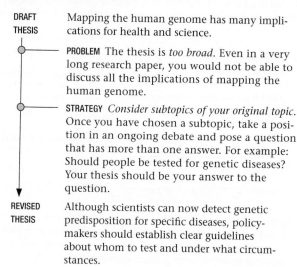

DRAFT THESIS — Mapping the human genome has many implications for health and science.

PROBLEM The thesis is *too broad*. Even in a very long research paper, you would not be able to discuss all the implications of mapping the human genome.

STRATEGY *Consider subtopics of your original topic.* Once you have chosen a subtopic, take a position in an ongoing debate and pose a question that has more than one answer. For example: Should people be tested for genetic diseases? Your thesis should be your answer to the question.

REVISED THESIS — Although scientists can now detect genetic predisposition for specific diseases, policy-makers should establish clear guidelines about whom to test and under what circumstances.

A thesis also should not be too narrow.

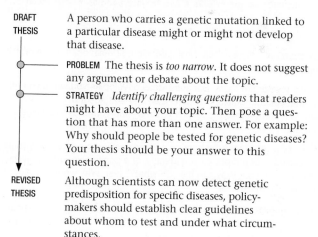

DRAFT THESIS — A person who carries a genetic mutation linked to a particular disease might or might not develop that disease.

PROBLEM The thesis is *too narrow*. It does not suggest any argument or debate about the topic.

STRATEGY *Identify challenging questions* that readers might have about your topic. Then pose a question that has more than one answer. For example: Why should people be tested for genetic diseases? Your thesis should be your answer to this question.

REVISED THESIS — Although scientists can now detect genetic predisposition for specific diseases, policy-makers should establish clear guidelines about whom to test and under what circumstances.

Understanding the comment

When a teacher or tutor points out that your thesis is unclear, the comment often signals that readers may have a hard time identifying your essay's main point.

> Fathers are more involved in the lives of their children today than they used to be. In the past, the father's primary role was as the provider; child care was most often left to the mother or other relatives. However, today's father drives to dance lessons, coaches his child's baseball team, hosts birthday parties, and provides homework help. <u>Do more involved fathers help or hinder the development of their children?</u>

Unclear thesis

One student wrote this introductory paragraph in response to an assignment that asked her to analyze the changing roles of mothers or fathers.

A writer's thesis, or main point, should be phrased as a statement, not a question. To revise, the student could answer the question she has posed, or she could pose a new question and answer it. After considering her evidence, she needs to decide what position she wants to take, state this position clearly, and show readers *why* this position—her thesis—matters.

Similar comments: vague thesis • state your position • your main point?

Revising when *your* thesis is unclear

1. *Ask questions.* What is the thesis, position, or main point of the draft? Can you support it with the available evidence?

2. *Reread your entire draft.* Because ideas develop as you write, you may find that your conclusion contains a clearer statement of your main point than your current thesis does. Or you may find your thesis elsewhere in your draft.

3. *Try revising your thesis* by framing it as an answer to a question you pose, the resolution of a problem you identify, or a position you take in a debate. And put your thesis to the "So what?" test: Why would a reader be interested in this thesis?

More help with writing a clear thesis: **1c** and **1e**

A thesis should be sharply focused, not too vague. Avoid fuzzy, hard-to-define words such as *interesting, good*, or *disgusting*.

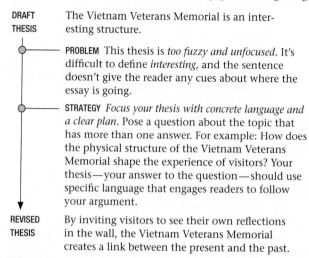

DRAFT THESIS — The Vietnam Veterans Memorial is an interesting structure.

PROBLEM This thesis is *too fuzzy and unfocused*. It's difficult to define *interesting*, and the sentence doesn't give the reader any cues about where the essay is going.

STRATEGY *Focus your thesis with concrete language and a clear plan*. Pose a question about the topic that has more than one answer. For example: How does the physical structure of the Vietnam Veterans Memorial shape the experience of visitors? Your thesis—your answer to the question—should use specific language that engages readers to follow your argument.

REVISED THESIS — By inviting visitors to see their own reflections in the wall, the Vietnam Veterans Memorial creates a link between the present and the past.

EXERCISE 1–3 In each of the following pairs, which sentence might work well as a thesis for a short paper? What is the problem with the other one? Is it too factual? Too broad? Too vague?

1. a. By networking with friends, a single parent can manage to strike a balance among work, school, a social life, and family.
    b. Single parents face many challenges as they try to juggle all of their responsibilities.
2. a. At the Special Olympics, athletes with disabilities show that, with hard work and support from others, they can accomplish anything—that they can indeed be winners.
    b. Working with the Special Olympics program is rewarding.
3. a. History 201, taught by Professor Brown, is offered at 10:00 a.m. on Tuesdays and Thursdays.
    b. Whoever said that history is nothing but polishing tombstones must have missed History 201, because in Professor Brown's class history is very much alive.
4. a. So far, research suggests that zero-emissions vehicles are not a sensible solution to the problem of steadily increasing air pollution.

    b. Because air pollution is of serious concern to many people today, several US government agencies have implemented plans to begin solving the problem.

5.   a. Anorexia nervosa is a dangerous and sometimes deadly eating disorder occurring mainly in young, upper-middle-class teens.

    b. The eating disorder anorexia nervosa is rarely cured by one treatment alone; only by combining drug therapy with psychotherapy and family therapy can the patient begin the long, torturous journey to wellness.

hackerhandbooks.com/bedhandbook > **Writing exercises** > E-ex 1–5 to 1–7

1f Draft the body.

The body of the essay develops support for your thesis, so it's important to have at least a working thesis before you start writing. What does your thesis promise readers? Try to keep your response to that question in mind as you draft the body.

You may already have written an introduction that includes your thesis. If not, as long as you have a thesis you can begin developing the body and return later to the introduction. If your thesis suggests a plan (see 1e) or if you have sketched a preliminary outline, try to block out your paragraphs accordingly. Draft the body of your essay by writing a paragraph about each supporting point you listed in the planning stage. If you do not have a plan, pause for a few moments and sketch one (see 1d).

Keep in mind that often you might not know what you want to say until you have written a draft. It is possible to begin without a plan—assuming you are prepared to treat your first attempt as a "discovery draft" that will be radically rewritten once you discover what you really want to say. Whether or not you have a plan when you begin drafting, you can often figure out a workable order for your ideas by stopping each time you start a new paragraph to think about what your readers will need to know to follow your train of thought.

For more detailed advice about paragraphs in the body of an essay, see 3.

Understanding the comment

When a teacher or tutor indicates that you need to "be specific," the comment often signals that you could strengthen your writing with additional details.

There are many cultural differences between the United States and Italy. Italian citizens do not share many of the same (attitudes) or (values) as American citizens. Such (differences) make it hard for some Italian students to feel comfortable coming to the United States for extended periods of time, even for an academic year.

Be specific!

In this body paragraph, a student responds to an assignment that asked him to interview a group of international students and describe the challenges of studying in the United States.

The paragraph presents a student's claim but doesn't include specific examples or evidence to support the claim. To revise, the student might focus on *one* specific example of cultural differences between the United States and Italy. The student might then ask: What vivid details illustrate this cultural difference? The answer to that question will provide specific evidence to inform and persuade readers.

Similar comments: need examples • too general • evidence?

Strategies for revising when *your* writing needs to be more specific

1. *Reread your topic sentence* to understand the focus of the paragraph.

2. *Ask questions.* Does the paragraph contain claims that need support? Have you provided evidence—specific examples, vivid details and illustrations, statistics and facts—to help readers understand your ideas and find them persuasive?

3. *Choose exact, active, and engaging words* as you shape your evidence. And remember that details and examples don't speak for themselves. You'll need to interpret your evidence to show readers how it supports your claims.

More help with using specific evidence: **5e**

33

TIP: As you draft, keep careful notes and records of all the sources you read and consult. (See 48b.) If you quote, paraphrase, or summarize a source, include a citation, even in your draft. You will save time and avoid plagiarism if you follow the rules of citation and documentation while drafting.

1g Draft a conclusion.

A conclusion should remind readers of the essay's main idea without repeating it. Often the concluding paragraph can be relatively short. By the end of the essay, readers should already understand your main point; your conclusion drives it home and, perhaps, gives readers something more to consider.

In addition to echoing your main idea, a conclusion might briefly summarize the essay's key points, propose a course of action, offer advice, discuss the topic's wider significance, or pose a question for future study. To conclude an essay analyzing the shifting roles of women in the military, one student discusses her topic's implications for society as a whole.

> As the military continues to train women in jobs formerly reserved for men, our understanding of women's roles in society will no doubt continue to change. When news reports of women training for and taking part in combat operations become commonplace, reports of women becoming CEOs, police chiefs, and even president of the United States will cease to surprise us. Or perhaps we have already reached this point. —Rosa Broderick, student

To make the conclusion memorable, you might include a detail, an example, or an image from the introduction to bring readers full circle; a quotation or a bit of dialogue; an anecdote; or a witty or ironic comment. To conclude an essay explaining how credit card companies hook college students, one student brings readers full circle by echoing his thesis and ending with a familiar phrase borrowed from popular culture.

> Credit cards are a convenient part of life, and there is nothing wrong with having one or two of them. Before signing up for a particular card, however, college students should

take time to read the fine print and do some comparison shopping. Students also need to learn to resist the many seductive offers that credit card companies extend to them after they have signed up. Students who can't "just say no" to temptations such as high credit limits and revolving balances could well become hooked on a cycle of debt from which there is no easy escape.   —Matt Watson, student

Whatever concluding strategy you choose, keep in mind that an effective conclusion is decisive and unapologetic. Avoid introducing wholly new ideas at the end of an essay. And because the conclusion is so closely tied to the rest of the essay in both content and tone, be prepared to rework it (or even replace it) when you revise.

2   Make global revisions; then revise sentences.

For most experienced writers, revising is rarely a one-step process. Global matters—focus, purpose, organization, content, and overall strategy—generally receive attention first. Improvements in sentence structure, word choice, grammar, punctuation, and mechanics come later.

Many of us resist making global revisions because we find it difficult to view our work from our audience's perspective. To distance yourself from a draft, put it aside for a while, preferably overnight or even longer. When you return to it, try to play the role of your audience as you read. Ask questions like the following:

> **Making the most of your handbook**
>
> Seeking and using feedback are critical steps in revising a college paper.
>
> ▶ Checklist for global revision: page 40
> ▶ Guidelines for peer reviewers: page 38
> ▶ Tips on using feedback: page 42

- Would readers disagree with my thesis? If so, how might I address their counterarguments?
- Would readers be confused by my organization?
- Have I provided enough evidence to inform or persuade readers?

EXAMPLE OF GLOBAL REVISIONS

Big Box Stores Aren't So Bad

In her essay *Big Box Stores Are Bad for Main Street*, Betsy Taylor shifts the focus away from the economic effects of these stores to the effects these stores have on the "soul" of America. She claims that stores like Home Depot and Target are bad for America, they draw people out of downtown shopping districts and cause them to focus on consumption. She believes that small businesses are good for America because they provide personal attention, encourage community interaction, and make each city different from the other ones. But Taylor's argument is not strong because it is based on nostalgic images rather than true assumptions about the roles that businesses play in consumers lives and communities. Taylor reveals that she has a nostalgic view of American society and does not understand economic realities. ~~She focuses~~ on idealized shoppers and shopkeepers interacting on Main Street ~~rather than the economic realities of the situation.~~ As a result, she incorrectly assumes that simply getting rid of big box stores would have a positive effect on us.

For example, in her first paragraph she refers to a big box store as a "25-acre slab of concrete with a 100,000 square foot box of stuff" that lands on a town, evoking images of something strong and powerful conquering something small and weak. But she oversimplifies a complex issue. She ignores the complex economic relationship between large chain stores and the communities in which they exist.

EXAMPLE OF SENTENCE-LEVEL REVISIONS

Rethinking Big-Box Stores
~~Big Box Stores Aren't So Bad~~ (no italics)

In her essay (Big Box Stores Are Bad for Main Street), Betsy Taylor ~~shifts~~ focuses not on ~~the focus away from~~ the economic effects of ~~these~~ large chain stores ~~to~~ but on the effects these stores have on the "soul" of America. She ~~claims~~ argues that stores like Home Depot, ~~and~~ Wal-Mart ~~Target,~~ and Target are bad for America because they draw people out of downtown shopping districts and cause them to focus on consumption. ~~She~~ In contrast, she believes that small businesses are good for America because they provide personal attention, encourage community interaction, and make each city ~~different from the other ones.~~ unique. But Taylor's argument is ~~not strong~~ unconvincing because it is based on ~~nostalgic images~~ nostalgia —on idealized ~~shoppers and shopkeepers interacting on~~ images of Main Street—rather than ~~true assumptions about~~ on the roles that businesses play in consumers' lives and communities. ~~She ignores~~ By ignoring the complex economic relationship between large chain stores and ~~the~~ their communities, ~~in which they exist. As a result, she~~ Taylor incorrectly assumes that simply getting rid of big-box stores would have a positive effect on ~~us.~~ America's communities. ~~Taylor~~ Taylor's colorful use of language reveals that she has a nostalgic view of American society and does not understand economic realities. ~~For example, in~~ In her first paragraph, ~~she~~ Taylor refers to a big-box store as a "25-acre slab of concrete with a 100,000 square foot box of stuff" that lands on a town, evoking images of ~~something strong and powerful conquering something small and weak.~~ a powerful monster crushing the American way of life (1011). But she oversimplifies a complex issue.

Guidelines for peer reviewers

View yourself as a coach, not a judge.

Think of yourself as proposing possibilities, not dictating revisions. It is the writer, after all, who will have to grapple with the task of improving the essay. Work with the writer to identify the strengths and limitations of the draft.

Restate the writer's main ideas.

It's helpful for the writer to see if you understand the main point of the essay. Restate the thesis for the writer. And try to paraphrase each paragraph of the draft to help the writer see if the essay's points are clearly expressed.

Where possible, give specific compliments.

Vague compliments (such as "I liked your essay") sound insincere—and they aren't helpful. Point out specific successes. For example, you might mention that you particularly admire how the writer examines the opposing viewpoint in the second paragraph before challenging it in the third.

Link suggestions for improvement to the writer's goals.

Criticism is constructive when it is offered in the right spirit. For example, you might advise the writer to put the most dramatic example last, where it will have the maximum impact on readers. Or you might suggest that a passage would gain power if the writer replaced abstractions with concrete details.

Ask questions and tell the writer where you would like to hear more.

Note passages that you found either confusing or interesting. By asking for clarification, you will help the writer see what needs to be revised. Indicating an interest in hearing more about a topic will often inspire the writer to come up with useful and vivid details.

Express interest in reading the next draft.

When your interest is sincere, expressing it can be a powerful motivation for a writer.

If possible, enlist friends or family to play the role of audience for you, or perhaps visit your school's writing center to go over your draft with a writing tutor. Ask your reviewers to focus on the larger issues of writing, not on word- or sentence-level issues.

2a Approach global revision in cycles.

Making major revisions can be difficult, sometimes even painful. You might discover, for example, that an essay's first three paragraphs are merely padding, that its central argument tilts the wrong way, and that you sound pompous. But the fact that you can see such problems in your own writing is a sign of hope. Those opening paragraphs can be dropped, the argument's slant realigned, the voice made more approachable.

Because the process of global revision can be overwhelming, approach it in cycles. Five common cycles of global revision are discussed in this section:

- Engaging the audience
- Sharpening the focus
- Improving the organization
- Strengthening the content
- Clarifying the point of view

You can handle these cycles in nearly any order or even skip or combine some. See the chart on page 40.

Engaging the audience

Considerations of audience can contribute to global revision. Sometimes a rough draft needs an overhaul because it is directed at no audience at all for no apparent purpose. Readers are put off by such writing because they don't know *why* they are reading. A good question to ask yourself is the toughest question a reader might ask: "So what?" If your draft can't pass the "So what?" test, you may need to rethink your entire approach; in fact, you may even decide to scrap the draft and start over.

Checklist for global revision

Audience

- Does the draft address a question, a problem, or an issue that is of interest to readers?
- Is the tone diplomatic and respectful?

Focus

- Is the thesis clear? Is it prominently placed?
- If there is no thesis, is there a good reason for omitting one?
- Are any ideas obviously off the point?

Organization and paragraphing

- Are there enough organizational cues for readers (such as topic sentences and headings)?
- Are ideas presented in a logical order?
- Are any paragraphs too long or too short for easy reading?

Content

- Is the supporting material relevant and persuasive?
- Which ideas need further development?
- Are the parts proportioned sensibly? Do major ideas receive enough attention?
- Where might material be deleted?

Point of view

- Is the draft free of distracting shifts in point of view (from *I* to *you*, for example, or from *it* to *they*)?
- Is the dominant point of view—*I, we, you, he, she, it, one,* or *they*—appropriate?

Once you have made sure that your draft is directed at an audience—readers who stand to benefit in some way by reading it—you may still need to refine your tone. The tone of a piece of writing expresses the writer's feelings toward the audience, so it is important to get it right. If the tone seems too self-centered or too flippant, stuffy, bossy, patronizing, opinionated, or hostile, modify it.

For example, the following paragraph was drafted by a student who hoped to persuade his audience to buy organic produce.

A PARAGRAPH THAT ALIENATES READERS

If you choose to buy organic produce, you are supporting local farmers as well as demonstrating your opposition to chemical pesticides. As more and more supermarkets carry organic fruits and vegetables, consumers have fewer reasons not to buy organic. Some consumers do not buy organic produce because they are not willing to spend the extra money. But if you care at all about the environment or the small farmer, you should be willing to support organic farms in your area.

When he reviewed this draft, the writer saw the need to be more diplomatic. He didn't want to alienate his readers by accusing them of being unwilling to spend money or uninterested in helping the environment. He revised the paragraph to offer readers positive reasons to support his cause.

A PARAGRAPH THAT RESPECTS READERS

By choosing to buy organic produce, you have the opportunity to support local farmers, to oppose the use of chemical pesticides, and to taste some of the freshest produce available. Because more supermarkets carry organic produce than ever, you won't even have to miss out on any of your favorite fruits or vegetables. Although organic produce can be more expensive than conventional produce, the costs are not prohibitive. For example, a pound of organic bananas at my local grocery store is eighty-nine cents, while the conventional bananas are sixty-nine cents a pound. If you can afford this small price difference, you will have the opportunity to make a difference for the environment and for the small farmer.   —Leon Nage, student

Guidelines for using reviewers' comments

Don't take criticism personally.

Your reader is responding to your essay, not to you. It may be frustrating to hear that you still have more work to do, but taking feedback seriously will make your essay stronger.

Pay attention to ideas that contradict your own.

If comments show that a reviewer doesn't understand what you're trying to do, don't be defensive. Instead, consider why your reader is confused and figure out how to clarify your point. Responding to readers' objections—instead of dismissing them—will strengthen your ideas and make your essay more persuasive.

Look for global concerns.

Your reviewers will probably make more suggestions than you can use. To keep things manageable, focus on the comments that relate to your thesis, organization, and evidence. Do your readers understand your main idea? Can they follow your train of thought? Are they looking for more supporting ideas or facts?

Weigh feedback carefully.

As you begin revising, you may find yourself sorting through suggestions from many people, including instructors, writing tutors, and peer reviewers. Sometimes these readers will agree, but often their advice will differ. It's important to sort through all the comments you receive with your original goals in mind—otherwise you'll be facing the impossible task of trying to incorporate everyone's advice.

Keep a revision and editing log.

Make a clear and simple list of the global and sentence-level concerns that keep coming up in most of your reviewers' comments. That list can serve as a starting point each time you revise a paper. When you take charge of your own writing in this way, comments will become a valuable resource rather than something to dread.

Sharpening the focus

A clearly focused draft fixes readers' attention on one central idea and does not stray from that idea. You can sharpen the focus of a draft by clarifying the introduction (especially the thesis) and by deleting any text that is off the point.

Clarifying the introduction   Check to see whether the introduction clearly states the essay's main point. Does it let readers know what to expect as they read on? Does it make the significance of the subject clear so that readers will want to read on?

Can readers tell where the introduction stops and the body of the essay begins? Have you perhaps included material in the introduction that really belongs in the body? Is your introduction too broad or unfocused?

The most important sentence in the introduction is the thesis. (See 1e.) If your thesis is poorly focused or if it doesn't accurately state the real point of the essay, revise it. If your essay lacks a thesis, add one now or have a good reason for not including one.

Deleting text that is off the point   Compare the introduction, particularly the thesis sentence, with the body of the essay. Does the body fulfill the promise of the introduction? If not, you will need to adjust one or the other. Either rebuild the introduction to fit the body or keep the introduction and delete any body sentences or paragraphs that stray from its point.

Improving the organization

A draft is well organized when its major divisions are logical and easy to follow. To improve the organization of your draft, you may need to take one or more of the following actions: adding or sharpening topic sentences, moving blocks of text, and inserting headings.

Adding or sharpening topic sentences Topic sentences state the main ideas of the paragraphs in the body of an essay. (See 3a.) You can review the organization of a draft by reading only the topic sentences. Do they clearly support the essay's main idea? Do they make a reasonable sentence outline of the paper? If your draft lacks topic sentences, either add them or have a good reason for omitting them.

Moving blocks of text Improving the organization of a draft can be as simple as moving a few sentences from one paragraph to another or reordering paragraphs. You may also find that you can clarify the organization of a draft by combining choppy paragraphs or by dividing those that are too long for easy reading. (See 3e.) Often, however, the process is more complex. As you move blocks of text, you may need to supply transitions to make them fit smoothly in the new positions; you may also need to rework topic sentences to make your new organization clear.

Before moving text, consider sketching a revised outline. Divisions in the outline might become topic sentences in the restructured essay. (See 1d.)

Inserting headings In long documents, such as complex research papers or business reports, headings can help readers follow your organization. Typically, headings are presented as phrases, declarative or imperative sentences, or questions. To draw attention to headings, you can center them, put them in boldface, underline them, use all capital letters, or do some combination of these. (See also 58b.)

TIP: Construct an outline of your draft after you have written it (see 1d). By going through your draft paragraph by paragraph and listing the most important ideas in an outline, you can see how the parts work together and whether each paragraph has a clear focus.

Strengthening the content

In reviewing the content of a draft, first consider whether your argument is sound. You may need to rethink your argument

Understanding the comment

When a teacher or tutor points out that your introduction needs to be "narrowed," the comment often signals that the beginning sentences of your essay are not specific or focused.

> Sports fans are an interesting breed. They have many ways of showing support for the team they love. Many fans perform elaborate rituals before, during, or after a sporting event. These rituals are performed both privately in homes with family or friends and at the stadiums and arenas where the games take place. Experiencing a sports competition where the fans are participating in rituals to support the team makes the game exciting. Some fans even believe that rituals are necessary and that their actions influence the outcome of a game. However, some fans go beyond cheering, and their actions, verbal harassment, and chanted slurs reveal a darker side of sports.
>
> *Narrow your introduction*

One student wrote this introductory paragraph in response to an assignment that asked her to analyze a ritual.

This opening begins with such general statements that the purpose of the essay is unclear. To revise, the student might delete her first few sentences — generalizations about sports fans and rituals — and focus on one specific sports ritual. She might describe how fans who wear lucky clothes, eat certain foods, or chant a particular expression think they can influence the outcome of a game. Using a quotation, a vivid example, or a startling statistic, the student might show how a particular ritual not only unites fans but also reveals a dark side of sports. Whatever "hook" she chooses should lead readers to her thesis.

Similar comments: focus your intro • too general • engage your readers

Revising when you need to narrow *your* introduction

1. *Reread your introduction and ask questions.* Are the sentences leading to your thesis specific enough to engage readers and communicate your purpose? Do these sentences lead logically to your thesis? Do they spark your readers' curiosity and offer them a reason to continue reading?

2. *Try revising your introduction with a "hook"* that will engage readers — a question, quotation, paradoxical statement, or vivid example.

More advice on writing introductions: **1e**

as you revise. Second, consider whether any text (sentences, paragraphs, or longer passages) should be added or deleted, keeping in mind your readers' needs. Finally, if your purpose is to argue a point, consider how persuasively you have proved your point to an intelligent, discerning audience.

Rethinking your argument   A first draft presents you with an opportunity for rethinking your argument. You can often deepen your ideas about a subject by asking yourself some hard questions: Is your claim more sweeping than the evidence allows? Have you left out an important step in the argument? Have you dealt fairly with the arguments of the opposition? Is your draft free of faulty reasoning? The more challenging your subject, the more likely you will find yourself adjusting your early thoughts. (For more about writing arguments, see 5.)

Adding text   If any paragraphs or sections of the essay are too skimpy to be clear and convincing (a common flaw in rough drafts), add specific facts, details, and examples. You may need to go back to the beginning of the writing process: listing specifics, brainstorming ideas with friends or classmates, perhaps doing more research.

Deleting text   Look for sentences and paragraphs that can be cut without serious loss of meaning. Perhaps you have repeated yourself or strayed from your point. Maybe you have given too much emphasis to minor ideas. Cuts may also be necessitated by word limits, such as those imposed by a college assignment or by the realities of the business world, where readers are often pressed for time.

Clarifying the point of view

If the point of view of a draft shifts confusingly or if it seems not quite appropriate for your purpose, audience, and subject, consider adjusting it.

There are three basic points of view: the first person (*I* or *we*), the second person (*you*), and the third person (*he, she, it, one*, or *they*). Each point of view is appropriate in at least some contexts, and you may need to experiment before deciding which one best suits your needs.

The third-person point of view Much academic and professional writing is best presented from the third-person point of view (*he*, *she*, *it*, *one*, or *they*), which puts the subject in the foreground. The *I* point of view is usually inappropriate in such contexts because, by focusing attention on the writer, it pushes the subject to the background. Consider one student's first-draft description of the behavior of a species of frog he had observed in the field.

> **INAPPROPRIATE FIRST PERSON**
> Each frog that *I* was able to locate in trees remained in its tree during *my* observation period. However, *I* noticed that there was considerable movement within the home tree.

Here the *I* point of view is distracting. The student's revision focuses more on the frogs and less on himself.

> **APPROPRIATE THIRD PERSON**
> Each frog located in a tree remained in that tree throughout the observation period. The frogs moved about considerably, however, within their home trees.

Just as the first-person *I* can draw too much attention to the writer, the second-person *you* can focus unnecessarily on the reader. In the following sentence from a memo, a supervisor writing to a sales manager needlessly draws attention to the reader.

> **INAPPROPRIATE SECOND PERSON**
> When *you* look at the numbers, *you* can clearly see that travel expenses must be cut back.

This sentence is clearer and more direct when it is revised without the distracting *you* point of view.

APPROPRIATE THIRD PERSON

The numbers clearly show that travel expenses must be cut back.

Although the third-person point of view is often a better choice than the *I* or *you* point of view, it is not trouble-free. Writers can run into problems when their writing requires many singular pronouns. Using the pronoun *he* to include both men and women is no longer acceptable, and using *one* as a gender-neutral alternative can sound stuffy. Writers should be aware of the awkwardness that third-person singular pronouns create and should try to find graceful alternatives (see 17f and 22a).

The second-person point of view The *you* point of view, which puts the reader in the foreground, is appropriate for advising readers directly, as in giving tips or instructions. All imperative sentences, such as the advice for writers in this book, are written from the *you* point of view, although the word itself is frequently omitted. "Sketch a plan" means "*You* should sketch a plan." (See 62a.)

In the course of giving advice or instructions, the actual word *you* may be appropriate and even desired. In a pamphlet designed to motivate students to vote, the second-person *you* is effective.

APPROPRIATE SECOND PERSON

If *you* have ideas about how the Student Senate should be run and *you* want *your* voice to be heard, vote on October 15 at the field house.

Written in the third-person point of view, the call to vote is far less motivating.

INAPPROPRIATE THIRD PERSON

Students who have ideas about how the Student Senate should be run and who want their voices to be heard should vote on October 15 at the field house.

Indefinite uses of *you* are inappropriate in formal writing. (See 23d.) The third person is usually more appropriate.

INAPPROPRIATE SECOND PERSON

Young Japanese women wired together electronic products on a piece-rate system: The more *you* wired, the more *you* were paid.

APPROPRIATE THIRD PERSON

The more *they* wired, the more *they* were paid.

The first-person point of view   If much of a writer's material comes from personal experience, the *I* point of view will be most natural.

Writers who are aware that the first-person point of view is sometimes seen as inappropriate in academic writing often go to extreme lengths to avoid it.

INAPPROPRIATE THIRD PERSON

Mama read with such color and detail that *one* could fancy *oneself* as the hero of the story.

Because the paper in which this sentence appeared was a personal reminiscence, the entire paper sounded more natural when the writer allowed himself to use the word *I*.

APPROPRIATE FIRST PERSON

Mama read with such color and detail that *I* could fancy *myself* as the hero of the story.

TIP: As you write in various disciplines and for a range of audiences, pay attention to the ways in which writers use the first-person or third-person point of view. For guidelines on point of view in various disciplines, see the chart on page 134.

hackerhandbooks.com/bedhandbook > **Writing exercises** > E-ex 2–1 and 2–2

2b Revise and edit sentences; proofread the final draft.

When you revise sentences, you focus on effectiveness; when you edit, you check for correctness. Proofreading is a slow and careful reading in search of spelling errors, typos, and other obvious mistakes.

Revising and editing sentences

Parts III–VIII in this book offer advice on revising sentences for clarity and on editing them for grammar, punctuation, and mechanics.

Some writers handle sentence-level revisions directly at the computer, experimenting on-screen with a variety of possible improvements. Other writers prefer to print out a hard copy of the draft, mark it up, and then return to the computer to enter their revisions. Here, for example, is a rough-draft paragraph as one student edited it on-screen for a variety of sentence-level problems.

Although some cities have found creative ways to improve access to public transportation for passengers with physical disabilities, ~~and to fund other programs, there have been problems in~~ our city has struggled with ~~due to the need to address~~ budget constraints and competing ~~needs~~ priorities. ~~This~~ The budget crunch has led citizens to question how funds are distributed.~~?~~ For example, last year ~~when~~ city officials voted to use available funds to support ~~had to choose between allocating funds for accessible transportation or allocating funds to~~ after-school programs rather than transportation upgrades. ~~, they voted for the after-school programs.~~ It is not clear to some citizens why ~~these~~ after-school programs are more important.

The original paragraph was flawed by wordiness, a problem that can be addressed through any number of revisions. The following revision would also be acceptable.

Some cities have funded improved access to public transportation for passengers with physical disabilities. Because of budget constraints, our city chose to fund after-school programs rather than transportation programs. As a result, citizens have begun to question how funds are distributed and why certain programs are more important than others.

Some of the paragraph's improvements do not involve choice and must be fixed in any revision. The hyphen in *after-school programs* is necessary; a noun must be substituted for the pronoun *these* in the last sentence; and the question mark in the second sentence must be changed to a period.

Grammar checkers can help with some but by no means all of the sentence-level problems in a typical draft. Many problems—such as faulty parallelism and misplaced modifiers—require an understanding of grammatical structure that computer programs lack. Even if the grammar checker makes a suggestion for revision, it is your responsibility to decide whether the suggestion is more effective than your original.

Proofreading

After revising and editing, you are ready to prepare the final manuscript. (See 59 for guidelines.) Make sure to allow yourself enough time for proofreading—the final and most important step in manuscript preparation.

Proofreading is a special kind of reading: a slow and methodical search for misspellings, typographical mistakes, and omitted words or word endings. Such errors can be difficult to spot in your own work because you may read what you intended to write, not what is actually on the page. To fight this tendency, try proofreading out loud, articulating each word as it is actually written. You might also try proofreading your sentences in reverse order, a strategy that takes your attention away from the meanings you intended and forces you to think about surface features instead.

Although proofreading may be dull, it is crucial. Errors strewn throughout an essay are distracting and annoying. If the writer doesn't care about this piece of writing, thinks the reader, why should I? A carefully proofread essay, however, sends a positive message: It shows that you value your writing and respect your readers.

Spell checkers are more reliable than grammar checkers, but they too must be used with caution. Many typographical errors (such as *quiet* for *quite*) and misused words (such as *effect* for *affect*) slip past the spell checker because it flags only words not found in its dictionary.

Student essay

Matt Watson wrote the essay "Hooked on Credit Cards" (pp. 56–59) in response to the following assignment.

> In an essay of 500–1,000 words, discuss a significant problem facing today's college students. Assume that your audience consists of general readers, not simply college students.
>
> If you use any sources, document them with in-text citations and a list of works cited in MLA style (see section 53 in *The Bedford Handbook*).

When he received the assignment, Watson considered several possibilities before settling on the topic of credit cards. He already knew something about the topic because

SAMPLE NOTES

Ideas for college problem essay

Phone call with Rebecca Watson, 3.3.01

- Easy to get hooked on credit cards and run up huge debts

- Why do credit card companies try to sign up students? Aren't we a bad risk? But they must be profiting, or they'd stop.

- High interest rates

- Ads for credit cards appear all over campus and on the Web

- Using plastic doesn't seem like spending money

- Tactics used by the companies—offering low interest rates at first, setting high credit limits, allowing a revolving balance

- What happens to students who get in debt but don't have parents who can bail them out?

his older sister had run up large credit card bills while in college and was working hard to pay them off. Because the assignment required him to *discuss* a problem, he decided that a good strategy would be to identify a *how* or *why* question to answer.

To get started on his paper, Watson talked to his sister on the phone and typed some ideas on his laptop. (See p. 52.)

After he listed these ideas, Watson identified the question that would drive his essay:

Why do credit card companies put so many resources into soliciting students, who often have poor credit profiles?

Watson decided that his purpose would be to answer this question for himself and his audience. He wrote his first draft quickly, focusing more on ideas than on grammar, style, and mechanics. Then he made some additions and deletions and fixed a few typos before submitting the draft for peer review. Here is the draft he submitted, together with the most helpful comments he received from classmates. The peer reviewers were asked to comment on global issues—audience appeal, focus, organization, content, and point of view—and to ignore any problems with grammar and punctuation.

ROUGH DRAFT

Hooked on Credit Cards

Credit card companies love to extend credit to college students. You see ads for these cards on campus bulletin boards and also on the Web. Why do companies market their product to a population that has no job and lacks a substantial credit history? They seem to be trying to hook us on their cards; unfortunately many of us do get hooked on a cycle of spending that leads to financial ruin.

Banks require applicants for a loan to demonstrate a good credit history and some evidence of a source of

Good question. Is there more to the answer than you've written here? That is, why are these companies trying to hook us? (Mark)

Some students do have jobs. (Sara)

The assignment asks for a general audience; your thesis shouldn't be about "us." (Sara)

Shouldn't your thesis also explain *how* the companies hook students? (Tim)

Good point. I never thought of it that way. (Sara)

Mention the solicitors who show up during orientation? (Mark)

This sentence sounds less formal than the rest of your essay. (Tim)

I like this example. (Mark)

Why not give us some numbers here? Just how low and how high? (Sara)

The shift to "you" seems odd. (Sara)

Maybe you could search LexisNexis for some statistical information. (Mark)

This paragraph seems sort of skimpy. (Tim)

This would be more convincing if you provided some evidence to back up your claim. (Mark)

You shift from "you" to "I" here. (Sara)

Cite this? (Sara)

income, but credit card companies don't. On campus, students are bombarded with offers of preapproved credit cards. Then there are the Web sites. Sites with lots of student traffic are plastered with banner ads like this one: "To get a credit card, you need to establish credit. To establish credit, you need a credit card. Stop the vicious cycle! Apply for our student MasterCard."

Credit card companies often entice students with low interest rates, then they jack up the rates later. A student may not think about the cost of interest. That new stereo or back-to-school wardrobe can get pretty expensive at 17.9% interest if it's compounded over several months. Would you have bought that $600 item if you knew it would end up costing you $900?

Most cards allow the holder to keep a revolving balance, which means that they don't have to pay the whole bill, they just pay a minimum amount. The minimum is usually not too much, but a young person may be tempted to keep running up debt. The companies also give students an unrealistically high credit limit. I've heard of undergraduates who had a limit as high as $4,000.

Card companies make money not just from high interest rates. Often they charge fees for late payments. I've heard of penalties for going over the credit limit too.

Often students discover too late that they are thoroughly trapped. Some drop out of school, others graduate and then can't find a good job because they have a poor credit rating. There are psychological problems too. Your parents may bail you out of debt, but you'll probably feel guilty. On a Web site, I read that two students felt so bad they committed suicide.

Credit cards are a part of life these days, and everyone is probably wise to have a charge account for emergencies. But college students must take a hard look at their financial picture. The very things that make those cards so convenient and easy to use can lead to a mountain of debt that will take years to pay off.

Your paper focuses on the tactics that the companies use, but your conclusion doesn't mention them. (Tim)

After rereading his draft and considering the feedback from his classmates, Watson realized that he needed to develop his thesis further. He set out some goals for revising his essay.

MATT WATSON'S REVISION GOALS

Answer Mark's question about what credit card companies gain by hooking students.

Expand explanation of both why and how credit card companies market cards to students.

Include evidence to back up claims about how credit card companies hook students. Look at reputable Web sites: student loan provider Nellie Mae and the Consumer Federation of America.

Rework introduction to explain why credit card companies profit from students who have no steady source of income.

Adjust point of view so that essay is appropriate for a general audience, not just for other students.

When he was more or less satisfied with the paper as a whole, Watson worked to polish his sentences. His final draft begins on the next page.

Watson 1

Matt Watson

Professor Mills

English 101

12 March 2001

Hooked on Credit Cards

Credit card companies love to extend credit to college students, especially those just out of high school. Ads for credit cards line campus bulletin boards, flash across commercial Web sites for students, and get stuffed into shopping bags at college bookstores. Why do the companies market their product so vigorously to a population that lacks a substantial credit history and often has no steady source of income? The answer is that significant profits can be earned through high interest rates and assorted penalties and fees. By granting college students liberal lending arrangements, credit card companies often hook them on a cycle of spending that can ultimately lead to financial ruin.

Whereas banks require applicants for a loan to demonstrate a good credit history and some evidence of income, credit card companies make no such demands on students. On campus, students find themselves bombarded with offers of preapproved cards—and not just on flyers pinned to bulletin boards. Many campuses allow credit card vendors to solicit applications during orientation week. In addition to offering preapproved cards, these vendors often give away T-shirts or CDs to entice students to apply. Some companies even offer rewards program bonuses based on a student's GPA. Students are bombarded on the Web as well. Sites with heavy student traffic are emblazoned with banner ads like this one: "To get a credit card, you need to establish credit. To establish credit, you need a credit card. Stop the vicious cycle! Apply for our student MasterCard."

Marginal annotations:

Introduction hooks readers with interesting details.

Introduction poses a question that leads readers to the thesis.

Thesis announces Watson's main point.

Clear topic sentences guide readers through the body of the paper.

Essay is double-spaced throughout.

Marginal annotations indicate MLA-style formatting and effective writing.

Watson 2

Credit card companies often entice students with low "teaser" interest rates of 13% and later raise those rates to 18% or even higher. Others charge high rates up front, trusting that students won't read the fine print. Some young people don't think about the cost of interest, let alone the cost of interest compounding month after month. That back-to-school wardrobe can get pretty expensive at 17.9% interest compounded over several months. A $600 trip to Fort Lauderdale is not such a bargain when in the long run it costs $900 or more.

In addition to charging high interest rates, credit card companies try to maximize the amount of interest generated. One tactic is to extend an unreasonably high credit limit to students. According to Nellie Mae statistics, in 1998 undergraduates were granted an average credit limit of $3,683; for graduate students, the figure jumped to $15,721. Nearly 10% of the students in the Nellie Mae study carried balances near or exceeding these credit limits (Blair).

Another tactic is to allow students to maintain a revolving balance. A revolving balance permits the debtor to pay only part of a current bill, often an amount just a little larger than the accumulated interest. The indebted student is tempted to keep on charging, paying a minimum amount every month, because there aren't any immediate consequences to doing so.

Once a student is hooked on a cycle of debt, the companies profit even further by assessing a variety of fees and penalties. According to a press release issued by Consumer Action and the Consumer Federation of America, many credit card companies charge late fees and "over the limit" penalties as high as $29 per month. In addition, grace periods are often shortened to ensure that late fees kick in earlier. Many companies also raise interest rates for those who fail to pay on time or who exceed the credit limit. Those "penalty" rates can climb as high as 25% (1-2).

Body paragraphs are developed with details and examples.

Transition serves as a bridge between paragraphs.

Summary of the source is in Watson's own words.

Source is documented with an MLA in-text citation.

Watson cites a Web article from a reputable source.

Watson 3

Often students discover too late that they are thoroughly hooked. The results can be catastrophic. Some students are forced to drop out of school and take low-paying full-time jobs. Others, once they graduate, have difficulty landing good jobs because of their poor credit rating. Many students suffer psychologically as well. Even those who have parents willing to bail them out of debt often experience a great deal of anxiety and guilt. Two students grew so stressed by their accumulating debt that they committed suicide (Consumer Federation of Amer. 3).

Conclusion echoes Watson's main idea.

Credit cards are a convenient part of life, and there is nothing wrong with having one or two of them. Before signing up for a particular card, however, college students should take time to read the fine print and do some comparison shopping. Students also need to learn to resist the many seductive offers that credit card companies extend to them after they have signed up. Students who can't "just say no" to temptations such as high credit limits and revolving balances could well become hooked on a cycle of debt from which there is no easy escape.

Watson 4

Works Cited

Blair, Alan D. "A High Wire Act: Balancing Student Loan and Credit
Card Debt." *Credit World* 86.2 (1997): 15-17. *Business Source
Premier*. Web. 4 Mar. 2001.

Consumer Action and Consumer Federation of America. "Card Issuers Hike
Fees and Rates to Bolster Profits." *Consumer Federation of America*.
Consumer Federation of Amer., 5 Nov. 1998. Web. 4 Mar. 2001.

Consumer Federation of America. "Credit Card Debt Imposes Huge Costs
on Many College Students." *Consumer Federation of America*.
Consumer Federation of Amer., 8 June 1999. Web. 4 Mar. 2001.

Works cited page
follows MLA
format.

2c Prepare a portfolio; reflect on your writing.

At the end of the semester, your instructor may expect you
to submit a portfolio, or collection, of your writing. A writing portfolio often consists of drafts, revised pieces, and reflective entries that demonstrate a writer's thinking and
learning processes or that showcase the writer's best work.
Your instructor may give you the choice of submitting a paper
portfolio, often maintained and submitted in a folder or
binder, or an e-portfolio, maintained and submitted as a Web
site or as a collection of files on a flash drive or a CD.

Your instructor may distinguish between a *process portfolio*
and an *evaluation portfolio* (sometimes called an *assessment
portfolio*). A process portfolio allows you to demonstrate your
development as a writer; in it you will collect notes, outlines,
brainstorming, reflective journal or blog entries, multiple
drafts—in short, the messy stuff. In an evaluation portfolio,
you will include a few select final pieces that have perhaps
been revised multiple times, along with early drafts of those
pieces. At the end of the semester, you may be asked to re-
shape your process portfolio into an evaluation portfolio.

As early in the course as possible, be sure you know the answers to the following questions:

- Should the portfolio be a paper collection or an electronic one? Is it your choice?
- Will the portfolio be a process portfolio, an evaluation portfolio, or some combination of the two?
- Will the portfolio be checked or assessed before the end of the term? If so, when or how often?
- Are you free to choose any or all of the pieces to include?
- Are you free to include a variety of items (not just rough and final drafts of papers), such as outlines and notes, journal entries, photographs or other visuals, comments from readers, sound files, or video clips?
- Will your instructor be the primary or only audience for the portfolio? Or will the portfolio be shared with peers or with other instructors?
- Who will evaluate the portfolio?

Reflection—the process of stepping back periodically to examine your decisions, preferences, strengths, and challenges as a writer—is the backbone of portfolio keeping. Many instructors require writers to submit a number of reflective entries throughout the semester.

When you submit your portfolio for a final evaluation or reading, you may be asked to include a reflective opening statement—a cover letter, an introduction, a preface, or an essay. Whatever form your reflective piece takes, it could be your most important writing in the course. You will need to show that you can identify the strengths and weaknesses of your writing, comment on the progress you've made in the course, understand your own writing process, and make good writing decisions. Your instructor or other evaluator will expect you to reflect on how the specific pieces in the portfolio show your development as a writer.

Writing a reflective opening statement for your portfolio

Your instructor may require a reflective document in which you introduce the pieces in your portfolio and comment on your development as a writer throughout the course. Your document may take the form of an essay, a cover letter, or another introductory statement. Check with your instructor about the form this document should take.

For an effective portfolio cover document, you might try one or more of the following strategies:

- Discuss, in depth, your best entry. Explain why it is your best and how it reflects what you learned in the course.

- Discuss each piece of writing you've included, touching on its strengths.

- Describe in detail the revisions you've made to one key piece and the improvements and changes you want others to notice. Include specific passages from the piece.

- Demonstrate what this portfolio illustrates about you as a writer, student, researcher, or critical thinker.

- Acknowledge the readers or reviewers who have influenced your portfolio and describe their influence.

- Reflect on what you've learned about writing, reading, or other topics of the course.

- Acknowledge an important challenge you faced in your writing and show how you worked to overcome it. Where possible, include specific references to one or more pieces in your portfolio.

- Reflect on how you plan to take the skills and experiences from your writing course into other courses where writing will be assigned.

Keep in mind that it is critical to write multiple drafts of the reflective cover document, perhaps getting feedback from a peer, a tutor, or your instructor between drafts.

3 Build effective paragraphs.

Except for special-purpose paragraphs, such as introductions and conclusions (see 1e and 1g), paragraphs are clusters of information supporting an essay's main point (or advancing a story's action). Aim for paragraphs that are clearly focused, well developed, organized, coherent, and neither too long nor too short for easy reading.

3a Focus on a main point.

A paragraph should be unified around a main point. The point should be clear to readers, and all sentences in the paragraph should relate to it.

Stating the main point in a topic sentence

As readers move into a paragraph, they need to know where they are—in relation to the whole essay—and what to expect in the sentences to come. A good topic sentence, a one-sentence summary of the paragraph's main point, acts as a signpost pointing in two directions: backward toward the thesis of the essay and forward toward the body of the paragraph.

Like a thesis sentence (see 1c and 1e), a topic sentence is more general than the material supporting it. Usually the topic sentence (italicized in the following example) comes first in the paragraph.

> *All living creatures manage some form of communication.* The dance patterns of bees in their hive help to point the way to distant flower fields or announce successful foraging. Male stickleback fish regularly swim upside-down to indicate outrage in a courtship contest. Male deer and lemurs mark territorial ownership by rubbing their own body secretions on boundary stones or trees. Everyone has seen a frightened dog put his tail between his legs and run in panic. We, too, use gestures, expressions, postures, and movement to give our words point. [Italics added.] —Olivia Vlahos, *Human Beginnings*

Sometimes the topic sentence is introduced by a transitional sentence linking it to earlier material. In the following paragraph, the topic sentence has been delayed to allow for a transition.

But flowers are not the only source of spectacle in the wilderness. *An opportunity for late color is provided by the berries of wildflowers, shrubs, and trees.* Baneberry presents its tiny white flowers in spring but in late summer bursts forth with clusters of red berries. Bunchberry, a ground-cover plant, puts out red berries in the fall, and the red berries of wintergreen last from autumn well into the winter. In California, the bright red, fist-sized clusters of Christmas berries can be seen growing beside highways for up to six months of the year. [Italics added.]   —James Crockett et al., *Wildflower Gardening*

Occasionally the topic sentence may be withheld until the end of the paragraph—but only if the earlier sentences hang together so well that readers perceive their direction, if not their exact point. The opening sentences of the following paragraph state facts, so they are supporting material rather than topic sentences, but they strongly suggest a central idea. The topic sentence at the end is hardly a surprise.

Tobacco chewing starts as soon as people begin stirring. Those who have fresh supplies soak the new leaves in water and add ashes from the hearth to the wad. Men, women, and children chew tobacco and all are addicted to it. Once there was a shortage of tobacco in Kạobawä's village and I was plagued for a week by early morning visitors who requested permission to collect my cigarette butts in order to make a wad of chewing tobacco. Normally, if anyone is short of tobacco, he can request a share of someone else's already chewed wad, or simply borrow the entire wad when its owner puts it down somewhere. *Tobacco is so important to them that their word for "poverty" translates as "being without tobacco."* [Italics added.]
—Napoleon A. Chagnon, *Yanomamö: The Fierce People*

You will find that some professional writers, especially journalists and informal essayists, do not always use clear

Making the most of your handbook

Topic sentences let your reader know how a body paragraph relates to your essay's thesis.

▶ Effective thesis statements: 1e

topic sentences. In college writing, however, topic sentences are often necessary for clarifying the lines of an argument or reporting the research in a field. In business writing, topic sentences (along with headings) are essential because readers often scan for information.

Sticking to the point

Sentences that do not support the topic sentence destroy the unity of a paragraph. If the paragraph is otherwise focused, such sentences can simply be deleted or perhaps moved elsewhere. In the following paragraph describing the inadequate facilities in a high school, the information about the chemistry instructor (in italics) is clearly off the point.

> As the result of tax cuts, the educational facilities of Lincoln High School have reached an all-time low. Some of the books date back to 1990 and have long since shed their covers. The few computers in working order must share one printer. The lack of lab equipment makes it necessary for four or five students to work at one table, with most watching rather than performing experiments. *Also, the chemistry instructor left to have a baby at the beginning of the semester, and most of the students don't like the substitute.* As for the furniture, many of the upright chairs have become recliners, and the desk legs are so unbalanced that they play seesaw on the floor. [Italics added.]

Sometimes the solution for a disunified paragraph is not as simple as deleting or moving material. Writers often wander into uncharted territory because they cannot think of enough evidence to support a topic sentence. Feeling that it is too soon to break into a new paragraph, they move on to new ideas for which they have not prepared the reader. When this happens, the writer is faced with a choice: Either find more evidence to support the topic sentence or adjust the topic sentence to mesh with the evidence that is available.

Revising with comments | More than one point in this paragraph

Understanding the comment

When a teacher or tutor tells you that you have "more than one point in this paragraph," the comment often signals that not all sentences in your paragraph support the topic sentence.

> Bringing casino gaming to Massachusetts would benefit the state in a number of ways. First, it would provide needed property tax relief for many of the state's towns and cities. Casino gaming would also bring in revenue needed to fix the state's roads and bridges. The speaker of the House of Representatives is blocking the governor's proposal because he believes the social costs are greater than the economic benefits. Many people agree with the speaker. Most important, casino gaming would provide jobs in areas of the state that have suffered economically in recent years. *More than one point in this paragraph*

One student wrote this body paragraph in response to an assignment that asked him to take a position on a current issue.

The topic sentence promises a discussion of benefits, but the detour into risks strays from the point. To revise, the student should focus on the key word in his topic sentence—*benefit*—because that signals to readers that the paragraph will examine the advantages of casino gaming. He might focus his paragraph by providing specific examples of benefits and deleting references to risks, perhaps using risks as counterpoints in a separate paragraph.

Similar comments: unfocused • lacks unity • hard to follow

Strategies for revising when *you* have more than one point in a paragraph

1. *Reread your paragraph and ask questions.* What is the main point of the paragraph? Is there a topic sentence that signals to readers what to expect in the rest of the paragraph? Does each sentence support the topic sentence and logically follow from the one before? Have you included sentences that perhaps belong elsewhere in your paper?

2. *Remember the purpose of topic sentences*; they serve as important signposts for readers. Make sure that the wording of your topic sentence is precise and that you have enough evidence to support it in the paragraph.

More advice on unifying paragraphs: **3d**

65

EXERCISE 3–1 Underline the topic sentence in the following paragraph and cross out any material that does not clarify or develop the central idea.

Quilt making has served as an important means of social, political, and artistic expression for women. In the nineteenth century, quilting circles provided one of the few opportunities for women to forge social bonds outside of their families. Once a week or more, they came together to sew as well as trade small talk, advice, and news. They used dyed cotton fabrics much like the fabrics quilters use today; surprisingly, quilters' basic materials haven't changed that much over the years. Sometimes the women joined their efforts in support of a political cause, making quilts that would be raffled to raise money for temperance societies, hospitals for sick and wounded soldiers, and the fight against slavery. Quilt making also afforded women a means of artistic expression at a time when they had few other creative outlets. Within their socially acceptable roles as homemakers, many quilters subtly pushed back at the restrictions placed on them by experimenting with color, design, and technique.

hackerhandbooks.com/bedhandbook > Writing exercises > E-ex 3–2

3b Develop the main point.

Though an occasional short paragraph is fine, particularly if it functions as a transition or emphasizes a point, a series of brief paragraphs suggests inadequate development. How much development is enough? That varies, depending on the writer's purpose and audience.

For example, when health columnist Jane Brody wrote a paragraph attempting to convince readers that it is impossible to lose fat quickly, she knew that she would have to present a great deal of evidence because many dieters want to believe the opposite. She did *not* write only the following:

When you think about it, it's impossible to lose—as many diets suggest—10 pounds of *fat* in ten days, even on a total fast. Even a moderately active person cannot lose so much weight so fast. A less active person hasn't a prayer.

This three-sentence paragraph is too skimpy to be convincing. But the paragraph that Brody did write contains enough evidence to convince even skeptical readers.

> When you think about it, it's impossible to lose—as many . . . diets suggest—10 pounds of *fat* in ten days, even on a total fast. A pound of body fat represents 3,500 calories. To lose 1 pound of fat, you must expend 3,500 more calories than you consume. Let's say you weigh 170 pounds and, as a moderately active person, you burn 2,500 calories a day. If your diet contains only 1,500 calories, you'd have an energy deficit of 1,000 calories a day. In a week's time that would add up to a 7,000-calorie deficit, or 2 pounds of real fat. In ten days, the accumulated deficit would represent nearly 3 pounds of lost body fat. Even if you ate nothing at all for ten days and maintained your usual level of activity, your caloric deficit would add up to 25,000 calories. . . . At 3,500 calories per pound of fat, that's still only 7 pounds of lost fat.
> —Jane Brody, *Jane Brody's Nutrition Book*

3c Choose a suitable pattern of organization.

Although paragraphs (and indeed whole essays) may be patterned in any number of ways, certain patterns of organization occur frequently, either alone or in combination: examples and illustrations, narration, description, process, comparison and contrast, analogy, cause and effect, classification and division, and definition. These patterns (sometimes called *methods of development*) have different uses, depending on the writer's subject and purpose.

Examples and illustrations

Examples, perhaps the most common pattern of development, are appropriate whenever the reader might be tempted to ask, "For example?" Though examples are just selected instances, not a complete catalog, they are enough to suggest the truth of many topic sentences, as in the following paragraph.

> Normally my parents abided scrupulously by "The Budget," but several times a year Dad would dip into his battered black strongbox and splurge on some irrational, totally satisfying luxury. Once he bought over a hundred comic books at a flea market, doled out to us thereafter at the tantalizing rate of two a week. He always got a whole flat of pansies, Mom's favorite flower, for us to give her on Mother's Day. One day a boy stopped at our house selling fifty-cent raffle tickets on a sailboat and Dad bought every ticket the boy had left—three books' worth. —Connie Hailey, student

Illustrations are extended examples, frequently presented in story form. Because they require several sentences apiece, they are used more sparingly than examples. When well selected, however, they can be a vivid and effective means of developing a point. The writer of the following paragraph uses illustrations to demonstrate that Harriet Tubman, the underground railroad's most famous conductor, was a genius at eluding her pursuers.

> Part of [Harriet Tubman's] strategy of conducting was, as in all battle-field operations, the knowledge of how and when to retreat. Numerous allusions have been made to her moves when she suspected that she was in danger. When she feared the party was closely pursued, she would take it for a time on a train southward bound. No one seeing Negroes going in this direction would for an instant suppose them to be fugitives. Once on her return she was at a railroad station. She saw some men reading a poster and she heard one of them reading it aloud. It was a description of her, offering a reward for her capture. She took a southbound train to avert suspicion. At another time when Harriet heard men talking about her, she pretended to read a book which she carried. One man remarked, "This can't be the woman. The one we want can't read or write." Harriet devoutly hoped the book was right side up. —Earl Conrad, *Harriet Tubman*

Narration

A paragraph of narration tells a story or part of a story. Narrative paragraphs are usually arranged in chronological order, but they may also contain flashbacks, interruptions that take the story back to an earlier time. The following paragraph, from Jane Goodall's *In the Shadow of Man*, recounts one of the author's experiences in the African wild.

> One evening when I was wading in the shallows of the lake to pass a rocky outcrop, I suddenly stopped dead as I saw the sinuous black body of a snake in the water. It was all of six feet long, and from the slight hood and the dark stripes at the back of the neck I knew it to be a Storm's water cobra— a deadly reptile for the bite of which there was, at that time, no serum. As I stared at it an incoming wave gently deposited part of its body on one of my feet. I remained motionless, not even breathing, until the wave rolled back into the lake, drawing the snake with it. Then I leaped out of the water as fast as I could, my heart hammering.
>
> —Jane Goodall, *In the Shadow of Man*

Description

A descriptive paragraph sketches a portrait of a person, place, or thing by using concrete and specific details that appeal to one or more of our senses—sight, sound, smell, taste, and touch. Consider, for example, the following description of the grasshopper invasions that devastated the midwestern landscape in the late 1860s.

> They came like dive bombers out of the west. They came by the millions with the rustle of their wings roaring overhead. They came in waves, like the rolls of the sea, descending with a terrifying speed, breaking now and again like a mighty surf. They came with the force of a williwaw and they formed a huge, ominous, dark brown cloud that eclipsed the sun. They dipped and touched earth, hitting objects and people like hailstones. But they were not hail. These were *live* demons. They popped, snapped, crackled, and roared. They were dark brown, an inch or longer in length, plump in the middle and tapered at the ends. They had transparent wings, slender legs, and two black eyes that flashed with a fierce intelligence.
>
> —Eugene Boe, "Pioneers to Eternity"

Process

A process paragraph is structured in chronological order. A writer may choose this pattern either to describe how something is made or done or to explain to readers, step by step, how to do something. The following paragraph describes what happens when water freezes.

> In school we learned that with few exceptions the solid phase of matter is more dense than the liquid phase. Water, alone among common substances, violates this rule. As water begins to cool, it contracts and becomes more dense, in a perfectly typical way. But about four degrees above the freezing point, something remarkable happens. It ceases to contract and begins expanding, becoming less dense. At the freezing point the expansion is abrupt and drastic. As water turns to ice, it adds about one-eleventh to its liquid volume.
> —Chet Raymo, "Curious Stuff, Water and Ice"

Here is a paragraph explaining how to perform a "roll cast," a popular fly-fishing technique.

> Begin by taking up a suitable stance, with one foot slightly in front of the other and the rod pointing down the line. Then begin a smooth, steady draw, raising your rod hand to just above shoulder height and lifting the rod to the 10:30 or 11:00 position. This steady draw allows a loop of line to form between the rod top and the water. While the line is still moving, raise the rod slightly, then punch it rapidly forward and down. The rod is now flexed and under maximum compression, and the line follows its path, bellying out slightly behind you and coming off the water close to your feet. As you power the rod down through the 3:00 position, the belly of line will roll forward. Follow through smoothly so that the line unfolds and straightens above the water.
> —*The Dorling Kindersley Encyclopedia of Fishing*

Comparison and contrast

To compare two subjects is to draw attention to their similarities, although the word *compare* also has a broader meaning that includes a consideration of differences. To contrast is to focus only on differences.

Whether a paragraph stresses similarities or differences, it may be patterned in one of two ways. The two subjects may be presented one at a time, as in the following paragraph of contrast.

> So Grant and Lee were in complete contrast, representing two diametrically opposed elements in American life. Grant was the modern man emerging; beyond him, ready to come on the stage, was the great age of steel and machinery, of crowded cities and a restless, burgeoning vitality. Lee might have ridden down from the old age of chivalry, lance in hand, silken banner fluttering over his head. Each man was the perfect champion of his cause, drawing both his strengths and his weaknesses from the people he led.
> —Bruce Catton, "Grant and Lee: A Study in Contrasts"

Or a paragraph may proceed point by point, treating the two subjects together, one aspect at a time. The following paragraph uses the point-by-point method to contrast speeches given by Abraham Lincoln in 1860 and Barack Obama in 2008.

> Two men, two speeches. The men, both lawyers, both from Illinois, were seeking the presidency, despite what seemed their crippling connection with extremists. Each was young by modern standards for a president. Abraham Lincoln had turned fifty-one just five days before delivering his speech. Barack Obama was forty-six when he gave his. Their political experience was mainly provincial, in the Illinois legislature for both of them, and they had received little exposure at the national level—two years in the House of Representatives for Lincoln, four years in the Senate for Obama. Yet each was seeking his party's nomination against a New York senator of longer standing and greater prior reputation—Lincoln against Senator William Seward, Obama against Senator Hillary Clinton. They were both known for having opposed an initially popular war—Lincoln against President Polk's Mexican War, raised on the basis of a fictitious provocation;

Obama against President Bush's Iraq War, launched on false claims that Saddam Hussein possessed WMDs [weapons of mass destruction] and had made an alliance with Osama bin Laden. —Garry Wills, "Two Speeches on Race"

Analogy

Analogies draw comparisons between items that appear to have little in common. Writers turn to analogies for a variety of reasons: to make the unfamiliar seem familiar, to provide a concrete understanding of an abstract topic, to argue a point, or to provoke fresh thoughts or changed feelings about a subject. In the following paragraph, physician Lewis Thomas draws an analogy between the behavior of ants and that of humans.

Ants are so much like human beings as to be an embarrassment. They farm fungi, raise aphids as livestock, launch armies into wars, use chemical sprays to alarm and confuse enemies, capture slaves. The families of weaver ants engage in child labor, holding their larvae like shuttles to spin out the thread that sews the leaves together for their fungus gardens. They exchange information ceaselessly. They do everything but watch television.

—Lewis Thomas, "On Societies as Organisms"

Although analogies can be a powerful tool for illuminating a subject, they should be used with caution in arguments. Just because two things may be alike in one respect, we cannot conclude that they are alike in all respects. (See "false analogy," p. 121.)

Cause and effect

When causes and effects are a matter of argument, they are too complex to be reduced to a simple pattern (see p. 121). However, if a writer wishes merely to describe a cause-and-effect relationship that is generally accepted, then the effect may be stated in the topic sentence, with the causes listed in the body of the paragraph.

The fantastic water clarity of the Mount Gambier sinkholes results from several factors. The holes are fed from aquifers holding rainwater that fell decades—even centuries—ago, and that has been filtered through miles of limestone. The high level of calcium that limestone adds causes the silty detritus from dead plants and animals to cling together and settle quickly to the bottom. Abundant bottom vegetation in the shallow sinkholes also helps bind the silt. And the rapid turnover of water prohibits stagnation.

—Hillary Hauser, "Exploring a Sunken Realm in Australia"

Or the paragraph may move from cause to effects, as in this paragraph from a student paper on the effects of the industrial revolution on American farms.

The rise of rail transport in the nineteenth century forever changed American farming—for better and for worse. Farmers who once raised crops and livestock to sustain just their own families could now make a profit by selling their goods in towns and cities miles away. These new markets improved the living standard of struggling farm families and encouraged them to seek out innovations that would increase their profits. On the downside, the competition fostered by the new markets sometimes created hostility among neighboring farm families where there had once been a spirit of cooperation. Those farmers who couldn't compete with their neighbors left farming forever, facing poverty worse than they had ever known.

—Chris Mileski, student

Classification and division

Classification is the grouping of items into categories according to some consistent principle. For example, an elementary school teacher might classify children's books according to their level of difficulty, but a librarian might group them by subject matter. The principle of classification that a writer chooses ultimately depends on the purpose of the classification. The following paragraph classifies species of electric fish.

Scientists sort electric fishes into three categories. The first comprises the strongly electric species like the marine electric rays or the freshwater African electric catfish and South American electric eel. Known since the dawn of history, these deliver a punch strong enough to stun a human. In recent years, biologists have focused on a second category: weakly electric fish in the South American and African rivers that use tiny voltages for communication and navigation. The third group contains sharks, nonelectric rays, and catfish, which do not emit a field but possess sensors that enable them to detect the minute amounts of electricity that leak out of other organisms.

—Anne and Jack Rudloe, "Electric Warfare: The Fish That Kill with Thunderbolts"

Division takes one item and divides it into parts. As with classification, division should be made according to some consistent principle. The following passage describes the components that make up a baseball.

Like the game itself, a baseball is composed of many layers. One of the delicious joys of childhood is to take apart a baseball and examine the wonders within. You begin by removing the red cotton thread and peeling off the leather cover—which comes from the hide of a Holstein cow and has been tanned, cut, printed, and punched with holes. Beneath the cover is a thin layer of cotton string, followed by several hundred yards of woolen yarn, which makes up the bulk of the ball. Finally, in the middle is a rubber ball, or "pill," which is a little smaller than a golf ball. Slice into the rubber and you'll find the ball's heart—a cork core. The cork is from Portugal, the rubber from southeast Asia, the covers are American, and the balls are assembled in Costa Rica.

—Dan Gutman, *The Way Baseball Works*

Definition

A definition puts a word or concept into a general class and then provides enough details to distinguish it from others in the same class. In the following paragraph, the writer defines *envy* as a special kind of desire.

Envy is so integral and so painful a part of what animates behavior in market societies that many people have forgotten the full meaning of the word, simplifying it into one of the synonyms of desire. It is that, which may be why it flourishes in market societies: democracies of desire, they might be called, with money for ballots, stuffing permitted. But envy is more or less than desire. It begins with an almost frantic sense of emptiness inside oneself, as if the pump of one's heart were sucking on air. One has to be blind to perceive the emptiness, of course, but that's just what envy is, a selective blindness. *Invidia*, Latin for envy, translates as "non-sight," and Dante has the envious plodding along under cloaks of lead, their eyes sewn shut with leaden wire. What they are blind to is what they have, God-given and humanly nurtured, in themselves.
—Nelson W. Aldrich Jr., *Old Money*

3d Make paragraphs coherent.

When sentences and paragraphs flow from one to another without discernible bumps, gaps, or shifts, they are said to be coherent. Coherence can be improved by strengthening the ties between old information and new. A number of techniques for strengthening those ties are detailed in this section.

Linking ideas clearly

Readers expect to learn a paragraph's main point in a topic sentence early in the paragraph. Then, as they move into the body of the paragraph, they expect to encounter specific details, facts, or examples that support the topic sentence—either directly or indirectly. In the following paragraph, all of the sentences following the topic sentence directly support it.

A passenger list of the early years [of the Orient Express] would read like a *Who's Who of the World*, from art to politics. Sarah Bernhardt and her Italian counterpart Eleonora Duse used the train to thrill the stages of Europe. For musicians there were Toscanini and Mahler. Dancers Nijinsky and Pavlova were there, while lesser performers like Harry Houdini and the girls of the Ziegfeld Follies also rode the rails.

> Violinists were allowed to practice on the train, and occasionally one might see trapeze artists hanging like bats from the baggage racks. —Barnaby Conrad III, "Train of Kings"

If a sentence does not support the topic sentence directly, readers expect it to support another sentence in the paragraph and therefore to support the topic sentence indirectly. The following paragraph begins with a topic sentence. The italicized sentences are direct supports, and the rest of the sentences are indirect supports.

> Though the open-space classroom works for many children, it is not practical for my son, David. *First, David is hyperactive.* When he was placed in an open-space classroom, he became distracted and confused. He was tempted to watch the movement going on around him instead of concentrating on his own work. *Second, David has a tendency to transpose letters and numbers, a tendency that can be overcome only by individual attention from the instructor.* In the open classroom he was moved from teacher to teacher, with each one responsible for a different subject. No single teacher worked with David long enough to diagnose the problem, let alone help him with it. *Finally, David is not a highly motivated learner.* In the open classroom, he was graded "at his own level," not by criteria for a certain grade. He could receive a B in reading and still be a grade level behind, because he was doing satisfactory work "at his own level." [Italics added.]
> —Margaret Smith, student

Repeating key words

Repetition of key words is an important technique for gaining coherence. To prevent repetitions from becoming dull, you can use variations of a key word (*hike, hiker, hiking*), pronouns referring to the word (*gamblers . . . they*), and synonyms (*run, spring, race, dash*). In the following paragraph describing plots among indentured servants in the seventeenth century, historian Richard Hofstadter binds sentences together by repeating the key word *plots* and echoing it with a variety of synonyms (which are italicized).

Plots hatched by several servants to run away together occurred mostly in the plantation colonies, and the few recorded servant *uprisings* were entirely limited to those colonies. Virginia had been forced from its very earliest years to take stringent steps against *mutinous plots*, and severe punishments for *such behavior* were recorded. Most servant *plots* occurred in the seventeenth century: a contemplated *uprising* was nipped in the bud in York County in 1661; apparently led by some left-wing offshoots of the *Great Rebellion*, servants *plotted* an *insurrection* in Gloucester County in 1663, and four leaders were condemned and executed; some discontented servants apparently joined *Bacon's Rebellion* in the 1670's. In the 1680's the planters became newly apprehensive of discontent among the servants "owing to their great necessities and want of clothes," and it was feared they would *rise up* and *plunder* the storehouses and ships; in 1682 there were plant-cutting *riots* in which servants and laborers, as well as some planters, took part. [Italics added.]

—Richard Hofstadter, *America at 1750*

Using parallel structures

Parallel structures are frequently used within sentences to underscore the similarity of ideas (see 9). They may also be used to bind together a series of sentences expressing similar information. In the following passage describing folk beliefs, anthropologist Margaret Mead presents similar information in parallel grammatical form.

Actually, almost every day, even in the most sophisticated home, something is likely to happen that evokes the memory of some old folk belief. The salt spills. A knife falls to the floor. Your nose tickles. Then perhaps, with a slightly embarrassed smile, the person who spilled the salt tosses a pinch over his left shoulder. Or someone recites the old rhyme, "Knife falls, gentleman calls." Or as you rub your nose you think, That means a letter. I wonder who's writing?

—Margaret Mead, "New Superstitions for Old"

Maintaining consistency

Coherence suffers whenever a draft shifts confusingly from one point of view to another or from one verb tense to another. (See 13.) In addition, coherence can suffer when new information is introduced with the subject of each sentence. As a rule, a sentence's subject should echo a subject or an object in the previous sentence.

The following rough-draft paragraph is needlessly hard to read because so few of the sentences' subjects are tied to earlier subjects or objects. The subjects appear in italics.

> *One* goes about trapping in this manner. At the very outset *one* acquires a "trapping" state of mind. A *library* of books must be read, and preferably *someone* with experience should educate the novice. *Preparing* for the first expedition takes several steps. The *purchase* of traps is first. A *pair* of rubber gloves, waterproof *boots*, and the grubbiest *clothes* capable of withstanding human use come next to outfit the trapper for his adventure. Finally, the *decision* has to be made on just what kinds of animals to seek, what sort of bait to use, and where to place the traps. [Italics added.]

Although the writer repeats a number of key words, such as *trapping*, the paragraph seems disconnected because new information is introduced with the subject of each sentence.

To improve the paragraph, the writer used the first-person pronoun as the subject of every sentence. The revision is much easier to read.

> *I* went about trapping in this manner. To acquire a "trapping" state of mind, *I* read a library of books and talked at length with an experienced trapper, my father. Then *I* purchased the traps and outfitted myself by collecting a pair of rubber gloves, waterproof boots, and the grubbiest clothes capable of withstanding human use. Finally, *I* decided just what kinds of animals to seek, what sort of bait to use, and where to place my traps. [Italics added.]
> —John Clyde Thatcher, student

Notice that Thatcher combined some of his original sentences. By doing so, he was able to avoid excessive repetitions of the pronoun *I*. Notice, too, that he varied his sentence openings (most sentences do not begin with *I*) so that readers are not likely to find the repetitions tiresome.

Providing transitions

Transitions are bridges between what has been read and what is about to be read. Transitions help readers move from sentence to sentence; they also alert readers to more global connections of ideas—those between paragraphs or even larger blocks of text.

Academic English   Choose transitions carefully and vary them appropriately. Each transition has a different meaning (see the chart on p. 81). If you do not use a transition with an appropriate meaning, you might confuse your readers.

▶ **Although taking eight o'clock classes may seem**

   unappealing, coming to school early has its advan-
   For example,
   tages. ~~Moreover~~, students who arrive early typically

   avoid the worst traffic and find the best parking spaces.

Sentence-level transitions   Certain words and phrases signal connections between (or within) sentences. Frequently used transitions are included in the chart on page 81.

Skilled writers use transitional expressions with care, making sure, for example, not to use *consequently* when *also* would be more precise. They are also careful to select transitions with an appropriate tone, perhaps preferring *so* to *thus* in an informal piece, *in summary* to *in short* for a scholarly essay.

In the following paragraph, taken from an argument that dinosaurs had the "'right-sized' brains for reptiles of their body

Understanding the comment

When a teacher or tutor points out that you "need a transition," the comment often signals that readers need bridges—transitional words—to follow the progression from one idea to the next.

> The United States of America is one of many countries in the world that were created by immigration. This essential characteristic is perhaps America's greatest weakness and its greatest strength. Our country has the potential to be swallowed up by the diverse beliefs, values, and social practices of its immigrants so that nothing is common to anyone. America can benefit from embracing the amazing cultural diversity within itself. ? Need a transition

In this body paragraph, a student responded to an assignment that asked him to analyze a central feature of American identity.

Transitional words or phrases help readers follow the connections between sentences and ideas. To revise, the student might begin by asking: What idea is expressed in each sentence? Does each sentence point clearly back to the previous one? If not, what words or phrases might be added to help readers see how one idea moves to the next? The answers to these questions will help the student recognize that his last two sentences contrast with each other (one about weaknesses, one about strengths) but that he needs to provide a transitional word or phrase, such as *however*, before the last sentence to make the contrast clear.

Similar comments: something missing? • missing connection • transition?

Revising when *you* need a transition between sentences

1. *Read your paragraph aloud* to a peer or a tutor. Ask your listeners what is missing between sentences that would help them follow the progression from one idea to the next.

2. *Ask questions.* What words or phrases might be added to help readers move from sentence to sentence? For instance, do you need transitions to show addition (*furthermore*), to give examples (*specifically*), to compare (*similarly*), to contrast (*however*), or to summarize (*in summary*)?

3. *Revise with an appropriate transition* to show connections between ideas.

More help with transitions: pages **79–83**

Common transitions

To show addition: and, also, besides, further, furthermore, in addition, moreover, next, too, first, second

To give examples: for example, for instance, to illustrate, in fact, specifically

To compare: also, in the same manner, similarly, likewise

To contrast: but, however, on the other hand, in contrast, nevertheless, still, even though, on the contrary, yet, although

To summarize or conclude: in short, in summary, in conclusion, to sum up, therefore

To show time: after, as, before, next, during, later, finally, meanwhile, then, when, while, immediately

To show place or direction: above, below, beyond, nearby, opposite, close, to the left

To indicate logical relationship: if, so, therefore, consequently, thus, as a result, for this reason, because, since

size," biologist Stephen Jay Gould uses transitions (italicized) with skill.

> I don't wish to deny that the flattened, minuscule head of large bodied Stegosaurus houses little brain from our subjective, top-heavy perspective, *but* I do wish to assert that we should not expect more of the beast. *First of all*, large animals have relatively smaller brains than related, small animals. The correlation of brain size with body size among kindred animals (all reptiles, all mammals, *for example*) is remarkably regular. *As* we move from small to large animals, from mice to elephants or small lizards to Komodo dragons, brain size increases, *but* not so fast as body size. *In other words*, bodies grow faster than brains, *and* large animals have low ratios of brain weight to body weight. *In fact*, brains grow only about two-thirds as fast as bodies. *Since* we have no reason to believe that large animals are consistently stupider than their smaller relatives, we must conclude that large animals require

relatively less brain to do as well as smaller animals. *If* we do not recognize this relationship, we are likely to underestimate the mental power of very large animals, dinosaurs *in particular.* [Italics added.]
—Stephen Jay Gould, "Were Dinosaurs Dumb?"

hackerhandbooks.com/bedhandbook > Writing exercises > E-ex 3–3

Paragraph-level transitions   Paragraph-level transitions usually link the *first* sentence of a new paragraph with the *first* sentence of the previous paragraph. In other words, the topic sentences signal global connections.

Look for opportunities to allude to the subject of a previous paragraph (as summed up in its topic sentence) in the topic sentence of the next one. In his essay "Little Green Lies," Jonathan H. Alder uses this strategy in the following topic sentences, which appear in a passage describing the benefits of plastic packaging.

> Consider aseptic packaging, the synthetic packaging for the "juice boxes" so many children bring to school with their lunch. One criticism of aseptic packaging is that it is nearly impossible to recycle, yet on almost every other count, aseptic packaging is environmentally preferable to the packaging alternatives. Not only do aseptic containers not require refrigeration to keep their contents from spoiling, but their manufacture requires less than one-10th the energy of making glass bottles.
>
> What is true for juice boxes is also true for other forms of synthetic packaging. The use of polystyrene, which is commonly (and mistakenly) referred to as "Styrofoam," can reduce food waste dramatically due to its insulating properties. (Thanks to these properties, polystyrene cups are much preferred over paper for that morning cup of coffee.) Polystyrene also requires significantly fewer resources to produce than its paper counterpart.

Transitions between blocks of text   In long essays, you will need to alert readers to connections between blocks of text that are more than one paragraph long. You can do this by inserting transitional sentences or short paragraphs at key points in the essay. Here, for example, is a transitional paragraph from a student research paper. It announces that the first part of the paper has come to a close and the second part is about to begin.

> Although the great apes have demonstrated significant language skills, one central question remains: Can they be taught to use that uniquely human language tool we call grammar, to learn the difference, for instance, between "ape bite human" and "human bite ape"? In other words, can an ape create a sentence?

Another strategy to help readers move from one block of text to another is to insert headings in your essay. Headings, which usually sit above blocks of text, allow you to announce a new topic boldly, without the need for subtle transitions. (See 58b.)

3e If necessary, adjust paragraph length.

Most readers feel comfortable reading paragraphs that range between one hundred and two hundred words. Shorter paragraphs require too much starting and stopping, and longer ones strain readers' attention span. There are exceptions to this guideline, however. Paragraphs longer than two hundred words frequently appear in scholarly writing, where scholars explore complex ideas. Paragraphs shorter than one hundred words occur in newspapers because of narrow columns; in informal essays to quicken the pace; and in business writing and Web sites, where readers routinely skim for main ideas.

In an essay, the first and last paragraphs will ordinarily be the introduction and the conclusion. These special-purpose paragraphs are likely to be shorter than the paragraphs in the body of the essay. Typically, the body paragraphs will follow the essay's outline: one paragraph per point in short essays, several paragraphs per point in longer ones. Some ideas require more development than others, however, so it is best to be flexible. If an idea stretches to a length unreasonable for a paragraph, you should divide the paragraph, even if you have presented comparable points in the essay in single paragraphs.

Paragraph breaks are not always made for strictly logical reasons. Writers use them for the following reasons as well.

REASONS FOR BEGINNING A NEW PARAGRAPH

- to mark off the introduction and the conclusion
- to signal a shift to a new idea
- to indicate an important shift in time or place
- to emphasize a point (by placing it at the beginning or the end, not in the middle, of a paragraph)
- to highlight a contrast
- to signal a change of speakers (in dialogue)
- to provide readers with a needed pause
- to break up text that looks too dense

Beware of using too many short, choppy paragraphs, however. Readers want to see how your ideas connect, and they become irritated when you break their momentum by forcing them to pause every few sentences. Here are some reasons you might have for combining some of the paragraphs in a rough draft.

REASONS FOR COMBINING PARAGRAPHS

- to clarify the essay's organization
- to connect closely related ideas
- to bind together text that looks too choppy

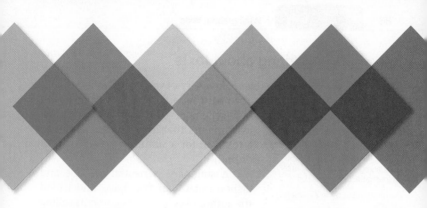

Part II
Academic Writing

4 Writing about texts

The word *texts* can refer to a variety of works, including essays, periodical articles, government reports, books, Web sites, and even visuals such as advertisements and photographs. Most assignments that ask you to respond to a text call for a summary or an analysis or both.

A summary is neutral in tone and demonstrates that you have understood the author's key ideas. Assignments calling for an analysis of a text vary widely, but they usually ask you to look at how the text's parts contribute to its central argument or purpose, often with the aim of judging its evidence or overall effect.

When you write about a written text, you will need to read it several times to digest its full meaning. Two techniques will help you move beyond a superficial first reading: (1) annotating the text with your observations and questions and (2) outlining the text's key points. The same techniques will help you analyze visual texts.

> **Making the most of your handbook**
>
> Knowing the expectations for a writing assignment is a key first step in drafting.
>
> ▶ Understanding an assignment: page 9

4a Read actively: Annotate the text.

Read actively by jotting down your questions and thoughts in the margins of the text or visual or in a notebook. When you annotate a text as you read, you are engaging with the work, not just letting the words slip past you. Use a pencil instead of a highlighter; with a pencil you can underline key concepts, mark points, or circle elements that intrigue you. If you change your mind, you can erase your early annotations and replace them with new ones. (See the chart on the following page for advice about active reading.)

On pages 88 and 89 are an article from a consumer-oriented newsletter and a magazine advertisement, both annotated by students. The students, Emilia Sanchez and Albert Lee, were assigned to write both a summary and an analysis. Each began by annotating the text.

Guidelines for active reading

Familiarize yourself with the basic features and structure of a text.

- What kind of text are you reading? An essay? An editorial? A scholarly article? An advertisement? A photograph?
- What is the author's purpose? To inform? To persuade? To call to action?
- Who is the audience? How does the author appeal to the audience?
- What is the author's thesis? What question does the text attempt to answer?
- What evidence does the author provide to support the thesis?

Note details that surprise, puzzle, or intrigue you.

- Has the author revealed a fact or made a point that runs counter to your assumptions? What exactly is surprising?
- Has the author made a generalization you disagree with? Can you think of evidence that would challenge the generalization?
- Are there any contradictions or inconsistencies in the text?
- Does the text contain words, statements, or phrases that you don't understand? If so, what reference materials could you consult?

Read and reread to discover meaning.

- What do you notice on a second or third reading that you didn't notice earlier?
- Does the text raise questions that it does not resolve?
- If you could address the author directly, what questions would you pose? Where do you agree and disagree with the author? Why?

Apply critical thinking strategies to visual texts.

- What first strikes you about the visual text? What elements do you notice immediately?
- Who or what is the main subject of the visual text?
- What colors and textures dominate?
- What is in the background? In the foreground?
- What role, if any, do words play in the visual text?

ANNOTATED ARTICLE

Big Box Stores Are Bad for Main Street

BETSY TAYLOR

[margin note: pening rategy— he problem not x, it's y.]

There is plenty of reason to be concerned about the proliferation of Wal-Marts and other so-called "big box" stores. The question, however, is not whether or not these types of stores create jobs (although several studies claim they produce a net job loss in local communities) or whether they ultimately save consumers money. The real concern about having a 25-acre slab of concrete with a 100,000 square foot box of stuff land on a town is whether it's good for a community's soul.

[margin note: entimental— hat is a ommunity's oul?]

[margin note: umps all big oxes together.]

The worst thing about "big boxes" is that they have a tendency to produce Ross Perot's famous "big sucking sound"—sucking the life out of cities and small towns across the country. On the other hand, small businesses are great for a community. They offer more personal service; they won't threaten to pack up and leave town if they don't get tax breaks, free roads and other blandishments; and small-business owners are much more responsive to a customer's needs. (Ever try to complain about bad service or poor quality products to the president of Home Depot?)

[margin note: ssumes ll small usinesses re attentive.]

[margin note: ogic problem? Vhy couldn't ustomer complain to store nanager?]

Yet, if big boxes are so bad, why are they so successful? One glaring reason is that we've become a nation of hyper-consumers, and the big-box boys know this. Downtown shopping districts comprised of small businesses take some of the efficiency out of overconsumption. There's all that hassle of having to travel from store to store, and having to pull out your credit card so many times. Occasionally, we even find ourselves chatting with the shopkeeper, wandering into a coffee shop to visit with a friend or otherwise wasting precious time that could be spent on acquiring more stuff.

[margin note: rue?]

[margin note: lostalgia for a ime that is ong gone or never was.]

But let's face it—bustling, thriving city centers are fun. They breathe life into a community. They allow cities and towns to stand out from each other. They provide an atmosphere for people to interact with each other that just cannot be found at Target, or Wal-Mart or Home Depot.

[margin note: Community vs. conomy. What about prices?]

Is it anti-American to be against having a retail giant set up shop in one's community? Some people would say so. On the other hand, if you board up Main Street, what's left of America?

[margin note: Ends with emotional appeal.]

ANNOTATED ADVERTISEMENT

What signals is
McDonald's giving
customers about its menu?

Is McDonald's trying
to remake its image
with lettuce?

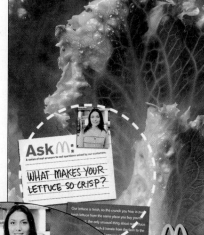

A real
customer?

Repetition
of "real."

Ask M:

A series of real answers to real questions asked by our customers.

WHAT MAKES YOUR
LETTUCE SO CRISP?

Our lettuce is fresh, so the crunch you hear is pure,
fresh lettuce from the same place you buy yours.
Simply put, the only unusual thing about our lettuce
is the speed at which it travels from the farm to the
restaurant. For more real answers to real questions,
give us a call at 1-877-623-3663 or write us at
mcdonalds.com.

Local vs.
corporation,
McDonald's
as family
restaurant.

Open, nothing
to hide.

Trying to show
its commitment to
customer service.

i'm lovin' it

4b Sketch a brief outline of the text.

After reading, rereading, and annotating a text, attempt to outline it. Seeing how the author has constructed a text can help you understand it. As you sketch an outline, pay special attention to the text's thesis (central idea) and its topic sentences. The thesis of a written text usually appears in the introduction, often in the first or second paragraph. Topic sentences often can be found at the beginning of body paragraphs, where they announce a shift to a new topic. (See 1e and 3a.)

In your outline, put the author's thesis and key points in your own words. Here, for example, is the outline that Emilia Sanchez developed as she prepared to write her summary and analysis of the text printed on page 88. Notice that the outline does not simply trace the author's ideas paragraph by paragraph; instead, it sums up the article's central points.

OUTLINE OF "BIG BOX STORES ARE BAD FOR MAIN STREET"

Thesis: Whether or not they take jobs away from a community or offer low prices to consumers, we should be worried about "big-box" stores like Wal-Mart, Target, and Home Depot because they harm communities by taking the life out of downtown shopping districts.

I. Small businesses are better for cities and towns than big-box stores are.
   A. Small businesses offer personal service, and big-box stores do not.
   B. Small businesses don't make demands on community resources as big-box stores do.
   C. Small businesses respond to customer concerns, and big-box stores do not.

II. Big-box stores are successful because they cater to consumption at the expense of benefits to the community.
   A. Buying everything in one place is convenient.
   B. Shopping at small businesses may be inefficient, but it provides opportunities for socializing.
   C. Downtown shopping districts give each city or town a special identity.

Conclusion: Although some people say that it's anti-American to oppose big-box stores, actually these stores threaten the communities that make up America by encouraging buying at the expense of the traditional interactions of Main Street.

A visual often doesn't state an explicit thesis or an explicit line of reasoning. Instead, you must sometimes infer the meaning beneath the image's surface and interpret its central point and supporting ideas from the elements of its design. One way to outline a visual text is to try to define its purpose and sketch a list of its key elements. Here, for example, are the key features that Albert Lee identified for the advertisement printed on page 89.

OUTLINE OF MCDONALD'S ADVERTISEMENT

Purpose: To persuade readers that McDonald's is concerned about its customers' health.

Key features:
- A close-up of a fresh, green lettuce leaf makes up the entire background.
- Near the center is a comment card with a handwritten question from a "real" McDonald's customer: "What makes your lettuce so crisp?"
- A photograph of a smiling woman is clipped to the card.
- Beneath the comment card is the company's response, which emphasizes the farm-fresh quality and purity of its vegetables and urges customers to ask other candid questions.
- At the bottom of the ad is the McDonald's slogan "I'm lovin' it."

4c Summarize to demonstrate your understanding.

Your goal in summarizing a text is to state the work's main ideas and key points simply, briefly, and accurately in your own words. If you have sketched a brief outline of the text (see 4b), refer to it as you draft your summary.

Summarizing a written text

To summarize a written text, first find the author's central idea—the thesis. Then divide the whole piece into a few major and perhaps minor ideas. Since a summary must be fairly short, you must make judgments about what is most important. Following is Emilia Sanchez's summary of the article that is printed on page 88.

Making the most of your handbook

Knowing how to summarize a source is a key research skill.

▶ Using summaries in researched writing: 48c

In her essay "Big Box Stores Are Bad for Main Street," Betsy Taylor argues that chain stores harm communities by taking the life out of downtown shopping districts. Explaining that a community's "soul" is more important than low prices or consumer convenience, she argues that small businesses are better than stores like Wal-Mart, Target, and Home Depot because they emphasize personal interactions and don't place demands on a community's resources. Taylor asserts that big-box stores are successful because "we've become a nation of hyper-consumers" (1011), although the convenience of shopping in these stores comes at the expense of benefits to the community. She concludes by suggesting that it's not "anti-American" to oppose big-box stores because the damage they inflict on downtown shopping districts extends to America itself.

Summarizing a visual text

To summarize a visual text, begin with essential information such as who created the visual, who the intended audience is, where the visual appeared, and when it was created. Then, in a few sentences, explain the visual's main point or purpose and describe the image by pointing to its key features.

Following is Albert Lee's summary of the McDonald's advertisement printed on page 89.

An advertisement for McDonald's in the July-August 2004 issue of *Men's Health* magazine represents an attempt by the restaurant chain to remake its image. The implicit reason for the ad is that McDonald's world-famous fast food has come under increasingly harsh attack for

Guidelines for writing a summary

- In the first sentence, mention the title of the text, the name of the author, and the author's thesis or the visual's central point.
- Maintain a neutral tone; be objective.
- Use the third-person point of view and the present tense: *Taylor argues*. . . .
- Keep your focus on the text. Don't state the author's ideas as if they were your own.
- Put all or most of your summary in your own words; if you borrow a phrase or a sentence from the text, put it in quotation marks and give the page number in parentheses.
- Limit yourself to presenting the text's key points.
- Be concise; make every word count.

unhealthful processing and preparation. The fresh, spring-green lettuce that dominates this ad is a signal to customers that McDonald's has changed its menu and now offers food as fresh and healthful as any found in a supermarket. By publicizing this new direction, McDonald's clearly hopes to attract health-conscious customers. Moreover, by framing this advertisement as a response to an individual customer's question, McDonald's attempts to show that the vast size of the chain does not prevent it from tending personally to its customers' concerns.

4d Analyze to demonstrate your critical thinking.

When you analyze, you separate the whole to study the parts. Whereas a summary most often answers the question of *what* a text says, an analysis looks at *how* a text makes its point. When an assignment calls for an analysis, read the whole

Making the most of your handbook

Writing about a text often requires you to quote directly from the text.

▶ Guidelines for using quotation marks: 48c

Making the most of your handbook

When you analyze a text, you weave words and ideas from the source into your own writing.

▶ Quoting or paraphrasing: 51 (MLA), 56b (APA), 57b (*Chicago*)

▶ Using signal phrases: 52b (MLA), 56c (APA), 57c (*Chicago*)

▶ Using details for support: 50c (MLA), 56a (APA), 57a (*Chicago*)

▶ Analyzing literature: 55

assignment carefully, along with any models provided, to see what your instructor expects.

Typically, an analysis takes the form of an essay that makes its own argument about a text. Include an introduction that briefly summarizes the text, a thesis that states your own judgment about the text, and body paragraphs that support your thesis with evidence. If you are analyzing a visual, examine it as a whole and then reflect on how the individual elements contribute to its overall meaning. If you have written a summary of the text or visual, you may find it useful to refer to the main points of the summary as you write your analysis.

Within your body paragraphs, include and interpret individual passages from the text to help support your overall analysis of the text. The following steps can help you do this:

1. In a topic sentence, include a claim about the author's text.

2. Use a signal phrase to introduce exact language or ideas from the text. Place any exact language in quotation marks.

3. Follow the quotation or ideas with your interpretation. To interpret the text, you may explain its significance, define one of its important terms, or point out what the author is assuming or implying in the passage.

4. Provide a transition to the claim in your next paragraph. (See 3d.)

Using interpretation in an analysis

In her paper analyzing the article by Betsy Taylor that appears on page 88, student writer Emilia Sanchez begins by

Guidelines for analyzing a text

Written texts

Instructors who ask you to analyze an essay or an article often expect you to address some of the following questions.

- What is the author's thesis or central idea? Who is the audience?
- What questions does the author address (implicitly or explicitly)?
- How does the author structure the text? What are the key parts, and how do they relate to one another and to the thesis?
- What strategies has the author used to generate interest in the argument and to persuade readers of its merit?
- What evidence does the author use to support the thesis? How persuasive is the evidence (5e)?
- Does the author anticipate objections and counter opposing views (see 6c)?
- Does the author fall prey to any faulty reasoning (see 6a)?

Visual texts

If you are analyzing a visual text, the following additional questions will help you evaluate an image's purpose and meaning.

- What surprises, perplexes, or intrigues you about the image?
- What clues suggest the visual text's intended audience? How does the image appeal to its audience?
- If the text is an advertisement, what product is it selling? Does it attempt to sell an idea or a message as well?
- If the visual text includes words, how do the words contribute to its meaning?
- How do design elements—colors, shapes, perspective, background, foreground—shape the visual text's meaning or serve its purpose?

Understanding the comment

When a teacher or tutor points out that you need to "summarize less, analyze more," the comment often signals that your readers want to hear your interpretation of a text, not a summary of the text itself.

> Growing up as a borderlander, I have always considered myself bilingual. Reading "How to Tame a Wild Tongue" by Gloria Anzaldúa made me rethink that label. In the *"El lenguaje de la frontera"* section of the essay, Anzaldúa explains the origins of Chicano Spanish, a "border tongue" (326). Then she says that most Chicanos actually speak as many as eight languages. Anzaldúa lists these languages and then tells which languages she speaks with which people in her life. For example, she speaks Tex-Mex with friends, Chicano Texas Spanish with her mother, and working-class English at school (327). Finally, she talks about her experience with speaking made-up languages.

Summarize less, analyze more

One student wrote this body paragraph in response to an assignment that asked students to analyze Gloria Anzaldúa's essay "How to Tame a Wild Tongue."

The student writer needs to go beyond summary to offer his insights about Anzaldúa's text. To revise this paragraph, the student might begin by underlining the verbs in his own sentences: *explains, says, lists, tells,* and *talks*. These sentences simply restate what Anzaldúa has written. Although the student needs a brief summary to help his readers understand the basis of his analysis, he should move quickly to exploring the meaning of Anzaldúa's text. In his analysis, the student might ask questions about Anzaldúa's strategies. For instance, why does she combine Spanish with English? Or why does she list the eight separate languages that most Chicanos speak?

Similar comments: too much summary • show, don't tell • go deeper

Revising when *you* need to summarize less and analyze more

1. *Reread your paragraph* and highlight the sentences that summarize. Then, in a different color, highlight the sentences that contain your analysis.

(Think about the differences between summary and analysis: Summary answers the question of *what* a text says; analysis offers a judgment or interpretation of the text.)

2. *Reread the text* (or passages of the text) that you are analyzing, paying attention to the language and structure of the text.

3. *Ask questions.* What strategies does the author use? How do these strategies convey the meaning of the text? What insights can you convey to your readers about the text? How can you deepen your readers' understanding of the text?

More advice on analyzing a text: **4d** and **55b**

summarizing Taylor's argument. She then states her own thesis, or claim, which offers her judgment of Taylor's article, and begins her analysis. In her first body paragraph, Sanchez interprets Taylor's use of language.

Topic sentence includes Sanchez's claim.

Quoted material shows the author's language in quotation marks.

Transition to Sanchez's next point.

Taylor's use of colorful language reveals that she has a nostalgic view of American society and does not understand economic realities. In her first paragraph, Taylor refers to a big-box store as a "25-acre slab of concrete with a 100,000 square foot box of stuff" that "land[s] on a town," evoking images of a powerful monster crushing the American way of life (1011). But she oversimplifies a complex issue. Taylor does not consider. . . .

Signal phrase introduces a quotation from the text.

Quotation is followed by Sanchez's interpretation of the author's language.

4e Sample student essay: Analysis of an article

Following is Emilia Sanchez's complete essay. Sanchez used Modern Language Association (MLA) style to format her paper and cite the source.

97

Sanchez 1

Emilia Sanchez

Professor Goodwin

English 10

23 October 2009

Rethinking Big-Box Stores

Opening briefly summarizes the article's purpose and thesis.

In her essay "Big Box Stores Are Bad for Main Street," Betsy Taylor focuses not on the economic effects of large chain stores but on the effects these stores have on the "soul" of America. She argues that stores like Home Depot, Target, and Wal-Mart are bad for America because they draw people out of downtown shopping districts and cause them to focus on consumption. In contrast, she believes that small businesses are good for America because they provide personal attention, encourage community interaction, and make each city

Sanchez begins to analyze Taylor's argument.

unique. But Taylor's argument is unconvincing because it is based on nostalgia—on idealized images of a quaint Main Street—rather than on the roles that businesses play in consumers' lives and communities.

Thesis expresses Sanchez's judgment of Taylor's article.

By ignoring the complex economic relationship between large chain stores and their communities, Taylor incorrectly assumes that simply getting rid of big-box stores would have a positive effect on America's communities.

Taylor's use of colorful language reveals that she has a nostalgic view of American society and does not understand economic realities.

Signal phrase introduces quotations from the source; Sanchez uses an MLA in-text citation.

In her first paragraph, Taylor refers to a big-box store as a "25-acre slab of concrete with a 100,000 square foot box of stuff" that "land[s] on a town," evoking images of a powerful monster crushing the American way of life (1011). But she oversimplifies a complex issue. Taylor does not consider that many downtown business districts failed

Sanchez begins to identify and challenge Taylor's assumptions.

long before chain stores moved in, when factories and mills closed and workers lost their jobs. In cities with struggling economies, big-box

Marginal annotations indicate MLA-style formatting and effective writing.

Sanchez 2

stores can actually provide much-needed jobs. Similarly, while Taylor blames big-box stores for harming local economies by asking for tax breaks, free roads, and other perks, she doesn't acknowledge that these stores also enter into economic partnerships with the surrounding communities by offering financial benefits to schools and hospitals.

Transition to another point in Sanchez's analysis.

Taylor's assumption that shopping in small businesses is always better for the customer also seems driven by nostalgia for an old-fashioned Main Street rather than by the facts. While she may be right that many small businesses offer personal service and are responsive to customer complaints, she does not consider that many customers appreciate the service at big-box stores. Just as customer service is better at some small businesses than at others, it is impossible to generalize about service at all big-box stores. For example, customers depend on the lenient return policies and the wide variety of products at stores like Target and Home Depot.

Clear topic sentence announces a shift to a new topic.

Sanchez refutes Taylor's claim.

Taylor blames big-box stores for encouraging American "hyper-consumerism," but she oversimplifies by equating big-box stores with bad values and small businesses with good values. Like her other points, this claim ignores the economic and social realities of American society today. Big-box stores do not force Americans to buy more. By offering lower prices in a convenient setting, however, they allow consumers to save time and purchase goods they might not be able to afford from small businesses. The existence of more small businesses would not change what most Americans can afford, nor would it reduce their desire to buy affordable merchandise.

Taylor may be right that some big-box stores have a negative impact on communities and that small businesses offer certain advantages. But she ignores the economic conditions that support big-box stores as well as the fact that Main Street was in decline before

Sanchez treats the author fairly.

Sanchez 3

Conclusion returns to the thesis and shows the wider significance of Sanchez's analysis.

the big-box store arrived. Getting rid of big-box stores will not bring back a simpler America populated by thriving, unique Main Streets; in reality, Main Street will not survive if consumers cannot afford to shop there.

Sanchez 4

Work Cited

Work cited page is in MLA style.

Taylor, Betsy. "Big Box Stores Are Bad for Main Street." *CQ Researcher* 9.44 (1999): 1011. Print.

4f Sample student essay: Analysis of an advertisement

On the following pages is Albert Lee's analysis of the McDonald's ad that appears on page 89.

Lee 1

Albert Lee

Professor McIntosh

English 101

4 November 2009

The Golden Arches Go Green: McDonald's and Real Lettuce

Dominating a McDonald's advertisement in the July-August 2004 issue of *Men's Health* magazine is a highly magnified head of lettuce, the centerpiece of a healthful menu that McDonald's was promoting. The lettuce looms over the ad's two other elements, a comment card from a smiling female customer with a question about lettuce and a friendly note in reply from McDonald's. For a restaurant chain known for its supersized meals of Double Quarter Pounders with Cheese, the close-up of a lettuce leaf might come as a surprise. A superficial interpretation of the McDonald's ad would point out that the fast-food giant is attempting to remake its image into a health-conscious restaurant. After all, the greening of the Golden Arches follows a shift in public attitudes toward diet and a sometimes environmentally unfriendly food industry.

Less obvious are the associations that the ad creates to persuade people that McDonald's is committed to a product—an entire experience—not usually offered by fast-food restaurants. If fast food has become synonymous in many consumers' minds with the impersonal and artificial conditions of modern life—from assembly-line food to robotic exchanges at the counter or drive-through window—then the McDonald's ad seeks to replace those associations with images of authenticity and familiarity.

The ad's underlying message emphasizes for viewers the real over the artificial, a quality in both McDonald's food and its relationship with its customers. Through vivid graphics McDonald's shows, rather than tells, viewers that its ingredients are wholesome. The head of lettuce

Lee briefly summarizes the content of the ad.

Lee suggests a simple interpretation to highlight his more compelling interpretation.

Lee's thesis offers his analysis of the ad's message.

Marginal annotations indicate MLA-style formatting and effective writing.

Lee 2

Lee describes the dominant image in the visual text.

that creates the ad's entire background is the picture of mouthwatering wholesomeness. Enlarged to many times its natural size, the lettuce reveals its sharp, spring-green edges and beads of water standing on its leaves, presumably from recent washing. The fast-food chain could have bombarded the public with nutritional statistics about its food items, as many other restaurants do, but it seems to recognize that numbers can begin to read like cold data from a science textbook. Instead, McDonald's invites us to take a closer look at its ingredients, a chance to verify for ourselves that the lettuce is as "pure" and "fresh" as it claims. The lettuce does in fact look "so crisp" that we can easily believe it would produce a "crunch" if we bit into it, just as McDonald's reports.

Lee quotes words from the text.

Clear topic sentence announces a shift to a new topic.

The ad's copy suggests that McDonald's wishes to convince viewers that its commitment to serving customers' needs is as genuine as its lettuce. The prominent repetition of the word *real* in the tagline expresses McDonald's policy of plain dealing with individual customers. The picture of a supposedly real customer, a paper clip holding her photograph, and the ragged left edge of the comment card all contribute to a sense that this exchange between customer and McDonald's is as real, as "pure," as McDonald's claims its lettuce is.

Lee analyzes the ad's language.

Indeed, the heading to the comment card, "Ask M," gives McDonald's a personal identity, which intensifies the impression of the company's accessibility. "Ask M" conjures up the image of a straight-shooting, small-town newspaper advice columnist. McDonald's lettuce, "M" says, comes "from the same place you buy yours." This comparison with the neighborhood market emphasizes the local presence of the restaurant by association. The lettuce we eat at McDonald's, the ad suggests, is in fact the very same we would feel confident putting on our family's plate at home. The opening phrase of the second sentence, "Simply put," is a signal that McDonald's earnestly desires to explain its operations to its

Lee 3

customers. As with the close-up of the lettuce, the wording suggests that the company has nothing to hide.

It might be difficult to imagine that people will be persuaded to abandon their local markets for McDonald's. But then again, we cannot easily forget the ad's image of lettuce, its curling, serrated edges and finely branched veins, enlarged to a slightly unsettling size. And if this green image conjures up in our minds a golden "M"—a place where we can reconnect with real people and the bounty of the land—then maybe one of the most successful companies in history has done it again.

Lee concludes with his interpretation of the ad's overall effect.

Lee 4

Work Cited

McDonald's Corporation. Advertisement. *Men's Health* July-
     Aug. 2004: 95. Print.

Work cited page is in MLA style.

5 Constructing reasonable arguments

In writing an argument, you take a stand on a debatable issue. The question being debated might be a matter of public policy:

> Should religious groups be allowed to meet on public school property?
>
> What is the least dangerous way to dispose of hazardous waste?
>
> Should a state require its citizens to have health insurance?

On such questions, reasonable people may disagree.

Reasonable men and women also disagree about many scholarly issues. Psychologists debate the role of genes and environment in determining behavior; historians interpret the causes of the Civil War quite differently; biologists challenge one another's predictions about the effects of global warming.

When you construct a *reasonable* argument, your goal is not simply to win or to have the last word. Your aim is to explain your understanding of the truth about a subject or to propose the best solution available for solving a problem—without being needlessly combative. In constructing your argument, you join a conversation with other writers and readers. Your aim is to convince readers to reconsider their opinions by offering new reasons to question an old viewpoint.

5a Examine your issue's social and intellectual contexts.

Arguments appear in social and intellectual contexts. Public policy debates obviously arise in social contexts, conducted among groups with competing values and interests. For example, the debate over offshore oil drilling has been renewed in the United States in light of skyrocketing energy costs

Academic English   Some cultures value writers who argue with force; other cultures value writers who argue subtly or indirectly. Academic audiences in the United States will expect your writing to be assertive and confident—neither aggressive nor passive. You can create an assertive tone by acknowledging different opinions and supporting your view with specific evidence.

TOO AGGRESSIVE   Of course prayer should be discouraged in public schools. Only foolish people think that organized prayer is good for everyone.

TOO PASSIVE   I might be wrong, but I think that organized prayer should be discouraged in public schools.

ASSERTIVE TONE   Organized prayer should be discouraged in public schools because it violates the religious freedom guaranteed by the First Amendment.

If you are uncertain about the tone of your work, ask for help at your school's writing center.

and terrorism concerns—with environmentalists, policymakers, and consumers all weighing in on the argument. Most public policy debates also have intellectual dimensions that address scientific or theoretical questions. In the case of the

Making the most of your handbook

Supporting your claims with evidence from sources can make your argument more effective.

▶ Conducting research: 46

drilling issue, geologists, oceanographers, and economists all contribute their expertise.

Scholarly debates clearly play themselves out in intellectual contexts, but they have a social dimension too. Scholars respond to the contributions of other specialists in the field, often building on others' views and refining them, but at times challenging them.

Because many of your readers will be aware of the social and intellectual contexts in which your issue is grounded, you will be at a serious disadvantage if you are not informed. That's why it is a good idea to conduct some research before preparing your argument; consulting even a few sources can help. For example, the student whose paper appears on pages 115–18 became more knowledgeable about his issue—the ethics of performance-enhancing procedures in sports—after consulting several brief sources.

5b View your audience as a panel of jurors.

Do not assume that your audience already agrees with you; instead, envision skeptical readers who, like a panel of jurors, will make up their minds after listening to all sides of the argument. If you are arguing a public policy issue, aim your paper at readers who represent a variety of opinions. In the case of the debate over offshore drilling, for example, imagine a jury representative of those who have a stake in the matter: environmentalists, policymakers, and consumers.

> **Making the most of your handbook**
>
> You may need to consider a specific audience for your argument.
>
> ▶ Analyzing your audience: 1a
>
> ▶ Writing in a particular discipline, such as business or psychology: 7

At times, you can deliberately narrow your audience. If you are working within a word limit, for example, you might not have the space in which to address all the concerns surrounding the offshore drilling debate. Or you might be primarily interested in reaching one segment of a general audience, such as consumers. In such instances, you can still view your audience as a panel of jurors; the jury will simply be a less diverse group.

In the case of scholarly debates, you will be addressing readers who share your interest in a discipline such as literature or psychology. Such readers belong to a group with an agreed-upon way of investigating and talking about issues. Though they generally agree about procedures, scholars in an academic discipline often disagree about particular issues. Once you see how they disagree about your issue, you should be able to imagine a jury that reflects the variety of opinions they hold.

5c In your introduction, establish credibility and state your position.

When you are constructing an argument, make sure your introduction contains a thesis sentence that states your position on the issue you have chosen to debate. In the sentences leading up to the thesis, establish your credibility with readers by showing that you are knowledgeable and fair-minded. If possible, build common ground with readers who may not at first agree with your views, and show them why they should consider your thesis.

> **Making the most of your handbook**
>
> When you write an argument, you state your position in a thesis.
>
> ▶ Writing effective thesis statements: 1c, 1e

In the following introduction, student Kevin Smith presents himself as someone worth listening to. Because Smith introduces both sides of the debate, readers are likely to approach his essay with an open mind.

Writer is fair-minded, presenting the views of both sides.

Although the Supreme Court has ruled against prayer in public schools on First Amendment grounds, many people still feel that prayer should be allowed. Such people value prayer as a practice central to their faith and believe that prayer is a way for schools to reinforce moral principles. They also compellingly point out a paradox in the First Amendment itself: at what point does the separation of church and state restrict the freedom of those who wish to practice their religion? What proponents of school prayer fail to realize, however, is that the Supreme Court's decision, although it was made on legal grounds, makes sense on religious grounds as well. Prayer is too important to be trusted to our public schools.   —Kevin Smith, student

Smith shows that he is familiar with the legal issues surrounding school prayer.

Smith's thesis builds common ground.

TIP: A good way to test a thesis while drafting and revising is to imagine a counterargument to your argument (see 5f). If you can't think of an opposing point of view, rethink your thesis or ask a classmate to respond to your argument.

5d Back up your thesis with persuasive lines of argument.

Arguments of any complexity contain lines of argument that, when taken together, might reasonably persuade readers that the thesis has merit. The following, for example, are the main lines of argument that Jamal Hammond used in his paper on performance-enhancing practices in sports (see pp. 115–18).

CENTRAL CLAIM	Thesis: Athletes who use any type of biotechnology give themselves an unfair advantage and disrupt the sense of fair play, and they should be banned from competition.
SUPPORTING CLAIMS	• Athletic achievement nowadays increasingly results from biological and high-tech intervention rather than strictly from hard work.
	• There is a difference between the use of state-of-the-art equipment and the modification of the body itself.
	• If the rules that guarantee an even playing field are violated, competitors and spectators alike are deprived of a sound basis of comparison on which to judge athletic effort and accomplishment.
	• If we let athletes alter their bodies through biotechnology, we might as well dispense with the human element altogether.

If you sum up your main lines of argument, as Hammond did, you will have a rough outline of your essay. In your paper, you will provide evidence for each of these claims.

5e Support your claims with specific evidence.

You will need to support your central claim and any subordinate claims with evidence: facts, statistics, examples and illustrations, expert opinion, and so on. Most debatable topics require that you consult some written sources. As you read through the sources, you will learn more about the arguments and counter-arguments at the center of your debate.

Remember that you must document your sources. Documentation gives credit to the authors and shows readers how to locate a source in case they want to assess its credibility or explore the issue further.

Using facts and statistics

A fact is something that is known with certainty because it has been objectively verified: The capital of Wyoming is Cheyenne. Carbon has an atomic weight of 12. John F. Kennedy was assassinated on November 22, 1963. Statistics are collections of numerical facts: Alcohol abuse is a factor in nearly 40 percent of traffic fatalities. More than four in ten businesses in the United States are owned by women. As of 2007, more than 50 percent of US households owned a digital television.

> **Making the most of your handbook**
>
> Sources, when used responsibly, can provide evidence to support an argument.
>
> ▶ Paraphrasing, summarizing, and quoting sources: 48c
>
> ▶ Punctuating direct quotations: 37a
>
> ▶ Citing sources: 51 (MLA), 56b (APA), 57b (*Chicago*)

Most arguments are supported at least to some extent by facts and statistics. For example, in the following passage the writer uses statistics to show that college students carry unreasonably high credit card debt.

> A 2001 study by Nellie Mae revealed that while the average credit card debt per college undergraduate is $2,327, more than 20% of undergraduates who have at least one credit card maintain a much higher debt level, from $3,000 to $7,000 (Barrett).

Writers often use statistics in selective ways to bolster their own views. If you suspect that a writer's handling of statistics is not quite fair, read authors with opposing views, who may give you a fuller understanding of the numbers, or track down the original sources for those statistics.

Using examples and illustrations

Examples and illustrations (extended examples, often in story form) rarely prove a point by themselves, but when used in combination with other forms of evidence they flesh out an argument and bring it to life. Because they often have an emotional dimension, they can reach readers in ways that statistics cannot.

Understanding the comment

When a teacher or tutor suggests that you "develop more," the comment often signals that you stopped short of providing a full and detailed discussion of your idea.

> Distancing ourselves from our family is a natural part of growing up. There are many ways in which we try doing so. For essayist Richard Rodriguez, it was his drive for academic success that separated him from his parents and his past (195). In his desire to become educated, he (removed himself) from his family and (distanced himself) from his culture. In his essay "The Achievement of Desire," he admits regretting the separation from his family and acknowledges the particular challenges of growing up between two cultures.

Develop more

In this body paragraph, a student responded to an assignment that asked her to explore one theme in Richard Rodriguez's essay "The Achievement of Desire."

The student has not included enough evidence or developed a thorough analysis of that evidence. To revise, she might look for specific examples and details from Rodriguez's essay to support her claim that Rodriguez "removed . . . and distanced himself" from his family. Then she might develop the claim by analyzing *how* and *why* Rodriguez's "desire to become educated" removed him from his family.

Similar comments: undeveloped • give examples • explain • expand

Revising when *you* need to develop more

1. *Read your paragraph to a peer or a tutor* and ask specific questions: What more is needed? More evidence? If so, what kind of evidence — specific examples, vivid details, statistics, or facts? Or more analysis? If so, how might you explain the meaning of the evidence you provide?

2. *Keep your purpose in mind.* You aren't being asked to restate what you've already written or what the author has written.

3. *Consider including more evidence* from the text and a more thorough exploration of why or how your evidence supports your claims.

More advice on using specific evidence: **5e**

110

In a paper arguing that any athletes who use gene therapy should be banned from competition, Jamal Hammond gives a thought-provoking example of how running with genetically modified limbs is no different from riding a motorcycle in a footrace.

Citing expert opinion

Although they are no substitute for careful reasoning of your own, the views of an expert can contribute to the force of your argument. For example, to help him make the case that biotechnology could degrade the meaning of sports, Jamal Hammond quotes the remarks of an expert.

> Thomas Murray, chair of the ethics advisory panel for the World Anti-Doping Agency, says he hopes, not too optimistically, for an "alternative future . . . where we still find meaning in great performances as an alchemy of two factors, natural talents . . . and virtues" (qtd. in Jenkins D11).

When you rely on expert opinion, make sure that your source is an expert in the field you are writing about. In some cases, you may need to provide credentials showing why your source is worth listening to. When including expert testimony in your paper, you can summarize or paraphrase the expert's opinion or you can quote the expert's exact words. You will of course need to document the source, as Hammond did in the example just given.

5f Anticipate objections; counter opposing arguments.

Readers who already agree with you need no convincing, but indifferent or skeptical readers may resist your arguments. To be willing to give up a position that seems reasonable, a reader has to see that there is an even more reasonable one. In addition to presenting your own case, therefore, you should review the opposing arguments and attempt to counter them.

It might seem at first that drawing attention to an opposing point of view or contradictory evidence would weaken your argument. But by anticipating and countering objections to your argument, you show yourself as a reasonable and well-informed writer. You also establish your purpose, demonstrate the significance of the issue you are debating, and ultimately strengthen your argument.

There is no best place in an essay to deal with opposing views. Often it is useful to summarize the opposing position early in your essay. After stating your thesis but before developing your own arguments, you might have a paragraph that takes up the most important counterargument. Or you can anticipate objections paragraph by paragraph as you develop your case. Wherever you decide to deal with opposing arguments,

Anticipating and countering objections

To anticipate a possible objection, consider the following questions:

- Could a reasonable person draw a different conclusion from your facts or examples?
- Might a reader question any of your assumptions?
- Could a reader offer an alternative explanation of this issue?
- Is there any evidence that might weaken your position?

The following questions may help you respond to a potential objection:

- Can you concede the point to the opposition but challenge the point's importance or usefulness?
- Can you explain why readers should consider a new perspective or question a piece of evidence?
- Should you explain your position in light of contradictory evidence?
- Can you suggest a different interpretation of the evidence?

When you write, use phrasing to signal to readers that you're about to present an objection. Often the signal phrase can go in the lead sentence of a paragraph:

Critics of this view argue that. . . .

Some readers might point out that. . . .

But isn't it possible that . . . ?

Understanding the comment

When a teacher or tutor suggests that you "consider opposing viewpoints," the comment often signals that you need to recognize and respond to possible objections to your argument.

> For many American workers, drug testing is a routine part of their working life. In her book *Nickel and Dimed*, Barbara Ehrenreich observes how random drug testing leads to a hostile work environment (128). In addition, researchers Shepard and Clifton have found that companies using drug-testing programs are likelier to have lower productivity levels than those that have not adopted such practices (1). Drug testing in the workplace has shown no benefits for employers or employees.

consider opposing viewpoints

In response to an assignment about changes in the workplace, one student wrote this body paragraph.

The student jumps to a conclusion too quickly without recognizing any opposing points of view. To revise, the student might begin by reading two or more sources to gain a different perspective and to learn more about the debate surrounding her topic. As she reads more sources, she might ask: What evidence do those in favor of drug testing provide to support their point of view? How would they respond to my conclusion against drug testing? By anticipating and countering opposing views, she will show herself as a fair and reasonable writer.

Similar comments: what about the other side? • counterargument?

Revising when *you* need to consider other points of view

1. *Read more* to learn about the debates surrounding the topic. Ask questions: Are there other sides to the issue? Would a reasonable person offer an alternative explanation for the evidence or provide counterevidence?

2. *Be open-minded.* Although it might seem counterintuitive to introduce opposing arguments, you'll show your knowledge of the topic by recognizing that not everyone draws the same conclusion.

3. *Try these (or similar) phrases* to introduce and counter objections: "Some readers might point out that . . ." or "Critics of this view argue that. . . ."

4. *Revise your thesis,* if necessary, to account for multiple points of view.

More advice on considering opposing viewpoints: **5f** and **6c**

113

do your best to explain the arguments of others accurately and fairly (see 6c).

5g Build common ground.

As you counter opposing arguments, try to seek out one or two assumptions you might share with readers who do not initially agree with your views. If you can show that you share their concerns, your readers will be more likely to acknowledge the validity of your argument. For example, to persuade people opposed to shooting deer, a state wildlife commission would have to show that it too cares about preserving deer and does not want them to die needlessly. Having established these values in common, the commission might be able to persuade critics that a carefully controlled hunting season is good for the deer population because reducing the total number of deer prevents starvation caused by overpopulation.

People believe that intelligence and decency support their side of an argument. To be persuaded, they must see these qualities in your argument. Otherwise they will persist in their opposition.

5h Sample argument paper

In the paper that begins on the following page, student Jamal Hammond argues that athletes who enhance their performance through biotechnology should be banned from athletic competition. Notice that he is careful to present opposing views fairly before providing his counterarguments.

In writing the paper, Hammond consulted three newspaper articles, two in print and one online. When he quotes or uses information from a source, he cites the source with an MLA (Modern Language Association) in-text citation. Citations in the paper refer readers to the list of works cited at the end of the paper. (See 53.)

hackerhandbooks.com/bedhandbook > Model papers
  > MLA argument papers: Hammond; Lund; Sanghvi
  > MLA papers: Orlov; Daly; Levi

Hammond 1

Jamal Hammond
Professor Paschal
English 102
19 March 2007

Performance Enhancement through Biotechnology

Has No Place in Sports

The debate over athletes' use of performance-enhancing
substances is getting more complicated as biotechnologies such as
gene therapy become a reality. The availability of these new methods
of boosting performance will force us to decide what we value most in
sports—displays of physical excellence developed through hard work
or victory at all costs. For centuries, spectators and athletes have
cherished the tradition of fairness in sports. While sports competition
is, of course, largely about winning, it is also about the means
by which a player or team wins. Athletes who use any type of
biotechnology give themselves an unfair advantage and disrupt the
sense of fair play, and they should be banned from competition.

Researchers are experimenting with techniques that could
manipulate an athlete's genetic code to build stronger muscles or
increase endurance. Searching for cures for diseases like Parkinson's
and muscular dystrophy, scientists at the University of Pennsylvania
have created "Schwarzenegger mice," rodents that grew larger-than-
normal muscles after receiving injections with a gene that stimulates
growth protein. The researchers also found that a combination of gene
manipulation and exercise led to a 35% increase in the strength of rats'
leg muscles (Lamb 13).

Such therapies are breakthroughs for humans suffering from
muscular diseases; for healthy athletes, they could mean new world
records in sports involving speed and endurance—but at what cost to

Opening sentences provide background for Hammond's thesis.

Thesis states the main point.

Hammond establishes his credibility by summarizing medical research.

Source is cited in MLA style.

Marginal annotations indicate MLA-style formatting and effective writing.

Hammond 2

Hammond uses specific evidence to support his thesis.

the integrity of athletic competition? The International Olympic Committee's World Anti-Doping Agency has become so alarmed about the possible effects of new gene technology on athletic competition that it has banned the use of gene therapies and urged researchers to devise a test for detecting genetic modification (Lamb 13).

Opposing views are presented fairly.

Some bioethicists argue that this next wave of performance enhancement is an acceptable and unavoidable feature of competition. As Dr. Andy Miah, who supports the regulated use of gene therapies in sports, claims, "The idea of the naturally perfect athlete is romantic nonsense. . . . An athlete achieves what he or she achieves through

"Qtd. in" is used for an indirect source: words quoted in another source.

all sorts of means—technology, sponsorship, support and so on" (qtd. in Rudebeck). Miah, in fact, sees athletes' imminent turn to genetic modification as "merely a continuation of the way sport works; it allows us to create more extraordinary performances" (qtd. in Rudebeck). Miah's approval of "extraordinary performances" as the goal of competition reflects our culture's tendency to demand and reward new heights

Hammond counters opposing arguments.

of athletic achievement. The problem is that achievement nowadays increasingly results from biological and high-tech intervention rather than strictly from hard work.

Better equipment, such as aerodynamic bicycles and fiberglass poles for pole vaulting, have made it possible for athletes to record achievements unthinkable a generation ago. But athletes themselves must put forth the physical effort of training and practice—they must still build

Hammond develops the thesis.

their skills (Jenkins D11). There is a difference between the use of state-of-the-art equipment and the modification of the body itself. Athletes who use medical technology, including drugs, to alter their bodies can bypass the hard work of training by taking on the powers of a machine. If they set new records this way, we lose the opportunity to witness sports as a spectacle of human effort and are left marveling at scientific advances, which have little relation to the athletic tradition of fair play.

Hammond 3

Such a tradition has long defined athletic competition. Sports rely on equal conditions to ensure fair play, from regulations that demand similar equipment to referees who evenhandedly apply the rules to all participants. If the rules that guarantee an even playing field are violated, competitors and spectators alike are deprived of a sound basis of comparison on which to judge athletic effort and accomplishment. When major league baseball rules call for solid-wood bats, the player who uses a corked bat enhances his hitting statistics at the expense of players who use regulation equipment. When Ben Johnson tested positive for steroids after setting a world record in the 100-meter dash in the 1988 Olympics, his "achievement" devalued the intense training that his competitors had undergone to prepare for the event. The International Olympic Committee responded by stripping Johnson of his medal and his world record. Likewise, athletes who use gene therapy to alter their bodies and enhance their performance will create an uneven playing field.

Transition moves from the writer's main argument to specific examples.

If we let athletes alter their bodies through biotechnology, we might as well dispense with the human element altogether. Instead of watching the 100-meter dash to see who the fastest runner in the world is, we might just as well watch the sprinters mount motorcycles and race across the finish line. The absurdity of such an example, however, points to the damage that we will do to sports if we allow these therapies. Thomas Murray, chair of the ethics advisory panel for the World Anti-Doping Agency, says he hopes, not too optimistically, for an "alternative future . . . where we still find meaning in great performances as an alchemy of two factors, natural talents . . . and virtues" (qtd. in Jenkins D11).

A vivid example helps the writer make his point.

Unless we are willing to organize separate sporting events and leagues—an Olympics, say, for athletes who have opted for a boost from

Conclusion echoes the thesis without dully repeating it.

Hammond 4

the test tube and another for athletes who have chosen to keep their
bodies natural—we should ask from our athletes that they dazzle us less
with extraordinary performance and more with the fruits of their hard work.

Hammond 5

Works Cited

Works cited page
uses MLA style.

Jenkins, Sally. "The First Item in a Pandora's Box of Moral
Ambiguities." *Washington Post* 4 Dec. 2004: D11. Print.

Lamb, Gregory M. "Will Gene-Altered Athletes Kill Sports?" *Christian
Science Monitor* 23 Aug. 2004: 12-13. Print.

Rudebeck, Clare. "The Eyes Have It." *Independent* [London]. Independent
News and Media, 27 Apr. 2005. Web. 1 Mar. 2007.

6 Evaluating arguments

In your reading and in your own writing, evaluate all arguments
for logic and fairness. Many arguments can stand up to critical
scrutiny. Often, however, a line of argument that at first seems
reasonable turns out to be illogical, unfair, or both.

6a Distinguish between reasonable and fallacious argumentative tactics.

A number of unreasonable argumentative tactics are known as
logical fallacies. Most of the fallacies—such as hasty generalizations and false analogies—are misguided or dishonest uses
of legitimate argumentative strategies. The examples in this
section suggest when such strategies are reasonable and when
they are not.

Generalizing (inductive reasoning)

Writers and thinkers generalize all the time. We look at a sample of data and conclude that data we have not observed will most likely conform to what we have seen. From a spoonful of soup, we conclude just how salty the whole bowl will be. After numerous bad experiences with an airline, we decide to book future flights with a competitor.

When we draw a conclusion from an array of facts, we are engaged in inductive reasoning. Such reasoning deals in probability, not certainty. For a conclusion to be highly probable, it must be based on evidence that is sufficient, representative, and relevant. (See the chart on p. 120.)

The fallacy known as *hasty generalization* is a conclusion based on insufficient or unrepresentative evidence.

HASTY GENERALIZATION

In a single year, scores on standardized tests in California's public schools rose by ten points. Therefore, more children than ever are succeeding in America's public school systems.

Data from one state do not justify a conclusion about the whole United States.

A *stereotype* is a hasty generalization about a group. Here are a few examples.

STEREOTYPES

Women are bad bosses.

Politicians are corrupt.

Asian students are exceptionally intelligent.

Stereotyping is common because of our human tendency to perceive selectively. We tend to see what we want to see; we notice evidence confirming our already formed opinions and fail to notice evidence to the contrary. For example, if you have concluded that politicians are corrupt, your stereotype will be confirmed by news reports of legislators being indicted—even though every day the media describe conscientious officials serving the public honestly and well.

Testing inductive reasoning

Though inductive reasoning leads to probable and not absolute truth, you can assess a conclusion's likely probability by asking three questions. This chart shows how to apply those questions to a sample conclusion based on a survey.

CONCLUSION The majority of students on our campus would volunteer at least five hours a week in a local organization if the school provided a placement service for volunteers.

EVIDENCE In a recent survey, 723 of 1,215 students questioned said they would volunteer at least five hours a week in a local organization if the school provided a placement service for volunteers.

1. Is the evidence sufficient?
   That depends. On a small campus (say, 3,000 students), the pool of students surveyed would be sufficient for market research, but on a large campus (say, 30,000), 1,215 students are only 4 percent of the population. If that 4 percent were known to be truly representative of the other 96 percent, however, even such a small sample would be sufficient (see question 2).

2. Is the evidence representative?
   The evidence is representative if those responding to the survey reflect the characteristics of the entire student population: age, sex, race, field of study, overall number of extracurricular commitments, and so on. If most of those surveyed are majors in fields like social work or counseling, however, the researchers would be wise to question the survey's conclusion.

3. Is the evidence relevant?
   Yes. The results of the survey are directly linked to the conclusion. A question about the number of hours students work for pay, by contrast, would not be relevant because it would not be about *choosing to volunteer*.

Academic English Many hasty generalizations contain words such as *all*, *ever*, *always*, and *never*, when qualifiers such as *most*, *many*, *usually*, and *seldom* would be more accurate.

Drawing analogies

An analogy points out a similarity between two things that are otherwise different. Analogies can be an effective means of arguing a point. Our system of judicial decision making, or case law, which relies heavily on previous decisions, makes extensive use of reasoning by analogy. One lawyer may point out, for example, that specific facts or circumstances resemble those from a previous case and will thus argue for a similar result or decision. In response, the opposing lawyer may maintain that such facts or circumstances bear only a superficial resemblance to those in the previous case and that in legally relevant respects they are quite different and thus require a different result or decision.

It is not always easy to draw the line between a reasonable and an unreasonable analogy. At times, however, an analogy is clearly off base, in which case it is called a *false analogy*.

FALSE ANALOGY

If we can send a spacecraft to Pluto, we should be able to find a cure for the common cold.

The writer has falsely assumed that because two things are alike in one respect, they must be alike in others. Exploring the outer reaches of the solar system and finding a cure for the common cold are both scientific challenges, but the problems confronting medical researchers are quite different from those solved by space scientists.

Tracing causes and effects

Demonstrating a connection between causes and effects is rarely simple. For example, to explain why a chemistry course has a high failure rate, you would begin by listing possible causes: inadequate preparation of students, poor teaching, lack of qualified tutors, and so on. Next you would investigate each possible cause. Only after investigating the possible causes would you be able to weigh the relative impact of each cause and suggest appropriate remedies.

Because cause-and-effect reasoning is so complex, it is not surprising that writers frequently oversimplify it. In particular, writers sometimes assume that because one event follows another, the first is the cause of the second. This common fallacy is known as *post hoc*, from the Latin *post hoc, ergo propter hoc*, meaning "after this, therefore because of this."

> *POST HOC* FALLACY
> Since Governor Cho took office, unemployment among minorities in the state has decreased by 7 percent. Governor Cho should be applauded for reducing unemployment among minorities.

The writer must show that Governor Cho's policies are responsible for the decrease in unemployment; it is not enough to show that the decrease followed the governor's taking office.

Weighing options

Especially when reasoning about problems and solutions, writers must weigh options. To be fair, a writer should mention the full range of options, showing why one is superior to the others or might work well in combination with others.

It is unfair to suggest that there are only two alternatives when in fact there are more. Writers who set up a false choice between their preferred option and one that is clearly unsatisfactory are guilty of the *either . . . or* fallacy.

> *EITHER . . . OR* FALLACY
> Our current war against drugs has not worked. Either we should legalize drugs or we should turn the drug war over to our armed forces and let them fight it.

Clearly there are other options, such as increased funding for drug abuse prevention and treatment.

Making assumptions

An assumption is a claim that is taken to be true—without the need of proof. Most arguments are based to some extent on assumptions, since writers rarely have the time and space to prove all of the conceivable claims on which their argument is based. For example, someone arguing about the best means of limiting population growth in developing countries might well assume that the goal of limiting population growth is worthwhile. For most audiences, there would be no need to articulate this assumption or to defend it. Some religious audiences, however, argue that bringing children into the world is an act of faith. It is a good idea to think through your own assumptions and imagine where they might conflict with those of your audience.

There is a danger in failing to spell out and prove a claim that is clearly controversial. Consider the following short argument, in which a key claim is missing.

ARGUMENT WITH MISSING CLAIM
Violent crime is increasing. Therefore, we should vigorously enforce the death penalty.

The writer seems to be assuming that the death penalty deters violent criminals—and that most audiences will agree. The writer also assumes that the death penalty is a fair punishment for violent crimes. These are not safe assumptions.

When a missing claim is an assertion that few would agree with, we say that a writer is guilty of a *non sequitur* (Latin for "does not follow").

NON SEQUITUR
Leah loves good food; therefore, she will be an excellent chef.

Few people would agree with the missing claim—that lovers of good food always make excellent chefs.

Deducing conclusions (deductive reasoning)

When we deduce a conclusion, we—like Sherlock Holmes—put things together. We establish that a general principle is true, that a specific case is an example of that principle, and that therefore a particular conclusion about that case is a certainty. In real life, such absolute reasoning rarely happens. Approximations of it, however, sometimes occur.

Deductive reasoning can often be structured in a three-step argument called a *syllogism*. The three steps are the major premise, the minor premise, and the conclusion.

1. Anything that increases radiation in the environment is dangerous to public health. (Major premise)
2. Nuclear reactors increase radiation in the environment. (Minor premise)
3. Therefore, nuclear reactors are dangerous to public health. (Conclusion)

The major premise is a generalization. The minor premise is a specific case. The conclusion follows from applying the generalization to the specific case.

Deductive arguments break down if one of the premises is not true or if the conclusion does not logically follow from the premises. In the following short argument, the major premise is very likely untrue.

UNTRUE PREMISE

The police do not give speeding tickets to people driving less than five miles per hour over the limit. Sam is driving fifty-nine miles per hour in a fifty-five-mile-per-hour zone. Therefore, the police will not give Sam a speeding ticket.

The conclusion is true only if the premises are true. If the police sometimes give tickets for driving less than five miles per hour over the limit, Sam cannot safely conclude that he will avoid a ticket.

In the following argument, both premises might be true, but the conclusion does not follow logically from them.

CONCLUSION DOES NOT FOLLOW

All members of our club ran in this year's Boston Marathon.
Jay ran in this year's Boston Marathon. Therefore, Jay is a
member of our club.

The fact that Jay ran the race is no guarantee that he is a member of the club. Presumably, many runners are nonmembers.

Assuming that both premises are true, the following argument holds up.

CONCLUSION FOLLOWS

All members of our club ran in this year's Boston Marathon.
Jay is a member of our club. Therefore, Jay ran in this year's
Boston Marathon.

6b Distinguish between legitimate and unfair emotional appeals.

There is nothing wrong with appealing to readers' emotions.
After all, many issues worth arguing about have an emotional
as well as a logical dimension. Even the Greek logician Aristotle lists *pathos* (emotion) as a legitimate argumentative tactic. For example, in an essay criticizing big-box stores, writer
Betsy Taylor has a good reason for tugging at readers' emotions: Her subject is the decline of city and town life. In her
conclusion, Taylor appeals to readers' emotions by invoking
their national pride.

LEGITIMATE EMOTIONAL APPEAL

Is it anti-American to be against having a retail giant set up
shop in one's community? Some people would say so. On
the other hand, if you board up Main Street, what's left of
America?

As we all know, however, emotional appeals are frequently
misused. Many of the arguments we see in the media, for instance, strive to win our sympathy rather than our intelligent
agreement. A TV commercial suggesting that you will be thin
and sexy if you drink a certain diet beverage is making a pitch

to emotions. So is a political speech that recommends electing a candidate because he is a devoted husband and father who serves as a volunteer firefighter.

The following passage illustrates several types of unfair emotional appeals.

UNFAIR EMOTIONAL APPEALS

This progressive proposal to build a ski resort in the state park has been carefully researched by Western Trust, the largest bank in the state; furthermore, it is favored by a majority of the local merchants. The only opposition comes from narrow-minded, do-gooder environmentalists who care more about trees than they do about people; one of their leaders was actually arrested for disturbing the peace several years ago.

Words with strong positive or negative connotations, such as *progressive* and *do-gooder*, are examples of *biased language*. Attacking the persons who hold a belief (environmentalists) rather than refuting their argument is called *ad hominem*, a Latin term meaning "to the man." Associating a prestigious name (Western Trust) with the writer's side is called *transfer*. Claiming that an idea should be accepted because a large number of people (the majority of merchants) are in favor of it is called the *bandwagon appeal*. Bringing in irrelevant issues (the arrest) is a *red herring*, named after a trick used in fox hunts to mislead the dogs by dragging a smelly fish across the trail.

6c Judge how fairly a writer handles opposing views.

The way in which a writer deals with opposing views is telling. Some writers address the arguments of the opposition fairly, conceding points when necessary and countering others, all in a civil spirit. Other writers will do almost anything to win an argument: either ignoring opposing views altogether or misrepresenting such views and attacking their proponents.

In your own writing, you build credibility by addressing opposing arguments fairly. (See also 5f.) In your reading, you can assess the credibility of your sources by looking at how they deal with views not in agreement with their own.

Describing the views of others

Writers and politicians often deliberately misrepresent the views of others. One way they do this is by setting up a "straw man," a character so weak that he is easily knocked down. The *straw man* fallacy consists of an oversimplification or outright distortion of opposing views. For example, in a California debate over attempts to control the mountain lion population, pro-lion groups characterized their opponents as trophy hunters bent on shooting harmless lions and sticking them on the walls of their dens. In truth, such hunters were only one faction of those who saw a need to control the lion population.

During the District of Columbia's struggle for voting representation, some politicians set up a straw man, as shown in the following example.

STRAW MAN FALLACY
Washington, DC, residents are lobbying for statehood. Giving a city such as the District of Columbia the status of a state would be unfair.

The straw man wanted statehood. In fact, most District citizens lobbied for voting representation in any form, not necessarily through statehood.

Quoting opposing views

Writers often quote the words of writers who hold opposing views. In general, this is a good idea, for it assures some level of fairness and accuracy. At times, though, both the fairness and the accuracy are an illusion.

A source may be misrepresented when it is quoted out of context. All quotations are to some extent taken out of context, but a fair writer will explain the context to readers. To select a provocative sentence from a source and to ignore the more moderate sentences surrounding it is both unfair and misleading. Sometimes a writer deliberately distorts a source through the device of ellipsis dots. Ellipsis dots tell readers that words have been omitted from the original source. When those words are crucial to an author's meaning, omitting them is obviously unfair. (See also 39d.)

ORIGINAL SOURCE

Johnson's *History of the American West* is riddled with inaccuracies and astonishing in its blatantly racist description of the Indian wars.　　　　　　　　—B. R., reviewer

MISLEADING QUOTATION

According to B. R., Johnson's *History of the American West* is "astonishing in its . . . description of the Indian wars."

EXERCISE 6–1　Explain what is illogical in the following brief arguments. It may be helpful to identify the logical fallacy or fallacies by name. Answers to lettered sentences appear in the back of the book.

a. My roommate, who is an engineering major, is taking a course called Structures of Tall Buildings. All engineers have to know how to design tall buildings.

b. If you're old enough to vote, you're old enough to drink. Therefore, the drinking age should be lowered to eighteen.

c. Cable stations that rely on nauseating reality shows, annoying infomercials for useless products, idiotic talk shows, and second-rate movies should have their licenses pulled.

d. Most young people can't afford to buy a house in Silicon Valley because they spend too much money on new clothes and computer games.

e. If you're not part of the solution, you're part of the problem.

1. Whenever I wash my car, it rains. I have discovered a way to end all droughts—get all the people to wash their cars.

2. Either you can learn how to build a Web site or you won't be able to get a decent job after college.

3. College professors tend to be sarcastic. Three of my five professors this semester make sarcastic remarks.

4. Although Bell's book on Joe DiMaggio was well researched, I doubt that an Australian historian can contribute much to our knowledge of an American baseball player.
5. Slacker co-workers and crazy, big-mouthed clients make our spineless managers impose ridiculous workloads on us hard-working, conscientious employees.
6. If professional sports teams didn't pay athletes such high salaries, we wouldn't have so many kids breaking their legs at hockey and basketball camps.
7. Ninety percent of the students oppose a tuition increase; therefore, the board of trustees should not pass the proposed increase.
8. If more people would take a long, close look at businesses like Microsoft and Amazon, they could reorganize their family lives to run successfully.
9. A mandatory ten-cent deposit on bottles and cans will eliminate litter because everyone I know will return the containers for the money rather than throw them away.
10. Researching what voters think during an election campaign is useless because most citizens don't vote anyway.

7 Writing in the disciplines

Writing is a fact of college life. No matter what you study, you will be expected to write for a variety of audiences in a variety of formats. College courses expose you to the thinking of scholars in many disciplines, such as the humanities (literature, music, art), the social sciences (psychology, anthropology, sociology), and the sciences (biology, physics, chemistry). Writing in any discipline provides the opportunity to practice the methods used by scholars in these fields and to enter into their debates. Each field has its own questions, evidence, language, and conventions, but all disciplines share certain expectations for good writing.

7a Find commonalities across disciplines.

If you understand the features that are common to writing in all disciplines, you will have an easier time sorting out the unique aspects of writing in a particular field.

Making the most of your handbook

When writing for any course, keep in mind the steps needed to write a strong academic paper.

▶ Communicating a purpose: 1a

▶ Determining your audience: 1a

▶ Asking an academic question: 7b

▶ Making and supporting a claim: 5c, 5e

▶ Citing sources: 51 (MLA), 56b (APA), 57b (*Chicago*)

In every discipline, scholars write about texts. For example, in the humanities scholars write about texts such as novels, poems, paintings, and music. In the social sciences, texts include journal articles, books and field accounts by researchers, census reports, case studies, and reports on experiments. In the sciences, researchers write about data taken from reports that other researchers have published and about data drawn from site results, site surveys, and laboratory experiments.

A good paper in any field needs to communicate a writer's purpose to an audience and to explore an engaging question about a subject. Effective writers make an argument and support their claims with evidence. Writers in most fields need to show readers the thesis they're developing (or, in the sciences, the hypothesis they're testing) and how they counter the opposing explanations or objections of other writers. In some fields, such as nursing and business, writers may not put forth an explicit claim or thesis but will still communicate a clear purpose and use evidence to support their ideas. All disciplines require writers to document where they found their evidence and from whom they borrowed ideas.

7b Recognize the questions that writers in a discipline ask.

Disciplines are characterized by the kinds of questions their scholars attempt to answer. Social scientists, who analyze human behavior, might ask about the factors that cause people to act in certain ways. Humanities scholars interpret texts within their cultural contexts; they ask questions about the society at the time a text was written or about the connections between an author's life and work. Historians, who seek an understanding of the past, ask questions about the causes and effects of events and about connections between current and past events. Scientists collect data and ask questions to help them interpret the data.

One way to understand how disciplines ask different questions is to look at assignments on the same topic in various fields. Many disciplines, for example, might be interested in the subject of disasters. The following are some questions that writers in different fields might ask about this subject.

EDUCATION
Should the elementary school curriculum teach students how to cope in disaster situations?

FILM
How has the disaster film genre changed since the advent of computer-generated imagery (CGI) in the early 1970s?

HISTORY
How did the formation of the American Red Cross change this country's approach to natural disasters?

ENGINEERING
What recent innovations in levee design are most promising?

PSYCHOLOGY
What are the most effective ways to identify and treat post-traumatic stress disorder (PTSD) in disaster survivors?

The questions you ask in any discipline will form the basis of the thesis for your paper. The questions themselves don't communicate a central idea, but they may lead you to one. For an education paper, for example, you might begin with the question "Should the elementary school curriculum teach students how to cope in disaster situations?" After considering the issues involved, you might draft the following thesis.

School systems should adopt age-appropriate curriculum units that introduce children to the risks of natural and human-made disasters and that allow children to practice coping strategies.

Whenever you write for a college course, try to determine the kinds of questions scholars in the field might ask about a topic. You can find clues in assigned readings, lecture or discussion topics, e-mail discussion groups, and the paper assignment itself. When in doubt, ask your instructor for guidance.

7c Understand the kinds of evidence that writers in a discipline use.

Regardless of the discipline in which you are writing, you must support any claims you make with evidence—facts, statistics, examples and illustrations, expert opinion, and so on. Familiarize yourself with the kinds of evidence most writers use to support claims in your field.

- For an English paper that examines three types of parent-child relationships in Shakespeare's *King Lear*, you would look closely at lines from the play.

- For a psychology paper on the connection between certain medications and suicidal impulses, you might study the results of clinical trials.

- For a nursing practice paper about the medical condition of a particular patient, you would review the patient's chart as well as any relevant medical literature.

- For a history paper on Renaissance attitudes toward marriage, you might examine historical documents such as letters, diaries, and church records.

The kinds of evidence used in different disciplines often overlap. Students of geography, media studies, and political science, for example, might use census data to explore different topics. The evidence that one discipline values, however, might not be sufficient to support an interpretation or a conclusion in another field. You might use anecdotes or interviews in an anthropology paper, for example, but such evidence would be irrelevant in a biology lab report. The chart

Evidence typically used in various disciplines

Humanities: Literature, art, film, music, philosophy

- Passages of text or lines of a poem
- Details from an image or a work of art
- Passages of a musical composition
- Critical essays that analyze original works

Humanities: History

- Primary sources such as photographs, letters, maps, and government documents
- Scholarly books and articles that interpret evidence

Social sciences: Psychology, sociology, political science, anthropology

- Data from original experiments
- Results of field research such as interviews, observations, or surveys
- Statistics from government agencies
- Scholarly books and articles that interpret data from original experiments and from other researchers' studies

Sciences: Biology, chemistry, physics

- Data from original experiments
- Scholarly articles that report findings from experiments

at the top of this page lists the kinds of evidence accepted in various disciplines.

7d Become familiar with a discipline's language conventions.

Every discipline has a specialized vocabulary. As you read the articles and books in a field, you'll notice certain words and phrases that come up repeatedly. Sociologists, for example,

Point of view and verb tense in academic writing

Point of view

- Writers of analytical or research essays in the humanities usually use the third-person point of view: *Austen presents . . .* or *Castel describes the battle as. . . .*

- Scientists and most social scientists, who depend on quantitative research to present findings, tend to use the third-person point of view: *The results indicated. . . .*

- Writers in the humanities and in some social sciences occasionally use the first person in discussing their personal experience or in writing a personal narrative: *After spending two years interviewing families affected by the war, I began to understand that . . .* or *Every July as we approached the Cape Cod Canal, we could sense. . . .*

Present or past tense

- Literature scholars use the present tense to discuss a text: *Hughes effectively dramatizes different views of minority assertiveness.* (See 52b.)

- Science and social science writers use the past tense to describe experiments and the present tense to discuss the findings: *In 2003, Berkowitz released the first double-blind placebo study. . . . These results paint a murky picture.* (See 56c.)

- Writers in history use the present tense or the present perfect tense to discuss a text: *Shelby Foote describes the scene like this . . .* or *Shelby Foote has described the scene like this. . . .* (See 57c.)

use terms such as *independent variables, political opportunity resources,* and *dyads* to describe social phenomena; computer scientists might refer to *algorithm design* and *loop invariants* to describe programming methods. Practitioners in health fields such as nursing use terms like *treatment plan* and *systemic assessment* to describe patient care. Use discipline-specific terms only when you are certain that you and your readers fully understand their meaning.

In addition to vocabulary, many fields of study have developed specialized conventions for point of view and verb tense. See the chart at the top of the previous page.

7e Use a discipline's preferred citation style.

In any discipline, you must give credit to those whose ideas or words you have borrowed. Whenever you write, it is your responsibility to avoid plagiarism by citing sources honestly and accurately.

While all disciplines emphasize careful documentation, each follows a particular system of citation that its members have agreed on. Writers in the humanities usually use the system established by the Modern Language Association (MLA). Scholars in some social sciences, such as psychology and anthropology, follow the style guidelines of the American Psychological Association (APA); scholars in history and some humanities typically follow *The Chicago Manual of Style*.

> **Making the most of your handbook**
>
> You will need to document your sources in the style preferred by your discipline.
>
> ▶ Documenting sources: MLA (humanities), 53; APA (social sciences), 56d; *Chicago* (history), 57d; CSE (sciences), online at hackerhandbooks .com/resdoc

7f Respond to writing assignments in the disciplines.

When you are asked to write in a specific discipline, become familiar with the distinctive features of the writing in that discipline. Then read the assignment carefully and try to identify the purpose of the assignment and the type of evidence you are expected to use.

On the following pages are examples of assignments in four disciplines—psychology, business, biology, and nursing—along with excerpts from student papers that were written in response to the assignments.

Psychology

ASSIGNMENT: LITERATURE REVIEW

Write a literature review in which you report on and
evaluate the published research on a behavioral disorder.

1 Key terms

2 Purpose: to report on and evaluate a body of evidence

3 Evidence: research of other psychologists

ADHD in Boys vs. Girls   1

Always Out of Their Seats (and Fighting):

Why Are Boys Diagnosed with ADHD More Often Than Girls?

Background and explanation of writer's purpose.

Attention deficit hyperactivity disorder (ADHD) is a commonly diagnosed disorder in children that affects social, academic, or occupational functioning. As the name suggests, its hallmark characteristics are hyperactivity and lack of attention as well as impulsive behavior. For decades, studies have focused on the causes, expression, prevalence, and outcome of the disorder, but until recently very little research investigated gender differences. In fact, until the early 1990s most research focused exclusively on boys (Brown, Madan-Swain, & Baldwin, 1991), perhaps because many more boys than girls are diagnosed with ADHD. Researchers have speculated on the possible explanations for the disparity, citing reasons such as true sex differences in the manifestation of the disorder's symptoms, gender biases in those who refer children to clinicians, and possibly even the diagnostic procedures themselves (Gaub & Carlson, 1997). But the most persuasive reason is that ADHD is often a comorbid condition—that is, it coexists with other behavior disorders that are not diagnosed properly and that do exhibit gender differences.

Evidence from research the writer has reviewed.

APA citations and specialized language (*ADHD, comorbid*).

Thesis: writer's argument.

Marginal annotations indicate appropriate formatting and effective writing.

Business

ASSIGNMENT: PROPOSAL

Write a proposal, as a memo, for improving or adding a service at a company where you have worked. Address the pros and cons of your proposal; draw on relevant studies, research, and your knowledge of the company.

1 Key terms

2 Purpose: to analyze certain evidence and make a proposal based on that analysis

3 Appropriate evidence: relevant studies

Memorandum

To: Jay Crosson, Senior Vice President, Human Resources

From: Kelly Ratajczak, Intern, Purchasing Department

Subject: Proposal to Add a Wellness Program

Date: April 24, 2009

Health care costs are rising. In the long run, implementing a wellness program in our corporate culture will decrease the company's health care costs.

Research indicates that nearly 70% of health care costs are from common illnesses related to high blood pressure, overweight, lack of exercise, high cholesterol, stress, poor nutrition, and other preventable health issues (Hall, 2006). Health care costs are a major expense for most businesses, and they do not reflect costs due to the loss of productivity or absenteeism. A wellness program would address most, if not all, of these health care issues and related costs.

Writer's main idea.

Data from recent study as support for claim.

APA citation style, typical in business.

Business terms familiar to readers (costs, productivity, absenteeism).

Biology

ASSIGNMENT: LABORATORY REPORT

Write a report on an experiment you conduct on the distribution pattern of a plant species indigenous to the Northeast. Describe your methods for collecting data and interpret your experiment's results.

1   Key terms
2   Purpose: to interpret the results of an experiment
3   Evidence: data collected during the experiment

CSE style, typical in sciences.

Distribution Pattern of Dandelion 1

Distribution Pattern of Dandelion (*Taraxacum officinale*)
on an Abandoned Golf Course

ABSTRACT

Abstract: an overview of hypothesis, experiment, and results.

This paper reports our study of the distribution pattern of the common dandelion (*Taraxacum officinale*) on an abandoned golf course in Hilton, New York, on 10 July 2005. An area of 6 ha was sampled with 111 randomly placed $1 \times 1\ m^2$ quadrats. The dandelion count

Specialized language (*aggregated*, *random*, *uniformly distributed*, and so on).

from each quadrat was used to test observed frequencies against expected frequencies based on a hypothesized random distribution. [Abstract continues.]

INTRODUCTION

Introduction: context and purpose of experiment. Instead of a thesis, or main claim, a lab report interprets the data in a later Discussion section.

Theoretically, plants of a particular species may be aggregated, random, or uniformly distributed in space [1]. The distribution type may be determined by many factors, such as availability of nutrients, competition, distance of seed dispersal, and mode of reproduction [2].

The purpose of this study was to determine if the distribution pattern of the common dandelion (*Taraxacum officinale*) on an abandoned golf course was aggregated, random, or uniform.

Nursing

ASSIGNMENT: NURSING PRACTICE PAPER

Write a client history, a nursing diagnosis, recommendations for care, your rationales, and expected and actual outcomes. Use interview notes, the client's health records, and relevant research findings.

1 Key terms

2 Purpose: to provide client history, diagnosis, recommendations, and outcomes

3 Evidence: interviews, health records, and research findings

---

ALL and HTN in One Client   1

Acute Lymphoblastic Leukemia and Hypertension in One Client:
A Nursing Practice Paper

Physical History

E.B. is a 16-year-old white male 5'10" tall weighing 190 lb. He was admitted to the hospital on April 14, 2006, due to decreased platelets and a need for a PRBC transfusion. He was diagnosed in October 2005 with T-cell acute lymphoblastic leukemia (ALL), after a 2-week period of decreased energy, decreased oral intake, easy bruising, and petechia. The client had experienced a 20-lb weight loss in the previous 6 months. At the time of diagnosis, his CBC showed a WBC count of 32, an H & H of 13/38, and a platelet count of 34,000. His initial chest X-ray showed an anterior mediastinal mass. Echocardiogram showed a structurally normal heart. He began induction chemotherapy on October 12, 2005, receiving vincristine, 6-mercaptopurine, doxorubicin, intrathecal methotrexate, and then high-dose methotrexate per protocol. During his hospital stay, he

Evidence from client's medical chart for overall assessment.

Specialized nursing language (*echocardiogram, chemotherapy*, and so on).

Instead of a thesis, or main claim, the writer gives a diagnosis, recommendations for care, and expected outcomes, all supported by evidence from observations and client records.

required packed red cells and platelets on two different occasions. He was diagnosed with hypertension (HTN) due to systolic blood pressure readings consistently ranging between 130s and 150s and was started on nifedipine. E.B. has a history of mild ADHD, migraines, and deep vein thrombosis (DVT). He has tolerated the induction and consolidation phases of chemotherapy well and is now in the maintenance phase, in which he receives a daily dose of mercaptopurine, weekly doses of methotrexate, and intermittent doses of steroids.

hackerhandbooks.com/bedhandbook > Model papers
> APA literature review: Charat
> APA business proposal: Ratajczak
> CSE laboratory report: Johnson and Arnold
> APA nursing practice paper: Riss

Part III
Clear Sentences

8   Prefer active verbs.

As a rule, choose an active verb and pair it with a subject that names the person or thing doing the action. Active verbs express meaning more emphatically and vigorously than their weaker counterparts—forms of the verb *be* or verbs in the passive voice.

PASSIVE	The pumps *were destroyed* by a surge of power.
BE VERB	A surge of power *was* responsible for the destruction of the pumps.
ACTIVE	A surge of power *destroyed* the pumps.

Verbs in the passive voice lack strength because their subjects receive the action instead of doing it. Forms of the verb *be* (*be, am, is, are, was, were, being, been*) lack vigor because they convey no action.

Although passive verbs and the forms of *be* have legitimate uses, choose an active verb if it can carry your meaning. Even among active verbs, some are more active—and therefore more vigorous and colorful—than others. Carefully selected verbs can energize a piece of writing.

▶ The goalie crouched low, ~~reached~~ *swept* out his stick, and ~~sent~~ *hooked* the rebound away from the mouth of the net.

> **Academic English**   Although you may be tempted to avoid the passive voice completely, keep in mind that some writing situations call for it, especially scientific writing. For appropriate uses of the passive voice, see page 144; for advice about forming the passive voice, see 28c and 62c.

Grammar checkers are fairly good at flagging passive verbs, such as *is used* or *had been tried*. However, because passive verbs are sometimes appropriate, you—not the computer program—must decide whether to change a verb from passive to active.

8a Use the active voice unless you have a good reason for choosing the passive.

In the active voice, the subject does the action; in the passive voice, the subject receives the action (see also 62c). Although both voices are grammatically correct, the active voice is usually more effective because it is simpler and more direct.

ACTIVE   Hernando *caught* the fly ball.

PASSIVE   The fly ball *was caught* by Hernando.

Passive sentences often identify the actor in a *by* phrase, as in the preceding example. Sometimes, however, that phrase is omitted, and who or what is responsible for the action becomes unclear: *The fly ball was caught.*

Most of the time, you will want to emphasize the actor, so you should use the active voice. To replace a passive verb with an active one, make the actor the subject of the sentence.

▶ A bolt of lightning struck the transformer.
~~The transformer was struck by a bolt of lightning.~~

The active verb (*struck*) makes the point more forcefully than the passive verb (*was struck*).

▶ The settlers stripped the land of timber before realizing
~~The land was stripped of timber before the settlers realized~~

the consequences of their actions.

The revision emphasizes the actors (*settlers*) by naming them in the subject.

> ~~The~~ debris ~~was removed~~ from the construction site.

The contractor removed the (inserted above)

Sometimes the actor does not appear in a passive-voice sentence. To turn such a sentence into the active voice, the writer must determine an appropriate subject, in this case *contractor*.

Appropriate uses of the passive

The passive voice is appropriate if you wish to emphasize the receiver of the action or to minimize the importance of the actor.

APPROPRIATE   Many Hawaiians *were forced* to leave their homes
PASSIVE   after the earthquake.

APPROPRIATE   As the time for harvest approaches, the tobacco
PASSIVE   plants *are sprayed* with a chemical to retard the growth
              of suckers.

The writer of the first sentence wished to emphasize the receiver of the action, *Hawaiians*. The writer of the second sentence wished to focus on the tobacco plants, not on the people spraying them.

In much scientific writing, the passive voice properly emphasizes the experiment or process being described, not the researcher. Check with your instructor for the preference in your discipline.

APPROPRIATE   The solution *was heated* to the boiling point, and
PASSIVE   then it was reduced in volume by 50 percent.

8b Replace *be* verbs that result in dull or wordy sentences.

Not every *be* verb needs replacing. The forms of *be* (*be, am, is, are, was, were, being, been*) work well when you want to link a subject to a noun that clearly renames it or to an adjective that describes it: *Orchard House was the home of Louisa May Alcott. The harvest will be bountiful after the summer rains.* And *be* verbs are essential as helping verbs before present participles (*is flying, are disappearing*) to express ongoing action: *Derrick was fighting the fire when his wife went into labor.* (See 27f.)

If using a *be* verb makes a sentence needlessly dull and wordy, however, consider replacing it. Often a phrase following the verb will contain a noun or an adjective (such as *violation, resistant*) that suggests a more vigorous, active verb (*violate, resist*).

▶ Burying nuclear waste in Antarctica would ~~be in violation of~~ *violate*

 an international treaty.

 Violate is less wordy and more vigorous than *be in violation of.*

▶ When Rosa Parks ~~was resistant to~~ *resisted* giving up her seat on the

 bus, she became a civil rights hero.

 Resisted is stronger than *was resistant to.*

> **Grammar checkers** usually do not flag wordiness caused by *be* verbs. Only you can find ways to strengthen your sentences by using vigorous, active verbs in place of *be.*

8c As a rule, choose a subject that names the person or thing doing the action.

In weak, unemphatic prose, both the actor and the action may be buried in sentence elements other than the subject and the verb. In the following sentence, for example, both the actor and the action appear in prepositional phrases, word groups that do not receive much attention from readers.

WEAK	The institution of the New Deal had the effect of reversing some of the economic inequalities of the Great Depression.
EMPHATIC	The New Deal reversed some of the economic inequalities of the Great Depression.

Consider the subjects and verbs of the two versions—*institution had* versus *New Deal reversed.* The latter expresses the writer's point more emphatically.

▶ ~~The use of~~ pure oxygen can ~~cause~~ healing ~~in~~ wounds that

are otherwise untreatable.

(editing marks: P inserted above "pure"; caret mark showing "heal" inserted)

In the original sentence, the subject and verb—*use can cause*—express the point blandly. *Pure oxygen can heal* makes the point more emphatically and directly.

Writing with sources

Chicago-style citation

▶ In 1813, a large mill ~~was built by Francis Lowell~~ along the

(handwritten insertion: Francis Lowell built)

Charles River in Waltham, Massachusetts.[1]

When you are writing about historical events, naming the actor in the subject is the clearest and most direct way to get your point across. Instead of burying the actor (*Francis Lowell*) in a prepositional phrase, the writer has made *Francis Lowell* the subject and has changed the verb *was built* from passive to active voice. (See also 8a on active voice and 57d on *Chicago* documentation style.)

EXERCISE 8–1 Revise any weak, unemphatic sentences by replacing be verbs or passive verbs with active alternatives and, if necessary, by naming in the subject the person or thing doing the action. Some sentences are emphatic; do not change them. Revisions of lettered sentences appear in the back of the book. Example:

(handwritten insertion: The ranger doused the campfire before giving us)

~~The campfire was doused by the ranger before we were given~~

a ticket for unauthorized use of a campsite.

a. The Prussians were victorious over the Saxons in 1745.
b. The entire operation is managed by Ahmed, the producer.
c. The sea kayaks were expertly paddled by the tour guides.
d. At the crack of rocket and mortar blasts, I jumped from the top bunk and landed on my buddy below, who was crawling on the floor looking for his boots.
e. There were shouting protesters on the courthouse steps.

1. A strange sound was made in the willow tree by the monkey that had escaped from the zoo.
2. Her letter was in acknowledgment of the student's participation in the literacy program.
3. The bomb bay doors rumbled open, and freezing air whipped through the plane.

4. The work of Paul Oakenfold and Sandra Collins was influential in my choice of music for my audition.
5. The only responsibility I was given by my parents was putting my little brother to bed when they had to work late.

hackerhandbooks.com/bedhandbook > Grammar exercises > Clear sentences
> E-ex 8–2 to 8–5

9 Balance parallel ideas.

If two or more ideas are parallel, they are easier to grasp when expressed in parallel grammatical form. Single words should be balanced with single words, phrases with phrases, clauses with clauses.

A kiss can be a comma, a question mark, or an exclamation

point. —Mistinguett

This novel is not to be tossed lightly aside, but to be hurled

with great force. —Dorothy Parker

In matters of principle, stand like a rock; in matters of taste,

swim with the current. —Thomas Jefferson

Writers often use parallelism to create emphasis. (See p. 190.)

> **Grammar checkers** only occasionally flag faulty parallelism because they cannot assess whether ideas are parallel in grammatical form.

9a Balance parallel ideas in a series.

Readers expect items in a series to appear in parallel grammatical form. When one or more of the items violate readers' expectations, a sentence will be needlessly awkward.

▶ Children who study music also learn confidence,

discipline, and ~~they are creative.~~
creativity.

The revision presents all the items in the series as nouns: *confidence*, *discipline*, and *creativity*.

▶ Impressionist painters believed in focusing on ordinary

subjects, capturing the effects of light on those subjects,

and ~~to use~~ short brushstrokes.
using

The revision uses *-ing* forms for all the items in the series: *focusing*, *capturing*, and *using*.

▶ Racing to get to work on time, Sam drove down the middle

of the road, ran one red light, and two stop signs.
ignored

The revision adds a verb to make the three items parallel: *drove*, *ran*, and *ignored*.

In headings and lists, aim for as much parallelism as the content allows. (See 58b and 58c.)

9b Balance parallel ideas presented as pairs.

When pairing ideas, underscore their connection by expressing them in similar grammatical form. Paired ideas are usually connected in one of these ways:

- with a coordinating conjunction such as *and*, *but*, or *or*
- with a pair of correlative conjunctions such as *either . . . or* or *not only . . . but also*
- with a word introducing a comparison, usually *than* or *as*

Parallel ideas linked with coordinating conjunctions

Coordinating conjunctions (*and*, *but*, *or*, *nor*, *for*, *so*, and *yet*) link ideas of equal importance. When those ideas are closely parallel in content, they should be expressed in parallel grammatical form.

▶ **Emily Dickinson's poetry features the use of dashes and** the capitalization of
~~capitalizing~~ **common words.**

The revision balances the nouns *use* and *capitalization.*

▶ **Many states are reducing property taxes for home owners** extending
and ~~extend~~ financial aid in the form of tax credits to

renters.

The revision balances the verb *reducing* with the verb *extending.*

Parallel ideas linked with correlative conjunctions

Correlative conjunctions come in pairs: *either . . . or, neither . . . nor, not only . . . but also, both . . . and, whether . . . or.* Make sure that the grammatical structure following the second half of the pair is the same as that following the first half.

▶ **Thomas Edison was not only a prolific inventor but also ~~was~~**

a successful entrepreneur.

The words *a prolific inventor* follow *not only,* so *a successful entrepreneur* should follow *but also.* Repeating *was* creates an unbalanced effect.

▶ **The clerk told me either to change my flight or** to **take the train.**

To change my flight, which follows *either,* should be balanced with *to take the train,* which follows *or.*

Comparisons linked with than or as

In comparisons linked with *than* or *as,* the elements being compared should be expressed in parallel grammatical structure.

▶ **It is easier to speak in abstractions than** to ground ~~grounding~~ **one's**

thoughts in reality.

To speak is balanced with *to ground.*

▶ In Pueblo culture, according to Silko, ~~to write~~ down the [*writing*]

stories of a tribe is not the same as "keeping track of all the

stories" (290).

When you are quoting from a source, parallel grammatical
structure—such as *writing . . . keeping*—helps create continuity
between your sentence and the words from the source.

Comparisons should also be logical and complete. (See
10c.)

9c Repeat function words to clarify parallels.

Function words such as prepositions (*by*, *to*) and subordinating conjunctions (*that*, *because*) signal the grammatical nature of the word groups to follow. Although you can
sometimes omit them, be sure to include them whenever
they signal parallel structures that readers might otherwise
miss.

▶ Our study revealed that left-handed students were more likely

to have trouble with classroom desks and rearranging [*that*]

desks for exam periods was useful.

A second subordinating conjunction helps readers sort out the two
parallel ideas: *that* left-handed students have trouble with classroom desks and *that* rearranging desks was useful.

EXERCISE 9–1 Edit the following sentences to correct faulty parallelism. Revisions of lettered sentences appear in the back of the
book. Example:

Rowena began her workday by pouring a cup of coffee and
~~checked~~ her e-mail. [*checking*]

a. Police dogs are used for finding lost children, tracking criminals, and the detection of bombs and illegal drugs.

b. Hannah told her rock-climbing partner that she bought a new harness and of her desire to climb Otter Cliffs.

c. It is more difficult to sustain an exercise program than starting one.

d. During basic training, I was not only told what to do but also what to think.

e. Jan wanted to drive to the wine country or at least Sausalito.

1. Camp activities include fishing trips, dance lessons, and computers.

2. Arriving at Lake Powell in a thunderstorm, the campers found it safer to remain in their cars than setting up their tents.

3. The streets were not only too steep but also were too narrow for anything other than pedestrian traffic.

4. More digital artists in the show are from the South Shore than the North Shore.

5. To load her toolbox, Anika the Clown gathered hats of different sizes, put in two tubes of face paint, arranged a bundle of extra-long straws, added a bag of colored balloons, and a battery-powered hair dryer.

hackerhandbooks.com/bedhandbook > Grammar exercises > Clear sentences
> E-ex 9–2 to 9–5

10 Add needed words.

Do not omit words necessary for grammatical or logical completeness. Readers need to see at a glance how the parts of a sentence are connected.

> **ESL** Languages sometimes differ in the need for certain words. In particular, be alert for missing articles, verbs, subjects, or expletives. See 29, 30a, and 30b.

> **Grammar checkers** do not flag the vast majority of missing words. They can, however, catch some missing verbs (see 27e). Although they can flag some missing articles (*a, an,* and *the*), they often suggest that an article is missing when in fact it is not. (See also 29.)

10a Add words needed to complete compound structures.

In compound structures, words are often left out for economy: *Tom is a man who means what he says and* [*who*] *says what he means.* Such omissions are acceptable as long as the omitted words are common to both parts of the compound structure.

If a sentence defies grammar or idiom because an omitted word is not common to both parts of the compound structure, the simplest solution is to put the word back in.

▶ **Successful advertisers target customers whom they identify**
  who
  through demographic research or have purchased their

  product in the past.

  The word *who* must be included because *whom . . . have purchased* is not grammatically correct.

  accepted
▶ **Mayor Davis never has and never will accept a bribe.**

  Has . . . accept is not grammatically correct.

  in
▶ **Many South Pacific islanders still believe and live by ancient**

  laws.

  Believe . . . by is not idiomatic in English. (For a list of common idioms, see 18d.)

NOTE: Even when the omitted word is common to both parts of the compound structure, occasionally it must be inserted to avoid ambiguity.

  My favorite *professor* and *mentor* influenced my choice of a career. [Professor and mentor are the same person.]

  My favorite *professor* and *my mentor* influenced my choice of a career. [Professor and mentor are two different people; *my* must be repeated.]

10b Add the word *that* if there is any danger
of misreading without it.

If there is no danger of misreading, the word *that* may be
omitted when it introduces a subordinate clause. *The value
of a principle is the number of things* [*that*] *it will explain.*
Occasionally, however, a sentence might be misread without
that.

▶ **In his famous obedience experiments, psychologist Stanley**
  that
  Milgram discovered ordinary people were willing to inflict

  physical pain on strangers.

  Milgram didn't discover ordinary people; he discovered that
  ordinary people were willing to inflict pain on strangers. The word
  that tells readers to expect a clause, not just *ordinary people*, as the
  direct object of *discovered.*

10c Add words needed to make comparisons
logical and complete.

Comparisons should be made between items that are alike. To
compare unlike items is illogical and distracting.

▶ **The forests of North America are much more extensive than**
  those of
  Europe.

  Forests must be compared with forests, not with all of Europe.

▶ ~~**The death rate of**~~ **ınfantry soldiers in the Vietnam War** ~~**was**~~   *died*
  at a   *rate*
  much higher than the other combat troops.

  The death rate cannot logically be compared with troops. The
  writer could revise the sentence by inserting *that of* after *than*, but
  the preceding revision is more concise.

▶ Some say that Ella Fitzgerald's renditions of Cole Porter's
songs are better than any other ~~singer.~~ *singer's.*

Ella Fitzgerald's renditions cannot logically be compared with a
singer. The revision uses the possessive form *singer's,* with the word
renditions being implied.

Sometimes the word *other* must be inserted to make a
comparison logical.

▶ Jupiter is larger than any *other* planet in our solar system.

Jupiter is a planet, and it cannot be larger than itself.

Sometimes the word *as* must be inserted to make a comparison grammatically complete.

▶ The city of Lowell is as old, *as* if not older than, the neighboring
city of Lawrence.

The construction *as old* is not complete without a second *as: as old
as . . . the neighboring city of Lawrence.*

Comparisons should be complete enough to ensure clarity.
The reader should understand what is being compared.

INCOMPLETE   Brand X is less salty.

COMPLETE   Brand X is less salty than Brand Y.

Finally, comparisons should leave no ambiguity for readers. If more than one interpretation is possible, revise the
sentence to state clearly which interpretation you intend. In
the following ambiguous sentence, two interpretations are
possible.

AMBIGUOUS   Ken helped me more than my roommate.

CLEAR   Ken helped me more than *he helped* my roommate.

CLEAR   Ken helped me more than my roommate *did.*

10d Add the articles *a*, *an*, and *the* where necessary for grammatical completeness.

It is not always necessary to repeat articles with paired items: *We bought a computer and printer.* However, if one of the items requires *a* and the other requires *an*, both articles must be included.

▶ We bought a computer and ᵃⁿ antivirus program.

Articles are sometimes omitted in recipes and other instructions that are meant to be followed while they are being read. Such omissions are inappropriate, however, in nearly all other forms of writing, whether formal or informal.

> **ESL**   Choosing and using articles can be challenging for multilingual writers. See 29.

EXERCISE 10–1   Add any words needed for grammatical or logical completeness in the following sentences. Revisions of lettered sentences appear in the back of the book. Example:

The officer feared ᵗʰᵃᵗ the prisoner would escape.

a.   A grapefruit or orange is a good source of vitamin C.
b.   The women entering VMI can expect haircuts as short as the male cadets.
c.   Looking out the family room window, Sarah saw her favorite tree, which she had climbed as a child, was gone.
d.   The graphic designers are interested and knowledgeable about producing posters for the balloon race.
e.   Reefs are home to more species than any ecosystem in the sea.

1.   Very few black doctors were allowed to serve in the Civil War, and their qualifications had to be higher than white doctors.
2.   Rachel is interested and committed to working at a school in Ecuador next semester.
3.   Vassily likes mathematics more than his teacher.

4. The inspection team saw many historic buildings had been damaged by the earthquake.
5. Lila knows seven languages, but she found English harder to learn than any language.

hackerhandbooks.com/bedhandbook > Grammar exercises > Clear sentences
> E-ex 10–2 to 10–4

11 Untangle mixed constructions.

A mixed construction contains sentence parts that do not sensibly fit together. The mismatch may be a matter of grammar or of logic.

> **Grammar checkers** can flag *is when, is where,* and *reason . . . is because* constructions (11c), but they fail to identify nearly all other mixed constructions, including sentences as tangled as this one: *Depending on our method of travel and our destination determines how many suitcases we are allowed to pack.*

11a Untangle the grammatical structure.

Once you head into a sentence, your choices are limited by the range of grammatical patterns in English. (See 62 and 63.) You cannot begin with one grammatical plan and switch without warning to another. Often you must rethink the purpose of the sentence and revise.

MIXED   For most drivers who have a blood alcohol content of .05 percent double their risk of causing an accident.

The writer begins the sentence with a long prepositional phrase and makes it the subject of the verb *double.* But a prepositional phrase can serve only as a modifier; it cannot be the subject of a sentence.

REVISED   For most drivers who have a blood alcohol content of .05 percent, the risk of causing an accident is doubled.

REVISED   Most drivers who have a blood alcohol content of .05 percent double their risk of causing an accident.

In the first revision, the writer begins with the prepositional phrase and finishes the sentence with a proper subject and verb (*risk . . . is doubled*). In the second revision, the writer stays with the original verb (*double*) and heads into the sentence another way, making *drivers* the subject of *double*.

▶ ~~When the country elects~~ *Electing* a president is the most important

responsibility in a democracy.

The adverb clause *When the country elects a president* cannot serve as the subject of the verb *is*. The revision replaces the adverb clause with a gerund phrase, a word group that can function as a subject. (See 63e and 63b.)

▶ Although the United States is one of the wealthiest nations

in the world, ~~but~~ more than twelve million of our children

live in poverty.

The coordinating conjunction *but* cannot link a subordinate clause (*Although the United States . . .*) with an independent clause (*more than twelve million of our children live in poverty*).

Occasionally a mixed construction is so tangled that it defies grammatical analysis. When this happens, back away from the sentence, rethink what you want to say, and then rewrite the sentence.

MIXED   In the whole-word method, children learn to recognize entire words rather than by the phonics method in which they learn to sound out letters and groups of letters.

REVISED   The whole-word method teaches children to recognize entire words; the phonics method teaches them to sound out letters and groups of letters.

ESL English does not allow double subjects, nor does it allow an object or an adverb to be repeated in an adjective clause. Unlike some other languages, English does not allow a noun and a pronoun to be repeated in a sentence if they have the same grammatical function. See 30c and 30d.

▶ My father ~~he~~ moved to Peru before he met my mother.

▶ ~~The final exam~~ I should really study for ~~it~~ *the final exam* to pass the

course.

11b Straighten out the logical connections.

The subject and the predicate (the verb and its modifiers) should make sense together; when they don't, the error is known as *faulty predication*.

▶ We decided that ~~Tiffany's welfare~~ *Tiffany* would not be safe living

with her mother.

Tiffany, not her welfare, may not be safe.

▶ Under the revised plan, the elderly, ~~who now receive a double~~

~~personal exemption,~~ *double personal exemption for the* will be abolished.

The exemption, not the elderly, will be abolished.

An appositive is a noun that renames a nearby noun. When an appositive and the noun it renames are not logically equivalent, the error is known as *faulty apposition*. (See 63c.)

▶ ~~The tax accountant,~~ *Tax accounting,* a very lucrative profession, requires

intelligence, patience, and attention to mathematical detail.

The tax accountant is a person, not a profession.

11c Avoid *is when*, *is where*, and *reason . . . is because* constructions.

In formal English, many readers object to *is when*, *is where*, and *reason . . . is because* constructions on either grammatical or logical grounds. Grammatically, the verb *is* (as well as *are*, *was*, and *were*) should be followed by a noun that renames the subject or by an adjective that describes the subject, not by an adverb clause beginning with *when*, *where*, or *because*. (See 62b and 63e.) Logically, the words *when*, *where*, and *because* suggest relations of time, place, and cause—relations that do not always make sense with *is*, *are*, *was*, or *were*.

▶ Anorexia nervosa is ~~where people~~ a disorder suffered by people who think they are too

fat and diet to the point of starvation.

Where refers to places. Anorexia nervosa is a disorder, not a place.

▶ The ~~reason the~~ experiment failed ~~is~~ because conditions in

the lab were not sterile.

The writer might have changed *because* to *that* (*The reason the experiment failed is that conditions in the lab were not sterile*), but the preceding revision is more concise.

EXERCISE 11–1 Edit the following sentences to untangle mixed constructions. Revisions of lettered sentences appear in the back of the book. Example:

Taking
~~By taking~~ the oath of allegiance made Ling a US citizen.

a. Using surgical gloves is a precaution now worn by dentists to prevent contact with patients' blood and saliva.
b. A physician, the career my brother is pursuing, requires at least ten years of challenging work.
c. The reason the pharaohs had bad teeth was because tiny particles of sand found their way into Egyptian bread.

d. Recurring bouts of flu among team members set a record for number of games forfeited.
e. In this box contains the key to your future.

1. Early diagnosis of prostate cancer is often curable.
2. Depending on our method of travel and our destination determines how many suitcases we are allowed to pack.
3. Dyslexia is where people have a learning disorder that impairs reading ability.
4. Even though Ellen had heard French spoken all her life, yet she could not speak it.
5. In understanding artificial intelligence code is a critical skill for computer game designers.

hackerhandbooks.com/bedhandbook > Grammar exercises > Clear sentences
> E-ex 11–2 to 11–4

12 Repair misplaced and dangling modifiers.

Modifiers, whether they are single words, phrases, or clauses, should point clearly to the words they modify. As a rule, related words should be kept together.

> **Grammar checkers** can flag split infinitives, such as *to carefully and thoroughly sift* (12d). However, they don't alert you to other misplaced modifiers (*I only ate three radishes*) or dangling modifiers (*When a boy, my mother enrolled me in tap dance classes*).

12a Put limiting modifiers in front of the words they modify.

Limiting modifiers such as *only*, *even*, *almost*, *nearly*, and *just* should appear in front of a verb only if they modify the verb: *At first, I couldn't even touch my toes, much less grasp them.* If they limit the meaning of some other word in the sentence, they should be placed in front of that word.

▶ The literature reveals that students ~~only~~ learn new vocabulary
  only
words when they are encouraged to read.

Only limits the meaning of the *when* clause.

▶ St. Vitus Cathedral, commissioned by Charles IV in the
  almost
mid-fourteenth century, ~~almost~~ took six centuries to

complete.

Almost limits the meaning of *six centuries*, not *took*.

  just
▶ If you ~~just~~ interview chemistry majors, your picture of the

student body's response to the new grading policies will

be incomplete.

The adverb *just* limits the meaning of *chemistry majors*, not *interview*.

When the limiting modifier *not* is misplaced, the sentence
usually suggests a meaning the writer did not intend.

  not
▶ In the United States in 1860, all black southerners were ~~not~~

slaves.

The original sentence says that no black southerners were slaves.
The revision makes the writer's real meaning clear: Some (but not
all) black southerners were slaves.

12b Place phrases and clauses so that readers can see at a glance what they modify.

Although phrases and clauses can appear at some distance
from the words they modify, make sure your meaning is clear.
When phrases or clauses are oddly placed, absurd misreadings
can result.

MISPLACED The soccer player returned to the clinic where he had undergone emergency surgery in 2004 in a limousine sent by Adidas.

REVISED Traveling in a limousine sent by Adidas, the soccer player returned to the clinic where he had undergone emergency surgery in 2004.

The revision corrects the false impression that the soccer player underwent emergency surgery in a limousine.

▶ ~~There~~ are many pictures of comedians who have performed *On the walls*^ at Gavin's ~~on the walls.~~

The comedians weren't performing on the walls; the pictures were on the walls.

▶ The robber was described as a six-foot-tall man with a heavy *170-pound,*^ mustache ~~weighing 170 pounds.~~

The robber, not the mustache, weighed 170 pounds.

Occasionally the placement of a modifier leads to an ambiguity—a squinting modifier. In such a case, two revisions will be possible, depending on the writer's intended meaning.

AMBIGUOUS The exchange students we met for coffee occasionally questioned us about our latest slang.

CLEAR The exchange students we occasionally met for coffee questioned us about our latest slang.

CLEAR The exchange students we met for coffee questioned us occasionally about our latest slang.

In the original version, it was not clear whether the meeting or the questioning happened occasionally. Both revisions eliminate the ambiguity.

12c Move awkwardly placed modifiers.

As a rule, a sentence should flow from subject to verb to object, without lengthy detours along the way. When a long adverbial word group separates a subject from its verb, a verb from its object, or a helping verb from its main verb, the result is often awkward.

▶ ~~Hong Kong,~~ *A* after more than 150 years of British rule, was *Hong Kong*

transferred back to Chinese control in 1997.

> There is no reason to separate the subject, *Hong Kong*, from the verb, *was transferred*, with a long phrase.

▶ ~~Jeffrey Meyers discusses,~~ in his biography of F. Scott *Jeffrey Meyers discusses* Fitzgerald, the writer's "fascination with the superiority, the selfishness, and the emptiness of the rich" (166).

Writing with sources

MLA-style citation

> When you quote from a source, the phrase or clause that you use to introduce the source should be as straightforward as possible. There is no reason to separate the verb, *discusses*, from its object, *fascination*, with two prepositional phrases.

EXCEPTION: Occasionally a writer may choose to delay a verb or an object to create suspense. In the following passage, for example, Robert Mueller inserts the *after* phrase between the subject *women* and the verb *walk* to heighten the dramatic effect.

> I asked a Burmese why women, after centuries of following their men, now walk ahead. He said there were many unexploded land mines since the war. —Robert Mueller

> **ESL** English does not allow an adverb to appear between a verb and its object. See 30f.
>
> *easily*
> ▶ Yolanda lifted ~~easily~~ the fifty-pound weight.

12d Avoid split infinitives when they are awkward.

An infinitive consists of *to* plus the base form of a verb: *to think, to breathe, to dance.* When a modifier appears between *to* and the verb, an infinitive is said to be "split": *to carefully balance, to completely understand.*

When a long word or a phrase appears between the parts of the infinitive, the result is usually awkward.

▶ ~~The~~ *If possible, the* patient should try to ~~if possible~~ avoid going up and down stairs.

Attempts to avoid split infinitives can result in equally awkward sentences. When alternative phrasing sounds unnatural, most experts allow—and even encourage—splitting the infinitive.

AWKWARD   We decided actually to enforce the law.
BETTER   We decided to actually enforce the law.

At times, neither the split infinitive nor its alternative sounds particularly awkward. In such situations, it is usually better to unsplit the infinitive, especially in formal writing.

▶ Nursing students learn to ~~accurately~~ record a patient's vital signs/ *accurately.*

EXERCISE 12–1 Edit the following sentences to correct misplaced or awkwardly placed modifiers. Revisions of lettered sentences appear in the back of the book. Example:

Answering questions can be annoying. *in a telephone survey* ~~in a telephone survey.~~

a. More research is needed to effectively evaluate the risks posed by volcanoes in the Pacific Northwest.

b. Many students graduate with debt from college totaling more than fifty thousand dollars.
c. It is a myth that humans only use 10 percent of their brains.
d. A coolhunter is a person who can find in the unnoticed corners of modern society the next wave of fashion.
e. All geese do not fly beyond Narragansett for the winter.

1. The flood nearly displaced half of the city's residents, who packed into several overcrowded shelters.
2. Most lions at night hunt for medium-size prey, such as zebra.
3. Several recent studies have encouraged heart patients to more carefully watch their cholesterol levels.
4. The garden's centerpiece is a huge sculpture that was carved by three women called *Walking in Place*.
5. The old Marlboro ads depicted a man on a horse smoking a cigarette.

hackerhandbooks.com/bedhandbook > Grammar exercises > Clear sentences
> E-ex 12–3 to 12–5

12e Repair dangling modifiers.

A dangling modifier fails to refer logically to any word in the sentence. Dangling modifiers are easy to repair, but they can be hard to recognize, especially in your own writing.

Recognizing dangling modifiers

Dangling modifiers are usually word groups (such as verbal phrases) that suggest but do not name an actor. When a sentence opens with such a modifier, readers expect the subject of the next clause to name the actor. If it doesn't, the modifier dangles.

▶ Understanding the need to create checks and balances on
  the framers of
power, the Constitution divided the government into three
   ^
branches.

The framers of the Constitution (not the document itself) understood the need for checks and balances.

▶ After completing seminary training, ~~women's~~ access to the *women have often been denied*

priesthood. ~~has often been denied.~~

Women (not their access to the priesthood) complete the training.

The following sentences illustrate four common kinds of dangling modifiers.

DANGLING   *Deciding to join the navy*, the recruiter enthusiastically pumped Joe's hand. [Participial phrase]

DANGLING   *Upon entering the doctor's office*, a skeleton caught my attention. [Preposition followed by a gerund phrase]

DANGLING   *To satisfy her mother*, the piano had to be practiced every day. [Infinitive phrase]

DANGLING   *Though not eligible for the clinical trial*, the doctor was willing to prescribe the drug for Ethan on compassionate grounds. [Elliptical clause with an understood subject and verb]

These dangling modifiers falsely suggest that the recruiter decided to join the navy, that the skeleton entered the doctor's office, that the piano intended to satisfy the mother, and that the doctor was not eligible for the clinical trial.

Although most readers will understand the writer's intended meaning in such sentences, the inadvertent humor can be distracting.

Repairing dangling modifiers

To repair a dangling modifier, you can revise the sentence in one of two ways:

- Name the actor in the subject of the sentence.
- Name the actor in the modifier.

Checking for dangling modifiers

Does an opening phrase suggest an action without naming the actor? —NO→ No problem

YES ↓

Does the subject of the sentence name the actor? —YES→ No problem

NO ↓

Revise the dangling modifier.

Depending on your sentence, one of these revision strategies may be more appropriate than the other.

ACTOR NAMED IN SUBJECT

► Upon entering the doctor's office, a skeleton. ~~caught my~~ *I noticed*

~~attention.~~

► To satisfy her mother, the piano ~~had to be practiced~~ *Jing-mei had to practice*

every day.

ACTOR NAMED IN MODIFIER

► ~~Deciding~~ *When Joe decided* to join the navy, the recruiter enthusiastically

pumped ~~Joe's~~ *his* hand.

▶ Though not eligible for the clinical trial, the doctor *(Ethan was)* was willing to prescribe the drug for ~~Ethan~~ *him* on compassionate grounds.

NOTE: You cannot repair a dangling modifier just by moving it. Consider, for example, the sentence about the skeleton. If you put the modifier at the end of the sentence (*A skeleton caught my attention upon entering the doctor's office*), you are still suggesting—absurdly, of course—that the skeleton entered the office. The only way to avoid the problem is to put the word *I* in the sentence, either as the subject or in the modifier.

▶ Upon entering the doctor's office, a skeleton. *I noticed* ~~caught my attention.~~

▶ *As I entered* ~~Upon entering~~ the doctor's office, a skeleton caught my attention.

EXERCISE 12–2 Edit the following sentences to correct dangling modifiers. Most sentences can be revised in more than one way. Revisions of lettered sentences appear in the back of the book. Example:

To acquire a degree in almost any field, two science courses *a student must complete*. ~~must be completed.~~

a. Though only sixteen, UCLA accepted Martha's application.
b. To replace the gear mechanism, attached is a form to order the part by mail.
c. Settled in the cockpit, the pounding of the engine was muffled only slightly by my helmet.
d. After studying polymer chemistry, computer games seemed less complex to Phuong.
e. When a young man, my mother enrolled me in tap dance classes.

1. While working as a ranger in Everglades National Park, a Florida panther crossed the road in front of my truck one night.
2. By following the new recycling procedure, the city's landfill costs will be reduced significantly.
3. Serving as president of the missionary circle, one of Sophia's duties is to raise money for the church.
4. After buying an album by Ali Farka Toure, the rich and rolling rhythms of Malian music made more sense to Silas.
5. Opening the window to let out a huge bumblebee, the car swerved into an oncoming truck.

hackerhandbooks.com/bedhandbook > Grammar exercises > Clear sentences > E-ex 12–6 to 12–8

13 Eliminate distracting shifts.

Grammar checkers usually do not flag shifts in point of view or in verb tense, mood, or voice. Even obvious errors, like the following shift in tense, slip right past the grammar checker: *My three-year-old fell into the pool and to my surprise she swims to the shallow end.*

Sometimes grammar checkers mark a shift from a direct to an indirect question or quotation but do not make any suggestions for revision. You must decide where the structure is faulty and how to fix it.

13a Make the point of view consistent in person and number.

The point of view of a piece of writing is the perspective from which it is written: first person (*I* or *we*), second person (*you*), or third person (*he, she, it, one, they,* or any noun).

The *I* (or *we*) point of view, which emphasizes the writer, is a good choice for informal letters and writing based primarily on personal experience. The *you* point of view, which emphasizes the reader, works well for giving advice or explaining how to do something. The third-person point of view, which emphasizes the subject, is appropriate in formal academic and professional writing.

Writers who are having difficulty settling on an appropriate point of view sometimes shift confusingly from one to another. The solution is to choose a suitable perspective and then stay with it.

▶ Our class practiced rescuing a victim trapped in a wrecked

car. We learned to dismantle the car with the essential

tools. ~~You~~ We were graded on ~~your~~ our speed and ~~your~~ our skill in

freeing the victim.

The writer should have stayed with the *we* point of view. *You* is inappropriate because the writer is not addressing readers directly. *You* should not be used in a vague sense meaning "anyone." (See 23d.)

▶ ~~One needs~~ You need a password and a credit card number to access

the database. You will be billed at an hourly rate.

You is an appropriate choice because the writer is giving advice directly to readers.

Writing with sources

APA-style citation

▶ According to the National Institute of Mental Health

(2007), ~~a child~~ children with attention deficit hyperactivity disorder

may have trouble sitting still and may gradually stop

paying attention to their teachers (Symptoms section,

para. 2).

In describing reports or results of studies, writers are often tempted to generalize with singular nouns, such as *child*, and then later in the passage find themselves shifting from singular to plural. Here the writer might have changed *their* to the singular *his or her* to agree with *child*, but the revision making both terms plural is more concise. (See also 17f and 22a.)

EXERCISE 13–1 Edit the following paragraph to eliminate distracting shifts in point of view (person and number).

When online dating first became available, many people thought that it would simplify romance. We believed that you could type in a list of criteria—sense of humor, college education, green eyes, good job—and a database would select the perfect mate. Thousands of people signed up for services and filled out their profiles, confident that true love was only a few mouse clicks away. As it turns out, however, virtual dating is no easier than traditional dating. I still have to contact the people I find, exchange e-mails and phone calls, and meet him in the real world. Although a database might produce a list of possibilities and screen out obviously undesirable people, you can't predict chemistry. More often than not, people who seem perfect online just don't click in person. Electronic services do help a single person expand their pool of potential dates, but it's no substitute for the hard work of romance.

hackerhandbooks.com/bedhandbook > Grammar exercises > Clear sentences
> E-ex 13–5

13b Maintain consistent verb tenses.

Consistent verb tenses clearly establish the time of the actions being described. When a passage begins in one tense and then shifts without warning and for no reason to another, readers are distracted and confused.

▶ There was no way I could fight the current and win. Just as I

was losing hope, a stranger ~~jumps~~ *jumped* off a passing boat and

~~swims~~ *swam* toward me.

The writer thought that the present tense (*jumps, swims*) would convey immediacy and drama. But having begun in the past tense (*could fight, was losing*), the writer should follow through in the past tense.

Writers often encounter difficulty with verb tenses when writing about literature. Because fictional events occur outside the time frames of real life, the past tense and the present tense may seem equally appropriate. The literary convention, however, is to describe fictional events consistently in the present tense. (See 55.)

▶ The scarlet letter is a punishment sternly placed on Hester's
breast by the community, and yet it ~~was~~ a fanciful and
$\overset{is}{\wedge}$
imaginative product of Hester's own needlework.

EXERCISE 13–2 Edit the following paragraphs to eliminate distracting shifts in tense.

The English colonists who settled in Massachusetts received assistance at first from the local Indian tribes, but by 1675 there had been friction between the English and the Indians for many years. On June 20 of that year, Metacomet, whom the colonists called Philip, leads the Wampanoag tribe in the first of a series of attacks on the colonial settlements. The war, known today as King Philip's War, rages on for more than a year and leaves three thousand Indians and six hundred colonists dead. Metacomet's attempt to retain power in his native land failed. Finally he too is killed, and the victorious colonists sell his wife and children into slavery.

The Indians did not leave records of their encounters with the English settlers, but the settlers recorded some of their experiences at the hands of the Indians. One of the few accounts to survive was written by a captured colonist, Mrs. Mary Rowlandson. She is a minister's wife who is kidnapped by an Indian war party and held captive for eleven weeks in 1676. Her history, *A Narrative of the Captivity and Restoration of Mrs. Mary Rowlandson,* tells the story of her experiences with the Wampanoags. Although it did not paint a completely balanced picture of the Indians, Rowlandson's narrative, which is considered a classic early American text, showed its author to be a keen observer of life in an Indian camp.

13c Make verbs consistent in mood and voice.

Unnecessary shifts in the mood of a verb can be distracting and confusing to readers. There are three moods in English: the *indicative,* used for facts, opinions, and questions; the *imperative,* used for orders or advice; and the *subjunctive,* used in certain contexts to express wishes or conditions contrary to fact (see 27g).

The following passage shifts confusingly from the indicative to the imperative mood.

▶ **The counselor advised us to spread out our core requirements** ~~She also suggested that we~~ **over two or three semesters. ~~Also,~~ pay attention to prerequisites for elective courses.**

The writer began by reporting the counselor's advice in the indicative mood (*counselor advised*) and switched to the imperative mood (*pay attention*); the revision puts both sentences in the indicative.

A verb may be in either the active voice (with the subject doing the action) or the passive voice (with the subject receiving the action). (See 8a.) If a writer shifts without warning from one to the other, readers may be left wondering why.

▶ **Each student completes a self-assessment,** *gives it* **~~The self-assessment is then given~~ to the teacher, and a copy** *exchanges* **~~is exchanged~~ with a classmate.**

Because the passage began in the active voice (*student completes*) and then switched to the passive (*self-assessment is given, copy is exchanged*), readers are left wondering who gives the self-assessment to the teacher and the classmate. The active voice, which is clearer and more direct, leaves no ambiguity.

13d Avoid sudden shifts from indirect to direct questions or quotations.

An indirect question reports a question without asking it: *We asked whether we could visit Miriam.* A direct question asks directly: *Can we visit Miriam?* Sudden shifts from indirect to direct questions are awkward. In addition, sentences containing such shifts are impossible to punctuate because indirect questions must end with a period and direct questions must end with a question mark. (See 38b.)

▶ I wonder whether Karla knew of the theft and, if so, ~~did~~
   whether she reported
   ~~she report~~ it to the police~~?~~.

> The revision poses both questions indirectly. The writer could also ask both questions directly: *Did Karla know of the theft and, if so, did she report it to the police?*

An indirect quotation reports someone's words without quoting word for word: *Annabelle said that she is a Virgo.* A direct quotation presents the exact words of a speaker or writer, set off with quotation marks: *Annabelle said, "I am a Virgo."* Unannounced shifts from indirect to direct quotations are distracting and confusing, especially when the writer fails to insert the necessary quotation marks, as in the following example.

▶ The patient said she had been experiencing heart palpitations
   asked me to   *was*
   and ~~please~~ run as many tests as possible to find out what~~'s~~
   wrong.

> The revision reports the patient's words indirectly. The writer also could quote the words directly: *The patient said, "I have been experiencing heart palpitations. Please run as many tests as possible to find out what's wrong."*

EXERCISE 13–3 Edit the following sentences to make the verbs consistent in mood and voice and to eliminate distracting shifts from indirect to direct questions or quotations. Revisions of lettered sentences appear in the back of the book. Example:

> As a public relations intern, I wrote press releases, managed
> the Web site, and ~~all phone calls were fielded by me.~~ *fielded all phone calls.*

a. An incredibly talented musician, Ray Charles mastered R&B, soul, and gospel styles. Even country music was performed well by him.

b. Environmentalists point out that shrimp farming in Southeast Asia is polluting water and making farmlands useless. They warn that action must be taken by governments before it is too late.

c. The samples were observed for five days before we detected any growth.

d. In his famous soliloquy, Hamlet contemplates whether death would be preferable to his difficult life and, if so, is he capable of committing suicide?

e. The lawyer told the judge that Miranda Hale was innocent and allow her to prove the allegations false.

1. When the photographs were taken on the beach at sunset, I intentionally left the foreground out of focus.

2. If the warning sirens sound, evacuate at once. It is not advised that you return to the building until the alarm has stopped.

3. Most baby products warn parents not to leave children unattended. Also, follow all directions carefully.

4. The advertisement promised that results would be seen in five days or consumers could return the product for a full refund.

5. Investigators first need to determine whether there was a forceful entry and then what was the motive?

EXERCISE 13–4 Edit the following sentences to eliminate distracting shifts. Revisions of lettered sentences appear in the back of the book. Example:

> For many first-year engineering students, adjusting to a
> rigorous course load can be so challenging that ~~you~~ *they*
> sometimes feel overwhelmed.

a. A courtroom lawyer has more than a touch of theater in their blood.
b. The interviewer asked if we had brought our proof of citizenship and did we bring our passports?
c. The reconnaissance scout often has to make fast decisions and use sophisticated equipment to keep their team from being detected.
d. After the animators finish their scenes, the production designer arranges the clips according to the storyboard. Synchronization notes must also be made for the sound editor and the composer.
e. Madame Defarge is a sinister figure in Dickens's *A Tale of Two Cities*. On a symbolic level, she represents fate; like the Greek Fates, she knitted the fabric of individual destiny.

1. Everyone should protect yourself from the sun, especially on the first day of extensive exposure.
2. Our neighbors told us that the island was being evacuated because of the coming storm. Also, take the northern route to the mainland.
3. Rescue workers put water on her face and lifted her head gently onto a pillow. Finally, she opens her eyes.
4. In my first tai chi class, the instructor asked if I had ever done yoga stretches and did I have good balance?
5. The artist has often been seen as a threat to society, especially when they refuse to conform to conventional standards of taste.

hackerhandbooks.com/bedhandbook > Grammar exercises > Clear sentences
> E-ex 13–7 to 13–9

14 Emphasize key ideas.

Within each sentence, emphasize your point by expressing it in the subject and verb of an independent clause, the words that receive the most attention from readers (see 14a–14e).

Within longer stretches of prose, you can draw attention to ideas deserving special emphasis by using a variety of techniques, often involving an unusual twist or some element of surprise (see 14f).

14a Coordinate equal ideas; subordinate minor ideas.

When combining two or more ideas in one sentence, you have two choices: coordination or subordination. Choose coordination to indicate that the ideas are equal or nearly equal in importance. Choose subordination to indicate that one idea is less important than another.

> **Grammar checkers** do not catch the problems with coordination and subordination discussed in this section. Not surprisingly, computer programs have no way of sensing the relative importance of ideas.

Coordination

Coordination draws attention equally to two or more ideas. To coordinate single words or phrases, join them with a coordinating conjunction or with a pair of correlative conjunctions: *bananas and strawberries*; *not only a lackluster plot but also inferior acting* (see 61g).

To coordinate independent clauses—word groups that express a complete thought and that can stand alone as a sentence—join them with a comma and a coordinating conjunction or with a semicolon:

, and	, but	, or	, nor
, for	, so	, yet	;

The semicolon is often accompanied by a conjunctive adverb such as *moreover, furthermore, therefore,* or *however* or by a transitional phrase such as *for example, in other words,* or *as a matter of fact.* (For a longer list, see p. 179.)

Assume, for example, that your intention is to draw equal attention to the following two ideas.

> Web sites like *Facebook* and *MySpace* offer ways for people to connect in the virtual world. They do not replace traditional forms of social interaction.

To coordinate these ideas, you can join them with a comma and the coordinating conjunction *but* or with a semicolon and the conjunctive adverb *however*.

> Web sites like *Facebook* and *MySpace* offer ways for people to connect in the virtual world, but they do not replace traditional forms of social interaction.

> Web sites like *Facebook* and *MySpace* offer ways for people to connect in the virtual world; however, they do not replace traditional forms of social interaction.

It is important to choose a coordinating conjunction or conjunctive adverb appropriate to your meaning. In the preceding example, the two ideas contrast with each other, calling for *but* or *however*. (For specific coordination strategies, see the chart on p. 179.)

Subordination

To give unequal emphasis to two or more ideas, express the major idea in an independent clause and place any minor ideas in subordinate clauses or phrases. (For specific subordination strategies, see the chart on p. 180.)

Let your intended meaning determine which idea you emphasize. Consider the two ideas about social networking Web sites.

> Web sites like *Facebook* and *MySpace* offer ways for people to connect in the virtual world. They do not replace traditional forms of social interaction.

If your purpose is to stress the ways that people can connect in the virtual world rather than the limitations of these connections, subordinate the idea about the limitations.

> Although they do not replace traditional forms of social interaction, Web sites like *Facebook* and *MySpace* offer ways for people to connect in the virtual world.

Using coordination to combine sentences of equal importance

1. Consider using a comma and a coordinating conjunction. (See 32a.)

, and	, but	, or	, nor
, for	, so	, yet	

▶ In Orthodox Jewish funeral ceremonies, the shroud is
a simple linen vestment. ~~The~~ *and the* coffin is plain wood.

2. Consider using a semicolon with a conjunctive adverb or transitional phrase. (See 34b.)

also	however	next
as a result	in addition	now
besides	in fact	of course
consequently	in other words	otherwise
finally	in the first place	still
for example	meanwhile	then
for instance	moreover	therefore
furthermore	nevertheless	thus

▶ Alicia scored well on the SAT; *moreover, she* ~~She also~~ had excellent

grades and a record of community service.

3. Consider using a semicolon alone. (See 34a.)

▶ In youth we learn; *in* ~~In~~ age we understand.

To focus on the limitations of the virtual world, subordinate the idea about the Web sites.

Although Web sites like *Facebook* and *MySpace* offer ways for people to connect in the virtual world, they do not replace traditional forms of social interaction.

Using subordination to combine sentences of unequal importance

1. Consider putting the less important idea in a subordinate clause beginning with one of the following words. (See 63e.)

after	before	that	which
although	even though	unless	while
as	if	until	who
as if	since	when	whom
because	so that	where	whose

▶ *When*
Elizabeth Cady Stanton proposed a convention to discuss the status of women in America/, Lucretia Mott agreed.

▶ My sister owes much of her recovery to a yoga program/ ~~She~~ *that she* began ~~the program~~ three years ago.

2. Consider putting the less important idea in an appositive phrase. (See 63c.)

▶ Karate, ~~is~~ a discipline based on the philosophy of nonviolence/, ~~It~~ teaches the art of self-defense.

3. Consider putting the less important idea in a participial phrase. (See 63b.)

▶ *Noticing*
~~I noticed~~ the EpiPen in her tote bag/, I asked her if she has food allergies.

▶ ~~American essayist Cheryl Peck was~~ *E*ncouraged by friends to *American essayist Cheryl Peck*
write about her life/, ~~She~~ began combining humor and irony in her essays about being overweight.

EXERCISE 14–1 Use the coordination or subordination technique in brackets to combine each pair of independent clauses. Revisions of lettered sentences appear in the back of the book. Example:

> **Ted Williams was one of the best hitters in the history of**
> *baseball, but he*
> **baseball. He never won a World Series ring.** [*Use a comma*
>
> *and a coordinating conjunction.*]

a. Williams played for the Boston Red Sox from 1939 to 1960. He managed the Washington Senators and Texas Rangers for several years after retiring as a player. [*Use a comma and a coordinating conjunction.*]

b. In 1941, Williams finished the season with a batting average of .406. No player has hit over .400 for a season since then. [*Use a semicolon.*]

c. Williams acknowledged that Joe DiMaggio was a better all-around player. Williams felt that he was a better hitter than DiMaggio. [*Use the subordinating conjunction* although.]

d. Williams was a stubborn man. He always refused to tip his cap to the crowd after a home run because he claimed that fans were fickle. [*Use a semicolon and the transitional phrase* for example].

e. Williams's relationship with the media was unfriendly at best. He sarcastically called baseball writers the "knights of the keyboard" in his memoir. [*Use a semicolon.*]

1. Williams took time out from his baseball career to serve in the Marines during World War II. He went on active duty a second time during the Korean War. [*Use a semicolon and the transitional phrase* in addition.]

2. Williams was named most valuable player twice in his career. He was listed as the eighth-best baseball player of all time by the *Sporting News* in 1999. [*Use the relative pronoun* who.]

3. Williams hit a home run in his final at bat in September 1960. Then he retired as a player. [*Use a comma and a coordinating conjunction.*]

4. Williams surprised many people with his 1966 Hall of Fame induction speech. It called for recognition of Negro League players and their inclusion in the Hall of Fame. [*Use the relative pronoun* which.]

5. At the 1999 All-Star game, Ted Williams returned to Fenway Park in Boston to throw out the ceremonial first pitch. For the first time he waved his hat to the cheering fans. [*Use a comma and a coordinating conjunction.*]

14b Combine choppy sentences.

Short sentences demand attention, so you should use them primarily for emphasis. Too many short sentences, one after the other, make for a choppy style.

If an idea is not important enough to deserve its own sentence, try combining it with a sentence close by. Put any minor ideas in subordinate structures such as phrases or subordinate clauses. (See 63.)

▶ The Parks Department keeps the use of insecticides to a
because the
minimum/ ~~The~~ city is concerned about the environment.

The writer wanted to emphasize that the Parks Department minimizes its use of chemicals, so she put the reason in a subordinate clause beginning with *because*.

▶ The Chesapeake and Ohio Canal, ~~is~~ a 184-mile waterway

constructed in the 1800s,/ ~~It~~ was a major source of

transportation for goods during the Civil War.

A minor idea is now expressed in an appositive phrase (*a 184-mile waterway constructed in the 1800s*).

▶ ~~Sister Consilio was~~ Énveloped in a black robe with only her
Sister Consilio
face and hands visible,/ ~~She~~ was an imposing figure.

Because Sister Consilio's overall impression was more important to the writer's purpose, the writer put the description of the clothing in a participial phrase beginning with *Enveloped*.

Although subordination is ordinarily the most effective technique for combining short, choppy sentences, coordination is appropriate when the ideas are equal in importance.

▶ At 3:30 p.m., Forrest displayed a flag of truce/ ~~Forrest~~ sent *and*

in a demand for unconditional surrender.

Combining two short sentences by joining their predicates (*displayed . . . sent*) is an effective coordination technique.

ESL Unlike some other languages, English does not repeat objects or adverbs in adjective clauses. The relative pronoun (*that, which, whom*) or relative adverb (*where*) in the adjective clause represents the object or adverb. See 30d.

▶ The apartment that we rented ~~it~~ needed repairs.

The pronoun *it* cannot repeat the relative pronoun *that*.

▶ The small town where my grandfather was born ~~there~~ is

now a big city.

The adverb *there* cannot repeat the relative adverb *where*.

EXERCISE 14–2 Combine the following sentences by subordinating minor ideas or by coordinating ideas of equal importance. You must decide which ideas are minor because the sentences are given out of context. Revisions of lettered sentences appear in the back of the book. Example:

Agnes, ~~was another girl I worked with/~~ ~~She~~ was a hyper-

active child.

a. The X-Men comic books and Japanese woodcuts of kabuki dancers were part of Marlena's research project on popular culture. They covered the tabletop and the chairs.

b. Our waitress was costumed in a kimono. She had painted her face white. She had arranged her hair in a lacquered beehive.

c. Students can apply for a spot in the leadership program. The program teaches thinking and communication skills.

d. Shore houses were flooded up to the first floor. Beaches were washed away. Brant's Lighthouse was swallowed by the sea.

e. Laura Thackray is an engineer at Volvo Car Corporation. She addressed women's safety needs. She designed a pregnant crash-test dummy.

1. I noticed that the sky was glowing orange and red. I bent down to crawl into the bunker.

2. The Market Inn is located on North Wharf. It doesn't look very impressive from the outside. The food, however, is excellent.

3. He walked up to the pitcher's mound. He dug his toe into the ground. He swung his arm around backward and forward. Then he threw the ball and struck the batter out.

4. Eryn and Maeve have decided to start a business. They have known each other since kindergarten. They will renovate homes for people with disabilities.

5. The first football card set was released by the Goudey Gum Company in 1933. The set featured only three football players. They were Red Grange, Bronko Nagurski, and Knute Rockne.

hackerhandbooks.com/bedhandbook > Grammar exercises > Clear sentences
> E-ex 14–5 and 14–6

14c Avoid ineffective or excessive coordination.

Coordinate structures are appropriate only when you intend to draw readers' attention equally to two or more ideas: *Professor Sakellarios praises loudly, and she criticizes softly.* If one idea is more important than another—or if a coordinating conjunction does not clearly signal the relationship between the ideas—you should subordinate the less important idea.

INEFFECTIVE COORDINATION	Closets were taxed as rooms, and most colonists stored their clothes in chests or clothespresses.
IMPROVED WITH SUBORDINATION	Because closets were taxed as rooms, most colonists stored their clothes in chests or clothespresses.

The revision subordinates the less important idea (*closets were taxed as rooms*) by putting it in a subordinate clause. Notice that the subordinating conjunction *Because* signals the relation between the ideas more clearly than the coordinating conjunction *and*.

Because it is so easy to string ideas together with *and*, writers often rely too heavily on coordination in their rough drafts. The cure for excessive coordination is simple: Look for opportunities to tuck minor ideas into subordinate clauses or phrases.

▶ ~~Shareholders~~ When shareholders exchanged investment tips at the company's annual meeting, ~~and~~ they learned that different approaches can yield similar results.

The minor idea has become a subordinate clause beginning with *When*.

▶ My uncle, ~~noticed~~ noticing my frightened look, ~~and~~ told me that Aunt Edna had to feel my face because she was blind.

The less important idea has become a participial phrase modifying the noun *uncle*.

▶ ~~Four hours went by, and~~ After four hours, a rescue truck finally arrived, but by that time we had been evacuated in a helicopter.

Three independent clauses were excessive. The least important idea has become a prepositional phrase.

EXERCISE 14–3 The following sentences show coordinated ideas (ideas joined with a coordinating conjunction or a semicolon). Restructure the sentences by subordinating minor ideas. You must decide which ideas are minor because the sentences are given out of context. Revisions of lettered sentences appear in the back of the book. Example:

The rowers returned to shore, ~~and~~ had a party on the beach *where they* ~~and celebrated~~ the start of the season. *to celebrate*

a. These particles are known as "stealth liposomes," and they can hide in the body for a long time without detection.
b. Irena is a competitive gymnast and majors in biochemistry; her goal is to apply her athletic experience and her science degree to a career in sports medicine.
c. Students, textile workers, and labor unions have loudly protested sweatshop abuses, so apparel makers have been forced to examine their labor practices.
d. IRC (Internet relay chat) was developed in a European university; it was created as a way for a group of graduate students to talk about projects from their dorm rooms.
e. The cafeteria's new menu has an international flavor, and it includes everything from enchiladas and pizza to pad thai and sauerbraten.

1. Victor switched on his remote-control lawn mower, and it began to shudder and emit clouds of smoke.
2. Iguanas are dependent on ultraviolet rays from the sun, so in the winter months they must be put under ultraviolet-coated lights that can be purchased at most pet stores.
3. The Civil War Trust was founded in 1991; it spearheads a nationwide campaign to protect America's Civil War battlefields.
4. We did not expect to receive so many large orders so quickly, and we are short on inventory.
5. Mother spread her love equally among us all, but she made each of us feel special in our own way.

14d Do not subordinate major ideas.

If a sentence buries its major idea in a subordinate construction, readers may not give the idea enough attention. Make sure to express your major idea in an independent clause and to subordinate any minor ideas.

▶ Harry S. Truman, who was the unexpected winner of the

1948 presidential election,. ~~defeated Thomas E. Dewey.~~

(inserted above: defeated Thomas E. Dewey,*)*

The writer wanted to focus on Truman's unexpected victory, but the original sentence buried this information in an adjective clause. The revision puts the more important idea in an independent clause and tucks the less important idea into an adjective clause (*who defeated Thomas E. Dewey*).

▶ *(inserted:* As*)* I was driving home from my new job, heading down

Ranchitos Road, ~~when~~ my car suddenly overheated.

The writer wanted to emphasize that the car overheated, not the fact of driving home. The revision expresses the major idea in an independent clause and places the less important idea in an adverb clause (*As I was driving home from my new job*).

14e Do not subordinate excessively.

In attempting to avoid short, choppy sentences, writers sometimes go to the opposite extreme, putting more subordinate ideas into a sentence than its structure can bear. If a sentence collapses of its own weight, occasionally it can be restructured. More often, however, such sentences must be divided.

▶ In *Animal Liberation*, Peter Singer argues that animals possess

nervous systems and can feel pain. ~~and that~~ *(inserted:* H*)* he therefore

believes that "the ethical principle on which human

equality rests requires us to extend equal consideration to

animals" (1).

Writing with sources

MLA-style citation

Excessive subordination makes it difficult for the reader to focus on the quoted passage. By splitting the original sentence into two separate sentences, the writer draws attention to Peter Singer's main claim, that animals should be given "equal consideration" to humans.

EXERCISE 14–4 In each of the following sentences, the idea that the writer wished to emphasize is buried in a subordinate construction. Restructure each sentence so that the independent clause expresses the major idea, as indicated in brackets, and lesser ideas are subordinated. Revisions of lettered sentences appear in the back of the book. Example:

Although
Catherine has weathered many hardships, ~~although~~ she has rarely become discouraged. [*Emphasize that Catherine has rarely become discouraged.*]

a. Gina worked as an aide for the relief agency, distributing food and medical supplies. [*Emphasize distributing food and medical supplies.*]

b. Janbir spent every Saturday learning tabla drumming, noticing with each hour of practice that his memory for complex patterns was growing stronger. [*Emphasize Janbir's memory.*]

c. The rotor hit, gouging a hole about an eighth of an inch deep in my helmet. [*Emphasize that the rotor gouged a hole in the helmet.*]

d. My grandfather, who raised his daughters the old-fashioned way, was born eighty years ago in Puerto Rico. [*Emphasize how the grandfather raised his daughters.*]

e. The Narcan reversed the depressive effect of the drug, saving the patient's life. [*Emphasize that the patient's life was saved.*]

1. Fatima, who studied Persian miniature painting after college, majored in early childhood education. [*Emphasize Fatima's studies after college.*]

2. I was losing consciousness when my will to live kicked in. [*Emphasize the will to live.*]

3. Using a sliding compound miter saw, the carpenter made intricate edges on the cabinets. [*Emphasize the carpenter's use of the saw.*]

4. Ernie was using origami to solve some tricky manufacturing problems when he decided to leave engineering and become an artist. [*Emphasize Ernie's decision.*]

5. As the undulating waves glinted in the sun, the paddlers synchronized their strokes. [*Emphasize the brightness of the waves.*]

hackerhandbooks.com/bedhandbook > Grammar exercises > Clear sentences > E-ex 14–7 and 14–8

14f Experiment with techniques for gaining special emphasis.

By experimenting with certain techniques, usually involving some element of surprise, you can draw attention to ideas that deserve special emphasis. Use such techniques sparingly, however, or they will lose their punch. The writer who tries to emphasize everything ends up emphasizing nothing.

Using sentence endings for emphasis

You can highlight an idea simply by withholding it until the end of a sentence. The technique works something like a punch line. In the following example, the sentence's meaning is not revealed until its very last word.

> The only completely consistent people are the dead.
> —Aldous Huxley

Two types of sentences that withhold information until the end are the inversion and the periodic sentence. The *inversion* reverses the normal subject-verb order, placing the subject at the end, where it receives unusual emphasis. (Also see 15c.)

> In golden pots are hidden the most deadly poisons.
> —Thomas Draxe

The *periodic* sentence opens with a pile-up of modifiers and withholds the subject and verb until the end. It draws attention to itself because it contrasts with the cumulative sentence, which is used more frequently. A *cumulative* sentence begins with the subject and verb and adds modifying elements at the end.

PERIODIC
Twenty-five years ago, at the age of thirteen, while hiking in the mountains near my hometown of Vancouver, Washington, I came face-to-face with a legend.   —Tom Weitzel, student

CUMULATIVE

A metaphysician is one who goes into a dark cellar at midnight without a light, looking for a black cat that is not there.
—Baron Bowan of Colwood

Using parallel structure for emphasis

Parallel grammatical structure draws special attention to paired ideas or to items in a series. (See 9.) When parallel ideas are paired, the emphasis falls on words that underscore comparisons or contrasts, especially when they occur at the end of a phrase or clause.

We must *stop talking* about the *American dream* and *start listening* to the *dreams of Americans*. —Reubin Askew

In a parallel series, the emphasis falls at the end, so it is generally best to end with the most dramatic or climactic item in the series.

Sister Charity enjoyed passing out writing punishments: translate the Ten Commandments into Latin, type a thousand-word essay on good manners, copy the New Testament with a quill pen. —Marie Visosky, student

Using punctuation for emphasis

Obviously the exclamation point can add emphasis, but you should not overuse it. As a rule, the exclamation point is more appropriate in dialogue than in ordinary prose.

I oozed a glob of white paint onto my palette, whipped some medium into it, loaded my brush, and announced to the class, "Move over, Michelangelo. Here I come!"
—Carolyn Goff, student

A dash or a colon may be used to draw attention to word groups worthy of special attention. (See 35a, 35b, and 39a.)

The middle of the road is where the white line is — and that's the worst place to drive. —Robert Frost

I turned to see what the anemometer read: The needle had pegged out at 106 knots.   —Jonathan Shilk, student

Occasionally, a pair of dashes may be used to highlight a word or an idea.

They carried the land itself—Vietnam, the place, the soil—a powdery orange-red dust that covered their boots and fatigues and faces.   —Tim O'Brien

Using an occasional short sentence for emphasis

Too many short sentences in a row will fast become monotonous (see 14b), but an occasional short sentence, when played off against longer sentences in the same passage, will draw attention to an idea.

The great secret, known to internists and learned early in marriage by internists' wives [or husbands], but still hidden from the general public, is that most things get better by themselves. Most things, in fact, are better by morning.
                    —Lewis Thomas

15 Provide some variety.

When a rough draft is filled with too many sentences that begin the same way or have the same structure, try injecting some variety—as long as you can do so without sacrificing clarity or ease of reading.

15a Vary your sentence openings.

Most sentences in English begin with the subject, move to the verb, and continue to the object, with modifiers tucked in along the way or put at the end. For the most part, such sentences are fine. Put too many of them in a row, however, and they become monotonous.

Adverbial modifiers are easily movable when they modify verbs; they can often be inserted ahead of the subject. Such modifiers might be single words, phrases, or clauses.

▶ A few drops of sap ~~eventually~~ began to trickle into the

bucket.

Eventually a (inserted before "A few drops")

Like most adverbs, *eventually* does not need to appear close to the verb it modifies (*began*).

▶ A pair of black ducks flew over the pond. ~~just as the sun was coming up.~~

Just as the sun was coming up, a (inserted at beginning)

The adverb clause, which modifies the verb *flew*, is as clear at the beginning of the sentence as it is at the end.

Adjectives and participial phrases can frequently be moved to the beginning of a sentence without loss of clarity.

▶ Edward/ ~~dejected and withdrawn,~~ nearly gave up his search

for a job.

Dejected and withdrawn, (inserted at beginning)

▶ ~~John and I,~~ A anticipating a peaceful evening, *John and I* sat down at the

campfire to brew a cup of coffee.

TIP: When beginning a sentence with an adjective or a participial phrase, make sure that the subject of the sentence names the person or thing described in the introductory phrase. If it doesn't, the phrase will dangle. (See 12e.)

15b Use a variety of sentence structures.

A writer should not rely too heavily on simple sentences and compound sentences, for the effect tends to be both monotonous and choppy. (See 14b and 14c.) Too many complex or compound-complex sentences, however, can be equally monotonous. If your style tends to one or the other extreme, try to achieve a better mix of sentence types.

The major sentence types are illustrated in the following sentences, all taken from Flannery O'Connor's "The King of the Birds," an essay describing the author's pet peafowl.

SIMPLE	Frequently the cock combines the lifting of his tail with the raising of his voice.
COMPOUND	Any chicken's dusting hole is out of place in a flower bed, but the peafowl's hole, being the size of a small crater, is more so.
COMPLEX	The peacock does most of his serious strutting in the spring and summer when he has a full tail to do it with.
COMPOUND-COMPLEX	The cock's plumage requires two years to attain its pattern, and for the rest of his life, this chicken will act as though he designed it himself.

For a fuller discussion of sentence types, see 64a.

15c Try inverting sentences occasionally.

A sentence is inverted if it does not follow the normal subject-verb-object pattern (see 62c). Many inversions sound artificial and should be avoided except in the most formal contexts. But if an inversion sounds natural, it can provide a welcome touch of variety.

▶ Opposite the produce section is a ~~A~~ refrigerated case of mouthwatering cheeses; ~~is opposite the produce section;~~ a friendly attendant will cut off just the amount you want.

The revision inverts the normal subject-verb order by moving the verb, *is*, ahead of its subject, *case*.

> *Set at the top two corners of the stage were huge*
> ~~Huge~~ lavender hearts outlined in bright white lights. ~~were~~
>
> ~~set at the top two corners of the stage.~~

In the revision, the subject, *hearts*, appears after the verb, *were set*. Notice that the two parts of the verb are also inverted—and separated from each other (*Set . . . were*)—without any awkwardness or loss of meaning.

Inverted sentences are used for emphasis as well as for variety (see 14f).

15d Consider adding an occasional question or quotation.

An occasional question can provide a change of pace, especially at the beginning of a paragraph, where it engages the reader's interest.

> Virginia Woolf, in her book *A Room of One's Own*, wrote that in order for a woman to write fiction she must have two things, certainly: a room of her own (with key and lock) and enough money to support herself.
> *What then are we to make of Phillis Wheatley, a slave, who owned not even herself?* This sickly, frail black girl who required a servant of her own at times—her health was so precarious—and who, had she been white, would have been easily considered the intellectual superior of all the women and most of the men in the society of her day. [Italics added.]
> —Alice Walker

Quotations can also provide variety, for they add other people's voices to your own. These other voices might be bits of dialogue.

> When we got back upstairs, Dr. Haney and Captain Shiller, the head nurse, were waiting for us by the elevator. As the nurse hurried off, pushing Todd, the doctor explained to us what would happen next.

"Mrs. Barrus," he began, "this last test is one we do only when absolutely necessary. It is very painful and hard on the patient, but we have no other choice." Apologetically, he went on. "I cannot give him an anesthetic." He waited for the statement to sink in. —Celeste L. Barrus, student

Or they might be quotations from written sources.

Even when she enters the hospital on the brink of death, the anorexic will refuse help from anyone and will continue to deny needing help, especially from a doctor. At this point, reports Dr. Steven Levenkron, the anorexic is most likely "a frightened, cold, lonely, starved, and physically tortured, exhausted person—not unlike an actual concentration camp inmate" (29). In this condition she is ultimately force-fed through a tube inserted in the chest. —Jim Drew, student

Notice that the quotation from a written source is documented with a citation in parentheses. (See 53a.)

EXERCISE 15–1 Improve sentence variety in each of the following sentences by using the technique suggested in brackets. Revisions of lettered sentences appear in the back of the book. Example:

To protect endangered marine turtles, fishing
~~Fishing~~ crews place turtle excluder devices in fishing nets.

~~to protect endangered marine turtles.~~ [*Begin the sentence with the adverbial infinitive phrase.*]

a. The exhibits for insects and spiders are across the hall from the fossils exhibit. [*Invert the sentence.*]
b. Sayuri becomes a successful geisha after growing up desperately poor in Japan. [*Move the adverb clause to the beginning of the sentence.*]
c. It is interesting to consider what caused Mount St. Helens to erupt. Researchers believe that a series of earthquakes in the area was a contributing factor. [*Change the first sentence to a question.*]
d. Ice cream typically contains 10 percent milk fat. Premium ice cream may contain up to 16 percent milk fat and has

considerably less air in the product. [*Combine the two sentences as a compound sentence.*]

e. The economy may recover more quickly than expected if home values climb. [*Move the adverb clause to the beginning of the sentence.*]

1. The Dust Bowl farmers, looking wearily into the cameras of US government photographers, represented the harshest effects of the Great Depression. [*Move the participial phrase to the beginning of the sentence.*]

2. The Trans Alaska Pipeline was completed in 1977. It has moved more than fifteen billion barrels of oil since 1977. [*Combine the two sentences into a complex sentence.*]

3. Mr. Guo habitually dresses in loose clothing and canvas shoes for his wushu workout. [*Move the adverb to the beginning of the sentence.*]

4. A number of obstacles are strategically placed throughout a firefighter training maze. [*Invert the sentence.*]

5. Ian McKellen is a British actor who made his debut in 1961 and was knighted in 1991, and he played Gandalf in the movie trilogy *The Lord of the Rings*. [*Make a simple sentence. See also 64a.*]

EXERCISE 15–2 Edit the following paragraph to increase sentence variety.

Making architectural models is a skill that requires patience and precision. It is an art that illuminates a design. Architects come up with a grand and intricate vision. Draftspersons convert that vision into blueprints. The model maker follows the blueprints. The model maker builds a miniature version of the structure. Modelers can work in traditional materials like wood and clay and paint. Modelers can work in newer materials like Styrofoam and liquid polymers. Some modelers still use cardboard, paper, and glue. Other modelers prefer glue guns, deformable plastic, and thin aluminum and brass wire. The modeler may seem to be making a small mess in the early stages of model building. In the end the modeler has completed a small-scale structure. Architect Rem Koolhaas has insisted that plans reveal the logic of a design. He has argued that models expose the architect's vision. The model maker's art makes this vision real.

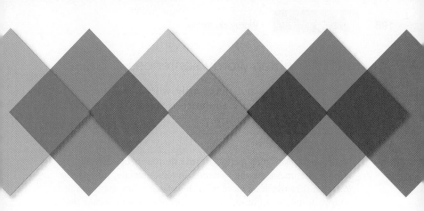

Part IV
Word Choice

197

16　Tighten wordy sentences.

Long sentences are not necessarily wordy, nor are short sentences always concise. A sentence is wordy if it can be tightened without loss of meaning.

> **Grammar checkers** flag wordy constructions only occasionally. They sometimes alert you to common redundancies, such as *true fact*, but they overlook more than they catch. They may miss empty or inflated phrases, such as *in my opinion* and *in order that*, and they rarely identify sentences with needlessly complex structures. Grammar checkers are very good, however, at flagging and suggesting revisions for wordy constructions beginning with *there is* and *there are*.

16a Eliminate redundancies.

Writers often repeat themselves unnecessarily, thinking that expressions such as *cooperate together*, *yellow in color*, or *basic essentials* add emphasis to their writing. In reality, such redundancies do just the opposite. There is no need to say the same thing twice.

▶ Twentysomethings are often ~~thought of or~~ stereotyped as

apathetic even though many are active in political and

service groups.

▶ Daniel ~~is now employed~~ works at a private rehabilitation center

~~working~~ as a registered physical therapist.

Though modifiers ordinarily add meaning to the words they modify, occasionally they are redundant.

▶ Sylvia ~~very hurriedly~~ scribbled her name, address, and phone

number on a greasy napkin.

The word *scribbled* already suggests that Sylvia wrote *very hurriedly.*

▶ Gabriele Muccino's film *The Pursuit of Happyness* tells the

story of a single father determined ~~in his mind~~ to pull

himself and his son out of homelessness.

The word *determined* contains the idea that his resolution formed in his mind.

16b Avoid unnecessary repetition of words.

Though words may be repeated deliberately, for effect, repetitions will seem awkward if they are clearly unnecessary. When a more concise version is possible, choose it.

▶ Our fifth patient, in room six, is a mentally ill. ~~patient.~~

▶ The best teachers help each student ~~become a better~~ grow

~~student~~ both academically and emotionally.

▶ A study by the Henry J. Kaiser Family Foundation (2004)

~~studied~~ measured the effects of diet and exercise on childhood

obesity.

Writing with sources

APA-style citation

The repetition of *study . . . studied* is awkward and redundant. By using the descriptive verb *measured* instead, the writer conveys more precisely the purpose of the study and suggests its function in her paper.

16c Cut empty or inflated phrases.

An empty phrase can be cut with little or no loss of meaning. Common examples are introductory word groups that weaken the writer's authority by apologizing or hedging: *in my opinion, I think that, it seems that, one must admit that,* and so on.

▶ ~~In my opinion,~~ Our current immigration policy is misguided.

Readers understand without being told that they are hearing the writer's opinion.

Inflated phrases can be reduced to a word or two without loss of meaning.

INFLATED	CONCISE
along the lines of	like
as a matter of fact	in fact
at all times	always
at the present time	now, currently
at this point in time	now, currently
because of the fact that	because
by means of	by
by virtue of the fact that	because
due to the fact that	because
for the purpose of	for
for the reason that	because
have the ability to	be able to, can
in light of the fact that	because
in order to	to
in spite of the fact that	although, though
in the event that	if
in the final analysis	finally
in the nature of	like
in the neighborhood of	about
until such time as	until

► ~~At this point in time~~ M̂y skills and experience are a perfect

match for the position of assistant manager.

16d Simplify the structure.

If the structure of a sentence is needlessly indirect, try simplifying it. Look for opportunities to strengthen the verb.

► The financial analyst claimed that because of volatile market

conditions she could not ~~make an~~ estimate ~~of~~ the company's

future profits.

The verb *estimate* is more vigorous and concise than *make an estimate of.*

The colorless verbs *is*, *are*, *was*, and *were* frequently generate excess words.

▶ Investigators ~~were involved in studying~~ studied the effect of classical music on unborn babies.

The revision is more direct and concise. The action (*studying*), originally appearing in a subordinate structure, has become a strong verb, *studied*.

The expletive constructions *there is* and *there are* (or *there was* and *there were*) can also generate excess words. The same is true of expletive constructions beginning with *it*. (See 62c.)

▶ ~~There is~~ Another module ~~that~~ tells the story of Charles Darwin and introduces the theory of evolution.

▶ ~~It is imperative that~~ All night managers must follow strict procedures when locking the safe.

Finally, verbs in the passive voice may be needlessly indirect. When the active voice expresses your meaning as effectively, use it. (See 8a.)

▶ All too often, our coaches have recruited athletes with marginal academic skills. ~~have been recruited by our coaches.~~

16e Reduce clauses to phrases, phrases to single words.

Word groups functioning as modifiers can often be made more compact. Look for any opportunities to reduce clauses to phrases or phrases to single words.

▶ We took a side trip to Monticello, ~~which was~~ the home of

Thomas Jefferson.

▶ In ~~the~~ essay, *this* ~~that follows,~~ I argue against Immanuel

Kant's claim that we should not lie under any *problematic*

circumstances. ~~which is a problematic claim.~~

EXERCISE 16–1　Edit the following sentences to reduce wordiness. Revisions of lettered sentences appear in the back of the book. Example:

The Wilsons moved into the house ~~in spite of the fact that~~ *even though*

the back door was only ten yards from the train tracks.

a. Martin Luther King Jr. was a man who set a high standard for future leaders to meet.

b. Alice has been deeply in love with cooking since she was little and could first peek over the edge of a big kitchen tabletop.

c. In my opinion, Bloom's race for the governorship is a futile exercise.

d. It is pretty important in being a successful graphic designer to have technical knowledge and at the same time an eye for color and balance.

e. Your task will be the delivery of correspondence to all employees in the company.

1. Seeing the barrels, the driver immediately slammed on his brakes.

2. A really well-stocked bookshelf should have classical literature on it as well as important modern works of the current day.

3. China's enormously huge workforce has an effect on the global world of high-tech manufacturing of things.

4. A typical autocross course consists of at least two straightaways, and the rest of the course is made up of numerous slaloms and several sharp turns.

5. At breakfast time, Mehrdad always started his day with cantaloupe, lemon yogurt, and black coffee.

EXERCISE 16–2 Edit the following business memo to reduce wordiness.

To: District managers
From: Margaret Davenport, Vice President
Subject: Customer database

It has recently been brought to my attention that a percentage of our sales representatives have been failing to log reports of their client calls in our customer database each and every day. I have also learned that some representatives are not checking the database on a routine basis.

Our clients sometimes receive a multiple number of sales calls from us when a sales representative is not cognizant of the fact that the client has been contacted at a previous time. Repeated telephone calls from our representatives annoy our customers. These repeated telephone calls also portray our company as one that is lacking in organization.

Effective as of immediately, direct your representatives to do the following:

- Record each and every customer contact in the customer database at the end of each day, without fail.
- Check the database at the very beginning of each day to ensure that telephone communications will not be initiated with clients who have already been called.

Let me extend my appreciation to you for cooperating in this important matter.

hackerhandbooks.com/bedhandbook > Grammar exercises > Word choice
> E-ex 16–3 to 16–6

17 Choose appropriate language.

Language is appropriate when it suits your subject, engages your audience, and blends naturally with your own voice.

To some extent, your choice of language will be governed by the conventions of the genre in which you are writing. When in doubt about the conventions of a particular genre—lab reports, informal essays, business memos, and so on—consult your instructor or look at models written by experts in the field.

17a Stay away from jargon.

Jargon is specialized language used among members of a trade, profession, or group. Use jargon only when readers will be familiar with it; even then, use it only when plain English will not do as well.

Sentences filled with jargon are likely to be long and lumpy. To revise such sentences, you must rewrite them, usually in fewer words.

JARGON   For years, the indigenous body politic of South Africa attempted to negotiate legal enfranchisement without result.

REVISED   For years, the indigenous people of South Africa negotiated unsuccessfully for the right to vote.

Though a political scientist might feel comfortable with the original version, jargon such as *body politic* and *legal enfranchisement* is needlessly complicated for most readers.

Broadly defined, jargon includes puffed-up language designed more to impress readers than to inform them. The following are common examples from business, government, higher education, and the military, with plain English alternatives in parentheses.

ameliorate (improve)   indicator (sign)
commence (begin)   optimal (best, most favorable)
components (parts)   parameters (boundaries, limits)
endeavor (try)   peruse (read, look over)
exit (leave)   prior to (before)
facilitate (help)   utilize (use)
impact (v.) (affect)   viable (workable)

Sentences filled with jargon are hard to read, and they are often wordy as well.

▶ All ~~employees functioning in the capacity of~~ work-study
        must prove that they are currently enrolled.
students ~~are required to give evidence of current enrollment.~~
        ^

▶ The CEO should ~~dialogue~~ _talk_ with investors about ~~partnering~~ _working_
with clients to ~~purchase~~ _buy_ land in ~~economically deprived zones.~~ _poor neighborhoods._

17b Avoid pretentious language, most euphemisms, and "doublespeak."

Hoping to sound profound or poetic, some writers embroider their thoughts with large words and flowery phrases, language that in fact sounds pretentious. Pretentious language is so ornate and often so wordy that it obscures the thought that lies beneath.

▶ Taylor's ~~employment of multihued means of expression draws~~ _use of colorful language reveals that she has a_
~~back the curtains and lets slip the~~ nostalgic ~~vantage point~~ _view of_
~~from which she observes~~ American society ~~as well as her lack~~ _and does not_
~~of comprehension of~~ _understand_ economic realities.

The writer of the original sentence had turned to a thesaurus (a dictionary of synonyms and antonyms) in an attempt to sound authoritative. When such a writer gains enough confidence to speak in his or her own voice, pretentious language disappears.

Related to pretentious language are euphemisms, nice-sounding words or phrases substituted for words thought to sound harsh or ugly. Like pretentious language, euphemisms are wordy and indirect. Unlike pretentious language, they are sometimes appropriate. It is our social custom, for example, to use euphemisms when speaking or writing about excretion (_I have to go to the bathroom_), sexual intercourse (_They did not sleep together until they were married_), and the like. We may also use euphemisms out of concern for someone's feelings. Telling parents, for example, that their daughter is "unmotivated" is more sensitive than saying she's lazy. Tact or politeness, then, can justify an occasional euphemism.

Most euphemisms, however, are needlessly evasive or even deceitful. Like pretentious language, they obscure the intended meaning.

EUPHEMISM	PLAIN ENGLISH
adult entertainment	pornography
preowned automobile	used car
economically deprived	poor
negative savings	debts
strategic withdrawal	retreat or defeat
revenue enhancers	taxes
chemical dependency	drug addiction
downsize	lay off, fire
correctional facility	prison

The term *doublespeak* applies to any deliberately evasive or deceptive language, including euphemisms. Doublespeak is especially common in politics and business. A military retreat is described as "tactical redeployment," "enhanced interrogation" is a euphemism for "torture," and "downsizing" really means "firing employees."

> **Grammar checkers** rarely identify jargon and only occasionally flag pretentious language, so you should be alert to your own use of jargon and pretentious language and simplify it whenever possible.

EXERCISE 17–1   Edit the following sentences to eliminate jargon, pretentious or flowery language, euphemisms, and doublespeak. You may need to make substantial changes in some sentences. Revisions of lettered sentences appear in the back of the book. Example:

After two weeks in the legal department, Sue has ~~worked~~ *mastered* ~~into~~ the routine, ~~of the office,~~ and her ~~functional and self-management skills have~~ *office* *performance has* exceeded all expectations.

a. In my youth, my family was under the constraints of difficult financial circumstances.

b. In order that I may increase my expertise in the area of delivery of services to clients, I feel that participation in this conference will be beneficial.

c. The prophetic meteorologist cautioned the general populace regarding the possible deleterious effects of the impending tempest.

d. Governmentally sanctioned investigations into the continued value of after-school programs indicate a perceived need in the public realm at large.

e. Passengers should endeavor to finalize the customs declaration form prior to exiting the aircraft.

1. We learned that the mayor had been engaging in a creative transfer of city employees' pension funds.

2. After a cursory examination of brand-new research findings on textiles, Patricia and the members of her team made the decision to engage in a series of visits to fashion manufacturers in the local vicinity.

3. The nurse announced that there had been a negative patient-care outcome due to a therapeutic misadventure on the part of the surgeon.

4. A generally leisurely pace at the onset of tai chi exercises can yield a variety of beneficial points within a short period of time.

5. The bottom line is that the company is experiencing a negative cash flow.

EXERCISE 17–2 Edit the following e-mail message to eliminate jargon.

Dear Ms. Jackson:

We members of the Nakamura Reyes team value our external partnering arrangements with Creative Software, and I look forward to seeing you next week at the trade show in Fresno. Per Mr. Reyes, please let me know when you'll have some downtime there so that he and I can conduct a strategizing session with you concerning our production schedule. It's crucial that we all be on the same page re our 2009–2010 product release dates.

Before we have some face time, however, I have some findings to share. Our customer-centric approach to the new products will necessitate that user testing periods trend upward. The enclosed data should help you effectuate any adjustments to your timeline; let me know ASAP if you require any additional information to facilitate the above.

Before we convene in Fresno, Mr. Reyes and I will agendize any further talking points. Thanks for your help.

Sincerely,

Sylvia Nakamura

hackerhandbooks.com/bedhandbook > Grammar exercises > Word choice
> E-ex 17–6

17c Avoid obsolete and invented words.

Although dictionaries list obsolete words such as *recomfort* and *reechy*, these words are not appropriate for current use. Invented words (called *neologisms*) are too recently created to be part of standard English. Many invented words fade out of use without becoming standard. *Bling* and *blogosphere* are neologisms that may not last. *Prequel* and *e-mail* are no longer neologisms; they have become standard English. Avoid using invented words in formal writing unless they are given in the dictionary as standard or unless no other word expresses your meaning.

17d In most contexts, avoid slang, regional expressions, and nonstandard English.

Slang is an informal and sometimes private vocabulary that expresses the solidarity of a group such as teenagers, rock musicians, or football fans; it is subject to more rapid change than standard English. For example, the slang teenagers use to express approval changes every few years; *cool, groovy, neat, awesome, phat,* and *sick* have replaced one another within the last three decades. Sometimes slang becomes so widespread that it is accepted as standard vocabulary. *Jazz,* for example, started out as slang but is now a standard term for a style of music.

Although slang has a certain vitality, it is a code that not everyone understands, and it is very informal. Therefore, it is inappropriate in most written work.

▶ When the server crashed unexpectedly, three hours of ~we lost~

unsaved data. ~went down the tubes.~

▶ The government's "filth" guidelines for food will ~gross you~ ~disgust you.~

~out.~

Regional expressions are common to a group in a geographic area. *Let's talk with the bark off* (for *Let's speak frankly*) is an expression in the southern United States, for example. Regional expressions have the same limitations as slang and are therefore inappropriate in most writing.

▶ John was four blocks from the house before he remembered
to ~cut~ the headlights. ~on.~ *turn on*

▶ Seamus wasn't ~for~ sure, but he thought the whales might

be migrating during his visit to Oregon.

Standard English is the language used in all academic, business, and professional fields. Nonstandard English is spoken by people with a common regional or social heritage. Although nonstandard English may be appropriate when spoken within a close group, it is out of place in most formal and informal writing.

▶ The governor said he ~don't~ know if he will approve the *doesn't*

budget without the clean air provision.

If you speak a nonstandard dialect, try to identify the ways in which your dialect differs from standard English. Look especially for the following features of nonstandard English, which commonly cause problems in writing.

Misusing verb forms such as *began* and *begun* (See 27a.)

Leaving -*s* endings off verbs (See 27c.)

Leaving -*ed* endings off verbs (See 27d.)

Leaving out necessary verbs (See 27e.)

Using double negatives (See 26d.)

17e Choose an appropriate level of formality.

In deciding on a level of formality, consider both your subject and your audience. Does the subject demand a dignified treatment, or is a relaxed tone more suitable? Will readers be put off if you assume too close a relationship with them, or might you alienate them by seeming too distant?

For most college and professional writing, some degree of formality is appropriate. In a job application letter, for example, it is a mistake to sound too breezy and informal.

TOO INFORMAL   I'd like to get that sales job you've got in the paper.

MORE FORMAL   I would like to apply for the position of sales associate advertised in the *Peoria Journal Star*.

Informal writing is appropriate for private letters, personal e-mail and text messages, and business correspondence between close associates. Like spoken conversation, informal writing allows contractions (*don't, I'll*) and colloquial words (*kids, kinda*). Vocabulary and sentence structure are rarely complex.

In choosing a level of formality, above all be consistent. When a writer's voice shifts from one level of formality to another, readers receive mixed messages.

▶ Once a pitcher for the Blue Jays, Jorge shared with me

the secrets of his trade. His lesson ~~commenced~~ *began* with his

famous curveball, ~~implemented~~ *thrown* by tucking the little finger

behind the ball. Next he ~~elucidated~~ *revealed* the mysteries of the

sucker pitch, a slow ball coming behind a fast windup.

Words such as *commenced* and *elucidated* are inappropriate for the subject matter, and they clash with informal terms such as *sucker pitch* and *fast windup*.

Grammar checkers rarely flag slang and informal language. They do, however, flag contractions. If your ear tells you that a contraction such as *isn't* or *doesn't* strikes the right tone, stay with it.

EXERCISE 17–3   Revise the following passage so that the level of formality is appropriate for a letter to the editor of a major newspaper.

In pop culture, college grads who return home to live with the folks are seen as good-for-nothing losers who mooch off their families. And many older adults seem to feel that the trend of moving back home after school, which was rare in their day, is becoming too commonplace today. But society must realize that times have changed. Most young adults want to live on their own ASAP, but they graduate with heaps of debt and need some time to get back on their feet. College tuition and the cost of housing have increased way more than salary increases in the past fifty years. Also, the job market is tighter and more jobs require advanced degrees than in the past. So before people go off on college graduates who move back into their parents' house for a spell, they'd better consider all the facts.

17f Avoid sexist language.

Sexist language is language that stereotypes or demeans women or men. Using nonsexist language is a matter of courtesy—of respect for and sensitivity to the feelings of others.

Recognizing sexist language

Some sexist language is easy to recognize because it reflects genuine contempt for women: referring to a woman as a "chick," for example, or calling a lawyer a "lady lawyer."

Other forms of sexist language are less blatant. The following practices, while they may not result from conscious sexism, reflect stereotypical thinking: referring to members of one profession as exclusively male or exclusively female (teachers as women or computer engineers as men, for instance), using different conventions when naming or identifying women and men, or assuming that all of one's readers are men.

STEREOTYPICAL LANGUAGE

After a nursing student graduates, *she* must face a difficult state board examination. [Not all nursing students are women.]

Running for city council are Boris Stotsky, an attorney, and *Mrs.* Cynthia Jones, a professor of English and *mother of three*. [The title *Mrs.* and the phrase *mother of three* are irrelevant.]

All executives' *wives* are invited to the welcome dinner. [Not all executives are men.]

Still other forms of sexist language result from outdated traditions. The pronouns *he*, *him*, and *his*, for instance, were traditionally used to refer generically to persons of either sex. Nowadays, to avoid that sexist usage, some writers use *she*, *her*, and *hers* generically or substitute the female pronouns alternately with the male pronouns.

GENERIC PRONOUNS

A journalist is stimulated by *his* deadline.

A good interior designer treats *her* clients' ideas respectfully.

But both forms are sexist—for excluding one sex entirely and for making assumptions about the members of particular professions.

Similarly, the nouns *man* and *men* were once used to refer generically to persons of either sex. Current usage demands gender-neutral terms for references to both men and women.

INAPPROPRIATE	APPROPRIATE
chairman	chairperson, moderator, chair, head
clergyman	member of the clergy, minister, pastor
congressman	member of Congress, representative, legislator
fireman	firefighter
foreman	supervisor
mailman	mail carrier, postal worker, letter carrier
to man	to operate, to staff
mankind	people, humans
manpower	personnel, staff
policeman	police officer
salesman	salesperson, sales associate, salesclerk
weatherman	forecaster, meteorologist
workman	worker, laborer

> **Grammar checkers** are good at flagging obviously sexist terms, such as *mankind* and *fireman*, but they do not flag language that might be demeaning (*woman doctor*) or stereotypical. They also have no way of identifying the generic use of *he* or *she*. You must use your common sense to tell when a word or a construction is offensive.

Revising sexist language

When revising sexist language, you may be tempted to substitute *he or she* and *his or her*. These terms are inclusive but wordy; fine in small doses, they can become awkward when repeated throughout an essay. A better revision strategy is to write in the plural; yet another strategy is to recast the sentence so that the problem does not arise (see p. 214).

SEXIST

A journalist is stimulated by *his* deadline.

A good interior designer treats *her* clients' ideas respectfully.

ACCEPTABLE BUT WORDY

A journalist is stimulated by *his or her* deadline.

A good interior designer treats *his or her* clients' ideas respectfully.

BETTER: USING THE PLURAL

Journalists are stimulated by *their* deadlines.

Good interior designers treat *their* clients' ideas respectfully.

BETTER: RECASTING THE SENTENCE

A journalist is stimulated by *a* deadline.

A good interior designer treats clients' ideas respectfully.

For more examples of these revision strategies, see 22.

EXERCISE 17–4 Edit the following sentences to eliminate sexist language or sexist assumptions. Revisions of lettered sentences appear in the back of the book. Example:

Scholarship athletes
A scholarship athlete must be as concerned about his
                                                  their
academic performance as he is about his athletic
                              they are   their
performance.

a. Mrs. Geralyn Farmer, who is the mayor's wife, is the chief surgeon at University Hospital. Dr. Paul Green is her assistant.
b. Every applicant wants to know how much he will earn.
c. An elementary school teacher should understand the concept of nurturing if she intends to be effective.
d. An obstetrician needs to be available to his patients at all hours.
e. If man does not stop polluting his environment, mankind will perish.

1. A fireman must always be on call even when he is off duty.
2. The chairman for the new program in digital art is Ariana Tamlin, an accomplished portrait painter, computer programmer, and cookie baker.
3. In the governor's race, Lena Weiss, a defense lawyer and mother of two, easily defeated Harvey Tower, an architect.
4. Recent military history has shown that lady combat helicopter pilots are as skilled, reliable, and resourceful as men.
5. An emergency room head nurse must know how to use sophisticated digital equipment if she is to keep track of all her patients' data and guide her medical team.

EXERCISE 17–5 Eliminate sexist language or sexist assumptions in the following job posting for an elementary school teacher.

> We are looking for qualified women for the position of elementary school teacher. The ideal candidate should have a bachelor's degree, a state teaching certificate, and one year of student teaching. She should be knowledgeable in all elementary subject areas, including science and math. While we want our new teacher to have a commanding presence in the classroom, we are also looking for motherly characteristics such as patience and trustworthiness. She must be able to both motivate an entire classroom and work with each student one-on-one to assess his individual needs. She must also be comfortable communicating with the parents of her students. For salary and benefits information, including maternity leave policy, please contact the Martin County School Board. Any qualified applicant should submit her résumé by March 15.

hackerhandbooks.com/bedhandbook > Grammar exercises > Word choice
> E-ex 17–7 and 17–8

17g Revise language that may offend groups of people.

Obviously it is impolite to use offensive terms such as *Polack* and *redneck*, but biased language can take more subtle forms. Because language evolves over time, names once thought acceptable may become offensive. When describing groups of people, choose names that the groups currently use to describe themselves.

▶ North Dakota takes its name from the ~~Indian~~ Lakota word meaning "friend" or "ally."

▶ Many ~~Oriental~~ Asian immigrants have recently settled in our town.

Negative stereotypes (such as "drives like a teenager" or "sour as a spinster") are of course offensive. But you should avoid stereotyping a person or a group even if you believe your generalization to be positive.

▶ It was no surprise that Greer, ~~a Chinese American,~~ was *an excellent math and science student,* selected for the honors chemistry program.

18　Find the exact words.

Two reference works (or their online equivalents) will help you find words to express your meaning exactly: a good dictionary, such as *The American Heritage Dictionary* or *Merriam-Webster's Collegiate Dictionary*, and a collection of synonyms and antonyms, such as *Roget's International Thesaurus*.

TIP: Do not turn to a thesaurus in search of flowery or impressive words. Look instead for words that exactly express your meaning.

> **Grammar checkers** flag some nonstandard idioms but few clichés. They do not identify commonly confused words, such as *principal* and *principle*, or misused word forms, such as *significance* and *significant*. You must be alert for such words and use your dictionary if you are unsure of the correct form. Grammar checkers are of little help with the other problems discussed in 18.

18a Select words with appropriate connotations.

In addition to their strict dictionary meanings (or *denotations*), words have *connotations*, emotional colorings that affect how readers respond to them. The word *steel* denotes "commercial iron that contains carbon," but it also calls up a cluster of images associated with steel. These associations give the word its connotations—cold, hard, smooth, unbending.

If the connotation of a word does not seem appropriate for your purpose, your audience, or your subject matter, you should change the word. When a more appropriate synonym does not come quickly to mind, consult a dictionary or a thesaurus.

▶ When American soldiers returned home after World War II,

many women ~~abandoned~~ *left* their jobs in favor of marriage.

The word *abandoned* is too negative for the context.

▶ As I covered the boats with marsh grass, the ~~perspiration~~ *sweat* I

had worked up evaporated in the wind, and the cold

morning air seemed even colder.

The term *perspiration* is too dainty for the context, which suggests vigorous exercise.

EXERCISE 18–1 Use a dictionary and a thesaurus to find at least four synonyms for each of the following words. Be prepared to explain any slight differences in meaning.

1. decay (verb)
2. difficult (adjective)
3. hurry (verb)
4. pleasure (noun)
5. secret (adjective)
6. talent (noun)

18b Prefer specific, concrete nouns.

Unlike general nouns, which refer to broad classes of things, specific nouns point to particular items. *Film*, for example, names a general class, *fantasy film* names a narrower class, and *The Golden Compass* is more specific still. Other examples: *team, football team, Denver Broncos; music, symphony, Beethoven's Ninth.*

Unlike abstract nouns, which refer to qualities and ideas (*justice, beauty, realism, dignity*), concrete nouns point to immediate, often sensory experience and to physical objects (*steeple, asphalt, lilac, stone, garlic*).

Specific, concrete nouns express meaning more vividly than general or abstract ones. Although general and abstract language is sometimes necessary to convey your meaning, use specific, concrete words whenever possible.

▶ The senator spoke about the challenges of the future: *pollution, dwindling resources, and terrorism.* ~~the environment and world peace.~~

Nouns such as *thing*, *area*, *aspect*, *factor*, and *individual* are especially dull and imprecise.

▶ Toni Morrison's *Beloved* is about slavery, *motherhood, and memory.* ~~among other things.~~

▶ Try pairing a trainee with an *experienced technician.* ~~individual with technical experience.~~

18c Do not misuse words.

If a word is not in your active vocabulary, you may find yourself misusing it, sometimes with embarrassing consequences. When in doubt, check the dictionary.

▶ The fans were *climbing* ~~migrating~~ up the bleachers in search of seats.

▶ The Internet has so *permeated* ~~diffused~~ our culture that it touches all segments of society.

Writing with sources

MLA-style citation

▶ Marie Winn *argues* ~~quarrels~~ that television viewing is bad for families because it "serves to anesthetize parents into accepting their family's diminished state" (357).

When you are introducing a quotation with a signal phrase, be sure to choose a verb that clearly reflects the source's intention. *Quarrel* suggests a heated or angry dispute; *argue* is a more neutral word. (Also see 52b on using signal phrases.)

Be especially alert for misused word forms—using a noun such as *absence*, *significance*, or *persistence*, for example, when your meaning requires the adjective *absent*, *significant*, or *persistent*.

► Most dieters are not ~~persistence~~ persistent enough to make a permanent

change in their eating habits.

EXERCISE 18–2 Edit the following sentences to correct misused words. Revisions of lettered sentences appear in the back of the book. Example:

These days the training required for a ballet dancer

is ~~all-absorbent.~~ all-absorbing.

a. We regret this delay; thank you for your patients.
b. Ada's plan is to require education and experience to prepare herself for a position as property manager.
c. Tiger Woods, the penultimate competitor, has earned millions of dollars just in endorsements.
d. Many people take for granite that public libraries have up-to-date computer systems.
e. The affect of Gao Xinjian's novels on Chinese exiles is hard to gauge.

1. Because Anne Tyler often writes about family loyalties, her illusions to *King Lear* are not surprising.
2. Designers of handheld devices understand that changes in ambience temperatures can damage the tiny circuit boards.
3. The Keweenaw Peninsula is surrounded on three sides by Lake Superior.
4. At the cooking school in Tuscany, I learned that rosemary is a perfect compliment to lamb.
5. The person who complained to the human resources manager wishes to remain unanimous.

hackerhandbooks.com/bedhandbook > Grammar exercises > Word choice > E-ex 18–5

18d Use standard idioms.

Idioms are speech forms that follow no easily specified rules. The English say "Bernice went *to hospital*," an idiom strange to American ears, which are accustomed to hearing *the* in front of *hospital*. Native speakers of a language seldom have problems

with idioms, but prepositions (such as *with*, *to*, *at*, and *of*) sometimes cause trouble, especially when they follow certain verbs
and adjectives. When in doubt, consult a dictionary.

UNIDIOMATIC	IDIOMATIC
abide with (a decision)	abide by (a decision)
according with	according to
agree to (an idea)	agree with (an idea)
angry at (a person)	angry with (a person)
capable to	capable of
comply to	comply with
desirous to	desirous of
different than (a person or thing)	different from (a person or thing)
intend on doing	intend to do
off of	off
plan on doing	plan to do
preferable than	preferable to
prior than	prior to
superior than	superior to
sure and	sure to
try and	try to
type of a	type of

> **ESL** Because idioms follow no particular rules, you must
> learn them individually. You may find it helpful to keep a list of
> idioms that you frequently encounter in conversation and in
> reading.

EXERCISE 18–3 Edit the following sentences to eliminate errors in
the use of idiomatic expressions. If a sentence is correct, write "correct" after it. Answers to lettered sentences appear in the back of the
book. Example:

We agreed to abide ~~with~~ *by* the decision of the judge.

a. Queen Anne was so angry at Sarah Churchill that she refused
to see her again.

b. Jean-Pierre's ambitious travel plans made it impossible for him to comply with the residency requirement for in-state tuition.
c. The parade moved off of the street and onto the beach.
d. The frightened refugees intend on making the dangerous trek across the mountains.
e. What type of a wedding are you planning?

1. Be sure and report on the danger of releasing genetically engineered bacteria into the atmosphere.
2. Why do you assume that embezzling bank assets is so different than robbing the bank?
3. The wilderness guide seemed capable to show us where the trail of petroglyphs was located.
4. In Evan's cautious mind, packing his own parachute seemed preferable to letting an indifferent teenager fold all that silk and cord into a small pack.
5. Andrea plans on joining the Peace Corps after graduation.

hackerhandbooks.com/bedhandbook > Grammar exercises > Word choice > E-ex 18–6

18e Do not rely heavily on clichés.

The pioneer who first announced that he had "slept like a log" no doubt amused his companions with a fresh and unlikely comparison. Today, however, that comparison is a cliché, a saying that has lost its dazzle from overuse. No longer can it surprise.

To see just how dully predictable clichés are, put your hand over the right-hand column in the following list and then finish the phrases on the left.

cool as a	cucumber
beat around	the bush
blind as a	bat
busy as a	bee, beaver
crystal	clear
dead as a	doornail
out of the frying pan and	into the fire
light as a	feather
like a bull	in a china shop

playing with	fire
nutty as a	fruitcake
selling like	hotcakes
starting out at the bottom	of the ladder
water under the	bridge
white as a	sheet, ghost
avoid clichés like the	plague

The solution for clichés is simple: Just delete them or rewrite them.

▶ **When I received a full scholarship from my second-choice**
        felt squeezed to settle for second best.
school, I ~~found myself between a rock and a hard place.~~

Sometimes you can write around a cliché by adding an element of surprise. One student, for example, who had written that she had butterflies in her stomach, revised her cliché like this:

If all of the action in my stomach is caused by butterflies, there must be a horde of them, with horseshoes on.

The image of butterflies wearing horseshoes is fresh and unlikely, not predictable like the original cliché.

18f Use figures of speech with care.

A figure of speech is an expression that uses words imaginatively (rather than literally) to make abstract ideas concrete. Most often, figures of speech compare two seemingly unlike things to reveal surprising similarities.

In a *simile*, the writer makes the comparison explicitly, usually by introducing it with *like* or *as*: *By the time cotton had to be picked, Grandfather's neck was as red as the clay he plowed.* In a *metaphor*, the *like* or *as* is omitted, and the comparison is implied. For example, in the Old Testament Song of Solomon, a young woman compares the man she loves to a fruit tree: *With great delight I sat in his shadow, and his fruit was sweet to my taste.*

Although figures of speech are useful devices, writers sometimes use them without thinking through the images they evoke. The result is sometimes a *mixed metaphor*, the combination of two or more images that don't make sense together.

▶ Crossing Utah's salt flats in his new convertible, my father flew
at jet speed.
~~under a full head of steam.~~

Flew suggests an airplane, whereas *under a full head of steam* suggests a steamboat or a train. To clarify the image, the writer should stick with one comparison or the other.

▶ Our business manager decided to put all controversial

issues ~~in a holding pattern~~ on a back burner until after the

annual meeting.

Here the writer is mixing airplanes and stoves. Simply deleting one of the images corrects the problem.

EXERCISE 18–4 Edit the following sentences to replace worn-out expressions and clarify mixed figures of speech. Revisions of lettered sentences appear in the back of the book. Example:

the color drained from his face.
When he heard about the accident, ~~he turned white as a~~

~~sheet.~~

a. John stormed into the room like a bull in a china shop.
b. Some people insist that they'll always be there for you, even when they haven't been before.
c. The Cubs easily beat the Mets, who were in the soup early in the game today at Wrigley Field.
d. We ironed out the sticky spots in our relationship.
e. My mother accused me of beating around the bush when in fact I was just talking off the top of my head.

1. Priscilla was used to burning the candle at both ends to get her assignments done.

2. No matter how many books he reads, André can never seem to quench his thirst for knowledge.
3. In an era of cutbacks and outsourcing, the best tech-savvy workers discover that being a jack of all trades is a solid gold key to continued success.
4. Too many cooks are spoiling the broth at corporate headquarters.
5. Juanita told Kyle that keeping skeletons in the closet would be playing with fire.

hackerhandbooks.com/bedhandbook > Grammar exercises > Word choice > E-ex 18–7

Part V
Grammatical Sentences

19 Repair sentence fragments.

A sentence fragment is a word group that pretends to be a sentence. Sentence fragments are easy to recognize when they appear out of context, like these:

> When the cat leaped onto the table.

> Running for the bus.

> And immediately popped their flares and life vests.

When fragments appear next to related sentences, however, they are harder to spot.

> We had just sat down to dinner. When the cat leaped onto the table.

> I tripped and twisted my ankle. Running for the bus.

> The pilots ejected from the burning plane, landing in the water not far from the ship. And immediately popped their flares and life vests.

Recognizing sentence fragments

To be a sentence, a word group must consist of at least one full independent clause. An independent clause includes a subject and a verb, and it either stands alone or could stand alone.

To test whether a word group is a complete sentence or a fragment, use the flowchart on page 227. By using the flowchart, you can see exactly why *When the cat leaped onto the table* is a fragment: It has a subject (*cat*) and a verb (*leaped*), but it begins with a subordinating word (*When*). *Running for the bus* is a fragment because it lacks a subject and a verb (*Running* is a verbal, not a verb). *And immediately popped their flares and life vests* is a fragment because it lacks a subject. (See also 63b and 63e.)

Test for fragments

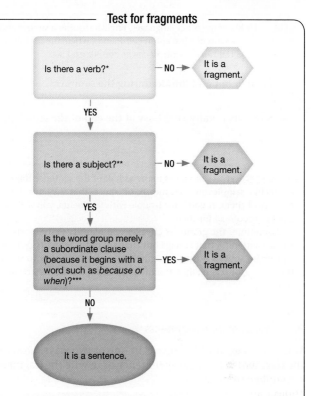

* Do not mistake verbals for verbs. A verbal is a verb form (such as *walking, to act*) that does not function as a verb of a clause. (See 63b.)

** The subject of a sentence may be *you*, understood but not present in the sentence. (See 62a.)

*** A sentence may open with a subordinate clause, but the sentence must also include an independent clause. (See 19a and 64a.)

If you find any fragments, try one of these methods of revision (see 19a–19c):

1. Attach the fragment to a nearby sentence.

2. Rewrite the fragment as a complete sentence.

ESL　Unlike some other languages, English requires a subject and a verb in every sentence (except in commands, where the subject *you* is understood but not present: *Sit down*). See 30a and 30b.

▶ ~~Is~~ *It is* often hot and humid during the summer.

▶ Students usually *are* very busy at the end of the semester.

Grammar checkers can flag as many as half of the sentence fragments in a sample; but that means, of course, that they miss half or more of them. If you have trouble with fragments, you will still need to proofread for them.

Sometimes the grammar checker will identify "false positives," sentences that it flags but that are not fragments. When a program spots a possible fragment, you should check to see if the word group is really a fragment by using the flowchart on page 227.

Repairing sentence fragments

You can repair most fragments in one of two ways: Either pull the fragment into a nearby sentence or rewrite the fragment as a complete sentence.

▶ We had just sat down to dinner/ ~~When~~ *when* the cat leaped onto the table.

▶ *Running for the bus,* I tripped and twisted my ankle. ~~Running for the bus.~~

▶ The pilots ejected from the burning plane, landing in the water not far from the ship. ~~And~~ *They* immediately popped their flares and life vests.

19a Attach fragmented subordinate clauses or turn them into sentences.

A subordinate clause is patterned like a sentence, with both a subject and a verb, but it begins with a word that marks it as subordinate. The following words commonly introduce subordinate clauses.

after	before	so that	until	while
although	even though	than	when	who
as	how	that	where	whom
as if	if	though	whether	whose
because	since	unless	which	why

Subordinate clauses function within sentences as adjectives, as adverbs, or as nouns. They cannot stand alone. (See 63e.)

Most fragmented clauses beg to be pulled into a sentence nearby.

▶ Americans have come to fear the West Nile virus/ ~~Because~~ *because*

it is transmitted by the common mosquito.

Because introduces a subordinate clause, so it cannot stand alone. (For punctuation of subordinate clauses appearing at the end of a sentence, see 33f.)

▶ Although psychiatrist Peter Kramer expresses concerns

about Prozac/, ~~Many~~ *many* other doctors believe that the

benefits of antidepressants outweigh the risks.

Although introduces a subordinate clause, so it cannot stand alone. (For punctuation of subordinate clauses at the beginning of a sentence, see 32b.)

If a fragmented clause cannot be attached to a nearby sentence or if you feel that attaching it would be awkward, try turning the clause into a sentence. The simplest way to do this is to delete the opening word or words that mark it as subordinate.

▶ Population increases and uncontrolled development are

taking a deadly toll on the environment. ~~So that across~~ the
                                          Across

globe, fragile ecosystems are collapsing.

19b Attach fragmented phrases or turn them into sentences.

Like subordinate clauses, phrases function within sentences as adjectives, as adverbs, or as nouns. They cannot stand alone. Fragmented phrases are often prepositional or verbal phrases; sometimes they are appositives, words or word groups that re-name nouns or pronouns. (See 63a, 63b, and 63c.)

Often a fragmented phrase may simply be pulled into a nearby sentence.

▶ The archaeologists worked slowly, ~~Examining~~ and
                                      examining

labeling every pottery shard they uncovered.

The word group beginning with *Examining* is a verbal phrase.

▶ The patient displayed symptoms of ALS, ~~A~~ neuro-
                                          a

degenerative disease.

A neurodegenerative disease is an appositive renaming the noun *ALS*. (For punctuation of appositives, see 32e.)

If a fragmented phrase cannot be pulled into a nearby sentence effectively, turn the phrase into a sentence. You may need to add a subject, a verb, or both.

▶ In the training session, Jamie explained how to access our
                           She also taught us
new database. ~~Also~~ how to submit expense reports and

request vendor payments.

The revision turns the fragmented phrase into a sentence by add-ing a subject and a verb.

19c Attach other fragmented word groups or turn them into sentences.

Other word groups that are commonly fragmented include parts of compound predicates, lists, and examples introduced by *for example*, *in addition*, or similar expressions.

Parts of compound predicates

A predicate consists of a verb and its objects, complements, and modifiers (see 62b). A compound predicate includes two or more predicates joined with a coordinating conjunction such as *and*, *but*, or *or*. Because the parts of a compound predicate have the same subject, they should appear in the same sentence.

▶ The woodpecker finch of the Galápagos Islands carefully

    selects a twig of a certain size and shape/. ~~And~~ *and* then uses this

    tool to pry out grubs from trees.

    The subject is *finch*, and the compound predicate is *selects . . . and . . . uses*. (For punctuation of compound predicates, see 33a.)

Lists

To correct a fragmented list, often you can attach it to a nearby sentence with a colon or a dash. (See 35a and 39a.)

▶ It has been said that there are only three indigenous

    American art forms/: ~~Musical~~ *musical* comedy, jazz, and soap opera.

Sometimes terms like *especially*, *namely*, *like*, and *such as* introduce fragmented lists. Such fragments can usually be attached to the preceding sentence.

▶ In the twentieth century, the South produced some great

    American writers/, ~~Such~~ *such* as Flannery O'Connor, William

    Faulkner, Alice Walker, Tennessee Williams, and Thomas

    Wolfe.

Examples introduced by for example, in addition, *or similar expressions*

Other expressions that introduce examples or explanations can lead to unintentional fragments. Although you may begin a sentence with some of the following words or phrases, make sure that what follows has a subject and a verb.

also	for example	mainly
and	for instance	or
but	in addition	that is

Often the easiest solution is to turn the fragment into a sentence.

▶ **In his memoir, Primo Levi describes the horrors of living in a concentration camp. For example, ~~working~~** he worked **without food and ~~suffering~~** suffered **emotional abuse.**

The writer corrected this fragment by adding a subject—*he*—and substituting verbs for the verbals *working* and *suffering*.

▶ **Deborah Tannen's research reveals that men and women**

Writing with sources

MLA-style citation

have different ideas about communication. For example, Tannen explains **that a woman "expects her husband to be a new and improved version of her best friend" (441).**

A quotation must be part of a complete sentence. *That a woman "expects her husband to be a new and improved version of her best friend"* is a fragment—a subordinate clause. In this case, adding a signal phrase that includes a subject and a verb (*Tannen explains*) corrects the fragment and clarifies that the quotation is from Tannen.

19d Exception: Occasionally a fragment may be used deliberately, for effect.

Skilled writers occasionally use sentence fragments for the following special purposes.

FOR EMPHASIS   Following the dramatic Americanization of their children, even my parents grew more publicly confident. *Especially my mother.*

                                 —Richard Rodriguez

TO ANSWER   Are these new drug tests 100 percent
A QUESTION   reliable? *Not in the opinion of most experts.*

TRANSITIONS   *And now the opposing arguments.*

EXCLAMATIONS   *Not again!*

IN ADVERTISING   *Fewer carbs. Improved taste.*

Although fragments are sometimes appropriate, writers and readers do not always agree on when they are appropriate. That's why you will find it safer to write in complete sentences.

EXERCISE 19–1 Repair any fragment by attaching it to a nearby sentence or by rewriting it as a complete sentence. If a word group is correct, write "correct" after it. Revisions of lettered sentences appear in the back of the book. Example:

One Greek island that should not be missed is Mykonos, A

vacation spot for Europeans and a playground for the rich

and famous.

a. Listening to the CD her sister had sent, Mia was overcome with a mix of emotions. Happiness, homesickness, nostalgia.
b. Cortés and his soldiers were astonished when they looked down from the mountains and saw Tenochtitlán. The magnificent capital of the Aztecs.
c. Although my spoken Spanish is not very good. I can read the language with ease.
d. There are several reasons for not eating meat. One reason being that dangerous chemicals are used throughout the various stages of meat production.
e. To learn how to sculpt beauty from everyday life. This is my intention in studying art and archaeology.

1. The panther lay motionless behind the rock. Waiting silently for its prey.
2. Aunt Mina loved to play all my favorite games. Cat's cradle, Uno, mancala, and even four square.
3. With machetes, the explorers cut their way through the tall grasses to the edge of the canyon. Then they began to lay out the tapes for the survey.
4. The owners of the online grocery store rented a warehouse in the Market district. An area catering to small businesses.
5. If a woman from the desert tribe showed anger toward her husband, she was whipped in front of the whole village. And shunned by the rest of the women.

EXERCISE 19–2   Repair each fragment in the following passage by attaching it to a sentence nearby or by rewriting it as a complete sentence.

Digital technology has revolutionized information delivery. Forever blurring the lines between information and entertainment. Yesterday's readers of books and newspapers are today's readers of e-books and news blogs. Countless readers have moved on from print information entirely. Choosing instead to point, click, and scroll their way through a text on their Amazon Kindle or in an online forum. Once a nation of people spoon-fed television commercials and the six o'clock evening news. We are now seemingly addicted to *YouTube*. Remember the family trip when Dad or Mom wrestled with a road map? On the way to St. Louis or Seattle? No wrestling is required with a slick GPS navigator by the driver's side. Unless it's Mom and Dad wrestling over who gets to program the address. Accessing information now seems to be America's favorite pastime. John Horrigan, associate director for research at the Pew Internet and American Life Project, reports that 31 percent of American adults are "elite" users of technology. Who are "highly engaged" with digital content. As a country, we embrace information and communication technologies. Which include iPods, cell phones, laptops, and handheld devices. Among children and adolescents, Internet and other personal technology use is on the rise. For activities like socializing, gaming, and information gathering.

hackerhandbooks.com/bedhandbook > Grammar exercises > Grammatical sentences
> E-ex 19–3 to 19–6

20 Revise run-on sentences.

Run-on sentences are independent clauses that have not been joined correctly. An independent clause is a word group that can stand alone as a sentence. (See 64a.) When two independent clauses appear in one sentence, they must be joined in one of these ways:

- with a comma and a coordinating conjunction (*and, but, or, nor, for, so, yet*)
- with a semicolon (or occasionally with a colon or a dash)

Recognizing run-on sentences

There are two types of run-on sentences. When a writer puts no mark of punctuation and no coordinating conjunction between independent clauses, the result is called a *fused sentence.*

FUSED   INDEPENDENT CLAUSE
Air pollution poses risks to all humans it can be
INDEPENDENT CLAUSE
deadly for asthma sufferers.

A far more common type of run-on sentence is the *comma splice*—two or more independent clauses joined with a comma but without a coordinating conjunction. In some comma splices, the comma appears alone.

COMMA   Air pollution poses risks to all humans, it can be
SPLICE   deadly for asthma sufferers.

In other comma splices, the comma is accompanied by a joining word that is *not* a coordinating conjunction. There are only seven coordinating conjunctions in English: *and, but, or, nor, for, so,* and *yet.*

COMMA   Air pollution poses risks to all humans, however, it can
SPLICE   be deadly for asthma sufferers.

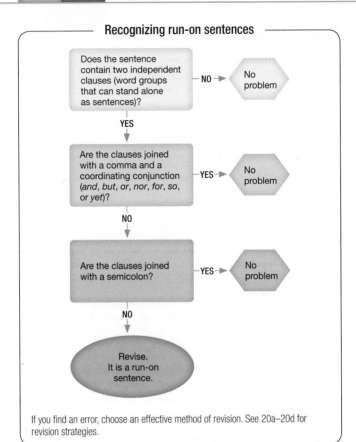

Recognizing run-on sentences

Does the sentence contain two independent clauses (word groups that can stand alone as sentences)? — NO → No problem

YES

Are the clauses joined with a comma and a coordinating conjunction (*and, but, or, nor, for, so,* or *yet*)? — YES → No problem

NO

Are the clauses joined with a semicolon? — YES → No problem

NO

Revise. It is a run-on sentence.

If you find an error, choose an effective method of revision. See 20a–20d for revision strategies.

Grammar checkers flag fewer than half the run-on sentences in a sample and may suggest inappropriate revision strategies. The flowchart above can help you identify run-on sentences in your own writing.

However is a transitional expression, not a coordinating conjunction, and cannot be used with only a comma to join two independent clauses (see 20b).

Revising run-on sentences

To revise a run-on sentence, you have four choices.

1. Use a comma and a coordinating conjunction (*and, but, or, nor, for, so, yet*).

▶ **Air pollution poses risks to all humans, *but* it can be deadly for asthma sufferers.**

2. Use a semicolon (or, if appropriate, a colon or a dash). A semicolon may be used alone; it can also be accompanied by a transitional expression.

▶ **Air pollution poses risks to all humans*/;* it can be deadly for asthma sufferers.**

▶ **Air pollution poses risks to all humans*/; however,* it can be deadly for asthma sufferers.**

3. Make the clauses into separate sentences.

▶ **Air pollution poses risks to all humans*/. It* can be deadly for asthma sufferers.**

4. Restructure the sentence, perhaps by subordinating one of the clauses.

▶ ***Although air* ~~Air~~ pollution poses risks to all humans, it can be deadly for asthma sufferers.**

One of these revision techniques usually works better than the others for a particular sentence. The fourth technique, the one requiring the most extensive revision, is often the most effective.

20a Consider separating the clauses with a comma and a coordinating conjunction.

There are seven coordinating conjunctions in English: *and, but, or, nor, for, so,* and *yet*. When a coordinating conjunction joins independent clauses, it is usually preceded by a comma. (See 32a.)

▶ Some lesson plans include exercises, ^but^ completing them

should not be the focus of all class periods.

▶ Many government officials privately admit that the poly-

graph is unreliable, ^yet^ ~~however,~~ they continue to use it as a

security measure.

However is a transitional expression, not a coordinating conjunction, so it cannot be used with only a comma to join independent clauses. (See also 20b.)

20b Consider separating the clauses with a semicolon (or, if appropriate, with a colon or a dash).

When the independent clauses are closely related and their relation is clear without a coordinating conjunction, a semicolon is an acceptable method of revision. (See 34a.)

▶ Tragedy depicts the individual confronted with the fact

of death^/;^ comedy depicts the adaptability of human

society.

A semicolon is required between independent clauses that have been linked with a transitional expression (such as *however*, *therefore*, *moreover*, *in fact*, or *for example*). For a longer list, see 34b.

▶ The timber wolf looks like a large German shepherd/; however, the wolf has longer legs, larger feet, and a wider head.

▶ In his film adaptation of the short story "Killings," director Todd Field changed key details of the plot/; as a matter of fact, he added whole scenes that do not appear in the story.

A colon or a dash may be more appropriate if the first independent clause introduces the second or if the second clause summarizes or explains the first. (See 35b and 39a.) In formal writing, the colon is usually preferred to the dash.

▶ Nuclear waste is hazardous: ~~this~~ This is an indisputable fact.

▶ The female black widow spider is often a widow of her own making/she has been known to eat her partner after mating.

A colon is an appropriate method of revision if the first independent clause introduces a quoted sentence.

▶ Nobel Peace Prize winner Al Gore had this to say about climate change/: "The truth is that our circumstances are not only new; they are completely different than they have ever been in all of human history."

20c Consider making the clauses into separate sentences.

▶ Why should we spend money on expensive space

   exploration/? ~~we~~ ^{We} have enough underfunded programs here

   on Earth.

Since one independent clause is a question and the other is a statement, they should be separate sentences.

Writing with sources

APA-style citation

▶ Some studies have suggested that the sexual relationships

   of bonobos set them apart from common chimpanzees/.

   ^A~~a~~ccording to Stanford (1998), these differences have been

   exaggerated.

Using a comma to join two independent clauses creates a comma splice. In this example, an effective revision is to separate the first independent clause (*Some studies . . .*) from the second independent clause (*these differences . . .*) and to keep the signal phrase with the second clause. (See also 56c.)

NOTE: When two quoted independent clauses are divided by explanatory words, make each clause its own sentence.

▶ "It's always smart to learn from your mistakes," quipped my

   supervisor/. ^{"It's}"~~it's~~ even smarter to learn from the mistakes of

   others."

20d Consider restructuring the sentence, perhaps by subordinating one of the clauses.

If one of the independent clauses is less important than the other, turn it into a subordinate clause or phrase. (For more about subordination, see 14, especially the chart on p. 180.)

► One of the most famous advertising slogans is Wheaties

cereal's "Breakfast of Champions," ~~it~~ *which* was penned in 1933.

► *Although many*
~~Many~~ scholars dismiss the abominable snowman of the

Himalayas as a myth, others claim it may be a kind of ape.

► Mary McLeod Bethune , ~~was~~ the seventeenth child of former

slaves, ~~she~~ founded the National Council of Negro Women

in 1935.

Minor ideas in these sentences are now expressed in subordinate
clauses or phrases.

EXERCISE 20–1 Revise the following run-on sentences using the
method of revision suggested in brackets. Revisions of lettered sentences appear in the back of the book. Example:

Because
Orville had been obsessed with his weight as a teenager, he

rarely ate anything sweet. [*Restructure the sentence.*]

a. The city had one public swimming pool, it stayed packed with
children all summer long. [*Restructure the sentence.*]
b. The building is being renovated, therefore at times we have
no heat, water, or electricity. [*Use a comma and a coordinating
conjunction.*]
c. The view was not what the travel agent had described, where
were the rolling hills and the shimmering rivers? [*Make two
sentences.*]
d. All those gnarled equations looked like toxic insects, maybe I
was going to have to rethink my major. [*Use a semicolon.*]
e. City officials had good reason to fear a major earthquake, most
of the business district was built on landfill. [*Use a colon.*]

1. The car was hardly worth trading, the frame was twisted and
the block was warped. [*Restructure the sentence.*]
2. The next time an event is canceled because of bad weather, don't
blame the meteorologist, blame nature. [*Make two sentences.*]

3. Ray was fluent in American Sign Language he could sign as easily as he could speak. [*Restructure the sentence.*]
4. Susanna arrived with a stack of her latest hats she hoped the gift shop would place a big winter order. [*Restructure the sentence.*]
5. There was one major reason for John's wealth, his grandfather had been a multimillionaire. [*Use a colon.*]

EXERCISE 20–2 Revise any run-on sentences using a technique that you find effective. If a sentence is correct, write "correct" after it. Revisions of lettered sentences appear in the back of the book. Example:

> Crossing so many time zones on an eight-hour flight, I knew
> I would be tired when I arrived, ~~however,~~ *but* I was too excited
> to sleep on the plane.

a. Wind power for the home is a supplementary source of energy, it can be combined with electricity, gas, or solar energy.
b. Aidan viewed Sofia Coppola's *Lost in Translation* three times and then wrote a paper describing the film as the work of a mysterious modern painter.
c. In the Middle Ages, the streets of London were dangerous places, it was safer to travel by boat along the Thames.
d. "He's not drunk," I said, "he's in a state of diabetic shock."
e. Are you able to endure extreme angle turns, high speeds, frequent jumps, and occasional crashes, then supermoto racing may be a sport for you.

1. Death Valley National Monument, located in southern California and Nevada, is one of the hottest places on Earth, temperatures there have soared as high as 134 degrees Fahrenheit.
2. Anamaria opened the boxes crammed with toys, out sprang griffins, dragons, and phoenixes.
3. Subatomic physics is filled with strange and marvelous particles, tiny bodies of matter that shiver, wobble, pulse, and flatten to no thickness at all.
4. As his first major project, Frederick Law Olmsted designed New York City's Central Park, one of the most beautiful urban spaces in the United States.
5. The neurosurgeon explained that the medication could have one side effect, it might cause me to experience temporary memory loss.

EXERCISE 20–3 In the following rough draft, revise any run-on sentences.

Some parents and educators argue that requiring uniforms in public schools would improve student behavior and performance. They think that uniforms give students a more professional attitude toward school, moreover, they believe that uniforms help create a sense of community among students from diverse backgrounds. But parents and educators should consider the drawbacks to requiring uniforms in public schools.

Uniforms do create a sense of community, they do this, however, by stamping out individuality. Youth is a time to express originality, it is a time to develop a sense of self. One important way young people express their identities is through the clothes they wear. The self-patrolled dress code of high school students may be stricter than any school-imposed code, nevertheless, trying to control dress habits from above will only lead to resentment or to mindless conformity.

If children are going to act like adults, they need to be treated like adults, they need to be allowed to make their own choices. Telling young people what to wear to school merely prolongs their childhood. Requiring uniforms undermines the educational purpose of public schools, which is not just to teach facts and figures but to help young people grow into adults who are responsible for making their own choices.

hackerhandbooks.com/bedhandbook > Grammar exercises > Grammatical sentences
> E-ex 20–4 to 20–7

21   Make subjects and verbs agree.

In the present tense, verbs agree with their subjects in number (singular or plural) and in person (first, second, third): *I sing, you sing, he sings, she sings, we sing, they sing.* Even if your ear recognizes the standard subject-verb combinations presented in 21a, you will no doubt encounter tricky situations such as those described in 21b–21k.

21a Consult this section for standard subject-verb combinations.

This section describes the basic guidelines for making present-tense verbs agree with their subjects. The present-tense ending -*s* (or -*es*) is used on a verb if its subject is third-person singular (*he*, *she*, *it*, and singular nouns); otherwise the verb takes no ending. Consider, for example, the present-tense forms of the verbs *love* and *try*, given at the beginning of the chart on the following page.

The verb *be* varies from this pattern; unlike any other verb, it has special forms in *both* the present and the past tense. These forms appear at the end of the chart.

If you aren't confident that you know the standard forms, use the charts on pages 245 and 246 as you proofread for subject-verb agreement. You may also want to look at 27c on -*s* endings of regular and irregular verbs.

> **Grammar checkers** are fairly good at flagging subject-verb agreement problems. But they occasionally flag a correct sentence, usually because they misidentify the subject, the verb, or both. Sometimes they miss an agreement problem because they don't recognize a pronoun's antecedent (see 21i).

21b Make the verb agree with its subject, not with a word that comes between.

Word groups often come between the subject and the verb. Such word groups, usually modifying the subject, may contain a noun that at first appears to be the subject. By mentally stripping away such modifiers, you can isolate the noun that is in fact the subject.

The *samples* on the tray in the lab *need* testing.

Subject-verb agreement at a glance

Present-tense forms of *love* and *try* (typical verbs)

	SINGULAR		PLURAL	
FIRST PERSON	I	love	we	love
SECOND PERSON	you	love	you	love
THIRD PERSON	he/she/it*	loves	they**	love

	SINGULAR		PLURAL	
FIRST PERSON	I	try	we	try
SECOND PERSON	you	try	you	try
THIRD PERSON	he/she/it*	tries	they**	try

Present-tense forms of *have*

	SINGULAR		PLURAL	
FIRST PERSON	I	have	we	have
SECOND PERSON	you	have	you	have
THIRD PERSON	he/she/it*	has	they**	have

Present-tense forms of *do* (including negative forms)

	SINGULAR		PLURAL	
FIRST PERSON	I	do/don't	we	do/don't
SECOND PERSON	you	do/don't	you	do/don't
THIRD PERSON	he/she/it*	does/doesn't	they**	do/don't

Present-tense and past-tense forms of *be*

	SINGULAR		PLURAL	
FIRST PERSON	I	am/was	we	are/were
SECOND PERSON	you	are/were	you	are/were
THIRD PERSON	he/she/it*	is/was	they**	are/were

*And singular nouns (*child*, *Roger*)
**And plural nouns (*children*, *the Mannings*)

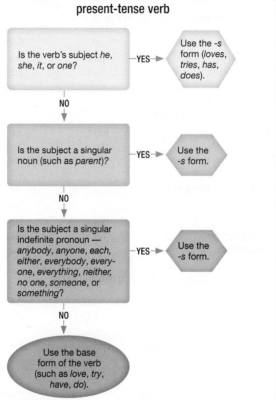

When to use the -s (or -es) form of a present-tense verb

Is the verb's subject *he, she, it,* or *one*? —YES→ Use the *-s* form (*loves, tries, has, does*).

NO ↓

Is the subject a singular noun (such as *parent*)? —YES→ Use the *-s* form.

NO ↓

Is the subject a singular indefinite pronoun — *anybody, anyone, each, either, everybody, everyone, everything, neither, no one, someone,* or *something*? —YES→ Use the *-s* form.

NO ↓

Use the base form of the verb (such as *love, try, have, do*).

EXCEPTION: Choosing the correct present-tense form of *be* (*am, is,* or *are*) is not quite so simple. See the chart on the previous page for both present- and past-tense forms of *be.*

ESL TIP: Do not use the *-s* form of a verb if it follows a modal verb such as *can, must,* or *should* or another helping verb. (See 28b.)

▶ High levels of air pollution causes damage to the respiratory

tract.

The subject is *levels*, not *pollution*. Strip away the phrase *of air pollution* to hear the correct verb: *levels cause*.

▶ The slaughter of pandas for their pelts ~~have~~ *has* caused the

panda population to decline drastically.

The subject is *slaughter*, not *pandas* or *pelts*.

NOTE: Phrases beginning with the prepositions *as well as, in addition to, accompanied by, together with,* and *along with* do not make a singular subject plural.

▶ The governor as well as his press secretary ~~were~~ *was* on

the plane.

To emphasize that two people were on the plane, the writer could use *and* instead: *The governor and his press secretary were on the plane.*

21c Treat most subjects joined with *and* as plural.

A subject with two or more parts is said to be compound. If the parts are connected with *and*, the subject is nearly always plural.

Leon and Jan often *jog* together.

▶ The Supreme Court's willingness to hear the case and its

affirmation of the original decision ~~has~~ *have* set a new

precedent.

EXCEPTIONS: When the parts of the subject form a single unit or when they refer to the same person or thing, treat the subject as singular.

> Strawberries and cream was a last-minute addition to the menu.

> Sue's friend and adviser was surprised by her decision.

When a compound subject is preceded by *each* or *every*, treat it as singular.

> Each tree, shrub, and vine needs to be sprayed.

> Every car, truck, and van is required to pass inspection.

This exception does not apply when a compound subject is followed by *each*: *Alan and Marcia each have different ideas*.

21d With subjects joined with *or* or *nor* (or with *either . . . or* or *neither . . . nor*), make the verb agree with the part of the subject nearer to the verb.

> A driver's *license* or credit *card is* required.

> A driver's *license* or two credit *cards are* required.

▶ If an infant or a child ~~are~~ *is* having difficulty breathing, seek medical attention immediately.

▶ Neither the chief financial officer nor the marketing managers ~~was~~ *were* able to convince the client to reconsider.

The verb must be matched with the part of the subject closer to it: *child is* in the first sentence, *managers were* in the second.

NOTE: If one part of the subject is singular and the other is plural, put the plural one last to avoid awkwardness.

21e Treat most indefinite pronouns as singular.

Indefinite pronouns are pronouns that do not refer to specific persons or things. The following commonly used indefinite pronouns are singular.

anybody	each	everyone	nobody	somebody
anyone	either	everything	no one	someone
anything	everybody	neither	nothing	something

Many of these words appear to have plural meanings, and they are often treated as such in casual speech. In formal written English, however, they are nearly always treated as singular.

Everyone on the team *supports* the coach.

▶ Each of the furrows ~~have~~ ^{has} been seeded.

▶ Nobody who participated in the clinical trials ~~were~~ ^{was} given a placebo.

The subjects of these sentences are *Each* and *Nobody.* These indefinite pronouns are third-person singular, so the verbs must be *has* and *was.*

A few indefinite pronouns (*all, any, none, some*) may be singular or plural depending on the noun or pronoun they refer to.

Some of our *luggage was* lost. *None* of his *advice makes* sense.

Some of the *rocks are* slippery. *None* of the *eggs were* broken.

NOTE: When the meaning of *none* is emphatically "not one," *none* may be treated as singular: *None* [meaning "Not one"] *of the eggs was broken.* However, some experts advise using *not one* instead: *Not one of the eggs was broken.*

21f Treat collective nouns as singular unless the meaning is clearly plural.

Collective nouns such as *jury, committee, audience, crowd, troop, family,* and *couple* name a class or a group. In American English, collective nouns are nearly always treated as singular: They emphasize the group as a unit. Occasionally, when there is some reason to draw attention to the individual members of the group, a collective noun may be treated as plural. (See also 22b.)

SINGULAR   The *class respects* the teacher.

PLURAL   The *class are* debating among themselves.

To underscore the notion of individuality in the second sentence, many writers would add a clearly plural noun.

PLURAL   The class *members are* debating among themselves.

▶ The board of trustees ~~meet~~ meets in Denver twice a year.

   The board as a whole meets; there is no reason to draw attention to its individual members.

▶ A young couple ~~was~~ were arguing about politics while holding

   hands.

   The meaning is clearly plural. Only separate individuals can argue and hold hands.

NOTE: The phrase *the number* is treated as singular, *a number* as plural.

SINGULAR   *The number* of school-age children *is* declining.

PLURAL   *A number* of children *are* attending the wedding.

NOTE: In general, when fractions or units of measurement are used with a singular noun, treat them as singular; when they are used with a plural noun, treat them as plural.

SINGULAR   *Three-fourths* of the salad *has* been eaten.

SINGULAR   Twenty *inches* of wallboard *was* covered with mud.

PLURAL   *One-fourth* of the drivers *were* texting.

PLURAL   Two *pounds* of blueberries *were* used to make the pie.

21g Make the verb agree with its subject even when the subject follows the verb.

Verbs ordinarily follow subjects. When this normal order is reversed, it is easy to become confused. Sentences beginning with *there is* or *there are* (or *there was* or *there were*) are inverted; the subject follows the verb.

There *are* surprisingly few *children* in our neighborhood.

▶ There ~~was~~ a social worker and a neighbor at the scene of the

accident.
> were

The subject, *worker and neighbor*, is plural, so the verb must be *were*.

Occasionally you may decide to invert a sentence for variety or effect. When you do so, check to make sure that your subject and verb agree.

▶ Of particular concern ~~is~~ penicillin and tetracycline,
> are

antibiotics used to make animals more resistant to disease.

The subject, *penicillin and tetracycline*, is plural, so the verb must be *are*.

21h Make the verb agree with its subject, not with a subject complement.

One basic sentence pattern in English consists of a subject, a linking verb, and a subject complement: *Jack is a securities lawyer.* Because the subject complement (*lawyer*) names or describes the subject (*Jack*), it is sometimes mistaken for the subject. (See 62b on subject complements.)

These *exercises are* a way to test your ability to perform under pressure.

▶ A tent and a sleeping bag ~~is~~ are the required equipment for all campers.

Tent and bag is the subject, not *equipment.*

▶ A major force in today's economy ~~are~~ is children—as consumers, decision makers, and trend spotters.

Force is the subject, not *children.* If the corrected version seems too awkward, make *children* the subject: *Children are a major force in today's economy—as consumers, decision makers, and trend spotters.*

21i *Who*, *which*, and *that* take verbs that agree with their antecedents.

Like most pronouns, the relative pronouns *who*, *which*, and *that* have antecedents, nouns or pronouns to which they refer. Relative pronouns used as subjects of subordinate clauses take verbs that agree with their antecedents.

ANT   PN   V

Take a *course that prepares* you for classroom management.

One of the

Constructions such as *one of the students who* [or *one of the things that*] cause problems for writers. Do not assume that the antecedent must be *one*. Instead, consider the logic of the sentence.

▶ Our ability to use language is one of the things that sets us

apart from animals.

The antecedent of *that* is *things*, not *one*. Several things set us apart from animals.

Only one of the

When the word *only* comes before *one*, you are safe in assuming that *one* is the antecedent of the relative pronoun.

▶ Veronica was the only one of the first-year Spanish
                                           was
students who ~~were~~ fluent enough to apply for the exchange
              ^

program.

The antecedent of *who* is *one*, not *students*. Only one student was fluent enough.

21j Words such as *athletics*, *economics*, *mathematics*, *physics*, *politics*, *statistics*, *measles*, and *news* are usually singular, despite their plural form.

        is
▶ Politics ~~are~~ among my mother's favorite pastimes.
          ^

EXCEPTION: Occasionally some of these words, especially *economics*, *mathematics*, *politics*, and *statistics*, have plural meanings: *Office politics often sway decisions about hiring and promotion. The economics of the building plan are prohibitive.*

21k Titles of works, company names, words mentioned as words, and gerund phrases are singular.

▶ *Lost Cities* ~~describe~~ *describes* the discoveries of fifty ancient

civilizations.

▶ Delmonico Brothers ~~specialize~~ *specializes* in organic produce and

additive-free meats.

▶ *Controlled substances* ~~are~~ *is* a euphemism for illegal drugs.

A gerund phrase consists of an *-ing* verb form followed by any objects, complements, or modifiers (see 63b). Treat gerund phrases as singular.

▶ Encountering long hold times ~~make~~ *makes* customers impatient

with telephone tech support.

EXERCISE 21–1 For each sentence in the following passage, underline the subject (or compound subject) and then select the verb that agrees with it. (If you have trouble identifying the subject, consult 62a.)

Loggerhead sea turtles (migrate / migrates) thousands of miles before returning to their nesting location every two to three years. The nesting season for loggerhead turtles (span / spans) the hottest months of the summer. Although the habitat of Atlantic loggerheads (range / ranges) from Newfoundland to Argentina, nesting for these turtles (take / takes) place primarily along the southeastern coast of the United States. Female turtles that have reached sexual maturity (crawl / crawls) ashore at night to lay their eggs. The cavity that serves as a nest for the eggs (is / are) dug out with the female's strong flippers. Deposited into each nest (is / are) anywhere from fifty to two hundred spherical eggs, also known as a *clutch*. After a two-month incubation period, all eggs in the clutch (begin / begins) to hatch, and within a few days the young turtles attempt to make their way into the ocean. A major cause of the loggerhead's decreasing numbers (is / are) natural predators such as raccoons, birds, and crabs. Beach erosion and coastal development also (threaten / threatens) the turtles' survival. For example, a crowd of curious humans or lights from beachfront residences (is / are) enough to make the female abandon her nesting plans and return to the ocean. Since only one in one thousand loggerheads survives to adulthood, special care should be taken to protect this threatened species.

EXERCISE 21–2 Edit the following sentences to eliminate problems with subject-verb agreement. If a sentence is correct, write "correct" after it. Answers to lettered sentences appear in the back of the book. Example:

> *were*
> Jack's first days in the infantry ~~was~~ grueling.

a. One of the main reasons for elephant poaching are the profits received from selling the ivory tusks.
b. Not until my interview with Dr. Hwang were other possibilities opened to me.
c. A number of students in the seminar was aware of the importance of joining the discussion.
d. Batik cloth from Bali, blue and white ceramics from Delft, and a bocce ball from Turin has made Angelie's room the talk of the dorm.
e. The board of directors, ignoring the wishes of the neighborhood, has voted to allow further development.

1. Measles is a contagious childhood disease.
2. Adorning a shelf in the lab is a Vietnamese figurine, a set of Korean clay gods, and an American plastic village.
3. The presence of certain bacteria in our bodies is one of the factors that determines our overall health.
4. Sheila is the only one of the many applicants who has the ability to step into this job.
5. Neither the explorer nor his companions was ever seen again.

22 Make pronouns and antecedents agree.

A pronoun is a word that substitutes for a noun. (See 61b.) Many pronouns have antecedents, nouns or pronouns to which they refer. A pronoun and its antecedent agree when they are both singular or both plural.

SINGULAR *Dr. Ava Berto* finished *her* rounds.

PLURAL The hospital *interns* finished *their* rounds.

> **ESL** The pronouns *he, his, she, her, it,* and *its* must agree in gender (masculine, feminine, or neuter) with their antecedents, not with the words they modify.
>
>   *Steve* visited *his* [not *her*] sister in Seattle.

> Grammar checkers rarely flag problems with pronoun-antecedent agreement. It takes a human eye to see that a plural pronoun does not agree with a singular noun. When grammar checkers do flag agreement problems, they often suggest (correctly) substituting the singular phrase *his or her* for the plural pronoun *their.* For other revision strategies that avoid the wordy *his or her* construction, see the chart on page 259.

22a Do not use plural pronouns to refer to singular antecedents.

Writers are frequently tempted to use plural pronouns to refer to two kinds of singular antecedents: indefinite pronouns and generic nouns.

Indefinite pronouns

Indefinite pronouns refer to nonspecific persons or things. Even though some of the following indefinite pronouns may seem to have plural meanings, treat them as singular in formal English.

anybody	each	everyone	nobody	somebody
anyone	either	everything	no one	someone
anything	everybody	neither	nothing	something

Everyone performs at *his or her* [not *their*] own fitness level.

When a plural pronoun refers mistakenly to a singular indefinite pronoun, you can usually choose one of three options for revision:

1. Replace the plural pronoun with *he or she* (or *his or her*).

2. Make the antecedent plural.

3. Rewrite the sentence so that no problem of agreement exists.

▶ When someone travels outside the United States for the
first time, ~~they need~~ *he or she needs* to apply for a passport several months

in advance.

▶ When ~~someone travels~~ *people travel* outside the United States for the

first time, they need to apply for a passport several months

in advance.

▶ ~~When someone~~ *Anyone who* travels outside the United States for the
first time, ~~they need~~ *needs* to apply for a passport several months

in advance.

Because the *he or she* construction is wordy, often the second or third revision strategy is more effective. Using *he* (or *his*) to refer to persons of either sex, while less wordy, is considered sexist, as is using *she* (or *her*) for all persons. Some writers alternate male and female pronouns throughout a text, but the result is often awkward. See 17f and the chart on page 259 for strategies that avoid sexist usage.

NOTE: If you change a pronoun from singular to plural (or vice versa), check to be sure that the verb agrees with the new pronoun (see 21e).

Generic nouns

A generic noun represents a typical member of a group, such as a typical student, or any member of a group, such as any lawyer. Although generic nouns may seem to have plural meanings, they are singular.

Every *runner* must train rigorously if *he or she wants* [not *they want*] to excel.

When a plural pronoun refers mistakenly to a generic noun, you will usually have the same three revision options as mentioned on page 257 for indefinite pronouns.

▶ A medical student must study hard if ~~they want~~ to succeed. *he or she wants*

▶ ~~A medical student~~ must study hard if they want to succeed. *Medical students*

▶ A medical student must study hard ~~if they want~~ to succeed.

22b Treat collective nouns as singular unless the meaning is clearly plural.

Collective nouns such as *jury, committee, audience, crowd, class, troop, family, team,* and *couple* name a group. Ordinarily the group functions as a unit, so the noun should be treated as

Choosing a revision strategy that avoids sexist language

Because many readers object to sexist language, avoid using *he*, *him*, and *his* (or *she*, *her*, and *hers*) to refer to both men and women. Also try to avoid the wordy expressions *he or she* and *his or her*. More graceful alternatives are usually possible.

Use an occasional *he or she* (or *his or her*).

▶ In our office, everyone works at ~~their~~ *his or her* own pace.

Make the antecedent plural.

▶ ~~An employee~~ *Employees* on extended disability leave may continue their life insurance.

Recast the sentence.

▶ The amount of vacation time a federal worker may accrue depends on ~~their~~ length of service.

▶ ~~If~~ *A* ~~a~~ child ~~is~~ born to parents who are both bipolar~~, they~~ *has* ~~have~~ a high chance of being bipolar.

▶ A year later someone finally admitted ~~that they were~~ *to being* involved in the kidnapping.

▶ In his autobiography, Benjamin Franklin suggests that anyone can achieve success ~~as long as they live~~ *by living* a virtuous life and ~~work~~ *working* hard.

singular; if the members of the group function as individuals, however, the noun should be treated as plural. (See also 21f.)

AS A UNIT   The *committee* granted *its* permission to build.

AS INDIVIDUALS   The *committee* put *their* signatures on the document.

When treating a collective noun as plural, many writers prefer to add a clearly plural antecedent such as *members* to the sentence: *The members of the committee put their signatures on the document.*

▶ **Defense attorney Clarence Darrow surprisingly urged the**

jury to find his client, John Scopes, guilty so that he could

appeal the case to a higher court. The jury complied,

                    its
returning ~~their~~ verdict in only nine minutes.

There is no reason to draw attention to the individual members of the jury, so *jury* should be treated as singular.

22c Treat most compound antecedents joined with *and* as plural.

In 1987, *Reagan and Gorbachev* held a summit where *they* signed the Intermediate-Range Nuclear Forces Treaty.

22d With compound antecedents joined with *or* or *nor* (or with *either . . . or* or *neither . . . nor*), make the pronoun agree with the nearer antecedent.

Either *Bruce* or *Tom* should receive first prize for *his* poem.

Neither the *mouse* nor the *rats* could find *their* way through the maze.

NOTE: If one of the antecedents is singular and the other plural, as in the second example, put the plural one last to avoid awkwardness.

EXCEPTION: If one antecedent is male and the other female, do not follow the traditional rule. The sentence *Either Bruce or Elizabeth should receive first prize for her short story* makes no sense. The best solution is to recast the sentence: *The prize for best short story should go to either Bruce or Elizabeth.*

EXERCISE 22–1 Edit the following sentences to eliminate problems with pronoun-antecedent agreement. Most of the sentences can be revised in more than one way, so experiment before choosing a solution. If a sentence is correct, write "correct" after it. Revisions of lettered sentences appear in the back of the book. Example:

> *Recruiters*
> ~~The recruiter~~ may tell the truth, but there is much that they
> choose not to tell.

a. Every presidential candidate must appeal to a wide variety of ethnic and social groups if they want to win the election.
b. David lent his motorcycle to someone who allowed their friend to use it.
c. The aerobics teacher motioned for everyone to move their arms in wide, slow circles.
d. The parade committee was unanimous in its decision to allow all groups and organizations to join the festivities.
e. The applicant should be bilingual if they want to qualify for this position.

1. If a driver refuses to take a blood or breath test, he or she will have their licenses suspended for six months.
2. Why should anyone learn a second language? One reason is to sharpen their minds.
3. The Department of Education issued guidelines for school security. They were trying to anticipate problems and avert disaster.
4. The logger in the Northwest relies on the old forest growth for their living.
5. If anyone notices any suspicious activity, they should report it to the police.

EXERCISE 22–2 Edit the following paragraph to eliminate problems with pronoun-antecedent agreement or sexist language.

A common practice in businesses is to put each employee in their own cubicle. A typical cubicle resembles an office, but their walls don't reach the ceiling. Many office managers feel that a cubicle floor plan has its advantages. Cubicles make a large area feel spacious. In addition, they can be moved around so that each new employee can be accommodated in his own work area. Of course, the cubicle model also has problems. The typical employee is not as happy with a cubicle as they would be with a traditional office. Also, productivity can suffer. Neither a manager nor a frontline worker can ordinarily do their best work in a cubicle because of noise and lack of privacy. Each worker can hear his neighbors tapping on computer keyboards, making telephone calls, and muttering under their breath.

hackerhandbooks.com/bedhandbook > Grammar exercises > Grammatical sentences > E-ex 22–3 to 22–5

23 Make pronoun references clear.

Pronouns substitute for nouns; they are a kind of shorthand. In a sentence like *After Andrew intercepted the ball, he kicked it as hard as he could*, the pronouns *he* and *it* substitute for the nouns *Andrew* and *ball*. The word a pronoun refers to is called its *antecedent*.

> Grammar checkers do not flag problems with faulty pronoun reference. Although a computer program can identify pronouns, it has no way of knowing which words, if any, they refer to. Only you can determine whether your readers will be confused.

23a Avoid ambiguous or remote pronoun reference.

Ambiguous pronoun reference occurs when a pronoun could refer to two possible antecedents.

> The pitcher broke when Gloria set it
> ▶ When Gloria set the pitcher on the glass-topped table, it broke.

identifying what the pronoun refers to •
this, that, which, it
ref 23b 263

▶ Tom told James, ~~that he had~~ "You have won the lottery."

What broke—the pitcher or the table? Who won the lottery—Tom or James? The revisions eliminate the ambiguity.

Remote pronoun reference occurs when a pronoun is too far away from its antecedent for easy reading.

▶ After the court ordered my ex-husband to pay child support,
he refused. Approximately eight months later, we were back
in court. This time the judge ordered him to make payments
directly to the Support and Collections Unit, which would in
turn pay me. For the first six months, I received regular payments, but then they stopped. Again ~~he~~ *my ex-husband* was summoned to
appear in court; he did not respond.

The pronoun *he* was too distant from its antecedent, *ex-husband*, which appeared several sentences earlier.

23b Generally, avoid broad reference of *this, that, which*, and *it*.

For clarity, the pronouns *this, that, which,* and *it* should ordinarily refer to specific antecedents rather than to whole ideas
or sentences. When a pronoun's reference is needlessly broad,
either replace the pronoun with a noun or supply an antecedent to which the pronoun clearly refers.

▶ By advertising on television, pharmaceutical companies
gain exposure for their prescription drugs. Patients
respond to ~~this~~ *the ads* by requesting drugs they might not need.

For clarity, the writer substituted the noun *ads* for the pronoun *this*, which referred broadly to the idea expressed in the preceding sentence.

▶ Romeo and Juliet were both too young to have acquired

  much wisdom, ~~and~~ that accounts for their rash actions.

  (inserted above: a fact*)*

  The writer added an antecedent (*fact*) that the pronoun *that* clearly refers to.

EXCEPTION: Many writers view broad reference as acceptable when the pronoun refers clearly to the sense of an entire clause.

  If you pick up a starving dog and make him prosperous, he will not bite you. *This* is the principal difference between a dog and a man.   —Mark Twain

23c Do not use a pronoun to refer to an implied antecedent.

A pronoun should refer to a specific antecedent, not to a word that is implied but not present in the sentence.

▶ After braiding Ann's hair, Sue decorated ~~them~~ with ribbons.

  (inserted above: the braids*)*

  The pronoun *them* referred to Ann's braids (implied by the term *braiding*), but the word *braids* did not appear in the sentence.

Modifiers, such as possessives, cannot serve as antecedents. A modifier may strongly imply the noun that a pronoun might logically refer to, but it is not itself that noun.

Writing with sources

MLA-style citation

▶ In ~~Jamaica Kincaid's~~ "Girl," ~~she~~ describes the advice a

  (inserted above: Jamaica Kincaid*)*

  mother gives her daughter, including the mysterious

  warning not to be "the kind of woman who the baker won't

  let near the bread" (454).

  Using the possessive form of an author's name to introduce a source leads to a problem later in this sentence: The pronoun *she* cannot refer logically to a possessive modifier (*Jamaica Kincaid's*). The revision substitutes the noun *Jamaica Kincaid* for the pronoun *she*, thereby eliminating the problem.

23d Avoid the indefinite use of *they*, *it*, and *you*.

Do not use the pronoun *they* to refer indefinitely to persons who have not been specifically mentioned. *They* should always refer to a specific antecedent.

▶ In 2001, ~~they~~ shut down all government agencies for more

than a month until the budget crisis was finally resolved.

(edit: they → Congress)

The word *it* should not be used indefinitely in constructions such as *It is said on television . . .* or *In the article, it says that. . . .*

▶ ~~In the~~ encyclopedia ~~it~~ states that male moths can smell

female moths from several miles away.

(edit: In the → The)

The pronoun *you* is appropriate only when the writer is addressing the reader directly: *Once you have kneaded the dough, let it rise in a warm place.* Except in informal contexts, however, *you* should not be used to mean "anyone in general." Use a noun instead. (See pp. 48–49.)

▶ Ms. Pickersgill's *Guide to Etiquette* stipulates that ~~you~~

should not arrive at a party too early or leave too late.

(edit: you → a guest)

23e To refer to persons, use *who*, *whom*, or *whose*, not *which* or *that*.

In most contexts, use *who*, *whom*, or *whose* to refer to persons, *which* or *that* to refer to animals or things. *Which* is reserved only for animals or things, so it is impolite to use it to refer to persons.

▶ All thirty-two women in the study, half of ~~which~~ were

unemployed for more than six months, reported higher

self-esteem after job training.

(edit: which → whom)

Although *that* is sometimes used to refer to persons, many readers will find such references dehumanizing. It is more polite to use a form of *who*—a word reserved only for people.

▶ During the two-day festival El Día de los Muertos (Day of the

Dead), Mexican families celebrate loved ones ~~that~~ have died.
                                               who

NOTE: Occasionally *whose* may be used to refer to animals and things to avoid the awkward *of which* construction.

▶ A local school, ~~the~~ name ~~of which~~ will be in tomorrow's
                          whose

paper, has received the Governor's Gold Medal for out-

standing community service.

EXERCISE 23–1 Edit the following sentences to correct errors in pronoun reference. In some cases, you will need to decide on an antecedent that the pronoun might logically refer to. Revisions of lettered sentences appear in the back of the book. Example:

Although Apple makes the most widely recognized MP3

player, other companies have gained a share of the market.
                  The competition
~~This~~ has kept prices from skyrocketing.

a. They say that engineering students should have hands-on experience with dismantling and reassembling machines.
b. She had decorated her living room with posters from chamber music festivals. This led her date to believe that she was interested in classical music. Actually she preferred rock.
c. In my high school, you didn't need to get all A's to be considered a success; you just needed to work to your ability.
d. Marianne told Jenny that she was worried about her mother's illness.
e. Though Lewis cried for several minutes after scraping his knee, eventually it subsided.

1. Our German conversation group is made up of six people, three of which I had never met before.
2. Many people believe that the polygraph test is highly reliable if you employ a licensed examiner.
3. Parent involvement is high at Mission San Jose High School. They participate in many committees and activities that affect all aspects of school life.
4. Because of Paul Robeson's outspoken attitude toward fascism, he was labeled a Communist.
5. In the report, it points out that the bald eagle, after several decades of protection, was removed from the endangered species list in 1997.

EXERCISE 23–2   Edit the following passage to correct errors in pronoun reference. In some cases, you will need to decide on an antecedent that the pronoun might logically refer to.

Since the Internet's inception in the 1980s, it has grown to be one of the largest communications forums in the world. The Internet was created by a team of academics who were building on a platform that government scientists had started developing in the 1950s. They initially viewed it as a noncommercial enterprise that would serve only the needs of the academic and technical communities. But with the introduction of user-friendly browser technology in the 1990s, it expanded tremendously. By the late 1990s, many businesses were connecting to the Internet with high-speed broadband and fiber-optic connections, which is also true of many home users today. Accessing information, shopping, and communicating are easier than ever before. This, however, can lead to some possible downfalls. You can be bombarded with spam and pop-up ads or attacked by harmful viruses and worms. They say that the best way to protect home computers from harm is to keep antivirus protection programs up-to-date and to shut them down when not in use.

hackerhandbooks.com/bedhandbook > Grammar exercises > Grammatical sentences > E-ex 23–3 to 23–5

24 Distinguish between pronouns such as *I* and *me*.

The personal pronouns in the following chart change what is known as *case form* according to their grammatical function in a sentence. Pronouns functioning as subjects or subject complements appear in the *subjective* case; those functioning as objects appear in the *objective* case; and those showing ownership appear in the *possessive* case.

	SUBJECTIVE CASE	OBJECTIVE CASE	POSSESSIVE CASE
SINGULAR	I	me	my
	you	you	your
	he/she/it	him/her/it	his/her/its
PLURAL	we	us	our
	you	you	your
	they	them	their

Pronouns in the subjective and objective cases are frequently confused. Most of the rules in this section specify when to use one or the other of these cases (*I* or *me*, *he* or *him*, and so on). Section 24g explains a special use of pronouns and nouns in the possessive case.

> **Grammar checkers** sometimes flag incorrect pronouns and suggest using the correct form. But they miss more incorrect pronouns than they catch, and their suggestions for revision are sometimes off the mark, especially with pronouns following *than* or *as* (see 24d).

24a Use the subjective case (*I*, *you*, *he*, *she*, *it*, *we*, *they*) for subjects and subject complements.

When personal pronouns are used as subjects, ordinarily your ear will tell you the correct pronoun. Problems sometimes arise, however, with compound word groups containing a pronoun, so it is not always safe to trust your ear.

▶ Joel ran away from home because his stepfather and ~~him~~ *he* had

quarreled.

His stepfather and he is the subject of the verb *had quarreled*. If we
strip away the words *his stepfather and*, the correct pronoun becomes clear: *he had quarreled* (not *him had quarreled*).

When a pronoun is used as a subject complement (a word
following a linking verb), your ear may mislead you, since the
incorrect form is frequently heard in casual speech. (See "subject complement," 62b.)

▶ During the Lindbergh trial, Bruno Hauptmann repeatedly

denied that the kidnapper was ~~him.~~ *he.*

If *kidnapper was he* seems too stilted, rewrite the sentence: *During
the Lindbergh trial, Bruno Hauptmann repeatedly denied that he was
the kidnapper.*

24b Use the objective case (*me, you, him, her, it, us, them*) for all objects.

When a personal pronoun is used as a direct object, an indirect object, or the object of a preposition, ordinarily your ear
will lead you to the correct pronoun. When an object is compound, however, you may occasionally become confused.

▶ Janice was indignant when she realized that the salesclerk

was insulting her mother and ~~she.~~ *her.*

Her mother and her is the direct object of the verb *was insulting*.
Strip away the words *her mother and* to hear the correct pronoun:
was insulting her (not *was insulting she*).

▶ The most traumatic experience for her father and ~~I~~ *me* occurred

long after her operation.

Her father and me is the object of the preposition *for*. Strip away the
words *her father and* to test for the correct pronoun: *for me* (not *for I*).

When in doubt about the correct pronoun, some writers try to avoid making the choice by using a reflexive pronoun such as *myself*. Using a reflexive pronoun in such situations is nonstandard.

▶ The Indian cab driver gave my cousin and ~~myself~~ *me* some

good tips on traveling in New Delhi.

My cousin and me is the indirect object of the verb *gave*. For correct uses of *myself*, see the Glossary of Usage.

▶ The independent film company hired my sister and ~~myself~~ *me*

as marketing consultants.

My sister and me is the direct object of the verb *hired*. For correct uses of *myself*, see the Glossary of Usage.

24c Put an appositive and the word to which it refers in the same case.

Appositives are noun phrases that rename nouns or pronouns. A pronoun used as an appositive has the same function (usually subject or object) as the word(s) it renames.

▶ The chief strategists, Dr. Bell and ~~me,~~ *I,* could not agree on a

plan.

The appositive *Dr. Bell and I* renames the subject, *strategists*. Test: *I could not agree* (not *me could not agree*).

▶ The reporter interviewed only two witnesses, the bicyclist

and ~~I.~~ *me.*

The appositive *the bicyclist and me* renames the direct object, *witnesses*. Test: *interviewed me* (not *interviewed I*).

24d Following *than* or *as*, choose the pronoun that expresses your meaning.

When a comparison begins with *than* or *as*, your choice of a pronoun will depend on your intended meaning. Consider, for example, the difference in meaning between these sentences.

My roommate likes football more than I.

My roommate likes football more than me.

Finish each sentence mentally and its meaning becomes clear: *My roommate likes football more than I [do]. My roommate likes football more than [he likes] me.*

▶ In our position paper supporting nationalized health care

in the United States, we argued that Canadians are much

better off than ~~us.~~ we.

We is the subject of the verb *are*, which is understood: *Canadians are much better off than we [are].* If the correct English seems too formal, you can always add the verb.

▶ We respected no other candidate for the city council

as much as ~~she.~~ her.

This sentence means that we respected no other candidate as much as *we respected her. Her* is the direct object of the understood verb *respected*.

24e For *we* or *us* before a noun, choose the pronoun that would be appropriate if the noun were omitted.

▶ ~~Us~~ We tenants would rather fight than move.

▶ Management is shortchanging ~~we~~ us tenants.

No one would say *Us would rather fight than move* or *Management is shortchanging we.*

24f Use the objective case for subjects and objects of infinitives.

An infinitive is the word *to* followed by the base form of a verb. (See 63b.) Subjects of infinitives are an exception to the rule that subjects must be in the subjective case. Whenever an infinitive has a subject, it must be in the objective case. Objects of infinitives also are in the objective case.

▶ Ms. Wilson asked John and ~~I~~ *me* to drive the senator and ~~she~~ *her* to

the airport.

John and me is the subject of the infinitive *to drive*; *senator and her* is the direct object of the infinitive.

24g Use the possessive case to modify a gerund.

A pronoun that modifies a gerund or a gerund phrase should be in the possessive case (*my, our, your, his, her, its, their*). A gerund is a verb form ending in *-ing* that functions as a noun. Gerunds frequently appear in phrases; when they do, the whole gerund phrase functions as a noun. (See 63b.)

▶ The chances of ~~you~~ *your* being hit by lightning are about two

million to one.

Your modifies the gerund phrase *being hit by lightning*.

Nouns as well as pronouns may modify gerunds. To form the possessive case of a noun, use an apostrophe and an *-s* (*victim's*) or just an apostrophe (*victims'*). (See 36a.)

▶ The old order in France paid a high price for the ~~aristocracy~~ *aristocracy's*

exploiting the lower classes.

The possessive noun *aristocracy's* modifies the gerund phrase *exploiting the lower classes*.

Gerund phrases should not be confused with participial phrases, which function as adjectives, not as nouns: *We saw him driving a yellow convertible.* Here *driving a yellow convertible* is a participial phrase modifying the pronoun *him.* (See 63b.)

The choice between the objective and the possessive case depends on your meaning; sometimes the distinction is subtle.

> We watched *them* dancing.
>
> We watched *their* dancing.

In the first sentence, the emphasis is on the people; we watched *them*, and they happened to be dancing. In the second sentence, the emphasis is on the dancing; we watched the *dancing*—a noun form modified by the possessive *their.*

NOTE: Do not use the possessive if it creates an awkward effect. Try to reword the sentence instead.

AWKWARD   The president agreed to the applications' being reviewed by a faculty committee.

REVISED   The president agreed that the applications could be reviewed by a faculty committee.

REVISED   The president agreed that a faculty committee could review the applications.

EXERCISE 24–1 Edit the following sentences to eliminate errors in pronoun case. If a sentence is correct, write "correct" after it. Answers to lettered sentences appear in the back of the book. Example:

> **Grandfather cuts down trees for neighbors much younger than ~~him.~~ he.**

a. Rick applied for the job even though he heard that other candidates were more experienced than he.

b. The volleyball team could not believe that the coach was she.

c. She appreciated him telling the truth in such a difficult situation.

d. The director has asked you and I to draft a proposal for a new recycling plan.

e. Five close friends and myself rented a station wagon, packed it with food, and drove two hundred miles to Mardi Gras.

1. The squawk of the brass horns nearly overwhelmed us oboe and bassoon players.
2. Ushio, the last rock climber up the wall, tossed Teri and she the remaining pitons and carabiners.
3. The programmer realized that her and the interface designers were creating an entirely new Web application.
4. My desire to understand classical music was aided by me working as an usher at Symphony Hall.
5. The shower of sinking bricks caused he and his diving partner to race away from the collapsing seawall.

EXERCISE 24–2 In the following paragraph, choose the correct pronoun in each set of parentheses.

We may blame television for the number of products based on characters in children's TV shows—from Big Bird to Sponge-Bob—but in fact merchandising that capitalizes on a character's popularity started long before television. Raggedy Ann began as a child's rag doll, and a few years later books about (she / her) and her brother, Raggedy Andy, were published. A cartoonist named Johnny Gruelle painted a cloth face on a family doll and applied for a patent in 1915. Later Gruelle began writing and illustrating stories about Raggedy Ann, and in 1918 (he / him) and a publisher teamed up to publish the books and sell the dolls. He was not the only one to try to sell products linked to children's stories. Beatrix Potter published the first of many Peter Rabbit picture books in 1902, and no one was better than (she / her) at making a living from spin-offs. After Peter Rabbit and Benjamin Bunny became popular, Potter began putting pictures of (they / them) and their little animal friends on merchandise. Potter had fans all over the world, and she understood (them / their) wanting to see Peter Rabbit not only in books but also on teapots and plates and lamps and other furnishings for the nursery. Potter and Gruelle, like countless others before and since, knew that entertaining children could be a profitable business.

hackerhandbooks.com/bedhandbook > Grammar exercises > Grammatical sentences
> E-ex 24–3 and 24–4
> E-ex 25–3 and 25–4 (pronoun review)

25 Distinguish between *who* and *whom*.

The choice between *who* and *whom* (or *whoever* and *whomever*) occurs primarily in subordinate clauses and in questions. *Who* and *whoever*, subjective-case pronouns, are used for subjects and subject complements. *Whom* and *whomever*, objective-case pronouns, are used for objects. (See 25a and 25b.)

An exception to this general rule occurs when the pronoun functions as the subject of an infinitive (see 25c). See also 24f.

Consult the chart on page 278 for a summary of the trouble spots with *who* and *whom*.

> Grammar checkers catch misuses of *who* and *whom* (or *whoever* and *whomever*) only about half the time. Pay special attention to sentences that include *who* or *whom* as you edit your writing.

25a In subordinate clauses, use *who* and *whoever* for subjects and subject complements, *whom* and *whomever* for all objects.

When *who* and *whom* (or *whoever* and *whomever*) introduce subordinate clauses, their case is determined by their function *within the clause they introduce*. To choose the correct pronoun, you must isolate the subordinate clause and then decide how the pronoun functions within it. (See "subordinate clauses," 63e.)

In the following two examples, the pronouns *who* and *whoever* function as the subjects of the clauses they introduce.

▶ First prize goes to the runner ~~whom~~ who earns the most

points.

The subordinate clause is *who earns the most points*. The verb of the clause is *earns*, and its subject is *who*.

▶ Maya Angelou's *I Know Why the Caged Bird Sings* should be

read by ~~whomever~~ *whoever* is interested in the effects of racial

prejudice on children.

> The writer selected the pronoun *whomever*, thinking that it was
> the object of the preposition *by*. However, the object of the prepo-
> sition is the entire subordinate clause *whoever is interested in the
> effects of racial prejudice on children*. The verb of the clause is *is*, and
> the subject of the verb is *whoever*.

Who occasionally functions as a subject complement in a
subordinate clause. Subject complements occur with linking
verbs (usually *be, am, is, are, was, were, being,* and *been*). When
who is a subject complement, it appears in inverted order, before the subject and verb. (See 62b.)

▶ From your social security number, anyone can find out

~~whom~~ *who* you are.

> The subordinate clause is *who you are*. Its subject is *you*, and its
> subject complement is *who*.

When functioning as an object in a subordinate clause,
whom (or *whomever*) also appears out of order, before the subject and verb. To choose the correct pronoun, you can mentally restructure the clause.

▶ You will work with our senior traders, ~~who~~ *whom* you will meet

later.

> The subordinate clause is *whom you will meet later*. The subject of
> the clause is *you* and the verb is *will meet*. *Whom* is the direct ob-
> ject of the verb. The correct choice becomes clear if you mentally
> restructure the clause: *you will meet whom*.

When functioning as the object of a preposition in
a subordinate clause, *whom* is often separated from its
preposition.

▶ The tutor ~~who~~ *whom* I was assigned to was very supportive.

Whom is the object of the preposition *to*. In this sentence, the writer might choose to drop *whom*: *The tutor I was assigned to was very supportive.*

NOTE: Inserted expressions such as *they know*, *I think*, and *she says* should be ignored in determining whether to use *who* or *whom*.

▶ The speech pathologist reported a particularly difficult

session with a stroke patient ~~whom~~ *who* she knew was suffering

from aphasia.

Who is the subject of *was suffering*, not the object of *knew*.

25b In questions, use *who* and *whoever* for subjects, *whom* and *whomever* for all objects.

When *who* and *whom* (or *whoever* and *whomever*) are used to open questions, their case is determined by their function within the question. In the following example, *who* functions as the subject of the question.

▶ ~~Whom~~ *Who* was responsible for creating that computer virus?

Who is the subject of the verb *was*.

When *whom* functions as the object of a verb or the object of a preposition in a question, it appears out of normal order. To choose the correct pronoun, you can mentally restructure the question.

▶ ~~Who~~ *Whom* did the Democratic Party nominate in 2004?

Whom is the direct object of the verb *did nominate*. This becomes clear if you restructure the question: *The Democratic Party did nominate whom in 2004?*

Checking for problems with *who* and *whom*

In subordinate clauses (25a)

Isolate the subordinate clause. Then read its subject, verb, and any objects, restructuring the clause if necessary. Some writers find it helpful to substitute *he* for *who* and *him* for *whom*.

Samuels hoped to become the business partner of (whoever/whomever) found the treasure.

TEST: . . . *whoever* found the treasure. [. . . *he* found the treasure.]

Ada always seemed to be bestowing a favor on (whoever/whomever) she worked for.

TEST: . . . she worked for *whomever*. [. . . she worked for *him*.]

In questions (25b)

Read the subject, verb, and any objects, rearranging the sentence structure if necessary.

(Who/Whom) conferred with Roosevelt and Stalin at Yalta in 1945?

TEST: *Who* conferred . . . ?

(Who/Whom) did the committee nominate?

TEST: The committee did nominate *whom*?

                        Whom
► ~~Who~~ did you enter into the contract with?
      ^

Whom is the object of the preposition *with*, as is clear if you recast the question: *You did enter into the contract with whom?*

25c Use *whom* for subjects or objects of infinitives.

An infinitive is the word *to* followed by the base form of a verb. (See 63b.) Subjects of infinitives are an exception to the rule that subjects must be in the subjective case. The subject of an infinitive must be in the objective case. Objects of infinitives also are in the objective case.

▶ **When it comes to money, I know ~~who~~ to believe.** *[whom written above who]*

> The infinitive phrase *whom to believe* is the direct object of the verb *know*, and *whom* is the subject of the infinitive *to believe*.

NOTE: In spoken English, *who* is frequently used when the correct *whom* sounds too stuffy. Even educated speakers are likely to say *Who* [not *Whom*] *did Joe replace?* Although some readers will accept such constructions in informal written English, it is safer to use *whom* in formal English: *Whom did Joe replace?*

EXERCISE 25–1   Edit the following sentences to eliminate errors in the use of *who* and *whom* (or *whoever* and *whomever*). If a sentence is correct, write "correct" after it. Answers to lettered sentences appear in the back of the book. Example:

> **What is the address of the artist ~~who~~ Antonio hired?** *[whom written above who]*

a.   The roundtable featured scholars who I had never heard of.
b.   Arriving late for rehearsal, we had no idea who was supposed to dance with whom.
c.   Whom did you support for student government president?
d.   Daniel always gives a holiday donation to whomever needs it.
e.   So many singers came to the audition that Natalia had trouble deciding who to select for the choir.

1.   My cousin Sylvie, who I am teaching to fly a kite, watches us every time we compete.
2.   Who decided to research the history of Hungarians in New Brunswick?
3.   According to Greek myth, the Sphinx devoured those who could not answer her riddles.
4.   The people who ordered their medications from Canada were retirees whom don't have health insurance.
5.   Who did the committee select?

hackerhandbooks.com/bedhandbook > Grammar exercises > Grammatical sentences
                    > E-ex 25–2
                    > E-ex 25–3 and 25–4 (pronoun review)

26 Choose adjectives and adverbs with care.

Adjectives modify nouns or pronouns. They usually come before the word they modify; occasionally they function as complements following the word they modify. Adverbs modify verbs, adjectives, or other adverbs. (See 61d and 61e.)

Many adverbs are formed by adding -*ly* to adjectives (*normal, normally; smooth, smoothly*). But don't assume that all words ending in -*ly* are adverbs or that all adverbs end in -*ly*. Some adjectives end in -*ly* (*lovely, friendly*), and some adverbs don't (*always, here, there*). When in doubt, consult a dictionary.

> **ESL** Placement of adjectives and adverbs can be a tricky matter for multilingual writers. See 30f and 30h.

26a Use adjectives to modify nouns.

Adjectives ordinarily precede the nouns they modify. But they can also function as subject complements or object complements, following the nouns they modify.

> **ESL** In English, adjectives are not pluralized to agree with the words they modify: *The red* [not *reds*] *roses were a surprise.*

Subject complements

A subject complement follows a linking verb and completes the meaning of the subject. (See 62b.) When an adjective functions as a subject complement, it describes the subject.

Justice is *blind.*

Problems can arise with verbs such as *smell*, *taste*, *look*, and *feel*, which sometimes, but not always, function as linking verbs. If the word following one of these verbs describes the subject, use an adjective; if the word following the verb modifies the verb, use an adverb.

ADJECTIVE   The detective looked *cautious*.

ADVERB   The detective looked *cautiously* for fingerprints.

The adjective *cautious* describes the detective; the adverb *cautiously* modifies the verb *looked*.

Linking verbs suggest states of being, not actions. Notice, for example, the different meanings of *looked* in the preceding examples. To look cautious suggests the state of being cautious; to look cautiously is to perform an action in a cautious way.

▶ The lilacs in our backyard smell especially ~~sweetly~~ sweet this year.

The verb *smell* suggests a state of being, not an action. Therefore, it should be followed by an adjective, not an adverb.

▶ The drawings looked ~~well~~ good after the architect made a few

changes.

The verb *looked* is a linking verb suggesting a state of being, not an action. The adjective *good* is appropriate following the linking verb to describe *drawings*. (See also 26c.)

Object complements

An object complement follows a direct object and completes its meaning. (See 62b.) When an adjective functions as an object complement, it describes the direct object.

Sorrow makes *us wise*.

Object complements occur with verbs such as *call*, *consider*, *create*, *find*, *keep*, and *make*. When a modifier follows the direct object of one of these verbs, use an adjective to describe the direct object; use an adverb to modify the verb.

ADJECTIVE   The referee called the plays *perfect*.

ADVERB   The referee called the plays *perfectly*.

The first sentence means that the referee considered the plays to be perfect; the second means that the referee did an excellent job of calling the plays.

▶ **In terms of sharpness, Ray considers cheddar and Swiss** equal. ~~equally.~~

The adjective *equal* is an object complement describing the direct object *cheddar and Swiss*.

> **Grammar checkers** sometimes flag problems with adjectives and adverbs: some misuses of *bad* or *badly* and *good* or *well*; some double comparisons, such as *more meaner*; some absolute comparisons, such as *most unique*; and some double negatives, such as *can't hardly*. However, the programs miss more problems than they find.

26b Use adverbs to modify verbs, adjectives, and other adverbs.

When adverbs modify verbs (or verbals), they nearly always answer the question When? Where? How? Why? Under what conditions? How often? or To what degree? When adverbs modify adjectives or other adverbs, they usually qualify or intensify the meaning of the word they modify. (See 61e.)

Adjectives are often used incorrectly in place of adverbs in casual or nonstandard speech.

▶ **The transportation arrangement worked out** perfectly ~~perfect~~ **for**

everyone.

▶ The manager must see that the office runs ~~smooth~~ *smoothly* and
~~efficient.~~ *efficiently*.

The adverb *perfectly* modifies the verb *worked out*; the adverbs
smoothly and *efficiently* modify the verb *runs*.

▶ The chance of recovering any property lost in the fire looks
~~real~~ *really* slim.

Only adverbs can modify adjectives or other adverbs. *Really* intensifies
the meaning of the adjective *slim*.

26c Distinguish between *good* and *well*, *bad* and *badly*.

Good is an adjective (*good performance*). *Well* is an adverb when
it modifies a verb (*speak well*). The use of the adjective *good* in
place of the adverb *well* to modify a verb is nonstandard and
especially common in casual speech.

▶ We were glad that Sanya had done ~~good~~ *well* on the CPA exam.

The adverb *well* modifies the verb *had done*.

Confusion can arise because *well* is an adjective when it
modifies a noun or pronoun and means "healthy" or "satisfac-
tory" (*The babies were well and warm*).

▶ Adrienne did not feel ~~good,~~ *well,* but she made her presentation

anyway.

As an adjective following the linking verb *did feel*, *well* describes
Adrienne's health.

Bad is always an adjective and should be used to describe a
noun; *badly* is always an adverb and should be used to modify
a verb. The adverb *badly* is often used inappropriately to describe a noun, especially following a linking verb.

▶ The sisters felt ~~badly~~ *bad* when they realized they had left their

brother out of the planning.

The adjective *bad* is used after the linking verb *felt* to describe the noun *sisters*.

26d Use comparatives and superlatives with care.

Most adjectives and adverbs have three forms: the positive, the comparative, and the superlative.

POSITIVE	COMPARATIVE	SUPERLATIVE
soft	softer	softest
fast	faster	fastest
careful	more careful	most careful
bad	worse	worst
good	better	best

Comparative versus superlative

Use the comparative to compare two things, the superlative to compare three or more.

▶ Which of these two low-carb drinks is ~~best?~~ *better?*

▶ Though Shaw and Jackson are impressive, Hobbs is the ~~more~~ *most* qualified of the three candidates running for mayor.

Forming comparatives and superlatives

To form comparatives and superlatives of most one- and two-syllable adjectives, use the endings *-er* and *-est*: *smooth, smoother, smoothest; easy, easier, easiest.* With longer adjectives, use *more* and *most* (or *less* and *least* for downward comparisons): *exciting, more exciting, most exciting; helpful, less helpful, least helpful.*

Some one-syllable adverbs take the endings -er and -est
(*fast, faster, fastest*), but longer adverbs and all of those ending
in -ly form the comparative and superlative with *more* and *most*
(or *less* and *least*).

The comparative and superlative forms of some adjectives
and adverbs are irregular: *good, better, best; well, better, best; bad,
worse, worst; badly, worse, worst.*

▶ The Kirov is the ~~talentedest~~ ballet company we have seen.
  most talented

▶ According to our projections, sales at local businesses will

  be ~~worser~~ than those at the chain stores this winter.
  worse

Double comparatives or superlatives

Do not use double comparatives or superlatives. When you
have added -er or -est to an adjective or adverb, do not also use
more or *most* (or *less* or *least*).

▶ Of all her family, Julia is the ~~most~~ happiest about the move.

▶ All the polls indicated that Gore was more ~~likelier~~ to win
  likely

  than Bush.

Absolute concepts

Avoid expressions such as *more straight, less perfect, very round*,
and *most unique.* Either something is unique or it isn't. It is illogical to suggest that absolute concepts come in degrees.

▶ That is the most ~~unique~~ wedding gown I have ever seen.
  unusual

▶ The painting would have been even more ~~priceless~~ had it
  valuable

  been signed.

26e Avoid double negatives.

Standard English allows two negatives only if a positive meaning is intended: *The orchestra was not unhappy with its performance* (meaning that the orchestra was happy). Using a double negative to emphasize a negative meaning is nonstandard.

Negative modifiers such as *never*, *no*, and *not* should not be paired with other negative modifiers or with negative words such as *neither*, *none*, *no one*, *nobody*, and *nothing*.

▶ Management is not doing ~~nothing~~ *anything* to see that the trash is

picked up.

The double negative *not . . . nothing* is nonstandard.

The modifiers *hardly*, *barely*, and *scarcely* are considered negatives in standard English, so they should not be used with negatives such as *not*, *no one*, or *never*.

▶ Maxine is so weak that she ~~can't~~ *can* hardly climb stairs.

EXERCISE 26–1 Edit the following sentences to eliminate errors in the use of adjectives and adverbs. If a sentence is correct, write "correct" after it. Answers to lettered sentences appear in the back of the book. Example:

We weren't surprised by how ~~good~~ *well* the sidecar racing team

flowed through the tricky course.

a. Did you do good on last week's chemistry exam?
b. With the budget deadline approaching, our office hasn't hardly had time to handle routine correspondence.
c. Some flowers smell surprisingly bad.

d. The customer complained that he hadn't been treated nice.
e. Of all my relatives, Uncle Roberto is the most cleverest.

1. When you answer the phone, speak clear and courteous.
2. Who was more upset about the loss? Was it the coach or the quarterback or the owner of the team?
3. To a novice skateboarder, even the basic ollie seems real challenging.
4. After checking how bad I had been hurt, my sister dialed 911.
5. If the college's Web page had been updated more regular, students would have learned about the new course offerings.

EXERCISE 26–2   Edit the following passage to eliminate errors in the use of adjectives and adverbs.

Doctors recommend that to give skin the most fullest protection from ultraviolet rays, people should use plenty of sunscreen, limit sun exposure, and wear protective clothing. The commonest sunscreens today are known as "broad spectrum" because they block out both UVA and UVB rays. These lotions don't feel any differently on the skin from the old UVA-only types, but they work best at preventing premature aging and skin cancer. Many sunscreens claim to be waterproof, but they won't hardly provide adequate coverage after extended periods of swimming or perspiring. To protect good, even waterproof sunscreens should be reapplied liberal and often. All areas of exposed skin, including ears, backs of hands, and tops of feet, need to be coated good to avoid burning or damage. Some people's skin reacts bad to PABA, or para-aminobenzoic acid, so PABA-free (hypoallergenic) sunscreens are widely available. In addition to recommending sunscreen, doctors almost unanimously agree that people should stay out of the sun when rays are the most strongest—between 10:00 a.m. and 3:00 p.m.—and should limit time in the sun. They also suggest that people wear long-sleeved shirts, broad-brimmed hats, and long pants whenever possible.

hackerhandbooks.com/bedhandbook > Grammar exercises > Grammatical sentences > E-ex 26–3 and 26–4

27 Choose appropriate verb forms, tenses, and moods in standard English.

In speech, some people use verb forms and tenses that match a home dialect or variety of English. In writing, use standard English verb forms unless you are quoting nonstandard speech or using alternative forms for literary effect. (See 17d.)

Except for the verb *be*, all verbs in English have five forms. The following list shows the five forms and provides a sample sentence in which each might appear.

BASE FORM	Usually I (*walk, ride*).
PAST TENSE	Yesterday I (*walked, rode*).
PAST PARTICIPLE	I have (*walked, ridden*) many times before.
PRESENT PARTICIPLE	I am (*walking, riding*) right now.
-S FORM	He/she/it (*walks, rides*) regularly.

Both the past-tense and past-participle forms of regular verbs end in *-ed* (*walked, walked*). Irregular verbs form the past tense and past participle in other ways (*rode, ridden*).

The verb *be* has eight forms instead of the usual five: *be, am, is, are, was, were, being, been.*

> Grammar checkers sometimes flag misused irregular verbs in sentences. But you cannot rely on grammar checkers to identify problems with irregular verbs—they miss about twice as many errors as they find.

27a Choose standard English forms of irregular verbs.

For all regular verbs, the past-tense and past-participle forms are the same (ending in *-ed* or *-d*), so there is no danger of confusion. This is not true, however, for irregular verbs, such as the following.

BASE FORM	PAST TENSE	PAST PARTICIPLE
go	went	gone
break	broke	broken
fly	flew	flown

The past-tense form always occurs alone, without a helping verb. It expresses action that occurred entirely in the past: *I rode to work yesterday. I walked to work last Tuesday*. The past participle is used with a helping verb. It forms the perfect tenses with *has*, *have*, or *had*; it forms the passive voice with *be*, *am*, *is*, *are*, *was*, *were*, *being*, or *been*. (See 61c for a complete list of helping verbs and 27f for a survey of tenses.)

PAST TENSE	Last July, we *went* to Paris.
HELPING VERB + PAST PARTICIPLE	We *have gone* to Paris twice.

The list of common irregular verbs beginning on the next page will help you distinguish between the past tense and the past participle. Choose the past-participle form if the verb in your sentence requires a helping verb; choose the past-tense form if the verb does not require a helping verb. (See verb tenses in 27f.)

▶ Yesterday we ~~seen~~ saw a documentary about Isabel Allende.

The past-tense *saw* is required because there is no helping verb.

▶ The truck was apparently ~~stole~~ stolen while the driver ate lunch.

▶ By Friday, the stock market had ~~fell~~ fallen two hundred points.

Because of the helping verbs *was* and *had*, the past-participle forms are required: *was stolen*, *had fallen*.

When in doubt about the standard English forms of irregular verbs, consult the list on pages 290–92 or look up the base form of the verb in the dictionary, which also lists any irregular forms. (If no additional forms are listed in the dictionary, the verb is regular, not irregular.)

Common irregular verbs

BASE FORM	PAST TENSE	PAST PARTICIPLE
arise	arose	arisen
awake	awoke, awaked	awaked, awoke, awoken
be	was, were	been
beat	beat	beaten, beat
become	became	become
begin	began	begun
bend	bent	bent
bite	bit	bitten, bit
blow	blew	blown
break	broke	broken
bring	brought	brought
build	built	built
burst	burst	burst
buy	bought	bought
catch	caught	caught
choose	chose	chosen
cling	clung	clung
come	came	come
cost	cost	cost
deal	dealt	dealt
dig	dug	dug
dive	dived, dove	dived
do	did	done
drag	dragged	dragged
draw	drew	drawn
dream	dreamed, dreamt	dreamed, dreamt
drink	drank	drunk
drive	drove	driven
eat	ate	eaten
fall	fell	fallen
fight	fought	fought
find	found	found
fly	flew	flown
forget	forgot	forgotten, forgot
freeze	froze	frozen
get	got	gotten, got
give	gave	given
go	went	gone

BASE FORM	PAST TENSE	PAST PARTICIPLE
grow	grew	grown
hang (execute)	hanged	hanged
hang (suspend)	hung	hung
have	had	had
hear	heard	heard
hide	hid	hidden
hurt	hurt	hurt
keep	kept	kept
know	knew	known
lay (put)	laid	laid
lead	led	led
lend	lent	lent
let (allow)	let	let
lie (recline)	lay	lain
lose	lost	lost
make	made	made
prove	proved	proved, proven
read	read	read
ride	rode	ridden
ring	rang	rung
rise (get up)	rose	risen
run	ran	run
say	said	said
see	saw	seen
send	sent	sent
set (place)	set	set
shake	shook	shaken
shoot	shot	shot
shrink	shrank	shrunk
sing	sang	sung
sink	sank	sunk
sit (be seated)	sat	sat
slay	slew	slain
sleep	slept	slept
speak	spoke	spoken
spin	spun	spun
spring	sprang	sprung
stand	stood	stood
steal	stole	stolen
sting	stung	stung

BASE FORM	PAST TENSE	PAST PARTICIPLE
strike	struck	struck, stricken
swear	swore	sworn
swim	swam	swum
swing	swung	swung
take	took	taken
teach	taught	taught
throw	threw	thrown
wake	woke, waked	waked, woken
wear	wore	worn
wring	wrung	wrung
write	wrote	written

27b Distinguish among the forms of *lie* and *lay*.

Writers and speakers frequently confuse the various forms of *lie* (meaning "to recline or rest on a surface") and *lay* (meaning "to put or place something"). *Lie* is an intransitive verb; it does not take a direct object: *The tax forms lie on the table.* The verb *lay* is transitive; it takes a direct object: *Please lay the tax forms on the table.* (See 62b.)

In addition to confusing the meaning of *lie* and *lay*, writers and speakers are often unfamiliar with the standard English forms of these verbs.

BASE FORM	PAST TENSE	PAST PARTICIPLE	PRESENT PARTICIPLE
lie ("recline")	lay	lain	lying
lay ("put")	laid	laid	laying

▶ Sue was so exhausted that she ~~laid~~ *lay* down for a nap.

The past-tense form of *lie* ("to recline") is *lay*.

▶ The patient had ~~laid~~ *lain* in an uncomfortable position all night.

The past-participle form of *lie* ("to recline") is *lain*. If the correct English seems too stilted, recast the sentence: *The patient had been lying in an uncomfortable position all night.*

▶ The prosecutor ~~lay~~ *laid* the pistol on a table close to the jurors.

The past-tense form of *lay* ("to place") is *laid*.

▶ Letters dating from the Civil War were ~~laying~~ *lying* in the corner of the chest.

The present participle of *lie* ("to rest on a surface") is *lying*.

EXERCISE 27–1 Edit the following sentences to eliminate problems with irregular verbs. If a sentence is correct, write "correct" after it. Answers to lettered sentences appear in the back of the book. Example:

The ranger ~~seen~~ *saw* the forest fire ten miles away.

a. When I get the urge to exercise, I lay down until it passes.
b. Grandmother had drove our new hybrid to the sunrise church service on Savage Mountain, so we were left with the station wagon.
c. A pile of dirty rags was laying at the bottom of the stairs.
d. How did the computer know that the gamer had went from the room with the blue ogre to the hall where the gold was heaped?
e. Abraham Lincoln took good care of his legal clients; the contracts he drew for the Illinois Central Railroad could never be broke.

1. The burglar must have gone immediately upstairs, grabbed what looked good, and took off.
2. Have you ever dreamed that you were falling from a cliff or flying through the air?
3. Tomás reached for the pen, signed the title page of his novel, and then laid the book on the table for the first customer in line.
4. In her junior year, Cindy run the 440-yard dash in 51.1 seconds.
5. Larry claimed that he had drank too much soda, but Esther suspected the truth.

hackerhandbooks.com/bedhandbook > Grammar exercises > Grammatical sentences
> E-ex 27–4 and 27–5

27c Use -*s* (or -*es*) endings on present-tense verbs that have third-person singular subjects.

All singular nouns (*child, tree*) and the pronouns *he, she,* and *it* are third-person singular; indefinite pronouns such as *everyone* and *neither* are also third-person singular. When the subject of a sentence is third-person singular, its verb takes an -*s* or -*es* ending in the present tense. (See also 21.)

	SINGULAR		PLURAL	
FIRST PERSON	I	know	we	know
SECOND PERSON	you	know	you	know
THIRD PERSON	he/she/it	knows	they	know
	child	knows	parents	know
	everyone	knows		

▶ My neighbor ~~drive~~ drives to Marco Island every weekend in the summer.

▶ Sulfur dioxide ~~turn~~ turns leaves yellow, ~~dissolve~~ dissolves marble, and ~~eat~~ eats away iron and steel.

The subjects *neighbor* and *sulfur dioxide* are third-person singular, so the verbs must end in -*s*.

TIP: Do not add the -*s* ending to the verb if the subject is not third-person singular. The writers of the following sentences, knowing they sometimes dropped -*s* endings from verbs, over-corrected by adding the endings where they don't belong.

▶ I prepare~~s~~ program specifications and logic diagrams for every installation.

The writer mistakenly concluded that the -*s* ending belongs on present-tense verbs used with *all* singular subjects, not just *third-person* singular subjects. The pronoun *I* is first-person singular, so its verb does not require the -*s*.

▶ **The dirt floors requires continual sweeping.**

The writer mistakenly thought that the verb needed an -s ending because of the plural subject. But the -s ending is used only on present-tense verbs with third-person *singular* subjects.

Has *versus* have

In the present tense, use *has* with third-person singular subjects; all other subjects require *have*.

	SINGULAR		PLURAL	
FIRST PERSON	I	have	we	have
SECOND PERSON	you	have	you	have
THIRD PERSON	he/she/it	has	they	have

▶ **This respected musician almost always ~~have~~ a message to**
                                        has

convey in his work.

▶ **The retirement program ~~have~~ finally been established.**
                        has

The subjects *musician* and *program* are third-person singular, so the verb should be *has* in each case.

TIP: Do not use *has* if the subject is not third-person singular.

▶ **My law classes ~~has~~ helped me understand contracts.**
                 have

▶ **I ~~has~~ much to be thankful for.**
   have

The subjects of these sentences—*classes* and *I*—are third-person plural and first-person singular, so standard English requires *have*. *Has* is used only with third-person singular subjects.

Does *versus* do *and* doesn't *versus* don't

In the present tense, use *does* and *doesn't* with third-person singular subjects; all other subjects require *do* and *don't*.

	SINGULAR		PLURAL	
FIRST PERSON	I	do/don't	we	do/don't
SECOND PERSON	you	do/don't	you	do/don't
THIRD PERSON	he/she/it	does/doesn't	they	do/don't

▶ Grandfather really ~~don't~~ *doesn't* have a place to call home.

▶ ~~Do~~ *Does* she know the correct procedure for setting up the

experiment?

Grandfather and *she* are third-person singular, so the verbs should be *doesn't* and *Does*.

Am, is, and are; was and were

The verb *be* has three forms in the present tense (*am, is, are*) and two in the past tense (*was, were*).

	SINGULAR		PLURAL	
FIRST PERSON	I	am/was	we	are/were
SECOND PERSON	you	are/were	you	are/were
THIRD PERSON	he/she/it	is/was	they	are/were

▶ Judy wanted to borrow Tim's notes, but she ~~were~~ *was* too shy to

ask for them.

The subject *she* is third-person singular, so the verb should be *was*.

▶ Did you think you ~~was~~ *were* going to drown?

The subject *you* is second-person singular, so the verb should be *were*.

Grammar checkers are fairly good at catching missing *-s* endings on verbs and some misused *-s* forms of the verb. Also see the grammar checker advice on page 244.

27d Do not omit *-ed* endings on verbs.

Speakers who do not fully pronounce *-ed* endings sometimes omit them unintentionally in writing. Failure to pronounce *-ed* endings is common in many dialects and in informal speech even in standard English. In the following frequently used words and phrases, for example, the *-ed* ending is not always fully pronounced.

advised	developed	prejudiced	supposed to
asked	fixed	pronounced	used to
concerned	frightened	stereotyped	

When a verb is regular, both the past tense and the past participle are formed by adding *-ed* (or *-d*) to the base form of the verb.

Past tense

Use the ending *-ed* or *-d* to express the past tense of regular verbs. The past tense is used when the action occurred entirely in the past.

▶ Over the weekend, Ed ~~fix~~ fixed his brother's skateboard and tuned

up his mother's 1991 Fiat.

▶ Last summer, my counselor ~~advise~~ advised me to ask my chemistry

instructor for help.

Past participles

Past participles are used in three ways: (1) following *have, has,* or *had* to form one of the perfect tenses; (2) following *be, am, is, are, was, were, being,* or *been* to form the passive voice; and (3) as adjectives modifying nouns or pronouns. The perfect tenses are listed on page 301, and the passive voice is discussed in 8a. For a discussion of participles as adjectives, see 63b.

▶ Robin has ~~ask~~ *asked* for more housing staff for next year.

Has asked is present perfect tense (*have* or *has* followed by a past participle).

▶ Though it is not a new phenomenon, domestic violence is now ~~publicize~~ *publicized* more than ever.

Is publicized is a verb in the passive voice (a form of *be* followed by a past participle).

▶ All aerobics classes end in a cool-down period to stretch ~~tighten~~ *tightened* muscles.

The past participle *tightened* functions as an adjective modifying the noun *muscles*.

Grammar checkers flag missing *-ed* endings on verbs more often than not. Unfortunately, they often suggest an *-ing* ending (*passing*) rather than the missing *-ed* ending (*passed*), when they encounter a sentence like this: *The law was pass last week.*

27e Do not omit needed verbs.

Although standard English allows some linking verbs and helping verbs to be contracted in informal contexts, it does not allow them to be omitted.

Linking verbs, used to link subjects to subject complements, are frequently a form of *be*: *be, am, is, are, was, were, being, been.* (See 62b.) Some of these forms may be contracted (*I'm, she's, we're, you're, they're*), but they should not be omitted altogether.

▶ When we *are* quiet in the evening, we can hear crickets in the woods.

▶ Sherman Alexie ^is^ a Native American author whose stories

have been made into a film.

Helping verbs, used with main verbs, include forms of *be*, *do*, and *have* and the modal verbs *can*, *will*, *shall*, *could*, *would*, *should*, *may*, *might*, and *must*. (See 61c.) Some helping verbs may be contracted (*he's leaving*, *we'll celebrate*, *they've been told*), but they should not be omitted altogether.

▶ We ^have^ been in Chicago since last Thursday.

▶ Do you know someone who ^would^ be good for the job?

ESL Some languages do not require a linking verb between a subject and its complement. English, however, requires a verb in every sentence. See 30a.

▶ Every night, I read a short book to my daughter. When I ^am^

too busy, my husband reads to her.

Grammar checkers flag omitted verbs about half the time—but they often miss needed helping verbs. Proofread your work carefully to avoid leaving out helping verbs.

EXERCISE 27–2 Edit the following sentences to eliminate problems with *-s* and *-ed* verb forms and with omitted verbs. If a sentence is correct, write "correct" after it. Answers to lettered sentences appear in the back of the book. Example:

The Pell Grant sometimes ~~cover~~ ^covers^ the student's full tuition.

a. The glass sculptures of the Swan Boats was prominent in the brightly lit lobby.

b. Visitors to the glass museum were not suppose to touch the exhibits.
c. Our church has all the latest technology, even a close-circuit television.
d. Christos didn't know about Marlo's promotion because he never listens. He always talking.
e. Most psychologists agree that no one performs well under stress.

1. Have there ever been a time in your life when you were too depressed to get out of bed?
2. My days in this department have taught me to do what I'm told without asking questions.
3. We have change our plan and are waiting out the storm before leaving.
4. Winter training for search-and-rescue divers consist of building up a tolerance to icy water temperatures.
5. How would you feel if a love one had been a victim of a crime like this?

hackerhandbooks.com/bedhandbook > Grammar exercises > Grammatical sentences
> E-ex 27–6 and 27–7

27f Choose the appropriate verb tense.

Tenses indicate the time of an action in relation to the time of the speaking or writing about that action.

The most common problem with tenses—shifting confusingly from one tense to another—is discussed in section 13. Other problems with tenses are detailed in this section, after the following survey of tenses.

> **Grammar checkers** do not flag most problems with tense discussed in this section: special uses of the present tense, use of past versus past perfect tense, and sequence of tenses.

Survey of tenses

Tenses are classified as present, past, and future, with simple, perfect, and progressive forms for each.

Simple tenses The simple tenses indicate relatively simple time relations. The *simple present* tense is used primarily for actions occurring at the same time they are being discussed or for actions occurring regularly. The *simple past* tense is used for actions completed in the past. The *simple future* tense is used for actions that will occur in the future. In the following table, the simple tenses are given for the regular verb *walk*, the irregular verb *ride*, and the highly irregular verb *be*.

SIMPLE PRESENT

SINGULAR		PLURAL	
I	walk, ride, am	we	walk, ride, are
you	walk, ride, are	you	walk, ride, are
he/she/it	walks, rides, is	they	walk, ride, are

SIMPLE PAST

SINGULAR		PLURAL	
I	walked, rode, was	we	walked, rode, were
you	walked, rode, were	you	walked, rode, were
he/she/it	walked, rode, was	they	walked, rode, were

SIMPLE FUTURE

I, you, he/she/it, we, they	will walk, ride, be

Perfect tenses More complex time relations are indicated by the perfect tenses. A verb in one of the perfect tenses (a form of *have* plus the past participle) expresses an action that was or will be completed at the time of another action.

PRESENT PERFECT

I, you, we, they	have walked, ridden, been
he/she/it	has walked, ridden, been

PAST PERFECT

I, you, he/she/it, we, they	had walked, ridden, been

FUTURE PERFECT

I, you, he/she/it, we, they	will have walked, ridden, been

Progressive forms The simple and perfect tenses have progressive forms that describe actions in progress. A progressive verb consists of a form of *be* followed by a present participle. The progressive forms are not normally used with certain verbs, such as *believe, know, hear, seem,* and *think*.

PRESENT PROGRESSIVE

I	am walking, riding, being
he/she/it	is walking, riding, being
you, we, they	are walking, riding, being

PAST PROGRESSIVE

I, he/she/it	was walking, riding, being
you, we, they	were walking, riding, being

FUTURE PROGRESSIVE

I, you, he/she/it, we, they	will be walking, riding, being

PRESENT PERFECT PROGRESSIVE

I, you, we, they	have been walking, riding, being
he/she/it	has been walking, riding, being

PAST PERFECT PROGRESSIVE

I, you, he/she/it, we, they	had been walking, riding, being

FUTURE PERFECT PROGRESSIVE

I, you, he/she/it, we, they	will have been walking, riding, being

ESL See 28a for more specific examples of verb tenses that can be challenging for multilingual writers.

Special uses of the present tense

Use the present tense when expressing general truths, when writing about literature, and when quoting, summarizing, or paraphrasing an author's views.

General truths or scientific principles should appear in the present tense unless such principles have been disproved.

▶ Galileo taught that the earth ~~revolved~~ around the sun.
(revolves)

Because Galileo's teaching has not been discredited, the verb should be in the present tense. The following sentence, however, is acceptable: *Ptolemy taught that the sun revolved around the earth.*

When writing about a work of literature, you may be tempted to use the past tense. The convention, however, is to describe fictional events in the present tense.

▶ In Masuji Ibuse's *Black Rain*, a child ~~reached~~ for a *(reaches)*

pomegranate in his mother's garden, and a moment later

he ~~was~~ dead, killed by the blast of the atomic bomb.
(is)

When you are quoting, summarizing, or paraphrasing the author of a nonliterary work, use present-tense verbs such as *writes, reports, asserts,* and so on to introduce the source. This convention is usually followed even when the author is dead (unless a date or the context specifies the time of writing).

▶ Dr. Jerome Groopman ~~argued~~ that doctors are *(argues)*

"susceptible to the subtle and not so subtle efforts of the

pharmaceutical industry to sculpt our thinking" (9).

Writing with sources
MLA-style citation

In MLA style, signal phrases are written in the present tense, not the past tense. (See also 52b.)

APA NOTE: When you are documenting a paper with the APA (American Psychological Association) style of in-text citations, use past tense verbs such as *reported* or *demonstrated* or present perfect verbs such as *has reported* or *has demonstrated* to introduce the source.

E. Wilson (1994) reported that positive reinforcement alone was a less effective teaching technique than a mixture of positive reinforcement and constructive criticism.

The past perfect tense

The past perfect tense consists of a past participle preceded by *had* (*had worked, had gone*). This tense is used for an action already completed by the time of another past action or for an action already completed at some specific past time.

Everyone *had spoken* by the time I arrived.

I pleaded my case, but Paula *had made up* her mind.

Writers sometimes use the simple past tense when they should use the past perfect.

▶ We built our cabin high on a pine knoll, forty feet above an

abandoned quarry that ~~was~~ *had been* flooded in 1920 to create a lake.

The building of the cabin and the flooding of the quarry both occurred in the past, but the flooding was completed before the time of building.

▶ By the time dinner was served, the guest of honor *had* left.

The past perfect tense is needed because the action of leaving was already completed at a specific past time (when dinner was served).

Some writers tend to overuse the past perfect tense. Do not use the past perfect if two past actions occurred at the same time.

▶ When Ernest Hemingway lived in Cuba, he ~~had written~~ *wrote*

For Whom the Bell Tolls.

Sequence of tenses with infinitives and participles

An infinitive is the base form of a verb preceded by *to*. (See 63b.) Use the present infinitive to show action at the same time as or later than the action of the verb in the sentence.

▶ **The club had hoped to** ~~have raised~~ ^raise^ **a thousand dollars by**

April 1.

The action expressed in the infinitive (*to raise*) occurred later than
the action of the sentence's verb (*had hoped*).

Use the perfect form of an infinitive (*to have* followed by
the past participle) for an action occurring earlier than that of
the verb in the sentence.

▶ **Dan would like to** ~~join~~ ^have joined^ **the navy, but he did not pass the**

physical.

The liking occurs in the present; the joining would have occurred
in the past.

Like the tense of an infinitive, the tense of a participle is
governed by the tense of the sentence's verb. Use the present
participle (ending in *-ing*) for an action occurring at the same
time as that of the sentence's verb.

Hiking the Appalachian Trail in early spring, we spotted many
wildflowers.

Use the past participle (such as *given* or *helped*) or the present
perfect participle (*having* plus the past participle) for an action
occurring before that of the verb.

Discovered off the coast of Florida, the Spanish galleon yielded
many treasures.

Having worked her way through college, Lee graduated debt-free.

27g Use the subjunctive mood in the few contexts that require it.

There are three moods in English: the *indicative*, used for facts,
opinions, and questions; the *imperative*, used for orders or
advice; and the *subjunctive*, used in certain contexts to express

wishes, requests, or conditions contrary to fact. For many writers, the subjunctive causes the most problems.

Forms of the subjunctive

In the subjunctive mood, present-tense verbs do not change form to indicate the number and person of the subject (see 21). Instead, the subjunctive uses the base form of the verb (*be*, *drive*, *employ*) with all subjects.

> It is important that you *be* [not *are*] prepared for the interview.
>
> We asked that she *drive* [not *drives*] more slowly.

Also, in the subjunctive mood, there is only one past-tense form of *be*: *were* (never *was*).

> If I *were* [not *was*] you, I'd proceed more cautiously.

Uses of the subjunctive

The subjunctive mood appears only in a few contexts: in contrary-to-fact clauses beginning with *if* or expressing a wish; in *that* clauses following verbs such as *ask*, *insist*, *recommend*, *request*, and *suggest*; and in certain set expressions.

In contrary-to-fact clauses beginning with *if* When a subordinate clause beginning with *if* expresses a condition contrary to fact, use the subjunctive *were* in place of *was*.

▶ If I ~~was~~ a member of Congress, I would vote for that bill.
    were

▶ The astronomers would be able to see the moons of Jupiter tonight if the weather ~~was~~ clearer.
    were

The verbs in these sentences express conditions that do not exist: The writer is not a member of Congress, and the weather is not clear.

Do not use the subjunctive mood in *if* clauses expressing conditions that exist or may exist.

> If Dana *wins* the contest, she will leave for Barcelona in June.

In contrary-to-fact clauses expressing a wish   In formal English, use the subjunctive *were* in clauses expressing a wish or desire. While use of the indicative is common in informal speech, it is not appropriate in academic writing.

INFORMAL   I wish that Dr. Vaughn *was* my professor.

FORMAL   I wish that Dr. Vaughn *were* my professor.

In *that* clauses following verbs such as *ask*, *insist*, *request*, and *suggest*   Because requests have not yet become reality, they are expressed in the subjunctive mood.

▶ Professor Moore insists that her students ~~are~~ be on time.

▶ We recommend that Lambert ~~files~~ file form 1050 soon.

In certain set expressions   The subjunctive mood, once more widely used, remains in certain set expressions: *Be that as it may*, *as it were*, *far be it from me*, and so on.

> **Grammar checkers** only sometimes flag problems with the subjunctive mood. What they catch is very spotty, so you must be alert to the correct uses of the subjunctive in your own writing.

EXERCISE 27–3   Edit the following sentences to eliminate errors in verb tense or mood. If a sentence is correct, write "correct" after it. Answers to lettered sentences appear in the back of the book. Example:

After the path ~~was~~ had been plowed, we were able to walk through

the park.

a. The palace of Knossos in Crete is believed to have been destroyed by fire around 1375 BCE.
b. Watson and Crick discovered the mechanism that controlled inheritance in all life: the workings of the DNA molecule.

c. When city planners proposed rezoning the waterfront, did they know that the mayor promised to curb development in that neighborhood?
d. Tonight's concert begins at 9:30. If it were earlier, I'd consider going.
e. As soon as my aunt applied for the position of pastor, the post was filled by an inexperienced seminary graduate who had been so hastily snatched that his mortarboard was still in midair.

1. Don Quixote, in Cervantes's novel, was an idealist ill suited for life in the real world.
2. Visiting the technology museum inspired the high school seniors and had reminded them that science could be fun.
3. I would like to have been on the *Mayflower* but not to have experienced the first winter.
4. When the director yelled "Action!" I forgot my lines, even though I practiced my part every waking hour for three days.
5. If midday naps were a regular practice in American workplaces, employees would be far more productive.

hackerhandbooks.com/bedhandbook > Grammar exercises > Grammar
> E-ex 27–8 and 27–9

Part VI
Challenges for ESL and Multilingual Writers

Part VI of *The Bedford Handbook* is primarily for multilingual writers. You may find this section helpful if you learned English as a second language (ESL) or if you speak a language other than English with your friends and family.

hackerhandbooks.com/bedhandbook > ESL help
　　　　　　　　　　　　　　　 > Charts and study help
　　　　　　　　　　　　　　　 > Sample student paper (draft and final)
　　　　　　　　　　　　　　　 > Exercises
　　　　　　　　　　　　　　　 > Links to online resources

28　Verbs

Both native and nonnative speakers of English encounter challenges with verbs. Section 28 focuses on specific challenges that multilingual writers sometimes face. You can find more help with verbs in other sections in the book:

making subjects and verbs agree (21)

using irregular verb forms (27a, 27b)

leaving off verb endings (27c, 27d)

choosing the correct verb tense (27f)

avoiding inappropriate uses of the passive voice (8a)

28a Use the appropriate verb form and tense.

This section offers a brief review of English verb forms and tenses.

Basic verb forms

Every main verb in English has five forms, which are used to create all of the verb tenses in standard English. The chart at the top of page 311 shows these forms for the regular verb *help* and the irregular verbs *give* and *be*. See 27a for the forms of other common irregular verbs.

Basic verb forms

	REGULAR VERB $HELP$	IRREGULAR VERB $GIVE$	IRREGULAR VERB BE*
BASE FORM	help	give	be
PAST TENSE	helped	gave	was, were
PAST PARTICIPLE	helped	given	been
PRESENT PARTICIPLE	helping	giving	being
-S FORM	helps	gives	is

*Be also has the forms am and are, which are used in the present tense.

Verb tenses

Section 27f describes all the verb tenses in English, showing the forms of a regular verb, an irregular verb, and the verb be in each tense. The following chart provides more details about the tenses commonly used in the active voice in writing; the chart beginning on page 318 gives details about tenses commonly used in the passive voice.

Verb tenses commonly used in the active voice

For descriptions and examples of all verb tenses, see 27f. For verb tenses commonly used in the passive voice, see the chart on pages 318–19.

Simple tenses
For general facts, states of being, habitual actions

Simple present   **Base form or *-s* form**

- general facts — College students often *study* late at night.
- states of being — Water *becomes* steam at 100° centigrade.
- habitual, repetitive actions — We *donate* to a different charity each year.
- scheduled future events — The train *arrives* tomorrow at 6:30 p.m.

NOTE: For uses of the present tense in writing about literature, see page 303.

→

Verb tenses commonly used in the active voice, *continued*

Simple past	**Base form + *-ed* or *-d* or irregular form**
• completed actions at a specific time in the past	The storm *destroyed* their property. She *drove* to Montana three years ago.
• facts or states of being in the past	When I *was* young, I usually *walked* to school with my sister.
Simple future	***will* + base form**
• future actions, promises, or predictions	I *will exercise* tomorrow. The snowfall *will begin* around midnight.

Simple progressive forms
For continuing actions

Present progressive	***am*, *is*, *are* + present participle**
• actions in progress at the present time, not continuing indefinitely	The students *are taking* an exam in Room 105. The valet *is parking* the car.
• future actions (with *leave*, *go*, *come*, *move*, etc.)	I *am leaving* tomorrow morning.
Past progressive	***was*, *were* + present participle**
• actions in progress at a specific time in the past	They *were swimming* when the storm struck.
• *was going to*, *were going to* for past plans that did not happen	We *were going to* drive to Florida for spring break, but the car broke down.

NOTE: Some verbs are not normally used in the progressive: *appear*, *believe*, *belong*, *contain*, *have*, *hear*, *know*, *like*, *need*, *see*, *seem*, *taste*, *understand*, and *want*.

　　　　want
▶ I am wanting to see August Wilson's *Radio Golf*.

→

Perfect tenses
For actions that happened or will happen before another time

Present perfect   *has, have* + past participle
- repetitive or constant   I *have loved* cats since I was a child. Alicia *has*
  actions that began   *worked* in Kenya for ten years.
  in the past and
  continue to the
  present

- actions that happened   Stephen *has visited* Wales three times.
  at an unknown or
  unspecific time in the
  past

Past perfect   *had* + past participle
- actions that began   She *had* just *crossed* the street when the run-
  or occurred before   away car crashed into the building.
  another time in the
  past

NOTE: For more discussion of uses of the past perfect, see 27f. For uses of the
past perfect in conditional sentences, see 28e.

Perfect progressive forms
For continuous past actions before another time

Present perfect progressive   *has, have* + *been* + present participle
- continuous actions   Yolanda *has been trying* to get a job in Boston
  that began in the past   for five years.
  and continue to the
  present

Past perfect progressive   *had* + *been* + present participle
- actions that began   By the time I moved to Georgia, I *had been*
  and continued in the   *supporting* myself for five years.
  past until some other
  past action

EXERCISE 28–1   Revise the following sentences to correct errors in verb forms and verb tenses. You may need to look at 27a for the correct form of some irregular verbs and at 27f for help with tenses. Answers to lettered sentences appear in the back of the book. Example:

begins
The meeting ~~begin~~ tonight at 7:30.

a. In the past, tobacco companies deny any connection between smoking and health problems.
b. There is nothing in the world that TV has not touch on.
c. I am wanting to register for a summer tutoring session.
d. By the end of the year, the state will have test 139 birds for avian flu.
e. The benefits of eating fruits and vegetables have been promoting by health care providers.

1. By the time he was twelve years old, Mozart had compose an entire opera.
2. A serious accident was happened at the corner of Main Street and First Avenue last night.
3. My family has been gone to Sam's restaurant ever since we moved to this neighborhood.
4. I have ate Thai food only once before.
5. The bear is appearing to be sedated.

hackerhandbooks.com/bedhandbook > Grammar exercises > ESL challenges > E-ex 28–5

28b   Use the base form of the verb after a modal.

The modal verbs are *can, could, may, might, must, shall, should, will,* and *would*. (*Ought to* is also considered a modal verb.) The modals are used with the base form of a verb to show certainty, necessity, or possibility.

Modals and the verbs that follow them do not change form to indicate tense. For a summary of modals and their meanings, see the chart on pages 316–17. (See also 27e.)

launch
▶ **The art museum will ~~launches~~ its fundraising campaign**

next month.

The modal *will* must be followed by the base form *launch*, not the present tense *launches*.

▶ The translator could ~~spoke~~ speak many languages, so the ambassador hired her for the European tour.

The modal *could* must be followed by the base form *speak*, not the past tense *spoke*.

TIP: Do not use *to* in front of a main verb that follows a modal.

▶ Gina can ~~to~~ drive us home if we miss the last train.

For the use of modals in conditional sentences, see 28e.

EXERCISE 28–2 Edit the following sentences to correct errors in the use of verb forms with modals. You may find it helpful to consult the chart on pages 316–17. If a sentence is correct, write "correct" after it. Answers to lettered sentences appear in the back of the book. Example:

We should ~~to~~ order pizza for dinner.

a. A major league pitcher can to throw a baseball more than ninety-five miles per hour.
b. The writing center tutor will helps you revise your essay.
c. A reptile must adjusted its body temperature to its environment.
d. In some states, individuals may renew a driver's license online or in person.
e. My uncle, a cartoonist, could sketched a face in less than two minutes.

1. Working more than twelve hours a day might to contribute to insomnia, according to researchers.
2. A wasp will carry its immobilized prey back to the nest.
3. Hikers should not wandered too far from the trail.
4. Should we continued to submit hard copies of our essays?
5. Physical therapy may to help people after heart surgery.

Modals and their meanings

can

- general ability (present)

  Ants *can survive* anywhere, even in space. Jorge *can run* a marathon faster than his brother.

- informal requests or permission

  Can you *tell* me where the light is? Sandy *can borrow* my calculator.

could

- general ability (past)

  Lea *could read* when she was only three years old.

- polite, informal requests or permission

  Could you *give* me that pen?

may

- formal requests or permission

  May I *see* the report? Students *may park* only in the yellow zone.

- possibility

  I *may try* to finish my homework tonight, or I *may wake up* early and *finish* it tomorrow.

might

- possibility

  The population of New Delhi *might reach* thirteen million by 2013.

NOTE: *Might* usually expresses a stronger possibility than *may*.

must

- necessity (present or future)

  To be effective, welfare-to-work programs *must provide* access to job training.

- strong probability

  Amy *must be* sick. [She is probably sick.]

- near certainty (present or past)

  I *must have left* my wallet at home. [I almost certainly left my wallet at home.]

should

- suggestions or advice

  Diabetics *should drink* plenty of water every day.

- obligations or duties

  The government *should protect* citizens' rights.

- expectations

  The books *should arrive* soon. [We expect the books to arrive soon.]

→

will	
• certainty	If you don't leave now, you *will be* late.
• requests	*Will* you *help* me study for my test?
• promises and offers	Jonah *will arrange* the carpool.
would	
• polite requests	*Would* you *help* me carry these books? I *would like* some coffee. [*Would like* is more polite than *want*.]
• habitual or repeated actions (past)	Whenever Elena needed help with sewing, she *would call* her aunt.

28c To write a verb in the passive voice, use a form of *be* with the past participle.

When a sentence is written in the passive voice, the subject receives the action instead of doing it. (See 62c.)

The solution *was measured* by the lab assistant.

Melissa *was taken* to the hospital.

To form the passive voice, use a form of *be*—*am, is, are, was, were, being, be,* or *been*—followed by the past participle of the main verb: *was chosen, are remembered*. (Sometimes a form of *be* follows another helping verb: *will be stopped, could have been broken*.)

> *Dreaming in Cuban* was ~~writing~~ written by Cristina García.

In the passive voice, the past participle *written*, not the present participle *writing*, must follow *was* (the past tense of *be*).

> Senator Dixon will be defeated.

The passive voice requires a form of *be* before the past participle.

Verb tenses commonly used in the passive voice

For details about verb tenses in the active voice, see pages 311–13.

Simple tenses (passive voice)

Simple present   *am*, *is*, *are* + past participle
- general facts   Meals *are served* by students in the hotel
                                    management program.

- habitual, repetitive   The receipts *are counted* every night.
  actions

Simple past   *was*, *were* + past participle
- completed past actions   He *was punished* for being late.

Simple future   *will be* + past participle
- future actions,   The decision *will be made* by the committee
  promises, or predictions   next week.

Simple progressive forms (passive voice)

Present progressive   *am*, *is*, *are* + *being* + past participle
- actions in progress at   The new stadium *is being built* with private
  the present time   money.

- future actions (with *leave*,   Jo *is being moved* to a new class next month.
  go, *come*, *move*, etc.)

Past progressive   *was*, *were* + *being* + past participle
- actions in progress at a   We thought we *were being followed*.
  specific time in the past

Perfect tenses (passive voice)

Present perfect   *has*, *have* + *been* + past participle
- actions that began in   The flight *has been delayed* because of violent
  the past and continue   storms in the Midwest.
  to the present

- actions that happened   Wars *have been fought* throughout history.
  at an unknown or un-
  specific time in the past   →

Past perfect	*had* + *been* + past participle
• actions that began or occurred before another time in the past	He *had been given* all the hints he needed to complete the puzzle.

NOTE: Future progressive, future perfect, and perfect progressive forms are not used in the passive voice.

▶ The child was being ~~tease.~~ teased.

The past participle *teased*, not the base form *tease*, must be used with *was being* to form the passive voice.

For details on forming the passive in various tenses, consult the chart beginning on page 318. (For appropriate uses of the passive voice, see 8a.)

NOTE: Only transitive verbs, those that take direct objects, may be used in the passive voice. Intransitive verbs such as *occur, happen, sleep, die, become,* and *fall* are not used in the passive. (See 62b.)

▶ The accident ~~was~~ happened suddenly.

▶ Stock prices ~~were fallen~~ fell all week.

28d To make negative verb forms, add *not* in the appropriate place.

If the verb is the simple present or past tense of *be* (*am, is, are, was, were*), add *not* after the verb.

Mario *is not* a member of the club.

For simple present-tense verbs other than *be*, use *do* or *does* plus *not* before the base form of the verb. (For the correct forms of *do* and *does*, see the chart in 21a.)

▶ Mariko ~~no~~ want more dessert. *(does not)*

▶ Mariko does not ~~wants~~ more dessert.

For simple past-tense verbs other than *be*, use *did* plus *not* before the base form of the verb.

▶ They did not ~~planted~~ corn this year. *(plant)*

In a verb phrase consisting of one or more helping verbs and a present or past participle (*is watching, were living, has played, could have been driven*), use the word *not* after the first helping verb.

▶ Inna should have ~~not~~ gone dancing last night. *(not)*

▶ Bonnie is ~~no~~ singing this weekend. *(not)*

NOTE: English allows only one negative in an independent clause to express a negative idea; using more than one is an error known as a *double negative* (see 26e).

▶ We could not find ~~no~~ books about the history of our *(any)*

school.

28e In a conditional sentence, choose verb tenses according to the type of condition expressed in the sentence.

Conditional sentences contain two clauses: a subordinate clause (usually starting with *if, when,* or *unless*) and an independent clause. The subordinate clause (sometimes called the *if* or *unless* clause) states the condition or cause; the independent clause states the result or effect. In each example in this section, the subordinate clause (*if* clause) is marked SUB, and the independent clause is marked IND. (See 63e on clauses.)

Factual

Factual conditional sentences express factual relationships. If the relationship is a scientific truth, use the present tense in both clauses.

```
       ┌──────── SUB ─────────┐  ┌── IND ──┐
       If water cools to 32° Fahrenheit, it freezes.
```

If the sentence describes a condition that is (or was) habitually true, use the same tense in both clauses.

```
       ┌──────── SUB ─────────┐  ┌──────── IND ────────┐
       When Sue jogs along the canal, her dog runs ahead of her.
```

```
       ┌──────── SUB ─────────┐  ┌──── IND ────┐
       Whenever the coach asked for help, I volunteered.
```

Predictive

Predictive conditional sentences are used to predict the future or to express future plans or possibilities. To form a predictive sentence, use a present-tense verb in the subordinate clause; in the independent clause, use the modal *will, can, may, should,* or *might* plus the base form of the verb.

```
       ┌──────── SUB ────────┐  ┌──────── IND ────────┐
       If you practice regularly, your tennis game should improve.
```

```
       ┌──────── IND ────────┐  ┌──── SUB ────┐
       We will lose our remaining wetlands unless we act now.
```

TIP: In all types of conditional sentences (factual, predictive, and speculative), *if* or *unless* clauses do not use the modal verb *will.*

▶ If Jenna ~~will pass~~ her history test, she will graduate this year.
  _{passes}

Speculative

Speculative conditional sentences express unlikely, contrary-to-fact, or impossible conditions. English uses the past or past perfect tense in the *if* clause, even for conditions in the present or the future.

Unlikely possibilities If the condition is possible but unlikely in the present or the future, use the past tense in the subordinate clause; in the independent clause, use *would*, *could*, or *might* plus the base form of the verb.

┌────── SUB ──────┐ ┌────── IND ──────┐
If I *won* the lottery, I *would travel* to Egypt.

The writer does not expect to win the lottery. Because this is a possible but unlikely present or future situation, the subordinate clause uses the past tense.

Conditions contrary to fact In conditions that are currently unreal or contrary to fact, use the past-tense verb *were* (not *was*) in the *if* clause for all subjects. (See also 27g, on the subjunctive mood.)

      were
▶ If I ~~was~~ president, I would make children's issues a priority.

The writer is not president, so *were* is correct in the *if* clause.

Events that did not happen In a conditional sentence that speculates about an event that did not happen or was impossible in the past, use the past perfect tense in the *if* clause; in the independent clause, use *would have*, *could have*, or *might have* with the past participle. (See also past perfect tense, p. 313.)

┌────── SUB ──────┐ ┌────── IND ──────┐
If I *had saved* more money, I *would have visited* Laos last year.

The writer did not save more money and did not travel to Laos. This sentence shows a possibility that did not happen.

┌────── SUB ──────┐ ┌── IND ──┐
If Aunt Grace *had been* alive for your graduation, she *would*

┌──────────────┐
have been very proud.

Aunt Grace was not alive at the time of the graduation. This sentence shows an impossible situation in the past.

EXERCISE 28–3 Edit the following conditional sentences to correct problems with verbs. In some cases, more than one revision is possible. Suggested revisions of lettered sentences appear in the back of the book. Example:

> had
> If I ~~have~~ time, I would study both French and Russian next
> semester.

a. The electrician might have discovered the broken circuit if she went through the modules one at a time.
b. If Verena wins a scholarship, she would go to graduate school.
c. Whenever there is a fire in our neighborhood, everybody came out to watch.
d. Sarah will take the paralegal job unless she would get a better offer.
e. If I live in Budapest with my cousin Szusza, she would teach me Hungarian cooking.

1. If the science fiction festival starts Monday, we wouldn't need to plan entertainment for our visitors.
2. If everyone has voted in the last election, the results would have been very different.
3. The tenants will not pay the rent unless the landlord fixed the furnace.
4. When dark gray clouds appeared on a hot summer afternoon, a thunderstorm often follows.
5. Our daughter would have drowned if Officer Blake didn't risk his life to save her.

hackerhandbooks.com/bedhandbook > Grammar exercises > ESL challenges
> E-ex 28–7

28f Become familiar with verbs that may be followed by gerunds or infinitives.

A gerund is a verb form that ends in *-ing* and is used as a noun: *sleeping, dreaming.* (See 63b.) An infinitive is the word *to* plus the base form of the verb: *to sleep, to dream.* (The word *to* is an infinitive marker, not a preposition, in this use.)

A few verbs may be followed by either a gerund or an infinitive; others may be followed by a gerund but not by an infinitive; still others may be followed by an infinitive but not by a gerund.

Verb + gerund or infinitive (no change in meaning)

The following commonly used verbs may be followed by a gerund or an infinitive, with little or no difference in meaning:

begin	hate	love
continue	like	start

I love *skiing*. I love *to ski*.

Verb + gerund or infinitive (change in meaning)

With a few verbs, the choice of a gerund or an infinitive changes the meaning dramatically:

forget   remember   stop   try

She stopped *speaking* to Lucia. [She no longer spoke to Lucia.]

She stopped *to speak* to Lucia. [She paused so that she could speak to Lucia.]

Verb + gerund

These verbs may be followed by a gerund but not by an infinitive:

admit	enjoy	postpone	resist
appreciate	escape	practice	risk
avoid	finish	put off	suggest
deny	imagine	quit	tolerate
discuss	miss	recall	

Bill enjoys *playing* [not *to play*] the piano.

Jamie quit *smoking*.

Verb + infinitive

These verbs may be followed by an infinitive but not by a gerund:

agree	expect	need	refuse
ask	help	offer	wait
beg	hope	plan	want
claim	manage	pretend	wish
decide	mean	promise	would like

Jill has offered *to water* [not *watering*] the plants while we are away.

Joe finally managed *to find* a parking space.

The man refused *to join* the rebellion.

A few of these verbs may be followed either by an infinitive directly or by a noun or pronoun plus an infinitive:

ask	help	promise	would like
expect	need	want	

We asked *to speak* to the congregation.

We asked *Rabbi Abrams to speak* to our congregation.

Alex expected *to get* the lead in the play.

Ira expected *Alex to get* the lead in the play.

Verb + noun or pronoun + infinitive

With certain verbs in the active voice, a noun or pronoun must come between the verb and the infinitive that follows it. The noun or pronoun usually names a person who is affected by the action of the verb.

advise	convince	order	tell
allow	encourage	persuade	urge
cause	have ("own")	remind	warn
command	instruct	require	

The class encouraged Luis to tell the story of his escape.

The counselor *advised Haley to take* four courses instead of five.

Professor Howlett *instructed us to write* our names on the left side of the paper.

Verb + noun or pronoun + unmarked infinitive

An unmarked infinitive is an infinitive without *to*. A few verbs (often called *causative verbs*) may be followed by a noun or pronoun and an unmarked infinitive.

> have ("cause")   let ("allow")
>
> help   make ("force")
>
> Jorge *had the valet park* his car.

▶ Please let me ~~to~~ pay for the tickets.

▶ Frank made me ~~to~~ carry his book for him.

NOTE: *Help* can be followed by a noun or pronoun and either an unmarked or a marked infinitive.

> Emma *helped Brian wash* the dishes.
>
> Emma *helped Brian to wash* the dishes.

EXERCISE 28–4   Form sentences by adding gerund or infinitive constructions to the following sentence openings. In some cases, more than one kind of construction is possible. Possible answers to lettered items appear in the back of the book. Example:

> **Please remind** your sister to call me.

a.   I enjoy
b.   The tutor told Samantha
c.   The team hopes
d.   Ricardo and his brothers miss
e.   The babysitter let

1.   Pollen makes
2.   The club president asked
3.   Next summer we plan
4.   My supervisor intends
5.   Please stop

29 Articles

Articles (*a*, *an*, *the*) are part of a category of words known as *noun markers* or *determiners*.

29a Be familiar with articles and other noun markers.

Standard English uses noun markers to help identify the nouns that follow. In addition to articles (*a*, *an*, and *the*), noun markers include

- possessive nouns, such as *Elena's* (See 36a.)
- possessive pronoun/adjectives: *my, your, his, her, its, our, their* (See 61b.)
- demonstrative pronoun/adjectives: *this, that, these, those* (See 61b.)
- quantifiers: *all, any, each, either, every, few, many, more, most, much, neither, several, some,* and so on (See 29d.)
- numbers: *one, twenty-three,* and so on

Using articles and other noun markers

Articles and other noun markers always appear before nouns; sometimes other modifiers, such as adjectives, come between a noun marker and a noun.

<pre>   ART N</pre>
Felix is reading a book about mythology.

<pre>   ART ADJ   N</pre>
We took an exciting trip to Alaska last summer.

<pre>NOUN
MARKER ADV   ADJ   N</pre>
That very delicious meal was expensive.

In most cases, do not use an article with another noun marker.

▶ ~~The~~ **Natalie's older brother lives in Wisconsin.**

Expressions like *a few, the most,* and *all the* are exceptions: *a few potatoes, all the rain.* See also 29d.

Types of articles and types of nouns

To choose an appropriate article for a noun, you must first determine whether the noun is *common* or *proper*, *count* or *noncount*, *singular* or *plural*, and *specific* or *general*. The chart on pages 329–30 describes the types of nouns.

Articles are classified as *indefinite* and *definite*. The indefinite articles, *a* and *an*, are used with general nouns. The definite article, *the*, is used with specific nouns. (The last section of the chart on p. 330 explains general and specific nouns.)

A and *an* both mean "one" or "one among many." Use *a* before a consonant sound: *a banana, a tree, a picture, a happy child, a united family.* Use *an* before a vowel sound: *an eggplant, an occasion, an uncle, an honorable person.* (See also *a, an* in the Glossary of Usage.)

The shows that a noun is specific; use *the* with one or more than one specific thing: *the newspaper, the soldiers.*

29b Use *the* with most specific common nouns.

The definite article, *the*, is used with most nouns—both count and noncount—that the reader can identify specifically. Usually the identity will be clear to the reader for one of the following reasons. (See also the chart on p. 332.)

1. The noun has been previously mentioned.

▶ A truck cut in front of our van. When ^the^ truck skidded a few seconds later, we almost crashed into it.

> The article *A* is used before *truck* when the noun is first mentioned. When the noun is mentioned again, it needs the article *the* because readers can now identify which truck skidded—the one that cut in front of the van.

2. A phrase or clause following the noun restricts its identity.

▶ Bryce warned me that ^the^ computer on his desk had just crashed.

> The phrase *on his desk* identifies the specific computer.

Types of nouns

Common or proper

Common nouns
- name general persons, places, things, or ideas
- begin with lowercase

Examples

religion   beauty
knowledge   student
rain   country

Proper nouns
- name specific persons, places, things, or ideas
- begin with capital letter

Examples

Hinduism   President Adams
Philip   Washington Monument
Vietnam   Renaissance

Count or noncount (common nouns only)

Count nouns
- name persons, places, things, or ideas that can be counted
- have plural forms

Examples

girl, girls
city, cities
goose, geese
philosophy, philosophies

Noncount nouns
- name things or abstract ideas that cannot be counted
- cannot be made plural

Examples

water   patience
silver   knowledge
furniture   air

NOTE: See the chart on page 333 for commonly used noncount nouns.

Singular or plural (both common and proper)

Singular nouns (count and noncount)
- represent one person, place, thing, or idea

Examples

backpack   rain
country   beauty
woman   Nile River
achievement Block Island

→

Types of nouns, *continued*

Plural nouns
(count only)

	Examples	
• represent more than one person, place, thing, or idea	backpacks countries women	Ural Mountains Falkland Islands achievements
• must be count nouns		

Specific (definite) or general (indefinite) (count and noncount)

Specific nouns

• name persons, places, things, or ideas that can be identified within a group of the same type

Examples

The students in Professor Martin's *class* should study.

The airplane carrying *the senator* was late.

The furniture in *the truck* was damaged.

General nouns

• name categories of persons, places, things, or ideas (often plural)

Examples

Students should study.

Books bridge *gaps* between *cultures*.

The airplane has made commuting between cities easy.

NOTE: Descriptive adjectives do not necessarily make a noun specific. A specific noun is one that readers can identify within a group of nouns of the same type.

▶ If I win the lottery, I will buy ~~the~~ *a* brand-new bright red sports car.

The reader cannot identify which specific brand-new bright red sports car the writer will buy. Even though *car* has many adjectives in front of it, it is a general noun in this sentence.

3. A superlative adjective such as *best* or *most intelligent* makes the noun's identity specific. (See also 26d on comparatives and superlatives.)

▶ Our petite daughter dated *the* tallest boy in her class.

The superlative *tallest* makes the noun *boy* specific. Although there might be several tall boys, only one boy can be the tallest.

4. The noun describes a unique person, place, or thing.

▶ During an eclipse, one should not look directly at *the* sun.

There is only one sun in our solar system, so its identity is clear.

5. The context or situation makes the noun's identity clear.

▶ Please don't slam *the* door when you leave.

Both the speaker and the listener know which door is meant.

6. The noun is singular and refers to a scientific class or category of items (most often animals, musical instruments, and inventions).

▶ ~~Microchip~~ *The microchip* has transformed nearly everyone's life.

The writer is referring to the microchip as an invention.

29c Use *a* (or *an*) with common singular count nouns that refer to "one" or "any."

If a count noun refers to one unspecific item (not a whole category), use the indefinite article, *a* or *an*. *A* and *an* usually mean "one among many" but can also mean "any one." (See the chart on p. 332.)

▶ My English professor asked me to bring *a* dictionary to class.

The noun *dictionary* refers to "one unspecific dictionary" or "any dictionary."

Choosing articles for common nouns

Use *the*

- if the reader has enough information to identify the noun specifically

COUNT: Please turn on *the lights*. We're going to *the lake* tomorrow.

NONCOUNT: *The food* in Italy is excellent.

Use *a* or *an*

- if the noun refers to one item

and

- if the item is singular but not specific

COUNT: Bring *a pencil* to class. Charles wrote *an essay* about his first job.

NOTE: Do not use *a* or *an* with plural or noncount nouns.

Use a quantifier (*enough, many, some*, etc.)

- if the noun represents an unspecified amount of something

- if the amount is more than one but not all items in a category

COUNT (plural): Amir showed us *some photos* of India. *Many turtles* return to the same nesting site each year.

NONCOUNT: We expect *some rain* this evening.

NOTE: Sometimes no article conveys an unspecified amount: *Amir showed us photos of India*.

Use no article

- if the noun represents all items in a category

- if the noun represents a category in general

COUNT (plural): *Students* can attend the show for free.

NONCOUNT: *Coal* is a natural resource.

NOTE: *The* is occasionally used when a singular count noun refers to all items in a class or a specific category: *The bald eagle is no longer endangered in the United States*.

Commonly used noncount nouns

Food and drink

beef, bread, butter, candy, cereal, cheese, cream, meat, milk, pasta, rice, salt, sugar, water, wine

Nonfood substances

air, cement, coal, dirt, gasoline, gold, paper, petroleum, plastic, rain, silver, snow, soap, steel, wood, wool

Abstract nouns

advice, anger, beauty, confidence, courage, employment, fun, happiness, health, honesty, information, intelligence, knowledge, love, poverty, satisfaction, wealth

Other

biology (and other areas of study), clothing, equipment, furniture, homework, jewelry, luggage, machinery, mail, money, news, poetry, pollution, research, scenery, traffic, transportation, violence, weather, work

NOTE: A few noncount nouns (such as *love*) can also be used as count nouns: *He had two loves: music and archery.*

> *an*
> ▶ We want to rent ‸ apartment close to the lake.

The noun *apartment* refers to "any apartment close to the lake," not a specific apartment.

29d Use a quantifier such as *some* or *more*, not *a* or *an*, with a noncount noun to express an approximate amount.

Do not use *a* or *an* with noncount nouns. Also do not use numbers or words such as *several* or *many* because they must be used with plural nouns, and noncount nouns do not have plural forms. (See the chart on p. 333 for a list of commonly used noncount nouns.)

▶ Dr. Snyder gave us ~~an~~ information about the Peace Corps.

▶ Do you have ~~many~~ money with you?

You can use quantifiers such as *enough, less,* and *some* to suggest approximate amounts or nonspecific quantities of noncount nouns: *a little salt, any homework, enough wood, less information, much pollution.*

▶ Vincent's mother told him that she had ~~a~~ ^{some} news that

would surprise him.

29e Do not use articles with nouns that refer to all of something or something in general.

When a noncount noun refers to all of its type or to a concept in general, it is not marked with an article.

▶ ~~The~~ kindness is a virtue. *(Kindness)*

The noun represents kindness in general; it does not represent a specific type of kindness.

▶ In some parts of the world, ~~the~~ rice is preferred to all other

grains.

The noun *rice* represents rice in general, not a specific type or serving of rice.

In most cases, when you use a count noun to represent a general category, make the noun plural. Do not use unmarked singular count nouns to represent whole categories.

▶ ~~Fountain is~~ an expensive element of landscape design. *(Fountains are)*

Fountains is a count noun that represents fountains in general.

EXCEPTION: In some cases, *the* can be used with singular count nouns to represent a class or specific category: *The Chinese alligator is smaller than the American alligator.* See also number 6 in 29b.

29f Do not use articles with most singular proper nouns. Use *the* with most plural proper nouns.

Since singular proper nouns are already specific, they typically do not need an article: *Prime Minister Brown, Jamaica, Lake Huron, Mount Etna.*

There are, however, many exceptions. In most cases, if the proper noun consists of a common noun with modifiers (adjectives or an *of* phrase), use *the* with the proper noun.

▶ We visited $\overset{the}{\wedge}$ Great Wall of China last year.

▶ Rob wants to be a translator for $\overset{the}{\wedge}$ Central Intelligence Agency.

The is used with most plural proper nouns: *the McGregors, the Bahamas, the Finger Lakes, the United States.*

Geographic names create problems because there are so many exceptions to the rules. When in doubt, consult the chart on page 336, check a dictionary, or ask a native speaker.

EXERCISE 29–1   Edit the following sentences for proper use of articles and nouns. If a sentence is correct, write "correct" after it. Answers to lettered sentences appear in the back of the book. Example:

~~The~~ Josefina's dance routine was flawless.

a.   Doing volunteer work often brings a satisfaction.
b.   As I looked out the window of the plane, I could see the Cape Cod.
c.   Melina likes to drink her coffees with lots of cream.
d.   Recovering from abdominal surgery requires patience.
e.   I completed the my homework assignment quickly.

1.   The attorney argued that her client should receive a money for emotional suffering.

Using *the* with geographic nouns

When to omit *the*

streets, squares, parks	Ivy Street, Union Square, Denali National Park
cities, states, counties	Miami, New Mexico, Bee County
most countries, continents	Italy, Nigeria, China, South America, Africa
bays, single lakes	Tampa Bay, Lake Geneva
single mountains, islands	Mount Everest, Crete

When to use *the*

country names with *of* phrase	the United States (of America), the People's Republic of China
large regions, deserts	the East Coast, the Sahara
peninsulas	the Baja Peninsula, the Sinai Peninsula
oceans, seas, gulfs	the Pacific Ocean, the Dead Sea, the Persian Gulf
canals and rivers	the Panama Canal, the Amazon
mountain ranges	the Rocky Mountains, the Alps
groups of islands	the Solomon Islands

2. Please check to see if there is a mail in the mailbox.
3. The Times Square in New York City is known for its billboards and theaters.
4. A cement is one of the components of concrete.
5. I took all the boys on the roller coaster after lunch.

EXERCISE 29–2 Articles have been omitted from the following description of winter weather. Insert the articles *a*, *an*, and *the* where English requires them and be prepared to explain the reasons for your choices.

Many people confuse terms *hail, sleet,* and *freezing rain.* Hail normally occurs in thunderstorm and is caused by strong updrafts that lift growing chunks of ice into clouds. When chunks of ice, called hailstones, become too heavy to be carried by updrafts, they fall to ground. Hailstones can cause damage to crops, windshields, and people. Sleet occurs during winter storms and is caused by snowflakes falling from layer of cold air into warm layer, where they become raindrops, and then into another cold layer. As they fall through last layer of cold air, raindrops freeze and become small ice pellets, forming sleet. When it hits car windshield or windows of house, sleet can make annoying racket. Driving and walking can be hazardous when sleet accumulates on roads and sidewalks. Freezing rain is basically rain that falls onto ground and then freezes after it hits ground. It causes icy glaze on trees and any surface that is below freezing.

hackerhandbooks.com/bedhandbook > Grammar exercises > ESL challenges > E-ex 29–3 to 29–5

30 Sentence structure

Although their structure can vary widely, sentences in English generally flow from subject to verb to object or complement: *Bears eat fish.* This section focuses on the major challenges that multilingual students face when writing sentences in English. For more details on the parts of speech and the elements of sentences, consult sections 61–64.

30a Use a linking verb between a subject and its complement.

Some languages, such as Russian and Turkish, do not use linking verbs (*is, are, was, were*) between subjects and complements (nouns or adjectives that rename or describe the subject). Every English sentence, however, must include a verb. For more on linking verbs, see 27e.

▶ Jim *is* intelligent.

▶ Many streets in San Francisco *are* very steep.

30b Include a subject in every sentence.

Some languages, such as Spanish and Japanese, do not require a subject in every sentence. Every English sentence, however, needs a subject. Commands are an exception: The subject *you* is understood but not present (*Give me the book*).

▶ Your aunt is very energetic. ~~Seems~~ young for her age.
   She seems

The word *it* is used as the subject of a sentence describing the weather or temperature, stating the time, indicating distance, or suggesting an environmental fact.

▶ ~~Is~~ raining in the valley and snowing in the mountains.
   It is

▶ In July, is very hot in Arizona.
   it

▶ ~~Is~~ 9:15 a.m.
   It is

In most English sentences, the subject appears before the verb. Some sentences, however, are inverted: The subject comes after the verb. In these sentences, a placeholder called an *expletive* (*there* or *it*) often comes before the verb.

EXP V ┌── S ──┐   ┌── S ──┐ V
There are many people here today. (Many people are here today.)

▶ ~~Is~~ an apple in the refrigerator.
   There is

▶ As you know, many religious sects in India.
   there are

Notice that the verb agrees with the subject that follows it: *apple is, sects are*. (See 21g.)

Sometimes an inverted sentence has an infinitive (*to work*) or a noun clause (*that she is intelligent*) as the subject. In such sentences, the placeholder *it* is needed before the verb. (Also see 63b and 63e.)

EXP V ⎡—S—⎤ ⎡—S—⎤ V
It is important to study daily. (To study daily is important.)

it
▶ Because the road is flooded, is necessary to change our route.
‸

TIP: The words *here* and *there* are not used as subjects. When they mean "in this place" (*here*) or "in that place" (*there*), they are adverbs, not nouns.

It
▶ I just returned from a vacation in Japan. ~~There~~ is very
‸
there.
beautiful/
‸

This school that school
▶ ~~Here~~ offers a master's degree in physical therapy; ~~there~~ has
‸ ‸
only a bachelor's program.

Grammar checkers can flag some sentences with a missing expletive, or placeholder (*there* or *it*), as in the sentence *Are many stores on Main Street.* But they often misdiagnose the problem because they cannot tell whether the sentence needs an expletive to make a statement (*There are many stores on Main Street*) or to ask a question (*Are there many stores on Main Street?*).

30c Do not use both a noun and a pronoun to perform the same grammatical function in a sentence.

English does not allow a subject to be repeated in its own clause.

▶ The doctor ~~she~~ advised me to cut down on salt.

The pronoun *she* cannot repeat the subject, *doctor*.

Do not add a pronoun even when a word group comes between the subject and the verb.

▶ **The watch that I lost on vacation i̶t̶ was in my**

backpack.

The pronoun *it* cannot repeat the subject, *watch*.

Some languages allow "topic fronting," placing a word or phrase (a "topic") at the beginning of a sentence and following it with an independent clause that explains something about the topic. This form is not allowed in English because the sentence seems to start with one subject but then introduces a new subject in an independent clause.

┌── TOPIC ──┐ ┌──────── IND CLAUSE ────────┐
INCORRECT The seeds I planted them last fall.

The sentence can be corrected by bringing the topic (*seeds*) into the independent clause.

the seeds
▶ T̶h̶e̶ ̶s̶e̶e̶d̶s̶ I planted t̶h̶e̶m̶ last fall.
                    ^

30d Do not repeat an object or an adverb in an adjective clause.

Adjective clauses begin with relative pronouns (*who, whom, whose, which, that*) or relative adverbs (*when, where*). Relative pronouns usually serve as subjects or objects in the clauses they introduce; another word in the clause cannot serve the same function. Relative adverbs should not be repeated by other adverbs later in the clause.

┌─────────── ADJ CLAUSE ───────────┐
The cat ran under the car that was parked on the street.

▶ **The cat ran under the car that i̶t̶ was parked on the street.**

The relative pronoun *that* is the subject of the adjective clause, so the pronoun *it* cannot be added as a subject.

▶ **Myrna enjoyed the investment seminars that she attended**

~~**them**~~ **last week.**

The relative pronoun *that* is the object of the verb *attended*. The pronoun *them* cannot also serve as an object.

Sometimes the relative pronoun is understood but not present in the sentence. In such cases, do not add another word with the same function as the omitted pronoun.

▶ **Myrna enjoyed the investment seminars she attended** ~~**them**~~

last week.

The relative pronoun *that* is understood after *seminars* even though it is not present in the sentence.

If the clause begins with a relative adverb, do not use another adverb with the same meaning later in the clause.

▶ **The office where I work** ~~**there**~~ **is one hour from the city.**

The adverb *there* cannot repeat the relative adverb *where*.

Grammar checkers are not much help with repeated subjects or objects. If they flag them at all, the programs often identify the problems incorrectly.

EXERCISE 30–1 In the following sentences, add needed subjects or expletives and delete any repeated subjects, objects, or adverbs. Answers to lettered sentences appear in the back of the book. Example:

The new geology professor is the one whom we saw ~~**him**~~ **on**

TV this morning.

a. Are some cartons of ice cream in the freezer.
b. I don't use the subway because am afraid.
c. The prime minister she is the most popular leader in my country.

d. We tried to get in touch with the same manager whom we spoke to him earlier.
e. Recently have been a number of earthquakes in Turkey.

1. We visited an island where several ancient ruins are being excavated there.
2. In this city is difficult to find a high-paying job.
3. Beginning knitters they are often surprised that their fingers are sore at first.
4. Is a banyan tree in our backyard.
5. The CD that teaches Italian for opera lovers it was stolen from my backpack.

hackerhandbooks.com/bedhandbook > Grammar exercises > ESL challenges > E-ex 30–5

30e Avoid mixed constructions beginning with *although* or *because*.

A word group that begins with *although* cannot be linked to a word group that begins with *but* or *however*. The result is an error called a *mixed construction* (see also 11a). Similarly, a word group that begins with *because* cannot be linked to a word group that begins with *so* or *therefore*.

If you want to keep *although* or *because*, drop the other linking word.

▶ Although Nikki Giovanni is best known for her poetry for

adults, ~~but~~ she has written several books for children.

▶ Because finance laws are not always enforced, ~~therefore~~

investing in the former Soviet Union can be risky.

If you want to keep the other linking word, omit *although* or *because*.

▶ ~~Although~~ Nikki Giovanni is best known for her poetry for

adults, but she has written several books for children.

> Finance
> ~~Because finance~~ laws are not always enforced/; therefore,
> investing in the former Soviet Union can be risky.

For advice about using commas and semicolons with linking words, see 32a and 34b.

30f Do not place an adverb between a verb and its direct object.

Adverbs modifying verbs can appear in various positions: at the beginning or end of a sentence, before or after a verb, or between a helping verb and its main verb.

Slowly, we drove along the rain-slick road.

Mia handled the teapot *very carefully*.

Martin *always* wins our tennis matches.

Christina is *rarely* late for our lunch dates.

My daughter has *often* spoken of you.

The election results were being *closely* followed by analysts.

However, an adverb cannot appear between a verb and its direct object.

> carefully
> Mother wrapped ~~carefully~~ the gift.

The adverb *carefully* cannot appear between the verb, *wrapped*, and its direct object, *the gift*.

EXERCISE 30–2 Edit the following sentences for proper sentence structure. If a sentence is correct, write "correct" after it. Answers to lettered sentences appear in the back of the book. Example:

slowly.
She peeled ~~slowly~~ the banana/

a. Although freshwater freezes at 32 degrees Fahrenheit, however ocean water freezes at 28 degrees Fahrenheit.

b. Because we switched cable packages, so our channel lineup has changed.
c. The competitor mounted confidently his skateboard.
d. My sister performs well the *legong*, a Balinese dance.
e. Because product development is behind schedule, we will have to launch the product next spring.

1. The teller counted methodically the stack of one-dollar bills.
2. I gasped when I saw lightning strike repeatedly the barn.
3. Although hockey is traditionally a winter sport, but many towns offer skills programs all year long.
4. Because salmon can survive in both freshwater and salt water, so they are classified as anadromous fish.
5. A surveyor determines precisely the boundaries of a piece of property.

hackerhandbooks.com/bedhandbook > Grammar exercises > ESL challenges > E-ex 30–6

30g Distinguish between present participles and past participles used as adjectives.

Both present and past participles may be used as adjectives. The present participle always ends in *-ing*. Past participles usually end in *-ed*, *-d*, *-en*, *-n*, or *-t*. (See 27a.)

PRESENT PARTICIPLES	confusing, speaking, boring
PAST PARTICIPLES	confused, spoken, bored

Like all other adjectives, participles can come before nouns; they also can follow linking verbs, in which case they describe the subject of the sentence. (See 62b.)

Use a present participle to describe a person or thing *causing or stimulating an experience*.

The *boring lecture* put us to sleep. [The lecture caused boredom.]

Use a past participle to describe a person or thing *undergoing an experience*.

The *audience* was *bored* by the lecture. [The audience experienced boredom.]

Participles that describe emotions or mental states often cause the most confusion.

annoying/annoyed	exhausting/exhausted
boring/bored	fascinating/fascinated
confusing/confused	frightening/frightened
depressing/depressed	satisfying/satisfied
exciting/excited	surprising/surprised

▶ Our hike was ~~exhausted.~~ *exhausting.*

Exhausting suggests that the hike caused exhaustion.

▶ The ~~exhausting~~ *exhausted* hikers reached the campground at

sunset.

Exhausted describes how the hikers felt.

Grammar checkers do not flag problems with present and past participles used as adjectives. Not surprisingly, the programs have no way of knowing the meaning a writer intends.

EXERCISE 30–3 Edit the following sentences for proper use of present and past participles. If a sentence is correct, write "correct" after it. Answers to lettered sentences appear in the back of the book. Example:

Danielle and Monica were very ~~exciting~~ *excited* to be going to a

Broadway show for the first time.

a. Listening to everyone's complaints all day was irritated.
b. The long flight to Singapore was exhausted.
c. His skill at chess is amazing.
d. After a great deal of research, the scientist made a fascinated discovery.
e. That blackout was one of the most frightened experiences I've ever had.

1. I couldn't concentrate on my homework because I was distracted.
2. The directions to the new board game seem extremely complicating.
3. How interested are you in visiting Civil War battlefields?
4. The aerial view of the devastated villages was depressing.
5. Even after the lecturer went over the main points again, the students were still confusing.

hackerhandbooks.com/bedhandbook > Grammar exercises > ESL challenges > E-ex 30–7

30h Place cumulative adjectives in an appropriate order.

Adjectives usually come before the nouns they modify and may also come after linking verbs. (See 61d and 62b.)

                    ADJ   N   V   ADJ
Janine wore a new necklace. Janine's necklace was new.

Cumulative adjectives, which cannot be joined by the word *and* or separated by commas, must come in a particular order. If you use cumulative adjectives before a noun, see the chart on page 347. The chart is only a guide; don't be surprised if you encounter exceptions. (See also 33d.)

▶ My dorm room has only a small desk and a ~~plastic red smelly~~ *smelly red plastic* chair.

▶ Nice weather, ~~blue clear~~ *clear blue* water, and ancient monuments attract many people to Italy.

EXERCISE 30–4 Using the chart on page 347, arrange the following modifiers and nouns in their proper order. Answers to lettered items appear in the back of the book. Example:

two new French racing bicycles
new, French, two, bicycles, racing

a. woman, young, an, Vietnamese, attractive
b. dedicated, a, priest, Catholic
c. old, her, sweater, blue, wool
d. delicious, Joe's, Scandinavian, bread
e. many, boxes, jewelry, antique, beautiful

1. oval, nine, brass, lamps, miniature
2. several, yellow, tulips, tiny
3. the, tree, gingko, yellow, ancient, Mongolian
4. courtyard, a, square, small, brick
5. charming, restaurants, Latvian, several

hackerhandbooks.com/bedhandbook > Grammar exercises > ESL challenges
> E-ex 30–8

Order of cumulative adjectives

FIRST   **ARTICLE OR OTHER NOUN MARKER** a, an, the, her, Joe's, two, many, some

EVALUATIVE WORD attractive, dedicated, delicious, ugly, disgusting

SIZE large, enormous, small, little

LENGTH OR SHAPE long, short, round, square

AGE new, old, young, antique

COLOR yellow, blue, crimson

NATIONALITY French, Peruvian, Vietnamese

RELIGION Catholic, Protestant, Jewish, Muslim

MATERIAL silver, walnut, wool, marble

LAST   **NOUN/ADJECTIVE** tree (as in *tree* house), kitchen (as in *kitchen* table)

THE NOUN MODIFIED house, sweater, bicycle, bread, woman, priest

My long green wool coat is in the attic.

Ana's collection includes *four small antique silver* coins.

31 Prepositions and idiomatic expressions

31a Become familiar with prepositions that show time and place.

The most frequently used prepositions in English are *at*, *by*, *for*, *from*, *in*, *of*, *on*, *to*, and *with*. Prepositions can be difficult to master because the differences among them are subtle and idiomatic. The chart on page 349 is limited to three troublesome prepositions that show time and place: *at*, *on*, and *in*.

Not every possible use is listed in the chart, so don't be surprised when you encounter exceptions and idiomatic uses that you must learn one at a time. For example, in English a person rides *in* a car but *on* a bus, plane, train, or subway.

▶ My first class starts ~~on~~ *at* 8:00 a.m.

▶ The farmers go to market ~~in~~ *on* Wednesday.

▶ I want to work at one of the biggest companies ~~on~~ *in* the world.

EXERCISE 31–1 In the following sentences, replace prepositions that are not used correctly. If a sentence is correct, write "correct" after it. Answers to lettered sentences appear in the back of the book. Example:

The play begins ~~on~~ *at* 7:20 p.m.

a. Whenever we eat at the Centerville Café, we sit at a small table on the corner of the room.
b. At the beginning of the dot-com wave, students created new businesses in record numbers.
c. In Thursday, Nancy will attend her first home repair class at the community center.
d. Alex began looking for her lost mitten in another location.
e. We decided to go to a restaurant because there was no fresh food on the refrigerator.

1. I like walking at my neighborhood in night.
2. If the train is on time, it will arrive on six o'clock at the morning.
3. In the corner of the room is a large bookcase with a pair of small Russian dolls standing at the top shelf.
4. She licked the stamp, stuck it in the envelope, put the envelope on her pocket, and walked to the nearest mailbox.
5. The mailbox was in the intersection of Laidlaw Avenue and Williams Street.

hackerhandbooks.com/bedhandbook > Grammar exercises > ESL challenges
> E-ex 31–2

At, on, *and* in *to show time and place*

Showing time

AT   *at* a specific time: *at* 7:20, *at* dawn, *at* dinner

ON   *on* a specific day or date: *on* Tuesday, *on* June 4

IN   *in* a part of a 24-hour period: *in* the afternoon, *in* the daytime
[but *at* night]

in a year or month: *in* 1999, *in* July

in a period of time: finished *in* three hours

Showing place

AT   *at* a meeting place or location: *at* home, *at* the club

at the edge of something: sitting *at* the desk

at the corner of something: turning *at* the intersection

at a target: throwing the snowball *at* Lucy

ON   *on* a surface: placed *on* the table, hanging *on* the wall

on a street: the house *on* Spring Street

on an electronic medium: *on* television, *on* the Internet

IN   *in* an enclosed space: *in* the garage, *in* an envelope

in a geographic location: *in* San Diego, *in* Texas

in a print medium: *in* a book, *in* a magazine

31b Use nouns (including *-ing* forms) after prepositions.

In a prepositional phrase, use a noun (not a verb) after the preposition. Sometimes the noun will be a gerund, the *-ing* verb form that functions as a noun (see 63b).

▶ Our student government is good at ~~save~~ money.

     saving

Distinguish between the preposition *to* and the infinitive marker *to*. If *to* is a preposition, it should be followed by a noun or a gerund.

▶ We are dedicated to ~~help~~ the poor.

     helping

If *to* is an infinitive marker, it should be followed by the base form of the verb.

▶ We want to ~~helping~~ the poor.

     help

To test whether *to* is a preposition or an infinitive marker, insert a word that you know is a noun after the word *to*. If the noun makes sense in that position, *to* is a preposition.

Zoe is addicted *to* _____.

They are planning *to* _____.

In the first case, a noun (such as *magazines*) makes sense after *to*, so *to* is a preposition and should be followed by a noun or a gerund.

Zoe is addicted *to magazines*.

Zoe is addicted *to reading*.

In the second case, a noun (such as *village*) does not make sense after *to*, so *to* is an infinitive marker and must be followed by the base form of the verb.

They are planning *to build* a new school.

31c Become familiar with common adjective + preposition combinations.

Some adjectives appear only with certain prepositions. These expressions are idiomatic and may be different from the combinations used in your native language.

▶ Paula is married ~~with~~ Jon.

   to

Check an ESL dictionary for combinations that are not listed in the chart at the bottom of this page.

31d Become familiar with common verb + preposition combinations.

Many verbs and prepositions appear together in idiomatic phrases. Pay special attention to the combinations that are different from the combinations used in your native language.

▶ Your success depends ~~of~~ your effort.

   on

Check an ESL dictionary for combinations that are not listed in the chart on page 352.

Adjective + preposition combinations

accustomed to	connected to	guilty of	preferable to
addicted to	covered with	interested in	proud of
afraid of	dedicated to	involved in	responsible for
angry with	devoted to	involved with	satisfied with
ashamed of	different from	known as	scared of
aware of	engaged to (*or*	known for	similar to
committed to	engaged in)	made of (*or*	tired of
concerned	excited about	made from)	worried about
about	familiar with	married to	
concerned with	full of	opposed to	

Verb + preposition combinations

agree with	compare with	forget about	speak to (or
apply to	concentrate on	happen to	speak with)
approve of	consist of	hope for	stare at
arrive at	count on	insist on	succeed at
arrive in	decide on	listen to	succeed in
ask for	depend on	participate in	take advantage of
believe in	differ from	rely on	take care of
belong to	disagree with	reply to	think about
care about	dream about	respond to	think of
care for	dream of	result in	wait for
compare to	feel like	search for	wait on

Part VII
Punctuation

32 The comma

The comma was invented to help readers. Without it, sentence parts can collide into one another unexpectedly, causing misreadings.

CONFUSING If you cook Elmer will do the dishes.

CONFUSING While we were eating a rattlesnake approached our campsite.

Add commas in the logical places (after *cook* and *eating*), and suddenly all is clear. No longer is Elmer being cooked, the rattlesnake being eaten.

Various rules have evolved to prevent such misreadings and to speed readers along through complex grammatical structures. Those rules are detailed in this section. (Section 33 explains when not to use commas.)

> Grammar checkers rarely flag missing or misused commas. They sometimes recognize that a comma belongs before a *which* clause but not before a *that* clause (see 32e). For all other uses of the comma covered in section 32, they are unreliable.

32a Use a comma before a coordinating conjunction joining independent clauses.

When a coordinating conjunction connects two or more independent clauses—word groups that could stand alone as separate sentences—a comma must precede it. There are seven coordinating conjunctions in English: *and, but, or, nor, for, so,* and *yet.*

A comma tells readers that one independent clause has come to a close and that another is about to begin.

▶ The department sponsored a seminar on college survival

skills during fall orientation$_{\wedge}$ and it also hosted a barbecue

to make new students feel at home.

EXCEPTION: If the two independent clauses are short and there is no danger of misreading, the comma may be omitted.

The plane took off and we were on our way.

TIP: As a rule, do *not* use a comma to separate compound elements that are not independent clauses. (See 33a.)

▶ A good money manager controls expenses/and invests

surplus dollars to meet future needs.

The word group following *and* is not an independent clause; it is the second half of a compound predicate (*controls . . . and invests*).

32b Use a comma after an introductory clause or phrase.

The most common introductory word groups are clauses and phrases functioning as adverbs. Such word groups usually tell when, where, how, why, or under what conditions the main action of the sentence occurred. (See 63a, 63b, and 63e.)

A comma tells readers that the introductory clause or phrase has come to a close and that the main part of the sentence is about to begin.

▶ When Irwin was ready to iron, his cat tripped on the

cord.

Without the comma, readers may have Irwin ironing his cat. The comma signals that *his cat* is the subject of a new clause, not part of the introductory one.

▶ Near a small stream at the bottom of the canyon, the park

rangers discovered an abandoned mine.

The comma tells readers that the introductory prepositional phrase has come to a close.

EXCEPTION: The comma may be omitted after a short adverb clause or phrase if there is no danger of misreading.

In no time we were at 2,800 feet.

Sentences also frequently begin with participial phrases describing the noun or pronoun immediately following them. The comma tells readers that they are about to learn the identity of the person or thing described; therefore, the comma is usually required even when the phrase is short. (See 63b.)

▶ Thinking his motorcade drive through Dallas was routine, President Kennedy smiled and waved at the crowds.

▶ Buried under layers of younger rocks, the earth's oldest rocks contain no fossils.

NOTE: Other introductory word groups include transitional expressions and absolute phrases (see 32f).

EXERCISE 32–1 Add or delete commas where necessary in the following sentences. If a sentence is correct, write "correct" after it. Answers to lettered sentences appear in the back of the book. Example:

Because we had been saving molding for a few weeks, we had enough wood to frame all thirty paintings.

a. Alisa brought the injured bird home, and fashioned a splint out of Popsicle sticks for its wing.

b. Considered a classic of early animation *The Adventures of Prince Achmed* used hand-cut silhouettes against colored backgrounds.

c. If you complete the enclosed evaluation form and return it within two weeks you will receive a free breakfast during your next stay.

d. After retiring from the New York City Ballet in 1965, legendary dancer Maria Tallchief went on to found the Chicago City Ballet.

e. Roger had always wanted a handmade violin but he couldn't afford one.

1. While I was driving a huge delivery truck ran through a red light.
2. He pushed the car beyond the tollgate, and poured a bucket of water on the smoking hood.
3. Lit by bright halogen lamps hundreds of origami birds sparkled like diamonds in sunlight.
4. As the first chord sounded, Aileen knew that her spirits were about to rise.
5. Many musicians of Bach's time played several instruments but few mastered them as early or played with as much expression as Bach.

EXERCISE 32–2 Add or delete commas where necessary in the following sentences. If a sentence is correct, write "correct" after it. Answers to lettered sentences appear in the back of the book. Example:

> The car had been sitting idle for a month$\overset{\wedge}{,}$ so the battery
>
> was completely dead.

a. J. R. R. Tolkien finished writing his draft of *The Lord of the Rings* trilogy in 1949 but the first book in the series wasn't published until 1954.
b. In the first two minutes of its ascent the space shuttle had broken the sound barrier and reached a height of over twenty-five miles.
c. German shepherds can be gentle guide dogs or they can be fierce attack dogs.
d. Some former professional cyclists claim that the use of performance-enhancing drugs is widespread in cycling and they argue that no rider can be competitive without doping.
e. As an intern, I learned most aspects of the broadcasting industry but I never learned about fundraising.

1. To be considered for the position candidates must demonstrate initiative and strong communication skills.
2. The cinematic lighting effect known as *chiaroscuro* was first used in German Expressionist filmmaking, and was later seen in American film noir.

3. Reptiles are cold-blooded and they are covered with scales.
4. Using a variety of techniques, advertisers grab the audience's attention and imprint their messages onto consumers' minds.
5. By the end of the first quarter the operating budget will be available online.

32c Use a comma between all items in a series.

When three or more items are presented in a series, those items should be separated from one another with commas. Items in a series may be single words, phrases, or clauses.

▶ Bubbles of air, leaves, ferns, bits of wood, and insects are

often found trapped in amber.

▶ Langston Hughes's poetry is concerned with racial pride,

social justice, and the diversity of the African American

experience.

Although some writers view the comma between the last two items as optional, most experts advise using the comma because its omission can result in ambiguity or misreading.

▶ Uncle David willed me all of his property, houses, and

warehouses.

Did Uncle David will his property *and* houses *and* warehouses—or simply his property, consisting of houses and warehouses? If the former meaning is intended, a comma is necessary to prevent ambiguity.

▶ The activities include touring the White House, visiting

the Air and Space Museum, attending a lecture about the

Founding Fathers, and kayaking on the Potomac River.

Without the comma, the activities might seem to include a lecture about kayaking, not participating in kayaking. The comma makes it clear that *kayaking on the Potomac River* is a separate item in the series.

32d Use a comma between coordinate adjectives not joined with *and*. Do not use a comma between cumulative adjectives.

When two or more adjectives each modify a noun separately, they are coordinate.

Roberto is a *warm, gentle, affectionate* father.

TEST: If the adjectives can be joined with *and*, the adjectives are coordinate, so you should use commas: *warm* and *gentle* and *affectionate* (*warm, gentle, affectionate*).

Adjectives that do not modify the noun separately are cumulative.

Three large gray shapes moved slowly toward us.

Beginning with the adjective closest to the noun *shapes*, these modifiers lean on one another, piggyback style, with each modifying a larger word group. *Gray* modifies *shapes*, *large* modifies *gray shapes*, and *three* modifies *large gray shapes*. Cumulative adjectives cannot be joined with *and* (not *three* and *large* and *gray shapes*).

COORDINATE ADJECTIVES

▶ Should patients with severe, irreversible brain damage

be put on life support systems?

Adjectives are coordinate if they can be connected with *and*: *severe and irreversible*.

CUMULATIVE ADJECTIVES

▶ Ira ordered a rich/chocolate/layer cake.

Ira didn't order a cake that was rich and chocolate and layer: He ordered a *layer cake* that was *chocolate*, a *chocolate layer cake* that was *rich*.

EXERCISE 32–3 Add or delete commas where necessary in the following sentences. If a sentence is correct, write "correct" after it. Answers to lettered sentences appear in the back of the book. Example:

> We gathered our essentials, took off for the great outdoors,
>
> and ignored the fact that it was Friday the 13th.

a. The cold impersonal atmosphere of the university was unbearable.
b. An ambulance threaded its way through police cars, fire trucks and irate citizens.
c. The *1812 Overture* is a stirring, magnificent piece of music.
d. After two broken arms, three cracked ribs and one concussion, Ken quit the varsity football team.
e. My cat's pupils had constricted to small black shining slits.

1. We prefer our staff to be orderly, prompt and efficient.
2. For breakfast the children ordered cornflakes, English muffins with peanut butter and cherry Cokes.
3. It was a small, unimportant part, but I was happy to have it.
4. Cyril was clad in a luminous orange rain suit and a brilliant white helmet.
5. Animation master Hironobu Sakaguchi makes computer-generated scenes look realistic, vivid and seductive.

EXERCISE 32–4 Add or delete commas where necessary in the following sentences. If a sentence is correct, write "correct" after it. Answers to lettered sentences appear in the back of the book. Example:

> Good social workers excel in patience, diplomacy, and
>
> positive thinking.

a. NASA's rovers on Mars are equipped with special cameras that can take close-up high-resolution pictures of the terrain.
b. A baseball player achieves the triple crown by having the highest batting average, the most home runs, and the most runs batted in during the regular season.
c. If it does not get enough sunlight, a healthy green lawn can turn into a shriveled brown mess within a matter of days.

d. Love, vengeance, greed and betrayal are common themes in Western literature.

e. Many experts believe that shark attacks on surfers are a result of the sharks' mistaking surfboards for small, injured seals.

1. In Sherman's march to the sea, the Union army set fire to all crops, killed all livestock and destroyed all roads and bridges in its path.

2. Milk that comes from grass-fed steroid-free cows has been gaining market share.

3. The film makes three main points about global warming: It is real, it is the result of human activity, and it should not be ignored.

4. The three, handmade, turquoise bracelets brought in the most money at the charity auction.

5. Matisse is well known for vibrant colorful prints that have been reproduced extensively on greeting cards and posters.

32e Use commas to set off nonrestrictive elements. Do not use commas to set off restrictive elements.

Certain word groups that modify nouns or pronouns can be restrictive or nonrestrictive—that is, essential or not essential to the meaning of a sentence. These word groups are usually adjective clauses, adjective phrases, or appositives.

Restrictive elements

A restrictive element defines or limits the meaning of the word it modifies; it is therefore essential to the meaning of the sentence and is not set off with commas. If you remove a restrictive modifier from a sentence, the meaning changes significantly, becoming more general than you intended.

RESTRICTIVE (NO COMMAS)

The campers need clothes *that are durable*.

Scientists *who study the earth's structure* are called geologists.

The writer of the first sentence does not mean that the campers need clothes in general. The intended meaning is more limited: The campers need durable clothes. The writer of the second sentence does not mean that scientists in general are called geologists; those scientists who specifically study the earth's structure are called geologists. The italicized word groups are essential and are therefore not set off with commas.

Nonrestrictive elements

A nonrestrictive modifier describes a noun or pronoun whose meaning has already been clearly defined or limited. Because the modifier contains nonessential or parenthetical information, it is set off with commas. If you remove a nonrestrictive element from a sentence, the meaning does not change dramatically. Some meaning is lost, to be sure, but the defining characteristics of the person or thing described remain the same.

NONRESTRICTIVE (WITH COMMAS)

The campers need sturdy shoes, *which are expensive.*

The scientists, *who represented eight different universities*, met to review applications for the prestigious O'Hara Award.

In the first sentence, the campers need sturdy shoes, and the shoes happen to be expensive. In the second sentence, the scientists met to review applications for the O'Hara Award; that they represented eight different universities is informative but not critical to the meaning of the sentence. The nonessential information in both sentences is enclosed in commas.

NOTE: Often it is difficult to tell whether a word group is restrictive or nonrestrictive without seeing it in context and considering the writer's meaning. Both of the following sentences are grammatically correct, but their meaning is slightly different.

The dessert made with fresh raspberries was delicious.

The dessert, made with fresh raspberries, was delicious.

In the first example, the phrase *made with fresh raspberries* tells readers which of two or more desserts the writer is referring to. In the example with commas, the phrase merely adds information about the dessert.

Adjective clauses

Adjective clauses are patterned like sentences, containing subjects and verbs, but they function within sentences as modifiers of nouns or pronouns. They always follow the word they modify, usually immediately. Adjective clauses begin with a relative pronoun (*who, whom, whose, which, that*) or with a relative adverb (*where, when*).

Nonrestrictive adjective clauses are set off with commas; restrictive adjective clauses are not.

NONRESTRICTIVE CLAUSE (WITH COMMAS)

▶ Ed's house, which is located on thirteen acres, was

completely furnished with bats in the rafters and mice in

the kitchen.

The adjective clause *which is located on thirteen acres* does not restrict the meaning of *Ed's house*; the information is nonessential and is therefore enclosed in commas.

RESTRICTIVE CLAUSE (NO COMMAS)

▶ The giant panda/ that was born at the San Diego Zoo in

2003/ was sent to China in 2007.

Because the adjective clause *that was born at the San Diego Zoo in 2003* identifies one particular panda out of many, the information is essential and is therefore not enclosed in commas.

NOTE: Use *that* only with restrictive (essential) clauses. Many writers prefer to use *which* only with nonrestrictive (nonessential) clauses, but usage varies.

Adjective phrases

Prepositional or verbal phrases functioning as adjectives may be restrictive or nonrestrictive. Nonrestrictive phrases are set off with commas; restrictive phrases are not.

NONRESTRICTIVE PHRASE (WITH COMMAS)

▶ The helicopter, with its million-candlepower spotlight

illuminating the area, circled above.

The *with* phrase is nonessential because its purpose is not to specify which of two or more helicopters is being discussed. The phrase is not required for readers to understand the meaning of the sentence.

RESTRICTIVE PHRASE (NO COMMAS)

▶ One corner of the attic was filled with newspapers/dating

from the early 1900s.

Dating from the early 1900s restricts the meaning of *newspapers*, so the comma should be omitted.

▶ The bill/proposed by the Illinois representative/would

lower taxes and provide services for middle-income families.

Proposed by the Illinois representative identifies exactly which bill is meant.

Appositives

An appositive is a noun or noun phrase that renames a nearby noun. Nonrestrictive appositives are set off with commas; restrictive appositives are not.

NONRESTRICTIVE APPOSITIVE (WITH COMMAS)

▶ Darwin's most important book, *On the Origin of Species,*

was the result of many years of research.

Most important restricts the meaning to one book, so the appositive *On the Origin of Species* is nonrestrictive and should be set off with commas.

RESTRICTIVE APPOSITIVE (NO COMMAS)

▶ The song/"Viva la Vida/" was blasted out of huge amplifiers at the concert.

Once they've read *song*, readers still don't know precisely which song the writer means. The appositive following *song* restricts its meaning, so the appositive should not be enclosed in commas.

EXERCISE 32–5 Add or delete commas where necessary in the following sentences. If a sentence is correct, write "correct" after it. Answers to lettered sentences appear in the back of the book. Example:

My youngest sister, who plays left wing on the soccer

team, now lives at The Sands, a beach house near

Los Angeles.

a. Choreographer Alvin Ailey's best-known work *Revelations* is more than just a crowd-pleaser.
b. Twyla Tharp's contemporary ballet *Push Comes to Shove* was made famous by the Russian dancer Baryshnikov. [Tharp has written more than one contemporary ballet.]
c. The glass sculptor sifting through hot red sand explained her technique to the other glassmakers. [There is more than one glass sculptor.]
d. A member of an organization, that provides job training for teens, was also appointed to the education commission.
e. Brian Eno who began his career as a rock musician turned to meditative compositions in the late seventies.

1. I had the pleasure of talking to a woman who had just returned from India where she had lived for ten years.
2. Patrick's oldest sister Fiona graduated from MIT with a degree in aerospace engineering.
3. The artist painting a portrait of Aung San Suu Kyi, the Burmese civil rights leader, was once a political prisoner himself.

4. *Jumanji*, the 1982 Caldecott Medal winner, is my nephew's favorite book.
5. The flame crawled up a few blades of grass to reach a low-hanging palmetto branch which quickly ignited.

32f Use commas to set off transitional and parenthetical expressions, absolute phrases, and elements expressing contrast.

Transitional expressions

Transitional expressions serve as bridges between sentences or parts of sentences. They include conjunctive adverbs such as *however*, *therefore*, and *moreover* and transitional phrases such as *for example*, *as a matter of fact*, and *in other words*. (For complete lists of these expressions, see 34b.)

When a transitional expression appears between independent clauses in a compound sentence, it is preceded by a semicolon and is usually followed by a comma. (See 34b.)

▶ Minh did not understand our language; moreover, he was

unfamiliar with our customs.

When a transitional expression appears at the beginning of a sentence or in the middle of an independent clause, it is usually set off with commas.

▶ As a matter of fact, American football was established

by fans who wanted to play a more organized game of

rugby.

▶ Natural foods are not always salt free; celery, for example,

contains more sodium than most people would imagine.

EXCEPTION: If a transitional expression blends smoothly with the rest of the sentence, calling for little or no pause in reading, it

does not need to be set off with a comma. Expressions such as
*also, at least, certainly, consequently, indeed, of course, moreover, no
doubt, perhaps, then,* and *therefore* do not always call for a pause.

Alice's bicycle is broken; *therefore* you will need to borrow Sue's.

NOTE: The conjunctive adverb *however* always calls for a pause.
It should not be confused with the adverb *however* meaning
"no matter how," which does not require a pause or a comma:
However hard Bill tried, he could not match his previous record.

Parenthetical expressions

Expressions that are distinctly parenthetical, providing only
supplemental information, should be set off with commas.
They interrupt the flow of a sentence or appear at the end as
afterthoughts.

▶ **Evolution, as far as we know, doesn't work this way.**

▶ **The bass weighed about twelve pounds, give or take a few**

ounces.

Absolute phrases

An absolute phrase, which modifies the whole sentence, usually consists of a noun followed by a participle or participial
phrase. (See 63d.) Absolute phrases may appear at the beginning or at the end of a sentence. Wherever they appear, they
should be set off with commas.

———————— ABSOLUTE PHRASE ————————
N   PARTICIPLE
The sun appearing for the first time in a week, we were at last
able to begin the archaeological dig.

▶ **Elvis Presley made music industry history in the 1950s, his**

records having sold more than ten million copies.

NOTE: Do not insert a comma between the noun and the participle in an absolute construction.

▶ The next contestant/being five years old, the emcee

adjusted the height of the microphone.

Contrasted elements

Sharp contrasts beginning with words such as *not*, *never*, and *unlike* are set off with commas.

▶ The Epicurean philosophers sought mental‸ not bodily‸

pleasures.

▶ Unlike Robert‸ Celia loved dance contests.

32g Use commas to set off nouns of direct address, the words *yes* and *no*, interrogative tags, and mild interjections.

▶ Forgive me‸ Angela‸ for forgetting your birthday.

▶ Yes‸ the loan will probably be approved.

▶ The film was faithful to the book‸ wasn't it?

▶ Well‸ cases like these are difficult to decide.

32h Use commas with expressions such as *he said* to set off direct quotations. (See also 37f.)

▶ In his "Letter from Birmingham Jail," Martin Luther King

Jr. wrote‸ "We know through painful experience that

freedom is never voluntarily given by the oppressor; it must

be demanded by the oppressed" (225).

▶ "Happiness in marriage is entirely a matter of chance,"

says Charlotte Lucas in *Pride and Prejudice*, a novel that

ends with two happy marriages (69; ch. 6).

See pages 528–29 on citing literary sources in MLA style.

32i Use commas with dates, addresses, titles, and numbers.

Dates

In dates, the year is set off from the rest of the sentence with a pair of commas.

▶ On December 12, 1890, orders were sent out for the arrest of

Sitting Bull.

EXCEPTIONS: Commas are not needed if the date is inverted or if only the month and year are given.

The security alert system went into effect on 15 April 2009.

January 2008 was an extremely cold month.

Addresses

The elements of an address or a place name are separated with commas. A zip code, however, is not preceded by a comma.

▶ John Lennon was born in Liverpool, England, in 1940.

▶ Please send the package to Greg Tarvin at 708 Spring Street,

Washington, IL 61571.

Titles

If a title follows a name, separate the title from the rest of the sentence with a pair of commas.

▶ Sandra Belinsky, MD, has been appointed to the board

of trustees.

Numbers

In numbers more than four digits long, use commas to separate the numbers into groups of three, starting from the right. In numbers four digits long, a comma is optional.

$$3,500 \text{ [or 3500]}$$
$$100,000$$
$$5,000,000$$

EXCEPTIONS: Do not use commas in street numbers, zip codes, telephone numbers, or years with four or fewer digits.

32j Use a comma to prevent confusion.

In certain contexts, a comma is necessary to prevent confusion. If the writer has omitted a word or phrase, for example, a comma may be needed to signal the omission.

▶ To err is human; to forgive, divine.

If two words in a row echo each other, a comma may be needed for ease of reading.

▶ All of the catastrophes that we had feared might happen,

happened.

Sometimes a comma is needed to prevent readers from grouping words in ways that do not match the writer's intention.

▶ Patients who can, walk up and down the halls several

times a day.

EXERCISE 32–6   This exercise covers the major uses of the comma described in 32a–32e. Add or delete commas where necessary. If a sentence is correct, write "correct" after it. Answers to lettered sentences appear in the back of the book. Example:

> **Even though Pavel had studied Nigella Lawson's recipes for a**
>
> **week⌄ he underestimated how long it would take to juice**
>
> **two hundred lemons.**

a. Cricket which originated in England is also popular in Australia, South Africa and India.
b. At the sound of the starting pistol the horses surged forward toward the first obstacle, a sharp incline three feet high.
c. After seeing an exhibition of Western art Gerhard Richter escaped from East Berlin, and smuggled out many of his notebooks.
d. Corrie's new wet suit has an intricate, blue pattern.
e. The cookies will keep for two weeks in sturdy airtight containers.

1. Research on Andean condors has shown that high levels of the pesticide chlorinated hydrocarbon can cause the thinning of eggshells.
2. Founded in 1868 Hampton University was one of the first colleges for African Americans.
3. Aunt Emilia was an impossible demanding guest.
4. The French Mirage, a high-tech fighter, is an astonishing machine to fly.
5. At the bottom of the ship's rusty hold sat several, well-preserved trunks, reminders of a bygone era of sea travel.

EXERCISE 32–7   This exercise covers all uses of the comma. Add or delete commas where necessary in the following sentences. If a sentence is correct, write "correct" after it. Answers to lettered sentences appear in the back of the book. Example:

> "Yes⌄ dear, you can have dessert," my mother said.

a. On January 15, 2008 our office moved to 29 Commonwealth Avenue, Mechanicsville VA 23111.
b. The coach having bawled us out thoroughly, we left the locker room with his harsh words ringing in our ears.

c. Ms. Carlson you are a valued customer whose satisfaction is very important to us.
d. Mr. Mundy was born on July 22, 1939 in Arkansas, where his family had lived for four generations.
e. Her board poised at the edge of the half-pipe, Nina waited her turn to drop in.

1. President Lincoln's original intention was to save the Union, not to destroy slavery.
2. For centuries people believed that Greek culture had developed in isolation from the world. Today however scholars are acknowledging the contributions made by Egypt and the Middle East.
3. Putting together a successful fundraiser, Patricia discovered, requires creativity and good timing.
4. Fortunately science is creating many alternatives to research performed on animals.
5. While the machine was printing the oversize paper jammed.

hackerhandbooks.com/bedhandbook > Grammar exercises > Punctuation
> E-ex 32–8 to 32–10

33 Unnecessary commas

Many common misuses of the comma result from an incomplete understanding of the major comma rules presented in 32. In particular, writers frequently form misconceptions about rules 32a–32e, either extending the rules inappropriately or misinterpreting them. Such misconceptions can lead to the errors described in 33a–33e; rules 33f–33h list other common misuses of the comma.

33a Do not use a comma between compound elements that are not independent clauses.

Though a comma should be used before a coordinating conjunction joining independent clauses (see 32a), this rule should not be extended to other compound word groups.

▶ Marie Curie discovered radium/and later applied her work

on radioactivity to medicine.

And links two verbs in a compound predicate: *discovered* and *applied*.

▶ Jake told us that his illness is serious/but that changes in

his lifestyle can improve his chances for survival.

The coordinating conjunction *but* links two subordinate clauses,
each beginning with *that*: *that his illness is serious* and *that changes
in his lifestyle. . . .*

33b Do not use a comma after a phrase that begins an inverted sentence.

Though a comma belongs after most introductory phrases
(see 32b), it does not belong after phrases that begin an inverted sentence. In an inverted sentence, the subject follows
the verb, and a phrase that ordinarily would follow the verb is
moved to the beginning (see 62c).

▶ At the bottom of the hill/sat the stubborn mule.

33c Do not use a comma before the first or after the last item in a series.

Though commas are required between items in a series (32c),
do not place them either before or after the whole series.

▶ Other causes of asthmatic attacks are/stress, change in

temperature, and cold air.

▶ Ironically, even novels that focus on horror, evil, and

alienation/often have themes of spiritual renewal and

redemption as well.

33d Do not use a comma between cumulative adjectives, between an adjective and a noun, or between an adverb and an adjective.

Commas are required between coordinate adjectives (those that can be joined with *and*), but they do not belong between cumulative adjectives (those that cannot be joined with *and*). (For a full discussion, see 32d.)

▶ In the corner of the closet we found an old/maroon hatbox

from Sears.

A comma should never be used between an adjective and the noun that follows it.

▶ It was a senseless, dangerous/mission.

Nor should a comma be used between an adverb and an adjective that follows it.

▶ The Hillside is a good home for severely/disturbed youths.

33e Do not use commas to set off restrictive or mildly parenthetical elements.

Restrictive elements are modifiers or appositives that restrict the meaning of the nouns they follow. Because they are essential to the meaning of the sentence, they are not set off with commas. (For a full discussion of restrictive and nonrestrictive elements, see 32e.)

▶ Drivers/who think they own the road/make cycling a

dangerous sport.

The modifier *who think they own the road* restricts the meaning of *Drivers* and is therefore essential to the meaning of the sentence. Putting commas around the *who* clause falsely suggests that all drivers think they own the road.

▶ Margaret Mead's book/*Coming of Age in Samoa*/stirred

up considerable controversy when it was published in 1928.

Since Mead wrote more than one book, the appositive contains information essential to the meaning of the sentence.

Although commas should be used with distinctly parenthetical expressions (see 32f), do not use them to set off elements that are only mildly parenthetical.

▶ Texting has/essentially/replaced e-mail for casual

communication.

33f Do not use a comma to set off a concluding adverb clause that is essential to the meaning of the sentence.

When adverb clauses introduce a sentence, they are nearly always followed by a comma (see 32b). When they conclude a sentence, however, they are not set off by commas if their content is essential to the meaning of the earlier part of the sentence. Adverb clauses beginning with *after*, *as soon as*, *because*, *before*, *if*, *since*, *unless*, *until*, and *when* are usually essential.

▶ Don't visit Paris at the height of the tourist season/unless

you have booked hotel reservations.

Without the *unless* clause, the meaning of the sentence might at first seem broader than the writer intended.

When a concluding adverb clause is nonessential, it should be preceded by a comma. Clauses beginning with *although*, *even though*, *though*, and *whereas* are usually nonessential.

▶ The lecture seemed to last only a short time‿although the

clock said it had gone on for more than an hour.

33g Do not use a comma to separate a verb from its subject or object.

A sentence should flow from subject to verb to object without unnecessary pauses. Commas may appear between these major sentence elements only when a specific rule calls for them.

▶ Zoos large enough to give the animals freedom to roam⁄are

becoming more popular.

The comma should not separate the subject, *Zoos*, from the verb, *are becoming*.

▶ The director explained to the board⁄that she was resigning

because of a conflict of interest.

The comma should not separate the verb, *explained*, from its object, the subordinate clause *that she was resigning because of a conflict of interest*.

▶ Maxine Hong Kingston writes⁄that many Chinese

American families struggle "to figure out how the invisible

world the emigrants built around our childhoods fits in

solid America" (107).

Writing with sources

MLA-style citation

The comma should not separate the verb, *writes*, from its object, the subordinate clause beginning with *that*. A signal phrase ending in a word like *writes* or *says* is followed by a comma only when a direct quotation immediately follows: *Kingston writes, "Those of us in the first American generations have had to figure out how the invisible world . . ." (107)*. (See also 37f.)

33h Avoid other common misuses of the comma.

Do not use a comma in the following situations.

AFTER A COORDINATING CONJUNCTION (*AND, BUT, OR, NOR, FOR, SO, YET*)

▶ Occasionally TV talk shows are performed live, but⁄more

often they are taped.

AFTER *SUCH AS* OR *LIKE*

▶ Shade-loving plants such as/begonias, impatiens, and
coleus can add color to a shady garden.

BEFORE *THAN*

▶ Touring Crete was more thrilling for us/than visiting the
Greek islands frequented by the rich.

AFTER *ALTHOUGH*

▶ Although/the air was balmy, the water was too cold for
swimming.

BEFORE A PARENTHESIS

▶ At InterComm, Sylvia began at the bottom/(with only
three and a half walls and a swivel chair), but within three
years she had been promoted to supervisor.

TO SET OFF AN INDIRECT (REPORTED) QUOTATION

▶ Samuel Goldwyn once said/that a verbal contract isn't
worth the paper it's written on.

WITH A QUESTION MARK OR AN EXCLAMATION POINT

▶ "Why don't you try it?/" she coaxed. "You can't do any
worse than the rest of us."

EXERCISE 33–1 Delete commas where necessary in the following
sentences. If a sentence is correct, write "correct" after it. Answers to
lettered sentences appear in the back of the book. Example:

In his Silk Road Project, Yo-Yo Ma incorporates work by

musicians such as/Kayhan Kahlor and Richard Danielpour.

a. After the morning rains cease, the swimmers emerge from their cottages.
b. Tricia's first artwork was a bright, blue, clay dolphin.
c. Some modern musicians, (trumpeter John Hassell is an example) blend several cultural traditions into a unique sound.
d. Myra liked hot, spicy foods such as, chili, kung pao chicken, and buffalo wings.
e. On the display screen, was a soothing pattern of light and shadow.

1. Mesquite, the hardest of the softwoods, grows primarily in the Southwest.
2. Jolie's parents encouraged independent thinking, but required respect for others' opinions.
3. The border guards told their sergeant, that their heat-sensing equipment was malfunctioning.
4. The streets that three hours later would be bumper to bumper with commuters, were quiet and empty except for a few prowling cats.
5. Some first-year architecture students, expect to design intricate structures immediately.

EXERCISE 33–2 Delete commas where necessary in the following passage.

Each spring since 1970, New Orleans has hosted the Jazz and Heritage Festival, an event that celebrates the music, food, and culture, of the region. Although, it is often referred to as "Jazz Fest," the festival typically includes a wide variety of musical styles such as, gospel, Cajun, blues, zydeco, and, rock and roll. Famous musicians who have appeared regularly at Jazz Fest, include Dr. John, B. B. King, and Aretha Franklin. Large stages are set up throughout the fairgrounds in a way, that allows up to ten bands to play simultaneously without any sound overlap. Food tents are located throughout the festival, and offer popular, local dishes like crawfish Monica, jambalaya, and fried, green tomatoes. In 2009, Jazz Fest marked its fortieth anniversary. Fans, who could not attend the festival, still enjoyed the music by downloading MP3 files, and watching performances online.

hackerhandbooks.com/bedhandbook > Grammar exercises > Punctuation
> E-ex 33–3 and 33–4

34 The semicolon

The semicolon is used to connect major sentence elements of equal grammatical rank.

> **Grammar checkers** flag some, but not all, misused semicolons (34d). In addition, they can alert you to some run-on sentences (34a). However, they miss more run-on sentences than they identify, and they sometimes flag correct sentences as possible run-ons.

34a Use a semicolon between closely related independent clauses not joined with a coordinating conjunction.

When related independent clauses appear in one sentence, they are ordinarily linked with a comma and a coordinating conjunction (*and*, *but*, *or*, *nor*, *for*, *so*, *yet*). The coordinating conjunction signals the relation between the clauses. If the clauses are closely related and the relation is clear without a conjunction, they may be linked with a semicolon instead.

> In film, a low-angle shot makes the subject look powerful; a high-angle shot does just the opposite.

A semicolon must be used whenever a coordinating conjunction has been omitted between independent clauses. To use merely a comma creates a type of run-on sentence known as a *comma splice*. (See 20.)

▶ In 1800, a traveler needed six weeks to get from New York

City to Chicago; in 1860, the trip by railroad took only

two days.

TIP: Do not overuse the semicolon as a means of revising run-on sentences. For other revision strategies, see 20a, 20c, and 20d.

34b Use a semicolon between independent clauses linked with a transitional expression.

Transitional expressions include conjunctive adverbs and transitional phrases.

CONJUNCTIVE ADVERBS

accordingly	furthermore	moreover	still
also	hence	nevertheless	subsequently
anyway	however	next	then
besides	incidentally	nonetheless	therefore
certainly	indeed	now	thus
consequently	instead	otherwise	
conversely	likewise	similarly	
finally	meanwhile	specifically	

TRANSITIONAL PHRASES

after all	even so	in fact
as a matter of fact	for example	in other words
as a result	for instance	in the first place
at any rate	in addition	on the contrary
at the same time	in conclusion	on the other hand

When a transitional expression appears between independent clauses, it is preceded by a semicolon and usually followed by a comma.

▶ Many corals grow very gradually/; in fact, the creation of a

coral reef can take centuries.

When a transitional expression appears in the middle or at the end of the second independent clause, the semicolon goes *between the clauses.*

▶ Biologists have observed laughter in primates other than

humans/; chimpanzees, however, sound more like they are

panting than laughing.

Transitional expressions should not be confused with the coordinating conjunctions *and, but, or, nor, for, so,* and *yet,* which are preceded by a comma when they link independent clauses. (See 32a.)

34c Use a semicolon between items in a series containing internal punctuation.

▶ Classic science fiction sagas are *Star Trek*, with Mr. Spock/;

  Battlestar Galactica, with its Cylons/; and *Star Wars,*

  with Han Solo, Luke Skywalker, and Darth Vader.

  Without the semicolons, the reader would have to sort out the major groupings, distinguishing between important and less important pauses according to the logic of the sentence. By inserting semicolons at the major breaks, the writer does this work for the reader.

34d Avoid common misuses of the semicolon.

Do not use a semicolon in the following situations.

BETWEEN A SUBORDINATE CLAUSE AND THE REST OF THE SENTENCE

▶ Although children's literature was added to the National

  Book Awards in 1969/; it has had its own award, the Newbery

  Medal, since 1922.

BETWEEN AN APPOSITIVE AND THE WORD IT REFERS TO

▶ The scientists were fascinated by the species *Argyroneta*

  aquatica/; a spider that lives underwater.

TO INTRODUCE A LIST

▶ Some of my favorite celebrities have their own blogs/;:

  Lindsay Lohan, Rosie O'Donnell, and Zach Braff.

BETWEEN INDEPENDENT CLAUSES JOINED BY *AND, BUT, OR, NOR, FOR, SO,* OR *YET*

▶ Five of the applicants had worked with spreadsheets;

but only one was familiar with database management.

EXCEPTIONS: If at least one of the independent clauses contains internal punctuation, you may use a semicolon even though the clauses are joined with a coordinating conjunction.

> As a vehicle [the model T] was hard-working, commonplace, and heroic; and it often seemed to transmit those qualities to the person who rode in it. —E. B. White

Although a comma would also be correct in this sentence, the semicolon is more effective, for it indicates the relative weights of the pauses.

Occasionally, a semicolon may be used to emphasize a sharp contrast or a firm distinction between clauses joined with a coordinating conjunction.

> We hate some persons because we do not know them; and we will not know them because we hate them.
> —Charles Caleb Colton

EXERCISE 34–1 Add commas or semicolons where needed in the following well-known quotations. If a sentence is correct, write "correct" after it. Answers to lettered sentences appear in the back of the book. Example:

> If an animal does something, we call it instinct; if we do
>
> the same thing, we call it intelligence. —Will Cuppy

a. Do not ask me to be kind just ask me to act as though I were.
   —Jules Renard
b. When men talk about defense they always claim to be protecting women and children but they never ask the women and children what they think. —Pat Schroeder
c. When I get a little money I buy books if any is left I buy food and clothes. —Desiderius Erasmus

d.   America is a country that doesn't know where it is going but is determined to set a speed record getting there.

—Lawrence J. Peter

e.   Wit has truth in it wisecracking is simply calisthenics with words.

—Dorothy Parker

1.   Standing in the middle of the road is very dangerous you get knocked down by the traffic from both sides.

—Margaret Thatcher

2.   I do not believe in an afterlife, although I am bringing a change of underwear.

—Woody Allen

3.   Once the children were in the house the air became more vivid and more heated every object in the house grew more alive.

—Mary Gordon

4.   We don't know what we want but we are ready to bite someone to get it.

—Will Rogers

5.   I've been rich and I've been poor rich is better.

—Sophie Tucker

EXERCISE 34–2   Edit the following sentences to correct errors in the use of the comma and the semicolon. If a sentence is correct, write "correct" after it. Answers to lettered sentences appear in the back of the book. Example:

> Love is blind; envy has its eyes wide open.

a.   Strong black coffee will not sober you up, the truth is that time is the only way to get alcohol out of your system.

b.   Margaret was not surprised to see hail and vivid lightning, conditions had been right for violent weather all day.

c.   There is often a fine line between right and wrong; good and bad; truth and deception.

d.   My mother always says that you can't learn common sense; either you're born with it or you're not.

e.   Severe, unremitting pain is a ravaging force, especially when the patient tries to hide it from others.

1.   Another delicious dish is the chef's special; a roasted duck rubbed with spices and stuffed with wild rice.

2.   Martin Luther King Jr. had not always intended to be a preacher, initially, he had planned to become a lawyer.

3. We all assumed that the thief had been Jean's boyfriend; even though we had seen him only from the back.
4. The Victorians avoided the subject of sex but were obsessed with death, a hundred years later, people were obsessed with sex but avoided thinking about death.
5. Some educators believe that African American history should be taught in separate courses, others prefer to see it integrated into survey courses.

hackerhandbooks.com/bedhandbook > Grammar exercises > Punctuation
> E-ex 34–3 and 34–4

35 The colon

The colon is used primarily to call attention to the words that follow it. In addition, the colon has some conventional uses.

> **Grammar checkers** are fairly good at flagging colons that incorrectly follow a verb (*The office work includes: typing, filing, and answering the phone*). They also point out semicolons used where colons are needed, although they don't suggest revisions.

35a Use a colon after an independent clause to direct attention to a list, an appositive, or a quotation.

A LIST

The daily routine should include at least the following: twenty knee bends, fifty sit-ups, fifteen leg lifts, and five minutes of running in place.

AN APPOSITIVE

My roommate is guilty of two of the seven deadly sins: gluttony and sloth.

A QUOTATION

Consider the words of Benjamin Franklin: "There never was a good war or a bad peace."

For other ways of introducing quotations, see "Introducing quoted material" on pages 396–97.

35b Use a colon between independent clauses if the second summarizes or explains the first.

Faith is like love: It cannot be forced.

NOTE: When an independent clause follows a colon, it may begin with a capital or a lowercase letter (see 45f).

35c Use a colon after the salutation in a formal letter, to indicate hours and minutes, to show proportions, between a title and subtitle, and between city and publisher in bibliographic entries.

Dear Sir or Madam:

5:30 p.m.

The ratio of women to men was 2:1.

The Glory of Hera: *Greek Mythology and the Greek Family*

Boston: Bedford, 2009

NOTE: In biblical references, a colon is ordinarily used between chapter and verse (Luke 2:14). The Modern Language Association (MLA) recommends a period instead (Luke 2.14).

35d Avoid common misuses of the colon.

A colon must be preceded by a full independent clause. Therefore, avoid using it in the following situations.

BETWEEN A VERB AND ITS OBJECT OR COMPLEMENT

▶ Some important vitamins found in vegetables are: vitamin A, thiamine, niacin, and vitamin C.

BETWEEN A PREPOSITION AND ITS OBJECT

▶ The heart's two pumps each consist of: an upper chamber,

or atrium, and a lower chamber, or ventricle.

AFTER *SUCH AS*, *INCLUDING*, OR *FOR EXAMPLE*

▶ The NCAA regulates college athletic teams, including:

basketball, baseball, softball, and football.

EXERCISE 35–1 Edit the following sentences to correct errors in the use of the comma, the semicolon, or the colon. If a sentence is correct, write "correct" after it. Answers to lettered sentences appear in the back of the book. Example:

Lifting the cover gently, Luca found the source of the odd

sound: a marble in the gears.

a. We always looked forward to Thanksgiving in Vermont: It was our only chance to see our Grady cousins.

b. If we have come to fight, we are far too few; if we have come to die, we are far too many.

c. The travel package includes: a round-trip ticket to Athens, a cruise through the Cyclades, and all hotel accommodations.

d. The news article portrays the land use proposal as reckless; although 62 percent of the town's residents support it.

e. Psychologists Kindlon and Thompson (2000) offer parents a simple starting point for raising male children, "Teach boys that there are many ways to be a man" (p. 256).

1. Harry Potter prevails against pain and evil for one reason, his heart is pure.

2. While traveling through France, Rose visited: the Loire Valley, Chartres, the Louvre, and the McDonald's stand at the foot of the Eiffel Tower.

3. There are three types of leave; annual leave, used for vacations, sick leave, used for medical appointments and illness, and personal leave, used for a variety of personal reasons.

4. American poet Carl Sandburg once asked these three questions, "Who paid for my freedom? What was the price? And am I somehow beholden?"
5. Amelie had four goals: to be encouraging, to be effective, to be efficient, and to be elegant.

hackerhandbooks.com/bedhandbook > Grammar exercises > Punctuation
> E-ex 35–2

36 The apostrophe

Grammar checkers flag only some missing or misused apostrophes. They catch missing apostrophes in contractions, such as *don't.* They also flag problems with possessives (*sled dogs feet, a babys eyes*), although they miss as many problems as they identify. Only you can decide when to add an apostrophe and whether to put it before or after the -*s* in possessives.

36a Use an apostrophe to indicate that a noun is possessive.

Possessive nouns usually indicate ownership, as in *Tim's hat, the lawyer's desk*, or *someone's glove.* Frequently, however, ownership is only loosely implied: *the tree's roots, a day's work.* If you are not sure whether a noun is possessive, try turning it into an *of* phrase: *the roots of the tree, the work of a day.*

When to add -'s

1. If the noun does not end in -*s*, add -*'s.*

   Luck often propels a rock musician's career.

   The Children's Defense Fund is a nonprofit organization that supports programs for poor and minority children.

2. If the noun is singular and ends in -s or an s sound, add -'s.

Lois's sister spent last year in India.

Her article presents an overview of Marx's teachings.

NOTE: To avoid potentially awkward pronunciation, some writers use only the apostrophe with a singular noun ending in -s: *Sophocles'*.

When to add only an apostrophe

If the noun is plural and ends in -s, add only an apostrophe.

Both diplomats' briefcases were searched by guards.

Joint possession

To show joint possession, use -'s or (-s') with the last noun only; to show individual possession, make all nouns possessive.

Have you seen Joyce and Greg's new camper?

John's and Marie's expectations of marriage couldn't have been more different.

Joyce and Greg jointly own one camper. John and Marie individually have different expectations.

Compound nouns

If a noun is compound, use -'s (or -s') with the last element.

My father-in-law's memoir about his childhood in Sri Lanka was published in October.

36b Use an apostrophe and -s to indicate that an indefinite pronoun is possessive.

Indefinite pronouns refer to no specific person or thing: *everyone, someone, no one, something.* (See 61b.)

Someone's raincoat has been left behind.

36c Use an apostrophe to mark omissions in contractions and numbers.

In a contraction, the apostrophe takes the place of one or more missing letters.

It's a shame that Frank can't go on the tour.

It's stands for *it is*, *can't* for *cannot*.

The apostrophe is also used to mark the omission of the first two digits of a year (*the class of '08*) or years (*the '60s generation*).

36d Do not use an apostrophe to form the plural of numbers, letters, abbreviations, and words mentioned as words.

An apostrophe typically is not used to pluralize numbers, letters, abbreviations, and words mentioned as words. Note the few exceptions and be consistent throughout your paper.

Plural numbers Omit the apostrophe in the plural of all numbers, including decades.

Oksana skated nearly perfect figure 8s.

The 1920s are known as the Jazz Age.

Plural letters Italicize the letter and use roman (regular) font style for the -s ending. Do not italicize academic grades.

Two large *J*s were painted on the door.

He received two Ds for the first time in his life.

EXCEPTIONS: To avoid misreading, use an apostrophe to form the plural of lowercase letters and the capital letters *A* and *I*: *p*'s, *A*'s.

Beginning readers often confuse *b*'s and *d*'s.

MLA NOTE: The Modern Language Association recommends using an apostrophe for the plural of both capital and lowercase letters: *J*'s, *p*'s.

Plural abbreviations Do not use an apostrophe to pluralize an abbreviation.

Harriet has thirty DVDs on her desk.

Marco earned two PhDs before his thirtieth birthday.

Plural of words mentioned as words Generally, omit the apostrophe to form the plural of words mentioned as words. If the word is italicized, the -s ending appears in roman (regular) type.

We've heard enough *maybe*s.

Words mentioned as words may also appear in quotation marks. When you choose this option, use the apostrophe.

We've heard enough "maybe's."

36e Avoid common misuses of the apostrophe.

Do not use an apostrophe in the following situations.

WITH NOUNS THAT ARE NOT POSSESSIVE

▶ Some ~~outpatient's~~ outpatients have special parking permits.

IN THE POSSESSIVE PRONOUNS *ITS*, *WHOSE*, *HIS*, *HERS*, *OURS*, *YOURS*, AND *THEIRS*

▶ Each area has ~~it's~~ its own conference room.

It's means "it is." The possessive pronoun *its* contains no apostrophe despite the fact that it is possessive.

▶ *The House on Mango Street* was written by Sandra Cisneros, ~~who's~~ whose work focuses on the Latino community in the United States.

Who's means "who is." The possessive pronoun is *whose*.

EXERCISE 36–1 Edit the following sentences to correct errors in the use of the apostrophe. If a sentence is correct, write "correct" after it. Answers to lettered sentences appear in the back of the book. Example:

> We rented an art studio above a barbecue restaurant, Poor
> ~~Richards~~ Ribs.
> *Richard's*

a. This diet will improve almost anyone's health.
b. The innovative shoe fastener was inspired by the designers young son.
c. Each days menu features a different European country's dish.
d. Sue worked overtime to increase her families earnings.
e. Ms. Jacobs is unwilling to listen to students complaints about computer failures.

1. Siddhartha sat by the river and listened to its many voices.
2. Three teenage son's can devour about as much food as four full-grown field hands. The only difference is that they dont do half as much work.
3. We handle contracts with NASA and many other government agency's.
4. Patience and humor are key tools in a travelers survival kit.
5. My sister-in-law's quilts are being shown at the Fendrick Gallery.

EXERCISE 36–2 Edit the following passage to correct errors in the use of the apostrophe.

> Its never too soon to start holiday shopping. In fact, some people choose to start shopping as early as January, when last seasons leftover's are priced at their lowest. Many stores try to lure customers in with promise's of savings up to 90 percent. Their main objective, of course, is to make way for next years inventory. The big problem with postholiday shopping, though, is that there isn't much left to choose from. Store's shelves have been picked over by last-minute shoppers desperately searching for gifts. The other problem is that its hard to know what to buy so far in advance. Next year's hot items are anyones guess. But proper timing, mixed with lot's of luck and determination, can lead to good purchases at great price's.

hackerhandbooks.com/bedhandbook > Grammar exercises > Punctuation
> E-ex 36–3 and 36–4

37 Quotation marks

> **Grammar checkers** are no help with quotation marks. They do not recognize direct and indirect quotations, they fail to identify quotation marks used incorrectly inside periods and commas, and they do not point out a missing quotation mark in a pair.

37a Use quotation marks to enclose direct quotations.

Direct quotations of a person's words, whether spoken or written, must be in quotation marks.

> "The contract negotiations are stalled," the airline executive told reporters, "but I am prepared to work night and day to bring both sides together."

Do not use quotation marks around indirect quotations. An indirect quotation reports someone's ideas without using that person's exact words.

> The airline executive told reporters that although contract negotiations were at a standstill, she was prepared to work hard with both labor and management to bring about a settlement.

NOTE: In academic writing, indirect quotation is called *paraphrase* or *summary*. See 48c.

In dialogue, begin a new paragraph to mark a change in speaker.

> "Mom, his name is Willie, not William. A thousand times I've told you, it's *Willie*."
> "Willie is a derivative of William, Lester. Surely his birth certificate doesn't have Willie on it, and I like calling people by their proper names."
> "Yes, it does, ma'am. My mother named me Willie K. Mason."   —Gloria Naylor

If a single speaker utters more than one paragraph, introduce each paragraph with quotation marks, but do not use closing quotation marks until the end of the speech.

37b Set off long quotations of prose or poetry by indenting.

The guidelines in this section are those of the Modern Language Association (MLA). The American Psychological Association (APA) and *The Chicago Manual of Style* have slightly different guidelines (see pp. 631–32 and 695–96).

When a quotation of prose runs to more than four typed lines in your paper, set it off by indenting one inch from the left margin. Quotation marks are not required because the indented format tells readers that the quotation is taken word-for-word from a source. Long quotations are ordinarily introduced by a sentence ending with a colon.

> After making an exhaustive study of the historical record, James Horan evaluates Billy the Kid like this:
>
> > The portrait that emerges of [the Kid] from the thousands of pages of affidavits, reports, trial transcripts, his letters, and his testimony is neither the mythical Robin Hood nor the stereotyped adenoidal moron and pathological killer. Rather Billy appears as a disturbed, lonely young man, honest, loyal to his friends, dedicated to his beliefs, and betrayed by our institutions and the corrupt, ambitious, and compromising politicians in his time. (158)

The number in parentheses is a citation handled according to MLA style. (See 53a.)

NOTE: When you quote two or more paragraphs from the source, indent the first line of each paragraph an additional one-quarter inch.

When you quote more than three lines of a poem, indent the quoted lines one inch from the left margin. Use no quotation marks unless they appear in the poem itself. (To quote two or three lines of poetry, see 39e.)

> Although many anthologizers "modernize" her punctuation, Emily Dickinson relied heavily on dashes, using them, perhaps, as a musical device. Here, for example, is the original version of the opening of one poem:
>> A narrow Fellow in the Grass
>> Occasionally rides —
>> You may have met Him — did you not
>> His notice sudden is — (1-4)

37c Use single quotation marks to enclose a quotation within a quotation.

> Megan Marshall notes that what Elizabeth Peabody "hoped to accomplish in her school was not merely 'teaching' but 'educating children morally and spiritually as well as intellectually from the first'" (107).

37d Use quotation marks around the titles of short works.

Short works include newspaper and magazine articles, poems, short stories, songs, episodes of television and radio programs, and chapters or subdivisions of books.

> James Baldwin's story "Sonny's Blues" tells the story of two brothers who come to understand each other's suffering.

NOTE: Titles of books, plays, Web sites, television and radio programs, films, magazines, and newspapers are put in italics.

37e Quotation marks may be used to set off words used as words.

Although words used as words are ordinarily italicized (see 42d), quotation marks are also acceptable. Be consistent throughout your paper.

The words "accept" and "except" are frequently confused.

The words *accept* and *except* are frequently confused.

37f Use punctuation with quotation marks according to convention.

This section describes the conventions used by American publishers in placing various marks of punctuation inside or outside quotation marks. It also explains how to punctuate when introducing quoted material.

Periods and commas

Place periods and commas inside quotation marks.

"I'm here as part of my service-learning project," I told the classroom teacher. "I'm hoping to become a reading specialist."

This rule applies to single quotation marks as well as double quotation marks. (See 37c.) It also applies to all uses of quotation marks: for quoted material, for titles of works, and for words used as words.

EXCEPTION: In the Modern Language Association's style of parenthetical in-text citations (see 53a), the period follows the citation in parentheses.

James M. McPherson comments, approvingly, that the Whigs "were not averse to extending the blessings of American liberty, even to Mexicans and Indians" (48).

Colons and semicolons

Put colons and semicolons outside quotation marks.

Harold wrote, "I regret that I am unable to attend the fundraiser for AIDS research"; his letter, however, came with a substantial contribution.

Question marks and exclamation points

Put question marks and exclamation points inside quotation marks unless they apply to the whole sentence.

> Contrary to tradition, bedtime at my house is marked by "Mommy, can I tell you a story now?"

> Have you heard the old proverb "Do not climb the hill until you reach it"?

In the first sentence, the question mark applies only to the quoted question. In the second sentence, the question mark applies to the whole sentence.

NOTE: In MLA style for a quotation that ends with a question mark or an exclamation point, the parenthetical citation and a period should follow the entire quotation.

> Rosie Thomas asks, "Is nothing in life ever straight and clear, the way children see it?" (77).

Introducing quoted material

After a word group introducing a quotation, choose a colon, a comma, or no punctuation at all, whichever is appropriate in context.

Formal introduction If a quotation is formally introduced, a colon is appropriate. A formal introduction is a full independent clause, not just an expression such as *he said* or *she remarked*.

> Thomas Friedman provides a challenging yet optimistic view of the future: "We need to get back to work on our country and on our planet. The hour is late, the stakes couldn't be higher, the project couldn't be harder, the payoff couldn't be greater" (25).

Expression such as *he said* If a quotation is introduced with an expression such as *he said* or *she remarked*—or if it is followed by such an expression—a comma is needed.

> About New England's weather, Mark Twain once declared, "In the spring I have counted one hundred and thirty-six different kinds of weather within four and twenty hours" (55).

"Unless another war is prevented it is likely to bring destruction on a scale never before held possible and even now hardly conceived," Albert Einstein wrote in the aftermath of the atomic bomb (29).

Blended quotation   When a quotation is blended into the writer's own sentence, either a comma or no punctuation is appropriate, depending on the way in which the quotation fits into the sentence structure.

The future champion could, as he put it, "float like a butterfly and sting like a bee."

Virginia Woolf wrote in 1928 that "a woman must have money and a room of her own if she is to write fiction; and that, as you will see, leaves the great problem of the true nature of woman and the true nature of fiction unsolved" (4).

Beginning of sentence   If a quotation appears at the beginning of a sentence, set it off with a comma unless the quotation ends with a question mark or an exclamation point.

"I've always thought of myself as a reporter," claimed American poet Gwendolyn Brooks (162).

"What is it?" she asked, bracing herself.

Interrupted quotation   If a quoted sentence is interrupted by explanatory words, use commas to set off the explanatory words.

"With regard to air travel," Stephen Ambrose notes, "Jefferson was a full century ahead of the curve" (53).

If two successive quoted sentences from the same source are interrupted by explanatory words, use a comma before the explanatory words and a period after them.

"Everyone agrees journalists must tell the truth," Bill Kovach and Tom Rosenstiel write. "Yet people are befuddled about what 'the truth' means" (37).

37g Avoid common misuses of quotation marks.

Do not use quotation marks to draw attention to familiar slang, to disown trite expressions, or to justify an attempt at humor.

▶ The economist estimated that single-family home prices

would decline another 5 percent by the end of the year,

emphasizing that this was only a ⁗ballpark figure.⁗

Do not use quotation marks around indirect quotations. (See also 37a.)

▶ After leaving the scene of the domestic quarrel, the officer

said that ⁗he was due for a coffee break.⁗

Do not use quotation marks around the title of your own essay.

EXERCISE 37–1   Add or delete quotation marks as needed and make any other necessary changes in punctuation in the following sentences. If a sentence is correct, write "correct" after it. Answers to lettered sentences appear in the back of the book. Example:

Gandhi once said, "An eye for an eye only ends up making

the whole world blind."

a. As for the advertisement "Sailors have more fun", if you consider chipping paint and swabbing decks fun, then you will have plenty of it.

b. Even after forty minutes of discussion, our class could not agree on an interpretation of Robert Frost's poem "The Road Not Taken."

c. After winning the lottery, Juanita said that "she would give half the money to charity."

d. After the movie, Vicki said, "The reviewer called this flick "trash of the first order." I guess you can't believe everything you read."

e. "Cleaning your house while your kids are still growing," said Phyllis Diller, "is like shoveling the walk before it stops snowing."

1. "That's the most beautiful seashell I've ever seen!", shouted Alexa.
2. "Get your head in the game, and the rest will come" advised the coach just before the whistle.
3. Gloria Steinem once twisted an old proverb like this, "A woman without a man is like a fish without a bicycle."
4. "Even when freshly washed and relieved of all obvious confections," says Fran Lebowitz, "children tend to be sticky."
5. Have you heard the Cowboy Junkies' cover of Hank Williams's "I'm So Lonesome I Could Cry?"

EXERCISE 37–2 Add or delete quotation marks as needed and make any other necessary changes in punctuation in the following passage. Citations should conform to MLA style (see 53a).

In his article The Moment of Truth, former vice president Al Gore argues that global warming is a genuine threat to life on Earth and that we must act now to avoid catastrophe. Gore calls our situation a "true *planetary emergency*" and cites scientific evidence of the greenhouse effect and its consequences (170-71). "What is at stake, Gore insists, is the survival of our civilization and the habitability of the Earth (197)." With such a grim predicament at hand, Gore questions why so many political and economic leaders are reluctant to act. "Is it simply more convenient to ignore the warnings," he asks (171)?

The crisis, of course, will not go away if we just pretend it isn't there. Gore points out that in Chinese two symbols form the character for the word crisis. The first of those symbols means "danger", and the second means "opportunity." The danger we face, he claims, is accompanied by "unprecedented opportunity." (172) Gore contends that throughout history we have won battles against seemingly unbeatable evils such as slavery and fascism and that we did so by facing the truth and choosing the moral high ground. Gore's final appeal is to our humanity:

"Ultimately, [the fight to end global warming] is not about any scientific discussion or political dialogue; it is about who we are as human beings. It is about our capacity to transcend our limitations, to rise to this new occasion. To see with our hearts, as well as our heads, the response that is now called for." (244)

Gore feels that the fate of our world rests in our own hands, and his hope is that we will make the choice to save the planet.

Quotations are from Al Gore, "The Moment of Truth," *Vanity Fair* May 2006: 170+; print.

hackerhandbooks.com/bedhandbook > Grammar exercises > Punctuation
> E-ex 37–3 and 37–4

38 End punctuation

> **Grammar checkers** occasionally flag sentences beginning with words like *Why* or *Are* and suggest that a question mark may be needed. On the whole, however, grammar checkers are of little help with end punctuation. Most notably, they neglect to tell you when your sentence is missing end punctuation.

38a The period

Use a period to end all sentences except direct questions or genuine exclamations. Also use periods in abbreviations according to convention.

To end sentences

Most sentences should end with a period. Problems sometimes arise when a writer must choose between a period and a question mark or between a period and an exclamation point.

If a sentence reports a question instead of asking it directly, it should end with a period, not a question mark.

▶ The professor asked whether talk therapy was more

beneficial than antidepressants?̸.

to end a sentence •
periods in abbreviations • question mark
.?! 38b 401

If a sentence is not a genuine exclamation, it should end with a period, not an exclamation point. (See also 38c.)

▶ After years of working her way through school, Geeta finally

graduated with high honors̶.

In abbreviations

A period is conventionally used in abbreviations of titles and Latin words or phrases, including the time designations for morning and afternoon.

Mr.	i.e.	a.m. (or AM)
Ms.	e.g.	p.m. (or PM)
Dr.	etc.	

NOTE: If a sentence ends with a period marking an abbreviation, do not add a second period.

Do not use a period with US Postal Service abbreviations for states: MD, TX, CA.

Current usage is to omit the period in abbreviations of organization names, academic degrees, and designations for eras.

NATO	UNESCO	UCLA	BS	BC
IRS	AFL-CIO	NIH	PhD	AD
USA	NAACP	SEC	RN	BCE

38b The question mark

A direct question should be followed by a question mark.

What is the horsepower of a 777 engine?

If a polite request is written in the form of a question, it may be followed by a period.

Would you please send me your catalog of lilies.

TIP: Do not use a question mark after an indirect question, one that is reported rather than asked directly. Use a period instead.

▶ He asked me who was teaching the mythology course

this year~~?~~.

NOTE: Questions in a series may be followed by question marks even when they are not complete sentences.

We wondered where Calamity had hidden this time. Under the sink? Behind the furnace? On top of the bookcase?

38c The exclamation point

Use an exclamation point after a word group or sentence to express exceptional feeling or to provide special emphasis. The exclamation point is rarely appropriate in academic writing.

When Gloria entered the room, I switched on the lights, and we all yelled, "Surprise!"

TIP: Do not overuse the exclamation point.

▶ In the fisherman's memory the fish lives on, increasing in

length and weight with each passing year, until at last it is

big enough to shade a fishing boat~~!~~.

This sentence doesn't need to be pumped up with an exclamation point. It is emphatic enough without it.

▶ Whenever I see my favorite hitter, Derek Lee, up at bat,

I dream of making it to the big leagues~~!~~. My team would

win every time!

The first exclamation point should be deleted so that the second one will have more force.

EXERCISE 38–1 Add appropriate end punctuation in the following paragraph.

Although I am generally rational, I am superstitious I never walk under ladders or put shoes on the table If I spill the salt, I go into frenzied calisthenics picking up the grains and tossing them over my left shoulder As a result of these curious activities, I've always wondered whether knowing the roots of superstitions would quell my irrational responses Superstition has it, for example, that one should never place a hat on the bed This superstition arises from a time when head lice were common and placing a guest's hat on the bed stood a good chance of spreading lice through the host's bed Doesn't this make good sense And doesn't it stand to reason that if I know that my guests don't have lice I shouldn't care where their hats go Of course it does It is fair to ask, then, whether I have changed my ways and place hats on beds Are you kidding I wouldn't put a hat on a bed if my life depended on it

39 Other punctuation marks: the dash, parentheses, brackets, the ellipsis mark, the slash

Grammar checkers rarely flag problems with the punctuation marks in this section: the dash, parentheses, brackets, the ellipsis mark, and the slash.

39a The dash

When typing, use two hyphens to form a dash (--). Do not put spaces before or after the dash. If your word processing program has what is known as an "em-dash" (—), you may use it instead, with no space before or after it. Dashes are used for the following purposes.

To set off parenthetical material that deserves emphasis

Everything that went wrong—from the peeping Tom at her window last night to my head-on collision today—we blamed on our move.

To set off appositives that contain commas

An appositive is a noun or noun phrase that renames a nearby noun. Ordinarily most appositives are set off with commas (32e), but when the appositive itself contains commas, a pair of dashes helps readers see the relative importance of all the pauses.

> In my hometown, the basic needs of people—food, clothing, and shelter—are less costly than in a big city like Los Angeles.

To prepare for a list, a restatement, an amplification, or a dramatic shift in tone or thought

> Along the wall are the bulk liquids—sesame seed oil, honey, safflower oil, and that half-liquid "peanuts only" peanut butter.

> In his last semester, Peter tried to pay more attention to his priorities—applying to graduate school and getting financial aid.

> Everywhere we looked there were little kids—a box of Cracker Jacks in one hand and mommy or daddy's sleeve in the other.

> Kiere took a few steps back, came running full speed, kicked a mighty kick—and missed the ball.

In the first two examples, the writer could also use a colon. (See 35a.) The colon is more formal than the dash and not quite as dramatic.

TIP: Unless there is a specific reason for using the dash, avoid it. Unnecessary dashes create a choppy effect.

▶ Insisting that students use computers as instructional

  tools ⁄ for information retrieval ⁄ makes good sense. Herding

  them ⁄ sheeplike ⁄ into computer technology does not.

39b Parentheses

Use parentheses to enclose supplemental material, minor digressions, and afterthoughts.

Nurses record patients' vital signs (temperature, pulse, and blood pressure) several times a day.

Use parentheses to enclose letters or numbers labeling items in a series.

Regulations stipulated that only the following equipment could be used on the survival mission: (1) a knife, (2) thirty feet of parachute line, (3) a book of matches, (4) two ponchos, (5) an E tool, and (6) a signal flare.

TIP: Do not overuse parentheses. Rough drafts are likely to contain more afterthoughts than necessary. As writers head into a sentence, they often think of additional details, occasionally working them in as best they can with parentheses. Usually such sentences should be revised so that the additional details no longer seem to be afterthoughts.

▶ Researchers have said that seventeen ~~million (estimates run~~ *from* ~~as high as~~ twenty-three million) Americans have diabetes. *to*

39c Brackets

Use brackets to enclose any words or phrases that you have inserted into an otherwise word-for-word quotation.

Audubon reports that "if there are not enough young to balance deaths, the end of the species [California condor] is inevitable."

The sentence quoted from the *Audubon* article did not contain the words *California condor* (since the context of the full article made clear what species was meant), so the writer needed to add the name in brackets.

The Latin word "sic" in brackets indicates that an error in a quoted sentence appears in the original source.

According to the review, Nelly Furtado's performance was brilliant, "exceding [sic] the expectations of even her most loyal fans."

Do not overuse "sic," however, since calling attention to others' mistakes can appear snobbish. The preceding quotation, for example, might have been paraphrased instead: *According to the review, even Nelly Furtado's most loyal fans were surprised by the brilliance of her performance.*

39d The ellipsis mark

The ellipsis mark consists of three spaced periods. Use an ellipsis mark to indicate that you have deleted words from an otherwise word-for-word quotation.

> Reuben reports that "when the amount of cholesterol circulating in the blood rises over . . . 300 milligrams per 100, the chances of a heart attack increase dramatically."

If you delete a full sentence or more in the middle of a quoted passage, use a period before the three ellipsis dots.

> "Most of our efforts," writes Dave Erikson, "are directed toward saving the bald eagle's wintering habitat along the Mississippi River. . . . It's important that the wintering birds have a place to roost, where they can get out of the cold wind."

TIP: Ordinarily, do not use the ellipsis mark at the beginning or at the end of a quotation. Readers will understand that the quoted material is taken from a longer passage. If you have cut some words from the end of the final quoted sentence, however, MLA requires an ellipsis mark, as in the third example on page 505.

In quoted poetry, use a full line of ellipsis dots to indicate that you have dropped a line or more from the poem, as in this example from "To His Coy Mistress" by Andrew Marvell:

> Had we but world enough, and time,
> This coyness, lady, were no crime.
> . . . .
> But at my back I always hear
> Time's wingèd chariot hurrying near; (1-2, 21-22)

The ellipsis mark may also be used to indicate a hesitation or an interruption in speech or to suggest unfinished thoughts.

"The apartment building next door . . . it's going up in flames!" yelled Marcia.

Before falling into a coma, the victim whispered, "It was a man with a tattoo on his . . . "

39e The slash

Use the slash to separate two or three lines of poetry that have been run into your text. Add a space both before and after the slash.

In the opening lines of "Jordan," George Herbert pokes gentle fun at popular poems of his time: "Who says that fictions only and false hair / Become a verse? Is there in truth no beauty?" (1-2).

More than three lines of poetry should be handled as an indented quotation. (See 37b.)

The slash may occasionally be used to separate paired terms such as *pass/fail* and *producer/director*. Do not use a space before or after the slash. Be sparing in this use of the slash. In particular, avoid the use of *and/or*, *he/she*, and *his/her*. Instead of using *he/she* and *his/her* to solve sexist language problems, you can usually find more graceful alternatives. (See 17f and 22a.)

EXERCISE 39–1   Edit the following sentences to correct errors in punctuation, focusing especially on appropriate use of the dash, parentheses, brackets, ellipsis mark, and slash. If a sentence is correct, write "correct" after it. Answers to lettered sentences appear in the back of the book. Example:

Social insects/— bees, for example/— are able to

communicate complicated messages to one another.

a.   A client has left his/her cell phone in our conference room.
b.   The films we made of Kilauea—on our trip to Hawaii Volcanoes National Park—illustrate a typical spatter cone eruption.

c. Greg selected the pass/fail option for Chemistry 101.

d. Masahiro poked through his backpack—laptop, digital camera, guidebook—to make sure he was ready for a day's study at the Ryoanji Temple garden.

e. Of three engineering fields, chemical, mechanical, and materials, Keegan chose materials engineering for its application to toy manufacturing.

1. The old Valentine verse we used to chant says it all: "Sugar is sweet, / And so are you."

2. In studies in which mothers gazed down at their infants in their cribs but remained facially unresponsive, for example, not smiling, laughing, or showing any change of expression, the infants responded with intense weariness and eventual withdrawal.

3. There are three points of etiquette in poker: 1. always allow someone else to cut the cards, 2. don't forget to ante up, and 3. never stack your chips.

4. In *Lifeboat*, Alfred Hitchcock appears [some say without his knowledge] in a newspaper advertisement for weight loss.

5. The writer Chitra Divakaruni explained her work with other Indian American immigrants: "Many women who came to Maitri [a women's support group in San Francisco] needed to know simple things like opening a bank account or getting citizenship. . . . Many women in Maitri spoke English, but their English was functional rather than emotional. They needed someone who understands their problems and speaks their language."

hackerhandbooks.com/bedhandbook > Grammar exercises > Punctuation > E-ex 39–2

Part VIII
Mechanics

409

40 Abbreviations

> **Grammar checkers** can flag a few inappropriate abbreviations, such as *Xmas* and e.*g.*, but do not assume that a program will catch all problems with abbreviations.

40a Use standard abbreviations for titles immediately before and after proper names.

TITLES BEFORE PROPER NAMES	TITLES AFTER PROPER NAMES
Mr. Rafael Zabala	William Albert Sr.
Ms. Nancy Linehan	Thomas Hines Jr.
Mrs. Edward Horn	Anita Lor, PhD
Dr. Margaret Simmons	Robert Simkowski, MD
Rev. John Stone	Margaret Chin, LLD
Prof. James Russo	Polly Stein, DDS

Do not abbreviate a title if it is not used with a proper name.

> My history ~~prof.~~ professor is an expert on race relations in South Africa.

Avoid redundant titles such as *Dr. Amy Day, MD*. Choose one title or the other: *Dr. Amy Day* or *Amy Day, MD*.

40b Use abbreviations only when you are sure your readers will understand them.

Familiar abbreviations, written without periods, are acceptable.

CIA	FBI	MD	NAACP
NBA	NEA	PhD	CD-ROM
YMCA	CBS	USA	ESL

Talk show host Conan O'Brien is a Harvard graduate with a BA in history.

The YMCA has opened a new gym close to my office.

NOTE: When using an unfamiliar abbreviation (such as NASW for National Association of Social Workers) throughout a paper, write the full name followed by the abbreviation in parentheses at the first mention of the name. Then use just the abbreviation throughout the rest of the paper.

40c Use *BC*, *AD*, *a.m.*, *p.m.*, *No.*, and *$* only with specific dates, times, numbers, and amounts.

The abbreviation BC ("before Christ") follows a date, and AD ("*anno Domini*") precedes a date. Acceptable alternatives are BCE ("before the common era") and CE ("common era"), both of which follow a date.

40 BC (or 40 BCE)	4:00 a.m. (or AM)	No. 12 (or no. 12)
AD 44 (or 44 CE)	6:00 p.m. (or PM)	$150

Avoid using *a.m.*, *p.m.*, *No.*, or *$* when not accompanied by a specific figure.

▶ The governor argued that the new sales tax would raise
    much-needed $ *money* for the state.

40d Be sparing in your use of Latin abbreviations.

Latin abbreviations are acceptable in footnotes and bibliographies and in informal writing for comments in parentheses.

cf. (Latin *confer*, "compare")
e.g. (Latin *exempli gratia*, "for example")
et al. (Latin *et alia*, "and others")
etc. (Latin *et cetera*, "and so forth")
i.e. (Latin *id est*, "that is")
N.B. (Latin *nota bene*, "note well")

Harold Simms et al., *The Race for Space*

Alfred Hitchcock directed many classic thrillers (e.g., *Psycho*, *Rear Window*, and *Vertigo*).

In formal writing, use the appropriate English phrases.

▶ **Many obsolete laws remain on the books. A law in**
   for example,
   Vermont, e.g., forbids an unmarried man and woman to

   sit closer than six inches apart on a park bench.

40e Avoid inappropriate abbreviations.

In formal writing, abbreviations for the following are not commonly accepted: personal names, units of measurement, days of the week, holidays, months, courses of study, divisions of written works, states, and countries (except in complete addresses and except Washington, DC). Do not abbreviate *Company* and *Incorporated* unless their abbreviated forms are part of an official name.

PERSONAL NAMES Charles (not Chas.)

UNITS OF MEASUREMENT feet (not ft.)

DAYS OF THE WEEK Monday (not Mon.)

HOLIDAYS Christmas (not Xmas)

MONTHS January, February, March (not Jan., Feb., Mar.)

COURSES OF STUDY political science (not poli. sci.)

DIVISIONS OF WRITTEN WORKS chapter, page (not ch., p.)

STATES AND COUNTRIES Massachusetts (not MA or Mass.)

PARTS OF A BUSINESS NAME Adams Lighting Company (not Adams Lighting Co.); Kim and Brothers (not Kim and Bros.)

▶ **The American Red Cross requires that blood donors be at**
   years   pounds,
   least seventeen yrs. old, weigh at least 110 lb., and not
                              weeks.
   have given blood in the past eight wks.

EXERCISE 40–1 Edit the following sentences to correct errors in abbreviations. If a sentence is correct, write "correct" after it. Answers to lettered sentences appear in the back of the book. Example:

This year ~~Xmas~~ will fall on a ~~Tues.~~
(^Christmas) (^Tuesday.)

a. Since its inception, the BBC has maintained a consistently high standard of radio and television broadcasting.
b. Some combat soldiers are trained by govt. diplomats to be sensitive to issues of culture, history, and religion.
c. Mahatma Gandhi has inspired many modern leaders, including Martin Luther King Jr.
d. How many lb. have you lost since you began running four miles a day?
e. Denzil spent all night studying for his psych. exam.

1. My favorite prof., Dr. Barker, is on sabbatical this semester.
2. When we visited NYU in early September, we were charmed by the lull of summer crickets in Washington Square Park.
3. Some historians think that the New Testament was completed by AD 100.
4. My mother's birthday was on Fri. the 13th this year.
5. Some first-time Flash users panic before the complex menus— i.e., they develop a blank stare and the tingling of a migraine.

hackerhandbooks.com/bedhandbook > Grammar exercises > Mechanics > E-ex 40–2

41 Numbers

> **Grammar checkers** can tell you to spell out certain numbers, such as *thirty-three* and numbers that begin a sentence, but they won't help you understand when it is acceptable to use numerals.

41a Follow the conventions in your discipline for spelling out or using numerals to express numbers.

In the humanities, which generally follow either Modern Language Association (MLA) style or *The Chicago Manual of Style*, use numerals only for specific numbers above one hundred: *353, 1,020*. Spell out numbers one hundred and below and large round numbers: *eleven, thirty-five, sixty, fifteen million*.

The social sciences and sciences, which follow American Psychological Association (APA) style or Council of Science Editors (CSE) style, use numerals for all but the numbers one through nine.

In all fields, treat related numbers in a passage consistently: *The survey found that 89 of 157 respondents had not taken any courses related to alcohol use.*

When one number immediately follows another, spelling out one number and using numerals for the other is usually effective: *three 100-meter events, 25 four-poster beds.*

▶ It's been 8 *eight* years since I visited Peru.

▶ Enrollment in the charter school in its first year will be limited to ~~three hundred forty~~ *340* students.

If a sentence begins with a number, spell out the number or rewrite the sentence.

▶ *One hundred fifty* ~~150~~ children in our program need expensive dental treatment.

Rewriting the sentence will also correct the error and may be less awkward if the number is long: *In our program, 150 children need expensive dental treatment.*

41b Use numerals according to convention in dates, addresses, and so on.

DATES July 4, 1776; 56 BC; AD 30

ADDRESSES 77 Latches Lane, 519 West 42nd Street

PERCENTAGES 55 percent (or 55%)

FRACTIONS, DECIMALS $\frac{1}{2}$, 0.047

SCORES 7 to 3, 21–18

STATISTICS average age 37, average weight 180

SURVEYS 4 out of 5

EXACT AMOUNTS OF MONEY $105.37, $106,000

DIVISIONS OF BOOKS volume 3, chapter 4, page 189

DIVISIONS OF PLAYS act 3, scene 3 (or act III, scene iii)

IDENTIFICATION NUMBERS serial number 10988675

TIME OF DAY 4:00 p.m., 1:30 a.m.

▶ The foundation raised ~~four hundred thirty thousand~~ $430,000

~~dollars~~ for cancer research.

NOTE: When not using *a.m.* or *p.m.*, write out the time in words (*two o'clock in the afternoon*, *twelve noon*, *seven in the morning*).

EXERCISE 41–1 Edit the following sentences to correct errors in the use of numbers. If a sentence is correct, write "correct" after it. Answers to lettered sentences appear in the back of the book. Example:

By the end of the evening, Ashanti had only ~~three dollars~~ $3.06

~~and six cents~~ left.

a. The carpenters located 3 maple timbers, 21 sheets of cherry, and 10 oblongs of polished ebony for the theater set.

b. The program's cost is well over one billion dollars.

c. The score was tied at 5–5 when the momentum shifted and carried the Standards to a decisive 12–5 win.

d. 8 students in the class had been labeled "learning disabled."

e. The Vietnam Veterans Memorial in Washington, DC, had fifty-eight thousand one hundred thirty-two names inscribed on it when it was dedicated in 1982.

1. One of my favorite scenes in Shakespeare is the property division scene in act 1 of *King Lear*.

2. The botany lecture will begin at precisely 3:30 p.m.

3. 40 percent of all gamers in the United States are women.

4. In two thousand twelve, the world population may reach 7 billion.

5. On a normal day, I spend at least 4 to 5 hours surfing the Internet.

42 Italics

This section describes conventional uses for italics. While italics is accepted by all three style guides covered in this handbook (MLA, APA, and *Chicago*), some instructors may prefer underlining in student papers. If that is the case in your course, simply substitute underlining for italics in the examples in this section.

Some computer and online applications do not allow for italics. To indicate words that should be italicized, you can use underscore marks or asterisks before and after the italic words.

I am planning to write my senior thesis on _Memoirs of a Geisha_.

NOTE: Excessive use of italics to emphasize words or ideas, especially in academic writing, is distracting and should be avoided.

42a Italicize the titles of works according to convention.

Titles of the following types of works, including electronic works, should be italicized.

TITLES OF BOOKS *The Color Purple, Middlesex, Encarta*

MAGAZINES *Time, Scientific American, Salon.com*

NEWSPAPERS the *Baltimore Sun,* the *Orlando Sentinel Online*

PAMPHLETS *Common Sense, Facts about Marijuana*

LONG POEMS *The Waste Land, Paradise Lost*

PLAYS *'Night Mother, Wicked*

FILMS *Casablanca, Do the Right Thing*

TELEVISION PROGRAMS *American Idol, Frontline*

RADIO PROGRAMS *All Things Considered*

MUSICAL COMPOSITIONS *Porgy and Bess*

CHOREOGRAPHIC WORKS *Brief Fling*

WORKS OF VISUAL ART *American Gothic*

ELECTRONIC DATABASES *InfoTrac*

WEB SITES *ZDNet, Google*

ELECTRONIC GAMES *Everquest, Guitar Hero*

The titles of other works, such as short stories, essays, episodes of radio and television programs, songs, and short poems, are enclosed in quotation marks. (See 37d.)

NOTE: Do not use italics when referring to the Bible, titles of books in the Bible (Genesis, not *Genesis*), or titles of legal documents (the Constitution, not the *Constitution*). Do not italicize the titles of computer software (Keynote, Photoshop). Do not italicize the title of your own paper.

42b Italicize the names of specific ships, spacecraft, and aircraft.

Queen Mary 2, Challenger, Spirit of St. Louis

The success of the Soviets' *Sputnik* energized the US space program.

42c Italicize foreign words used in an English sentence.

Shakespeare's Falstaff is a comic character known for both his excessive drinking and his general *joie de vivre.*

EXCEPTION: Do not italicize foreign words that have become a standard part of the English language—"laissez-faire," "fait accompli," "modus operandi," and "per diem," for example.

42d Italicize words mentioned as words, letters mentioned as letters, and numbers mentioned as numbers.

Tomás assured us that the chemicals could probably be safely mixed, but his *probably* stuck in our minds.

Some toddlers have trouble pronouncing the letter *s.*

A big *3* was painted on the stage door.

NOTE: Quotation marks may be used instead of italics to set off words mentioned as words. (See 37e.)

EXERCISE 42–1 Edit the following sentences to correct errors in the use of italics. If a sentence is correct, write "correct" after it. Answers to lettered sentences appear in the back of the book. Example:

> **We had a lively discussion about Gini Alhadeff's memoir**
>
> *The Sun at Midday. Correct*

a. Howard Hughes commissioned the Spruce Goose, a beautifully built but thoroughly impractical wooden aircraft.

b. The old man *screamed* his anger, *shouting* to all of us, "I will not leave my money to you worthless layabouts!"

c. I learned the Latin term ad infinitum from an old nursery rhyme about fleas: "Great fleas have little fleas upon their back to bite 'em, / Little fleas have lesser fleas and so on ad infinitum."

d. Cinema audiences once gasped at hearing the word *damn* in *Gone with the Wind*.

e. Neve Campbell's lifelong interest in ballet inspired her involvement in the film "The Company," which portrays a season with the Joffrey Ballet.

1. Yasmina spent a year painting white flowers in imitation of Georgia O'Keeffe's Calla Lilies.

2. On the monastery walls are murals depicting scenes from the book of Kings and the book of Proverbs.

3. My per diem allowance was two hundred dollars.

4. Cecily watched in amazement as the tattoo artist made angles and swooping loops into the Gothic letter G.

5. The blend of poetic lyrics and progressive instruments on Seal's "Human Being" makes it one of my favorite CDs.

hackerhandbooks.com/bedhandbook > Grammar exercises > Mechanics
> E-ex 42–2

43 Spelling

You learned to spell from repeated experience with words in both reading and writing, but especially writing. Words have a look, a sound, and even a feel to them as the hand moves across the page. As you proofread, you can probably tell if a word doesn't look quite right. In such cases, the solution is simple: Look up the word in the dictionary.

> **Spell checkers** are useful alternatives to a dictionary, but only to a point. A spell checker will not tell you how to spell words not listed in its dictionary; nor will it help you catch words commonly confused, such as *accept* and *except,* or some typographical errors, such as *own* for *won.* You will still need to proofread, and for some words you may need to turn to the dictionary.

43a Become familiar with your dictionary.

A good dictionary, whether print or online—such as *The American Heritage Dictionary of the English Language, The Random House College Dictionary,* or *Merriam-Webster's Collegiate Dictionary*—is an indispensable writer's aid.

A sample print dictionary entry, taken from *The American Heritage Dictionary,* appears on page 420. Labels show where various kinds of information about a word can be found in that dictionary.

A sample online dictionary entry, taken from *Merriam-Webster Online,* appears on page 421.

Spelling, word division, pronunciation

The main entry (*re•gard* in the sample entries) shows the correct spelling of the word. When there are two correct spellings of a word (as in *collectible, collectable,* for example), both are given, with the preferred spelling usually appearing first.

The main entry also shows how the word is divided into syllables. The dot between *re* and *gard* separates the two syllables and indicates where the word should be divided if it can't fit at the end of a line of type (see 44f). When a word is compound, the main entry shows how to write it: as one word (*crossroad*), as a hyphenated word (*cross-stitch*), or as two words (*cross section*).

The word's pronunciation is given just after the main entry. The accents indicate which syllables are stressed; the other marks are explained in the dictionary's pronunciation key. In print dictionaries, this key usually appears at the

PRINT DICTIONARY ENTRY

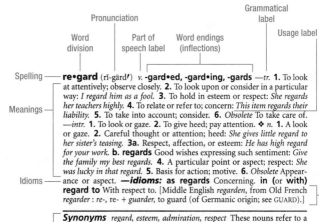

Synonyms — *Synonyms* regard, esteem, admiration, respect These nouns refer to a feeling based on perception of and approval for the worth of a person or thing. *Regard* is the most general: *"I once thought you had a kind of regard for her"* (George Borrow). *Esteem* connotes considered appraisal and positive regard: *"The near-unanimity of esteem he enjoyed during his lifetime has by no means been sustained since"* (Will Crutchfield). *Admiration* is a feeling of keen approbation: *"Greatness is a spiritual condition worthy to excite love, interest, and admiration"* (Matthew Arnold). *Respect* implies appreciative, often deferential regard resulting from careful assessment: *"I have a great respect for any man who makes his own way in life"* (Winston Churchill). See also synonyms at **consider.**

Usage note — *Usage Note* *Regard* is traditionally used in the singular in the phrase *in regard* (not *in regards*) *to. Regarding* and *as regards* are also standard in the sense "with reference to." In the same sense *with respect to* is acceptable, but *respecting* is not. • *Respects* is sometimes considered preferable to *regards* in the sense of "particulars": *In some respects* (not *regards*) *the books are alike.*

Word origin (etymology)

bottom of every page or every other page. Many online entries include an audio link to a person's voice pronouncing the word. And most online dictionaries have an audio pronunciation guide.

ONLINE DICTIONARY ENTRY

Merriam-Webster Online Dictionary

3 entries found for **regard**.
To select an entry, click on it.

Alternative entries — regard[1,noun] / regard[2,verb] / self-regard   Go

Spelling and word division —

Audio pronunciation link

Main Entry: ¹**re·gard** �})   Word origin (etymology)

Pronunciation — Pronunciation: ri-'gärd

Part of speech label — Function: *noun*

Etymology: Middle English, from Middle French, from Old French, from *regarder*

Usage label — **1** *archaic* : APPEARANCE

2 a : ATTENTION, CONSIDERATION <due *regard* should be given to all facets of the question> **b** : a protective interest : CARE <ought to have more *regard* for his health>

3 : LOOK, GAZE

4 a : the worth or estimation in which something or someone is held <a man of small *regard*> **b** (1) : a feeling of respect and affection : ESTEEM <his hard work won him the *regard* of his colleagues> (2) *plural* : friendly greetings implying such feeling <give him my *regards*>

Meanings (synonyms shown as hyperlinks) —

5 : a basis of action or opinion : MOTIVE

6 : an aspect to be taken into consideration : RESPECT <is a small school, and is fortunate in this *regard*>

7 *obsolete* : INTENTION

Idioms — **- in regard to** : with respect to : CONCERNING

- with regard to : in regard to

Word endings and grammatical labels

When a word takes endings to indicate grammatical functions (called *inflections*), the endings are listed in boldface, as with *-garded*, *-garding*, and *-gards* in the sample print entry (p. 420).

Labels for the parts of speech and for other grammatical terms are sometimes abbreviated, as they are in the print entry. The most commonly used abbreviations are these:

n.	noun	adj.	adjective
pl.	plural	adv.	adverb
sing.	singular	pron.	pronoun
v.	verb	prep.	preposition
tr.	transitive verb	conj.	conjunction
intr.	intransitive verb	interj.	interjection

Meanings, word origin, synonyms, and antonyms

Each meaning for the word is given a number. Occasionally a word's use is illustrated in a quoted sentence.

Sometimes a word can be used as more than one part of speech (*regard*, for instance, can be used as either a verb or a noun). In such a case, all the meanings for one part of speech are given before all the meanings for another, as in the sample entries. The entries also give idiomatic uses of the word.

The origin of the word, called its *etymology*, appears in brackets after all the meanings in the print version; in the online version, it appears before the meanings.

Synonyms, words similar in meaning to the main entry, are frequently listed. In the sample print entry, the dictionary draws distinctions in meaning among the various synonyms. In the online entry, synonyms appear as hyperlinks. Antonyms, which do not appear in the sample entries, are words having a meaning opposite from that of the main entry.

Usage

Usage labels indicate when, where, or under what conditions a particular meaning for a word is appropriately used. Common labels are *informal* (or *colloquial*), *slang*, *archaic*, *poetic*, *nonstandard*, *dialect*, *obsolete*, and *British*. In the sample print entry (p. 420), two meanings of *regard* are labeled *obsolete* because they are no longer in use. The sample online entry (p. 421) has meanings labeled both *archaic* and *obsolete*.

Dictionaries sometimes include usage notes as well. In the sample print entry, the dictionary offers advice on several uses of *regard* not specifically covered by the meanings. Such advice is based on the opinions of many experts and on actual usage in current magazines, newspapers, and books.

43b Discriminate between words that sound alike but have different meanings.

Words that sound alike or nearly alike but have different meanings and spellings are called *homophones*. The following sets of words are so commonly confused that a careful writer will double-check their every use.

affect (verb: to exert an influence)
effect (verb: to accomplish; noun: result)

its (possessive pronoun: of or belonging to it)
it's (contraction of *it is* or *it has*)

loose (adjective: free, not securely attached)
lose (verb: to fail to keep, to be deprived of)

principal (adjective: most important; noun: head of a school)
principle (noun: a fundamental guideline or truth)

their (possessive pronoun: belonging to them)
they're (contraction of *they are*)
there (adverb: that place or position)

who's (contraction of *who is* or *who has*)
whose (possessive form of *who*)

your (possessive pronoun: belonging to you)
you're (contraction of *you are*)

To check for correct use of these and other commonly confused words, see the Glossary of Usage (p. 789).

43c Become familiar with the major spelling rules.

i *before* e *except after* c

Use *i* before *e* except after *c* or when sounded like *ay*, as in *neighbor* and *weigh*.

I BEFORE *E*	relieve, believe, sieve, niece, fierce, frieze
E BEFORE *I*	receive, deceive, sleigh, freight, eight
EXCEPTIONS	seize, either, weird, height, foreign, leisure

Suffixes

Final silent -*e*   Generally, drop a final silent -*e* when adding a suffix that begins with a vowel. Keep the final -*e* if the suffix begins with a consonant.

combine, combination   achieve, achievement
desire, desiring   care, careful
prude, prudish   entire, entirety
remove, removable   gentle, gentleness

Words such as *changeable*, *judgment*, *argument*, and *truly* are exceptions.

Final -*y*   When adding -*s* or -*d* to words ending in -*y*, ordinarily change -*y* to -*ie* when the -*y* is preceded by a consonant but not when it is preceded by a vowel.

comedy, comedies   monkey, monkeys
dry, dried   play, played

With proper names ending in -*y*, however, do not change the -*y* to -*ie* even if it is preceded by a consonant: *the Dougherty family*, *the Doughertys*.

Final consonants   If a final consonant is preceded by a single vowel *and* the consonant ends a one-syllable word or a

stressed syllable, double the consonant when adding a suffix
beginning with a vowel.

bet, betting   occur, occurrence
commit, committed

Plurals

-*s* or -*es*   Add -*s* to form the plural of most nouns; add -*es* to
singular nouns ending in -*s*, -*sh*, -*ch*, and -*x*.

table, tables   church, churches
paper, papers   dish, dishes

Ordinarily add -*s* to nouns ending in -*o* when the -*o* is preceded by a vowel. Add -*es* when it is preceded by a consonant.

radio, radios   hero, heroes
video, videos   tomato, tomatoes

ESL   Spelling varies slightly among English-speaking countries.
This can prove particularly confusing for multilingual students in
the United States, who may have learned British English. Following
is a list of some common words spelled differently in American and
British English. Consult a dictionary for others.

AMERICAN	BRITISH
canceled, traveled	cancelled, travelled
color, humor	colour, humour
judgment	judgement
check	cheque
realize, apologize	realise, apologise
defense	defence
anemia, anesthetic	anaemia, anaesthetic
theater, center	theatre, centre
fetus	foetus
mold, smolder	mould, smoulder
civilization	civilisation
connection, inflection	connexion, inflexion
licorice	liquorice

Other plurals To form the plural of a hyphenated compound word, add -s to the chief word even if it does not appear at the end.

mother-in-law, mothers-in-law

English words derived from other languages such as Latin or French sometimes form the plural as they would in their original language.

medium, media   chateau, chateaux
criterion, criteria

43d Be alert to commonly misspelled words.

absence	benefited	eligible	independence
academic	bureau	embarrass	indispensable
accidentally	business	emphasize	inevitable
accommodate	calendar	entirely	intelligence
achievement	candidate	environment	irrelevant
acknowledge	cemetery	especially	irresistible
acquaintance	changeable	exaggerated	knowledge
acquire	column	exercise	library
address	commitment	exhaust	license
all right	committed	existence	lightning
amateur	committee	extraordinary	loneliness
analyze	competitive	extremely	maintenance
answer	completely	familiar	maneuver
apparently	conceivable	fascinate	marriage
appearance	conscience	February	mathematics
arctic	conscientious	foreign	mischievous
argument	conscious	forty	necessary
arithmetic	criticism	fourth	noticeable
arrangement	criticize	friend	occasion
ascend	decision	government	occurred
athlete	definitely	grammar	occurrence
athletics	descendant	guard	pamphlet
attendance	desperate	harass	parallel
basically	dictionary	height	particularly
beautiful	different	humorous	pastime
beginning	disastrous	incidentally	permanent
believe	eighth	incredible	permissible

perseverance	professor	schedule	tomorrow
phenomenon	pronunciation	seize	tragedy
physically	publicly	separate	transferred
playwright	quiet	sergeant	tries
practically	quite	siege	truly
precede	quizzes	similar	unnecessarily
preference	receive	sincerely	usually
preferred	recognize	sophomore	vacuum
prejudice	referred	strictly	vengeance
presence	restaurant	subtly	villain
prevalent	rhythm	succeed	weird
privilege	roommate	surprise	whether
proceed	sandwich	thorough	writing

EXERCISE 43–1 The following memo has been run through a spell checker. Proofread it carefully, editing the spelling and typographical errors that remain.

November 3, 2009

To: Patricia Wise
From: Constance Mayhew
Subject: Express Tours annual report

Thank you for agreeing to draft the annual report for Express Tours. Before you begin you're work, let me outline the initial steps.

First, its essential for you to include brief profiles of top management. Early next week, I'll provide profiles for all manages accept Samuel Heath, who's biographical information is being revised. You should edit these profiles carefully and than format them according to the enclosed instructions. We may ask you to include other employee's profiles at some point.

Second, you should arrange to get complete financial information for fiscal year 2009 from our comptroller, Richard Chang. (Helen Boyes, to, can provide the necessary figures.) When you get this information, precede according tot he plans we discuss in yesterday's meeting. By the way, you will notice from the figures that the sale of our Charterhouse division did not significantly effect net profits.

Third, you should submit first draft of the report by December 15. I assume that you won a laser printer, but if you don't, you can e-mail a file and we'll print out a draft here. Of coarse, you should proofread you writing.

I am quiet pleased that you can take on this project. If I can answers questions, don't hesitate to call.

44   The hyphen

> Spell checkers can flag some, but not all, missing or misused hyphens. For example, the programs can often tell you that a hyphen is needed in compound numbers, such as *sixty-four.* They can also tell you how to spell certain compound words, such as *breakup* (not *break-up*).

44a Consult the dictionary to determine how to treat a compound word.

The dictionary will tell you whether to treat a compound word as a hyphenated compound (*water-repellent*), one word (*waterproof*), or two words (*water table*). If the compound word is not in the dictionary, treat it as two words.

▶ The prosecutor chose not to cross–examine any witnesses.

▶ All students are expected to record their data in a small

   note book.

▶ Alice walked through the looking glass into a backward

   world.

44b Use a hyphen to connect two or more words functioning together as an adjective before a noun.

▶ Mrs. Douglas gave Toshiko a seashell and some newspaper–

   wrapped fish to take home to her mother.

▶ Richa Gupta is not yet a well-known candidate.

Newspaper-wrapped and *well-known* are adjectives used before the nouns *fish* and *candidate*.

Generally, do not use a hyphen when such compounds follow the noun.

▶ After our television campaign, Richa Gupta will be well/

known.

Do not use a hyphen to connect *-ly* adverbs to the words they modify.

▶ A slowly/moving truck tied up traffic.

NOTE: When two or more hyphenated adjectives in a row modify the same noun, you can suspend the hyphens.

Do you prefer first-, second-, or third-class tickets?

44c Hyphenate the written form of fractions and of compound numbers from twenty-one to ninety-nine.

▶ One-fourth of my income goes to pay my child care

expenses.

44d Use a hyphen with the prefixes *all-*, *ex-* (meaning "former"), and *self-* and with the suffix *-elect*.

▶ The private foundation is funneling more money into

self-help projects.

▶ The Student Senate bylaws require the president-elect to

attend all senate meetings between the election and the

official transfer of office.

44e Use a hyphen in certain words to avoid ambiguity or to separate awkward double or triple letters.

Without the hyphen, there would be no way to distinguish between words such as *re-creation* and *recreation*.

Bicycling in the city is my favorite form of recreation.

The film was praised for its astonishing re-creation of nineteenth-century London.

Hyphens are sometimes used to separate awkward double or triple letters in compound words (*anti-intellectual*, *cross-stitch*). Always check a dictionary for the standard form of the word.

44f Check for correct word breaks when words must be divided at the end of a line.

Some word processing programs and other computer applications automatically generate word breaks at the ends of lines. When you're writing an academic paper, it's best to set your computer application not to hyphenate automatically. Some hyphenation is inevitable, however, so you should be familiar with the following hyphenation conventions.

1. Words must be divided between syllables, and one-syllable words should not be divided.

   ▶ When I returned from my semester overseas, I didn't ~~reco-~~ rec-
   ~~ognize~~ *ognize*
   one face on the magazine covers.

   ▶ He didn't have the courage or the ~~stren-~~
   ~~gth~~ *strength*
   to open the door.

2. A single letter should not stand alone at the end of a line, and no fewer than three letters should begin a line.

   ▶ She'll bring her brother with her when she comes ~~a-~~
   ~~gain.~~ *again.*

▶ As audience to the play *The Mousetrap*, Hamlet is a ~~watch-~~
watcher
~~er~~ watching watchers.
  ^

3. Compound words should either be divided between the words that form the compound or not be divided at all.

▶ My niece Marielena is determined to become a long-~~dis-~~
distance
~~tance~~ runner when she grows up.
  ^

NOTE: E-mail addresses and URLs need special attention when they occur at the end of a line of text. You can't rely on your computer application to divide these terms correctly, so you must make a decision in each case. Do not insert a hyphen to divide e-mail addresses and URLs. Instead, break an e-mail address after the @ symbol or before a period. Break a URL after a slash or a double slash or before any other punctuation mark.

I repeatedly e-mailed Janine at janine.r.rose@dunbaracademy .org before I gave up and called her cell phone.

To find a zip code quickly, I always use the United States Postal Service Web site at http://zip4.usps.com/zip4/ welcome.jsp.

For breaks in URLs in MLA, APA, and *Chicago* documentation styles, see 54a, 56e, and 57e, respectively.

EXERCISE 44–1 Edit the following sentences to correct errors in hyphenation. If a sentence is correct, write "correct" after it. Answers to lettered sentences appear in the back of the book. Example:

Zola's first readers were scandalized by his slice–of–life novels.
                                                        ^   ^

a. Gold is the seventy-ninth element in the periodic table.
b. The swiftly-moving tugboat pulled alongside the barge and directed it away from the oil spill in the harbor.
c. The Moche were a pre-Columbian people who established a sophisticated culture in ancient Peru.
d. Your dog is well-known in our neighborhood.
e. Road-blocks were set up along all the major highways leading out of the city.

1. We knew we were driving too fast when our tires skidded on the rain slick surface.
2. The Black Death reduced the population of some medieval villages by two thirds.
3. Sewing forty-eight sequined tutus for the ballet recital nearly made Karyn cross-eyed.
4. Olivia had hoped to find a pay as you go plan to finance the construction of her observatory.
5. Gail Sheehy writes that at age twenty five many people assume that the choices they make are irrevocable.

hackerhandbooks.com/bedhandbook > Grammar exercises > Mechanics
> E-ex 44–2

45 Capitalization

In addition to the rules in this section, a good dictionary can tell you when to use capital letters.

> **Grammar checkers** remind you that sentences should begin with capital letters and that some words, such as *Cherokee*, are proper nouns. Many words, however, should be capitalized only in certain contexts, and you must determine when to do so.

45a Capitalize proper nouns and words derived from them; do not capitalize common nouns.

Proper nouns are the names of specific persons, places, and things. All other nouns are common nouns. The following types of words are usually capitalized: names of deities, religions, religious followers, sacred books; words of family relationship used as names; particular places; nationalities and their languages, races, tribes; educational institutions, departments, degrees, particular courses; government departments, organizations, political parties; historical movements, periods, events, documents; specific electronic sources; and trade names.

PROPER NOUNS	COMMON NOUNS
God (used as a name)	a god
Book of Common Prayer	a sacred book
Uncle Pedro	my uncle
Father (used as a name)	my father
Lake Superior	a picturesque lake
the Capital Center	a center for advanced studies
the South	a southern state
Wrigley Field	a baseball stadium
University of Wisconsin	a state university
Geology 101	geology
Environmental Protection Agency	a federal agency
Phi Kappa Psi	a fraternity
a Democrat	an independent
the Enlightenment	the eighteenth century
the Treaty of Versailles	a treaty
the World Wide Web, the Web	a home page
the Internet, the Net	a computer network
Advil	a painkiller

Months, holidays, and days of the week are treated as proper nouns; the seasons and numbers of the days of the month are not.

> Our academic year begins on a Tuesday in early September, right after Labor Day.

> Graduation is in early summer, on the second of June.

EXCEPTION: Capitalize Fourth of July (or July Fourth) when referring to the holiday.

Names of school subjects are capitalized only if they are names of languages. Names of particular courses are capitalized.

> This semester Austin is taking math, geography, geology, French, and English.

> Professor Obembe offers Modern American Fiction 501 to graduate students.

CAUTION: Do not capitalize common nouns to make them seem important: *Our company is currently hiring computer programmers* (not *Company, Computer Programmers*).

45b Capitalize titles of persons when used as part of a proper name but usually not when used alone.

Professor Margaret Barnes; Dr. Sinyee Sein; John Scott Williams Jr.

District Attorney Marshall was reprimanded for badgering the witness.

The district attorney was elected for a two-year term.

Usage varies when the title of an important public figure is used alone: *The president* [or *President*] *vetoed the bill.*

45c Capitalize the first, last, and all major words in titles and subtitles of works such as books, articles, songs, and online documents.

In both titles and subtitles, major words such as nouns, pronouns, verbs, adjectives, and adverbs should be capitalized. Minor words such as articles, prepositions, and coordinating conjunctions are not capitalized unless they are the first or last word of a title or subtitle. Capitalize the second part of a hyphenated term in a title if it is a major word but not if it is a minor word. Capitalize chapter titles and the titles of other major divisions of a work following the same guidelines used for titles of complete works.

Seizing the Enigma: The Race to Break the German U-Boat Codes
A River Runs through It
"I Want to Hold Your Hand"
The Canadian Green Page

To see why some of the titles in the list are italicized and some are put in quotation marks, see 42a and 37d.

45d Capitalize the first word of a sentence.

The first word of a sentence should be capitalized. When a sentence appears within parentheses, capitalize its first word unless the parentheses appear within another sentence.

Early detection of breast cancer significantly increases survival rates. (See table 2.)

Early detection of breast cancer significantly increases survival rates (see table 2).

45e Capitalize the first word of a quoted sentence but not a quoted phrase.

Robert Hughes writes, "There are only about sixty Watteau paintings on whose authenticity all experts agree" (102).

Russell Baker has written that in our country, sports are "the opiate of the masses" (46).

If a quoted sentence is interrupted by explanatory words, do not capitalize the first word after the interruption. (See 37f.)

"If you want to go out," he said, "tell me now."

When quoting poetry, copy the poet's capitalization exactly. Many poets capitalize the first word of every line of poetry; a few contemporary poets dismiss capitalization altogether.

it was the week   that
i felt the city's narrow breezes rush about
me   —Don L. Lee

45f Capitalize the first word after a colon if it begins an independent clause.

If a group of words following a colon could stand on its own as a complete sentence, capitalize the first word.

Clinical trials called into question the safety profile of the drug: A high percentage of participants reported hypertension and kidney problems.

Preferences vary among academic disciplines. See 54c, 56f, and 57f for MLA, APA, and *Chicago* style, respectively.

Always use lowercase for a list or an appositive that follows a colon.

Students were divided into two groups: residents and commuters.

45g Capitalize abbreviations according to convention.

Abbreviations for government agencies and other organizations as well as call numbers for radio and television stations are capitalized.

EPA, FBI, OPEC, IBM, WCRB, KNBC-TV

EXERCISE 45–1 Edit the following sentences to correct errors in capitalization. If a sentence is correct, write "correct" after it. Answers to lettered sentences appear in the back of the book. Example:

On our trip to the West, we visited the grand canyon and the great salt desert.

a. Assistant dean Shirin Ahmadi recommended offering more world language courses.

b. We went to the Mark Taper Forum to see a production of *Angels in America*.

c. Kalindi has an ambitious semester, studying differential calculus, classical hebrew, brochure design, and greek literature.

d. Lydia's Aunt and Uncle make modular houses as beautiful as modernist works of art.

e. We amused ourselves on the long flight by discussing how Spring in Kyoto stacks up against Summer in London.

1. When the Ducati will not start, I try a few tricks with the ignition key: Jiggling it to the left, pulling it out a quarter of an inch, and gently pulling down on it.

2. When you slowly bake a clove of garlic, the most amazing thing happens: It loses its bitter tang and becomes sweet and buttery.

3. After World War II, aunt Helena left Poland to study in Italy.

4. When we drove through the south last year, we enjoyed stopping at the peanut stands along the road.

5. Following in his sister's footsteps, Leonid is pursuing a degree in Marketing Research.

hackerhandbooks.com/bedhandbook > Grammar exercises > Mechanics > E-ex 45–2

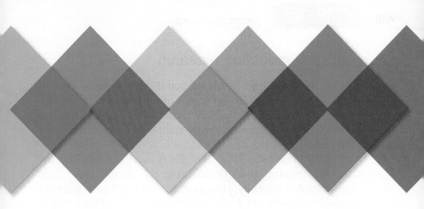

Part IX
Researched Writing

437

46 Conducting research

College research assignments ask you to pose a question worth exploring, to read widely in search of possible answers, to interpret what you read, to draw reasoned conclusions, and to support those conclusions with valid and well-documented evidence.

The process takes time: time for researching and time for drafting, revising, and documenting the paper in the style recommended by your instructor (see 49). Before beginning a research project, set a realistic schedule of deadlines. Think about how much time you might need for each step on the way to your final draft.

SAMPLE STEPS IN A RESEARCH ASSIGNMENT

Receive and analyze the assignment.

Pose questions you might explore.

Talk with a reference librarian and plan a search strategy.

Settle on a topic.

Locate sources.

Read and take notes.

Draft a working thesis and an outline.

Draft the paper.

Visit the writing center to discuss a revision plan.

Do additional research if needed.

Revise the paper; if necessary, revise the thesis.

Prepare a list of works cited.

Proofread the final draft.

Submit the final draft.

One student created a calendar to map out her tasks for a research paper assigned on October 3 and due October 31, keeping in mind that some tasks might overlap or need to be repeated. Notice that she has budgeted more than a week for

SAMPLE CALENDAR FOR A RESEARCH ASSIGNMENT

drafting and revising the paper. It's easy to spend too much time gathering sources; make sure you allow a significant portion of your schedule for drafting and revising your work.

Sections 46 and 47 include examples related to three sample student research papers:

- A paper on Internet surveillance in the workplace, written by a student in an English composition class (see pp. 583–88). The student, Anna Orlov, uses the MLA (Modern Language Association) style of documentation. (See highlights of Orlov's research process on pp. 573–82.)

- A paper on the limitations of medications to treat childhood obesity, written by a student in a psychology class (see pp. 674–83). The student, Luisa Mirano, uses the APA (American Psychological Association) style of documentation.

- A paper on the extent to which Civil War general Nathan Bedford Forrest can be held responsible for the Fort Pillow massacre, written by a student in a history class (see pp. 718–26). The student, Ned Bishop, uses the *Chicago Manual of Style* documentation system.

46a Pose questions you might explore.

Working within the guidelines of your assignment, pose a few questions that seem worth researching. Here, for example, are some preliminary questions jotted down by students enrolled in a variety of courses in different disciplines.

- Should the FCC broaden its definition of indecent programming to include violence?

- Which geological formations are the safest repositories for nuclear waste?

- What was Marcus Garvey's contribution to the fight for racial equality?

- How can governments and zoos help preserve Asia's endangered snow leopard?

- Why was amateur archaeologist Heinrich Schliemann such a controversial figure in his own time?

As you think about possible questions, make sure that they are appropriate lines of inquiry for a research paper. Choose questions that are narrow (not too broad), challenging (not too bland), and grounded (not too speculative).

Choosing a narrow question

If your initial question is too broad, given the length of the paper you plan to write, look for ways to restrict your focus (see the chart on p. 5). Here, for example, is how three students narrowed their initial questions.

TOO BROAD	NARROWER
What are the hazards of fad diets?	Why are low-carbohydrate diets hazardous?
What are the benefits of stricter auto emissions standards?	How will stricter auto emissions standards create new, more competitive auto industry jobs?
What causes depression?	How has the widespread use of antidepressant drugs affected teenage suicide rates?

Choosing a challenging question

Your research paper will be more interesting to both you and your audience if you base it on an intellectually challenging line of inquiry. Avoid bland questions that fail to provoke thought or engage readers in a debate.

TOO BLAND	CHALLENGING
What is obsessive-compulsive disorder?	Why is obsessive-compulsive disorder so difficult to treat?
Where is wind energy being used?	What makes wind farms economically viable?
How does DNA testing work?	How reliable is DNA testing?

You may need to address a bland question in the course of answering a more challenging one. For example, if you were writing about promising treatments for obsessive-compulsive disorder, you would no doubt answer the question "What is obsessive-compulsive disorder?" at some point in your paper. It would be a mistake, however, to use the bland question as the focus for the whole paper.

Choosing a grounded question

Finally, you will want to make sure that your research question is grounded, not too speculative. Although speculative questions—such as those that address philosophical, ethical, or religious issues—are worth asking and may receive some attention in a research paper, they are inappropriate central questions. The central argument of a research paper should be grounded in facts; it should not be based entirely on beliefs.

TOO SPECULATIVE	GROUNDED
Is it wrong to share music files on the Internet?	How has Internet file sharing affected the earning potential of musicians?
Do medical scientists have the right to experiment on animals?	How have technical breakthroughs made medical experiments on animals increasingly unnecessary?
Are youth sports too dangerous?	Why should school districts fund cardiac screening for all student athletes?

hackerhandbooks.com/bedhandbook > Research exercises > Researching
> E-ex 46–1

46b Map out a search strategy.

A search strategy is a systematic plan for tracking down sources. To create a search strategy appropriate for your research question, consult a reference librarian and take a look at your library's Web site, which will give you an overview of available resources.

Getting started

Reference librarians are information specialists who can save you time by steering you toward relevant and reliable sources. With the help of an expert, you can make the best use of electronic databases, Web search engines, your library's catalog, and other reference tools.

Before you ask a reference librarian for help, be sure you have thought through the following questions:

- What is your assignment?
- In which academic discipline are you writing?
- What is your tentative research question?
- How long will the paper be?
- How much time can you spend on the project?

It's a good idea to bring a copy of the assignment with you.

In addition to speaking with a reference librarian, take some time to explore your library's Web site. You will typically find links to the library's catalog and to a variety of databases and electronic sources that you can access from any networked computer. You may also find resources listed by subject, research guides, information about interlibrary loans, and links to Web sites selected by librarians for their quality. Many libraries offer online reference assistance to help you locate information and refine your search strategy.

NOTE FOR DISTANCE LEARNERS: Even if you are unable to visit the library, as an enrolled student you can still use its resources. Most libraries offer chat reference services and access to online databases, though you may have to follow special procedures to use them. Check your library's Web site for information for distance learners.

Including the library in your plan

You may be tempted to ignore your library's resources, but using them can save you time and money in the end. Libraries weed out questionable sources and make a wide range of quality materials readily available.

While a general Internet search might seem quick and convenient, it is often more time-consuming and can be less reliable than a search in a library's databases. Initial searches may generate thousands of results. Figuring out which of these

LIBRARY HOME PAGE

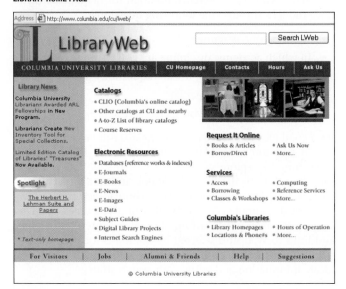

are credible, relevant, and worth further investigation can require many additional steps:

- Refining search terms to generate fewer results (See the chart on refining keyword searches on p. 449.)
- Narrowing the domain to include only .org, .gov, or .edu sites
- Weeding out any advertisements associated with results
- Determining which sites might present useful arguments by scanning their titles and, in some cases, viewing their content
- Visiting sites that seem promising to determine their currency and relevance
- Combing through sites to determine the credibility of their authors

Starting with your library's collection of databases to run the same search can save you time and effort. Library database searches will turn up a manageable number of results, most of which are relevant, even if your initial search is broader than it should be. Because these searches are limited to only academic databases, you can count on finding reliable sources. Not all of the results will be worth examining in detail, but most library searches automatically sort them into subject categories that allow you to view narrowed results with just one click.

Using library databases can also save money. Most college assignments will require using at least some books and scholarly journal articles. Internet search engines can help you locate such sources, but the published texts are often not free online. *Google Scholar*, for example, provides scholarly results, but often you have to pay a fee or purchase a subscription to access the full texts. Most libraries subscribe to databases that will give you unlimited access to many of these materials as well as scholarly resources that might not turn up outside of a database. You will be able to do some of your work from any computer that can connect to the campus network.

Choosing an appropriate search strategy

No single search strategy works for every topic. For some topics, it may be appropriate to search for information in newspapers, magazines, and Web sites. For others, the best sources might be found in scholarly journals and books and specialized reference works. Still other topics might be enhanced by field research—interviews, surveys, or direct observation.

With the help of a reference librarian, each of the students mentioned on page 440 constructed a search strategy appropriate for his or her research question.

Anna Orlov Anna Orlov's topic, Internet surveillance in the workplace, was current and influenced by technological changes, so she relied heavily on recent sources, especially those online. To find information on her topic, Orlov decided to

- search her library's general database for articles in magazines, newspapers, and journals
- check the library's catalog for recently published books
- use Web search engines, such as *Google*, to locate articles and government publications that might not show up in a database search

Luisa Mirano Luisa Mirano's topic, the limitations of medications for childhood obesity, is the subject of psychological studies as well as articles in the popular press (newspapers and magazines aimed at the general public). Thinking that both scholarly and popular works would be appropriate, Mirano decided to

- locate books through her library's catalog
- check a specialized encyclopedia, *Encyclopedia of Psychology*
- search a specialized database, *PsycINFO*, for scholarly articles
- search her library's general database for popular articles

Ned Bishop Ned Bishop's topic, Nathan Bedford Forrest's role in the Fort Pillow massacre, has been investigated and debated by professional historians. Given the nature of his historical topic, Bishop decided to

- locate books through his library's catalog
- locate scholarly articles by searching a specialized database, *America: History and Life*
- locate newspaper articles from 1864 by searching the historical archive at the *New York Times* Web site
- search the Web for other historical primary sources

46c To locate articles, search a database or consult a print index.

Libraries subscribe to a variety of electronic databases (sometimes called *periodical databases*) that give students access to articles and other materials without charge. Because many databases are limited to recent works, you may need to consult a print index as well.

What databases offer

Your library has access to databases that can lead you to articles in periodicals such as newspapers, magazines, and scholarly or technical journals. Some databases cover several subject areas; others cover one subject area in depth. Your library might subscribe to some of the following databases.

General databases College libraries typically subscribe to one or more general databases. The information in those databases is not restricted to a specific discipline or subject area. You may find searching a general database helpful in the early stages of your research process.

Academic Search Premier. An interdisciplinary database that indexes thousands of popular and scholarly journals on all subjects, offering many articles in full text.

Expanded Academic ASAP. An interdisciplinary database that indexes the contents of magazines, newspapers, and scholarly journals in all subject areas. It also includes many full-text articles.

JSTOR. A full-text archive of scholarly journals from many disciplines; unlike most databases, it includes articles published decades ago but does not include articles from the most recent issues of publications.

LexisNexis. A database that is particularly strong in coverage of news, business, legal, and political topics. Nearly all of the material is available in full text.

ProQuest. A database of periodical articles, many in full text. Through *ProQuest*, your library may subscribe to databases in subjects such as nursing, biology, and psychology.

Subject-specific databases Libraries have dozens of specialized databases covering many different subjects. Your library's

Web site will guide you to what's available. The following are examples of subject-specific databases.

ERIC. A database offering education-related documents and abstracts of articles published in education journals.

MLA Bibliography. A database of literary criticism, with citations to help researchers find articles, books, and dissertations.

PsycINFO. A comprehensive database of psychology research, including abstracts of articles in journals and books.

PubMed. A database offering millions of abstracts of medical research studies.

Many databases include the full text of at least some articles; others list only citations or citations with short summaries called *abstracts.* In the case of full-text articles, you may have the option to print an article, save it, or e-mail it to yourself.

When full text is not available, the citation will give you enough information to track down an article. Your library's Web site will help you determine which articles are available in your library, either in print or in electronic form. If the library does not own the item you want, you can usually request a copy through interlibrary loan; check with a librarian to find out how long it may take for the source to arrive.

Making the most of your handbook

Freewriting, listing, and clustering can help you come up with additional search terms.

▶ Exploring your subject: 1b

How to search a database

To find articles on your topic in a database, start with a keyword search. If the first keyword you try results in too few or no matches, experiment with synonyms or ask a librarian for suggestions. For example, if you're searching for sources on a

Refining keyword searches in databases and search engines

Although command terms and characters vary among electronic databases and Web search engines, some of the most commonly used functions are listed here.

- Use quotation marks around words that are part of a phrase: "gateway drug".

- Use AND to connect words that must appear in a document: hyperactivity AND children. In some search engines—*Google*, for example—*and* is assumed, so typing it is unnecessary. Other search engines require a plus sign instead: hyperactivity +children.

- Use NOT in front of words that must not appear in a document: shepherd NOT dog. Some search engines require a minus sign (hyphen) instead: shepherd -dog.

- Use OR if only one of the terms must appear in a document: "mountain lion" OR cougar.

- Use an asterisk as a substitute for letters that might vary: "marine biolog*" (to find *marine biology* or *marine biologist*, for example).

- Use parentheses to group a search expression and combine it with another: (standard OR student OR test*) AND reform.

NOTE: Many search engines and databases offer an advanced search option that makes it easy to refine your search.

topic related to education, you might also try the terms *teaching*, *learning*, *pedagogy*, and *curriculum*. If your keyword search results in too many matches, narrow it by using one of the strategies in the chart on this page.

For her paper on Internet surveillance in the workplace, Anna Orlov conducted a keyword search in a general periodical database. She typed "*internet use*" and *employee* and *surveillance* (see the database screen on p. 450). This search brought up twenty possible articles, some of which looked promising.

DATABASE SCREEN: KEYWORD SEARCH

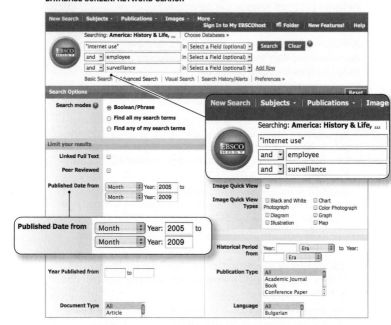

(See pp. 575–76 to view Orlov's annotated list of search results.) Orlov e-mailed several full-text articles to herself and printed citations to others so that she could locate them in the library.

When to use a print index

A print index to periodical articles is a useful tool when you are researching a historical topic, especially from the early to mid-twentieth century. The *Readers' Guide to Periodical Literature* or *Poole's Index to Periodical Literature* indexes magazine articles beginning around 1900, many of which are too old to appear in electronic databases. You can usually access the print articles themselves in your library's shelves, on microfilm or microfiche, or by interlibrary loan.

46d To locate books, consult the library's catalog.

The books your library owns are listed in its catalog, along with other resources such as videos. You can search the catalog by author, title, or subject keywords.

If your first search calls up too few results, try different keywords or search for books on broader topics. If your search gives you too many results, use the strategies in the chart on page 449 or try an advanced search tool to combine concepts and limit your results. If those strategies don't work, ask a librarian for suggestions.

When Luisa Mirano, whose topic was childhood obesity, entered the term *obesity* into the library's catalog, she was faced with an unmanageable number of hits. She narrowed her search by adding two specific terms to *obesity*: *child** (to include the terms *child*, *children*, and *childhood*) and *treatment*. When she still got too many results, she limited the first two terms to subject searches to find books with obesity in children as their primary subject. Mirano's advanced search and the seven records she retrieved are illustrated in screens 1 and 2.

**LIBRARY CATALOG SCREEN 1:
ADVANCED SEARCH**

LIBRARY CATALOG SCREEN 2: SEARCH RESULTS

MNCAT Twin Cities
Results for : All Subjects KW= (obesity) AND All Subjects KW= (child*) AND General Key
Sort options : ◦Author/Year(d)◦ Year(d)/Author ◦Author/Title ◦Title/Year(d) ◦Year(d)/Title

Records 1 - 7 of 7

#	Title	Author
1 ☐	Treatment of overweight children and adolescents : a needs assessment of health practitioners.	
2 ☐	Body image, eating disorders, and obesity in youth : assessment, prevention, and treatment /	Thompson, J. Kevin.
3 ☐	Childhood and adolescent obesity /	Styne, Dennis M.
4 ☐	Obesity : impact on cardiovascular disease /	Fletcher, Gerald F., 1935-
5 ☐	Obesity in childhood and adolescence : assessment, prevention and treatment : papers emanating from a conference held in Minneapolis, Minnesota, USA, May, 1997 /	Himes, J. H. (John H.)
6 ☐	Prevention and treatment of childhood obesity /	Williams, Christine L., 1943-
7 ☐	Treating childhood and adolescent obesity /	Kirschenbaum, Daniel S.,

LIBRARY CATALOG SCREEN 3: COMPLETE RECORD FOR A BOOK

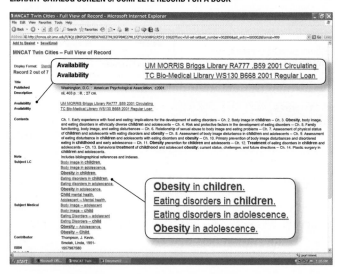

Once you have narrowed your search to a list of relevant sources, you can display or save the complete record for each source, which includes its bibliographic information (author, title, publication information) and a call number. Screen 3 shows the complete record for the second title on the list generated by Mirano's search. The call number, listed beside *Availability*, is the book's address on the library shelf. When you're retrieving a book from the shelf, take the time to scan other books in the area since they are likely to be on the same topic.

LIBRARIAN'S TIP: The catalog record for a book lists related subject headings. These headings are a good way to locate other books on your subject. For example, the record in screen 3 lists the terms *obesity in children* and *obesity in adolescence* as related subject headings. By clicking on these new terms, Mirano found a few more books on her subject. Subject headings can be useful terms for a database search as well.

46e To locate other sources, use a variety of online tools.

You can find a variety of reliable sources using online tools beyond those offered by your library. For example, most government agencies post information on their Web sites, and federal and state governments use Web sites to communicate with citizens. The sites of many private organizations, such as Doctors without Borders and the Sierra Club, contain useful information about current issues. Museums and libraries often post digital versions of primary sources, such as photographs, political speeches, and classic literary texts.

Although the Internet at large can be a rich source of information, some of which can't be found anywhere else, it lacks quality control. The material on many sites has not necessarily been reviewed by experts. So when you're not working with your library's tools to locate online sources, carefully evaluate what you find (see 47e).

This section describes the following general Web resources: search engines, directories, digital archives, government and news sites, blogs, and wikis.

hackerhandbooks.com/bedhandbook > Additional resources > Links Library
> Conducting research

Search engines

When using a search engine, such as *Google* or *Ask.com*, focus your search as narrowly as possible. You can refine your search by using many of the tips in the chart on page 449 or by using the search engine's advanced search form. For her paper on Internet surveillance in the workplace, Anna Orlov had difficulty restricting the number of hits. When she typed the words *internet*, *surveillance*, *workplace*, and *privacy* into a search engine, she got more than 80,000 matches. After examining the first page of results and viewing some that looked promising, Orlov grouped her search terms into the phrases "*internet surveillance*" and "*workplace privacy*" and added the term *employee* to narrow the focus. The result was 422 matches. To refine her search further, Orlov clicked on Advanced Search and restricted her search to sites with URLs ending in *.org* and to those updated in the last three months. (See the results screen on p. 455.)

Directories

If you want to find good resources on topics too broad for a search engine, try a directory. Unlike search engines, directories are put together by information specialists who choose reputable sites and arrange them by topic: education, health, politics, and so on.

Some directories are particularly useful for research. For example, links included in the *Internet Scout Project* are selected by an expert research team and include annotations that both describe and evaluate each site.

SEARCH ENGINE SCREEN: RESULTS OF AN ADVANCED SEARCH

Web Results 1 - 5 of about 9 over the past 3 months for "Internet surveillance" employee "workplace privacy"

Web Results 1 - 5 of about 9 over the past 3 months for "Internet surveillance" employee "workplace privacy" site:.org (0.44 seconds)

Tip: Try removing quotes from your search to get more results.

EPIC/PI - Privacy & Human Rights 2000
Now the supervision of **employee**'s performance, behavior and... [89]Information and Privacy Commissioner/Ontario, **Workplace Privacy**: The Need for a..
www.privacyinternational.org/survey/phr2000/threats.html - 131k Cached - Similar pages

Privacy and Human Rights 2003: Threats to Privacy
Other issues that raise **workplace privacy** concerns are employer requirements that **employees** complete medical tests, questionnaires, and polygraph tests..
www.privacyinternational.org/survey/phr2003/threats.htm - 279k Cached - Similar pages
[More results from www.privacyinternational.org]

[PDF] Monitoring **Employee** E-Mail And Internet Usage: Avoiding The..
File Format: PDF/Adobe Acrobat -View as HTML
Internet surveillance by employers in the American workplace. At present, US **employees** in the private workplace have no constitutional, common law or statu
lsr.nellco.org/cgi/viewcontent.cgi?article=1006&context=suffolk/lp - Similar pages

Previous EPIC Top News
The agencies plan to use RFID to track **employees**' movements and in ID cards... For more information on **workplace privacy**, see the EPIC **Workplace Privacy**...
www.epic.org/news/2005.html - 163k Cached - Similar pages

The following directories are especially useful for scholarly research:

Internet Scout Project <http://scout.wisc.edu/Archives>

Librarian's Internet Index <http://lii.org>

Open Directory Project <http://dmoz.org>

WWW Virtual Library <http://vlib.org>

Digital archives

Archives are a good place to find primary sources. They may contain the texts of poems, books, speeches, and historically significant documents; photographs; and political cartoons.

The materials in these sites are usually limited to official documents and older works because of copyright laws. The following online archives are impressive collections:

American Memory <http://memory.loc.gov>

Avalon Project <http://yale.edu/lawweb/avalon/avalon.htm>

Eurodocs <http://eudocs.lib.byu.edu>

Google Books <http:// books.google.com>

Google Scholar <http://scholar.google.com>

The Making of America <http://quod.lib.umich.edu/m/moagrp>

Online Books Page <http://onlinebooks.library.upenn.edu>

Government and news sites

For current topics, both government and news sites can prove useful. Many government agencies at every level provide online information. Government-maintained sites include resources such as legal texts, facts and statistics, government reports, and searchable reference databases. Here are just a few government sites:

Fedstats <http://www.fedstats.gov>

GPO Access <http://www.gpoaccess.gov>

United Nations <http://www.un.org>

University of Michigan Documents Center <http://www.lib.umich.edu/govdocs>

US Census Bureau <http://www.census.gov>

NOTE: You can access a state's Web site by putting the two-letter state abbreviation into a standard URL: <http://www.state .ga.us>. Substitute any state's two-letter abbreviation for the letters *ga*, which in this case stand for Georgia.

Many news organizations offer up-to-date information on the Web. Some require registration and may charge fees for some articles. Check with your library to see if it subscribes to online newspapers that you can access at no charge. The following are some free news sites:

BBC <http://www.bbc.co.uk>

Google News <http://news.google.com>

Kidon Media-Link <http://www.kidon.com/media-link>

New York Times <http://nytimes.com>

Blogs

A blog (short for *Weblog*) is a site that contains dated text or multimedia entries usually written and maintained by one person, with comments contributed by readers. Though some blogs are personal diaries and others are devoted to partisan politics, many journalists and academics maintain blogs that cover topics of interest to researchers. Some blogs feature short essays that provide useful insights or analysis; others point to new developments in an area of interest. Because blogs are frequently updated, you may want to subscribe to especially useful ones. The following Web sites can lead you to a wide range of blogs:

Academic Blog Portal <http://academicblogs.org>

Google Blog Search <http://www.google.com/blogsearch>

Science Blogs <http://scienceblogs.com>

Technorati <http://technorati.com>

Wikis

A wiki is a collaborative Web site with many contributors and with content that may change frequently. *Wikipedia*, the collaborative online encyclopedia, is one of the most frequently consulted wikis.

In general, *Wikipedia* may be helpful if you're checking for something that is common knowledge (facts available in multiple sources, such as dates and well-known historical events) or looking for very current information about a topic in contemporary culture that isn't covered elsewhere. However, many scholars do not consider *Wikipedia* and wikis in general to be appropriate sources for college research. Authorship is open to anyone, not limited to experts; articles may be written by enthusiastic amateurs who are not well informed. And because the articles can be changed by anyone, controversial texts are often altered to reflect a particular perspective and are especially susceptible to bias. When possible, locate and cite another, more reliable source for any useful information you find in a wiki. (Sometimes a wiki's own citations can lead you to such credible sources.) If you cannot find a second source, check with your instructor before integrating ideas from a wiki into your researched writing.

46f Use other search tools.

In addition to articles, books, and online sources, you may want to consult references such as encyclopedias and almanacs. Citations in scholarly works can also lead you to additional sources.

Reference works

The reference section of the library holds both general and specialized encyclopedias, dictionaries, almanacs, atlases, and biographical references, some available in electronic form through the library's Web site. Such works often provide a good overview of your subject and include references to the most significant works on a topic. Check with a reference librarian to see which works are most appropriate for your project.

General reference works General reference works are good places to check facts and get basic information. Here are a few frequently used general references:

American National Biography

National Geographic Atlas of the World

The New Encyclopaedia Britannica

The Oxford English Dictionary

Statistical Abstract of the United States

Although general encyclopedias are often a good place to find background about your topic, you should rarely use them in your final paper. Most instructors expect you to rely on more specialized sources.

Specialized reference works   Specialized reference works often explore a topic in depth, usually in the form of articles written by leading authorities. They offer a quick way to gain an expert's overview of a complex topic. Many specialized works are available, including these:

Contemporary Authors

Encyclopedia of Bioethics

Encyclopedia of Crime and Justice

Encyclopedia of Psychology

Encyclopedia of World Environmental History

International Encyclopedia of Communication

New Encyclopedia of Africa

Check with a reference librarian to see what specialized references are available for your topic.

hackerhandbooks.com/bedhandbook > Research and Documentation Online
> Finding sources

Bibliographies and scholarly citations as shortcuts

Scholarly books and articles list the works the author has cited, usually at the end. These lists are useful shortcuts to additional reliable sources on your topic. For example, most of the scholarly articles Luisa Mirano consulted contained citations to related research studies, selected by experts in the field; through these citations, she quickly located other sources related to her topic, treatments for childhood obesity. If you need help using an author's citations to find additional sources, ask a reference librarian.

46g Conduct field research, if appropriate.

Your own field research can enhance or be the focus of a writing project. For a composition class, for example, you might want to interview a local politician about a current issue, such as the use of alternative energy sources. For a sociology class, you might decide to conduct a survey regarding campus trends in community service. At work, you might need to learn how food industry executives have responded to reports that their products are contributing to health problems.

NOTE: Colleges and universities often require researchers to submit projects to an institutional review board (IRB) if the research involves human subjects outside of a classroom setting. Before administering a survey or conducting other fieldwork, check with your instructor to see if IRB approval is required.

Interviewing

Interviews can often shed new light on a topic. Look for an expert who has firsthand knowledge of the subject or seek out someone whose personal experience provides a valuable perspective on your topic.

When asking for an interview, be clear about who you are, what the purpose of the interview is, and how you would prefer to conduct it: via e-mail, over the phone, or in person. Plan for the interview by writing down a series of questions. Try to avoid questions with yes or no answers or those that encourage vague rambling. Instead, ask questions that lead to facts, anecdotes, and opinions that will add a meaningful dimension to your paper.

INEFFECTIVE INTERVIEW QUESTIONS

How many years have you spent studying childhood obesity?

Is your work interesting?

EFFECTIVE INTERVIEW QUESTIONS

What are some current interpretations of the causes of childhood obesity?

What treatments have you found to be most effective? Why do you think they work?

When quoting your source in your paper, be as accurate and fair as possible. To ensure accuracy, you might want to ask permission to record the interview; if you cannot record it, take careful notes or conduct it by e-mail.

Surveying opinion

For some topics, you may find it useful to survey opinions through written questionnaires, telephone or e-mail polls, or questions posted on a Web forum. Many people are reluctant to fill out long questionnaires or answer long-winded telephone pollsters, so if you want a good response rate, you will need to limit your questions and frame them carefully.

When possible, ask yes/no questions or give multiple-choice options. Surveys with such queries can be completed quickly, and they are easy to tabulate.

SAMPLE YES/NO QUESTION

Do you favor the use of Internet surveillance in the workplace?

You may also want to ask a few open-ended questions to elicit more individual responses, some of which may be worth quoting in your paper.

SAMPLE OPEN-ENDED QUESTION

What, if any, experiences have you had with Internet surveillance in the workplace?

Some online survey companies such as SurveyMonkey <http://www.surveymonkey.com> and Zoomerang <http://zoomerang.com> host Web-based surveys and provide for a limited number of questions and responses for free. They allow you to create easy-to-take online surveys and collate the results. See the note on page 460 if you intend to survey students on your campus.

Visiting and observing

Your firsthand observations of significant places, people, or events can enhance a paper in a variety of disciplines. For example, while researching trends in contemporary American folk art, a student in New York City went to an exhibit on folk art at the Museum of Modern Art. To gather information for a paper on nineteenth-century utopian experiments, a student in Peoria, Illinois, drove to nearby Bishop Hill, a commune founded in 1846 by Swedish refugees seeking religious freedom. For his political science paper on civic participation, a student in Salt Lake City attended a local school board meeting.

Contacting organizations

Many organizations, both public and private, have information on their Web sites and may provide literature in response to a phone call, an e-mail, or a letter. Although this literature sometimes contains up-to-date information, use it judiciously. Groups tend to promote their own interests; you can't always count on them to present a balanced view.

The Encyclopedia of Associations (available electronically and in print) lists groups by their concerns, such as the environment or health care, and provides addresses and phone numbers.

47 Evaluating sources

With electronic search tools, you can often locate dozens or even hundreds of potential sources for your topic—far more than you will have time to read. Your challenge will be to determine what kinds of sources you need and to zero in on a reasonable number of quality sources, those truly worth your time and attention.

Later, once you have decided on some sources worth consulting, your challenge will be to read them with an open mind and a critical eye.

47a Think about how sources might contribute to your writing.

How you plan to use sources will affect how you evaluate them. Not every source must directly support your thesis; sources can have other functions in a paper:

- provide background information or context for your topic
- explain terms or concepts that your readers might not understand
- provide evidence for your argument
- lend authority to your argument
- offer counterevidence and alternative interpretations to your argument

One student, for example, wrote an essay arguing that public funding for the arts should be granted on artistic merit alone and not on so-called decency standards. She used a 1998 Supreme Court decision (*National Endowment for the Arts v. Finley*) and the text of the First Amendment to provide background on the decency debate in the arts and to set her argument in context. She used published interviews given by controversial artists Karen Finley and Tim Miller to lend authority to her argument. She also used passages from a profile of conservative North Carolina senator Jesse Helms to represent an alternative point of view in the debate. With her overall purpose in mind, the student judged each source according to the specific role it would play in her argument. For more examples of how student writers use sources for a variety of purposes, see 50c, 56a, 57a, and page 574.

47b Select sources worth your time and attention.

Section 46 shows how to refine your searches in databases, in the library's book catalog, and in search engines. This section explains how to scan through the results for the most promising sources and how to preview them—without actually reading them—to see whether they are likely to live up to your expectations and meet your needs.

Scanning search results

As you scan through a list of search results, watch for clues indicating whether a source might be useful for your purposes or not worth pursuing. (For an annotated list of one student's search results, see pp. 575–76.) You will need to use somewhat different strategies when scanning search results from a database, a book catalog, and a Web search engine.

Databases Most databases, such as *Expanded Academic ASAP*, list at least the following information, which can help you decide if a source is relevant, current, scholarly enough (see the chart on p. 468), and a suitable length for your purposes.

Title and brief description (How relevant?)

Date (How current?)

Name of periodical (How scholarly?)

Length (How extensive in coverage?)

On the following page are just a few of the hits Ned Bishop came up with when he consulted a general database for articles on the Fort Pillow massacre, using the search term *Fort Pillow*.

Many databases allow you to sort your list of results by relevance or date; sorting may help you scan the information more efficiently. By scanning the titles in his search results, Bishop saw that only one contained the words *Fort Pillow*. The name of the periodical in which it appeared, *Journal of American History*, suggested that the source was scholarly. The

EVALUATING SEARCH RESULTS: LIBRARY DATABASE

☐ **Black, blue and gray: the other Civil War; African-American soldiers, sailors and spies were the** Mark **unsung heroes.** *Ebony* Feb 1991 v46 n4 p96(6) View text and retrieval choices	Popular magazine. Not relevant.
☐ **The Civil War.** (movie reviews) Lewis Cole. *The Nation* Dec 3, 1990 v251 n19 p694(5) Mark View text and retrieval choices	Movie review. Not relevant.
☐ **The hard fight was getting into the fight at all.** (black soldiers in the Civil War) Jack Fincher. Mark *Smithsonian* Oct 1990 v21 n7 p46(13) View text and retrieval choices	Subject too broad.
☑ **The Fort Pillow massacre: a statistical note.** John Cimprich, Robert C. Mainfort Jr.. *Journal of America* Mark *History* Dec 1989 v76 n3 p830(8) View extended citation and retrieval choices	Brief scholarly article. Matches the student's topic. Promising.

1989 publication date was not a problem, since currency is not necessarily a key issue for historical topics. The article's length (eight pages) is given in parentheses at the end of the citation. While the article may seem short, the topic—a statistical note—is narrow enough to ensure adequate depth of coverage. Bishop decided that the article was worth consulting. Because the other sources were irrelevant or too broad, he decided not to consult them.

Book catalogs   The library's book catalog usually lists basic information about books, enough for a first impression (see also p. 452). A book's title and date of publication will often be your first clues about whether the book is worth consulting. Be cautious about books that were published ten or more years ago; depending on the topic, they may be outdated. If a title looks interesting, you can click on it for information about the book's subject matter and its length. The table of contents may also be available, offering a glimpse of what's inside.

Web search engines   Because anyone can publish a Web site, legitimate sources and unreliable sources live side-by-side online. As you scan through search results, look for the following clues about the probable relevance, currency, and reliability of a site—but be aware that the clues are by no means foolproof.

The title, keywords, and lead-in text (How relevant?)

A date (How current?)

An indication of the site's sponsor or purpose (How reliable?)

The URL, especially the domain name extension: for example, .com, .edu, .gov, or .org (How relevant? How reliable?)

At the bottom of this page are a few of the results that Luisa Mirano retrieved after typing the keywords *childhood obesity* into a search engine; she limited her search to works with those words in the title.

Mirano found the first site, sponsored by a research-based organization, promising enough to explore for her paper. The second and fourth sites held less promise because they seemed to offer popular rather than scholarly information. In addition, the *KidSource* site was populated by distracting commercial advertisements. Mirano rejected the third source not because she doubted its reliability—in fact, research from the National Institutes of Health was what she hoped to find—but because a quick skim of its contents revealed that the information was too general for her purposes.

EVALUATING SEARCH RESULTS: INTERNET SEARCH ENGINE

Content from a research-based organization. Promising.

American **Obesity** Association - **Childhood Obesity**
Childhood Obesity. Obesity in children ... Note: The term "**childhood obesity**" may refer to both **children** and adolescents. In general, we ...
www.**obesity**.org/subs/**childhood**/ - 17k - Jan 8, 2005 - Cached - Similar pages

Popular rather than scholarly source. Not relevant.

Childhood Obesity
KS Logo, **Childhood Obesity**. advertisement. Source. ERIC Clearinghouse on Teaching and Teacher Education. Contents. ... Back to the Top Causes of **Childhood Obesity**. ...
www.kidsource.com/kidsource/content2/**obesity**.html - 18k - Cached - Similar pages

Content too general. Not relevant.

Childhood Obesity, June 2002 Word on Health - National Institutes ...
Childhood Obesity on the Rise, an article in the June 2002 edition of The NIH Word on Health - Consumer Information Based on Research from the National ...
www.nih.gov/news/WordonHealth/ jun2002/**childhoodobesity**.htm - 22k -
Cached - Similar pages

Popular and too general. Not relevant.

MayoClinic.com - **Childhood obesity**: Parenting advice
... **Childhood obesity**: Parenting advice By Mayo Clinic staff. ... Here are some other tips to help your **obese child** — and yourself: Be a positive role model. ...
www.mayoclinic.com/invoke.cfm?id=FL00058 - 42k - Jan 8, 2005 - Cached - Similar pages

Previewing sources

Once you have decided that a source looks promising, preview it quickly to see whether it lives up to its promise. If you can reject irrelevant or unreliable sources before actually reading them, you will save yourself time. Techniques for previewing an article from your library's subscription database or a book are relatively simple; strategies for investigating the likely worth of a Web site are more complicated.

Previewing an article The techniques for previewing an article are fairly straightforward. In researching her paper on childhood obesity, Luisa Mirano spent no more than a few minutes scanning an article before deciding whether it was worth her time.

Here are a few strategies for previewing an article:

- Consider the publication in which the article is printed. Is it a scholarly journal (see the chart on p. 468)? A popular magazine? A newspaper with a national reputation?

- For a magazine or journal article, look for an abstract or a statement of purpose at the beginning; also look for a summary at the end.

- For a newspaper article, focus on the headline and the opening paragraphs, known as the *lead*.

- Skim any headings and look at any visuals—charts, graphs, diagrams, or illustrations—that might indicate the article's focus and scope.

Previewing a book As you preview a book, keep in mind that even if the entire book is not worth your time, parts of it may prove useful. For example, by using the indexes of several books on Civil War history, Ned Bishop quickly located useful passages describing the Fort Pillow massacre.

Try any or all of the following techniques to preview a book:

- Glance through the table of contents, keeping your research question in mind.

- Skim the preface in search of a statement of the author's purposes.
- Use the index to look up a few words related to your topic.
- If a chapter looks useful, read its opening and closing paragraphs and skim any headings.
- Consider the author's style and approach. Does the style suggest enough intellectual depth, or is the book too specialized for your purposes? Does the author present ideas in an unbiased way?

Previewing a Web site It is a fairly quick and easy job to track down numerous potentially useful sources on the Web, but evaluating those sources can require some detective work.

Determining if a source is scholarly

For many college assignments, you will be asked to use scholarly sources. These are written by experts for a knowledgeable audience and usually go into more depth than books and articles written for a general audience. (Scholarly sources are sometimes called *refereed* or *peer-reviewed* because the work is evaluated by experts in the field before publication.) To determine if a source is scholarly, you should look for the following:

- Formal language and presentation
- Authors who are academics or scientists
- Footnotes or a bibliography documenting the works cited by the author in the source
- Original research and interpretation (rather than a summary of other people's work)
- Quotations from and analysis of primary sources (in humanities disciplines such as literature, history, and philosophy)
- A description of research methods or a review of related research (in the sciences and social sciences)

NOTE: In some databases, searches can be limited to refereed or peer-reviewed journals.

Web sites can be created by anyone, and their authors and purposes are not always apparent. In addition, there are no required standards for the design of Web sites, so you may need to do a fair amount of clicking and scrolling before you locate clues about a site's reliability. In researching her paper on Internet surveillance in the workplace, Anna Orlov spent considerable time previewing Web sites, many of which she rejected (see pp. 476–77).

As you preview a Web site, check for relevance, reliability, and currency:

- Browse the home page. Do its contents and links seem relevant to your research question?

- Ask yourself what the site is trying to do: Sell a product? Promote an idea? Inform the public? Is the site's purpose consistent with your research?

- Look for the name of an author or a Webmaster and, if possible, review his or her credentials. Often a site's author is named at the bottom of the home page. If you have landed on an internal page of a site and no author is evident, try navigating to the home page, either through a link or by truncating the URL (see the tip on p. 474).

- Check for a sponsor name, and consider possible motives the organization might have for sponsoring the site. Is the group likely to look at only one side of an issue?

- Find out when the site was created or last updated. Is it current enough for your purposes?

TIP: When conducting academic research, do not rely on sites that give very little information about authors or sponsors.

Distinguishing between primary and secondary sources

As you begin assessing evidence in a source, determine whether you are reading a primary or a secondary source. Primary sources are original documents such as letters, diaries, legislative bills, laboratory studies, field research reports, and eyewitness accounts.

Secondary sources are commentaries on primary sources—another writer's opinions about or interpretation of a primary source. A primary source for Ned Bishop was Nathan Bedford Forrest's official report on the battle at Fort Pillow. Bishop also consulted a number of secondary sources, some of which relied heavily on primary sources such as letters.

Although a primary source is not necessarily more reliable than a secondary source, it has the advantage of being a first-hand account. Naturally, you can better evaluate what a secondary source says if you have first read any primary sources it discusses.

47c Select appropriate versions of online sources.

An online source may appear as an abstract, an excerpt, or a full-text article or book. It is important to distinguish among these versions of sources and to use a complete version of a source, preferably one with page numbers, for your research.

Abstracts and excerpts are shortened versions of complete works. An abstract—a summary of a work's contents—might appear in a database record for a periodical article (see p. 471) and can give you clues about the usefulness of an article for your paper. Abstracts are brief (usually fewer than five hundred words) and usually do not contain enough information to function alone as sources in a research paper. Reading the complete article is the best way to understand the author's argument before referring to it in your own writing. When you determine that the full article is worth reading, scroll through the record to find a link to the complete text in your library's databases. If you cannot access the complete article from a database, see if the library has a print copy on the shelves. Ask a librarian for assistance if you are unsure whether your library keeps the periodical.

An excerpt is the first few sentences or paragraphs of a newspaper or magazine article and sometimes appears in a list of hits in an online search (see p. 472). From an excerpt, you can often determine whether the complete article would be useful for your paper. Sometimes, however, the thesis or topic sentence of the article is buried deeper in the article than the excerpt reveals. In these cases, the headline might be a clue to the relevance of the complete article. Be sure to retrieve and read the full text of any article you might want to cite. If you are working with an Internet search engine such as *Google*, you may find that your results lead to articles available only for a fee. Before paying a fee, see if you can get the article through your library system.

A full-text work may appear online as a PDF (portable document format) file or as an HTML file (sometimes called a *text file*). A PDF file is usually an exact copy of the pages of a periodical article as they appeared in print, including the page numbers. Some corporate and government reports are presented online as PDF files, and they are usually paginated. A full-text document that appears as an HTML or a text file is not paginated. If your source is available in both formats, choose the PDF file for your research because you will be able to cite specific page numbers.

DATABASE RECORD WITH AN ABSTRACT

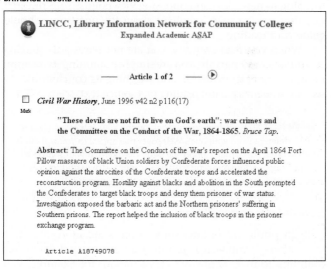

LINCC, Library Information Network for Community Colleges
Expanded Academic ASAP

—— Article 1 of 2 ——

☐ *Civil War History*, June 1996 v42 n2 p116(17)
Mark

"These devils are not fit to live on God's earth": war crimes and the Committee on the Conduct of the War, 1864-1865. *Bruce Tap*.

Abstract: The Committee on the Conduct of the War's report on the April 1864 Fort Pillow massacre of black Union soldiers by Confederate forces influenced public opinion against the atrocities of the Confederate troops and accelerated the reconstruction program. Hostility against blacks and abolition in the South prompted the Confederates to target black troops and deny them prisoner of war status. Investigation exposed the barbaric act and the Northern prisoners' suffering in Southern prisons. The report helped the inclusion of black troops in the prisoner exchange program.

Article A18749078

SEARCH RESULT WITH AN EXCERPT

▼ BOSTON GLOBE ARCHIVES

Your search for ((fort AND pillow AND massacre)) returned **1** article(s) matching your terms.
To purchase the full-text of an article, follow the link that says "Click for complete article."

| Perform a new search |

Your search results:

TALES OF BLACKS IN THE CIVIL WAR, FOR ALL AGES
Published on March 23, 1998
Author(s): Scott Alarik, Globe Correspondent

For African Americans, the Civil War was always two wars. It was, of course, the war to save the union and destroy slavery, but for the nearly 180,000 black soldiers who served in the Union Army, it was also a war to establish their rights as citizens and human beings in the United States. Their role in defeating the Confederacy is grandly chronicled in two new books, the massively complete "Like Men of War" and the superbly readable children's book "Black, Blue and
Click for complete article *(782 words)*

47d Read with an open mind and a critical eye.

As you begin reading the sources you have chosen, keep an open mind. Do not let your personal beliefs prevent you from listening to new ideas and opposing viewpoints. Your research question—not a snap judgment about the question—should guide your reading.

When you read critically, you are not necessarily judging an author's work harshly; you are simply examining its assumptions, assessing its evidence, and weighing its conclusions. (To see one student's careful reading of a source text, see p. 577.)

> **Academic English** When you research on the Web, it is easy to ignore views different from your own. Web pages that appeal to you will often link to other pages that support the same viewpoint. If your sources all seem to agree with you—and with one another—try to find sources with opposing views and evaluate them with an open mind.

Being alert for signs of bias

Both in print and online, some sources are more objective than others. If you were exploring the conspiracy theories surrounding John F. Kennedy's assassination, for example, you wouldn't look to a supermarket tabloid for answers. Even publications that are considered reputable can be editorially biased. For example, *USA Today*, *National Review*, and *Ms.* are all credible sources that are likely to interpret events quite differently from one another. If you are uncertain about a periodical's special interests, consult *Magazines for Libraries*. To check for bias in a book, see what book reviewers have written about it. A reference librarian can help you locate reviews and assess the credibility of both the book and the reviewers.

Like publishers, some authors are more objective than others. If you have reason to believe that a writer is particularly

Evaluating all sources

Checking for signs of bias

- Does the author or publisher endorse political or religious views that could affect objectivity?
- Is the author or publisher associated with a special-interest group, such as Greenpeace or the National Rifle Association, that might present only one side of an issue?
- Are alternative views presented and addressed? How fairly does the author treat opposing views? (See 6c.)
- Does the author's language show signs of bias? (See 6b.)

Assessing an argument

- What is the author's central claim or thesis?
- How does the author support this claim—with relevant and sufficient evidence or with just a few anecdotes or emotional examples?
- Are statistics consistent with those you encounter in other sources? Have they been used fairly? Does the author explain where the statistics come from? (It is possible to "lie" with statistics by using them selectively or by omitting mathematical details.)
- Are any of the author's assumptions questionable?
- Does the author consider opposing arguments and refute them persuasively? (See 6c.)
- Does the author fall prey to any logical fallacies? (See 6a.)

biased, you will want to assess his or her arguments with special care. For a list of questions worth asking, see the chart on page 473.

Assessing the author's argument

In nearly all subjects worth writing about, there is some element of argument, so don't be surprised to encounter experts who disagree. When you find areas of disagreement, you will want to read each source's arguments with special care, testing them with your own critical intelligence. The questions in the chart on page 473 can help you weigh the strengths and weaknesses of each author's arguments.

Making the most of your handbook

Good college writers read critically.

▶ Judging whether a source is reasonable: 6a

▶ Judging whether a source is fair: 6c

47e Assess Web sources with special care.

Web sources can provide valuable information, but verifying their credibility may take time. Before using a Web source in your paper, make sure you know who created the material and for what purpose.

TIP: If both the sponsorship and the authorship of a site are unclear, think twice about using the site for your research. To discover a site's sponsor, you may have to shorten the full URL to its domain name.

> FULL URL: http://www.bankofamerica.com/environment/dex
> .cfm?template=env_reports_speeches&context=smartgrowth
>
> DOMAIN NAME: http://www.bankofamerica.com
>
> SPONSOR: Bank of America

Many sophisticated-looking sites contain questionable information. Even a well-designed hate site may at first appear unbiased and informative. Sites with reliable information, however, can stand up to careful scrutiny. For a checklist on evaluating Web sources, see the chart on page 475.

Evaluating Web sources

Authorship

- Does the Web site or document have an author? You may need to do some clicking and scrolling to find the author's name. If you have landed directly on an internal page of a site, for example, you may need to navigate to the home page or find an "about this site" link to learn the name of the author.

- If there is an author, can you tell whether he or she is knowledgeable and credible? When the author's qualifications aren't listed on the site itself, look for links to the author's home page, which may provide evidence of his or her interests and expertise.

Sponsorship

- Who, if anyone, sponsors the site? The sponsor of a site is often named and described on the home page.

- What does the URL tell you? The domain name extension often indicates the type of group hosting the site: commercial (.com), educational (.edu), nonprofit (.org), governmental (.gov), military (.mil), or network (.net). URLs may also indicate a country of origin: .uk (United Kingdom) or .jp (Japan), for instance.

Purpose and audience

- Why was the site created: To argue a position? To sell a product? To inform readers?

- Who is the site's intended audience?

Currency

- How current is the site? Check for the date of publication or the latest update, often located at the bottom of the home page or at the beginning or end of an internal page.

- How current are the site's links? If many of the links no longer work, the site may be too dated for your purposes.

Ned Bishop came across unreliable Web sources while researching his topic, the Fort Pillow massacre. This topic is of great interest to Civil War buffs, who might not have scholarly backgrounds. One impressive-looking site turned out to have been created by a high school junior—an intelligent young man, no doubt, but by no means an authority on the subject.

In researching Internet surveillance and workplace privacy, Anna Orlov encountered sites that raised her suspicions.

EVALUATING A WEB SITE: CHECKING RELIABILITY

1 This article on Internet monitoring is on a site sponsored by the Massachusetts Nurses Association, a professional health care association and union whose staff and members advocate for nurses in the workplace. The URL ending .org marks this sponsor as a nonprofit organization.

2 Clear dates of publication show currency.

3 The author is a credible expert whose credentials can be verified.

In particular, some sites were authored by surveillance software companies, which have an obvious interest in focusing on the benefits of such software to company management.

Knowing that the creator of a site is an amateur or could be biased is not sufficient reason, however, to reject the site's information out of hand. For example, the surveillance software companies' Web sites provided some insight into why company management would want to monitor employees, and the high

EVALUATING A WEB SITE: CHECKING PURPOSE

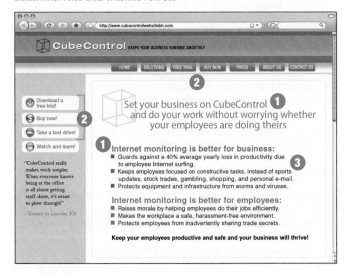

1   The site is sponsored by a company that specializes in employee monitoring software.

2   Repeated links for trial downloads and purchase suggest the site's intended audience: consumers seeking to purchase software (probably not researchers seeking detailed information about employees' use of the Internet in the workplace).

3   The site appears to provide information and even shows statistics from studies, but ultimately the purpose of the site is to sell a product.

school junior had intelligent things to say about the Fort Pillow massacre. Nevertheless, when you know something about the creator of a site and have a sense of a site's purpose, you will be in a good position to evaluate the likely worth of its information. Consider, for example, the two sites pictured on pages 476 and 477. Anna Orlov decided that the first Web site would be more useful for her project than sites like the second.

48 Managing information; avoiding plagiarism

An effective researcher is a good record keeper. Whether you decide to keep records on paper or on your computer—or both—your challenge as a researcher will be to find systematic ways of managing information. More specifically, you will need methods for maintaining a working bibliography (see 48a), keeping track of source materials (see 48b), and taking notes without plagiarizing your sources (see 48c). (For more on avoiding plagiarism, see 51 for MLA style, 56b for APA style, and 57b for *Chicago* style.)

48a Maintain a working bibliography.

Keep a record of any sources you decide to consult. You will need this record, called a *working bibliography*, when you compile the list of sources that will appear at the end of your paper. The format of this list depends on the documentation style you are using (for MLA style, see 53b; for APA style, see 56d; for *Chicago* style, see 57d). Using the proper style in your working bibliography will ensure that you have all the information you need to correctly cite any sources you use. Your working bibliography will probably contain more sources than you will actually include in the list of works cited in your final paper.

Most researchers save bibliographic information from the library's computer catalog, its periodical databases, and the Web. The information you need to collect is given in the chart on pages 480–81. If you download a visual, you must gather the same information as for a print source.

For Web sources, some bibliographic information may not be available, but spend time looking for it before assuming that it doesn't exist. When information isn't available on the home page, you may have to drill into the site, following links to interior pages. Look especially for the author's name, the date of publication (or latest update), and the name of any sponsoring organization. Do not omit such information unless it is genuinely unavailable.

Once you have created a working bibliography, you can annotate it. Writing several brief sentences summarizing key points of a source will help you identify how it relates to your argument and to your other sources. Clarifying the source's ideas at this stage will help you separate them from your own and avoid plagiarizing them later. Though annotated bibliographies can be informal writing in preparation for an essay, some instructors may require that you submit an annotated bibliography as a formal writing assignment.

SAMPLE ANNOTATED BIBLIOGRAPHY ENTRY (MLA STYLE)

Gonsalves, Chris. "Wasting Away on the Web." *eWeek.com*. Ziff Davis
Enterprise Holdings, 8 Aug. 2005. Web. 16 Feb. 2009.

Summarize the source.

    In this editorial, Gonsalves considers the implications of several surveys, including one in which 61% of respondents said that their companies have the right to spy on them. The author agrees with this majority, claiming that it's fine if his company chooses to monitor him as long as the company discloses its monitoring practices. He adds that he would prefer not to know the extent of the monitoring.

Annotations should be three to seven sentences long.

Interpret the relationship between this source and others in the bibliography.

This article, though not entirely objective, offers an employee's perspective on Internet surveillance in the workplace. It also contradicts some of my other sources, which claim that employees want to know and should know all the details of their company's monitoring procedures.

Evaluate the source for bias and relevance.

hackerhandbooks.com/bedhandbook > Model papers
> MLA annotated bibliography: Orlov
> APA annotated bibliography: Haddad

48b Keep track of source materials.

The best way to keep track of source materials is to save a copy of each one. Many database subscription services will allow you to e-mail, save, or print citations or full texts of articles, and you can easily download, copy, or take screen shots of information from the Web.

Working with photocopies, printouts, and electronic files — as opposed to relying on memory or hastily written notes — has several benefits. You save time spent in the library. You can highlight key passages, perhaps even color-coding them to reflect topics in your outline. You can annotate the source in the margins by hand or with your word processing program's comment fields and get a head start on note taking (for an example, see the annotated article on p. 577). Finally, you reduce the chances of unintentional plagiarism, since you will be able to compare your use of a source in your paper with the actual source, not just with your notes (see 48c).

NOTE: It's especially important to keep print or electronic copies of Web sources, which may change or even become

---

Information for a working bibliography

For an entire book

- All authors; any editors or translators
- Title and subtitle
- Edition (if not the first)
- Publication information: city, publisher, and date

For a periodical article

- All authors of the article
- Title and subtitle of the article
- Title of the magazine, journal, or newspaper
- Date; volume, issue, and page numbers

→

For a periodical article retrieved from a database (in addition to preceding information)

- Name of the database
- Name of the subscription service
- URL of the subscription service (for an online database)
- Accession number or other number assigned by the database
- Digital object identifier (DOI), if there is one
- Date you retrieved the source

NOTE: Use particular care when printing or saving articles in PDF files. The files themselves may not include some of the elements you need to cite the electronic source properly. You may need to record additional information from the database or Web site where you retrieved the PDF file.

For a Web source (including visuals)

- All authors, editors, or creators of the source
- Editor or compiler of the Web site, if there is one
- Title and subtitle of the source
- Title of the longer work, if applicable
- Title of the site
- Publication information for the source, if available
- Page or paragraph numbers, if any
- Date of online publication (or latest update)
- Sponsor of the site
- Date you accessed the source
- The site's URL

NOTE: For the exact bibliographic format to use in your working bibliography and in the final paper, see 53b (MLA), 56d (APA), or 57d (Chicago).

inaccessible over time. Make sure that your copy includes the site's URL and your date of access.

TIP: Your school may provide citation software, which allows researchers to download references directly from databases, import saved searches, or type in citations. Similarly, many databases format citations with a mouse click, and Web sites offer fill-in-the-blank forms for generating formatted citations. You must proofread these results carefully, however, because the programs sometimes provide incorrect results.

48c As you take notes, avoid unintentional plagiarism.

When you take notes and jot down ideas, be very careful not to borrow language from your sources. Even if you half-copy the author's sentences—either by mixing the author's phrases with your own without using quotation marks or by plugging your synonyms into the author's sentence structure—you are committing plagiarism, a serious academic offense. (For examples of this kind of plagiarism, see 51b, 56b, and 57b.)

To prevent unintentional borrowing, resist the temptation to look at the source as you take notes—except when you are quoting. Keep the source close by so you can check for accuracy, but don't try to put ideas in your own words with the source's sentences in front of you. When you need to quote the exact words of a source, make sure you copy the words precisely and put quotation marks around them.

For strategies for avoiding Internet plagiarism, see pages 485–87.

TIP: Be especially careful when using copy and paste functions in electronic files. Some researchers have unwittingly plagiarized their sources because they lost track of which words came from sources and which were their own. To prevent unintentional plagiarism, put quotation marks around any text that you plan to insert into your own work.

Academic English Even in the early stages of note taking, it is important to keep in mind that in the United States written texts are considered an author's property. (This "property" isn't a physical object, so it is often referred to as *intellectual property*.) The author (or publisher) owns the language as well as any original ideas contained in the writing, whether the source is published in print or electronic form. When you use another author's property in your own writing, you are required to follow certain conventions for citing the material, or you risk committing *plagiarism*.

There are three kinds of note taking: summarizing, paraphrasing, and quoting. Be sure to include exact page references for all three types of notes; you will need the page numbers later if you use the information in your paper.

Summarizing without plagiarizing

A summary condenses information, perhaps reducing a chapter to a short paragraph or a paragraph to a single sentence. A summary should be written in your own words; if you use phrases from the source, put them in quotation marks.

Here is a passage from a source about mountain lions. Following the passage is the student's summary. (The bibliographic information is recorded in MLA style.)

ORIGINAL SOURCE

In some respects, the increasing frequency of mountain lion encounters in California has as much to do with a growing *human* population as it does with rising mountain lion numbers. The scenic solitude of the western ranges is prime cougar habitat, and it is falling swiftly to the developer's spade. Meanwhile, with their ideal habitat already at its carrying capacity, mountain lions are forcing younger cats into less suitable terrain, including residential areas. Add that cougars have generally grown bolder under a lengthy ban on their being hunted, and an unsettling scenario begins to emerge.
—Rychnovsky, Ray. "Clawing into Controversy."
Outdoor Life Jan. 1995: 38-42. Print. [p. 40]

SUMMARY

Source: Rychnovsky, Ray. "Clawing into Controversy." *Outdoor Life* Jan.
1995: 38-42. Print. [p. 40]

Encounters between mountain lions and humans are on the rise in
California because increasing numbers of lions are competing for a
shrinking habitat. As the lions' wild habitat shrinks, older lions force
younger lions into residential areas. These lions have lost some of their
fear of humans because of a ban on hunting.

See page 579 for additional sample summaries in MLA style.

Paraphrasing without plagiarizing

Like a summary, a paraphrase is written in your own words;
but whereas a summary reports significant information in
fewer words than the source, a paraphrase retells the information in roughly the same number of words. If you retain occasional choice phrases from the source, use quotation marks so
that later you will know which phrases are not your own.

As you read the following paraphrase of the original
source (see p. 483), notice that the language is significantly
different from that in the original.

PARAPHRASE

Source: Rychnovsky, Ray. "Clawing into Controversy." *Outdoor Life* Jan.
1995: 38-42. Print. [p. 40]

Californians are encountering mountain lions more frequently because
increasing numbers of humans and a rising population of lions are
competing for the same territory. Humans have moved into
mountainous regions once dominated by the lions, and the wild
habitat that is left cannot sustain the current lion population.
Therefore, the older lions are forcing younger lions into residential
areas. And because of a ban on hunting, these younger lions have
become bolder—less fearful of encounters with humans.

See page 580 for an additional sample paraphrase in MLA style.

Using quotation marks to avoid plagiarizing

A quotation consists of the exact words from a source. In your notes, put all quoted material in quotation marks; do not assume that you will remember later which words, phrases, and passages you have quoted and which are your own. When you quote, be sure to copy the words of your source exactly, including punctuation and capitalization.

QUOTATION

Source: Rychnovsky, Ray. "Clawing into Controversy." *Outdoor Life* Jan. 1995: 38-42. Print. [p. 40]

Rychnovsky explains that as humans expand residential areas into mountain ranges, the cougar's natural habitat "is falling swiftly to the developer's spade" (40).

See page 581 for an additional sample quotation in MLA style.

Avoiding Internet plagiarism

Understand what plagiarism is. When you use another author's intellectual property—language, visuals, or ideas—in your own writing without giving proper credit, you commit a kind of academic theft called *plagiarism*.

Treat Web sources the same way you treat print sources. Any language that you find on the Internet must be carefully cited, even if the material is in the public domain or is publicly accessible on free sites. When you use material from Web sites sponsored by federal, state, or municipal governments (.gov sites) or by nonprofit organizations (.org sites), you must acknowledge that material, too, as intellectual property owned by those agencies.

Keep track of which words come from sources and which are your own. To prevent unintentional plagiarism when you copy and paste passages from Web sources to an electronic

Integrating and citing sources to avoid plagiarism

Source text

Our language is constantly changing. Like the Mississippi, it keeps forging new channels and abandoning old ones, picking up debris, depositing unwanted silt, and frequently bursting its banks. In every generation, there are people who deplore changes in the language and many who wish to stop the flow. But if our language stopped changing it would mean that American society had ceased to be dynamic, innovative, pulsing with life—that the river had frozen up.

—Robert MacNeil and William Cran,
Do You Speak American? p. 1

Avoiding plagiarism

If you are using an exact sentence from a source, with no changes at all . . .	→	. . . put quotation marks around the sentence. Use a signal phrase and include a page number in parentheses. MacNeil and Cran write, "Our language is constantly changing" (1). "Our language," according to MacNeil and Cran, "is constantly changing" (1).
If you are using a few exact words from the source but not an entire sentence . . .	→	. . . put quotation marks around the exact words that you have used from the source. Use a signal phrase and include a page number in parentheses. The English language, according to MacNeil and Cran, is "like the Mississippi" (1).
If you are using near-exact words from the source but changing some word forms (*I* to *she*, *walk* to *walked*) or adding words to	→	. . . put quotation marks around the quoted words and put brackets around the changes you have introduced. Use a signal phrase and include a page number in parentheses. MacNeil and Cran compare the English language to the Mississippi River, which "forg[es] new channels and abandon[s] old ones" (1). →

clarify and make the quotation flow with your own text . . .	"In every generation, there are people who deplore changes in the [English] language and many who wish to stop the flow," write MacNeil and Cran (1).
If you are paraphrasing or summarizing the source, using the author's ideas but not any of the author's exact words . . .	→ . . . introduce the ideas with a signal phrase and put the page number at the end of your sentence. Do not use quotation marks. (See 51, 56b, and 57b.) MacNeil and Cran argue that changes in the English language are natural and that they represent cultural progress (1).
If you have used the source's sentence structure but substituted a few synonyms for the author's words . . .	→ STOP! This is a form of plagiarism even if you use a signal phrase and a page number. Change your sentence by using one of the techniques given in this chart or in 52, 56c, or 57c. **PLAGIARIZED** MacNeil and Cran claim that, like a river, English creates new waterways and discards old ones. **INTEGRATED AND CITED CORRECTLY** MacNeil and Cran claim, "Like the Mississippi, [English] keeps forging new channels and abandoning old ones" (1).

NOTE: The examples in this chart follow MLA style (see 53). For information on APA and *Chicago* styles, see 56d and 57d, respectively.

file, put quotation marks around any text that you have inserted into your own work. In addition, during note taking and drafting, you might use a different color font or your word processing program's highlighting feature to draw attention to text taken from sources—so that material from articles, Web sites, and other sources stands out unmistakably as someone else's words.

Avoid Web sites that bill themselves as "research services" and sell essays. When you use Web search engines to research a topic, you will often see links to sites that appear to offer legitimate writing support but that actually sell college essays. Of course, submitting a paper that you have purchased is cheating, but even using material from such a paper is considered plagiarism.

For details on avoiding plagiarism while working with sources, see 51 (MLA style), 56b (APA style), and 57b (*Chicago* style).

49 Choosing a documentation style

The various academic disciplines use their own style for citing sources and for listing the works that are cited in a paper. *The Bedford Handbook* describes three commonly used styles:

Modern Language Association (MLA) in section 53

American Psychological Association (APA) in section 56d

Chicago Manual of Style (CMS) in section 57d

In researched writing, sources are cited for several reasons. First, it is important to acknowledge the contributions of others. If you fail to credit sources properly, you commit plagiarism, a serious academic offense. Second, choosing appropriate sources will add credibility to your work; in a sense, you are calling on authorities to serve as expert witnesses. The more care you have taken in choosing reliable sources, the stronger your argument will be. Finally—and most importantly—you are engaging in a scholarly conversation and showing readers where they can pursue your topic in greater depth.

All of the academic disciplines cite sources for these same reasons. However, the different styles for citing sources are based on the values and intellectual goals of scholars in different disciplines.

MLA and APA in-text citations

MLA style and APA style both use citations in the text of a paper that refer to a list of works at the end of the paper. The systems work somewhat differently, however, because MLA style was created for scholars in English composition and literature and APA style was created for researchers in the social sciences.

MLA IN-TEXT CITATION

Brandon Conran argues that the story is written from "a bifocal point of view" (111).

APA IN-TEXT CITATION

As researchers Yanovski and Yanovski (2002) have explained, obesity was once considered "either a moral failing or evidence of underlying psychopathology" (p. 592).

While MLA and APA styles work in a similar way, some basic disciplinary differences show up in these key elements:

author's name

date of publication

page numbers

verb tense in signal phrases

MLA style gives the author's full name on first mention, emphasizing authorship and interpretation. APA style, which uses last names only, gives a date after the author's name, reflecting the social scientist's concern with the currency of study findings. MLA style places the date in the works cited list but omits it in the text. While currency is important, what someone had to say a century ago may be as significant as the latest contribution to the field.

Both styles include page numbers for quotations. MLA style requires page numbers for summaries and paraphrases as well; with a page number, readers can easily find the original passage that has been summarized or paraphrased. While APA does not require page numbers for summaries and paraphrases, it recommends that writers use a page number if doing so would help readers find the passage in a longer work.

Finally, MLA style uses the present tense (such as *argues*) to introduce cited material (see 52b), whereas APA style uses the past or present perfect tense (such as *argued* or *has argued*) in signal phrases (see 56c). The present tense evokes the timelessness of a literary text; the past or present perfect tense emphasizes that research or experimentation occurred in the past.

Chicago-*style footnotes or endnotes*

Most historians and many scholars in the humanities use the style of footnotes or endnotes recommended by *The Chicago Manual of Style* (CMS). Historians base their work on a wide variety of primary and secondary sources, all of which must be cited. The *Chicago* note system has the virtue of being relatively unobtrusive; even when a paper or an article is thick with citations, readers will not be overwhelmed. In the text of the paper, only a raised number appears. Readers who are interested can consult the accompanying numbered note, which is given either at the foot of the page or at the end of the paper.

TEXT

Historian Albert Castel quotes several eyewitnesses on both the Union and the Confederate sides as saying that Forrest ordered his men to stop firing.[7]

NOTE

7. Albert Castel, "The Fort Pillow Massacre: A Fresh Examination of the Evidence," *Civil War History* 4, no. 1 (1958): 44-45.

The *Chicago* system gives as much information as the MLA or APA system, but less of that information appears in the text of the paper.

hackerhandbooks.com/resdoc > List of style manuals

Writing MLA papers

Brief directory

50 Supporting a thesis, 492

51 Citing sources; avoiding plagiarism, 498

52 Integrating sources, 504

53 MLA documentation style, 517
    Directory to MLA in-text citation models, 519
    Directory to MLA works cited models, 530

54 MLA manuscript format; student research process and sample paper, 569

55 Writing about literature, 589

Most English instructors and some humanities instructors will ask you to document your sources with the Modern Language Association (MLA) system of citations described in section 53.

When writing an MLA paper that is based on sources, you face three main challenges: (1) supporting a thesis, (2) citing your sources and avoiding plagiarism, and (3) integrating quotations and other source material.

Examples in sections 50–52 are drawn from a student's research related to online monitoring of employees' computer use. Anna Orlov's research paper, which argues that electronic surveillance in the workplace threatens employees' privacy, appears on pages 583–88. (See highlights of Anna Orlov's research process on pp. 573–82.)

If you are writing an MLA paper about literature (a short story, novel, play, film, or poem), see section 55.

NOTE: For advice on finding and evaluating sources and on managing information in all your college courses, see sections 46–49.

50 Supporting a thesis

Most research assignments ask you to form a thesis, or main idea, and to support that thesis with well-organized evidence. (See also 1c.) Remain flexible as you draft because you may need to revise your approach later. Writing about a subject is a way of learning about it; as you write, your understanding of your subject will almost certainly deepen.

50a Form a working thesis.

Once you have read a variety of sources and considered your issue from different perspectives, you are ready to form a working thesis: a one-sentence (or occasionally a two-sentence) statement of your central idea. (See also 1e and 50d.) Because it is a working, or tentative, thesis, it is flexible enough to change as your ideas develop. Ultimately, the thesis expresses not just your opinion but your informed, reasoned judgment.

In a research paper, your thesis will answer the central research question that you posed earlier (see 46a). Here, for example, are Anna Orlov's research question and working thesis.

RESEARCH QUESTION

Should employers monitor their employees' online activities in the workplace?

WORKING THESIS

Employers should not monitor their employees' online activities because electronic surveillance can compromise workers' privacy.

After you have written a rough draft and perhaps done more reading, you may decide to revise your thesis, as Orlov did.

REVISED THESIS

Although companies often have legitimate concerns that lead them to monitor employees' Internet usage—from expensive security breaches to reduced productivity—the benefits of electronic surveillance are outweighed by its costs to employees' privacy and autonomy.

The thesis usually appears at the end of the introductory paragraph. To read Anna Orlov's thesis in the context of her introduction, see page 583.

50b Organize ideas with a rough outline.

The body of your paper will consist of evidence in support of your thesis. Instead of getting tangled up in a complex, formal outline, sketch an informal plan that organizes your ideas in bold strokes. Anna Orlov, for example, used this simple plan to outline the structure of her argument:

- Compared with older types of surveillance, electronic surveillance allows employers to monitor workers more efficiently.
- Some experts argue that companies have important financial and legal reasons to monitor employees' Internet usage.
- But monitoring employees' Internet usage may lower worker productivity when the threat to privacy creates distrust.

Making the most of your handbook

It's helpful to start off with a working thesis and a rough outline—especially when writing from sources.

▶ Draft a working thesis: 1c

▶ Sketch a plan: 1d

- Current laws do little to protect employees' privacy rights, so
  employees and employers have to negotiate the potential risks and
  benefits of electronic surveillance.

After you have written a rough draft, a more formal outline can
be a useful way to shape the complexities of your argument.

hackerhandbooks.com/bedhandbook > Research exercises > MLA
> E-ex 50–1 and 50–2

50c Use sources to inform and support your argument.

Used thoughtfully, the source materials you have gathered
will make your argument more complex and convincing for
readers. Sources can play several different roles as you develop
your points.

Providing background information or context

You can use facts and statistics to support generalizations or to
establish the importance of your topic, as student writer Anna
Orlov does in her introduction.

> As the Internet has become an integral tool of businesses,
> company policies on Internet usage have become as common as
> policies regarding vacation days or sexual harassment. A 2005 study by
> the American Management Association and ePolicy Institute found that
> 76% of companies monitor employees' use of the Web, and the number
> of companies that block employees' access to certain Web sites has
> increased 27% since 2001 (1).

Explaining terms or concepts

If readers are unlikely to be familiar with a word or an idea
important to your topic, you must explain it for them. Quoting or paraphrasing a source can help you define terms and
concepts in accessible language.

One popular monitoring method is keystroke logging, which is done by means of an undetectable program on employees' computers. . . . As Lane explains, these programs record every key entered into the computer in hidden directories that can later be accessed or uploaded by supervisors; the programs can even scan for keywords tailored to individual companies (128-29).

Supporting your claims

As you draft your argument, make sure to back up your assertions with facts, examples, and other evidence from your research. (See also 5e.) Orlov, for example, uses an anecdote from one of her sources to support her claim that limiting computer access causes resentment among a company's staff.

Monitoring online activities can have the unintended effect of making employees resentful. . . . Kesan warns that "prohibiting personal use can seem extremely arbitrary and can seriously harm morale. . . . Imagine a concerned parent who is prohibited from checking on a sick child by a draconian company policy" (315-16). As this analysis indicates, employees can become disgruntled when Internet usage policies are enforced to their full extent.

Lending authority to your argument

Expert opinion can give weight to your argument. (See also 5e.) But don't rely on experts to make your arguments for you. Construct your argument in your own words and, when appropriate, cite the judgment of an authority in the field to support your position.

Additionally, many experts disagree with employers' assumption that online monitoring can increase productivity. Employment law attorney Joseph Schmitt argues that, particularly for employees who are paid a salary rather than an hourly wage, "a company shouldn't care whether employees spend one or 10 hours on the Internet as long as they are getting their jobs done—and provided that they are not accessing inappropriate sites" (qtd. in Verespej).

Anticipating and countering objections

Do not ignore sources that seem contrary to your position or that offer arguments different from your own. Instead, use them to give voice to opposing points of view and to state potential objections to your argument before you counter them (see 5f). Readers often have opposing points of view in mind already, whether or not they agree with you. Anna Orlov, for example, cites conflicting evidence to acknowledge that some readers may feel that unlimited Internet access in the workplace hinders productivity. In doing so, she creates an opportunity to counter that objection and persuade those readers.

Making the most of your handbook

Seeing how other writers use sources can help you think about your own writing.

▶ Highlights of one student's research process: 54b

> On the one hand, computers and Internet access give employees powerful tools to carry out their jobs; on the other hand, the same technology offers constant temptations to avoid work. As a 2005 study by *Salary.com* and *America Online* indicates, the Internet ranked as the top choice among employees for ways of wasting time on the job; it beat talking with co-workers—the second most popular method—by a margin of nearly two to one (Frauenheim).

50d Draft an introduction for your thesis.

In a research paper, readers are accustomed to seeing the thesis statement—the paper's main point—at the end of the first or second paragraph. The advantage of putting it in the first paragraph is that readers can immediately grasp your point. The advantage of delaying the thesis until the second paragraph is that you can provide a fuller context for your point.

As you draft your introduction, you may change your preliminary thesis, either because you have refined your thinking or because new wording fits more smoothly into the context you have provided for it.

In addition to stating your thesis and establishing a context for it, an introduction should hook readers (see 1e). For example, in your first sentence or two you might connect your topic to a recent news item or point to emerging trends in an academic discipline. Other strategies are to pose a puzzling problem or to cite a startling statistic. Anna Orlov begins her paper by using results from a recent study to show a significant trend in companies' electronic surveillance of employees (see p. 583).

50e Provide organizational cues.

Even if you are working with a good outline, your paper will appear disorganized unless you provide organizational cues: topic sentences, transitions between major sections of the paper, and perhaps headings. Anna Orlov's paper is easy to follow because she begins paragraphs with clear topic sentences and uses transitions to help readers move from one idea to the next (see pp. 583–88). For more about topic sentences, transitions, and headings, see 3a, 3d, and 58b.

50f Draft the paper in an appropriate voice.

A chatty, breezy voice is usually not appropriate in a research paper, but neither is a stuffy, pretentious style or a timid, unsure one.

TOO CHATTY

What's up with companies snooping around when their employees are surfing the Net? Employers who constantly spy on their workers' Internet habits are messing with people's rights.

MORE FORMAL

Although companies often have legitimate concerns that lead them to monitor employees' Internet usage, the benefits of electronic surveillance are outweighed by its costs to employees' privacy and autonomy.

TOO STUFFY

It has been concluded that an evident majority of companies undertake the monitoring of employees' utilization of the Internet.

MORE DIRECT

A recent study found that 76% of companies monitor employees' Internet use.

TOO TIMID

I may not be an expert, but it seems to me that monitoring online activities maybe has the unintended effect of making employees resentful.

MORE AUTHORITATIVE

Monitoring online activities can have the unintended effect of making employees resentful.

51 Citing sources; avoiding plagiarism

In a research paper, you will draw on the work of other writers, and you must document their contributions by citing your sources. Sources are cited for two reasons:

1. to tell readers where your information comes from—so that they can assess its reliability and, if interested, find and read the original source
2. to give credit to the writers from whom you have borrowed words and ideas

Borrowing another writer's language, sentence structures, or ideas without proper acknowledgment is a form of dishonesty known as *plagiarism*.

You must include a citation when you quote from a source, when you summarize or paraphrase, and when you borrow facts that are not common knowledge (see also 51b).

51a For most English papers, use the MLA system for citing sources.

Most English professors and some humanities professors require the MLA (Modern Language Association) system of in-text citations. Here, briefly, is how the MLA citation system usually works. (See 53 for more details and model citations.)

1. The source is introduced by a signal phrase that names its author.
2. The material being cited is followed by a page number in parentheses.
3. At the end of the paper, a list of works cited (arranged alphabetically by authors' last names) gives complete publication information for the source.

IN-TEXT CITATION

Legal scholar Jay Kesan points out that the law holds employers liable for employees' actions such as violations of copyright laws, the distribution of offensive or graphic sexual material, and illegal disclosure of confidential information (312).

ENTRY IN THE LIST OF WORKS CITED

Kesan, Jay P. "Cyber-Working or Cyber-Shirking? A First Principles Examination of Electronic Privacy in the Workplace." *Florida Law Review* 54.2 (2002): 289-332. Print.

This basic MLA format varies for different types of sources. For a detailed discussion and other models, see 53.

51b Avoid plagiarism when quoting, summarizing, and paraphrasing sources.

Your research paper is a collaboration between you and your sources. To be fair and ethical, you must acknowledge your debt to the writers of those sources. If you don't, you commit plagiarism, a serious academic offense. (See also 48c and 54b.)

In general, these three acts are considered plagiarism: (1) failing to cite quotations and borrowed ideas, (2) failing to enclose borrowed language in quotation marks, and (3) failing to put summaries and paraphrases in your own words. Definitions of plagiarism may vary; it's a good idea to find out how your school defines academic dishonesty.

Citing quotations and borrowed ideas

You must cite all direct quotations. You must also cite any ideas borrowed from a source: summaries and paraphrases; statistics and other specific facts; and visuals such as cartoons, graphs, and diagrams.

The only exception is common knowledge—information your readers could easily find in any number of general sources. For example, most encyclopedias will tell readers that Alfred Hitchcock directed *Notorious* in 1946 and that Emily Dickinson published only a handful of her many poems during her lifetime.

As a rule, when you have seen information repeatedly in your reading, you don't need to cite it. However, when information has appeared in only one or two sources, when it is highly specific (as with statistics), or when it is controversial, you should cite the source. If a topic is new to you and you are not sure what is considered common knowledge or what is controversial, ask your instructor or someone else with expertise. When in doubt, cite the source. (See 53 for details.)

Enclosing borrowed language in quotation marks

Making the most of your handbook

When you use exact language from a source, you need to show that it is a quotation.

▶ Quotation marks for direct quotations: 37a

▶ Setting off long quotations: 37b

To indicate that you are using a source's exact phrases or sentences, you must enclose them in quotation marks unless they have been set off from the text by indenting (see p. 506). To omit the quotation marks is to claim—falsely—that the language is your own. Such an omission is plagiarism even if you have cited the source.

ORIGINAL SOURCE

Without adequate discipline, the World Wide Web can be a tremendous time sink; no other medium comes close to matching the Internet's depth of materials, interactivity, and sheer distractive potential.

— Frederick Lane, *The Naked Employee*, p. 142

PLAGIARISM

Frederick Lane points out that if people do not have adequate discipline, the World Wide Web can be a tremendous time sink; no other medium comes close to matching the Internet's depth of materials, interactivity, and sheer distractive potential (142).

BORROWED LANGUAGE IN QUOTATION MARKS

Frederick Lane points out that for those not exercising self-control, "the World Wide Web can be a tremendous time sink; no other medium comes close to matching the Internet's depth of materials, interactivity, and sheer distractive potential" (142).

Putting summaries and paraphrases in your own words

Summaries and paraphrases are written in your own words. A summary condenses information from a source; a paraphrase uses roughly the same number of words as the original source to convey the information. When you summarize or paraphrase, it is not enough to name the source; you must restate the source's meaning using your own language. (See also 48c.) You commit plagiarism if you half-copy the author's sentences—either by mixing the author's phrases with your own without using quotation marks or by plugging your synonyms into the author's sentence structure.

The first paraphrase of the following source is plagiarized—even though the source is cited—because too much of its language is borrowed from the original. The underlined strings of words have been copied exactly (without quotation marks). In addition, the writer has closely echoed the sentence structure of the source, merely substituting some synonyms (*restricted* for *limited*, *modern era* for *computer age*, *monitoring* for *surveillance*, and *inexpensive* for *cheap*).

Understanding the comment

When a teacher or tutor asks "Your words?" the comment often signals that it's unclear whether certain words you've used are your own or those of your sources.

> Internet technology has made it possible for extremist groups to recruit and train members and carry out terrorist activity. The membership of these groups reaches beyond local geographic areas because of the Web. The world has become a cacophony of parochialisms where individuals seek association with coreligionists in a mystique of participation. Combating the influences of these groups is now harder than ever.

Your words?

One student wrote this body paragraph in a research paper on the Internet's role in facilitating terrorism.

Part of this paragraph doesn't sound like the student's voice. To revise, the student must determine which words are his own and which come from sources he consulted. If he chooses to include words or ideas from a source, he'll need to decide if he wants to quote, summarize, or paraphrase the source. He'll also need to properly cite the source in his paper.

Similar comments: source? • quotation? • who's talking here?

Revising when *your* readers wonder whose words they're reading

1. *Reread your sentences* to see if you have clearly marked the boundaries between your source material and your own words. Is every word your own? Or have you borrowed words from sources without properly acknowledging them?

2. *Use signal phrases* to introduce each source and provide context. Doing so prepares readers for a source's words.

3. *Use quotation marks* to enclose language that you borrow word-for-word from a source, and follow each quotation with a parenthetical citation.

4. *Put summaries and paraphrases in your own words* and always cite your sources.

More advice on citing quotations, paraphrases, and summaries: **51** (MLA); **56b** (APA); and **57b** (*Chicago*)

ORIGINAL SOURCE

In earlier times, surveillance was limited to the information that a supervisor could observe and record firsthand and to primitive counting devices. In the computer age surveillance can be instantaneous, unblinking, cheap, and, maybe most importantly, easy.

—Carl Botan and Mihaela Vorvoreanu, "What Do Employees Think about Electronic Surveillance at Work?" p. 126

PLAGIARISM: UNACCEPTABLE BORROWING

Scholars Carl Botan and Mihaela Vorvoreanu argue that in earlier times monitoring of employees was restricted to the information that a supervisor could observe and record firsthand. In the modern era, monitoring can be instantaneous, inexpensive, and, most importantly, easy.

To avoid plagiarizing an author's language, resist the temptation to look at the source while you are summarizing or paraphrasing. After you have read the passage you want to paraphrase, set the source aside. Ask yourself, "What is the author's meaning?" In your own words, state your understanding of the author's basic point. Return to the source and check that you haven't used the author's language or sentence structure or misrepresented the author's ideas. Following these steps will help you avoid plagiarizing the source. When you fully understand another writer's meaning, you can more easily and accurately represent those ideas in your own words.

ACCEPTABLE PARAPHRASE

Scholars Carl Botan and Mihaela Vorvoreanu claim that the nature of workplace surveillance has changed over time. Before the arrival of computers, managers could collect only small amounts of information about their employees based on what they saw or heard. Now, because computers are standard workplace technology, employers can monitor employees efficiently (126).

For more discussion of summary and paraphrase, see 48c and 54b.

52 Integrating sources

Quotations, summaries, paraphrases, and facts will help you develop your argument, but they cannot speak for you. You can use several strategies to integrate information from research sources into your paper while maintaining your own voice.

NOTE: If you are integrating quotations from a literary source, such as a poem or a short story, see 55f.

52a Use quotations appropriately.

In your academic writing, keep the emphasis on your ideas and your language; use your own words to summarize and to paraphrase your sources and to explain your points. Sometimes, however, quotations can be the most effective way to integrate a source's ideas.

WHEN TO USE QUOTATIONS
- When language is especially vivid or expressive
- When exact wording is needed for technical accuracy
- When it is important to let the debaters of an issue explain their positions in their own words
- When the words of an authority lend weight to an argument
- When the language of a source is the topic of your discussion (as in an analysis or interpretation)

Limiting your use of quotations

Although it is tempting to insert many quotations in your paper and to use your own words only for connecting passages, do not quote excessively. It is almost impossible to integrate numerous quotations smoothly into your own text.

It is not always necessary to quote full sentences from a source. To reduce your reliance on the words of others, you can often integrate language from a source into your own sentence structure.

> Kizza and Ssanyu observe that technology in the workplace has been accompanied by "an array of problems that needed quick answers," such as electronic monitoring to prevent security breaches (4).

Using the ellipsis mark and brackets

Two useful marks of punctuation, the ellipsis mark and brackets, allow you to keep quoted material to a minimum and to integrate it smoothly into your text.

The ellipsis mark   To condense a quoted passage, you can use the ellipsis mark (three periods, with spaces between) to indicate that you have left words out. What remains must be grammatically complete.

> Lane acknowledges the legitimate reasons that many companies have for monitoring their employees' online activities, particularly management's concern about preventing "the theft of information that can be downloaded to a . . . disk, e-mailed to oneself . . . , or even posted to a Web page for the entire world to see" (12).

The writer has omitted from the source the words *floppy or Zip* before *disk* and *or a confederate* after *oneself*.

On the rare occasions when you want to leave out one or more full sentences, use a period before the three ellipsis dots.

> Charles Lewis, director of the Center for Public Integrity, points out that "by 1987, employers were administering nearly 2,000,000 polygraph tests a year to job applicants and employees. . . . Millions of workers were required to produce urine samples under observation for drug testing . . ." (22).

Ordinarily, do not use an ellipsis mark at the beginning or at the end of a quotation. Your readers will understand that the quoted material is taken from a longer passage, so such marks are not necessary. The only exception occurs when you have dropped words at the end of the final quoted sentence. In such cases, put three ellipsis dots before the closing quotation mark and parenthetical reference, as in the previous example.

Make sure omissions and ellipsis marks do not distort the meaning of your source.

Brackets Brackets allow you to insert your own words into quoted material. You can insert words in brackets to clarify a confusing reference or to keep a sentence grammatical in your context. You also use brackets to indicate that you are changing a letter from capital to lowercase (or vice versa) to fit into your sentence.

> Legal scholar Jay Kesan notes that "[a] decade ago, losses [from employees' computer crimes] were already mounting to five billion dollars annually" (311).

This quotation began *A decade ago* . . . in the source, so the writer indicated the change to lowercase with brackets and inserted words in brackets to clarify the meaning of *losses*.

To indicate an error such as a misspelling in a quotation, insert the word "sic" in brackets right after the error.

> Johnson argues that "while online monitoring is often imagined as harmles [sic], the practice may well threaten employees' rights to privacy" (14).

Do not overuse "sic" to call attention to errors in a source. Sometimes paraphrasing is a better option. (See 39c.)

Setting off long quotations

When you quote more than four typed lines of prose or more than three lines of poetry, set off the quotation by indenting it one inch from the left margin.

Long quotations should be introduced by an informative sentence, usually followed by a colon. Quotation marks are

Understanding the comment

When a teacher or tutor responds "Cite your sources," the comment often signals that you need to acknowledge and give proper credit to the contributions of others.

> At the story's end, Edna Pontellier is described as a "naked . . . new-born creature" who, in the act of ending her own life, is experiencing a kind of re-birth.
>
> *Cite your sources*

One student wrote this sentence in an essay interpreting Kate Chopin's novel *The Awakening*.

The student has borrowed language from both a primary source and a secondary source without proper citation. To revise, she needs to consult her notes or return to the novel to locate the exact page number for the quotation she uses. In addition, she needs to include quotation marks around the words "a kind of re-birth," which come from a secondary source, and to provide a parenthetical citation.

Similar comments: cite this • documentation • source?

Revising when *you* need to cite your sources

1. *Reread your sentence and ask questions.* Have you properly acknowledged all the contributions—words, ideas, or facts—that you use as evidence? Have you given credit to the sources you quote, summarize, or paraphrase? Have you made it clear to readers how to locate the source if they want to consult it?

2. *Ask your instructor* which documentation style you are required to use—MLA, APA, or *Chicago*.

3. *Read your notes* or check the source itself to find the exact words. Make sure you have the author's name, the title, the date of publication, and the page number for each source you cite.

4. *Revise* by including an in-text citation for any words, ideas, or facts that you used as evidence—and by including quotation marks around any language borrowed word-for-word from a source.

More on citing sources: **53a** (MLA), **56d** (APA), and **57d** (*Chicago*) unnecessary because the indented format tells readers that the passage is taken word-for-word from the source.

> Botan and Vorvoreanu examine the role of gender in company practices of electronic surveillance:
>> There has never been accurate documentation of the extent of gender differences in surveillance, but by the middle 1990s, estimates of the proportion of surveilled employees that were women ranged from 75% to 85%. . . . Ironically, this gender imbalance in workplace surveillance may be evening out today because advances in surveillance technology are making surveillance of traditionally male dominated fields, such as long-distance truck driving, cheap, easy, and frequently unobtrusive. (127)

Notice that at the end of an indented quotation the parenthetical citation goes outside the final mark of punctuation. (When a quotation is run into your text, the opposite is true. See the sample citations on p. 505.)

52b Use signal phrases to integrate sources.

Whenever you include a paraphrase, summary, or direct quotation of another writer in your paper, prepare your readers for it with introductory words called a *signal phrase*. A signal phrase usually names the author of the source and often provides some context for the source material. (See also 52c and 54b.)

When you write a signal phrase, choose a verb that is appropriate for the way you are using the source (see 50c). Are you providing background, explaining a concept, supporting a claim, lending authority, or refuting a belief? See the chart on page 509 for a list of verbs commonly used in signal phrases.

Note that MLA style calls for verbs in the present or present perfect tense (*argues, has argued*) to introduce source material unless you include a date that specifies the time of the original author's writing.

Using signal phrases in MLA papers

To avoid monotony, try to vary both the language and the placement of your signal phrases.

Model signal phrases

In the words of researchers Greenfield and Davis, ". . ."

As legal scholar Jay Kesan has noted, ". . ."

The ePolicy Institute, an organization that advises companies about reducing risks from technology, reports that ". . ."

". . . ," writes Daniel Tynan, ". . ."

". . . ," attorney Schmitt claims.

Kizza and Ssanyu offer a persuasive counterargument: ". . ."

Verbs in signal phrases

acknowledges	comments	endorses	reasons
adds	compares	grants	refutes
admits	confirms	illustrates	rejects
agrees	contends	implies	reports
argues	declares	insists	responds
asserts	denies	notes	suggests
believes	disputes	observes	thinks
claims	emphasizes	points out	writes

Marking boundaries

Readers need to move from your words to the words of a source without feeling a jolt. Avoid dropping quotations into the text without warning. Instead, provide clear signal phrases, including at least the author's name, to indicate the boundary between your words and the source's words. (The signal phrase is underlined in the second example.)

DROPPED QUOTATION

Some experts have argued that a range of legitimate concerns justifies employer monitoring of employee Internet usage. "Employees could accidentally (or deliberately) spill confidential corporate information . . . or allow worms to spread throughout a corporate network" (Tynan).

QUOTATION WITH SIGNAL PHRASE

Some experts have argued that a range of legitimate concerns justifies employer monitoring of employee Internet usage. As *PC World* columnist Daniel Tynan points out, "Employees could accidentally (or deliberately) spill confidential corporate information . . . or allow worms to spread throughout a corporate network."

NOTE: Because this quotation is from an unpaginated Web source, no page number appears in parentheses after the quotation. See item 4 on page 520.

Establishing authority

Good research writing uses evidence from reliable sources. The first time you mention a source, include in the signal phrase the author's title, credentials, or experience—anything that would help your readers recognize the source's authority. (Signal phrases are underlined in the next two examples.)

SOURCE WITH NO CREDENTIALS

Jay Kesan points out that the law holds employers liable for employees' actions such as violations of copyright laws, the distribution of offensive or graphic sexual material, and illegal disclosure of confidential information (312).

SOURCE WITH CREDENTIALS

Legal scholar Jay Kesan points out that the law holds employers liable for employees' actions such as violations of copyright laws, the distribution of offensive or graphic sexual material, and illegal disclosure of confidential information (312).

When you establish your source's authority, as with the phrase *Legal scholar* in the previous example, you also signal to readers your own credibility as a responsible researcher who has located reliable sources.

Introducing summaries and paraphrases

Introduce most summaries and paraphrases with a signal phrase that names the author and places the material in the context of your argument. (See also 52c and 54b.) Readers will then understand that everything between the signal phrase and the parenthetical citation summarizes or paraphrases the cited source.

Without the signal phrase (underlined) in the following example, readers might think that only the quotation at the end is being cited, when in fact the whole paragraph is based on the source.

> <u>Frederick Lane believes</u> that the personal computer has posed new challenges for employers worried about workplace productivity. Whereas early desktop computers were primitive enough to prevent employees from using them to waste time, the machines have become so sophisticated that they now make non-work-related computer activities easy and inviting. Many employees spend considerable company time customizing features and playing games on their computers. But perhaps most problematic from the employer's point of view, Lane asserts, is giving employees access to the Internet, "roughly the equivalent of installing a gazillion-channel television set for each employee" (15-16).

There are times when a summary or a paraphrase does not require a signal phrase. When the context makes clear where the cited material begins, you may omit the signal phrase and include the author's last name in parentheses.

Using signal phrases with statistics and other facts

When you are citing a statistic or another specific fact, a signal phrase is often not necessary. In most cases, readers will understand that the citation refers to the statistic or fact (not the whole paragraph).

> Roughly 60% of responding companies reported disciplining employees who had used the Internet in ways the companies deemed inappropriate; 30% had fired their employees for those transgressions (Greenfield and Davis 347).

There is nothing wrong, however, with using a signal phrase to introduce a statistic or fact.

Putting source material in context

Readers should not have to guess why source material appears in your paper. A signal phrase can help you make the connection between your own ideas and those of another writer by clarifying how the source will contribute to your paper (see 47a).

If you use another writer's words, you must explain how they relate to your point. It's a good idea to embed a quotation between sentences of your own. In addition to introducing it with a signal phrase, follow it with interpretive comments that link the quotation to your paper's argument (see also 52c).

QUOTATION WITH EFFECTIVE CONTEXT

The difference, Lane argues, between old methods of data gathering and electronic surveillance involves quantity:

> Technology makes it possible for employers to gather enormous amounts of data about employees, often far beyond what is necessary to satisfy safety or productivity concerns. And the trends that drive technology—faster, smaller, cheaper—make it possible for larger and larger numbers of employers to gather ever-greater amounts of personal data. (3-4)

In an age when employers can collect data whenever employees use their computers—when they send e-mail, surf the Web, or even arrive at or depart from their workstations—the challenge for both employers and employees is to determine how much is too much.

52c Synthesize sources.

When you synthesize multiple sources in a research paper, you create a conversation about your research topic. You show readers that your argument is based on your active analysis

and integration of ideas, not just a list of quotations and paraphrases. Your synthesis will show how your sources relate to
one another; one source may support, extend, or counter the
ideas of another. Not every source has to "speak" to another
in a research paper, but readers should be able to see how each
one functions in your argument (see 47a).

Considering how sources relate to your argument

Before you integrate sources and show readers how they relate to one another, consider how each one might contribute
to your own argument. As student writer Anna Orlov became
more informed through her research about Internet surveillance in the workplace, she asked herself these questions:
*What do I think about monitoring employees online? Which sources
might support my ideas? Which sources might help extend or illustrate the points I want to make? What common or compelling
counterarguments do I need to address to strengthen my position?*
She annotated a passage from an *eWeek* article that challenged
the case she was building against Internet surveillance in the
workplace.

STUDENT NOTES ON THE ORIGINAL SOURCE

Catchy language — a good quotation.

Common examples — readers can relate.

While bosses can easily detect and interrupt water-
cooler chatter, the employee who is shopping at
Lands' End or IMing with fellow fantasy baseball
managers may actually appear to be working.
Thwarting the activity is a technology challenge,
and it's one that more and more enterprises are
taking seriously, despite resistance from privacy
advocates and some employees themselves.

    —Chris Gonsalves, "Wasting Away on the Web"

Strong case for surveillance, but I'm not convinced. Counter with use-ful workplace Web surfing?

Because Orlov felt that the Gonsalves article would convince many readers that Internet surveillance was good for
workplace productivity, she knew she needed to present and
counter his argument. The author's memorable language and

clear illustration seemed worth quoting, but she wanted to keep the emphasis on her own argument. So she quoted the passage from Gonsalves and then analyzed it, discussing and countering his view in her own writing. She also found other sources to support and extend her counterargument.

Placing sources in conversation

You can show readers how the ideas of one source relate to those of another by connecting and analyzing the ideas in your own voice. After all, you've done the research and thought through the issues, so you should control the conversation. When you effectively synthesize sources, the emphasis is still on your own writing; the thread of your argument should be easy to identify and to understand, with or without your sources.

SAMPLE SYNTHESIS (DRAFT)

Student writer Anna Orlov begins with a claim that needs support.

Signal phrases indicate how sources contribute to Orlov's paper and show that the ideas that follow are not her own.

Productivity is not easily measured in the wired workplace. As a result, employers find it difficult to determine how much freedom to allow their employees. On the one hand, computers and Internet access give employees powerful tools to carry out their jobs; on the other hand, the same technology offers constant temptations to avoid work. As a 2005 study by *Salary.com* and *America Online* indicates, the Internet ranked as the top choice among employees for ways of wasting time on the job (Frauenheim). Chris Gonsalves, an editor for *eWeek.com*, argues that technology has changed the terms between employers and employees: "While bosses can easily detect and interrupt water-cooler chatter," he writes, "the employee who is shopping at Lands' End or IMing with fellow fantasy baseball managers may actually appear to be working." The gap between observable behaviors and actual online activities has motivated some employers to invest in surveillance programs.

Student writer

Source 1

Source 2

Student writer

Orlov presents a counterposition to extend her argument. → Many experts, however, disagree with employers' assumption that online monitoring can increase productivity. Employment law attorney Joseph Schmitt argues that, particularly for salaried employees, "a company shouldn't care whether employees spend one or 10 hours on the Internet as long as they are getting their jobs done—and provided that they are not accessing inappropriate sites" (qtd. in Verespej). Other experts even argue that time spent on personal Internet browsing can actually be productive for companies. According to Bill Coleman, an executive at *Salary.com*, "Personal Internet use and casual office conversations often turn into new business ideas or suggestions for gaining operating efficiencies" (qtd. in Frauenheim). Employers, in other words, may benefit from showing more faith in their employees' ability to exercise their autonomy.

Student writer / *Source 3* / *Student writer* / *Source 4* / *Student writer*

Orlov builds her case—each quoted passage offers a more detailed claim or example in support of her larger claim.

In this draft, Orlov uses her own analyses to shape the conversation among her sources. She does not simply string quotations together or allow them to overwhelm her writing. The final sentence, written in her own voice, gives her an opportunity to explain to readers how the various sources support her argument.

When synthesizing sources in your own writing, ask yourself the following questions:

- Which sources inform, support, or extend your argument?
- Do you vary the functions of sources—to provide background information, explain terms or concepts, lend authority to your argument, and anticipate counterarguments?
- Do you explain to readers how your sources support your argument?
- Do you connect and analyze sources in your own voice?
- Is your own argument easy to identify and to understand, with or without your sources?

Reviewing an MLA paper: Use of sources

Use of quotations

- Is quoted material enclosed in quotation marks (unless it has been set off from the text)? (See 51b and p. 508.)

- Is quoted language word-for-word accurate? If not, do brackets or ellipsis marks indicate the changes or omissions? (See pp. 505–06.)

- Does a clear signal phrase (usually naming the author) prepare readers for each quotation and for the purpose the quotation serves? (See 52b.)

- Does a parenthetical citation follow each quotation? (See 53a.)

- Is each quotation put in context? (See 52c.)

Use of summaries and paraphrases

- Are summaries and paraphrases free of plagiarized wording — not copied or half-copied from the source? (See 51b.)

- Are summaries and paraphrases documented with parenthetical citations? (See 51b and 53a.)

- Do readers know where the cited material begins? In other words, does a signal phrase mark the boundary between your words and the summary or paraphrase? Or does the context alone make clear exactly what you are citing? (See 52b.)

- Does a signal phrase prepare readers for the purpose the summary or paraphrase has in your argument?

Use of statistics and other facts

- Are statistics and facts (other than common knowledge) documented with parenthetical citations? (See 51b and 53a.)

- If there is no signal phrase, will readers understand exactly which facts are being cited? (See 52b.)

53   MLA documentation style

In English and other humanities classes, you may be asked to use the MLA (Modern Language Association) system for documenting sources, which is set forth in the *MLA Handbook for Writers of Research Papers*, 7th ed. (New York: MLA, 2009).

MLA recommends in-text citations that refer readers to a list of works cited. An in-text citation names the author of the source, often in a signal phrase, and gives a page number in parentheses. At the end of the paper, a list of works cited provides publication information about the source; the list is alphabetized by authors' last names (or by titles for works without authors). There is a direct connection between the in-text citation and the alphabetical listing. In the following example, that connection is highlighted in orange.

IN-TEXT CITATION

Jay Kesan notes that even though many companies now routinely monitor employees through electronic means, "there may exist less intrusive safeguards for employers" (293).

ENTRY IN THE LIST OF WORKS CITED

Kesan, Jay P. "Cyber-Working or Cyber-Shirking? A First Principles Examination of Electronic Privacy in the Workplace." *Florida Law Review* 54.2 (2002): 289-332. Print.

For a list of works cited that includes this entry, see page 588.

53a   MLA in-text citations

MLA in-text citations are made with a combination of signal phrases and parenthetical references. A signal phrase introduces information taken from a source (a quotation, summary, paraphrase, or fact); usually the signal phrase includes the author's name. The parenthetical reference comes after the cited material, often at the end of the sentence. It includes at least a page number (except for unpaginated sources, such as those found online). In the models in 53a, the elements of the in-text citation are highlighted in color.

IN-TEXT CITATION

Kwon points out that the Fourth Amendment does not give employees any protections from employers' "unreasonable searches and seizures" (6).

Readers can look up the author's last name in the alphabetized list of works cited, where they will learn the work's title and other publication information. If readers decide to consult the source, the page number will take them straight to the passage that has been cited.

Basic rules for print and online sources

The MLA system of in-text citations, which depends heavily on authors' names and page numbers, was created with print sources in mind. Although many online sources have unclear authorship and lack page numbers, the basic rules are the same for both print and online sources.

The models in this section (items 1–5) show how the MLA system usually works and explain what to do if your source has no author or page numbers.

1. Author named in a signal phrase Ordinarily, introduce the material being cited with a signal phrase that includes the author's name. In addition to preparing readers for the source, the signal phrase allows you to keep the parenthetical citation brief.

Frederick Lane reports that employers do not necessarily have to use software to monitor how their employees use the Web: employers can "use a hidden video camera pointed at an employee's monitor" and even position a camera "so that a number of monitors [can] be viewed at the same time" (147).

Directory to MLA in-text citation models

Basic rules for print and online sources

1. Author named in a signal phrase, 518
2. Author named in parentheses, 519
3. Author unknown, 520
4. Page number unknown, 520
5. One-page source, 521

Variations on the basic rules

6. Two or three authors, 521
7. Four or more authors, 522
8. Organization as author, 522
9. Authors with the same last name, 522
10. Two or more works by the same author, 523
11. Two or more works in one citation, 523
12. Repeated citations from the same source, 523
13. Encyclopedia or dictionary entry, 524
14. Multivolume work, 524
15. Entire work, 525
16. Selection in an anthology, 525
17. Government document, 525
18. Historical document, 526
19. Legal source, 526
20. Visual such as a photograph, map, or chart, 526
21. E-mail, letter, or personal interview, 527
22. Web site or other electronic source, 527
23. Indirect source (source quoted in another source), 527

Literary works and sacred texts

24. Literary work without parts or line numbers, 528
25. Verse play or poem, 528
26. Novel with numbered divisions, 528
27. Sacred text, 529

The signal phrase—*Frederick Lane reports*—names the author; the parenthetical citation gives the page number of the book in which the quoted words may be found.

Notice that the period follows the parenthetical citation. When a quotation ends with a question mark or an exclamation point, leave the end punctuation inside the quotation mark and add a period at the end of your sentence: "... ?" (8). (See also the note on p. 396.)

2. Author named in parentheses If a signal phrase does not name the author, put the author's last name in parentheses along with the page number. Use no punctuation between the name and the page number.

Companies can monitor employees' every keystroke without legal penalty, but they may have to combat low morale as a result (Lane 129).

3. Author unknown Either use the complete title in a signal phrase or use a short form of the title in parentheses. Titles of books are italicized; titles of articles are put in quotation marks.

A popular keystroke logging program operates invisibly on workers' computers yet provides supervisors with details of the workers' online activities ("Automatically").

TIP: Before assuming that a Web source has no author, do some detective work. Often the author's name is available but is not easy to find. For example, it may appear at the end of the page, in tiny print. Or it may appear on another page of the site, such as the home page.

NOTE: If a source has no author and is sponsored by a corporation or government agency, name the corporation or agency as the author (see items 8 and 17 on pp. 522 and 525, respectively).

4. Page number unknown Do not include the page number if a work lacks page numbers, as is the case with many Web sources. Even if a printout from a Web site shows page numbers, treat the source as unpaginated in the in-text citation because not all printouts give the same page numbers. (When the pages of a Web source are stable, as in PDF files, supply a page number in your in-text citation.)

As a 2005 study by *Salary.com* and *America Online* indicates, the Internet ranked as the top choice among employees for ways of wasting time on the job; it beat talking with co-workers—the second most popular method—by a margin of nearly two to one (Frauenheim).

If a source has numbered paragraphs or sections, use "par." (or "pars.") or "sec." (or "secs.") in the parentheses: (Smith, par. 4). Notice that a comma follows the author's name in this case.

5. One-page source   If the source is one page long, MLA allows (but does not require) you to omit the page number. Many instructors will want you to supply the page number because without it readers may not know where your citation ends or, worse, may not realize that you have provided a citation at all.

NO PAGE NUMBER IN CITATION

Anush Yegyazarian reports that in 2000 the National Labor Relations Board's Office of the General Counsel helped win restitution for two workers who had been dismissed because their employers were displeased by the employees' e-mails about work-related issues. The case points to the ongoing struggle to define what constitutes protected speech in the workplace.

PAGE NUMBER IN CITATION

Anush Yegyazarian reports that in 2000 the National Labor Relations Board's Office of the General Counsel helped win restitution for two workers who had been dismissed because their employers were displeased by the employees' e-mails about work-related issues (62). The case points to the ongoing struggle to define what constitutes protected speech in the workplace.

Variations on the basic rules

This section describes the MLA guidelines for handling a variety of situations not covered by the basic rules in items 1–5. These rules for in-text citations are the same for both print and online sources.

6. Two or three authors   Name the authors in a signal phrase, as in the following example, or include their last names in the parenthetical reference: (Kizza and Ssanyu 2).

Kizza and Ssanyu note that "employee monitoring is a dependable, capable, and very affordable process of electronically or otherwise recording all employee activities at work" and elsewhere (2).

When three authors are named in the parentheses, separate the names with commas: (Alton, Davies, and Rice 56).

7. Four or more authors Name all of the authors or include only the first author's name followed by "et al." (Latin for "and others"). The format you use should match the format in your works cited entry (see item 3 on p. 533).

> The study was extended for two years, and only after results were reviewed by an independent panel did the researchers publish their findings (Blaine et al. 35).

8. Organization as author When the author is a corporation or an organization, name that author either in the signal phrase or in the parentheses. (For a government agency as author, see item 17 on p. 525.)

> According to a 2001 survey of human resources managers by the American Management Association, more than three-quarters of the responding companies reported disciplining employees for "misuse or personal use of office telecommunications equipment" (2).

In the list of works cited, the American Management Association is treated as the author and alphabetized under *A*. When you give the organization name in parentheses, abbreviate common words in the name: "Assn.," "Dept.," "Natl.," "Soc.," and so on.

> In a 2001 survey of human resources managers, more than three-quarters of the responding companies reported disciplining employees for "misuse or personal use of office telecommunications equipment" (Amer. Management Assn. 2).

9. Authors with the same last name If your list of works cited includes works by two or more authors with the same last name, include the author's first name in the signal phrase or first initial in the parentheses.

> Estimates of the frequency with which employers monitor employees' use of the Internet each day vary widely (A. Jones 15).

10. Two or more works by the same author Mention the title of the work in the signal phrase or include a short version of the title in the parentheses.

> The American Management Association and ePolicy Institute have tracked employers' practices in monitoring employees' e-mail use. The groups' 2003 survey found that one-third of companies had a policy of keeping and reviewing employees' e-mail messages ("2003 E-mail" 2); in 2005, more than 55% of companies engaged in e-mail monitoring ("2005 Electronic" 1).

Titles of articles and other short works are placed in quotation marks; titles of books are italicized.

In the rare case when both the author's name and a short title must be given in parentheses, separate them with a comma.

> A 2004 survey found that 20% of employers responding had employees' e-mail "subpoenaed in the course of a lawsuit or regulatory investigation," up 7% from the previous year (Amer. Management Assn. and ePolicy Inst., "2004 Workplace" 1).

11. Two or more works in one citation To cite more than one source in the parentheses, give the citations in alphabetical order and separate them with a semicolon.

> The effects of sleep deprivation among college students have been well documented (Cahill 42; Leduc 114; Vasquez 73).

Multiple citations can be distracting, so you should not overuse the technique. If you want to alert readers to several sources that discuss a particular topic, consider using an information note instead (see 53c).

12. Repeated citations from the same source When you are writing about a single work of fiction, you do not need to include the author's name each time you quote from or paraphrase the work. After you mention the author's name at the beginning of your paper, you may include just the page number in your parenthetical citations. (For specific guidelines for citing novels, plays, and poems, see 55f.)

> In Susan Glaspell's short story "A Jury of Her Peers," two women accompany their husbands and a county attorney to an isolated house where a farmer named John Wright has been choked to death in his bed with a rope. The chief suspect is Wright's wife, Minnie, who is in jail awaiting trial. The sheriff's wife, Mrs. Peters, has come along to gather some personal items for Minnie, and Mrs. Hale has joined her. Early in the story, Mrs. Hale sympathizes with Minnie and objects to the way the male investigators are "snoopin' round and criticizin'" her kitchen (200). In contrast, Mrs. Peters shows respect for the law, saying that the men are doing "no more than their duty" (201).

In a second citation from the same nonfiction source in one paragraph, you may omit the author's name in the signal phrase as long as it is clear that you are still referring to the same source.

13. Encyclopedia or dictionary entry   Unless an encyclopedia or a dictionary has an author, it will be alphabetized in the list of works cited under the word or entry that you consulted (see item 18 on p. 539). Either in your text or in your parenthetical citation, mention the word or entry. No page number is required, since readers can easily look up the word or entry.

> The word *crocodile* has a surprisingly complex etymology ("Crocodile").

14. Multivolume work   If your paper cites more than one volume of a multivolume work, indicate in the parentheses the volume you are referring to, followed by a colon and the page number.

> In his studies of gifted children, Terman describes a pattern of accelerated language acquisition (2: 279).

If you cite only one volume of a multivolume work, you will
include the volume number in the list of works cited and will
not need to include it in the parentheses. (See the second
example in item 17 on p. 539.)

15. Entire work   Use the author's name in a signal phrase or a
parenthetical citation. There is no need to use a page number.

> Lane explores the evolution of surveillance in the workplace.

16. Selection in an anthology   Put the name of the author of
the selection (not the editor of the anthology) in the signal
phrase or the parentheses.

> In "Love Is a Fallacy," the narrator's logical teachings disintegrate
> when Polly declares that she should date Petey because "[h]e's got a
> raccoon coat" (Shulman 379).

In the list of works cited, the work is alphabetized under *Shul-
man*, not under the name of the editor of the anthology.

> Shulman, Max. "Love Is a Fallacy." *Current Issues and Enduring
> Questions*. Ed. Sylvan Barnet and Hugo Bedau. 8th ed.
> Boston: Bedford, 2008. 371-79. Print.

17. Government document   When a government agency is
the author, you will alphabetize it in the list of works cited
under the name of the government, such as *United States* or
Great Britain (see item 73 on p. 563). For this reason, you must
name the government as well as the agency in your in-text
citation.

> Online monitoring by the United States Department of the
> Interior over a one-week period found that employees' use of
> "sexually explicit and gambling websites . . . accounted for over
> 24 hours of Internet use" and that "computer users spent over
> 2,004 hours accessing game and auction sites" during the same
> period (3).

18. Historical document For a historical document, such as the United States Constitution or the Canadian Charter of Rights and Freedoms, provide the document title, neither italicized nor in quotation marks, along with relevant article and section numbers. In parenthetical citations, use common abbreviations such as "art." and "sec." and abbreviations of well-known titles (US Const., art. 1, sec. 2).

> While the United States Constitution provides for the formation of new states (art. 4, sec. 3), it does not explicitly allow or prohibit the secession of states.

For other historical documents, cite as you would any other work, by the first element in the works cited entry (see item 74 on p. 564).

19. Legal source For legislative acts (laws) and court cases, name the act or case either in a signal phrase or in parentheses. Italicize the names of cases but not the names of acts.

> The Jones Act of 1917 granted US citizenship to Puerto Ricans.

> In 1857, Chief Justice Roger B. Taney declared in *Dred Scott v. Sandford* that blacks, whether enslaved or free, could not be citizens of the United States.

20. Visual such as a photograph, map, or chart To cite a visual that has a figure number in the source, use the abbreviation "fig." and the number in place of a page number in your parenthetical citation: (Manning, fig. 4). Spell out the word "figure" if you refer to it in your text.

To cite a visual that does not have a figure number in a print source, use the visual's title or a general description in your text and cite the author and page number as for any other source.

For a visual that is not contained in a source such as a book or periodical, identify the visual in your text and then cite it using the first element in the works cited entry: the photographer's or artist's name or the title of the work. (See item 69 on p. 562.)

Photographs such as *Woman Aircraft Worker* (Bransby) and *Women Welders* (Parks) demonstrate the US government's attempt to document the contributions of women on the home front during World War II.

21. E-mail, letter, or personal interview   Cite e-mail messages, personal letters, and personal interviews by the name listed in the works cited entry, as you would for any other source. Identify the type of source in your text if you feel it is necessary. (See item 53 on p. 557 and items 83 and 84 on p. 567.)

22. Web site or other electronic source   Your in-text citation for an electronic source should follow the same guidelines as for other sources. If the source lacks page numbers but has numbered paragraphs, sections, or divisions, use those numbers with the appropriate abbreviation in your in-text citation: "par.," "sec.," "ch.," "pt.," and so on. Do not add such numbers if the source itself does not use them. In that case, simply give the author or title in your in-text citation.

Julian Hawthorne points out profound differences between his father and Ralph Waldo Emerson but concludes that, in their lives and their writing, "together they met the needs of nearly all that is worthy in human nature" (ch. 4).

23. Indirect source (source quoted in another source)   When a writer's or a speaker's quoted words appear in a source written by someone else, begin the parenthetical citation with the abbreviation "qtd. in."

Researchers Botan and McCreadie point out that "workers are objects of information collection without participating in the process of exchanging the information . . ." (qtd. in Kizza and Ssanyu 14).

Literary works and sacred texts

Literary works and sacred texts are usually available in a variety of editions. Your list of works cited will specify which edition you are using, and your in-text citation will usually consist of a page number from the edition you consulted (see item 24). When possible, give enough information—such as book parts, play divisions, or line numbers—so that readers can locate the cited passage in any edition of the work (see items 25–27).

24. Literary work without parts or line numbers   Many literary works, such as most short stories and many novels and plays, do not have parts or line numbers. In such cases, simply cite the page number.

> At the end of Kate Chopin's "The Story of an Hour," Mrs. Mallard drops dead upon learning that her husband is alive. In the final irony of the story, doctors report that she has died of a "joy that kills" (25).

25. Verse play or poem   For verse plays, give act, scene, and line numbers that can be located in any edition of the work. Use arabic numerals and separate the numbers with periods.

> In Shakespeare's *King Lear*, Gloucester, blinded for suspected treason, learns a profound lesson from his tragic experience: "A man may see how this world goes / with no eyes" (4.2.148-49).

For a poem, cite the part, stanza, and line numbers, if it has them, separated by periods.

> The Green Knight claims to approach King Arthur's court "because the praise of you, prince, is puffed so high, / And your manor and your men are considered so magnificent" (1.12.258-59).

For poems that are not divided into numbered parts or stanzas, use line numbers. For a first reference, use the word "lines": (lines 5-8). Thereafter use just the numbers: (12-13).

26. Novel with numbered divisions   When a novel has numbered divisions, put the page number first, followed by a semicolon, and then the book, part, or chapter in which the passage may be found. Use abbreviations such as "pt." and "ch."

One of Kingsolver's narrators, teenager Rachel, pushes her vocabulary beyond its limits. For example, Rachel complains that being forced to live in the Congo with her missionary family is "a sheer tapestry of justice" because her chances of finding a boyfriend are "dull and void" (117; bk. 2, ch. 10).

27. Sacred text When citing a sacred text such as the Bible or the Qur'an, name the edition you are using in your works cited entry (see item 19 on p. 542). In your parenthetical citation, give the book, chapter, and verse (or their equivalent), separated by periods. Common abbreviations for books of the Bible are acceptable.

> Consider the words of Solomon: "If your enemy is hungry, give him bread to eat; and if he is thirsty, give him water to drink" (*Oxford Annotated Bible*, Prov. 25.21).

The title of a sacred work is italicized when it refers to a specific edition of the work, as in the preceding example. If you refer to the book in a general sense in your text, neither italicize it nor put it in quotation marks: "The Bible and the Qur'an provide allegories that help readers understand how to lead a moral life."

hackerhandbooks.com/bedhandbook > **Research exercises** > MLA > E-ex 53–1 to 53–3

53b MLA list of works cited

An alphabetized list of works cited, which appears at the end of your research paper, gives publication information for each of the sources you have cited in the paper. Include only sources that you have quoted, summarized, or paraphrased. (For information about preparing the list, see pp. 571–72; for a sample list of works cited, see p. 588.)

General guidelines for works cited in MLA style

In an MLA works cited entry, the first author's name is inverted (the last name comes first, followed by a comma and

Directory to MLA works cited models

Listing authors (print and online)

1. Single author, 532
2. Two or three authors, 532
3. Four or more authors, 533
4. Organization as author, 533
5. Unknown author, 533
6. Two or more works by the same author, 534

Books (print)

7. Basic format for a book, 535
8. Book with an author and an editor, 535
9. Book with an author and a translator, 535
10. Book with an editor, 535
11. Graphic narrative or illustrated book, 537
12. Book with an author using a pseudonym, 537
13. Book in a language other than English, 537
14. Entire anthology, 537
15. One or more selections from an anthology, 538
16. Edition other than the first, 539
17. Multivolume work, 539
18. Encyclopedia or dictionary entry, 539
19. Sacred text, 542
20. Foreword, introduction, preface, or afterword, 542
21. Book with a title in its title, 543
22. Book in a series, 543
23. Republished book, 543
24. Publisher's imprint, 543

Articles in periodicals (print)

25. Article in a journal (paginated by volume or by issue), 544
26. Article in a monthly magazine, 544
27. Article in a weekly magazine, 544
28. Article in a daily newspaper, 544
29. Abstract of a journal article, 545
30. Article with a title in its title, 545
31. Editorial or other unsigned article, 545
32. Letter to the editor, 545
33. Book or film review, 548

Online sources

34. Entire Web site, 548
35. Short work from a Web site, 549
36. Web site with an author using a pseudonym, 551
37. Article in an online scholarly journal, 553
38. Article in an online magazine, 553
39. Article in an online newspaper, 553
40. Work from a database, 553
41. Online book-length work, 554
42. Part of an online book, 554
43. Digital archives, 554
44. Entry in an online reference work, 555
45. Online poem, 555
46. Entire Weblog (blog), 555
47. Entry or comment in a Weblog (blog), 555
48. Academic course or department home page, 556
49. Online video clip, 556
50. Online abstract, 556

the first name), and all other names are in normal order. In titles of works, all words are capitalized except articles (*a, an, the*), prepositions (*to, from, between*, and so on), coordinating conjunctions (*and, but, or, nor, for, so, yet*), and the *to* in infinitives—unless they are the first or last word of the title or subtitle. Titles of periodical articles and other short works, such as brief documents from Web sites, are put in quotation marks; titles of books and other long works, such as entire Web sites, are italicized.

The city of publication is given without a state name. Publishers' names are shortened, usually to the first principal word ("Wiley" for "John Wiley and Sons," for instance), and "University" and "Press" are abbreviated "U" and "P" in the names of university publishers: UP of Florida. The date of publication is the date on the title page or the most recent date on the copyright page.

All works cited entries must include the medium in which a work was published, produced, or delivered. The medium usually appears at the end of the entry, capitalized but neither italicized nor in quotation marks. Typical designations for the medium are "Print," "Web," "Radio," "Television," "CD," "Audiocassette," "Film," "Videocassette," "DVD," "Photograph," "Performance," "Lecture," "MP3 file," and "PDF file." (See specific items throughout this section.)

Listing authors (print and online)

Alphabetize entries in the list of works cited by authors' last names (or by title if a work has no author). The author's name is important because citations in the text of the paper refer to it and readers will be looking for it at the beginning of an entry in the alphabetized list.

NAME CITED IN TEXT

According to Nancy Flynn, . . .

BEGINNING OF WORKS CITED ENTRY

Flynn, Nancy.

1. Single author

author: last name first — title (book) — city of publication — publisher — date — medium

Wood, James. *How Fiction Works*. New York: Farrar, 2008. Print.

2. Two or three authors

first author: last name first — second author: in normal order — title (book) — city of publication

Gourevitch, Philip, and Errol Morris. *Standard Operating Procedure*. New York:

publisher — date — medium

Penguin, 2008. Print.

first author: last name first | other authors: in normal order | title (newspaper article)

Farmer, John, John Azzarello, and Miles Kara. "Real Heroes, Fake Stories."

newspaper title | date of publication | page | medium

New York Times 14 Sept. 2008: WK10. Print.

3. Four or more authors   Name all the authors or name the first author followed by "et al." (Latin for "and others"). In an in-text citation, use the same form for the authors' names as you use in the works cited entry. See item 7 on page 522.

first author: last name first | other authors: in normal order | title (book)

Harris, Shon, Allen Harper, Chris Eagle, and Jonathan Ness. Gray Hat Hacking.

edition number | city of publication | publisher | date | medium

2nd ed. New York: McGraw, 2007. Print.

4. Organization as author

author: organization name, not abbreviated | title (book)

National Wildlife Federation. Rain Check: Conservation Groups Monitor Mercury

city of publication | publisher, with common abbreviations | date

Levels in Milwaukee's Rain. Ann Arbor: Natl. Wildlife Federation, 2001.

medium

Print.

For a publication by a government agency, see item 73. Your in-text citation should also treat the organization as the author (see item 8 on p. 522).

5. Unknown author

Article or other short work

title (newspaper article) | label | newspaper title | date of publication | page

"Poverty, by Outdated Numbers." Editorial. Boston Globe 20 Sept. 2008: A16.

medium

Print.

title (TV episode)　title (TV program)　producer　network　station　city of broadcast　date of broadcast
"Heat." *Frontline*. Prod. Martin Smith. PBS. KTWU, Topeka. 21 Oct. 2008.

medium
Television.

For other examples of an article with no author and a television program, see items 31 and 65, respectively.

Book, entire Web site, or other long work

title (book)　city of publication　publisher　date　medium
New Concise World Atlas. New York: Oxford UP, 2007. Print.

title (Web site)
Women of Protest: Photographs from the Records of the National Woman's Party.

sponsor of site　no date　medium　date of access
Lib. of Cong., n.d. Web. 29 Sept. 2008.

Before concluding that the author of an online source is unknown, check carefully (see the tip on p. 520). Also remember that an organization or a government may be the author (see items 4 and 73).

6. Two or more works by the same author If your list of works cited includes two or more works by the same author, first alphabetize the works by title (ignoring the article *A*, *An*, or *The* at the beginning of a title). Use the author's name for the first entry only; for subsequent entries, use three hyphens followed by a period. The three hyphens must stand for exactly the same name or names as in the first entry.

Knopp, Lisa. *Field of Vision*. Iowa City: U of Iowa P, 1996. Print.

---. *The Nature of Home: A Lexicon and Essays*. Lincoln: U of Nebraska P, 2002. Print.

Books (print)

Items 7–24 apply to print books. For online books, see items 41 and 42. For an illustrated citation of a print book, see page 536.

7. Basic format for a book

author: last name first / book title / city of publication / publisher

Sacks, Oliver. *Musicophilia: Tales of Music and the Brain*. New York: Knopf,

date / medium

2007. Print.

Take the information about the book from its title page and copyright page. Use a short form of the publisher's name; omit terms such as "Press," "Inc.," and "Co." except when naming university presses ("Harvard UP," for example). If the copyright page lists more than one date, use the most recent one.

8. Book with an author and an editor

author: last name first / book title / editor's name: in normal order / city of publication

Plath, Sylvia. *The Unabridged Journals of Sylvia Plath*. Ed. Karen V. Kukil. New York:

imprint-publisher / date / medium

Anchor-Doubleday, 2000. Print.

The abbreviation "Ed." means "Edited by," so it is the same for one or multiple editors.

9. Book with an author and a translator
"Trans." means "Translated by," so it is the same for one or multiple translators.

Scirocco, Alfonso. *Garibaldi: Citizen of the World*. Trans. Allan Cameron. Princeton: Princeton UP, 2007. Print.

10. Book with an editor
Begin with the editor's name. For one editor, use "ed." (for "editor") after the name; for multiple editors, use "eds." (for "editors"). See the example on page 537.

Citation at a glance | Book (MLA)

To cite a print book in MLA style, include the following elements:

1 Author
2 Title and subtitle
3 City of publication
4 Publisher
5 Date of publication
6 Medium

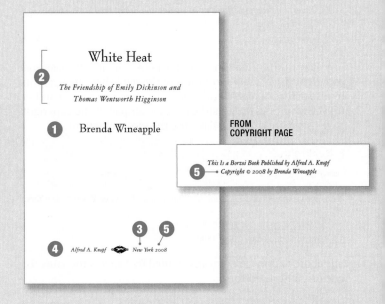

WORKS CITED ENTRY FOR A PRINT BOOK

Wineapple, Brenda. *White Heat: The Friendship of Emily Dickinson and Thomas Wentworth Higginson*. New York: Knopf, 2008. Print.

For more on citing print books in MLA style, see pages 535–43.

Lago, Mary, Linda K. Hughes, and Elizabeth MacLeod Walls, eds. *The BBC Talks of E. M. Forster, 1929-1960*. Columbia: U of Missouri P, 2008. Print.

11. Graphic narrative or illustrated book   For a book that combines text and illustrations, begin your citation with the person you wish to emphasize (writer, illustrator, artist) and list any other contributors after the title of the book. Use the abbreviation "illus." and other common labels to identify contributors. If the writer and illustrator are the same person, cite the work as you would a book, with no labels.

Weaver, Dustin, illus. *The Tenth Circle*. By Jodi Picoult. New York: Washington Square, 2006. Print.

Moore, Alan. *V for Vendetta*. Illus. David Lloyd. New York: Vertigo-DC Comics, 2008. Print.

Thompson, Craig. *Blankets*. Marietta: Top Shelf, 2005.

12. Book with an author using a pseudonym   Give the author's name as it appears on the title page (the pseudonym), and follow it with the author's real name in brackets.

Dinesen, Isak [Karen Blixen]. *Winter's Tales*. 1942. New York: Vintage, 1993. Print.

13. Book in a language other than English   If your readers are not familiar with the language of the book, include a translation of the title in brackets. Capitalize the title according to the conventions of the book's language, and give the original publication information.

Nemtsov, Boris, and Vladimir Milov. *Putin. Itogi. Nezavisimyi Ekspertnyi Doklad* [*Putin. The Results: An Independent Expert Report*]. Moscow: Novaya Gazeta, 2008. Print.

14. Entire anthology   An anthology is a collection of works on a common theme, often with different authors for the selections and usually with an editor for the entire volume. The abbreviation "eds." is for multiple editors. If the book has only one editor, use the singular "ed." after the editor's name.

Dumanis, Michael, and Cate Marvin, eds. *Legitimate Dangers: American
Poets of the New Century*. Louisville: Sarabande, 2006. Print.

15. One or more selections from an anthology

One selection from anthology

author of selection:
last name first   title of selection   title of anthology

Brouwer, Joel. "The Spots." *Legitimate Dangers: American Poets of the*

editor(s) of anthology: city of
name(s) in normal order   publication   publisher

New Century. Ed. Michael Dumanis and Cate Marvin. Louisville: Sarabande,

pages of
date   selection   medium

2006. 51-52. Print.

The abbreviation "Ed." means "Edited by," so it is the same for
one or multiple editors. For an illustrated citation of a selection from an anthology, see pages 540–41.

If you use two or more works from the same anthology in
your paper, provide an entry for the entire anthology (see item
14) and give a shortened entry for each selection. Cross-reference
the editor(s) of the anthology and give the page number(s) on
which the selection appears. Use the medium only in the entry
for the complete anthology. Alphabetize the entries in the list of
works cited by authors' or editors' last names, as shown here.

Two or more selections, with separate anthology entry

editor(s) of anthology: pages
author of selection   title of selection   last name(s) only   of selection

Brouwer, Joel. "The Spots." Dumanis and Marvin 51-52.

editor(s) of anthology   title of anthology

Dumanis, Michael, and Cate Marvin, eds. *Legitimate Dangers: American Poets of the*

city of
publication   publisher   date   medium

New Century. Louisville: Sarabande, 2006. Print.

author of
selection   title of selection   editor(s) of anthology: pages of
                               last name(s) only   selection

Keith, Sally. "Orphean Song." Dumanis and Marvin 195-96.

16. Edition other than the first Include the number of the
edition (1st, 2nd, 3rd, and so on). If the book has a translator
or an editor in addition to the author, give the name of the
translator or editor before the edition number, using the abbreviation "Trans." for "Translated by" (see item 9) or "Ed."
for "Edited by" (see item 10).

Auletta, Ken. *The Underclass*. 2nd ed. Woodstock: Overlook, 2000. Print.

17. Multivolume work Include the total number of volumes
before the city and publisher, using the abbreviation "vols."
If the volumes were published over several years, give the inclusive dates of publication. The abbreviation "Ed." means
"Edited by," so it is the same for one or multiple editors.

author: last   editor's name: total   city of
name first   title   in normal order   volumes   publication   publisher

Stark, Freya. *Letters*. Ed. Lucy Moorehead. 8 vols. Salisbury: Compton,

         inclusive
         dates   medium

    1974-82. Print.

If you cite only one of the volumes in your paper, include
the volume number before the city and publisher and give the
date of publication for that volume. After the date, give the medium of publication followed by the total number of volumes.

author: last   editor: in   volume   city of   date of
name first   title   normal order   cited   publication   publisher   volume

Stark, Freya. *Letters*. Ed. Lucy Moorehead. Vol. 5. Salisbury: Compton, 1978.

             total
    medium volumes

    Print. 8 vols.

18. Encyclopedia or dictionary entry List the author of the
entry (if there is one), the title of the entry, the title of the reference work, the edition number (if any), the date of the

Citation at a glance | Selection from an anthology (MLA)

To cite a selection from an anthology in MLA style, include the following elements:

1 Author of selection
2 Title of selection
3 Title and subtitle of anthology
4 Editor(s) of anthology
5 City of publication
6 Publisher
7 Date of publication
8 Page numbers of selection
9 Medium

FIRST PAGE OF SELECTION

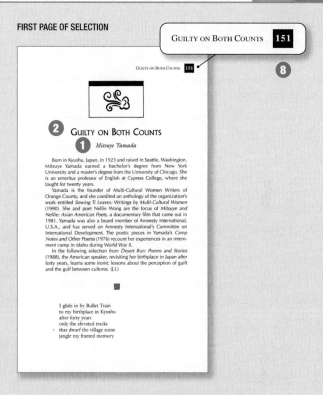

GUILTY ON BOTH COUNTS   151

2 GUILTY ON BOTH COUNTS

1 *Mitsuye Yamada*

Born in Kyushu, Japan, in 1923 and raised in Seattle, Washington, Mitsuye Yamada earned a bachelor's degree from New York University and a master's degree from the University of Chicago. She is an emeritus professor of English at Cypress College, where she taught for twenty years.

Yamada is the founder of Multi-Cultural Women Writers of Orange County, and she coedited an anthology of the organization's work entitled *Sowing Ti Leaves: Writings by Multi-Cultural Women* (1990). She and poet Nellie Wong are the focus of *Mitsuye and Nellie: Asian American Poets*, a documentary film that came out in 1981. Yamada was also a board member of Amnesty International, U.S.A., and has served on Amnesty International's Committee on International Development. The poetic pieces in Yamada's *Camp Notes and Other Poems* (1976) recount her experiences in an internment camp in Idaho during World War II.

In the following selection from *Desert Run: Poems and Stories* (1988), the American speaker, revisiting her birthplace in Japan after forty years, learns some ironic lessons about the perception of guilt and the gulf between cultures. (J.I.)

I glide in by Bullet Train
to my birthplace in Kyushu
after forty years
only the elevated tracks
that dwarf the village scene
jangle my framed memory.

WORKS CITED ENTRY FOR A SELECTION FROM AN ANTHOLOGY

Yamada, Mitsuye. "Guilty on Both Counts." *Asian-American Literature: An*

Anthology. Ed. Shirley Geok-lin Lim. Lincolnwood: NTC, 2000. 151-54.

Print.

For more on citing selections from anthologies in MLA style, see pages 537–39.

edition, and the medium. Volume and page numbers are not necessary because the entries in the source are arranged alphabetically and are therefore easy to locate.

Posner, Rebecca. "Romance Languages." *The Encyclopaedia Britannica: Macropaedia*. 15th ed. 1987. Print.

"Sonata." *The American Heritage Dictionary of the English Language*. 4th ed. 2000. Print.

19. Sacred text Give the title of the edition of the sacred text (taken from the title page), italicized; the editor's or translator's name (if any); publication information; and the medium. Add the name of the version, if there is one.

The Oxford Annotated Bible with the Apocrypha. Ed. Herbert G. May and Bruce M. Metzger. New York: Oxford UP, 1965. Print. Rev. Standard Vers.

The Qur'an: Translation. Trans. Abdullah Yusuf Ali. Elmhurst: Tahrike, 2000. Print.

20. Foreword, introduction, preface, or afterword

author of foreword: last name first | book part | book title
Bennett, Hal Zina. Foreword. *Shimmering Images: A Handy Little Guide to Writing*

author of book: in normal order | city of publication | imprint-publisher | date
Memoir. By Lisa Dale Norton. New York: Griffin-St. Martin's, 2008.

pages of foreword | medium
xiii-xvi. Print.

If the book part has a title, include it in quotation marks immediately after the author's name and before the label for the book part.

Ozick, Cynthia. "Portrait of the Essay as a Warm Body." Introduction. *The Best American Essays 1998*. Ed. Ozick. Boston: Houghton, 1998. xv-xxi. Print.

21. Book with a title in its title If the book title contains a title normally italicized, neither italicize the internal title nor place it in quotation marks.

Woodson, Jon. *A Study of Joseph Heller's* Catch-22: *Going Around Twice.*
New York: Lang, 2001. Print.

If the title within the title is normally put in quotation marks, retain the quotation marks and italicize the entire book title.

Millás, Juan José. *"Personality Disorders" and Other Stories.* Trans. Gregory
B. Kaplan. New York: MLA, 2007. Print. MLA Texts and Trans.

22. Book in a series After the publication information, give the medium of publication and then the series name as it appears on the title page, followed by the series number, if any.

Douglas, Dan. *Assessing Languages for Specific Purposes.* Cambridge:
Cambridge UP, 2000. Print. Cambridge Applied Linguistics Ser.

23. Republished book After the title of the book, give the original publication date, followed by the current publication information. If the republished book contains new material, such as an introduction or afterword, include information about the new material after the original date.

Trilling, Lionel. *The Liberal Imagination.* 1950. Introd. Louis Menand.
New York: New York Review of Books, 2008. Print.

24. Publisher's imprint If a book was published by an imprint (a division) of a publishing company, give the name of the imprint, a hyphen, and the name of the publisher.

Ackroyd, Peter. *The Fall of Troy.* New York: Talese-Doubleday, 2007. Print.

Articles in periodicals (print)

This section shows how to prepare works cited entries for articles in print magazines, journals, and newspapers. See "General guidelines" and "Listing authors" on pages 529 and 532 for how to handle basic parts of the entries. See also "Online sources" on page 548 for articles from Web sites and articles accessed through a library's database.

For articles appearing on consecutive pages, provide the range of pages (see items 25 and 26). When an article does not appear on consecutive pages, give the number of the first page followed by a plus sign: 32+. For dates requiring a month, abbreviate all but May, June, and July. For an illustrated citation of an article in a periodical, see pages 546–47.

25. Article in a journal (paginated by volume or by issue)

author: last name first — article title

Blackburn, Robin. "Economic Democracy: Meaningful, Desirable, Feasible?"

journal title — volume, issue — year — page range — medium

Daedalus 136.3 (2007): 36-45. Print.

26. Article in a monthly magazine

author: last name first — article title — magazine title — date: month(s) + year

Lanting, Frans. "Life: A Journey through Time." *Audubon* Nov.-Dec. 2006:

page range — medium

48-52. Print.

27. Article in a weekly magazine

author: last name first — article title — magazine title — date: day + month + year — page range — medium

von Drehle, David. "The Ghosts of Memphis." *Time* 7 Apr. 2008: 34-37. Print.

28. Article in a daily newspaper Give the page range of the article. If the article does not appear on consecutive pages, use a plus sign (+) after the first page number. If the city of publication is not obvious from the title of the newspaper, include the city in brackets after the name of the newspaper.

If sections are identified by letter, include the section letter as part of the page number. If sections are numbered, include the section number between the date and the page number, using the abbreviation "sec.": 14 Sept. 2008, sec. 2: 21.

Page number with section letter
Include the section letter as part of the page number.

author: last name first — article title — newspaper title — date: day + month + year

McKenna, Phil. "It Takes Just One Village." *New York Times* 23 Sept. 2008,

name of edition — page — medium

New England ed.: D1. Print.

Page number with section number
Include the section number immediately after the date, using the abbreviation "sec."

author: last name first — article title — newspaper title — city of publication

Knox, David Blake. "Lord Archer, Storyteller." *Sunday Independent* [Dublin]

date: inverted — section — page — medium

14 Sept. 2008, sec. 2: 9. Print.

29. Abstract of a journal article   Include the word "Abstract" after the title of the article.

Walker, Joyce. "Narratives in the Database: Memorializing September 11th
    Online." Abstract. *Computers and Composition* 24.2 (2007): 121. Print.

30. Article with a title in its title   Use single quotation marks around a title or another quoted term that appears in an article title. Italicize a title or term normally italicized.

Shen, Min. "'Quite a Moon!' The Archetypal Feminine in *Our Town*." *American
    Drama* 16.2 (2007): 1-14. Print.

31. Editorial or other unsigned article   Begin with the article title and alphabetize the entry by title in the list of works cited.

"Getting the Message: Communicating Electronically with Doctors Can Spur
    Honesty from Young Patients." Editorial. *Columbus* [OH] *Dispatch* 19
    June 2008: 10A. Print.

32. Letter to the editor

Morris, David. "Fiercely Proud." Letter. *Progressive* Feb. 2008: 6. Print.

Citation at a glance | Article in a periodical (MLA)

To cite an article in a print periodical in MLA style, include the following elements:

1 Author of article
2 Title and subtitle of article
3 Title of periodical
4 Volume and issue number (for scholarly journal)
5 Date or year of publication
6 Page numbers of article
7 Medium

FIRST PAGE OF ARTICLE

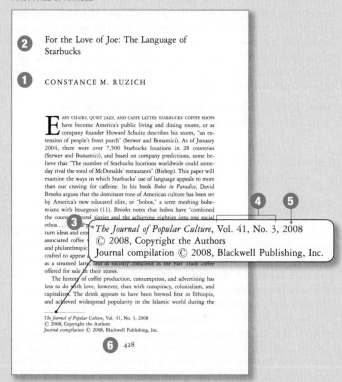

WORKS CITED ENTRY FOR AN ARTICLE IN A PRINT PERIODICAL

Ruzich, Constance M. "For the Love of Joe: The Language of Starbucks."

Journal of Popular Culture 41.3 (2008): 428-42. Print.

For more on citing print periodical articles in MLA style, see pages 543–48.

33. Book or film review   Name the reviewer and the title of the review, if any, followed by "Rev. of" and the title and author or director of the work reviewed. Add the publication information for the periodical in which the review appears. If the review has no author and no title, begin with "Rev. of" and alphabetize the entry by the first principal word in the title of the work reviewed.

Dodge, Chris. Rev. of *The Radical Jack London: Writings on War and Revolution*, ed. Jonah Raskni. *Utne Reader* Sept.-Oct. 2008: 35. Print.

Lane, Anthony. "Dream On." Rev. of *The Science of Sleep* and *Renaissance*, dir. Michel Gondry. *New Yorker* 25 Sept. 2006: 155-57. Print.

Online sources

MLA guidelines assume that readers can locate most online sources by entering the author, title, or other identifying information in a search engine or a database. Consequently, the *MLA Handbook* does not require a Web address (URL) in citations for online sources. Some instructors may require a URL; for an example, see the note at the end of item 34.

MLA style calls for a sponsor or a publisher for most online sources. If a source has no sponsor or publisher, use the abbreviation "N.p." (for "No publisher") in the sponsor position. If there is no date of publication or update, use "n.d." (for "no date") after the sponsor. For an article in an online journal or an article from a database, give page numbers if they are available; if they are not, use the abbreviation "n. pag." (See item 37.)

34. Entire Web site

Web site with author

author: last name first   title of Web site   sponsor of site (personal page)   update   medium

Peterson, Susan Lynn. *The Life of Martin Luther*. Susan Lynn Peterson, 2005. Web.

date of access: inverted

24 Jan. 2009.

Web site with organization (group) as author

organization name:
not abbreviated   title of Web site   sponsor:
abbreviated

American Library Association. *American Library Association*. ALA,

update medium   date of access:
inverted

2008. Web. 14 Jan. 2009.

Web site with no author

title of Web site   sponsor of site   update   medium

Margaret Sanger Papers Project. History Dept., New York U, 18 Oct. 2000. Web.

date of access:
inverted

6 Jan. 2009.

Web site with editor

See item 10 (p. 535) for listing the name(s) of editor(s).

Halsall, Paul, ed. *Internet Modern History Sourcebook*. Fordham U, 22 Sept.

2001. Web. 19 Jan. 2009.

Web site with no title

Use the label "Home page" or another appropriate description in place of a title.

Yoon, Mina. Home page. Oak Ridge Natl. Laboratory, 28 Dec. 2006. Web.

12 Jan. 2009.

NOTE: If your instructor requires a URL for Web sources, include the URL, enclosed in angle brackets, at the end of the entry. When a URL in a works cited entry must be divided at the end of a line, break it after a slash. Do not insert a hyphen.

Peterson, Susan Lynn. *The Life of Martin Luther*. Susan Lynn Peterson, 2005.

Web. 24 Jan. 2009. <http://www.susanlynnpeterson.com/index_files/
luther.htm>.

35. Short work from a Web site   Short works include articles, poems, and other documents that are not book length or that appear as internal pages on a Web site. For an illustrated citation of a short work from a Web site, see page 550.

Citation at a glance | Short work from a Web site (MLA)

To cite a short work from a Web site in MLA style, include the following elements:

1 Author of short work (if any)
2 Title of short work
3 Title of Web site
4 Sponsor of Web site ("N.p." if none)
5 Update date ("n.d." if none)
6 Medium
7 Date of access

INTERNAL PAGE OF WEB SITE

FOOTER ON HOME PAGE

the local area. It houses the most extensive collection of art, artifacts, and manuscripts pertaining to American whaling in the age of sail - late eighteenth century to the early twentieth, when sailing ships dominated merchant trade and whaling.

18 Johnny Cake Hill | New Bedford, MA | 02740-6398 | Tel. (508) 997-0046
Fax: (508) 997-0018 | Library Fax: (508) 207-1064

©Copyright 2006 Old Dartmouth Historical Society / New Bedford Whaling Museum

WORKS CITED ENTRY FOR A SHORT WORK FROM A WEB SITE

"Overview of American Whaling." *New Bedford Whaling Museum*. Old

Dartmouth Hist. Soc./New Bedford Whaling Museum, 2006. Web.

27 Oct. 2008.

For more on citing sources from Web sites in MLA style, see pages 548–49 and 551–58.

Short work with author

author: last name first — title of short work — title of Web site — sponsor — no update date

Shiva, Vandana. "Bioethics: A Third World Issue." *NativeWeb*. NativeWeb, n.d.

medium — date of access: inverted

Web. 22 Jan. 2007.

Short work with no author

title of short work — title of Web site — sponsor of site — update — medium — date of access: inverted

"Sister Aimee." *American Experience*. PBS Online, 2 Apr. 2007. Web. 30 Oct. 2008.

36. Web site with an author using a pseudonym Begin the entry with the pseudonym and add the author's or creator's real name, if known, in brackets. Follow with the information required for a Web site or a short work from a Web site (see item 34 or 35).

Grammar Girl [Mignon Fogarty]. "What Is the Plural of 'Mouse'?" *Grammar Girl: Quick and Dirty Tips for Better Writing*. Holtzbrinck, 16 Sept. 2008. Web. 10 Nov. 2008.

Citation at a glance | Article from a database (MLA)

To cite an article from a database in MLA style, include the following elements:

1 Author of article
2 Title of article
3 Title of periodical
4 Volume and issue numbers (for scholarly journal)
5 Date or year of publication
6 Page numbers of article ("n. pag." if there are none)
7 Name of database
8 Medium
9 Date of access

WORKS CITED ENTRY FOR AN ARTICLE FROM A DATABASE

Kranz, David L. "Tracking the Sounds of Franco Zeffirelli's *The Taming of the Shrew*." *Literature-Film Quarterly* 36.2 (2008): 94-112. *Academic OneFile*. Web. 28 Oct. 2008.

For more on citing articles from a database in MLA style, see pages 553–54.

37. Article in an online scholarly journal

author: last name first   article title

Mason, John Edwin. "'Mannenberg': Notes on the Making of an Icon and Anthem."

volume,   not   date of access:
journal title   issue year   paginated medium   inverted

African Studies Quarterly 9.4 (2007): n. pag. Web. 23 Sept. 2008.

38. Article in an online magazine Give the author; the title of the article, in quotation marks; the title of the magazine, italicized; the sponsor or publisher of the site (use "N.p." if there is none); the date of publication; the medium; and your date of access.

Burton, Robert. "The Certainty Epidemic." *Salon.com*. Salon Media Group,

    29 Feb. 2008. Web. 18 Jan. 2009.

39. Article in an online newspaper Give the author, the title of the article, in quotation marks; the title of the newspaper, italicized; the sponsor or publisher of the site (use "N.p." if there is none); the date of publication; the medium; and your date of access.

Smith, Andrew D. "Poll: More than 70% of US Workers Use Internet on the

    Job." *Dallasnews.com*. Dallas Morning News, 25 Sept. 2008. Web.

    29 Sept. 2008.

40. Work from a database For a source retrieved from a library's subscription database, first list the publication information for the source (see items 25–33) and then provide information about the database. For an illustrated citation of an article from a database, see page 552.

author of source: title of   volume,   page
last name first   article   journal title   issue   year   numbers

Heyen, William. "Sunlight." *American Poetry Review* 36.2 (2007): 55-56. *Expanded*

date of access:
database name   medium   inverted

    Academic ASAP. Web. 24 Sept. 2008.

Barrera, Rebeca María. "A Case for Bilingual Education." *Scholastic Parent and*

    Child Nov.-Dec. 2004: 72-73. *Academic Search Premier*. Web. 1 Feb. 2009.

Williams, Jeffrey J. "Why Today's Publishing World Is Reprising the Past."
Chronicle of Higher Education 13 June 2008: 8+. *LexisNexis Academic*.
Web. 29 Sept. 2008.

41. Online book-length work Cite a book or a book-length work, such as a play or a long poem, as you would a short work from a Web site (see item 35), but italicize the title of the work.

author: last name first | title of long poem | title of Web site | sponsor of site | update

Milton, John. *Paradise Lost: Book I. Poetryfoundation.org*. Poetry Foundation, 2008.

medium | date of access: inverted

Web. 14 Dec. 2008.

Give the print publication information for the work, if available (see items 7–24), followed by the title of the Web site, the medium, and your date of access.

author: last name first | book title

Jacobs, Harriet A. *Incidents in the Life of a Slave Girl: Written by Herself*. Ed.

editor of original book | city of publication | year | title of Web site | medium

L. Maria Child. Boston, 1861. *Documenting the American South*. Web.

date of access: inverted

3 Feb. 2009.

42. Part of an online book Begin as for a part of a print book (see item 20 on p. 542). If the online book part has no page numbers, use "N. pag." following the publication information. End with the Web site on which the work is found, the medium, and your date of access.

Adams, Henry. "Diplomacy." *The Education of Henry Adams*. Boston: Houghton,
1918. N. pag. *Bartleby.com: Great Books Online*. Web. 8 Jan. 2009.

43. Digital archives Digital archives are online collections of documents or records—books, letters, photographs, data—that have been converted to digital form. Cite publication information for the original document, if it is available, using the models throughout section 53b. Then give the location of the document, if any, neither italicized nor in quotation marks; the name of the archive, italicized; the medium ("Web"); and your date of access.

Fiore, Mark. *Shockwaves*. 18 Oct. 2001. *September 11 Digital Archive*. Web. 3 Apr. 2009.

Oblinger, Maggie. Letter to Charlie Thomas. 31 Mar. 1895. Nebraska State Hist. Soc. *Prairie Settlement: Nebraska Photographs and Family Letters, 1862-1912*. Web. 3 Apr. 2009.

WPA Household Census for 1047 W. 50th Street, Los Angeles County. 1939. USC Lib. Spec. Collections. *USC Libraries Digital Archive*. Web. 12 Mar. 2009.

44. Entry in an online reference work Give the title of the entry, in quotation marks; the title of the site; the sponsor and update date (use "n.d." if there is none); the medium; and your date of access.

"Native American Church." *Britannica*. Encyclopaedia Britannica, 2008. Web. 29 Jan. 2009.

45. Online poem Cite as you would a short work from a Web site (item 35) or part of an online book (item 42).

Bell, Acton [Anne Brontë]. "Mementos." *Poems by Currer, Ellis, and Acton Bell*. London, 1846. N. pag. *A Celebration of Women Writers*. Web. 18 Sept. 2008.

46. Entire Weblog (blog) Cite a blog as you would an entire Web site (see item 34).

Gristmill. Grist Magazine, 2008. Web. 19 Jan. 2009.

47. Entry or comment in a Weblog (blog) Cite an entry or a comment (a response to an entry) in a blog as you would a short work from a Web site (see item 35). If the comment or entry has no title, use the label "Weblog entry" or "Weblog comment." Follow with the remaining information as for an entire blog in item 46.

"Social Media: Facebook and MySpace as University Curricula." *Open Education*. Open Education.net, n.d. Web. 19 Sept. 2008.

Cindy. Weblog comment. *Open Education*. Open Education.net, 5 Sept. 2008. Web. 14 Aug. 2009.

48. Academic course or department home page Cite as a short work from a Web site (see item 35). For a course home page, begin with the name of the instructor and the title of the course or title of the page (use "Course home page" if there is no other title). For a department home page, begin with the name of the department and the label "Dept. home page."

Marrone, Carole. "355:301: College Writing and Research." *Rutgers School of Arts and Sciences*. Writing Program, Rutgers U, 2010. Web. 19 Sept. 2010.

Comparative Media Studies. Dept. home page. *Massachusetts Institute of Technology*. MIT, 2010. Web. 6 Oct. 2010.

49. Online video clip Cite as you would a short work from a Web site (see item 35).

author: last name first — video title — title of Web site — sponsor — update

Murphy, Beth. "Tips for a Good Profile Piece." *YouTube*. YouTube, 7 Sept. 2008.

medium — date of access: inverted

Web. 19 Apr. 2009.

50. Online abstract Cite as you would an abstract of a journal article (see item 29), giving whatever print information is available, followed by the medium and your date of access. If you found the abstract in an online periodical database, include the name of the database after the print publication information (see item 40).

Turner, Fred. "Romantic Automatism: Art, Technology, and Collaborative Labor in Cold War America." Abstract. *Journal of Visual Culture* 7.1 (2008): 5. Web. 25 Oct. 2008.

51. Online editorial or letter to the editor   Cite as you would an editorial or a letter to the editor in a print publication (see item 31 or 32), adding information for a short work from a Web site (see item 35).

"Compromise Is Key with Religion at Work." Editorial. *StarTribune.com*. Star Tribune, 18 June 2008. Web. 25 June 2008.

52. Online review   Begin the entry as you would for a review in a magazine or newspaper (see item 33). If the review is published in print as well as online, add publication information as for an article in a periodical (see items 25–28), the Web site on which the review appears, the medium, and your date of access. If the review is published only on the Web, add information as for a short work from a Web site (see item 35). If you found the review in a database, cite as in item 40.

Greer, W. R. "Who's the Fairest One of All?" Rev. of *Mirror, Mirror*, by Gregory Maguire. *Reviewsofbooks.com*. Reviewsofbooks.com, 2003. Web. 26 Oct. 2008.

53. E-mail message   Begin with the writer's name and the subject line. Then write "Message to" followed by the name of the recipient. End with the date of the message and the medium ("E-mail").

Lowe, Walter. "Review Questions." Message to the author. 15 Mar. 2009. E-mail.

54. Posting to an online discussion list   When possible, cite archived versions of postings. If you cannot locate an archived version, keep a copy of the posting for your records. Begin with the author's name, followed by the title or subject line, in quotation marks (use the label "Online posting" if the posting has no title). Then proceed as for a short work from a Web site (see item 35).

Fainton, Peter. "Re: Backlash against New Labour." *Media Lens Message Board*. Media Lens, 7 May 2008. Web. 2 June 2008.

55. Entry in a wiki   A wiki is an online reference that is openly edited by its users. Treat an entry in a wiki as you would a short work from a Web site (see item 35). Because wiki content is, by definition, collectively edited and can be updated frequently, do not include an author. Give the title of the entry; the name of the wiki, italicized; the sponsor or publisher of the wiki (use "N.p." if there is none); the date of the last update; the medium; and your date of access.

"Hip Hop Music." *Wikipedia*. Wikimedia Foundation, 26 Sept. 2008. Web. 18 Mar. 2009.

"Negation in Languages." *UniLang.org*. UniLang, 25 Oct. 2004. Web. 9 June 2009.

Audio and visual sources (including online versions)

56. Digital file   A digital file is any document or image that exists in digital form, independent of a Web site. To cite a digital file, begin with information required for the source (such as a photograph, a report, a sound recording, or a radio program), following the guidelines throughout 53b. Then for the medium, indicate the type of file: "JPEG file," "PDF file," "MP3 file," and so on.

photographer — photograph title — date of composition — location of photograph

Hine, Lewis W. *Girl in Cherryville Mill*. 1908. Prints and Photographs Div., Lib. of

medium: file type

Cong. JPEG file.

"Scenes from a Recession." *This American Life*. Narr. Ira Glass. NPR, 30 Mar. 2009. MP3 file.

National Institute of Mental Health. *What Rescue Workers Can Do*.

Washington: US Dept. of Health and Human Services, 2006. PDF file.

57. Podcast If you view or listen to a podcast online, cite it as you would a short work from a Web site (see item 35). If you download the podcast and view or listen to it on a computer or portable player, cite it as a digital file (see item 56).

Podcast online

"Calculating the Demand for Charter Schools." Narr. David Guenthner. *Texas PolicyCast*. Texas Public Policy Foundation, 28 Aug. 2008. Web. 10 Jan. 2009.

Podcast downloaded as digital file

"Calculating the Demand for Charter Schools." Narr. David Guenthner. *Texas PolicyCast*. Texas Public Policy Foundation, 28 Aug. 2008. MP3 file.

58. Musical score For both print and online versions, begin with the composer's name; the title of the work, italicized (unless it is named by form, number, and key); and the date of composition. For a print source, give the place of publication; the name of the publisher and date of publication; and the medium. For an online source, give the title of the Web site; the publisher or sponsor of the site; the date of Web publication; the medium; and your date of access.

Handel, G. F. *Messiah: An Oratorio*. N.d. *CCARH Publications: Scores and Parts*. Center for Computer Assisted Research in the Humanities, 2003. Web. 5 Jan. 2009.

59. Sound recording Begin with the name of the person you want to emphasize: the composer, conductor ("Cond."), or performer ("Perf."). For a long work, give the title, italicized (unless it is named by form, number, and key); the names of pertinent artists (such as performers, readers, or musicians); and the orchestra and conductor, if relevant. End with the manufacturer, the date, and the medium ("CD," "Audiocassette").

Bizet, Georges. *Carmen*. Perf. Jennifer Laramore, Thomas Moser, Angela Gheorghiu, and Samuel Ramey. Bavarian State Orch. and Chorus. Cond. Giuseppe Sinopoli. Warner, 1996. CD.

For a song, put the title in quotation marks. If you include the name of the album or CD, italicize it.

Blige, Mary J. "Be without You." *The Breakthrough*. Geffen, 2005. CD.

60. Film Typically, begin with the title, italicized, followed by the director and the lead actors ("Perf.") or narrator ("Narr."); the distributor; the year of the film's release; and the medium ("Film," "Videocassette"). If your paper emphasizes a person involved with the film, you may begin with that person, as in the first example in item 61.

movie title   director   major performers

Frozen River. Dir. Courtney Hunt. Perf. Melissa Leo, Charlie McDermott, and Misty

release
distributor date medium

Upham. Sony, 2008. Film.

61. DVD For a film on DVD, cite as you would a film, giving "DVD" as the medium. To cite the film as a whole, use the model in item 60. If your paper emphasizes a particular person, begin with that person's name and title, as shown here.

Forster, Marc, dir. *Finding Neverland*. Perf. Johnny Depp, Kate Winslet, Julie
    Christie, Radha Mitchell, and Dustin Hoffman. Miramax, 2004. DVD.

For any other work on DVD, such as an educational work or a game, cite as you would a film, giving information about the author, director, distributor, and so on.

Across the Drafts: Students and Teachers Talk about Feedback. Harvard
    Expository Writing Program, 2005. DVD.

62. Special feature on a DVD Begin with the title of the feature, in quotation marks, and the names of any important contributors, as for films or DVDs (item 60 or 61). End with information about the DVD, as in item 61, including the disc number, if any.

"Sweeney's London." Prod. Eric Young. *Sweeney Todd: The Demon Barber of
    Fleet Street*. Dir. Tim Burton. DreamWorks, 2007. DVD. Disc 2.

63. CD-ROM Treat a CD-ROM as you would any other source, but add the medium ("CD-ROM").

"Pimpernel." *The American Heritage Dictionary of the English Language.*
     4th ed. Boston: Houghton, 2000. CD-ROM.

64. Computer software or video game List the developer or author of the software (if any); the title, italicized; the distributor and date of publication; and the platform or medium.

Firaxis Games. *Sid Meier's Civilization Revolution.* Take-Two Interactive, 2008.
     Xbox 360.

65. Radio or television program Begin with the title of the radio segment or television episode (if there is one), in quotation marks. Then give the title of the program or series, italicized; relevant information about the program, such as the writer ("By"), director ("Dir."), performers ("Perf."), or narrator ("Narr."); the network; the local station (if any) and location; the date of broadcast; and the medium ("Television," "Radio"). For a program you accessed online, after the information about the program give the network, the original broadcast date, the title of the Web site, the medium ("Web"), and your date of access.

"Machines of the Gods." *Ancient Discoveries.* History Channel. 14 Oct. 2008.
     Television.

"Elif Shafak: Writing under a Watchful Eye." *Fresh Air.* Narr. Terry Gross. Natl.
     Public Radio, 6 Feb. 2007. *NPR.org.* Web. 22 Feb. 2009.

66. Radio or television interview Begin with the name of the person who was interviewed, followed by the word "Interview" and the interviewer's name, if relevant. End with the title of the program, the network, and other information about the program as in item 65.

De Niro, Robert, Barry Levinson, and Art Linson. Interview by Charlie Rose.
     Charlie Rose. PBS. WGBH, Boston, 13 Oct. 2008. Television.

67. Live performance For a live performance of a concert, a play, a ballet, or an opera, begin with the title of the work performed, italicized. Then give the author or composer of the work ("By"); relevant information such as the director ("Dir."), the choreographer ("Chor."), the conductor ("Cond."), or the major performers ("Perf."); the theater, ballet, or opera company, if any; the theater and location; the date of the performance; and the label "Performance."

The Brothers Size. By Tarell Alvin McCraney. Dir. Bijan Sheibani. Young Vic
    Theatre, London. 15 Oct. 2008. Performance.

Symphony no. 4 in G. By Gustav Mahler. Cond. Mark Wigglesworth. Perf.
    Juliane Banse and Boston Symphony Orch. Symphony Hall, Boston.
    17 Apr. 2009. Performance.

68. Lecture or public address Begin with the speaker's name, followed by the title of the lecture (if any), in quotation marks; the organization sponsoring the lecture; the location; the date; and a label such as "Lecture" or "Address."

Wellbery, David E. "On a Sentence of Franz Kafka." Franke Inst. for the
    Humanities. Gleacher Center, Chicago. 1 Feb. 2006. Lecture.

69. Work of art Cite the artist's name; the title of the artwork, italicized; the date of composition; the medium of composition (for instance, "Lithograph on paper," "Photograph," "Charcoal on paper"); and the institution and city in which the artwork is located. For artworks found online, omit the medium of composition and include the title of the Web site, the medium ("Web"), and your date of access.

Constable, John. *Dedham Vale*. 1802. Oil on canvas. Victoria and Albert
    Museum, London.

Hessing, Valjean. *Caddo Myth*. 1976. Joslyn Art Museum, Omaha. *Joslyn Art
    Museum*. Web. 19 Apr. 2009.

70. Cartoon Give the cartoonist's name; the title of the cartoon, if it has one, in quotation marks; the label "Cartoon" or "Comic strip"; publication information; and the medium. To cite an online cartoon, instead of publication information give the title of the Web site, the sponsor or publisher, the medium, and your date of access.

Keefe, Mike. "Content of Character." Cartoon. *Denverpost.com*. Denver Post,

28 Aug. 2008. Web. 12 Dec. 2008.

71. Advertisement   Name the product or company being advertised, followed by the word "Advertisement." Give publication information for the source in which the advertisement appears.

Truth by Calvin Klein. Advertisement. *Vogue* Dec. 2000: 95-98. Print.

Arbella Insurance. Advertisement. *Boston.com*. NY Times, n.d. Web. 3 June

2008.

72. Map or chart   Cite a map or a chart as you would a book or a short work within a longer work. Use the word "Map" or "Chart" following the title. Add the medium and, for an online source, the sponsor or publisher and the date of access.

Joseph, Lori, and Bob Laird. "Driving While Phoning Is Dangerous." Chart.

USA Today 16 Feb. 2001: 1A. Print.

"Serbia." Map. *Syrena Maps*. Syrena, 2 Feb. 2001. Web. 17 Mar. 2009.

Other sources (including online versions)

This section includes a variety of sources not covered elsewhere. For online sources, consult the appropriate model in this section and also see items 34–55.

73. Government document   Treat the government agency as the author, giving the name of the government followed by the name of the department and the agency, if any. For print sources, add the medium at the end of the entry. For online sources, follow the model for an entire Web site (item 34) or a short work from a Web site (item 35).

government   department   agency

United States. Dept. of the Interior. Office of Inspector General. "Excessive

document title

Indulgences: Personal Use of the Internet at the Department of the Interior."

                                          publication

    Web site title   publisher/sponsor   date   medium

Office of Inspector General. Dept. of the Interior, Sept. 1999. Web.

date of access:
inverted

20 May 2009.

Canada. Minister of Indian Affairs and Northern Dev. *Gathering Strength:*
     Canada's Aboriginal Action Plan. Ottawa: Minister of Public Works and
     Govt. Services Can., 2000. Print.

74. Historical document To cite a historical document, such
as the US Constitution or the Canadian Charter of Rights and
Freedoms, begin with the document author, if it has one, and
then give the document title, neither italicized nor in quotation marks, and the document date. For a print version, continue as for a selection in an anthology (see item 15) or for a
book (with the title not italicized). For an online version, cite
as a short work from a Web site (see item 35).

Jefferson, Thomas. First Inaugural Address. 1801. *The American Reader.*
     Ed. Diane Ravitch. New York: Harper, 1990. 42-44. Print.

The Virginia Declaration of Rights. 1776. *A Chronology of US*
     Historical Documents. U of Oklahoma Coll. of Law, 2008. Web.
     23 Feb. 2009.

75. Legal source

Legislative act (law)
Begin with the name of the act, neither italicized nor in quotation marks. Then provide the act's Public Law number; its
Statutes at Large volume and page numbers; its date of enact-
ment; and the medium of publication.

Electronic Freedom of Information Act Amendments of 1996. Pub. L.

104-231. 110 Stat. 3048. 2 Oct. 1996. Print.

Court case

Name the first plaintiff and the first defendant. Then give the volume, name, and page number of the law report; the court name; the year of the decision; and publication information. Do not italicize the name of the case. (In the text of the paper, the name of the case is italicized; see item 19 on p. 526.)

Utah v. Evans. 536 US 452. Supreme Court of the US. 2002. *Supreme Court
Collection*. Legal Information Inst., Cornell U Law School, n.d. Web.
30 Apr. 2008.

76. Pamphlet or brochure Cite as you would a book (see items 7–24).

Commonwealth of Massachusetts. Dept. of Jury Commissioner. *A Few Facts
about Jury Duty*. Boston: Commonwealth of Massachusetts, 2004.
Print.

77. Unpublished dissertation Begin with the author's name, followed by the dissertation title in quotation marks; the abbreviation "Diss."; the name of the institution; the year the dissertation was accepted; and the medium of the dissertation.

Jackson, Shelley. "Writing Whiteness: Contemporary Southern Literature in
Black and White." Diss. U of Maryland, 2000. Print.

78. Published dissertation For dissertations that have been published in book form, italicize the title. After the title and before the book's publication information, give the abbreviation "Diss.," the name of the institution, and the year the dissertation was accepted. Add the medium of publication at the end.

Damberg, Cheryl L. *Healthcare Reform: Distributional Consequences of an
Employer Mandate for Workers in Small Firms*. Diss. Rand Graduate
School, 1995. Santa Monica: Rand, 1996. Print.

79. Abstract of a dissertation Cite an abstract as you would an unpublished dissertation. After the dissertation date, give the abbreviation *DA* or *DAI* (for *Dissertation Abstracts* or *Dissertation Abstracts International*), followed by the volume and issue numbers; the year of publication; inclusive page numbers or, if the abstract is not numbered, the item number; and the medium of publication. For an abstract accessed in an online database, give the item number in place of the page number, followed by the name of the database, the medium, and your date of access.

Chen, Shu-Ling. "Mothers and Daughters in Morrison, Tan, Marshall, and
    Kincaid." Diss. U of Washington, 2000. *DAI* 61.6 (2000): AAT9975963.
    ProQuest Dissertations and Theses. Web. 22 Feb. 2009.

80. Published proceedings of a conference Cite as you would a book, adding the name, date, and location of the conference after the title.

Urgo, Joseph R., and Ann J. Abadie, eds. *Faulkner and Material Culture*.
    Proc. of Faulkner and Yoknapatawpha Conf., 25-29 July 2004, U of
    Mississippi. Jackson: UP of Mississippi, 2007. Print.

81. Paper in conference proceedings Cite as you would a selection in an anthology (see item 15), giving information about the conference after the title and editors of the conference proceedings (see item 80).

Henninger, Katherine R. "Faulkner, Photography, and a Regional Ethics of
    Form." *Faulkner and Material Culture*. Ed. Joseph R. Urgo and Ann
    J. Abadie. Proc. of Faulkner and Yoknapatawpha Conf., 25-29 July
    2004, U of Mississippi. Jackson: UP of Mississippi, 2007. 121-38.
    Print.

82. Published interview Name the person interviewed, followed by the title of the interview (if there is one). If the interview does not have a title, include the word "Interview" after the interviewee's name. Give publication information for the work in which the interview was published.

Simon, David. "Beyond the Choir: An Interview with David Simon." *Film Quarterly* 62.2 (2008/2009): 44-49.

If you wish to include the name of the interviewer, put it after the title of the interview (or after the name of the interviewee if there is no title).

Florida, Richard. "The Great Reset." Interview by Conor Clarke. *Atlantic*. Atlantic Monthly Group, Feb. 2009. Web. 28 Feb. 2010.

83. Personal interview To cite an interview that you conducted, begin with the name of the person interviewed. Then write "Personal interview" or "Telephone interview," followed by the date of the interview.

Akufo, Dautey. Personal interview. 11 Apr. 2009.

84. Personal letter To cite a letter that you received, begin with the writer's name and add the phrase "Letter to the author," followed by the date. Add the medium ("MS" for "manuscript," or a handwritten letter; "TS" for "typescript," or a typed letter).

Primak, Shoshana. Letter to the author. 6 May 2009. TS.

85. Published letter Begin with the writer of the letter, the words "Letter to" and the recipient, and the date of the letter (use "N.d." if the letter is undated). Then add the title of the collection and proceed as for a selection in an anthology (see item 15).

Wharton, Edith. Letter to Henry James. 28 Feb. 1915. *Henry James and Edith Wharton: Letters, 1900-1915*. Ed. Lyall H. Powers. New York: Scribner's, 1990. 323-26. Print.

86. Manuscript Give the author, a title or a description of the manuscript, and the date of composition, followed by the abbreviation "MS" for "manuscript" (handwritten) or "TS" for "typescript." Add the name and location of the institution housing the material. For a manuscript found online, give the preceding information but omit "MS" or "TS." Then list the title of the Web site, the medium ("Web"), and your date of access.

Arendt, Hannah. *Between Past and Presen*t. N.d. 1st draft. Hannah Arendt
Papers. MS Div., Lib. of Cong. *Manuscript Division, Library of Congress*.
Web. 24 Apr. 2009.

hackerhandbooks.com/bedhandbook > Research exercises > MLA > E-ex 53–4 to 53–8

53c MLA information notes (optional)

Researchers who use the MLA system of parenthetical documentation may also use information notes for one of two purposes:

1. to provide additional material that is important but might interrupt the flow of the paper
2. to refer to several sources or to provide comments on sources

Information notes may be either footnotes or endnotes. Footnotes appear at the foot of the page; endnotes appear on a separate page at the end of the paper, just before the list of works cited. For either style, the notes are numbered consecutively throughout the paper. The text of the paper contains a raised arabic numeral that corresponds to the number of the note.

TEXT

In the past several years, employees have filed a number of lawsuits against employers because of online monitoring practices.^{1}

NOTE

1. For a discussion of federal law applicable to electronic surveillance in the workplace, see Kesan 293.

54 MLA manuscript format; student research process and sample paper

The following guidelines are consistent with advice given in the *MLA Handbook for Writers of Research Papers*, 7th ed. (New York: MLA, 2009), and with typical requirements for student papers. For a sample MLA paper, see pages 583–88.

54a MLA manuscript format

Formatting the paper

Papers written in MLA style should be formatted as follows.

Materials and font   Use good-quality 8½″ × 11″ white paper. Avoid a font that is unusual or hard to read.

Title and identification   MLA does not require a title page. On the first page of your paper, place your name, your instructor's name, the course title, and the date on separate lines against the left margin. Then center your title. (See p. 583 for a sample first page.)

If your instructor requires a title page, ask for formatting guidelines. A format similar to the one on page 674 may be acceptable.

Pagination   Put the page number preceded by your last name in the upper right corner of each page, one-half inch below the top edge. Use arabic numerals (1, 2, 3, and so on).

Margins, line spacing, and paragraph indents Leave margins of one inch on all sides of the page. Left-align the text.

Double-space throughout the paper. Do not add extra space above or below the title of the paper or between paragraphs.

Indent the first line of each paragraph one-half inch from the left margin.

Capitalization and italics In titles of works, capitalize all words except articles (*a, an, the*), prepositions (*to, from, between,* and so on), coordinating conjunctions (*and, but, or, nor, for, so, yet*), and the *to* in infinitives—unless they are the first or last word of the title or subtitle. Follow these guidelines in your paper even if the title appears in all capital or all lowercase letters in the source.

In the text of an MLA paper, when a complete sentence follows a colon, lowercase the first word following the colon unless the sentence is a well-known expression or principle.

Italicize the titles of books and other long works, such as Web sites. Use quotation marks around the titles of periodical articles, short stories, poems, and other short works. (Some instructors may prefer underlining for the titles of long works. Be consistent throughout your paper.)

Long quotations When a quotation is longer than four typed lines of prose or three lines of verse, set it off from the text by indenting the entire quotation one inch from the left margin. Double-space the indented quotation, and do not add extra space above or below it.

Quotation marks are not needed when a quotation has been set off from the text by indenting. See page 584 for an example.

Web addresses When a Web address (URL) mentioned in the text of your paper must be divided at the end of a line, break it only after a slash and do not insert a hyphen. For MLA rules on dividing Web addresses in your list of works cited, see page 572.

Headings MLA neither encourages nor discourages the use of headings and provides no guidelines for their use. If you would like to insert headings in a long essay or research paper, check first with your instructor.

Visuals MLA classifies visuals as tables and figures (figures include graphs, charts, maps, photographs, and drawings). Label each table with an arabic numeral ("Table 1," "Table 2," and so on) and provide a clear caption that identifies the subject. Capitalize the caption as you would a title (see 45c); do not italicize the label and caption or place them in quotation marks. The label and caption should appear on separate lines above the table, flush with the left margin.

For a table that you have borrowed or adapted, give the source below the table in a note like the following:

Source: David N. Greenfield and Richard A. Davis; "Lost in Cyberspace: The Web @ Work"; *CyberPsychology and Behavior* 5.4 (2002): 349; print.

For each figure, place the figure number (using the abbreviation "Fig.") and a caption below the figure, flush left. Capitalize the caption as you would a sentence; include source information following the caption. (When referring to the figure in your paper, use the abbreviation "fig." in parenthetical citations; otherwise spell out the word.) See page 586 for an example of a figure in a paper.

Place visuals in the text, as close as possible to the sentences that relate to them, unless your instructor prefers them in an appendix.

Preparing the list of works cited

Begin the list of works cited on a new page at the end of the paper. Center the title Works Cited about one inch from the top of the page. Double-space throughout. See page 588 for a sample list of works cited.

Alphabetizing the list Alphabetize the list by the last names of the authors (or editors); if a work has no author or editor, alphabetize by the first word of the title other than *A*, *An*, or *The*.

If your list includes two or more works by the same author, use the author's name for the first entry only. For subsequent entries, use three hyphens followed by a period. List the titles in alphabetical order. (See item 6 on page 534.)

Indenting Do not indent the first line of each works cited entry, but indent any additional lines one-half inch. This technique highlights the names of the authors, making it easy for readers to scan the alphabetized list. See page 588.

Web addresses If you need to include a Web address (URL) in a works cited entry, do not insert a hyphen when dividing it at the end of a line. Break the URL only after a slash. Insert angle brackets around the URL. (See the note following item 34 on p. 549.) If your word processing program automatically turns Web addresses into links (by underlining them and changing the color), turn off this feature.

54b Highlights of one student's research process

The following pages describe key steps in student writer Anna Orlov's research process, from selecting a research question to documenting sources. At each step, cross-references in the margins point to more discussion and examples elsewhere in the handbook. Samples from Orlov's process illustrate strategies and skills she used to create an accurate and effective essay. See pages 583–88 for Orlov's final paper.

Making the most of your handbook
Highlights of one student's research process (MLA style)

Anna Orlov, a student in a composition class, was assigned a research essay related to technology and the American workplace. The assignment called for her to use a variety of print and electronic sources and to follow MLA style. Orlov immediately thought of her summer internship at an insurance company and her surprise at the strict employee Internet use policy in place there. As she thought about how to turn her experience into a research project, she developed some questions and strategies to guide her research and writing.

"How do I begin a research paper?"

Before getting started, Orlov worked with a writing tutor to break her research plan into several stages. (Section numbers in blue refer to relevant discussions throughout the book.)

- Ask worthwhile questions about my topic.   1b, 46a
- Talk with a reference librarian about useful types of sources and where to find them.   46b
- Consider how each source can contribute to my paper.   47a
- Decide which search results are worth a closer look.   47b
- Evaluate the sources.   47d, 47e
- Take notes and keep track of the sources.   48
- Write a working thesis.   1c, 50a
- Write a draft and integrate sources.   1e–1g, 52, 53a
- Document sources.   49, 53b

Orlov began by jotting down the research question she wanted to investigate: *Is Internet surveillance in the workplace fair or unfair to employees?* She thought the practice might be unfair but knew that she needed to consider all sides of the issue. Her instructor had explained that sources uncovered in the research process would both support and challenge her ideas and ultimately help shape the paper. Orlov knew she would have to be

1b and 46a: Posing questions for a research paper

open-minded and flexible and revisit her main ideas as she examined the information and arguments in her sources.

"What sources do I need, and where should I look for them?"

47a: Roles sources can play in a paper

Orlov planned to consider a variety of sources to help her focus her argument. Some sources might provide background information and context; others might provide evidence to help shape and support her developing ideas; still others might offer counterevidence and alternative interpretations that she would address when she built her argument. Orlov worked with a reference librarian to develop a search strategy.

Finding articles in journals, magazines, and newspapers with the library's online databases. Because her topic was current, Orlov wanted to search for up-to-date information. She turned to her library's subscription databases for trustworthy, scholarly writing. There she hoped to find recent articles with concrete examples of workplace Internet surveillance.

46b: Working with reference librarians

Searching the library's book catalog. For reliable sources covering legal, business, and labor issues, Orlov looked for recently published books in the library catalog. Books could offer in-depth context, including the history of online monitoring and the laws governing workplace surveillance. Orlov noticed that one book on the topic had the subject heading "electronic monitoring in the workplace." Using that heading as a search term, she found a more focused list of books. One book that provided a solid overview helped her identify issues and terms for further searches in databases and on the Web. She also found references to other sources that looked promising.

46c–46e: Searching databases, library catalogs, and the Web

Locating relevant sites, online articles, and government publications on the Web. Orlov decided to search for online articles and relevant Web sites as well, particularly those that might specialize in digital issues. She hoped to find explanations of the software used by employers and opinions held by those who use the Internet and e-mail in the workplace, including supervisors, employers, and employees who might disagree with her.

"What search terms should I use?"

Orlov thought that searches on her controversial topic might generate too many results if she started with an Internet search engine like *Google*. To save time, she asked a librarian to help her conduct a narrower search with her library's general periodical database. She could count on the database for fewer, more reliable results than an Internet search could provide.

Orlov's search terms	Date restrictions
employee	Past four years
internet use	**Number of results**
surveillance	20

46c and p. 449: Refining keyword searches, selecting search terms

"How do I select sources from my search results?"

Orlov used several criteria to decide which results of her general database search were worth a closer look. Would a source

- be relevant to her topic?
- provide authoritative support?
- provide background information?
- offer a range of views or evidence that Orlov could address when forming her argument?

47: Evaluating sources

DATABASE SCREEN: SEARCH RESULTS

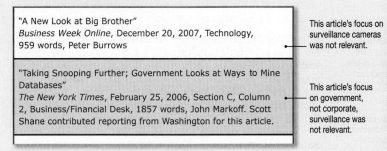

"A New Look at Big Brother"
Business Week Online, December 20, 2007, Technology, 959 words, Peter Burrows

This article's focus on surveillance cameras was not relevant.

"Taking Snooping Further; Government Looks at Ways to Mine Databases"
The New York Times, February 25, 2006, Section C, Column 2, Business/Financial Desk, 1857 words, John Markoff. Scott Shane contributed reporting from Washington for this article.

This article's focus on government, not corporate, surveillance was not relevant.

Orlov would want to respond to this survey if she argued that Internet surveillance is unfair.

"Wasting Away on the Web; More Employers Are Taking Workers' Web Use Seriously"
eWeek, August 8, 2005, 692 words, Chris Gonsalves

The *Wall Street Journal* is widely respected and might offer background for Orlov's topic.

"Snooping E-Mail by Software Is Now a Workplace Norm"
The Wall Street Journal Online, March 9, 2005, Pui-Wing Tam et al.

Orlov wondered if the *Progressive* had a political slant. She made a note to check for bias.

"Snooping Bosses; Electronic Surveillance Program"
The Progressive, February 1, 2006: 14, Barbara Ehrenreich.

Reviewed by legal experts, a law review article could provide legal context and lend credibility.

"Cyber-Working or Cyber-Shirking? A First Principles Examination of Electronic Privacy in the Workplace"
Florida Law Review 54.2 (2002): 289-332, Jay P. Kesan

"Should I consider using a blog?"

46e: Using blogs

Orlov was intrigued by a blog called *Today's Workplace*, which was critical of workplace surveillance. She remembered her instructor's caution about using blogs, since their credibility is difficult to establish. But her librarian had suggested that blogs can provide useful links to studies and to articles in reputable magazines and newspapers as well as compelling arguments of their own. Orlov knew that if the blog looked like a helpful source, she could check with her instructor before using it.

"How do I evaluate my sources?"

47: Assessing print and online sources

After Orlov had conducted several searches and narrowed down her list of promising search results, she downloaded her sources and began evaluating them. As she read, she tried to keep an open mind, knowing that some sources might make her reexamine her own views. Orlov wanted to see what evidence and claims she would need to address to strengthen her argument in progress.

p. 467: Previewing articles

She looked carefully at an article she found in *eWeek*, an online weekly business computing magazine. It was the kind of

ORLOV'S NOTES ON PASSAGES FROM AN ARTICLE

Wasting Away on the Web
Opinion: More employers are taking workers' Web use seriously.

Writer is sympathetic to employers?

By Chris Gonsalves
2005-08-08

SECTION: OPINION; Pg. 26

The issue of IT surveillance was driven home last month when
Salary.com and America Online released a survey of 10,000 American
workers, many of whom admitted that goofing off on the Internet was
their primary method of frittering away the workday. In a sign of the
times, it beat out socializing with co-workers, 45 percent to 23 percent.

Consider statistics. Is using work time for personal Internet use so bad?

While bosses can easily detect and interrupt water-cooler chatter, the
employee who is shopping at Lands' End or IMing with fellow fantasy
baseball managers may actually appear to be working. Thwarting the
activity is a technology challenge, and it's one that more and more
enterprises are taking seriously, despite resistance from privacy
advocates and some employees themselves.

Does the AMA side with employers? Survey results— good for background and counter-argument.

According to the American Management Association, 78 percent of large
U.S. employers are regularly checking workers' e-mail messages,
Internet use, computer files and phone calls. Nearly half of such
employers store employee e-mail messages for review. The AMA also
found that 65 percent of enterprises had disciplined employees for
misuse of e-mail or the Internet at work, and 27 percent had actually
fired someone over such offenses.

According to a recent poll of workers in technology-related fields
published by the executive recruiting company FPC, 61 percent said
they felt their bosses had the right to cyber-spy on them, but only with
consent. Just 28 percent felt IT had the right to monitor their activity
without consent, and only 1 percent said an employer never has the
right to monitor Internet use.

Employees want employers to be up-front about monitoring.

"It's not surprising that companies want to assure that their employees'
time is predominantly spent on work-related computer usage," said FPC
President Ron Herzog. "The majority of employees . . . would like to be
informed, so it is always in the company's best interest to have an
Internet usage policy clearly outlining the company's expectations,
which all employees sign upon hiring."

When is workplace surveillance unfair and when not?

As the stakes grow beyond a few wasted man-hours and some
misappropriated bandwidth, it grows increasingly important for IT to let
everyone in the company know they might be watched.

An extreme case. Does it justify Big Brother in the workplace?

Nowhere was that more evident than at the storied New York printing
company Bowne & Co. In June, Robert Johnson, the high-profile CEO of
Bowne and the former publisher of Newsday, was arrested and charged
with downloading child pornography to company PCs and laptops,
according to published reports. The case, which reportedly involved IT
tipping off Johnson to the investigation and ultimately resulted in the
dismissal of Bowne's CIO, illustrates the need for diligence in keeping
tabs on company computer use right up to the highest levels.

*Executive Editor/News Chris Gonsalves can be contacted at
chris_gonsalves@ziffdavis.com.*
LOAD-DATE: August 8, 2005
LANGUAGE: English

Copyright 2005 Ziff Davis Media Inc. All Rights Reserved

up-to-date, specialized publication that Orlov wanted to check for in-depth background information.

So that she would remember her thoughts about the author's text while drafting her argument, she made notes in the margins as she read. Taking good notes would help her to begin forming her own lines of argument and avoid plagiarism.

48a–48c:
Managing
your
information

"How do I integrate my sources into my paper?"

1c and 50a:
Writing a
working
thesis

After reading and evaluating a number of sources, Orlov wrote down her working thesis: *Though companies may have legitimate reasons to monitor employees' Internet usage, electronic surveillance is more unfair than beneficial to employees since it threatens their privacy.* She then sketched an informal plan to organize her ideas and began writing a rough draft. As she wrote and revised, she tried to integrate sources from her research that she had found useful.

1d–1g:
Planning and
drafting

For example, Orlov had selected a book on electronic surveillance in the workplace, written by Frederick Lane III. Because the American Management Association was the publisher, Orlov thought the book might be biased in favor of management's use of electronic surveillance. But by skimming the introduction, she saw that the author took the side of employees.

pp. 467–68:
Previewing
books

Orlov looked through the table of contents and selected a few chapters that seemed relevant to her working thesis. She read the chapters for ideas and information that she could paraphrase, summarize, or quote to provide background, support her argument, and help her counter the kind of pro-surveillance position that Chris Gonsalves takes in his *eWeek* article.

Summarizing a source

48c and 52b:
Summariz-
ing and
paraphrasing

Orlov turned to Lane's text for an authoritative explanation of how surveillance software typically works. Some passages contained more details than she could use, so she decided to summarize what she needed from the source.

ORIGINAL SOURCE PASSAGE (LANE, *THE NAKED EMPLOYEE*, 128-29)

relay chat, or instant messenger session that takes place on the computer.

Investigator could be monitoring activity on your office computer right now, but chances are, you'd never know if it's running or not. Eaton designed the program to be hidden in plain sight: An icon may appear in the system tray, but the various modules that make the program operate periodically change their name to make them more difficult to find. Similarly, the files that are used to hold the data that *Investigator* collects are given arbitrary names and dates so that they can't be easily located.

> Concrete example of monitoring software. Too much detail. Summarize?

Even if you know that *Investigator* is running on your office computer system, you may not realize the extent to which it is actively reporting on your activities. *Investigator* can be configured to surreptitiously send its collected data by e-mail to your boss on a regular basis or wait until it discovers certain preset keywords ("boss," "pornography," "kill," or the name of an unreleased product).

> Use key points about what software tells supervisors.

FIRST ATTEMPT AT SUMMARY

These programs record on-screen activity in the computer in hidden directories that can later be accessed or uploaded by supervisors; the programs can even scan for keywords tailored to individual companies and have employees receive warning e-mails from their bosses (128-29).

> Orlov condenses the original source passage in her own words.

This summary misrepresents the source.

A signal phrase credits the author with the explanation.

REVISED SUMMARY

As Lane explains, these programs record on-screen activity in the computer in hidden directories that can later be accessed or uploaded by supervisors; the programs can even scan for keywords tailored to individual companies (128-29).

> To avoid misrepresenting the source, Orlov removes the comment about e-mail warnings.

The page number and signal phrase show the boundaries of the source material.

Paraphrasing a source

48c and 51b:
Avoiding
plagiarism
when taking
notes and
paraphrasing

Orlov had photocopied the following passage from Lane's book because it contained broader claims about electronic surveillance in the workplace. To keep most of her paper in her own voice, she tried to paraphrase important ideas. She used quotations only when integrating especially effective language from Lane's writing.

ORIGINAL SOURCE PASSAGE (LANE, *THE NAKED EMPLOYEE*, 3-4)

Advanced
technology
= increased
surveillance.

Good
quotation,
but too much?
Paraphrase
this point and
quote last
sentence?

particularly as an employee, our cloak is at its thinnest and most revealing.

As we'll see in this chapter, there are a number of reasons — some of them quite compelling — for surveillance of employees. A major problem, however, is that technology makes it possible for employers to gather enormous amounts of data about employees, often far beyond what is necessary to satisfy safety or productivity concerns. And the trends that drive technology—faster, smaller, cheaper—make it possible for larger and larger numbers of employers to gather ever-greater amounts of personal data.

To date, the nation's legislatures and courts have made occasional efforts to reweave some threads of the privacy

Signal phrase shows where
Lane's idea begins.

ORLOV'S PARAPHRASE

Orlov uses her
own words,
avoiding Lane's
terms, phrasing,
and structure.

Lane notes that employers can use Internet surveillance technology to collect significantly more information from workers than they need (3-4).

The citation shows where to find this
information in Lane's book.

Selecting and integrating a quotation

52: Integrat-
ing sources

In the same photocopied passage, Orlov noted phrases that were striking and worth quoting.

ORIGINAL SOURCE PASSAGE (LANE, *THE NAKED EMPLOYEE*, 3-4)

particularly as an employee, our cloak is at its thinnest and most revealing.

As we'll see in this chapter, there are a number of reasons—some of them quite compelling—for surveillance of employees. A major problem, however, is that technology makes it possible for employers to gather enormous amounts of data about employees, often far beyond what is necessary to satisfy safety or productivity concerns. And the trends that drive technology—faster, smaller, cheaper—make it possible for larger and larger numbers of employers to gather ever-greater amounts of personal data.

Surveillance can go too far. "Faster, smaller, cheaper"—strong, surprising language for invasion of employee privacy.

ORLOV'S INTEGRATED QUOTATION

While surveillance of employees is not a new phenomenon, electronic surveillance allows employers to monitor workers with unprecedented efficiency. In his book *The Naked Employee*, Frederick Lane describes offline ways in which employers have been permitted to intrude on employees' privacy for decades, such as drug testing, background checks, psychological exams, lie detector tests, and in-store video surveillance. The difference, Lane argues, between these old methods of data gathering and electronic surveillance involves quantity. He notes that employers can use this technology to collect significantly more information from workers than they need. Lane also contends that "the trends that drive technology—faster, smaller, cheaper—make it possible for larger and larger numbers of employers to gather ever-greater amounts of personal data" (3-4).

The signal phrase shows that the idea that follows is not Orlov's.

Orlov uses the source to provide background information.

Orlov's summary points out a key contrast in Lane's argument.

Lane's striking and succinct language is worth quoting.

The citation shows where this passage can be found in the source.

Orlov was careful not to let her sources overwhelm her writing. To keep the emphasis on her ideas, she used her own analyses to shape the conversation among the sources she summarized, paraphrased, and quoted, creating an effective synthesis.

52c: Synthesizing and placing sources in conversation

"How do I document my sources?"

Throughout her research process, Orlov took careful notes about publication information and page numbers for source material she planned to use in her paper. Because she kept good records, she didn't need to hunt down information as she cited her sources. Managing her information also helped her avoid unintentional plagiarism.

48b: Keeping track of source materials

When it came time for her to document her sources in the paper, she followed the MLA (Modern Language Association) system. In addition to using in-text parenthetical citations, Orlov prepared an alphabetized list of works cited at the end of her paper. Entries in the works cited list gave publication information for the sources Orlov used in her paper and cited with page numbers in parentheses.

ENTRY IN WORKS CITED LIST

49 and 53a–53b: Documenting sources in MLA style

Lane, Frederick S., III. *The Naked Employee: How Technology Is Compromising Workplace Privacy.* New York: Amer. Management Assn., 2003. Print.

1 Author

2 Title and subtitle

3 City of publication

4 Publisher

5 Date of publication

6 Medium

54c Sample MLA research paper

On the following pages is a research paper on the topic of electronic surveillance in the workplace, written by Anna Orlov, a student in a composition class. Orlov's paper is documented with in-text citations and a list of works cited in MLA style. Annotations in the margins of the paper draw your attention to Orlov's use of MLA style and her effective writing. For highlights of Anna Orlov's research process, see pages 573–82.

hackerhandbooks.com/bedhandbook > Model papers
> MLA papers: Orlov; Daly; Levi
> MLA annotated bibliography: Orlov

keeping records • documenting
sources • sample MLA paper
MLA 54c 583

Orlov 1

Anna Orlov

Professor Willis

English 101

17 March 2009

Online Monitoring:

A Threat to Employee Privacy in the Wired Workplace

As the Internet has become an integral tool of businesses,
company policies on Internet usage have become as common as
policies regarding vacation days or sexual harassment. A 2005 study by
the American Management Association and ePolicy Institute found that
76% of companies monitor employees' use of the Web, and the number
of companies that block employees' access to certain Web sites has
increased 27% since 2001 (1). Unlike other company rules, however,
Internet usage policies often include language authorizing companies
to secretly monitor their employees, a practice that raises questions
about rights in the workplace. Although companies often have
legitimate concerns that lead them to monitor employees' Internet
usage—from expensive security breaches to reduced productivity—the
benefits of electronic surveillance are outweighed by its costs to
employees' privacy and autonomy.

While surveillance of employees is not a new phenomenon,
electronic surveillance allows employers to monitor workers with
unprecedented efficiency. In his book *The Naked Employee*, Frederick
Lane describes offline ways in which employers have been permitted
to intrude on employees' privacy for decades, such as drug testing,
background checks, psychological exams, lie detector tests, and in-store
video surveillance. The difference, Lane argues, between these old
methods of data gathering and electronic surveillance involves quantity:

Title is centered.

Opening sentences
provide background
for thesis.

Thesis asserts Orlov's
main point.

Summary and
long quotation are
introduced with a
signal phrase naming
the author.

Marginal annotations indicate MLA-style formatting and effective writing.

Orlov 2

Long quotation is set off from the text; quotation marks are omitted.

Technology makes it possible for employers to gather enormous amounts of data about employees, often far beyond what is necessary to satisfy safety or productivity concerns. And the trends that drive technology—faster, smaller, cheaper—make it possible for larger and larger numbers of employers to gather ever-greater amounts of personal data. (3-4)

Page number is given in parentheses after the final period.

In an age when employers can collect data whenever employees use their computers—when they send e-mail, surf the Web, or even arrive at or depart from their workstations—the challenge for both employers and employees is to determine how much is too much.

Clear topic sentences, like this one, are used throughout the paper.

Another key difference between traditional surveillance and electronic surveillance is that employers can monitor workers' computer use secretly. One popular monitoring method is keystroke logging, which is done by means of an undetectable program on employees' computers. The Web site of a vendor for Spector Pro, a popular keystroke logging program, explains that the software can be installed to operate in "Stealth" mode so that it "does not show up as an icon, does not appear in the Windows system tray, . . . [and] cannot be uninstalled without the Spector Pro password which YOU specify" ("Automatically"). As Lane explains, these programs record every key entered into the computer in hidden directories that can later be accessed or uploaded by supervisors; the programs can even scan for keywords tailored to individual companies (128-29).

Source with an unknown author is cited by a shortened title.

Orlov anticipates objections and provides sources for opposing views.

Some experts have argued that a range of legitimate concerns justifies employer monitoring of employee Internet usage. As *PC World* columnist Daniel Tynan points out, companies that don't monitor network traffic can be penalized for their ignorance: "Employees could accidentally (or deliberately) spill confidential information . . . or allow worms to spread throughout a corporate network." The ePolicy Institute, an organization that advises companies about reducing risks

Orlov 3

from technology, reported that breaches in computer security cost institutions $100 million in 1999 alone (Flynn). Companies also are held legally accountable for many of the transactions conducted on their networks and with their technology. Legal scholar Jay Kesan points out that the law holds employers liable for employees' actions such as violations of copyright laws, the distribution of offensive or graphic sexual material, and illegal disclosure of confidential information (312).

These kinds of concerns should give employers, in certain instances, the right to monitor employee behavior. But employers rushing to adopt surveillance programs might not be adequately weighing the effect such programs can have on employee morale. Employers must consider the possibility that employees will perceive surveillance as a breach of trust that can make them feel like disobedient children, not responsible adults who wish to perform their jobs professionally and autonomously.

Yet determining how much autonomy workers should be given is complicated by the ambiguous nature of productivity in the wired workplace. On the one hand, computers and Internet access give employees powerful tools to carry out their jobs; on the other hand, the same technology offers constant temptations to avoid work. As a 2005 study by *Salary.com* and *America Online* indicates, the Internet ranked as the top choice among employees for ways of wasting time on the job; it beat talking with co-workers—the second most popular method—by a margin of nearly two to one (Frauenheim). Chris Gonsalves, an editor for *eWeek.com*, argues that the technology has changed the terms between employers and employees: "While bosses can easily detect and interrupt water-cooler chatter," he writes, "the employee who is shopping at Lands' End or IMing with fellow fantasy baseball managers may actually appear to be working." The gap

Transition helps readers move from one paragraph to the next.

Orlov treats both sides fairly; she provides a transition to her own argument.

No page number is available for this Web source.

Orlov 4

Illustration has figure number, caption, and source information.

Fig. 1. This "Dilbert" comic strip suggests that personal Internet usage is widespread in the workplace (Adams 106).

between behaviors that are observable to managers and the employee's actual activities when sitting behind a computer has created additional motivations for employers to invest in surveillance programs. "Dilbert," a popular cartoon that spoofs office culture, aptly captures how rampant recreational Internet use has become in the workplace (see fig. 1).

Orlov counters opposing views and provides support for her argument.

But monitoring online activities can have the unintended effect of making employees resentful. As many workers would be quick to point out, Web surfing and other personal uses of the Internet can provide needed outlets in the stressful work environment; many scholars have argued that limiting and policing these outlets can exacerbate tensions between employees and managers. Kesan warns that "prohibiting personal use can seem extremely arbitrary and can seriously harm morale. . . . Imagine a concerned parent who is prohibited from checking on a sick child by a draconian company policy" (315-16). As this analysis indicates, employees can become disgruntled when Internet usage policies are enforced to their full extent.

Orlov uses a brief signal phrase to move from her argument to the words of a source.

Additionally, many experts disagree with employers' assumption that online monitoring can increase productivity. Employment law attorney Joseph Schmitt argues that, particularly for employees who

Orlov 5

are paid a salary rather than an hourly wage, "a company shouldn't care whether employees spend one or 10 hours on the Internet as long as they are getting their jobs done—and provided that they are not accessing inappropriate sites" (qtd. in Verespej). Other experts even argue that time spent on personal Internet browsing can actually be productive for companies. According to Bill Coleman, an executive at *Salary.com*, "Personal Internet use and casual office conversations often turn into new business ideas or suggestions for gaining operating efficiencies" (qtd. in Frauenheim). Employers, in other words, may benefit from showing more faith in their employees' ability to exercise their autonomy.

Orlov cites an indirect source: words quoted in another source.

Employees' right to privacy and autonomy in the workplace, however, remains a murky area of the law. Although evaluating where to draw the line between employee rights and employer powers is often a duty that falls to the judicial system, the courts have shown little willingness to intrude on employers' exercise of control over their computer networks. Federal law provides few guidelines related to online monitoring of employees, and only Connecticut and Delaware require companies to disclose this type of surveillance to employees (Tam et al.). "It is unlikely that we will see a legally guaranteed zone of privacy in the American workplace," predicts Kesan (293). This reality leaves employees and employers to sort the potential risks and benefits of technology in contract agreements and terms of employment. With continuing advances in technology, protecting both employers and employees will require greater awareness of these programs, better disclosure to employees, and a more public discussion about what types of protections are necessary to guard individual freedoms in the wired workplace.

Orlov sums up her argument and suggests a course of action.

Orlov 6

Heading is centered.

Works Cited

Adams, Scott. *Dilbert and the Way of the Weasel*. New York: Harper, 2002. Print.

List is alphabetized by authors' last names (or by title when a work has no author).

American Management Association and ePolicy Institute. "2005 Electronic Monitoring and Surveillance Survey." *American Management Association*. Amer. Management Assn., 2005. Web. 15 Feb. 2009.

"Automatically Record Everything They Do Online! Spector Pro 5.0 FAQ's." *Netbus.org*. Netbus.Org, n.d. Web. 17 Feb. 2009.

Abbreviation "n.d." indicates that the online source has no update date.

Flynn, Nancy. "Internet Policies." *ePolicy Institute*. ePolicy Inst., n.d. Web. 15 Feb. 2009.

Frauenheim, Ed. "Stop Reading This Headline and Get Back to Work." *CNET News.com*. CNET Networks, 11 July 2005. Web. 17 Feb. 2009.

First line of each entry is at the left margin; extra lines are indented ½".

Gonsalves, Chris. "Wasting Away on the Web." *eWeek.com*. Ziff Davis Enterprise Holdings, 8 Aug. 2005. Web. 16 Feb. 2009.

Kesan, Jay P. "Cyber-Working or Cyber-Shirking? A First Principles Examination of Electronic Privacy in the Workplace." *Florida Law Review* 54.2 (2002): 289-332. Print.

Double-spacing is used throughout.

Lane, Frederick S., III. *The Naked Employee: How Technology Is Compromising Workplace Privacy*. New York: Amer. Management Assn., 2003. Print.

A work with four authors is listed by the first author's name and the abbreviation "et al." (for "and others").

Tam, Pui-Wing, et al. "Snooping E-mail by Software Is Now a Workplace Norm." *Wall Street Journal* 9 Mar. 2005: B1+. Print.

Tynan, Daniel. "Your Boss Is Watching." *PC World*. PC World Communications, 6 Oct. 2004. Web. 17 Feb. 2009.

Verespej, Michael A. "Inappropriate Internet Surfing." *Industry Week*. Penton Media, 7 Feb. 2000. Web. 16 Feb. 2009.

55 Writing about literature

All good writing about literature attempts to answer a question, spoken or unspoken, about the text: "Why doesn't Hamlet kill his uncle sooner?" "How does street language function in Gwendolyn Brooks's 'We Real Cool'?" "What does Orwell's 'Shooting an Elephant' imply about the role the British played in imperial India?" "How do rhyme and meter support the meaning of Blake's 'The Tyger'?" "In what ways does Louise Erdrich's *Love Medicine* draw on oral narrative traditions?" The goal of a literature paper should be to answer such questions with a meaningful interpretation, presented forcefully and persuasively.

55a Get involved in the work; be an active reader.

Read the work closely and carefully. Think of the work as speaking to you: What is it telling you? Asking you? Trying to make you feel? If the work provides an introduction and footnotes, read them attentively. They may be a source of important information. Use the dictionary to look up words unfamiliar to you or words with subtle nuances that may affect the work's meaning.

Rereading is a central part of the process. You should read short works several times, first to get an overall impression and then again to focus on meaningful details. With longer works, such as novels or plays, read the most important chapters or scenes more than once while keeping in mind the work as a whole.

As you read and reread, interact with the work by posing questions and looking for answers. The chart on pages 594–95 suggests some questions about literature that may help you consider the composition and context of your reading. The chart on page 87 suggests strategies for active reading. The conclusions you draw in response to such questions shape and support your overall interpretation of the work (see 55b).

Annotating the work

Annotating the work is a way to focus your reading. The first time through, you may want to pencil a check mark next to passages you find especially significant. On a more careful rereading, pay particular attention to those passages and jot down your ideas and reactions in a notebook or (if you own the book) in the margins of the page.

Here is one student's annotation of a poem by Shakespeare:

Shall I compare <u>thee</u> to a summer's day? — *Who? (Must be a loved one.)*

Rhyming pattern of sonnet

Thou art more lovely and more <u>temperate</u>:

Rough winds do shake the darling buds of May, — *Pleasant-natured (like pleasant weather)?*

And summer's lease hath all too short a date.

Sometime <u>too hot</u> the eye of heaven shines,

Fair = beauty, or more than beauty?

And often is his <u>gold complexion dimmed</u>; — *Summer is fleeting and not always perfect. (But lover is perfect?)*

And every (fair) from (fair) sometimes declines,

By chance, or nature's changing course, untrimmed.

But thy eternal summer shall not fade,

What are "eternal lines to time"? Ask in class?

Nor lose possession of that fair thou ow'st

Nor shall death brag thou wand'rest in his shade, — *Death would be proud to claim the lover but can't?*

When in eternal lines to time thou grow'st.

Final couplet seems to signal a shift in thought.

So long as men can breathe or eyes can see,

So long lives <u>this</u>, and this gives life to thee.

This = the poem? (Art, like the writer's love, is eternal.)

Taking notes

Note taking is also an important part of rereading a work of literature. In your notes, you can try out ideas and develop your perspective on the work. Here are some notes one student took on a short story, "Chrysanthemums," by John Steinbeck. Notice that some of these notes pose questions for further thought. Such notes are the raw material out of which you will build an interpretation.

TAKING NOTES ON A LITERARY WORK

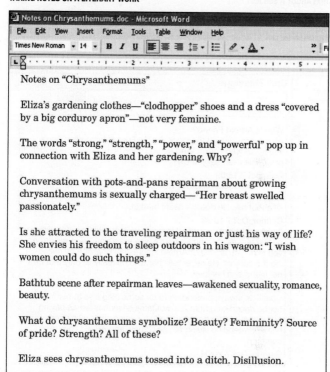

Notes on "Chrysanthemums"

Eliza's gardening clothes—"clodhopper" shoes and a dress "covered by a big corduroy apron"—not very feminine.

The words "strong," "strength," "power," and "powerful" pop up in connection with Eliza and her gardening. Why?

Conversation with pots-and-pans repairman about growing chrysanthemums is sexually charged—"Her breast swelled passionately."

Is she attracted to the traveling repairman or just his way of life? She envies his freedom to sleep outdoors in his wagon: "I wish women could do such things."

Bathtub scene after repairman leaves—awakened sexuality, romance, beauty.

What do chrysanthemums symbolize? Beauty? Femininity? Source of pride? Strength? All of these?

Eliza sees chrysanthemums tossed into a ditch. Disillusion.

Discussing the work

As you have no doubt discovered, class discussions can lead to interesting insights about a literary work, perhaps by calling attention to details in the work that you failed to notice on a first reading. Discussions don't always need to occur face-to-face. Many literature instructors encourage online discussion groups, where the class can post topics and explore ideas. Here, for example, is a series of postings about a character in Joyce Carol Oates's short story "Where Are You Going, Where Have You Been?"

CONVERSATION ABOUT A SUBJECT

Bay State University - Bay State University - Bay State University - Bay State

 The Composition Chat Room

User Name:

Password:

Log In

Forgot your password?

Help

Quit

Chat Message:

Submit

① **Who is Arnold Friend?**
At one point during the story, Arnold Friend demands, "Don't you know who I am?" Who do you think he is? Does the reader or Connie ever really know?

② **Zoë, Oct 7 18:09**
Everything about Arnold is weird, like his sunglasses and the way he talks. Connie has never seen him before, but he knows all about her. He doesn't seem human.

Connor, Oct 7 19:23
I think we're not supposed to know who Arnold Friend is. When he first arrives at Connie's house, she asks him, "Who the hell do you think you are?" but Arnold ignores her question by changing the subject. He never tells her who he really is, only that he's her friend and her lover.

Mirabel, Oct 7 19:47
Connie is always pretending to be something else to her friends, her boyfriends, and her family. Oates describes her as having two sides: one for home and one for when she's away from home. Pretending is something Connie and Arnold have in common.

Damon, Oct 7 20:04
I found a lot of parallels between Arnold and the wolf in "Little Red Riding Hood." For example, Connie notices Arnold's hair, his teeth, and his grin. It reminded me of that part when Little Red says, "Oh Grandmother, what big teeth you have!"

Yuko, Oct 7 23:11
I was thinking the same thing. Plus, Arnold seems like he's dressing up to hide who he is. Connie thinks that his hair is like a wig, and later that his face is a mask. It reminded me of when the wolf puts on the grandmother's clothing to trick Little Red Riding Hood, just like Arnold is trying to trick Connie.

1 Instructor's prompt

2 A series of students' responses to the prompt

55b Form an interpretation.

After rereading, jotting notes, and perhaps discussing the work, you are ready to start forming an interpretation. At this stage, try to focus on a single aspect of the work. Look through your notes and annotations for recurring questions and insights related to the aspect you have chosen.

Focusing on a central issue

In forming an interpretation, avoid trying to do everything at once. You may think, for example, that *Huckleberry Finn* is a great book because it contains brilliant descriptions of scenery, has many humorous moments, but also tells a serious story of one boy's development. These are legitimate responses to the work, but your job in writing an essay will be to close in on one issue that you can develop into a sustained, in-depth interpretation. For example, you might focus on how the runaway slave Jim uses humor to preserve his dignity. Or you might focus on ironic discrepancies between what Huck says and what his heart tells him.

Asking questions that lead to an interpretation

Think of your interpretation as answering a question about the work. Some interpretations answer questions about literary techniques, such as the writer's handling of plot, setting, or character. Others focus on questions about social context: what a work reveals about the time and culture in which it was written. You can find examples of both types of questions in the chart on pages 594–95.

Frequently you will find yourself writing about both technique and social context. For example, Margaret Peel, a student who wrote an essay on Langston Hughes's poem "Ballad of the Landlord" (see pp. 611–13), addressed the following question, which touches on both language and race:

How does the poem's language—through its four voices—dramatize the experience of a black man in a society dominated by whites?

Questions to ask about literature

Questions about technique

Plot: What central conflicts drive the plot? Are they internal (within a character) or external (between characters or between a character and a force)? How are conflicts resolved? Why are events revealed in a particular order?

Setting: Does the setting (time and place) create an atmosphere, offer insight into a character, suggest symbolic meanings, or hint at the theme of the work?

Character: What seems to motivate the central characters? Do any characters change significantly? If so, what—if anything—have they learned from their experiences? Do sharp contrasts between characters highlight important themes?

Point of view: Does the point of view—the perspective from which the story is narrated or the poem is spoken—affect the reader's understanding of events? Does the narration reveal character traits of the speaker, or does the speaker merely observe others? Is the narrator innocent, naive, or deceitful? Is the story told by multiple narrators?

Theme: Does the work have an overall theme (a central insight about people or a truth about life)? If so, how do details in the work illuminate this theme?

Language: Does language—such as formal or informal, standard or dialect, prosaic or poetic, cool or passionate—reveal the character of speakers? How do metaphors, similes, and sensory images contribute to the work? How do recurring images enrich the work and hint at its meaning? To what extent do sentence rhythms and sounds underscore the writer's meaning?

Questions about social context

Historical context: What does the work reveal about the time and place in which it was written? Does the work appear to promote or undermine a philosophy that was popular in its time, such as social Darwinism in the late nineteenth century or globalization in the late twentieth century?

Class: How does membership in a social class affect the characters' choices and their successes or failures? How does →

class affect the way characters view—or are viewed by—others?
What do economic struggles reveal about power relationships in
the society being depicted?

Race and culture: Are any characters portrayed as being caught
between cultures: between the cultures of home and work, for
example, or between a traditional and an emerging culture? Are
any characters struggling against society because of their race
or ethnic background? To what extent does the work celebrate a
specific culture and its traditions?

Gender: Are any characters' choices restricted because of
gender? What are the power relationships between the sexes, and
do these change during the course of the work? Do any characters
resist the gender roles that society has assigned to them? Do other
characters choose to conform to those roles?

Archetypes: Does a character, an image, or a plot fit a pattern—an
archetype—that has been repeated in stories throughout history and
across cultures? (For example, nearly every culture has stories about
heroes, quests, redemption, and revenge.) How does an archetypal
character, image, or plot line correspond to or differ from others like it?

In the introduction of your paper, you will usually announce
your interpretation in a one- or two-sentence thesis. The thesis
answers the central question that you posed. Here, for example,
is Margaret Peel's two-sentence thesis:

> Langston Hughes's "Ballad of the Landlord" is narrated through four
> voices, each with its own perspective on the poem's action. These
> opposing voices—of a tenant, a landlord, the police, and the press—
> dramatize a black man's experience in a society dominated by whites.

55c Draft a thesis and organize your ideas.

A thesis, which nearly always appears in the introduction, announces an essay's main point (see also 1c and 50a). In a literature paper, your thesis will answer the central question that you
have asked about the work. Putting your draft thesis and notes
into an informal outline can help you organize your ideas.

Drafting a thesis

In drafting your thesis, aim for a strong, assertive summary of your interpretation. Here, for example, are two successful thesis statements taken from student essays, together with the central question each student had posed.

QUESTION

What does Stephen Crane's short story "The Open Boat" reveal about the relation between humans and nature?

THESIS

In Stephen Crane's gripping tale "The Open Boat," four men lost at sea discover not only that nature is indifferent to their fate but also that their own particular talents make little difference as they struggle for survival.

QUESTION

In the Greek tragedy *Electra*, by Euripides, how do Electra and her mother, Clytemnestra, respond to the limitations society has placed on women?

THESIS

The experience of powerlessness has taught Electra and her mother two very different lessons: Electra has learned the value of traditional, conservative sex roles for women, but Clytemnestra has learned just the opposite.

As in other college papers, the thesis of a literature paper should not be too factual, too broad, or too vague (see 1e). For an essay on Mark Twain's *Huckleberry Finn*, the first three examples would all make poor thesis statements.

TOO FACTUAL

As a runaway slave, Jim is in danger from the law.

TOO BROAD

In *Huckleberry Finn*, Mark Twain criticizes mid-nineteenth-century American society.

TOO VAGUE

Huckleberry Finn is Twain's most exciting work.

The following thesis statement is sharply focused and presents a central idea that requires discussion and support.

ACCEPTABLE THESIS

Because Huckleberry Finn is a naive narrator, his comments on conventional religion are ironic at every turn, allowing Twain to poke fun at empty piety.

hackerhandbooks.com/bedhandbook > Research exercises > E-ex 55–1

Sketching an outline

Your thesis may strongly suggest a method of organization, in which case you will have little difficulty jotting down your essay's key points. Consider, for example, the following informal outline, based on a thesis that leads naturally to a three-part organization.

Thesis: George Bernard Shaw's *Major Barbara* depicts the ways in which three "religions" address the problem of poverty. The Established Church ignores poverty, the Salvation Army tries rather ineffectually to alleviate it, and a form of utopianism based on guns and money promises to eliminate it—but at a terrible cost.

- The Established Church (Lady Britomart)
- The Salvation Army (Major Barbara)
- Utopianism based on guns and money (Undershaft)

If your thesis does not by itself suggest a method of organization, turn to your notes and begin putting them into categories that relate to the thesis. For example, one student who was writing about Euripides's play *Medea* constructed the following formal outline from her notes.

Thesis: Although Medea professes great love for her children, Euripides gives us reason to suspect her sincerity: Medea does not hesitate to use the children as weapons in her bloody battle with Jason, and from the outset she displays little real concern for their fate.

I. From the very beginning of the play, Medea is a less than ideal mother.
   A. Her first words about the children are hostile.
   B. Her first actions suggest indifference.
II. In three scenes, Medea appears to be a loving mother, but in each of these scenes we have reason to doubt her sincerity.
III. Throughout the play, as Medea plots her revenge, her overriding concern is not her children but her reputation.
   A. Fearing ridicule, she is proud of her reputation as one who can "help her friends and hurt her enemies."
   B. Her obsession with reputation may stem from the Greek view of reputation as a means of immortality.
IV. After she kills her children, Medea reveals her real concern.
   A. She shows no remorse.
   B. She revels in Jason's agony over their death.

Whether to use a formal or an informal outline is to some extent a matter of personal preference. For most purposes, you will probably find that an informal outline is sufficient, perhaps even preferable. (See 1d.)

Drafting an introduction that announces your interpretation

The introduction to a literature paper is usually one paragraph long—and often begins with a few sentences that provide context for your thesis. The opening paragraph typically ends with your thesis, a single sentence that sums up your interpretation. Here, for example, is an introductory paragraph announcing one student's interpretation of one aspect of the play *Electra*. The first four sentences provide context for the thesis (underlined).

> In *Electra*, Euripides depicts two women who have had too little control over their lives. Electra, ignored by her mother, Clytemnestra, has been married off to a farmer and treated more or less like a slave. Clytemnestra has fared even worse. Her husband, Agamemnon, has slashed the throat of their daughter Iphigenia as a sacrifice to the gods. <u>The experience of powerlessness has taught Electra and her</u>

mother two very different lessons: Electra has learned the value of
traditional, conservative sex roles for women, but Clytemnestra has
learned just the opposite.

55d Support your interpretation with evidence from the work; avoid plot summary.

Your thesis and preliminary outline will point you toward details
in the work relevant to your interpretation. As you begin drafting the body of your paper, make good use of those details.

Supporting your interpretation

As a rule, the topic sentence of each paragraph in the body of
your paper should focus on some aspect of your overall interpretation. The rest of the paragraph should present details and
perhaps quotations from the work that back up your interpretation. In the following paragraph, which develops part of the organization sketched on page 597, the topic sentence comes first.
It sums up the religious views represented by Lady Britomart, a
character in George Bernard Shaw's play *Major Barbara*.

Lady Britomart, a member of the Established Church of England,
reveals her superficial attitude toward religion in a scene that takes
place in her fashionable London townhouse. Religion, according to
Lady Britomart, is a morbid topic of conversation. She admonishes
her daughter Barbara: "Really, Barbara, you go on as if religion were a
pleasant subject. Do have some sense of propriety" (1.686-87). Religion
is an unpleasant subject to Lady Britomart because, unlike Barbara, she
finds no joy or humor within her religion. It is not simply that she is a
humorless person, for she frequently displays a sharp wit. But in Lady
Britomart's upper-class world, religion has its proper place—a serious
place bound by convention and cut off from the real world. When
Undershaft suggests, for example, that religion can be a pleasant and
profoundly important subject, Lady Britomart replies, "Well if you are
determined to have it [religion], then I insist on having it in a proper
and respectable way. Charles: ring for prayers" (1.690-93).

Notice that the writer has quoted dialogue from the play to lend both flavor and substance to her interpretation (quotations are cited with the act and line numbers and are enclosed in quotation marks). Notice too that the writer is *interpreting* the work: She is not merely summarizing the plot.

Avoiding plot summary

In a literature paper, it is tempting to rely heavily on plot summary and avoid interpretation. You can resist this temptation by paying special attention to your topic sentences.

The following rough-draft topic sentence, for instance, led to a plot summary rather than an interpretation.

> As they drift down the river on a raft, Huck and the runaway slave Jim have many philosophical discussions.

The student's revised topic sentence announces an interpretation.

> The theme of dawning moral awareness is reinforced by the many philosophical discussions between Huck and Jim, the runaway slave, as they drift down the river on a raft.

Usually a little effort can make the difference between a plot summary that cannot be developed and a focused, forceful interpretation. As with all forms of writing, revision is key. To avoid simple plot summary, keep the following strategies in mind as you write.

- When you write for an academic audience, you can assume that readers have read the work. They don't need a summary but are interested instead in your ideas about the work.

- Pose questions that lead to an interpretation or judgment of the work rather than to a summary. The questions in the chart on pages 594–95 can help steer you away from summary and toward interpretation.

- Read your essay out loud. If you hear yourself listing events from the work, stop and revise.

- If organizing your paper according to the work's sequence of events is getting in the way of your own ideas, look again at your outline and consider other ways of arranging your material.

55e Observe the conventions of literature papers.

The academic discipline of English literature has certain conventions, or standard practices, that scholars in the field use when writing about literature. In your literature paper, it is important that you observe the conventions so that your readers' attention will be focused on your interpretation, not on the details of your presentation.

Referring to authors, titles, and characters according to convention

When referring to the author of a literary work or secondary source, such as a critical essay, you should give the author's full name the first time you mention it; in subsequent references, you may use the last name only. As a rule, do not use personal titles such as *Mr.* or *Ms.* or *Dr.* when referring to authors.

When you mention the title of a short story, an essay, or a short or medium-length poem, put the title in quotation marks (see 37d). Italicize the titles of novels, nonfiction books, plays, and long poems (see 42a).

Refer to each character by the name most often used for him or her in the work. If, for instance, a character's name is Lambert Strether and he is always referred to as "Strether," do not call him "Lambert" or "Mr. Strether." Similarly, write "Lady Macbeth," not "Mrs. Macbeth."

Using the present tense to describe fictional events

Perhaps because fictional events have not actually occurred in the past, the literary convention is to describe them in the present tense. Until you become used to this convention, you may find yourself shifting between present and past tense. As you revise your draft, make sure that you have used the present tense consistently.

INCONSISTENT USE OF TENSES

Octavia <u>demands</u> blind obedience from James and from all of her children. When James and Ty <u>caught</u> two redbirds in their trap, they <u>wanted</u> to play with them; Octavia, however, <u>had</u> other plans for the birds (89-90).

CONSISTENT USE OF THE PRESENT TENSE

Octavia <u>demands</u> blind obedience from James and from all of her children. When James and Ty <u>catch</u> two redbirds in their trap, they <u>want</u> to play with them; Octavia, however, <u>has</u> other plans for the birds (89-90).

NOTE: Also see pages 604–05 on avoiding shifts in tenses when you integrate quotations from a work into your own text.

55f Integrate quotations from the work.

Integrating quotations from a literary work can lend vivid support to your argument, but keep most quotations fairly short. Excessive use of long quotations interrupts the flow of your interpretation and can bore readers.

Integrating quotations smoothly into your own text can present a challenge. Because of the complexities of literature, do not be surprised to find yourself puzzling over the most graceful way to tuck in a short phrase or the clearest way to introduce a more extended passage from the work.

Using MLA style to cite and format passages quoted from the work

Unless your instructor suggests otherwise, use MLA (Modern Language Association) style for citing and formatting passages quoted from literary works.

MLA style typically requires that you name the author of the work quoted and give a page number for the exact location of the passage in the work. When writing about nonfiction articles and books, introduce a quotation with a signal phrase naming the author (*John Smith points out . . .*) or place the author's name and page number in parentheses at the end of the quoted passage: *. . . for all time" (Smith 22).*

When writing about a single work of fiction, you do not need to include the author's name each time you quote from the work. You will name the author in the introduction to your paper. Then, when you are quoting from the work, include just the page number in parentheses following the quotation (see the second example on p. 604). You may, of course, use the author's name in a signal phrase to highlight the author's role or technique, but you are not required to do so.

MLA guidelines for handling citations in the text of your paper differ somewhat for short stories or novels, poems, and plays, each of which is discussed in this section (see pp. 605–08). (If your instructor requires a works cited page, see p. 620.)

Introducing literary quotations

When introducing quotations from a literary work, make sure that you don't confuse the author with the narrator of a story, the speaker of a poem, or a character in a story or play. Instead of naming the author, you can refer to the narrator or speaker—or to the work itself.

INAPPROPRIATE

Poet Andrew Marvell describes his fear of death like this: "But at my back I always hear / Time's wingèd chariot hurrying near" (21-22).

APPROPRIATE

Addressing his beloved in an attempt to win her sexual favors, the speaker of the poem argues that death gives them no time to waste: "But at my back I always hear / Time's wingèd chariot hurrying near" (21-22).

APPROPRIATE

The poem "To His Coy Mistress" says as much about fleeting time and death as it does about sexual passion. Its most powerful lines are "But at my back I always hear / Time's wingèd chariot hurrying near" (21-22).

In the last example, you could mention the author as well: *Marvell's poem "To His Coy Mistress" says as much. . . .* Although the author is mentioned, readers will not confuse him with the speaker of the poem.

Providing context for quotations

When you quote the words of a narrator, speaker, or character in a literary work, you should name who is speaking and provide a context for the quoted words. In the following examples, the quoted dialogue is from Tennessee Williams's play *The Glass Menagerie* and Shirley Jackson's short story "The Lottery."

> Laura is so completely under Amanda's spell that when urged to make a wish on the moon, she asks, "What shall I wish for, Mother?" (1.5.140).

> When a neighbor suggests that the lottery should be abandoned, Old Man Warner responds, "There's *always* been a lottery" (284).

Avoiding shifts in tense when quoting

Because it is conventional to write about literature in the present tense (see pp. 601–02) and because literary works often use other tenses, you will need to exercise some care when weaving quotations into your own writing. A first-draft attempt may result in an awkward shift between your words and the quoted text, as it did for one student who was writing about Nadine Gordimer's short story "Friday's Footprint."

TENSE SHIFT

> When Rita sees Johnny's relaxed attitude, "she blushed, like a wave of illness" (159).

To avoid the distracting shift from present to past tense, the writer had two choices: to paraphrase the reference to Rita's blushing and reduce the length of the quotation or to change the verb in the quotation to the present tense, using brackets to indicate the change.

REVISED

When Rita sees Johnny's relaxed attitude, she is overcome with embarrassment, "like a wave of illness" (159).

REVISED

When Rita sees Johnny's relaxed attitude, "she blushe[s], like a wave of illness" (159).

Using brackets around just one letter of a word can seem fussy, so the writer chose the first revision. (For advice on using brackets to indicate changes in a quotation, see 39c.)

Using quotations within quotations

In writing about literature, you may sometimes want to use a quotation that has another quotation embedded in it—when you are integrating dialogue from a novel, for example. In such cases, set off the main quotation with double quotation marks, as you usually would, and set off the embedded quotation with single quotation marks. (See also 37c.) The following example from a student paper integrates lines from Amy Tan's novel *The Hundred Secret Senses*.

Early in the novel the narrator's half-sister Kwan sees—or thinks she sees—ghosts: "'Libby-ah,' she'll say to me. 'Guess who I see yesterday, you guess.' And I don't have to guess that she's talking about someone dead" (3).

Formatting quotations

MLA guidelines for formatting quotations differ somewhat for short stories or novels, poems, and plays.

Short stories or novels   To cite a passage from a short story or a novel, use a page number in parentheses after the quoted words.

The narrator of Eudora Welty's "Why I Live at the P.O.," known to us only as "Sister," makes many catty remarks about her enemies. For example, she calls Mr. Whitaker "this photographer with the pop-eyes" (46).

If a novel has numbered divisions, give the page number and a semicolon; then indicate the book, part, or chapter in which the passage is found. Use abbreviations such as "bk." and "ch."

> White relies on past authors to help retell the legend of King Arthur. The narrator does not provide specifics about Lancelot's tournament at Corbin, instead telling readers, "If you want to read about the Corbin tournament, Malory has it" (489; bk. 3, ch. 39).

When a quotation from a work of fiction takes up four or fewer typed lines, put it in quotation marks and run it into the text of your essay, as in the two previous examples. When a quotation is five lines or longer, set it off from the text by indenting one inch from the left margin; when you set a quotation off from the text, do not use quotation marks. Put the parenthetical citation after the final mark of punctuation.

> Sister's tale begins with "I," and she makes every event revolve around herself, even her sister's marriage:
>
>> I was getting along fine with Mama, Papa-Daddy, and Uncle Rondo until my sister Stella-Rondo just separated from her husband and came back home again. Mr. Whitaker! Of course I went with Mr. Whitaker first, when he first appeared here in China Grove, taking "Pose Yourself" photos, and Stella-Rondo broke us up. (46)

Poems To cite lines from a poem, use line numbers in parentheses at the end of the quotation. For the first reference, use the word "lines": (lines 1-2). Thereafter use just the numbers: (12-13).

> The opening lines of Frost's "Fire and Ice" strike a conversational tone: "Some say the world will end in fire, / Some say in ice" (1-2).

Enclose quotations of three or fewer lines of poetry in quotation marks within your text, and indicate line breaks with a slash, as in the example just given. (See also 39e and item 25 on p. 528.)

When you quote four or more lines of poetry, set the quotation off from the text by indenting one inch and omit the quotation marks. Put the line numbers in parentheses after the final mark of punctuation.

> In the second stanza of "A Noiseless Patient Spider," Whitman turns the spider's weaving into a metaphor for the activity of the human soul:
>
> > And you O my soul where you stand,
> > Surrounded, detached, in measureless oceans of space,
> > Ceaselessly musing, venturing, throwing, seeking the spheres
> > > to connect them,
> > Till the bridge you will need be form'd, till the ductile anchor
> > > hold,
> > Till the gossamer thread you fling catch somewhere, O my
> > > soul. (6-10)

NOTE: If any line of the poem takes up more than one line of your paper, carry the extra words to the next line of the paper and indent them an additional one-quarter inch, as in the previous example. Alternatively, you may indent the entire poem a little less than one inch to fit the long line.

Plays   To cite lines from a play, include the act number, scene number, and line numbers (as many of these as are available) in parentheses at the end of the quotation. Separate the numbers with periods, and use arabic numerals unless your instructor prefers roman numerals.

> Two attendants silently watch as the sleepwalking Lady Macbeth subconsciously struggles with her guilt: "Here's the smell of the blood still. All the perfumes of Arabia will not sweeten this little hand" (5.1.50-51).

If no act, scene, or line numbers are available, use a page number.

When a quotation from a play takes up four or fewer typed lines in your paper and is spoken by only one character, put quotation marks around it and run it into the text of your essay, as in the previous example. If the quotation consists of two or three lines from a verse play, use a slash for line breaks, as for poetry (see p. 606). When a dramatic quotation by a single character is five typed lines or longer (or more than three lines in a verse play), indent it one inch from the left margin and omit quotation marks. Include the citation in parentheses after the final mark of punctuation.

> Speaking to Electra, Clytemnestra complains about the sexual double standard that has allowed her husband to justify sacrificing her other daughter, Iphigenia, to the gods. She asks what would have happened if Menelaus, and not his wife Helen, had been seized by the Trojans:
>
>> If Menelaus had been raped from home on the sly, should I have had to kill Orestes so my sister's husband could be rescued? You think your father would have borne it? He would have killed me. Then why was it fair for him to kill what belonged to me and not be killed? (1041-45)

When quoting dialogue between two or more characters in a play, no matter how many lines you use, set the quotation off from the text. Type each character's name in all capital letters at a one-inch indent from the left margin. Indent subsequent lines under the character's name an additional one-quarter inch.

> Throughout *The Importance of Being Earnest*, Algernon criticizes romance and the institution of marriage, as in the scene when he learns of Jack's intention to marry Gwendolen:
>
>> ALGERNON. My dear fellow, the way you flirt with Gwendolen is perfectly disgraceful. It is almost as bad as the way Gwendolen flirts with you.
>>
>> JACK. I am in love with Gwendolen. I have come up to town expressly to propose to her.
>>
>> ALGERNON. I thought you had come up for pleasure? — I call that business. (act 1)

55g If you use secondary sources, document them appropriately and avoid plagiarism.

Many literature papers rely wholly on primary sources—the literary text under discussion. (For an example of an essay with only a primary source, see pp. 611–13.)

Other literature papers use some ideas from secondary sources, such as articles or books of literary criticism, biographies of the author, the author's own essays and autobiography, or histories of the era in which the work was written. (For an example of a paper that uses secondary sources, see pp. 615–20.) Even if you use secondary sources, your main goal should always be to develop your own understanding and interpretation of the literary work.

Whenever you use secondary sources, you must document them, and you must avoid plagiarism. Plagiarism is unacknowledged borrowing—whether intentional or unintentional—of a source's words or ideas. (See 51b.)

Documenting secondary sources

Most literature papers use the documentation system recommended by the Modern Language Association (MLA). This system of documentation is discussed in detail in 53.

MLA recommends in-text citations that refer readers to a list of works cited. An in-text citation names the author of the source, often in a signal phrase, and gives the page number in parentheses. At the end of the paper, a list of works cited provides publication information about the sources used in the paper.

SAMPLE MLA IN-TEXT CITATION

Arguing that fate has little to do with the tragedy that befalls Oedipus, Bernard Knox writes that "the catastrophe of Oedipus is that he discovers his own identity; and for his discovery he is first and last responsible" (6).

The signal phrase names the author of the secondary source; the number in parentheses is the page on which the quoted words appear.

Anyone interested in knowing additional information about the secondary source can consult the list of works cited at the end of the paper. Here, for example, is the works cited entry for the work referred to in the sample in-text citation.

SAMPLE ENTRY IN THE LIST OF WORKS CITED

Knox, Bernard. *Oedipus at Thebes: Sophocles' Tragic Hero and His Time*.
   New York: Norton, 1971. Print.

As you document secondary sources with in-text citations, consult 53a; as you construct your list of works cited, consult 53b.

Avoiding plagiarism

The rules about plagiarism are the same for literary papers as for other research writing (see 48c and 51 for important details). To be fair and ethical, you must acknowledge your debt to the writers of any sources you use. If an interpretation was suggested to you by another critic's work or if an obscure point was clarified by someone else's research, it is your responsibility to cite the source. If you have borrowed any phrases or sentences from your source, you must put them in quotation marks and credit the author.

55h Sample literature papers

Following are two sample essays. The first, by Margaret Peel, has no secondary sources. (Its primary source, Langston Hughes's "Ballad of the Landlord," appears on p. 614.) The second sample paper, by Dan Larson, uses secondary sources.

hackerhandbooks.com/bedhandbook > Model papers
                                 > MLA papers: Peel
                                 > MLA papers: Larson

Peel 1

Margaret Peel

Professor Lin

English 102

20 April 2005

Opposing Voices in "Ballad of the Landlord"

Langston Hughes's "Ballad of the Landlord" is narrated through

four voices, each with its own perspective on the poem's action. These

opposing voices—of a tenant, a landlord, the police, and the press—

dramatize a black man's experience in a society dominated by whites.

The main voice in the poem is that of the tenant, who, as the

last line tells us, is black. The tenant is characterized by his informal,

nonstandard speech. He uses slang ("Ten Bucks"), contracted words

(*'member*, *more'n*), and nonstandard grammar ("These steps is broken

down"). This colloquial English suggests the tenant's separation from

the world of convention, represented by the formal voices of the police

and the press, which appear later in the poem.

Although the tenant uses nonstandard English, his argument

is organized and logical. He begins with a reasonable complaint and

a gentle reminder that the complaint is already a week old: "My roof

has sprung a leak. / Don't you 'member I told you about it / Way last

week?" (lines 2-4). In the second stanza, he appeals diplomatically to

the landlord's self-interest: "These steps is broken down. / When you

come up yourself / It's a wonder you don't fall down" (6-8). In the

third stanza, when the landlord has responded to his complaints with

a demand for rent money, the tenant becomes more forceful, but his

voice is still reasonable: "Ten Bucks you say is due? / Well, that's Ten

Bucks more'n I'll pay you / Till you fix this house up new" (10-12).

The fourth stanza marks a shift in the tone of the argument.

At this point the tenant responds more emotionally, in reaction to

Marginal notes:

Thesis states Peel's main idea.

Details from the poem illustrate Peel's point.

The first citation of lines of the poem includes the word "lines." Subsequent citations from the poem are cited with line numbers alone.

Topic sentence focuses on an interpretation.

Marginal annotations indicate MLA-style formatting and effective writing.

Peel 2

the landlord's threats to evict him. By the fifth stanza, the tenant has unleashed his anger: "Um-huh! You talking high and mighty" (17). Hughes uses an exclamation point for the first time; the tenant is raising his voice at last. As the argument gets more heated, the tenant finally resorts to the language of violence: "You ain't gonna be able to say a word / If I land my fist on you" (19-20).

Transition prepares readers for the next topic.

These are the last words the tenant speaks in the poem. Perhaps Hughes wants to show how black people who threaten violence are silenced. When a new voice is introduced—the landlord's—the poem shifts to a frantic tone:

> *Police! Police!*
> *Come and get this man!*
> *He's trying to ruin the government*
> *And overturn the land!* (21-24)

This response is clearly an overreaction to a small threat. Instead of dealing with the tenant directly, the landlord shouts for the police. His hysterical voice—marked by repetitions and punctuated with exclamation points—reveals his disproportionate fear and outrage.

Peel interprets the landlord's response.

And his conclusions are equally excessive: this black man, he claims, is out to "ruin the government" and "overturn the land." Although the landlord's overreaction is humorous, it is sinister as well, because the landlord knows that, no matter how excessive his claims are, he has the police and the law on his side.

Peel shows how meter and rhyme support the poem's meaning.

In line 25, the regular meter and rhyme of the poem break down, perhaps showing how an arrest disrupts everyday life. The "voice" in lines 25-29 has two parts: the clanging sound of the police ("Copper's whistle! / Patrol bell!") and, in sharp contrast, the unemotional, factual tone of a police report ("Arrest. / Precinct Station. / Iron cell.").

Peel 3

The last voice in the poem is the voice of the press, represented in newspaper headlines: "MAN THREATENS LANDLORD/ TENANT HELD NO BAIL / JUDGE GIVES NEGRO 90 DAYS IN COUNTY JAIL" (31-33). Meter and rhyme return here, as if to show that once the tenant is arrested, life can go on as usual. The language of the press, like that of the police, is cold and distant, and it gives the tenant less and less status. In line 31, he is a "man"; in line 32, he has been demoted to a "tenant"; and in line 33, he has become a "Negro," or just another statistic.

By using four opposing voices in "Ballad of the Landlord," Hughes effectively dramatizes different views of minority assertiveness. To the tenant, assertiveness is informal and natural, as his language shows; to the landlord, it is a dangerous threat, as his hysterical response suggests. The police response is, like the language that describes it, short and sharp. Finally, the press's view of events, represented by the headlines, is distant and unsympathetic.

By the end of the poem, we understand the predicament of the black man. Exploited by the landlord, politically oppressed by those who think he's out "to ruin the government," physically restrained by the police and the judicial system, and denied his individuality by the press, he is saved only by his own sense of humor. The very title of the poem suggests his—and Hughes's—sense of humor. The tenant is singing a *ballad* to his oppressors, but this ballad is no love song. It portrays the oppressors, through their own voices, in an unflattering light: the landlord as cowardly and ridiculous, the police and press as dull and soulless. The tenant may lack political power, but he speaks with vitality, and no one can say he lacks dignity or the spirit to survive.

Peel sums up her interpretation.

Peel concludes with an analysis of the poem's political significance.

Ballad of the Landlord

LANGSTON HUGHES

Landlord, landlord,
My roof has sprung a leak.
Don't you 'member I told you about it
Way last week?

Landlord, landlord,
These steps is broken down.
When you come up yourself
It's a wonder you don't fall down.

Ten Bucks you say I owe you?
Ten Bucks you say is due?
Well, that's Ten Bucks more'n I'll pay you
Till you fix this house up new.

What? You gonna get eviction orders?
You gonna cut off my heat?
You gonna take my furniture and
Throw it in the street?

Um-huh! You talking high and mighty.
Talk on—till you get through.
You ain't gonna be able to say a word
If I land my fist on you.

Police! Police!
Come and get this man!
He's trying to ruin the government
And overturn the land!

Copper's whistle!
Patrol bell!
Arrest.

Precinct Station.
Iron cell.
Headlines in press:

MAN THREATENS LANDLORD
TENANT HELD NO BAIL
JUDGE GIVES NEGRO 90 DAYS IN COUNTY JAIL

Larson 1

Dan Larson

Professor Duncan

English 102

18 April 2005

The Transformation of Mrs. Peters:

An Analysis of "A Jury of Her Peers"

In Susan Glaspell's 1917 short story "A Jury of Her Peers," two women accompany their husbands and a county attorney to an isolated house where a farmer named John Wright has been choked to death in his bed with a rope. The chief suspect is Wright's wife, Minnie, who is in jail awaiting trial. The sheriff's wife, Mrs. Peters, has come along to gather some personal items for Minnie, and Mrs. Hale has joined her. Early in the story, Mrs. Hale sympathizes with Minnie and objects to the way the male investigators are "snoopin' round and criticizin'" her kitchen (200). In contrast, Mrs. Peters shows respect for the law, saying that the men are doing "no more than their duty" (201). By the end of the story, however, Mrs. Peters has joined Mrs. Hale in a conspiracy of silence, lied to the men, and committed a crime—hiding key evidence. What causes this dramatic change?

One critic, Leonard Mustazza, argues that Mrs. Hale recruits Mrs. Peters "as a fellow 'juror' in the case, moving the sheriff's wife away from her sympathy for her husband's position and towards identification with the accused woman" (494). While this is true, Mrs. Peters also reaches insights on her own. Her observations in the kitchen lead her to understand Minnie's grim and lonely plight as the wife of an abusive farmer, and her identification with both Minnie and Mrs. Hale is strengthened as the men conducting the investigation trivialize the lives of women.

The opening lines name the story and establish context.

Present tense is used to describe details from the story.

Quotations from the story are cited with page numbers in parentheses.

The opening paragraph ends with Larson's research question.

The thesis asserts Larson's main point.

Marginal annotations indicate MLA-style formatting and effective writing.

Larson 2

The first evidence that Mrs. Peters reaches understanding on her own surfaces in the following passage:

> The sheriff's wife had looked from the stove to the sink—to the pail of water which had been carried in from outside. . . . That look of seeing into things, of seeing through a thing to something else, was in the eyes of the sheriff's wife now. (203)

Something about the stove, the sink, and the pail of water connects with her own experience, giving Mrs. Peters a glimpse into the life of Minnie Wright. The details resonate with meaning.

Social historian Elaine Hedges argues that such details, which evoke the drudgery of a farm woman's work, would not have been lost upon Glaspell's readers in 1917. Hedges tells us what the pail and the stove, along with another detail from the story—a dirty towel on a roller—would have meant to women of the time. Laundry was a dreaded all-day affair. Water had to be pumped, hauled, and boiled; then the wash was rubbed, rinsed, wrung through a wringer, carried outside, and hung on a line to dry. "What the women see, beyond the pail and the stove," writes Hedges, "are the hours of work it took Minnie to produce that one clean towel" (56).

On her own, Mrs. Peters discovers clues about the motive for the murder. Her curiosity leads her to pick up a sewing basket filled with quilt pieces and then to notice something strange: a sudden row of badly sewn stitches. "What do you suppose she was so—nervous about?" asks Mrs. Peters (204). A short time later, Mrs. Peters spots another clue, an empty birdcage. Again she observes details on her own, in this case a broken door and hinge, suggesting that the cage has been roughly handled.

In addition to noticing details, both women draw conclusions from them and speculate on their significance. When Mrs. Hale finds the

A long quotation is set off by indenting with no quotation marks. Ellipsis dots indicate a sentence omitted from the source.

Larson summarizes ideas from a secondary source and then quotes from that source; he names the author in a signal phrase and gives a page number in parentheses.

Topic sentences focus on Larson's interpretation.

Larson 3

dead canary beneath a quilt patch, for example, the women conclude
that its neck has been wrung and understand who must have wrung it.

As the women speculate on the significance of the dead canary,
each connects the bird with her own experience. Mrs. Hale knows that
Minnie once sang in the church choir, an activity that Mr. Wright put a
stop to, just as he put a stop to the bird's singing. Also, as a farmer's
wife, Mrs. Hale understands the desolation and loneliness of life on the
prairie. She sees that the bird was both a thing of beauty and a
companion. "If there had been years and years of—nothing, then a
bird to sing to you," says Mrs. Hale, "it would be awful—still—after the
bird was still" (208). To Mrs. Peters, the stillness of the canary evokes
memories of the time when she and her husband homesteaded in the
northern plains. "I know what stillness is," she says, as she recalls the
death of her first child, with no one around to console her (208).

Details from the story provide evidence for the interpretation.

Elaine Hedges has written movingly of the isolation that women
experienced on late-nineteenth- and early-twentieth-century farms of
the West and Midwest:

> Women themselves reported that it was not unusual to
> spend five months in a log cabin without seeing another
> woman . . . or to spend one and a half years after arriving
> before being able to take a trip to town. . . . (54)

Ellipsis dots indicate omitted words within the sentence and at the end of the sentence.

To combat loneliness and monotony, says Hedges, many women
bought canaries and hung the cages outside their sod huts. The
canaries provided music and color, a spot of beauty that "might spell
the difference between sanity and madness" (60).

Mrs. Peters and Mrs. Hale understand—and Glaspell's readers
in 1917 would have understood—what the killing of the bird means
to Minnie. For Mrs. Peters, in fact, the act has a special significance.
When she was a child, a boy axed her kitten to death and, as she says,
"If they hadn't held me back I would have . . . hurt him" (207).

Larson 4

She has little difficulty comprehending Minnie's murderous rage, for she has felt it herself.

Transition serves as a bridge from one section of the paper to the next.

Although Mrs. Peters's growing empathy for Minnie stems largely from her observations, it is also prompted by her negative reaction to the patronizing comments of the male investigators. At several points in the story, her body language reveals her feelings. For example, when Mr. Hale remarks that "women are used to worrying over trifles," both women move closer together and remain silent. When the county attorney asks, "for all their worries, what would we do without the ladies?" the women do not speak, nor do they "unbend" (199). The fact that the women respond in exactly the same way reveals the extent to which they are bonding.

Both women are annoyed at the way in which the men criticize and trivialize the world of women. The men question the difficulty of women's work. For example, when the county attorney points to the dirty towel on the rack as evidence that Minnie wasn't much of a housekeeper, Mrs. Hale replies, "There's a great deal of work to be done on a farm" (199). Even the importance of women's work is questioned. The men kid the women for trying to decide if Minnie was going to quilt or knot patches together for a quilt and laugh about such trivial concerns. Those very quilts, of course, kept the men warm at night and cost them nothing beyond the price of thread.

The men also question the women's wisdom and intelligence. For example, when the county attorney tells the women to keep their eyes out for clues, Mr. Hale replies, "But would the women know a clue if they did come upon it?" (200). The women's response is to stand motionless and silent. The irony is that the men don't see the household clues that are right in front of them.

Larson gives evidence that Mrs. Peters has been transformed.

By the end of the story, Mrs. Peters has been so transformed that she risks lying to the men. When the district attorney walks into the kitchen and notices the birdcage the women have found, he asks

Larson 5

about the whereabouts of the bird. Mrs. Hale replies, "We think the cat got it," even though she knows from Mrs. Peters that Minnie was afraid of cats and would not have owned one. Instead of correcting the lie, Mrs. Peters elaborates on it, saying of cats, "They're superstitious, you know; they leave" (207). Clearly Mrs. Hale is willing to risk lying because she is confident that Mrs. Peters won't contradict her.

The Mrs. Peters character may have been based on a real sheriff's wife. Seventeen years before writing "A Jury of Her Peers," Susan Glaspell covered a murder case for the *Des Moines Daily News*. A farmer's wife, Margaret Hossack, was accused of murdering her sleeping husband with two axe blows to the head. In one of her newspaper reports, Glaspell wrote that the sheriff's wife sat next to Mrs. Hossack and "frequently applied her handkerchief to her eyes" (qtd. in Ben-Zvi 30).

Larson draws on a secondary source that gives background on Glaspell's life.

We do not know from the short story the ultimate fate of Minnie Wright, but Margaret Hossack, whose case inspired the story, was found guilty, though the case was later thrown out by the Iowa Supreme Court. However, as Linda Ben-Zvi points out, the women's guilt or innocence is not the issue:

> Whether Margaret Hossack or Minnie Wright committed murder is moot; what is incontrovertible is the brutality of their lives, the lack of options they had to redress grievances or to escape abusive husbands, and the complete disregard of their plight by the courts and by society. (38)

These are the issues that Susan Glaspell wished to stress in "A Jury of Her Peers."

These are also the issues that Mrs. Peters comes to understand as the story unfolds, with her understanding deepening as she identifies with Minnie and Mrs. Hale and is repulsed by male attitudes. Her transformation becomes complete when the men joke that she is "married to the law" and she responds by violating the law: hiding key evidence, the dead canary.

Larson's conclusion echoes his main point without dully repeating it.

Larson 6

Works Cited

The works cited page lists the primary source (Glaspell's story) and secondary sources.

Ben-Zvi, Linda. "'Murder, She Wrote': The Genesis of Susan Glaspell's *Trifles*." *Theatre Journal* 44.2 (1992): 141-62. Rpt. in *Susan Glaspell: Essays on Her Theater and Fiction*. Ed. Ben-Zvi. Ann Arbor: U of Michigan P, 1995. 19-48. Print.

Glaspell, Susan. "A Jury of Her Peers." *Literature and Its Writers: A Compact Introduction to Fiction, Poetry, and Drama*. Ed. Ann Charters and Samuel Charters. 3rd ed. Boston: Bedford, 2004. 194-210. Print.

Hedges, Elaine. "Small Things Reconsidered: 'A Jury of Her Peers.'" *Women's Studies* 12.1 (1986): 89-110. Rpt. in *Susan Glaspell: Essays on Her Theater and Fiction*. Ed. Linda Ben-Zvi. Ann Arbor: U of Michigan P, 1995. 49-69. Print.

Mustazza, Leonard. "Generic Translation and Thematic Shift in Susan Glaspell's *Trifles* and 'A Jury of Her Peers.'" *Studies in Short Fiction* 26.4 (1989): 489-96. Print.

Writing APA papers

56 APA papers

Brief Directory
56a Supporting a thesis, 621
56b Citing sources; avoiding plagiarism, 625
56c Integrating sources, 629
56d APA documentation style, 638
   Directory to APA in-text citation models, 640
   Directory to APA references, 645
56e APA manuscript format, 669
56f Sample APA research paper, 673

Many writing assignments in the social sciences are either reports of original research or reviews of the literature written about a research topic. Often an original research report contains a "review of the literature" section that places the writer's project in the context of previous research.

Most social science instructors will ask you to document your sources with the American Psychological Association (APA) system of in-text citations and references described in 56d. You face three main challenges when writing a social science paper that draws on sources: (1) supporting a thesis, (2) citing your sources and avoiding plagiarism, and (3) integrating quotations and other source material.

Examples in this section are drawn from one student's research for a review of the literature on treatments for childhood obesity. Luisa Mirano's paper appears on pages 674–83.

56a Supporting a thesis

Most assignments ask you to form a thesis, or main idea, and to support that thesis with well-organized evidence. (See also 1c.) In a paper reviewing the literature on a topic, the thesis analyzes the often competing conclusions drawn by a variety of researchers. Remain flexible as you draft because you may need to revise your approach later. Writing about a subject is a way of learning about it; as you write, your understanding of your subject will almost certainly deepen.

Forming a working thesis

Once you have read a variety of sources and considered your issue from different perspectives, you are ready to form a working thesis: a one-sentence (or occasionally a two-sentence) statement of your central idea. (See also 1c.) You will be reading articles and other sources that address the central research question you posed earlier (see 46c). Ultimately, your thesis will express not just your opinion but your informed, reasoned answer to that question, given the current state of research in the field. Here, for example, is a research question posed by Luisa Mirano, a student in a psychology class, followed by a thesis that answers the question.

RESEARCH QUESTION

Is medication the right treatment for the escalating problem of childhood obesity?

WORKING THESIS

Treating cases of childhood obesity with medication alone is too narrow an approach for this growing problem.

Notice that the thesis expresses a view on a debatable issue—an issue about which intelligent, well-meaning people might disagree. The writer's job is to convince such readers that this view is worth taking seriously.

Organizing your ideas

The American Psychological Association encourages the use of headings to help readers follow the organization of a paper. For an original research report, the major headings often follow a standard model: Method, Results, Discussion. The introduction is not given a heading; it consists of the material between the title of the paper and the first heading.

For a literature review, headings will vary. The student who wrote about treatments for childhood obesity used four questions to focus her research; the questions then became headings in her paper (see pp. 674–83).

> **Making the most of your handbook**
>
> When writing from sources, it helps to start with a working thesis and a rough outline.
>
> ▶ Draft a working thesis: 1c
>
> ▶ Sketch a plan: 1d

hackerhandbooks.com/bedhandbook > Research exercises > APA > E-ex 56–1 and 56–2

Using sources to inform and support your argument

Used thoughtfully, your source materials will make your argument more complex and convincing for readers. Sources can play several different roles as you develop your points.

Providing background information or context You can use facts and statistics to support generalizations or to establish the importance of your topic, as student writer Luisa Mirano does in her introduction.

> In March 2004, U.S. Surgeon General Richard Carmona called attention to a health problem in the United States that, until recently, has been overlooked: childhood obesity. Carmona said that the "astounding" 15% child obesity rate constitutes an "epidemic." Since the early 1980s, that rate has "doubled in children and tripled in adolescents." Now more than nine million children are classified as obese.

Explaining terms or concepts If readers are unlikely to be familiar with a word or an idea important to your topic, you must explain it for them. Quoting or paraphrasing a source can help you define terms and concepts in accessible language. Luisa Mirano uses a footnote in her paper to define the familiar word *obesity* in the technical sense used by researchers.

Obesity is measured in terms of body-mass index (BMI): weight in kilograms divided by square of height in meters. A child or an adolescent with a BMI in the 95th percentile for his or her age and gender is considered obese.

Supporting your claims As you draft your argument, make sure to back up your assertions with facts, examples, and other evidence from your research (see also 5e). Luisa Mirano, for example, uses one source's findings to support her central idea that the medical treatment of childhood obesity has limitations.

As journalist Greg Critser (2003) noted in his book *Fat Land*, use of weight-loss drugs is unlikely to have an effect without the proper "support system"—one that includes doctors, facilities, time, and money (p. 3).

Lending authority to your argument Including expert opinion can add credibility to your argument. (See also 5e.) But don't rely on experts to make your argument for you. Construct your argument in your own words and, when appropriate, cite the judgment of an authority in the field for support.

Both medical experts and policymakers recognize that solutions might come not only from a laboratory but also from policy, education, and advocacy. A handbook designed to educate doctors on obesity called for "major changes in some aspects of western culture" (Hoppin & Taveras, 2004, Conclusion section, para. 1).

Anticipating and countering alternative interpretations Do not ignore sources that seem contrary to your position or that offer interpretations different from your own. Instead, use them to give voice to opposing points of view before you counter them (see 5f). Readers often have objections in mind already, whether or not they agree with you. Mirano uses a source to acknowledge value in her opponents' position that medication alone can successfully treat childhood obesity.

As researchers Yanovski and Yanovski (2002) have explained, obesity was once considered "either a moral failing or evidence of underlying psychopathology" (p. 592). But this view has shifted: Many medical professionals now consider obesity a biomedical rather than a moral condition, influenced by both genetic and environmental factors. Yanovski and Yanovski have further noted that the development of weight-loss medications in the early 1990s showed that "obesity should be treated in the same manner as any other chronic disease . . . through the long-term use of medication" (p. 592).

56b Citing sources; avoiding plagiarism

In a research paper, you will draw on the work of other writers, and you must document their contributions by citing your sources. Sources are cited for two reasons:

- to tell readers where your information comes from—so that they can assess its reliability and, if interested, find and read the original source

- to give credit to the writers from whom you have borrowed words and ideas

Borrowing another writer's language, sentence structures, or ideas without proper acknowledgment is a form of dishonesty known as *plagiarism*.

You must include a citation when you quote from a source, when you summarize or paraphrase a source, and when you borrow facts that are not common knowledge. (See also "Avoiding plagiarism," p. 626.)

Using the APA system for citing sources

The American Psychological Association recommends an author-date style of citations. The following is a brief description of how the author-date system often works. (See 56d for more details and model citations.)

1. The source is introduced by a signal phrase that includes the last name of the author followed by the date of publication in parentheses.

2. The material being cited is followed by a page number in parentheses.

3. At the end of the paper, an alphabetized list of references gives complete publication information for the source.

IN-TEXT CITATION

As researchers Yanovski and Yanovski (2002) have explained, obesity was once considered "either a moral failing or evidence of underlying psychopathology" (p. 592).

ENTRY IN THE LIST OF REFERENCES

Yanovski, S. Z., & Yanovski, J. A. (2002). Drug therapy: Obesity. *The New England Journal of Medicine, 346,* 591-602.

This basic APA format varies for different types of sources. For a detailed discussion and other models, see 56d.

Avoiding plagiarism

Your research paper is a collaboration between you and your sources. To be fair and ethical, you must acknowledge your debt to the writers of those sources. If you don't, you commit plagiarism, a serious academic offense. (See also 48c.)

In general, these three acts are considered plagiarism: (1) failing to cite quotations and borrowed ideas, (2) failing to enclose borrowed language in quotation marks, and (3) failing to put summaries and paraphrases in your own words. Definitions of plagiarism may vary; it's a good idea to find out how your school defines academic dishonesty.

Citing quotations and borrowed ideas You must cite all direct quotations. You must also cite any ideas borrowed from a source: summaries and paraphrases; statistics and other specific facts; and visuals such as cartoons, graphs, and diagrams.

The only exception is common knowledge—information that your readers may know or could easily locate in any number of reference sources. For example, most general encyclopedias will tell readers that Sigmund Freud wrote *The Interpretation of Dreams* and that chimpanzees can learn American Sign Language.

As a rule, when you have seen certain information repeatedly in your reading, you don't need to cite it. However, when information has appeared in only a few sources, when it is highly specific (as with statistics), or when it is controversial, you should cite the source. If a topic is new to you and you are not sure what is considered common knowledge and what is considered controversial, ask your instructor or someone else with expertise. When in doubt, cite the source.

Enclosing borrowed language in quotation marks   To indicate that you are using a source's exact phrases or sentences, you must enclose them in quotation marks unless they have been set off from the text by indenting (see p. 631). To omit the quotation marks is to claim—falsely—that the language is your own. Such an omission is plagiarism even if you have cited the source.

ORIGINAL SOURCE

In an effort to seek the causes of this disturbing trend, experts have pointed to a range of important potential contributors to the rise in childhood obesity that are unrelated to media: a reduction in physical education classes and after-school athletic programs, an increase in the availability of sodas and snacks in public schools, the growth in the number of fast-food outlets across the country, the trend toward "super-sizing" food portions in restaurants, and the increasing number of highly processed high-calorie and high-fat grocery products.

—Henry J. Kaiser Family Foundation, "The Role of Media in Childhood Obesity" (2004), p. 1

PLAGIARISM

According to the Henry J. Kaiser Family Foundation (2004), experts have pointed to a range of important potential contributors to the rise in childhood obesity that are unrelated to media (p. 1).

BORROWED LANGUAGE IN QUOTATION MARKS

According to the Henry J. Kaiser Family Foundation (2004), "experts have pointed to a range of important potential contributors to the rise in childhood obesity that are unrelated to media" (p. 1).

Putting summaries and paraphrases in your own words Summaries and paraphrases are written in your own words. A summary condenses information; a paraphrase uses roughly the same number of words as the original source to convey the information. When you summarize or paraphrase, it is not enough to name the source; you must restate the source's meaning using your own language. (See also 48c.) You commit plagiarism if you half-copy the author's sentences—either by mixing the author's phrases with your own without using quotation marks or by plugging your own synonyms into the author's sentence structure. The following paraphrases are plagiarized—even though the source is cited—because their language and sentence structure are too close to those of the source.

ORIGINAL SOURCE

In an effort to seek the causes of this disturbing trend, experts have pointed to a range of important potential contributors to the rise in childhood obesity that are unrelated to media.
— Henry J. Kaiser Family Foundation, "The Role of Media in Childhood Obesity" (2004), p. 1

UNACCEPTABLE BORROWING OF PHRASES

According to the Henry J. Kaiser Family Foundation (2004), experts have indicated a range of significant potential contributors to the rise in childhood obesity that are not linked to media (p. 1).

UNACCEPTABLE BORROWING OF STRUCTURE

According to the Henry J. Kaiser Family Foundation (2004), experts have identified a variety of significant factors causing a rise in childhood obesity, factors that are not linked to media (p. 1).

To avoid plagiarizing an author's language, resist the temptation to look at the source while you are summarizing or paraphrasing. After you have read the passage you want to paraphrase, set the source aside. Ask yourself, "What is the author's meaning?" In your own words, state your understanding of the author's basic point. Return to the source and check that you haven't used the author's language or sentence structure or misrepresented the author's ideas. When you fully understand another writer's meaning, you can more easily and accurately represent those ideas in your own words.

ACCEPTABLE PARAPHRASE

A report by the Henry J. Kaiser Family Foundation (2004) described causes other than media for the childhood obesity crisis.

hackerhandbooks.com/bedhandbook > Research exercises > APA > E-ex 56–3 to 56–7

56c Integrating sources

Quotations, summaries, paraphrases, and facts will help you develop your argument, but they cannot speak for you. You can use several strategies to integrate information from sources into your paper while maintaining your own voice.

Using quotations appropriately

In your academic writing, keep the emphasis on your ideas and your language; use your own words to summarize and to paraphrase your sources and to explain your points. Sometimes, however, quotations can be the most effective way to integrate a source.

WHEN TO USE QUOTATIONS

- When language is especially vivid or expressive
- When exact wording is needed for technical accuracy
- When it is important to let the debaters of an issue explain their positions in their own words
- When the words of an authority lend weight to an argument
- When the language of a source is the topic of your discussion (as in an analysis or interpretation)

Limiting your use of quotations Although it is tempting to insert many quotations in your paper and to use your own words only for connecting passages, do not quote excessively. It is almost impossible to integrate numerous quotations smoothly into your own text.

It is not always necessary to quote full sentences from a source. To reduce your reliance on the words of others, you can often integrate language from a source into your own sentence structure.

> Carmona (2004) advised the subcommittee that the situation constitutes an "epidemic" and that the skyrocketing statistics are "astounding."

> As researchers continue to face a number of unknowns about obesity, it may be helpful to envision treating the disorder, as Yanovski and Yanovski (2002) suggested, "in the same manner as any other chronic disease" (p. 592).

Using the ellipsis mark To condense a quoted passage, you can use the ellipsis mark (three periods, with spaces between) to indicate that you have left words out. What remains must be grammatically complete.

> Roman (2003) reported that "social factors are nearly as significant as individual metabolism in the formation of . . . dietary habits of adolescents" (p. 345).

The writer has omitted the words *both healthy and unhealthy* from the source.

When you want to leave out one or more full sentences, use a period before the three ellipsis dots.

> According to Sothern and Gordon (2003), "Environmental factors may contribute as much as 80% to the causes of childhood obesity. . . . Research suggests that obese children demonstrate decreased levels of physical activity and increased psychosocial problems" (p. 104).

Ordinarily, do not use an ellipsis mark at the beginning or at the end of a quotation. Readers will understand that you have taken the quoted material from a longer passage, so such marks are not necessary. The only exception occurs when you have dropped words at the end of the final quoted sentence. In such cases, put three ellipsis dots before the closing quotation mark.

Make sure omissions and ellipsis marks do not distort the meaning of your source.

Using brackets   Brackets allow you to insert your own words into quoted material. You can insert words in brackets to clarify a confusing reference or to keep a sentence grammatical in your context.

> The cost of treating obesity currently totals $117 billion per year—a price, according to the surgeon general, "second only to the cost of [treating] tobacco use" (Carmona, 2004).

To indicate an error in a quotation, insert the word *sic* in brackets right after the error. Do not overuse *sic* to call attention to errors in a source. Sometimes paraphrasing is a better option. (See 39c.)

Setting off long quotations

When you quote forty or more words from a source, set off the quotation by indenting it one-half inch from the left margin. Use the normal right margin and do not single-space the quotation.

Long quotations should be introduced by an informative sentence, usually followed by a colon. Quotation marks are unnecessary because the indented format tells readers that the passage is taken word-for-word from the source.

> Yanovski and Yanovski (2002) have described earlier treatments for obesity that focused on behavior modification:
>
> > With the advent of behavioral treatments for obesity in the 1960s, hope arose that modification of maladaptive eating and exercise habits would lead to sustained weight loss, and that

> time-limited programs would produce permanent changes in
> weight. Medications for the treatment of obesity were proposed
> as short-term adjuncts for patients, who would presumably
> then acquire the skills necessary to continue to lose weight,
> reach "ideal body weight," and maintain a reduced weight
> indefinitely. (p. 592)

Notice that at the end of an indented quotation the parenthetical citation goes outside the final mark of punctuation. (When a quotation is run into your text, the opposite is true. See the sample citations on p. 630.)

Using signal phrases to integrate sources

Whenever you include a paraphrase, summary, or direct quotation of another writer in your paper, prepare your readers for it with introductory words called a *signal phrase*. A signal phrase usually names the author of the source and gives the publication year in parentheses and often provides context for the source material (see also p. 635).

When you write a signal phrase, choose a verb that is appropriate for the way you are using the source (see p. 623). Are you providing background, explaining a concept, supporting a claim, lending authority, or refuting a belief? By choosing an appropriate verb, you can make your source's role clear. See the chart on page 633 for a list of verbs commonly used in signal phrases.

APA requires using verbs in the past tense or present perfect tense (*noted* or *has noted*) to introduce quotations and other source material. Use the present tense only for discussing the results of an experiment (*the results show*) or knowledge that has clearly been established (*researchers agree*).

It is generally acceptable in the social sciences to call authors by their last name only, even on first mention. If your paper refers to two authors with same last name, use initials as well.

Marking boundaries Readers need to move from your words to the words of a source without feeling a jolt. Avoid dropping direct quotations into your text without warning. Instead, provide clear signal phrases, including at least the author's

signal phrases • introducing
sources • summary • paraphrase
APA 56c 633

name and the date of publication. Signal phrases mark the boundaries between source material and your own words; they can also tell readers why a source is worth quoting. (The signal phrase is underlined in the second example.)

DROPPED QUOTATION

Obesity was once considered in a very different light. "For many years, obesity was approached as if it were either a moral failing or evidence of underlying psychopathology" (Yanovski & Yanovski, 2002, p. 592).

QUOTATION WITH SIGNAL PHRASE

Obesity was once considered in a very different light. As researchers Yanovski and Yanovski (2002) have explained, obesity was widely thought of as "either a moral failing or evidence of underlying psychopathology" (p. 592).

Using signal phrases with summaries and paraphrases As with quotations, you should introduce most summaries and paraphrases with a signal phrase that mentions the author and the year and places the material in the context of your argument. Readers will then understand where the summary or paraphrase begins.

Without the signal phrase (underlined) in the following example, readers might think that only the last sentence is being cited, when in fact the whole paragraph is based on the source.

Carmona (2004) advised a Senate subcommittee that the problem of childhood obesity is dire and that the skyrocketing statistics—which put the child obesity rate at 15%—are cause for alarm. More than 9 million children, double the number in the early 1980s, are classified as obese. Carmona warned that obesity can cause myriad physical problems that only worsen as children grow older.

There are times, however, when a summary or a paraphrase does not require a signal phrase naming the author. When the context makes clear where the cited material begins, you may omit the signal phrase and include the author's

Using signal phrases in APA papers

To avoid monotony, try to vary both the language and the placement of your signal phrases.

Model signal phrases

In the words of Carmona (2004), ". . ."

As Yanovski and Yanovski (2002) have noted, ". . ."

Hoppin and Taveras (2004), medical researchers, pointed out that ". . ."

". . . ," claimed Critser (2003).

". . . ," wrote Duenwald (2004), ". . ."

Researchers McDuffie et al. (2003) have offered a compelling argument for this view: ". . ."

Hilts (2002) answered objections with the following analysis: ". . ."

Verbs in signal phrases

admitted	compared	insisted	rejected
agreed	confirmed	noted	reported
argued	contended	observed	responded
asserted	declared	pointed out	suggested
believed	denied	reasoned	thought
claimed	emphasized	refuted	wrote

name and the date in the parentheses. Unless the work is short, also include the page number in the parentheses.

Integrating statistics and other facts When you are citing a statistic or another specific fact, a signal phrase is often not necessary. In most cases, readers will understand that the citation refers to the statistic or fact (not the whole paragraph).

> In purely financial terms, the drugs cost more than $3 a day on average (Duenwald, 2004).

There is nothing wrong, however, with using a signal phrase to introduce a statistic or fact.

> Duenwald (2004) reported that the drugs cost more than $3 a day on average.

Putting source material in context   Readers should not have to guess why source material appears in your paper. A signal phrase can help you make the connection between your own ideas and those of another writer by clarifying how the source will contribute to your paper (see 47a).

If you use another writer's words, you must explain how they relate to your point. It's a good idea to embed a quotation between sentences of your own. In addition to introducing it with a signal phrase, follow it with interpretive comments that link the quotation to your paper's argument. (See also "Synthesizing sources," below.)

QUOTATION WITH EFFECTIVE CONTEXT

> A report by the Henry J. Kaiser Family Foundation (2004) outlined trends that may have contributed to the childhood obesity crisis, including food advertising for children as well as
>
> > a reduction in physical education classes . . . , an increase in the availability of sodas and snacks in public schools, the growth in the number of fast-food outlets . . . , and the increasing number of highly processed high-calorie and high-fat grocery products. (p. 1)
>
> Addressing each of these areas requires more than a doctor armed with a prescription pad; it requires a broad mobilization not just of doctors and concerned parents but of educators, food industry executives, advertisers, and media representatives.

hackerhandbooks.com/bedhandbook > Research exercises > APA > E-ex 56–8 to 56–11

Synthesizing sources

When you synthesize multiple sources in a research paper, you create a conversation about your research topic. You show readers that your argument is based on your active analysis and integration of ideas, not just a list of quotations and paraphrases. Your synthesis will show how your sources relate to one another. What one of your sources says may support, extend, or counter the ideas of another. Not every source has to "speak" to another in a research paper, but readers should be able to see how each one functions in your argument (see 47a).

Considering how sources relate to your argument Before you integrate sources and show readers how they relate to one another, consider how each one might contribute to your own argument. As student writer Luisa Mirano became more informed through her research about treatments for childhood obesity, she asked herself these questions: *What do I think about the various treatments for childhood obesity? Which sources might support my ideas? Which sources might help extend or illustrate the points I want to make? What common or compelling counterarguments do I need to address to strengthen my position?* She annotated a passage by journalist Greg Critser supporting her view that medication alone could not win the fight against childhood obesity.

STUDENT NOTES ON THE ORIGINAL SOURCE

Yet the more I contemplated my success [at losing weight], the more I came to see it not as a triumph of will, but as a triumph of my economic and social class. The weight loss medication Meridia, for example, had been effective not because it is such a good drug; even its purveyors freely admit it is far from effective for most people. What had made the drug work for me was the upper-middle-class support system that I had brought to it: a good physician who insisted on seeing me every two weeks, access to a safe park where I could walk and jog, friends who shared the value of becoming slender, healthy home-cooked food consumed with my wife, books about health, and medical journals about the latest nutritional breakthroughs. And money. And time.

Concrete examples — useful context.

Catchy term — good to quote

No easy fix for obesity. Critser had economic, educational, and medical support.

What about people without money and time? Even broader solution needed?

—Greg Critser, *Fat Land*, pp. 2–3

Critser's term *support system* offered Mirano a concise, visual way of referring to the extensive resources needed to fight obesity. His experience provided context and was a good choice for summary. Mirano planned to keep the emphasis on her own argument by analyzing Critser's text, discussing and expanding on his view in her own writing. She also looked for sources to support her view that larger-scale social and political change was needed to fight such a complex and widespread problem.

Placing sources in conversation   You can show readers how the ideas of one source relate to those of another by connecting and analyzing the ideas in your own voice. After all, you've done the research and thought through the issues, so you should control the conversation. When you synthesize sources, the emphasis is still on your own writing; the thread of your argument should be easy to identify and to understand, with or without your sources.

SAMPLE SYNTHESIS (DRAFT)

Student writer Luisa Mirano begins with a claim that needs support.

Signal phrases indicate how sources contribute to Mirano's paper and show that the ideas that follow are not her own.

Mirano interprets and connects sources. Each paragraph ends with her own thoughts.

Medical treatments have clear costs for individual patients, including unpleasant side effects, little information about long-term use, and uncertainty that they will yield significant weight loss. The financial burden is heavy as well; the drugs cost more than $3 a day on average (Duenwald, 2004). In each of the clinical trials, use of medication was accompanied by expensive behavioral therapies, including counseling, nutrition education, fitness advising, and monitoring. As Critser (2003) noted in his book *Fat Land*, use of weight-loss drugs is unlikely to have an effect without the proper "support system"—one that includes doctors, facilities, time, and money (p. 3). For many families, this level of care is prohibitively expensive.

Both medical experts and policymakers recognize that solutions might come not only from a laboratory but also from policy, education, and advocacy. A handbook designed to educate doctors on obesity called for "major changes in some aspects of western culture" (Hoppin & Taveras, 2004, Conclusion section, para. 1). Solving the childhood obesity problem will require broad mobilization of doctors and concerned parents and also of educators, food industry executives, advertisers, and media representatives.

Student writer

Source 1
Student writer

Source 2

Student writer

Source 3

Student writer

In this draft, Mirano uses her own analyses to shape the conversation among her quoted sources. She does not simply string quotations together or allow them to overwhelm her writing. The final sentence, written in her own voice, gives her an opportunity to explain to readers how the various sources support and extend her argument.

When synthesizing sources in your own writing, ask yourself the following questions:

- Which sources inform, support, or extend your argument?
- Do you vary the functions of sources—to provide background information, explain terms or concepts, lend authority to your argument, and anticipate counterarguments?
- Do you explain to readers how your sources support your argument?
- Do you control the conversation by connecting and analyzing sources in your own voice?
- Is your own argument easy to identify and to understand, with or without your sources?

56d APA documentation style

In most social science classes, you will be asked to use the APA system for documenting sources, which is set forth in the *Publication Manual of the American Psychological Association*, 6th ed. (Washington: APA, 2010). APA recommends in-text citations that refer readers to a list of references.

An in-text citation gives the author of the source (often in a signal phrase), the year of publication, and at times a page number in parentheses. At the end of the paper, a list of references provides publication information about the source (see p. 683 for a sample list of references). The direct link between the in-text citation and the entry in the reference list is highlighted in the following example.

Directory to APA in-text citation models

IN-TEXT CITATION

Yanovski and Yanovski (2002) reported that "the current state of the treatment for obesity is similar to the state of the treatment of hypertension several decades ago" (p. 600).

ENTRY IN THE LIST OF REFERENCES

Yanovski, S. Z., & Yanovski, J. A. (2002). Drug therapy: Obesity. *The New England Journal of Medicine, 346,* 591-602.

For a reference list that includes this entry, see page 683.

APA in-text citations

APA's in-text citations provide at least the author's last name and the year of publication. For direct quotations and some paraphrases, a page number is given as well.

NOTE: APA style requires the use of the past tense or the present perfect tense in signal phrases introducing cited material: *Smith (2005) reported, Smith (2005) has argued.*

1. Basic format for a quotation Ordinarily, introduce the quotation with a signal phrase that includes the author's last name followed by the year of publication in parentheses. Put the page number (preceded by "p.") in parentheses after the quotation.

Critser (2003) noted that despite growing numbers of overweight Americans, many health care providers still "remain either in ignorance or outright denial about the health danger to the poor and the young" (p. 5).

If the author is not named in the signal phrase, place the author's name, the year, and the page number in parentheses after the quotation: (Critser, 2003, p. 5).

NOTE: APA style requires the year of publication in an in-text citation. Do not include a month, even if the entry in the reference list includes the month.

2. Basic format for a summary or a paraphrase Include the author's last name and the year either in a signal phrase introducing the material or in parentheses following it. Give a page number to help readers find the passage. (For the use of paragraph numbers and headings in online sources, see "No page numbers" on pp. 643–44.)

Yanovski and Yanovski (2002) explained that sibutramine suppresses appetite by blocking the reuptake of the neurotransmitters serotonin and norepinephrine in the brain (p. 594).

Sibutramine suppresses appetite by blocking the reuptake of the neurotransmitters serotonin and norepinephrine in the brain (Yanovski & Yanovski, 2002, p. 594).

3. Work with two authors Name both authors in the signal phrase or the parentheses each time you cite the work. In the parentheses, use "&" between the authors' names; in the signal phrase, use "and."

According to Sothern and Gordon (2003), "Environmental factors may contribute as much as 80% to the causes of childhood obesity" (p. 104).

Obese children often engage in limited physical activity (Sothern & Gordon, 2003, p. 104).

4. Work with three to five authors Identify all authors in the signal phrase or the parentheses the first time you cite the source.

> In 2003, Berkowitz, Wadden, Tershakovec, and Cronquist concluded, "Sibutramine . . . must be carefully monitored in adolescents, as in adults, to control increases in [blood pressure] and pulse rate" (p. 1811).

In subsequent citations, use the first author's name followed by "et al." in either the signal phrase or the parentheses.

> As Berkowitz et al. (2003) advised, "Until more extensive safety and efficacy data are available, . . . weight-loss medications should be used only on an experimental basis for adolescents" (p. 1811).

5. Work with six or more authors Use the first author's name followed by "et al." in the signal phrase or the parentheses.

> McDuffie et al. (2002) tested 20 adolescents, aged 12-16, over a three-month period and found that orlistat, combined with behavioral therapy, produced an average weight loss of 4.4 kg, or 9.7 pounds (p. 646).

6. Work with unknown author If the author is unknown, mention the work's title in the signal phrase or give the first word or two of the title in the parenthetical citation. Titles of articles and chapters are put in quotation marks; titles of books and reports are italicized. (For online sources with no author, see item 12 on p. 643.)

> Children struggling to control their weight must also struggle with the pressures of television advertising that, on the one hand, encourages the consumption of junk food and, on the other, celebrates thin celebrities ("Television," 2002).

NOTE: In the rare case when "Anonymous" is specified as the author, treat it as if it were a real name: (Anonymous, 2001). In the list of references, also use the name Anonymous as author.

7. Organization as author If the author is a government agency or another organization, name the organization in the signal phrase or in the parenthetical citation the first time you cite the source.

> Obesity puts children at risk for a number of medical complications, including type 2 diabetes, hypertension, sleep apnea, and orthopedic problems (Henry J. Kaiser Family Foundation, 2004, p. 1).

If the organization has a familiar abbreviation, you may include it in brackets the first time you cite the source and use the abbreviation alone in later citations.

FIRST CITATION   (Centers for Disease Control and Prevention [CDC], 2009)

LATER CITATIONS   (CDC, 2009)

8. Authors with the same last name   To avoid confusion, use initials with the last names if your reference list includes two or more authors with the same last name.

> Research by E. Smith (1989) revealed that . . .

9. Two or more works by the same author in the same year   When your list of references includes more than one work by the same author in the same year, use lowercase letters ("a," "b," and so on) with the year to order the entries in the reference list. (See item 6 on p. 648.) Use those same letters with the year in the in-text citation.

> Research by Durgin (2003b) has yielded new findings about the role of counseling in treating childhood obesity.

10. Two or more works in the same parentheses   When your parenthetical citation names two or more works, put them in the same order that they appear in the reference list, separated with semicolons.

> Researchers have indicated that studies of pharmacological treatments for childhood obesity are inconclusive (Berkowitz et al., 2003; McDuffie et al., 2002).

11. Personal communication   Personal interviews, memos, letters, e-mail, and similar unpublished communications should be cited in the text only, not in the reference list. (Use the first initial with the last name in parentheses.)

One of Atkinson's colleagues, who has studied the effect of the media on children's eating habits, has contended that advertisers for snack foods will need to design ads responsibly for their younger viewers (F. Johnson, personal communication, October 20, 2009).

12. Electronic source   When possible, cite electronic sources, including online sources, as you would any other source, giving the author and the year.

Atkinson (2001) found that children who spent at least four hours a day watching TV were less likely to engage in adequate physical activity during the week.

Electronic sources sometimes lack authors' names, dates, or page numbers.

Unknown author
If no author is named, mention the title of the source in the signal phrase or give the first word or two of the title in the parentheses (see also item 6). (If an organization serves as the author, see item 7.)

The body's basal metabolic rate, or BMR, is a measure of its at-rest energy requirement ("Exercise," 2003).

Unknown date
When the date is unknown, use the abbreviation "n.d." (for "no date").

Attempts to establish a definitive link between television programming and children's eating habits have been problematic (Magnus, n.d.).

No page numbers
APA requires page numbers for quotations, summaries, and paraphrases. When an electronic source lacks stable numbered pages, include paragraph numbers or headings, if the source has them, to help readers locate the passage being cited.

If the source has numbered paragraphs, use the paragraph number preceded by the abbreviation "para.": (Hall, 2008, para. 5). If the source contains headings, cite the appropriate heading in parentheses; you may also indicate the paragraph under the heading that you are referring to, even if the paragraphs are not numbered.

> Hoppin and Taveras (2004) pointed out that several other medications were classified by the Drug Enforcement Administration as having the "potential for abuse" (Weight-Loss Drugs section, para. 6).

NOTE: Electronic files in portable document format (PDF) often have stable page numbers. For such sources, give the page number in the parenthetical citation.

13. Indirect source If you use a source that was cited in another source (a secondary source), name the original source in your signal phrase. List the secondary source in your reference list and include it in your parenthetical citation, preceded by the words "as cited in." In the following example, Satcher is the original source, and Critser is the secondary source, given in the reference list.

> Former surgeon general Dr. David Satcher described "a nation of young people seriously at risk of starting out obese and dooming themselves to the difficult task of overcoming a tough illness" (as cited in Critser, 2003, p. 4).

14. Sacred or classical text Identify the text, the version or edition you used, and the relevant part (chapter, verse, line). It is not necessary to include the source in the reference list.

> Peace activists have long cited the biblical prophet's vision of a world without war: "And they shall beat their swords into plowshares, and their spears into pruning hooks; nation shall not lift up sword against nation, neither shall they learn war any more" (Isaiah 2:4, Revised Standard Version).

hackerhandbooks.com/bedhandbook > Research exercises > APA > E-ex 56–12 to 56–14

Directory to APA references (bibliographic entries)

Directory to APA references (bibliographic entries)
(*continued*)

Other sources (including online versions)

51. Dissertation from a database, 665
52. Unpublished dissertation, 665
53. Government document, 666
54. Report from a private organization, 666
55. Legal source, 666
56. Conference proceedings, 666
57. Paper presented at a meeting or symposium (unpublished), 666
58. Poster session at a conference, 666
59. Map or chart, 667
60. Advertisement, 667
61. Published interview, 667
62. Lecture, speech, or address, 667
63. Work of art or photograph, 667
64. Brochure, pamphlet, or fact sheet, 667
65. Presentation slides, 667
66. Film or video (motion picture), 668
67. Television program, 668
68. Sound recording, 669
69. Computer software or video game, 669

APA list of references

In APA style, the alphabetical list of works cited, which appears at the end of the paper, is titled "References." For advice on preparing the reference list, see pages 672–73. For a sample reference list, see page 683.

Alphabetize entries in the list of references by authors' last names; if a work has no author, alphabetize it by its title. The first element of each entry is important because citations in the text of the paper refer to it and readers will be looking for it in the alphabetized list. The date of publication appears immediately after the first element of the citation.

In APA style, titles of books are italicized; titles of articles are neither italicized nor put in quotation marks. (For rules on capitalization of titles, see p. 670.)

General guidelines for listing authors (print and online)

In APA style, all authors' names are inverted (the last name comes first), and initials only are used for all first and middle names.

NAME AND DATE CITED IN TEXT

Duncan (2008) has reported that . . .

BEGINNING OF ENTRY IN THE LIST OF REFERENCES

Duncan, B. (2008).

1. Single author

author: last name
+ initial(s) | year | title (book)

Egeland, J. (2008). *A billion lives: An eyewitness report from the frontlines of*

place of
publication | publisher

humanity. New York, NY: Simon & Schuster.

2. Multiple authors List up to seven authors by last names followed by initials. Use an ampersand (&) before the name of the last author. If there are more than seven authors, list the first six followed by three ellipsis dots and the last author's name. (See pp. 640–41 for citing works with multiple authors in your paper.)

Two to seven authors

all authors:
last name + initial(s) | year | title (book) | place of publication

Musick, M. A., & Wilson, J. (2007). *Volunteers: A social profile.* Bloomington:

publisher

Indiana University Press.

all authors:
last name + initial(s) | year

Diessner, R., Solom, R. C., Frost, N. K., Parsons, L., & Davidson, J. (2008).

title (article)

Engagement with beauty: Appreciating natural, artistic, and moral beauty.

journal title | volume page range

The Journal of Psychology, 142, 303-329.

Eight or more authors

Mulvaney, S. A., Mudasiru, E., Schlundt, D. G., Baughman, C. L., Fleming, M.,
VanderWoude, A., . . . Rothman, R. (2008). Self-management in Type 2
diabetes: The adolescent perspective. *The Diabetes Educator, 34,* 118-127.

3. Organization as author

author:
organization name   year   title (book)

American Psychiatric Association. (1994). *Diagnostic and statistical manual of*

edition   place   organization as author
number   of publication   and publisher

mental disorders (4th ed.). Washington, DC: Author.

If the publisher is not the same as the author, give the publisher's name as you would for any other source.

4. Unknown author
Begin the entry with the work's title.

title (book)   year   place of publication   publisher

New concise world atlas. (2007). New York, NY: Oxford University Press.

title (article)   year + date (for weekly publication)   journal title   volume, issue   page range

Order in the jungle. (2008, March 15). *The Economist, 386*(8571), 83-85.

5. Two or more works by the same author
Use the author's name for all entries. List the entries by year, the earliest first.

Barry, P. (2007, December 8). Putting tumors on pause. *Science News, 172*, 365.

Barry, P. (2008, August 2). Finding the golden genes. *Science News, 174*, 16-21.

6. Two or more works by the same author in the same year
List the works alphabetically by title. In the parentheses, following the year add "a," "b," and so on. Use these same letters when giving the year in the in-text citation. (See also p. 672.)

Elkind, D. (2008a, Spring). Can we play? *Greater Good, 4*(4), 14-17.

Elkind, D. (2008b, June 27). The price of hurrying children [Web log post]. Retrieved from http://blogs.psychologytoday.com/blog /digital-children

Articles in periodicals (print)

Periodicals include scholarly journals, magazines, and newspapers. For a journal or a magazine, give only the volume number if the publication is paginated continuously through each volume; give the volume and issue numbers if each issue of the volume begins on page 1. Italicize the volume number and put the issue number, not italicized, in parentheses.

For all periodicals, when an article appears on consecutive pages, provide the range of pages. When an article does not appear on consecutive pages, give all page numbers: A1, A17. (See also "Online sources" beginning on p. 656 for online articles and articles accessed through a library's database.) For an illustrated citation of an article in a periodical, see page 650.

7. Article in a journal

author: last name + initial(s)   year   article title

Zhang, L.-F. (2008). Teachers' styles of thinking: An exploratory study. *The Journal*

journal title   volume   page range

   of Psychology, 142, 37-55.

8. Article in a magazine
Cite as a journal article, but give the year and the month for monthly magazines; add the day for weekly magazines.

McKibben, B. (2007, October). Carbon's new math. *National Geographic, 212*(4), 32-37.

9. Article in a newspaper

author: last name + initial(s)   year + month + day (for daily publication)   article title

Svoboda, E. (2008, October 21). Deep in the rain forest, stalking the next

newspaper title   page number

   pandemic. *The New York Times*, p. D5.

Citation at a glance | Article in a periodical (APA)

To cite an article in a print periodical in APA style, include the following elements:

1. Author
2. Year of publication
3. Title of article
4. Name of periodical
5. Volume number; issue number, if required (see p. 649)
6. Page numbers of article

REFERENCE LIST ENTRY FOR AN ARTICLE IN A PRINT PERIODICAL

Whitman, D. (2008). An appeal to authority: The new paternalism in urban

schools. *Education Next, 8*(4), 53-58.

For variations on citing articles in print periodicals in APA style, see pages 649–52.

Give the year, month, and day for daily and weekly newspapers. Use "p." or "pp." before page numbers.

10. Article with three to seven authors

Ungar, M., Brown, M., Liebenberg, L., Othman, R., Kwong, W. M., Armstrong, M., & Gilgun, J. (2007). Unique pathways to resilience across cultures. *Adolescence, 42,* 287-310.

11. Article with eight or more authors List the first six authors followed by three ellipsis dots and the last author.

Krippner, G., Granovetter, M., Block, F., Biggart, N., Beamish, T., Hsing, Y., . . . O'Riain, S. (2004). Polanyi Symposium: A conversation on embeddedness. *Socio-Economic Review, 2,* 109-135.

12. Abstract of a journal article

Lahm, K. (2008). Inmate-on-inmate assault: A multilevel examination of prison violence [Abstract]. *Criminal Justice and Behavior, 35*(1), 120-137.

13. Letter to the editor Letters to the editor appear in journals, magazines, and newspapers. Follow the appropriate model (see items 7–9), and insert the words "Letter to the editor" in brackets after the title of the letter. If the letter has no title, use the bracketed words as the title.

Park, T. (2008, August). Defining the line [Letter to the editor]. *Scientific American, 299*(2), 10.

14. Editorial or other unsigned article

The global justice movement [Editorial]. (2005). *Multinational Monitor, 26*(7/8), 6.

15. Newsletter article

Setting the stage for remembering. (2006, September). *Mind, Mood, and Memory, 2*(9), 4-5.

16. Review Give the author and title of the review (if any) and, in brackets, the type of work, the title, and the author for a book or the year for a motion picture. If the review has no author or title, use the material in brackets as the title.

Applebaum, A. (2008, February 14). A movie that matters [Review of the
motion picture *Katyn*, 2007]. *The New York Review of Books*, *55*(2), 13-15.

Agents of change. (2008, February 2). [Review of the book *The power of
unreasonable people: How social entrepreneurs create markets that
change the world,* by J. Elkington & P. Hartigan]. *The Economist,
386*(8565), 94.

Books (print)

Items 17–29 apply to print books. For online books, see items 36 and 37. For an illustrated citation of a print book, see page 653.

Take the information about a book from its title page and copyright page. If more than one place of publication is listed, use only the first. Give the city and state (abbreviated) for all US cities or the city and country (not abbreviated) for all non-US cities; also include the province (not abbreviated) for Canadian cities. Do not give a state if the publisher's name includes it (as in many university presses, for example).

17. Basic format for a book

author: last name + initial(s)   year of publication   book title

McKenzie, F. R. (2008). *Theory and practice with adolescents: An applied approach.*

place of publication   publisher

Chicago, IL: Lyceum Books.

18. Book with an editor

all editors: last name + initial(s)   year of publication   book title

Aronson, J., & Aronson, E. (Eds.). (2008). *Readings about the social animal*

edition number   place of publication   publisher

(10th ed.). New York, NY: Worth.

The abbreviation "Eds." is for multiple editors. If the book has one editor, use "Ed."

19. Book with an author and an editor

author: last name + initial(s) | year of publication | book title | name(s) of editor(s): in normal order

McLuhan, M. (2003). *Understanding me: Lectures and interviews* (S. McLuhan

place of publication (city, province, country) | publisher

& D. Staine, Eds.). Toronto, Ontario, Canada: McClelland & Stewart.

The abbreviation "Eds." is for multiple editors. If the book has one editor, use "Ed."

20. Book with an author and a translator
After the title, name the translator, followed by "Trans.," in parentheses. Add the original date of publication at the end of the entry.

Steinberg, M. D. (2003). *Voices of revolution, 1917* (M. Schwartz, Trans.). New Haven, CT: Yale University Press. (Original work published 2001)

21. Edition other than the first

O'Brien, J. A. (Ed.). (2006). *The production of reality: Essays and readings on social interaction* (4th ed.). Thousand Oaks, CA: Pine Forge Press.

22. Article or chapter in an edited book or an anthology

author of chapter: last name + initial(s) | year of publication | title of chapter

Denton, N. A. (2006). Segregation and discrimination in housing. In R. G.

book editor(s): in normal order | book title

Bratt, M. E. Stone, & C. Hartman (Eds.), *A right to housing: Foundation of*

page range for chapter | place of publication | publisher

a new social agenda (pp. 61-81). Philadelphia, PA: Temple University Press.

The abbreviation "Eds." is for multiple editors. If the book has one editor, use "Ed."

Citation at a glance | Book (APA)

To cite a print book in APA style, include the following elements:

1 Author
2 Year of publication
3 Title and subtitle
4 Place of publication
5 Publisher

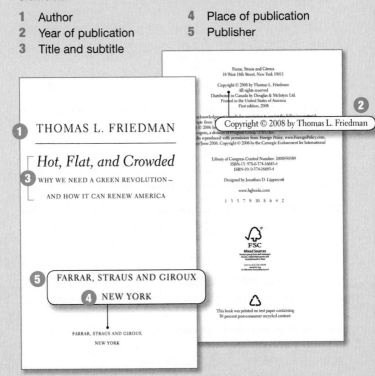

REFERENCE LIST ENTRY FOR A PRINT BOOK

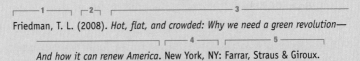

Friedman, T. L. (2008). *Hot, flat, and crowded: Why we need a green revolution—And how it can renew America*. New York, NY: Farrar, Straus & Giroux.

For more on citing print books in APA style, see pages 652–55.

23. Multivolume work   Give the number of volumes after the title.

Luo, J. (Ed.). (2005). *China today: An encyclopedia of life in the People's Republic* (Vols. 1-2). Westport, CT: Greenwood Press.

24. Introduction, preface, foreword, or afterword

Gore, A. (2000). Foreword. In B. Katz (Ed.), *Reflections on regionalism* (pp. ix-x). Washington, DC: Brookings Institution Press.

25. Dictionary or other reference work

Leong, F. T. L. (Ed.). (2008). *Encyclopedia of counseling* (Vols. 1-4). Thousand Oaks, CA: Sage.

26. Article in a reference work

Konijn, E. A. (2008). Affects and media exposure. In W. Donsbach (Ed.), *The international encyclopedia of communication* (Vol. 1, pp. 123-129). Malden, MA: Blackwell.

27. Republished book

Mailer, N. (2008). *Miami and the siege of Chicago: An informal history of the Republican and Democratic conventions of 1968*. New York, NY: New York Review Books. (Original work published 1968)

28. Book with a title in its title   If the book title contains another book title or an article title, neither italicize the internal title nor place it in quotation marks.

Marcus, L. (Ed.). (1999). *Sigmund Freud's* The interpretation of dreams: *New interdisciplinary essays*. Manchester, England: Manchester University Press.

29. Sacred or classical text   It is not necessary to list sacred works such as the Bible or the Qur'an or classical Greek and Roman works in your reference list. See item 14 on page 644 for how to cite these sources in the text of your paper.

Online sources

When citing an online article, include publication information as for a print periodical (see items 7–16) and add information about the online version (see items 30–35).

Online articles and books sometimes include a DOI (digital object identifier). APA uses the DOI, when available, in place of a URL in reference list entries.

Use a retrieval date for an online source only if the content is likely to change. Most of the examples in this section do not show a retrieval date because the content of the sources is stable; if you are unsure about whether to use a retrieval date, include the date or consult your instructor.

If you must break a DOI or a URL at the end of a line, break it after a double slash or before any other mark of punctuation; do not add a hyphen. Do not put a period at the end of the entry.

30. Article in an online journal

author: last name + initial(s)   year of publication   article title   journal title

Whitmeyer, J. M. (2000). Power through appointment. *Social Science Research,*

volume   page range   DOI

     29, 535-555. doi:10.1006/ssre.2000.0680

If there is no DOI, include the URL for the journal's home page.

Ashe, D. D., & McCutcheon, L. E. (2001). Shyness, loneliness, and attitude
     toward celebrities. *Current Research in Social Psychology, 6*, 124-133.
     Retrieved from http://www.uiowa.edu/~grpproc/crisp/crisp.html

31. Article in an online magazine   Treat as an article in a print magazine (see item 8), and add the URL for the magazine's home page.

Shelburne, E. C. (2008, September). The great disruption. *The Atlantic, 302*(2).
     Retrieved from http://www.theatlantic.com/

32. Article in an online newspaper Treat as an article in a print newspaper (see item 9), adding the URL for the newspaper's home page.

Watson, P. (2008, October 19). Biofuel boom endangers orangutan habitat.
Los Angeles Times. Retrieved from http://www.latimes.com/

33. Article published only online If an article in a journal, magazine, or newspaper appears only online, give whatever publication information is available in the source and add the description "Supplemental material" in brackets following the article title.

Samuel, T. (2009, March 27). Mind the wage gap [Supplemental material].
The American Prospect. Retrieved from http://www.prospect.org/

34. Article from a database Start with the publication information for the source (see items 7–16). If the database entry includes a DOI for the article, use the DOI number at the end. For an illustrated citation of a work from a database, see page 658.

all authors:
last name + initial(s)   year   article title
Eskritt, M., & McLeod, K. (2008). Children's note taking as a mnemonic tool.

                                                    page
            journal title   volume   range   DOI
Journal of Experimental Child Psychology, 101, 52-74. doi:10.1016

/jecp.2008.05.007

If there is no DOI, include the URL for the home page of the journal.

Howard, K. R. (2007). Childhood overweight: Parental perceptions and
readiness for change. *The Journal of School Nursing, 23*, 73-79.
Retrieved from http://jsn.sagepub.com/

Citation at a glance | Article from a database (APA)

To cite an article from a database in APA style, include the following elements:

1 Author(s)
2 Date of publication
3 Title of article
4 Name of periodical
5 Volume number; issue number, if required (see p. 649)
6 Page range
7 DOI (digital object identifier)
8 URL for journal's home page (if there is no DOI)

ON-SCREEN VIEW OF DATABASE RECORD

END OF DATABASE RECORD

REFERENCE LIST ENTRY FOR AN ARTICLE FROM A DATABASE

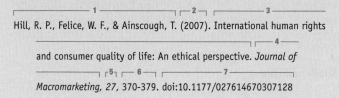

Hill, R. P., Felice, W. F., & Ainscough, T. (2007). International human rights

and consumer quality of life: An ethical perspective. *Journal of*

Macromarketing, 27, 370-379. doi:10.1177/027614670307128

For more on citing articles from a database in APA style, see item 34.

35. Abstract for an online article

Brockerhoff, E. G., Jactel, H., Parrotta, J. A., Quine, C. P., & Sayer, J. (2008). Plantation forests and biodiversity: Oxymoron or opportunity? [Abstract]. *Biodiversity and Conservation, 17,* 925-951. doi:10.1007/s10531-008 -9380-x

36. Online book

Adams, B. (2004). *The theory of social revolutions*. Retrieved from http://www.gutenberg.org/catalog/world/readfile?fk_files=44092 (Original work published 1913)

37. Chapter in an online book

Clinton, S. J. (1999). What can be done to prevent childhood obesity? In *Understanding childhood obesity* (pp. 81-98). Retrieved from http:// www.questia.com/

38. Online reference work

Swain, C. M. (2004). Sociology of affirmative action. In N. J. Smelser & P. B. Baltes (Eds.), *International encyclopedia of the social and behavioral sciences*. Retrieved from http://www.sciencedirect.com /science/referenceworks/9780080430768

Use a retrieval date only if the content of the work is likely to change.

39. Document from a Web site List as many of the following elements as are available: author's name, publication date (or "n.d." if there is no date), title (in italics), and URL. Give your retrieval date only if the content of the source is likely to change.

Source with date

all authors: last name + initial(s)   online publication date: year + month   document title

Cain, A., & Burris, M. (1999, April). *Investigation of the use of mobile*

URL

     phones while driving. Retrieved from http://www.cutr.usf.edu/pdf

     /mobile_phone_text.PDF

Source with no date

Archer, D. (n.d.). *Exploring nonverbal communication*. Retrieved from http://

     nonverbal.ucsc.edu

Source with no author

If a source has no author, begin with the title and follow it with the date in parentheses.

What causes Alzheimer's disease? (2008). Retrieved from http://

     www.memorystudy.org/alzheimers_causes.htm

40. Section in a Web document

author (organization)   year   title of section

National Institute on Media and the Family. (2009). Mobile networking.

title of Web document

     In *Guide to social networking: Risks*. Retrieved from http://www

URL

     .mediafamily.org/network_pdf/MediaWise_Guide_to_Social

     _Networking_Risks_09.pdf

For an illustrated citation of a section in a Web document, see page 662.

41. Document from a university Web site or government agency Name the organization or agency in your retrieval statement.

Cosmides, L., & Tooby, J. (1997). *Evolutionary psychology: A primer.*
Retrieved from University of California, Santa Barbara, Center for
Evolutionary Psychology website: http://www.psych.ucsb.edu
/research/cep/primer.html

42. Article in an online newsletter Cite as an online article (see items 30–32), giving the title of the newsletter and whatever other information is available, including volume and issue numbers.

In the face of extinction. (2008, May). *NSF Current.* Retrieved from http://
www.nsf.gov/news/newsletter/may_08/index.jsp

43. Podcast

organization as producer · · · · · · · date of posting
National Academies (Producer). (2007, June 6). Progress in preventing

· · · · · · · podcast title · · · · · · · · descriptive label
childhood obesity: How do we measure up? [Audio podcast].

· · · series title · · · · · · · · URL
The sounds of science podcast. Retrieved from http://media.nap.edu
/podcasts/

writer/
presenter · · · date of posting · · · · · · · · podcast title
Chesney, M. (2007, September 13). Gender differences in the use of

· · · · · · · · · podcast number · descriptive label
complementary and alternative medicine (No. 12827) [Audio podcast].

· · · Web site hosting podcast
Retrieved from University of California Television website:

· · · URL
http://www.uctv.tv/ondemand

Citation at a glance | Section in a Web document (APA)

To cite a section in a Web document in APA style, include the following elements:

1 Author
2 Date of publication or most recent update
3 Title of section
4 Title of document
5 URL of section or of document

BROWSER PRINTOUT OF WEB SITE

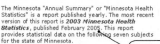

2003 Minnesota Health Statistics Annual Summary - Minneso... http://www.health.state.mn.us/divs/chs/03annsum/index.html

Minnesota Department of Health
Protecting, maintaining and improving the health of all Minnesotans

MDH

Minnesota Center for Health Statistics
- Home
- General statistics
  - Minnesota Vital Statistics Interactive Queries
  - Minnesota Vital Signs
  - Minnesota County Health Tables
  - Mini Profiles
  - Minnesota Health Statistics Annual Summary
  - Population Health Assessment Quarterly
- Topic-specific statistics
  - Induced Abortions in Minnesota Reports
  - Populations of Color Health Status Report
  - Tobacco Reports

2003 Minnesota Health Statistics Annual Summary

The Minnesota "Annual Summary" or "Minnesota Health Statistics" is a report published yearly. The most recent version of this report is *2003 Minnesota Health Statistics*, published February 2005. This report provides statistical data on the following seven subjects for the state of Minnesota.

published February 2005.

To view the PDF files, you will need Adobe Acrobat Reader or for screen reader accessibility Adobe Acrobat Access (free downloads from Adobe's Web site).

- **Overview of 2003 Annual Summary (PDF: 251KB/11 pages)**
- **Live Births (PDF: 608KB/21 pages)**
- **Fertility (PDF: 80KB/2 pages)**
- **Infant Mortality and Fetal Deaths (PDF: 414KB/15 pages)**
- **General Mortality (PDF: 581KB/40 pages)**
- **Marriage (PDF: 83KB/4 pages)**
- **Divorce (PDF: 62KB/3 pages)**
- **Population (PDF: 29KB/12 pages)**

Note: Induced abortion statistics previously reported in this publication are now published separately.
See > Report to the Legislature: Induced Abortions in Minnesota

See also> Minnesota Health Statistics Annual Summary Main Page

1of3   6/28/05 5:14 PM

ON-SCREEN VIEW OF DOCUMENT

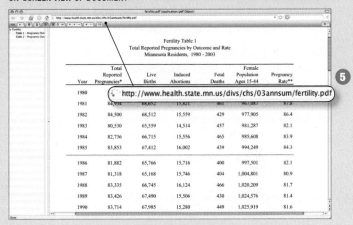

REFERENCE LIST ENTRY FOR A SECTION IN A WEB DOCUMENT

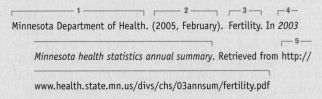

Minnesota Department of Health. (2005, February). Fertility. In *2003*

Minnesota health statistics annual summary. Retrieved from http://

www.health.state.mn.us/divs/chs/03annsum/fertility.pdf

For more on citing documents from Web sites in APA style, see pages 660–65.

44. Weblog (blog) post Give the writer's name, the date of the post, the subject, the label "Web log post," and the URL. For a response to a post, use the label "Web log comment."

Kellermann, M. (2007, May 23). Disclosing clinical trials [Web log post]. Retrieved from http://www.iq.harvard.edu/blog/sss /archives/2007/05

45. Online audio or video file Give the medium or a description of the source file in brackets following the title.

Chomsky, N. (n.d.). The new imperialism [Audio file]. Retrieved from http:// www.rhapsody.com/noamchomsky

Zakaria, F. (Host), & McCullough, C. (Writer). (2007, March 6). In focus: American teens, Rwandan truths [Video file]. Retrieved from http:// www.pulitzercenter.org/showproject.cfm?id=26

46. Entry in a wiki Begin with the title of the entry and the date of posting, if there is one (use "n.d." for "no date" if there is not). Then add your retrieval date and the URL for the wiki entry. Include the date of retrieval because the content of a wiki is often not stable. If an author or an editor is identified, include that name at the beginning of the entry.

Ethnomethodology. (n.d.). Retrieved August 22, 2008, from http:// en.stswiki.org/index.php/Ethnomethodology

47. Data set or graphic representation Give information about the type of source in brackets following the title. If there is no title, give a brief description of the content of the source in brackets in place of the title.

U.S. Department of Agriculture, Economic Research Service. (2009). *Eating and health module (ATUS): 2007 data* [Data set]. Retrieved from http:// www.ers.usda.gov/Data/ATUS/Data/2007/2007data.htm

Gallup. (2008, October 23). *No increase in proportion of first-time voters*
    [Graphs]. Retrieved from http://www.gallup.com/poll/111331
    /No-Increase-Proportion-First-Time-Voters.aspx

48. Conference hearing

Carmona, R. H. (2004, March 2). *The growing epidemic of childhood obesity*.
    Testimony before the Subcommittee on Competition, Foreign Commerce,
    and Infrastructure of the U.S. Senate Committee on Commerce, Science,
    and Transportation. Retrieved from http://www.hhs.gov/asl/testify
    /t040302.html

49. E-mail   E-mail messages, letters, and other personal communications are not included in the list of references. (See
p. 642 for citing these sources in the text of your paper.)

50. Online posting   If an online posting is not archived, cite
it as a personal communication in the text of your paper and
do not include it in the list of references. If the posting is archived, give the URL and the name of the discussion list if it
is not part of the URL.

McKinney, J. (2006, December 19). Adult education-healthcare
    partnerships [Electronic mailing list message]. Retrieved from http://
    www.nifl.gov/pipermail/healthliteracy/2006/000524.html

Other sources (including online versions)

51. Dissertation from a database

Hymel, K. M. (2009). *Essays in urban economics* (Doctoral dissertation). Available
    from ProQuest Dissertations and Theses database. (AAT 3355930)

52. Unpublished dissertation

Mitchell, R. D. (2007). *The Wesleyan Quadrilateral: Relocating the conversation*
    (Unpublished doctoral dissertation). Claremont School of Theology,
    Claremont, CA.

53. Government document

U.S. Census Bureau. (2006). *Statistical abstract of the United States*.
Washington, DC: Government Printing Office.

U.S. Census Bureau, Bureau of Economic Analysis. (2008, August). *U.S.
international trade in goods and services* (Report No. CB08-121,
BEA08-37, FT-900). Retrieved from http://www.census.gov
/foreign-trade/Press-Release/2008pr/06/ftdpress.pdf

54. Report from a private organization If the publisher and
the author are the same, begin with the publisher. For a print
source, use "Author" as the publisher at the end of the entry
(see item 3 on p. 648); for an online source, give the URL. If the
report has a number, put it in parentheses following the title.

Ford Foundation. (n.d.). *Helping citizens to understand and influence state
budgets*. Retrieved from http://www.fordfound.org/pdfs/impact
/evaluations/state_fiscal_initiative.pdf

55. Legal source

Sweatt v. Painter, 339 U.S. 629 (1950). Retrieved from Cornell University Law
School, Legal Information Institute website: http://www.law.cornell
.edu/supct/html/historics/USSC_CR_0339_0629_ZS.html

56. Conference proceedings

Stahl, G. (Ed.). (2002). *Proceedings of CSCL '02: Computer support for
collaborative learning*. Hillsdale, NJ: Erlbaum.

57. Paper presented at a meeting or symposium (unpublished)

Anderson, D. N. (2008, May). *Cab-hailing and the micropolitics of gesture*.
Paper presented at the Arizona Linguistics and Anthropology
Symposium, Tucson, AZ.

58. Poster session at a conference

Wang, Z., & Keogh, T. (2008, June). *A click away: Student response to clickers*.
Poster session presented at the annual conference of the American
Library Association, Anaheim, CA.

59. Map or chart

Ukraine [Map]. (2008). Retrieved from the University of Texas at Austin
    Perry-Castañeda Library Map Collection website: http://www.lib.utexas
    .edu/maps/cia08/ukraine_sm_2008.gif

60. Advertisement

Xbox 360 [Advertisement]. (2007, February). *Wired, 15*(2), 71.

61. Published interview

Murphy, C. (2007, June 22). As the Romans did [Interview by G. Hahn].
    Retrieved from http://www.theatlantic.com/

62. Lecture, speech, or address

Fox, V. (2008, March 5). *Economic growth, poverty, and democracy in Latin
    America: A president's perspective*. Address at the Freeman Spogli
    Institute, Stanford University, Stanford, CA.

63. Work of art or photograph

Weber, J. (1992). *Toward freedom* [Outdoor mural]. Sherman Oaks, CA.

Newkirk, K. (2006). *Gainer (part II)*. Museum of Contemporary Art, Chicago,
    IL.

64. Brochure, pamphlet, or fact sheet

National Council of State Boards of Nursing. (n.d.). *Professional boundaries*
    [Brochure]. Retrieved from https://www.ncsbn.org/Professional
    _Boundaries_2007_Web.pdf

World Health Organization. (2007, October). *Health of indigenous peoples*
    (No. 326) [Fact sheet]. Retrieved from http://www.who.int/mediacentre
    /factsheets/fs326/en/index.html

65. Presentation slides

Boeninger, C. F. (2008, August). *Web 2.0 tools for reference and
    instructional services* [Presentation slides]. Retrieved from http://
    libraryvoice.com/archives/2008/08/04/opal-20-conference
    -presentation-slides/

66. Film or video (motion picture) Give the director, producer, and other relevant contributors, followed by the year of the film's release, the title, the description "Motion picture" in brackets, the country where the film was made, and the studio. If you viewed the film on videocassette or DVD, indicate that medium in brackets in place of "Motion picture." If the original release date and the date of the DVD or videocassette are different, add "Original release" and that date in parentheses at the end of the entry. If the motion picture would be difficult for your readers to find, include instead the name and address of its distributor.

Guggenheim, D. (Director), & Bender, L. (Producer). (2006). *An inconvenient truth* [DVD]. United States: Paramount Home Entertainment.

Spurlock, M. (Director). (2004). *Super size me* [Motion picture].
Available from IDP Films, 1133 Broadway, Suite 926, New York, NY 10010

67. Television program List the producer and the date the program was aired. Give the title, followed by "Television broadcast" in brackets, the city, and the television network or service.

Pratt, C. (Executive producer). (2008, October 5). *Face the nation* [Television broadcast]. Washington, DC: CBS News.

For a television series, use the year in which the series was produced, and follow the title with "Television series" in brackets. For an episode in a series, list the writer and director and the year. After the episode title, put "Television series episode" in brackets. Follow with information about the series.

Fanning, D. (Executive producer). (2008). *Frontline* [Television series].
Boston, MA: WGBH.

Smith, M. (Writer/producer). (2008). Heat [Television series episode]. In
D. Fanning (Executive producer), *Frontline*. Boston, MA: WGBH.

68. Sound recording

Thomas, G. (1996). Breath. On *Didgeridoo: Ancient sound of the future* [CD]. Oxnard, CA: Aquarius International Music.

69. Computer software or video game Add the words "Computer software" (neither italicized nor in quotation marks) in brackets after the title of the program.

Sims 2 [Computer software]. (2005). New York, NY: Maxis.

hackerhandbooks.com/bedhandbook > Research exercises > APA > E–ex 56–15 to 56–19

56e APA manuscript format

The American Psychological Association makes a number of recommendations for formatting a paper and preparing a list of references. The following guidelines are consistent with advice given in the *Publication Manual of the American Psychological Association*, 6th ed. (Washington: APA, 2010), and typical requirements for undergraduate papers.

Formatting the paper

Many instructors in the social sciences require students to follow APA guidelines for formatting a paper.

The APA manual provides guidelines for papers prepared for publication in a scholarly journal; it does not provide separate guidelines for papers prepared for undergraduate classes. The formatting guidelines in this section and the sample paper on pages 674–83 can be used for either type of paper. The samples on page 684 show alternative formatting. If you are in doubt about which format is preferred or required in your course, ask your instructor.

Materials and font Use good-quality 8½" × 11" white paper. Avoid a font that is unusual or hard to read.

Title page At the top left, type the words "Running head," followed by a colon and the title of your paper (shortened to no more than fifty characters) in all capital letters. Put the page number 1 flush with the right margin. Halfway down the page, center the full title of your paper (capitalizing all words of four letters or more), your name, and your school's name. At the bottom of the page, you may add the heading "Author Note," centered, followed by a brief paragraph that lists information about the course or department or provides acknowledgments or contact information. See page 674 for a sample title page.

Some instructors may instead require a title page like the one on page 684. If in doubt about the requirements in your course, check with your instructor.

Page numbers and running head Number all pages with arabic numerals (1, 2, 3, and so on) in the upper right corner about one-half inch from the top of the page. The title page should be numbered 1.

On every page, in the upper left corner on the same line as the page number, place a running head consisting of the title of the paper (shortened to no more than fifty characters) in all capital letters. See pages 675–83. (See an alternative running head on p. 684.)

Margins, line spacing, and paragraph indents Use margins of one inch on all sides of the page. Left-align the text. Double-space throughout the paper. Indent the first line of each paragraph one-half inch.

Capitalization, italics, and quotation marks Capitalize all words of four letters or more in titles of works and in headings that appear in the text of the paper. Capitalize the first word after a colon if the word begins a complete sentence.

Italicize the titles of books and other long works, such as Web sites. Use quotation marks around the titles of periodical articles, short stories, poems, and other short works.

APA has different requirements for titles in the reference list. See page 673.

Long quotations and footnotes   When a quotation is longer than forty words, set it off from the text by indenting it one-half inch from the left margin. Double-space the quotation. Do not use quotation marks around a quotation that has been set off from the text. See page 682 for an example.

Place each footnote at the bottom of the page on which the text reference occurs. Double-space the footnote and indent the first line one-half inch. Begin the note with the superscript arabic numeral that corresponds to the number in the text. See page 676 for an example.

Abstract   If your instructor requires an abstract, include it immediately after the title page. Center the word Abstract one inch from the top of the page; double-space the abstract.

An abstract is a 100-to-150-word paragraph that provides readers with a quick overview of your essay. It should express your main idea and your key points; it might also briefly suggest any implications or applications of the research you discuss in the paper. See page 675 for an example.

Headings   Although headings are not always necessary, their use is encouraged in the social sciences. For most undergraduate papers, one level of heading will usually be sufficient.

In APA style, major headings are centered and boldface. Capitalize the first word of the heading, along with all words except articles, short prepositions, and coordinating conjunctions. See the sample paper on pages 674–83.

Visuals   APA classifies visuals as tables and figures (figures include graphs, charts, drawings, and photographs).

Label each table with an arabic numeral (Table 1, Table 2, and so on) and provide a clear title. Place the label and title on separate lines above the table, flush left and double-spaced.

Below the table, give its source in a note. If any data in the table require an explanatory footnote, use a superscript lowercase letter in the table and in a footnote following the source note. Double-space source notes and footnotes and do not indent the first line of each note. See page 679.

For each figure, place a label and a caption below the figure, flush left and double-spaced. The label and caption need not appear on separate lines.

In the text of your paper, discuss the most significant features of each visual. Place the visual as close as possible to the sentences that relate to it unless your instructor prefers it in an appendix.

Preparing the list of references

Begin your list of references on a new page at the end of the paper. Center the title References one inch from the top of the page. Double-space throughout. For a sample reference list, see page 683.

Indenting entries Use a hanging indent in the reference list: Type the first line of each entry flush left and indent any additional lines one-half inch, as shown on page 683.

Alphabetizing the list Alphabetize the reference list by the last names of the authors (or editors); when a work has no author or editor, alphabetize by the first word of the title other than *A*, *An*, or *The*.

If your list includes two or more works by the same author, arrange the entries by year, the earliest first. If your list includes two or more works by the same author in the same year, arrange the works alphabetically by title. Add the letters "a," "b," and so on within the parentheses after the year. Use only the year and the letter for articles in journals: (2002a). Use the full date and the letter for articles in magazines and newspapers in the reference list: (2005a, July 7). Use only the year and the letter in the in-text citation.

Authors' names Invert all authors' names and use initials instead of first names. With two or more authors, use an ampersand (&) before the last author's name. Separate the names with commas. Include names for the first seven authors; if there are eight or more authors, give the first six authors, three ellipsis dots, and the last author (see p. 647).

Titles of books and articles   Italicize the titles and subtitles of books. Do not use quotation marks around the titles of articles. Capitalize only the first word of the title and subtitle (and all proper nouns) of books and articles. Capitalize names of periodicals as you would capitalize them normally (see 45c).

Abbreviations for page numbers   Abbreviations for "page" and "pages" ("p." and "pp.") are used before page numbers of newspaper articles and articles in edited books (see item 9 on p. 649 and item 22 on p. 653) but not before page numbers of articles in magazines and scholarly journals (see items 7 and 8 on p. 649).

Breaking a URL   When a URL or a DOI (digital object identifier) must be divided, break it after a double slash or before any other mark of punctuation. Do not insert a hyphen, and do not add a period at the end.

For information about the exact format of each entry in your list, consult the models on pages 647–69.

56f Sample APA research paper

On the following pages is a research paper on the effectiveness of treatments for childhood obesity, written by Luisa Mirano, a student in a psychology class. Mirano's assignment was to write a literature review paper documented with APA-style citations and references.

hackerhandbooks.com/bedhandbook > Model papers
                                   > APA papers: Mirano
                                   > APA annotated bibliography: Haddad

A running head, which will be used in the printed journal article, consists of a title (shortened to no more than fifty characters) in all capital letters. On the title page, it is preceded by the label "Running head." Page numbers appear in the upper right corner.

Running head: CAN MEDICATION CURE OBESITY IN CHILDREN?   1

Full title, writer's name, and school name are centered halfway down the page.

Can Medication Cure Obesity in Children?

A Review of the Literature

Luisa Mirano

Northwest-Shoals Community College

An author's note lists specific information about the course or department and can provide acknowledgments and contact information.

Author Note

This paper was prepared for Psychology 108, Section B, taught by Professor Kang.

Marginal annotations indicate APA-style formatting and effective writing.

CAN MEDICATION CURE OBESITY IN CHILDREN? 2

Abstract

In recent years, policymakers and medical experts have expressed
alarm about the growing problem of childhood obesity in the United
States. While most agree that the issue deserves attention, consensus
dissolves around how to respond to the problem. This literature review
examines one approach to treating childhood obesity: medication. The
paper compares the effectiveness for adolescents of the only two drugs
approved by the Food and Drug Administration (FDA) for long-term
treatment of obesity, sibutramine and orlistat. This examination of
pharmacological treatments for obesity points out the limitations of
medication and suggests the need for a comprehensive solution that
combines medical, social, behavioral, and political approaches to this
complex problem.

Abstract appears on
a separate page.

CAN MEDICATION CURE OBESITY IN CHILDREN? 3

Full title, centered.

Can Medication Cure Obesity in Children?

A Review of the Literature

In March 2004, U.S. Surgeon General Richard Carmona called attention to a health problem in the United States that, until recently, has been overlooked: childhood obesity. Carmona said that the "astounding" 15% child obesity rate constitutes an "epidemic." Since the early 1980s, that rate has "doubled in children and tripled in adolescents." Now more than nine million children are classified as obese.[1] While the traditional response to a medical epidemic is to hunt for a vaccine or a cure-all pill, childhood obesity is more elusive. The lack of success of recent initiatives suggests that medication might not be the answer for the escalating problem. This literature review considers whether the use of medication is a promising approach for solving the childhood obesity problem by responding to the following questions:

Mirano sets up her organization by posing four questions.

1. What are the implications of childhood obesity?

2. Is medication effective at treating childhood obesity?

3. Is medication safe for children?

4. Is medication the best solution?

Mirano states her thesis.

Understanding the limitations of medical treatments for children highlights the complexity of the childhood obesity problem in the United States and underscores the need for physicians, advocacy groups, and policymakers to search for other solutions.

Headings, centered, help readers follow the organization.

What Are the Implications of Childhood Obesity?

Obesity can be a devastating problem from both an individual and a societal perspective. Obesity puts children at risk for a number of

Mirano uses a footnote to define an essential term that would be cumbersome to define within the text.

[1]Obesity is measured in terms of body-mass index (BMI): weight in kilograms divided by square of height in meters. A child or an adolescent with a BMI in the 95th percentile for his or her age and gender is considered obese.

CAN MEDICATION CURE OBESITY IN CHILDREN?   4

medical complications, including type 2 diabetes, hypertension, sleep
apnea, and orthopedic problems (Henry J. Kaiser Family Foundation,
2004, p. 1). Researchers Hoppin and Taveras (2004) have noted that
obesity is often associated with psychological issues such as
depression, anxiety, and binge eating (Table 4).

In a signal phrase, the word "and" links the names of two authors; the date is given in parentheses.

Obesity also poses serious problems for a society struggling
to cope with rising health care costs. The cost of treating obesity
currently totals $117 billion per year—a price, according to the
surgeon general, "second only to the cost of [treating] tobacco use"
(Carmona, 2004). And as the number of children who suffer from
obesity grows, long-term costs will only increase.

Because the author (Carmona) is not named in the signal phrase, his name and the date appear in parentheses.

Is Medication Effective at Treating Childhood Obesity?

The widening scope of the obesity problem has prompted
medical professionals to rethink old conceptions of the disorder
and its causes. As researchers Yanovski and Yanovski (2002) have
explained, obesity was once considered "either a moral failing or
evidence of underlying psychopathology" (p. 592). But this view
has shifted: Many medical professionals now consider obesity a
biomedical rather than a moral condition, influenced by both
genetic and environmental factors. Yanovski and Yanovski have
further noted that the development of weight-loss medications
in the early 1990s showed that "obesity should be treated in the
same manner as any other chronic disease . . . through the
long-term use of medication" (p. 592).

Ellipsis mark indicates omitted words.

The search for the right long-term medication has been
complicated. Many of the drugs authorized by the Food and Drug
Administration (FDA) in the early 1990s proved to be a
disappointment. Two of the medications—fenfluramine and
dexfenfluramine—were withdrawn from the market because of severe
side effects (Yanovski & Yanovski, 2002, p. 592), and several others

CAN MEDICATION CURE OBESITY IN CHILDREN? 5

were classified by the Drug Enforcement Administration as having the

In a parenthetical citation, an ampersand links the names of two authors.

"potential for abuse" (Hoppin & Taveras, 2004, Weight-Loss Drugs section, para. 6). Currently only two medications have been approved by the FDA for long-term treatment of obesity: sibutramine (marketed as Meridia) and orlistat (marketed as Xenical). This section compares studies on the effectiveness of each.

Sibutramine suppresses appetite by blocking the reuptake of the neurotransmitters serotonin and norepinephrine in the brain (Yanovski & Yanovski, 2002, p. 594). Though the drug won FDA approval in 1998, experiments to test its effectiveness for younger patients came considerably later. In 2003, University of Pennsylvania

Mirano draws attention to an important article.

researchers Berkowitz, Wadden, Tershakovec, and Cronquist released the first double-blind placebo study testing the effect of sibutramine on adolescents, aged 13-17, over a 12-month period. Their findings are summarized in Table 1.

After 6 months, the group receiving medication had lost 4.6 kg (about 10 pounds) more than the control group. But during the second half of the study, when both groups received sibutramine, the results were more ambiguous. In months 6-12, the group that continued to take sibutramine gained an average of 0.8 kg, or roughly 2 pounds; the control group, which switched from placebo to sibutramine, lost 1.3 kg, or roughly 3 pounds (p. 1808). Both groups received behavioral therapy covering diet, exercise, and mental health.

These results paint a murky picture of the effectiveness of the medication: While initial data seemed promising, the results after one year raised questions about whether medication-induced weight loss could be sustained over time. As Berkowitz et al. (2003) advised, "Until more extensive safety and efficacy data are available, . . . weight-loss medications should be used only on an experimental basis for adolescents" (p. 1811).

CAN MEDICATION CURE OBESITY IN CHILDREN? 6

Table 1

Effectiveness of Sibutramine and Orlistat in Adolescents

Mirano uses a table to summarize the findings presented in two sources.

Medication	Subjects	Treatment[a]	Side effects	Average weight loss/gain
Sibutramine	Control	0-6 mos.: placebo 6-12 mos.: sibutramine	Mos. 6-12: increased blood pressure; increased pulse rate	After 6 mos.: loss of 3.2 kg (7 lb) After 12 mos.: loss of 4.5 kg (9.9 lb)
	Medicated	0-12 mos.: sibutramine	Increased blood pressure; increased pulse rate	After 6 mos.: loss of 7.8 kg (17.2 lb) After 12 mos.: loss of 7.0 kg (15.4 lb)
Orlistat	Control	0-12 mos.: placebo	None	Gain of 0.67 kg (1.5 lb)
	Medicated	0-12 mos.: orlistat	Oily spotting; flatulence; abdominal discomfort	Loss of 1.3 kg (2.9 lb)

Note. The data on sibutramine are adapted from "Behavior Therapy and Sibutramine for the Treatment of Adolescent Obesity," by R. I. Berkowitz, T. A. Wadden, A. M. Tershakovec, & J. L. Cronquist, 2003, *Journal of the American Medical Association, 289*, pp. 1807-1809. The data on orlistat are adapted from *Xenical (Orlistat) Capsules: Complete Product Information*, by Roche Laboratories, December 2003, retrieved from http://www .rocheusa.com/products/xenical/pi.pdf

A note gives the source of the data.

[a]The medication and/or placebo were combined with behavioral therapy in all groups over all time periods.

A content note explains data common to all subjects.

CAN MEDICATION CURE OBESITY IN CHILDREN? 7

A study testing the effectiveness of orlistat in adolescents showed similarly ambiguous results. The FDA approved orlistat in 1999 but did not authorize it for adolescents until December 2003. Roche Laboratories (2003), maker of orlistat, released results of a one-year study testing the drug on 539 obese adolescents, aged 12-16. The drug, which promotes weight loss by blocking fat absorption in the large intestine, showed some effectiveness in adolescents: an average loss of 1.3 kg, or roughly 3 pounds, for subjects taking orlistat for one year, as opposed to an average gain of 0.67 kg, or 1.5 pounds, for the control group (pp. 8-9). See Table 1.

Short-term studies of orlistat have shown slightly more dramatic results. Researchers at the National Institute of Child Health and Human Development tested 20 adolescents, aged 12-16, over a three-month period and found that orlistat, combined with behavioral therapy, produced an average weight loss of 4.4 kg, or 9.7 pounds (McDuffie et al., 2002, p. 646). The study was not controlled against a placebo group; therefore, the relative effectiveness of orlistat in this case remains unclear.

For a source with six or more authors, the first author's surname followed by "et al." is used for the first and subsequent references.

Is Medication Safe for Children?

While modest weight loss has been documented for both medications, each carries risks of certain side effects. Sibutramine has been observed to increase blood pressure and pulse rate. In 2002, a consumer group claimed that the medication was related to the deaths of 19 people and filed a petition with the Department of Health and Human Services to ban the medication (Hilts, 2002). The sibutramine study by Berkowitz et al. (2003) noted elevated blood pressure as a side effect, and dosages had to be reduced or the medication discontinued in 19 of the 43 subjects in the first six months (p. 1809).

When this article was first cited, all four authors were named. In subsequent citations of a work with three to five authors, "et al." is used after the first author's name.

The main side effects associated with orlistat were abdominal discomfort, oily spotting, fecal incontinence, and nausea (Roche

CAN MEDICATION CURE OBESITY IN CHILDREN?   8

Laboratories, 2003, p. 13). More serious for long-term health is the concern that orlistat, being a fat-blocker, would affect absorption of fat-soluble vitamins, such as vitamin D. However, the study found that this side effect can be minimized or eliminated if patients take vitamin supplements two hours before or after administration of orlistat (p. 10). With close monitoring of patients taking the medication, many of the risks can be reduced.

Is Medication the Best Solution?

The data on the safety and efficacy of pharmacological treatments of childhood obesity raise the question of whether medication is the best solution for the problem. The treatments have clear costs for individual patients, including unpleasant side effects, little information about long-term use, and uncertainty that they will yield significant weight loss.

In purely financial terms, the drugs cost more than $3 a day on average (Duenwald, 2004). In each of the clinical trials, use of medication was accompanied by an expensive regime of behavioral therapies, including counseling, nutritional education, fitness advising, and monitoring. As journalist Greg Critser (2003) noted in his book *Fat Land*, use of weight-loss drugs is unlikely to have an effect without the proper "support system"—one that includes doctors, facilities, time, and money (p. 3). For some, this level of care is prohibitively expensive.

A third complication is that the studies focused on adolescents aged 12-16, but obesity can begin at a much younger age. Little data exist to establish the safety or efficacy of medication for treating very young children.

While the scientific data on the concrete effects of these medications in children remain somewhat unclear, medication is not the only avenue for addressing the crisis. Both medical experts and

Mirano develops the paper's thesis.

CAN MEDICATION CURE OBESITY IN CHILDREN? 9

policymakers recognize that solutions might come not only from a laboratory but also from policy, education, and advocacy. A handbook designed to educate doctors on obesity called for "major changes in some aspects of western culture" (Hoppin & Taveras, 2004, Conclusion section, para. 1). Cultural change may not be the typical realm of medical professionals, but the handbook urged doctors to be proactive and "focus [their] energy on public policies and interventions" (Conclusion section, para. 1).

Brackets indicate a word not in the original source.

The solutions proposed by a number of advocacy groups underscore this interest in political and cultural change. A report by the Henry J. Kaiser Family Foundation (2004) outlined trends that may have contributed to the childhood obesity crisis, including food advertising for children as well as

A quotation longer than forty words is indented without quotation marks.

> a reduction in physical education classes and after-school athletic programs, an increase in the availability of sodas and snacks in public schools, the growth in the number of fast-food outlets . . . , and the increasing number of highly processed high-calorie and high-fat grocery products. (p. 1)

Mirano interprets the evidence; she doesn't just report it.

Addressing each of these areas requires more than a doctor armed with a prescription pad; it requires a broad mobilization not just of doctors and concerned parents but of educators, food industry executives, advertisers, and media representatives.

The tone of the conclusion is objective.

The barrage of possible approaches to combating childhood obesity—from scientific research to political lobbying—indicates both the severity and the complexity of the problem. While none of the medications currently available is a miracle drug for curing the nation's 9 million obese children, research has illuminated some of the underlying factors that affect obesity and has shown the need for a comprehensive approach to the problem that includes behavioral, medical, social, and political change.

CAN MEDICATION CURE OBESITY IN CHILDREN?   10

References

Berkowitz, R. I., Wadden, T. A., Tershakovec, A. M., & Cronquist, J. L.
    (2003). Behavior therapy and sibutramine for the treatment of
    adolescent obesity. *Journal of the American Medical Association*,
    289, 1805-1812.

List of references begins on a new page. Heading is centered.

Carmona, R. H. (2004, March 2). *The growing epidemic of childhood
    obesity*. Testimony before the Subcommittee on Competition,
    Foreign Commerce, and Infrastructure of the U.S. Senate
    Committee on Commerce, Science, and Transportation. Retrieved
    from http://www.hhs.gov/asl/testify/t040302.html

List is alphabetized by authors' last names. All authors' names are inverted.

Critser, G. (2003). *Fat land*. Boston, MA: Houghton Mifflin.

Duenwald, M. (2004, January 6). Slim pickings: Looking beyond ephedra.
    The New York Times, p. F1. Retrieved from http://nytimes.com/

The first line of an entry is at the left margin; subsequent lines indent ½".

Henry J. Kaiser Family Foundation. (2004, February). *The role of media
    in childhood obesity*. Retrieved from http://www.kff.org
    /entmedia/7030.cfm

Hilts, P. J. (2002, March 20). Petition asks for removal of diet drug
    from market. *The New York Times*, p. A26. Retrieved from http://
    nytimes.com/

Hoppin, A. G., & Taveras, E. M. (2004, June 25). Assessment and
    management of childhood and adolescent obesity. *Clinical Update*.
    Retrieved from http://www.medscape.com/viewarticle/481633

Double-spacing is used throughout.

McDuffie, J. R., Calis, K. A., Uwaifo, G. I., Sebring, N. G., Fallon, E. M.,
    Hubbard, V. S., & Yanovski, J. A. (2002). Three-month tolerability
    of orlistat in adolescents with obesity-related comorbid condi-
    tions. *Obesity Research, 10*, 642-650.

Roche Laboratories. (2003, December). *Xenical (orlistat) capsules:
    Complete product information*. Retrieved from http://www
    .rocheusa.com/products/xenical/pi.pdf

Yanovski, S. Z., & Yanovski, J. A. (2002). Drug therapy: Obesity. *The New
    England Journal of Medicine, 346*, 591-602.

ALTERNATIVE APA TITLE PAGE

Short title and page number in the upper right corner on all pages.

Obesity in Children 1

Full title, centered.

Can Medication Cure Obesity in Children?

A Review of the Literature

Writer's name, course, instructor's name, and date, all centered at the bottom of the page.

Luisa Mirano

Psychology 108, Sector B

Professor Kang

October 31, 2004

ALTERNATIVE APA RUNNING HEAD

Obesity in Children 5

were classified by the Drug Enforcement Administration as having the "potential for abuse" (Hoppin & Taveras, 2004, Weight-Loss Drugs section, para. 6). Currently only two medications have been approved by the FDA for long-term treatment of obesity: sibutramine (marketed

Marginal annotations indicate APA-style formatting.

Writing *Chicago* papers

57 *Chicago* papers

Brief Directory

Most history instructors and some humanities instructors require you to document sources with footnotes or endnotes based on *The Chicago Manual of Style*, 16th ed. (Chicago: U of Chicago P, 2010). (See 57f.)

When you write a paper using sources, you face three main challenges: (1) supporting a thesis, (2) citing your sources and avoiding plagiarism, and (3) integrating quotations and other source material.

57a Supporting a thesis

Most research assignments ask you to form a thesis, or main idea, and to support that thesis with well-organized evidence. (See also 1c.) Remain flexible as you draft because you may need to revise your approach later. Writing about a subject is a way of learning about it; as you write, your understanding of your subject will almost certainly deepen.

Forming a working thesis

Once you have read a variety of sources and considered your issue from different perspectives, you are ready to form a working thesis: a one-sentence (or occasionally a two-sentence) statement of your central idea. (See also 1e.) Because it is a working, or tentative, thesis, it is flexible enough to change as your ideas develop. Ultimately, the thesis expresses not just your opinion but your informed, reasoned judgment.

Making the most of your handbook

When writing from sources, it helps to start with a working thesis and a rough outline.

▸ Draft a working thesis: 1c

▸ Sketch a plan: 1d

In a research paper, your thesis will answer the central research question that you posed earlier (see 46a). Here, for example, are student writer Ned Bishop's research question and working thesis statement.

RESEARCH QUESTION

To what extent was Confederate Major General Nathan Bedford Forrest responsible for the massacre of Union troops at Fort Pillow?

WORKING THESIS

By encouraging racism among his troops, Nathan Bedford Forrest was directly responsible for the massacre of Union troops at Fort Pillow.

Notice that the thesis expresses a view on a debatable issue—an issue about which intelligent, well-meaning people might disagree. The writer's job is to convince such readers that this view is worth taking seriously.

The thesis usually appears at the end of the introductory paragraph. To read Ned Bishop's thesis in the context of his introduction, see page 719.

Organizing your ideas

The body of your paper will consist of evidence in support of your thesis. Instead of getting tangled up in a complex, formal outline, sketch an informal plan that organizes your evidence in bold strokes. Ned Bishop, for example, used a simple outline to structure his ideas. In the paper itself, these points became headings that helped readers follow his line of argument.

What happened at Fort Pillow?

Did Forrest order the massacre?

Can Forrest be held responsible for the massacre?

hackerhandbooks.com/bedhandbook > **Research exercises**
> *Chicago* > E-ex 57–1 and 57–2

Using sources to inform and support your argument

Used thoughtfully, the source materials you have gathered will make your argument more complex and convincing for readers. Sources can play several different roles as you develop your points.

Providing background information or context　You can use facts and statistics to support generalizations or to establish the importance of your topic, as student writer Ned Bishop does early in his paper.

Fort Pillow, Tennessee, which sat on a bluff overlooking the Mississippi River, had been held by the Union for two years. It was garrisoned by 580 men, 292 of them from United States Colored Heavy and Light Artillery regiments, 285 from the white Thirteenth Tennessee Cavalry. Nathan Bedford Forrest commanded about 1,500 troops.[1]

Explaining terms or concepts　If readers are unlikely to be familiar with a word or an idea important to your topic, you must explain it for them. Quoting or paraphrasing a source can help you define terms and concepts clearly and concisely.

The Civil War practice of giving no quarter to an enemy—in other words, "denying [an enemy] the right of survival"—defied Lincoln's mandate for humane and merciful treatment of prisoners.[9]

Supporting your claims As you draft your argument, make sure to back up your assertions with facts, examples, and other evidence from your research. (See also 5e.) Ned Bishop, for example, uses an eyewitness report of the racially motivated violence perpetrated by Nathan Bedford Forrest's troops.

> The slaughter at Fort Pillow was no doubt driven in large part by racial hatred. . . . A Southern reporter traveling with Forrest makes clear that the discrimination was deliberate: "Our troops maddened by the excitement, shot down the ret[r]eating Yankees, and not until they had attained t[h]e water's edge and turned to beg for mercy, did any prisoners fall in [t]o our hands— Thus the whites received quarter, but the negroes were shown no mercy."^{19}

Lending authority to your argument Expert opinion can give weight to your argument. (See also 5e.) But don't rely on experts to make your argument for you. Construct your argument in your own words and, when appropriate, cite the judgment of an authority in the field to support your position.

> Fort Pillow is not the only instance of a massacre or threatened massacre of black soldiers by troops under Forrest's command. Biographer Brian Steel Wills points out that at Brice's Cross Roads in June 1864, "black soldiers suffered inordinately" as Forrest looked the other way and Confederate soldiers deliberately sought out those they termed "the damned negroes."^{21}

Anticipating and countering objections Do not ignore sources that seem contrary to your position or that offer arguments different from your own. Instead, use them to give voice to opposing points of view and to state potential objections to your arguments before you counter them (see 5f). Readers often have opposing points of view in mind already, whether or not they agree with you. Ned Bishop, for example, presents conflicting evidence to acknowledge that some readers may credit Nathan Bedford Forrest with stopping the massacre. In doing so, Bishop creates an opportunity to counter that objection and persuade those readers that Forrest can be held accountable.

> Hurst suggests that the temperamental Forrest "may have ragingly ordered a massacre and even intended to carry it out— until he rode inside the fort and viewed the horrifying result" and ordered it stopped.[15] While this is an intriguing interpretation of events, even Hurst would probably admit that it is merely speculation.

57b Citing sources; avoiding plagiarism

In a research paper, you will draw on the work of other writers, and you must document their contributions by citing your sources. Sources are cited for two reasons:

- to tell readers where your information comes from—so that they can assess its reliability and, if interested, find and read the original source
- to give credit to the writers from whom you have borrowed words and ideas

Borrowing another writer's language, sentence structures, or ideas without proper acknowledgment is a form of dishonesty known as *plagiarism*.

Using the Chicago system for citing sources

You must include a citation when you quote from a source, when you summarize or paraphrase a source, and when you borrow facts that are not common knowledge. (See also "Avoiding plagiarism" on p. 690.)

Chicago citations consist of superscript numbers in the text of the paper that refer readers to notes with corresponding numbers either at the foot of the page (footnotes) or at the end of the paper (endnotes).

TEXT

Governor John Andrew was not allowed to recruit black soldiers from out of state. "Ostensibly," writes Peter Burchard, "no recruiting was done outside Massachusetts, but it was an open secret that Andrew's agents were working far and wide."[1]

NOTE

1. Peter Burchard, *One Gallant Rush: Robert Gould Shaw and His Brave Black Regiment* (New York: St. Martin's, 1965), 85.

For detailed advice on using *Chicago*-style notes, see 57d. When you use footnotes or endnotes, you will usually need to provide a bibliography as well (see p. 716).

Avoiding plagiarism

Your research paper is a collaboration between you and your sources. To be fair and ethical, you must acknowledge your debt to the writers of those sources. If you don't, you commit plagiarism, a serious academic offense. (See also 48c.)

In general, these three acts are considered plagiarism: (1) failing to cite quotations and borrowed ideas, (2) failing to enclose borrowed language in quotation marks, and (3) failing to put summaries and paraphrases in your own words. Definitions of plagiarism may vary; it's a good idea to find out how your school defines academic dishonesty.

Citing quotations and borrowed ideas You must cite all direct quotations. You must also cite any ideas you borrow from a source: summaries and paraphrases; statistics and other specific facts; and visuals such as cartoons, graphs, and diagrams.

The only exception is common knowledge—information your readers could easily find in any number of general sources. For example, most encyclopedias will tell readers that the Korean War ended in 1953 and that President Theodore Roosevelt was the first American to receive the Nobel Prize.

As a rule, when you have seen certain general information repeatedly in your reading, you don't need to cite it. However, when information has appeared in only a few sources, when it is highly specific (as with statistics), or when it is controversial, you should cite the source. If a topic is new to you and you are not sure what is considered common knowledge or what is controversial, ask your instructor or someone else with expertise. When in doubt, cite the source. (See 57d for details.)

Enclosing borrowed language in quotation marks To indicate that you are using a source's exact phrases or sentences, you must enclose them in quotation marks unless they have been set off from the text by indenting (see p. 695). To omit the quotation marks is to claim—falsely—that the language is your own. Such an omission is plagiarism even if you have cited the source.

ORIGINAL SOURCE

For many Southerners it was psychologically impossible to see a black man bearing arms as anything but an incipient slave uprising complete with arson, murder, pillage, and rapine.
—Dudley Taylor Cornish, *The Sable Arm*, p. 158

PLAGIARISM

According to Civil War historian Dudley Taylor Cornish, for many Southerners it was psychologically impossible to see a black man bearing arms as anything but an incipient slave uprising complete with arson, murder, pillage, and rapine.[2]

BORROWED LANGUAGE IN QUOTATION MARKS

According to Civil War historian Dudley Taylor Cornish, "For many Southerners it was psychologically impossible to see a black man bearing arms as anything but an incipient slave uprising complete with arson, murder, pillage, and rapine."[2]

Putting summaries and paraphrases in your own words Summaries and paraphrases are written in your own words. A summary condenses information; a paraphrase uses roughly the same number of words as the original source to convey the information. When you summarize or paraphrase, it is not enough to name the source; you must restate the source's meaning using your own language. (See also 48c.) You commit plagiarism if you half-copy the author's sentences—either by mixing the author's phrases with your own without using quotation marks or by plugging your own synonyms into the author's sentence structure.

The first paraphrase of the following source is plagiarized—even though the source is cited—because too much of its language is borrowed from the original. The underlined strings of words have been copied exactly (without quotation marks). In addition, the writer has closely followed the sentence structure of the original source, merely making a few substitutions (such as *Fifty percent* for *Half* and *angered and perhaps frightened* for *enraged and perhaps terrified*).

ORIGINAL SOURCE

Half of the force holding Fort Pillow were Negroes, former slaves now enrolled in the Union Army. Toward them Forrest's troops had the fierce, bitter animosity of men who had been educated to regard the colored race as inferior and who for the first time had encountered that race armed and fighting against white men. The sight enraged and perhaps terrified many of the Confederates and aroused in them the ugly spirit of a lynching mob.

—Albert Castel, "The Fort Pillow Massacre," pp. 46–47

PLAGIARISM: UNACCEPTABLE BORROWING

Albert Castel suggests that much of the brutality at Fort Pillow can be traced to racial attitudes. Fifty percent of the troops holding Fort Pillow were Negroes, former slaves who had joined the Union Army. Toward them Forrest's soldiers displayed the savage hatred of men who had been taught the inferiority of blacks and who for the first time had confronted them armed and fighting against white men. The vision angered and perhaps frightened the Confederates and aroused in them the ugly spirit of a lynching mob.[3]

To avoid plagiarizing an author's language, resist the temptation to look at the source while you are summarizing or paraphrasing. After you have read the passage you want to paraphrase, set the source aside. Ask yourself, "What is the author's meaning?" In your own words, state your understanding of the author's basic point. Return to the source and check that you haven't used the author's language or sentence structure or misrepresented the author's ideas. Following these steps will help you avoid plagiarizing the source. When you fully understand another writer's meaning, you can more easily and accurately represent those ideas in your own words.

ACCEPTABLE PARAPHRASE

Albert Castel suggests that much of the brutality at Fort Pillow can be traced to racial attitudes. Fifty percent of the Union troops were blacks, men whom the Confederates had been raised to consider their inferiors. The shock and perhaps fear of facing armed ex-slaves in battle may well have unleashed the fury that led to the massacre.[3]

hackerhandbooks.com/bedhandbook > Research exercises
> *Chicago* > E-ex 57–3 to 57–7

57c Integrating sources

Quotations, summaries, paraphrases, and facts will support your argument, but they cannot speak for you. You can use several strategies to integrate information from research sources into your paper while maintaining your own voice.

Using quotations appropriately

In your academic writing, keep the emphasis on your ideas and your language; use your own words to summarize and to paraphrase your sources and to explain your points. Sometimes, however, quotations can be the most effective way to integrate a source.

WHEN TO USE QUOTATIONS

- When language is especially vivid or expressive
- When exact wording is needed for technical accuracy

- When it is important to let the debaters of an issue explain their positions in their own words
- When the words of an authority lend weight to an argument
- When the language of a source is the topic of your discussion (as in an analysis or interpretation)

Limiting your use of quotations Although it is tempting to insert many quotations in your paper and to use your own words only for connecting passages, do not quote excessively. It is almost impossible to integrate numerous quotations smoothly into your own text.

It is not always necessary to quote full sentences from a source. To reduce your reliance on the words of others, you can often integrate language from a source into your own sentence structure.

> As Hurst has pointed out, until "an outcry erupted in the Northern press," even the Confederates did not deny that there had been a massacre at Fort Pillow.[4]

> Union surgeon Dr. Charles Fitch testified that after he was in custody he "saw" Confederate soldiers "kill every negro that made his appearance dressed in Federal uniform."[20]

Using the ellipsis mark To condense a quoted passage, you can use the ellipsis mark (three periods, with spaces between) to indicate that you have left words out. What remains must be grammatically complete.

> Union surgeon Fitch's testimony that all women and children had been evacuated from Fort Pillow before the attack conflicts with Forrest's report: "We captured . . . about 40 negro women and children."[6]

The writer has omitted several words not relevant to the issue at hand: *164 Federals, 75 negro troops, and.*

When you want to leave out one or more full sentences, use a period before the three ellipsis dots. For an example, see the long quotation at the bottom of page 695.

Ordinarily, do not use the ellipsis mark at the beginning or at the end of a quotation. Readers will understand that the quoted material is taken from a longer passage, so such marks are not necessary. The only exception occurs when you have dropped words at the end of the final quoted sentence. In such cases, put three ellipsis dots before the closing quotation mark.

Make sure omissions and ellipsis marks do not distort the meaning of your source.

Using brackets Brackets allow you to insert words of your own into quoted material to clarify a confusing reference or to keep a sentence grammatical in your context.

> According to Albert Castel, "It can be reasonably argued that he [Forrest] was justified in believing that the approaching steamships intended to aid the garrison [at Fort Pillow]."[7]

NOTE: Use the word *sic* in brackets to indicate that an error in a quoted sentence appears in the original source. (An example appears on p. 696.) Do not overuse *sic* to call attention to errors in a source. Sometimes paraphrasing is a better option. (See 39c.)

Setting off long quotations *Chicago* style allows you some leeway in deciding whether to set off a long quotation or run it into your text. For emphasis, you may want to set off a quotation of more than four or five typed lines of text; almost certainly you should set off quotations of ten or more lines. To set off a quotation, indent it one-half inch from the left margin and use the normal right margin. Double-space the indented quotation.

Long quotations should be introduced by an informative sentence, usually followed by a colon. Quotation marks are unnecessary because the indented format tells readers that the passage is taken word-for-word from the source.

> In a letter home, Confederate officer Achilles V. Clark recounted what happened at Fort Pillow:
>
> > Words cannot describe the scene. The poor deluded negroes would run up to our men fall upon their knees and with uplifted hands

scream for mercy but they were ordered to their feet and then shot down. The whitte [*sic*] men fared but little better. . . . I with several others tried to stop the butchery and at one time had partially succeeded[,] but Gen. Forrest ordered them shot down like dogs[,] and the carnage continued.[8]

Using signal phrases to integrate sources

Whenever you include a paraphrase, summary, or direct quotation of another writer in your paper, prepare your readers for it with introductory words called a *signal phrase*. A signal phrase names the author of the source and often provides some context for the source material.

When you write a signal phrase, choose a verb that is appropriate for the way you are using the source (see p. 687). Are you providing background, explaining a concept, supporting a claim, lending authority, or refuting a belief? By choosing an appropriate verb, you can make your source's role clear. See the chart on page 697 for a list of verbs commonly used in signal phrases.

Note that *Chicago* style calls for verbs in the present or present perfect tense (*points out, has pointed out*) to introduce source material unless you include a date that specifies the time of the original author's writing.

The first time you mention an author, use the full name: *Shelby Foote argues*. . . . When you refer to the author again, you may use the last name only: *Foote raises an important question.*

Marking boundaries Readers should be able to move from your own words to the words you quote from a source without feeling a jolt. Avoid dropping quotations into the text without warning. Instead, provide clear signal phrases, usually including the author's name, to indicate the boundary between your words and the source's words. (The signal phrase is underlined in the second example.)

Using signal phrases in *Chicago* papers

To avoid monotony, try to vary both the language and the placement of your signal phrases.

Model signal phrases

In the words of historian James M. McPherson, "..."[1]

As Dudley Taylor Cornish has argued, "..."[2]

In a letter to his wife, a Confederate soldier who witnessed the massacre wrote that "..."[3]

"...," claims Benjamin Quarles.[4]

"...," writes Albert Castel, "..."[5]

Shelby Foote offers an intriguing interpretation: "..."[6]

Verbs in signal phrases

admits	compares	insists	rejects
agrees	confirms	notes	reports
argues	contends	observes	responds
asserts	declares	points out	suggests
believes	denies	reasons	thinks
claims	emphasizes	refutes	writes

DROPPED QUOTATION

Not surprisingly, those testifying on the Union and Confederate sides recalled events at Fort Pillow quite differently. Unionists claimed that their troops had abandoned their arms and were in full retreat. "The Confederates, however, all agreed that the Union troops retreated to the river with arms in their hands."[9]

QUOTATION WITH SIGNAL PHRASE

Not surprisingly, those testifying on the Union and Confederate sides recalled events at Fort Pillow quite differently. Unionists claimed that their troops had abandoned their arms and were in full retreat. "The Confederates, however," writes historian Albert Castel, "all agreed that the Union troops retreated to the river with arms in their hands."[9]

Using signal phrases with summaries and paraphrases Introduce most summaries and paraphrases with a signal phrase that mentions the author and places the material in the context of your argument. Readers will then understand where the summary or paraphrase begins.

Without the signal phrase (underlined) in the following example, readers might think that only the last sentence is being cited, when in fact the whole paragraph is based on the source.

> According to Jack Hurst, official Confederate policy was that black soldiers were to be treated as runaway slaves; in addition, the Confederate Congress decreed that white Union officers commanding black troops be killed. Confederate Lieutenant General Kirby Smith went one step further, declaring that he would kill all captured black troops. Smith's policy never met with strong opposition from the Richmond government.[10]

Integrating statistics and other facts When you are citing a statistic or another specific fact, a signal phrase is often not necessary. In most cases, readers will understand that the citation refers to the statistic or fact (not the whole paragraph).

> Of the 295 white troops garrisoned at Fort Pillow, 168 were taken prisoner. Black troops fared worse, with only 58 of 262 captured and most of the rest presumably killed or wounded.[12]

There is nothing wrong, however, with using a signal phrase to introduce a statistic or another fact.

Putting source material in context Readers should not have to guess why source material appears in your paper. A signal phrase can help you make the connection between your own ideas and those of another writer by setting up how a source will contribute to your paper (see 47a).

If you use another writer's words, you must explain how they relate to your point. It's a good idea to embed a quotation between sentences of your own. In addition to introducing it with a signal phrase, follow it with interpretive comments that link the source material to your paper's argument.

QUOTATION WITH EFFECTIVE CONTEXT

In a respected biography of Nathan Bedford Forrest, Hurst suggests that the temperamental Forrest "may have ragingly ordered a massacre and even intended to carry it out—until he rode inside the fort and viewed the horrifying result" and ordered it stopped.[15] While this is an intriguing interpretation of events, even Hurst would probably admit that it is merely speculation.

NOTE: When you bring other sources into a conversation about your research topic, you are synthesizing. For more on synthesis, see 52c.

hackerhandbooks.com/bedhandbook > Research exercises
                     > *Chicago* > E-ex 57–8 to 57–11

57d *Chicago* documentation style

In history and some humanities courses, you may be asked to use the documentation system set forth in *The Chicago Manual of Style*, 16th ed. (Chicago: U of Chicago P, 2010). In *Chicago* style, superscript numbers in the text of the paper refer readers to notes with corresponding numbers either at the foot of the page (footnotes) or at the end of the paper (endnotes). A bibliography is often required as well; it appears at the end of the paper and gives publication information for all the works cited in the notes.

TEXT

A Union soldier, Jacob Thompson, claimed to have seen Forrest order the killing, but when asked to describe the six-foot-two general, he called him "a little bit of a man."[12]

FOOTNOTE OR ENDNOTE

12. Brian Steel Wills, *A Battle from the Start: The Life of Nathan Bedford Forrest* (New York: HarperCollins, 1992), 187.

BIBLIOGRAPHY ENTRY

Wills, Brian Steel. *A Battle from the Start: The Life of Nathan Bedford Forrest*. New York: HarperCollins, 1992.

First and subsequent notes for a source

The first time you cite a source, the note should include publication information for that work as well as the page number on which the passage being cited may be found.

1. Peter Burchard, *One Gallant Rush: Robert Gould Shaw and His Brave Black Regiment* (New York: St. Martin's, 1965), 85.

For subsequent references to a source you have already cited, you may simply give the author's last name, a short form of the title, and the page or pages cited. A short form of the title of a book is italicized; a short form of the title of an article is put in quotation marks.

4. Burchard, *One Gallant Rush*, 31.

When you have two consecutive notes from the same source, you may use "Ibid." (meaning "in the same place") and the page number for the second note. Use "Ibid." alone if the page number is the same.

5. Jack Hurst, *Nathan Bedford Forrest: A Biography* (New York: Knopf, 1993), 8.

6. Ibid., 174.

Chicago-*style bibliography*

A bibliography, which appears at the end of your paper, lists every work you have cited in your notes; in addition, it may include works that you consulted but did not cite. For advice on constructing the list, see page 716. A sample bibliography appears on page 726.

NOTE: If you include a bibliography, *The Chicago Manual of Style* suggests that you shorten all notes, including the first reference to a source, as described on page 700. Check with your instructor, however, to see whether using an abbreviated note for a first reference to a source is acceptable.

Model notes and bibliography entries

The following models are consistent with guidelines set forth in *The Chicago Manual of Style*, 16th ed. For each type of source, a model note appears first, followed by a model bibliography entry. The note shows the format you should use when citing a source for the first time. For subsequent citations of a source, use shortened notes (see p. 700).

Some online sources, typically periodical articles, use a permanent locator called a digital object identifier (DOI). Use the DOI, when it is available, in place of a URL in your citations of online sources.

When a Web address (URL) or a DOI must break across lines, do not insert a hyphen or break at a hyphen if the URL or DOI contains one. Instead, break after a colon or a double slash or before any other mark of punctuation.

Books (print and online)

1. Basic format for a print book

1. Mary N. Woods, *Beyond the Architect's Eye: Photographs and the American Built Environment* (Philadelphia: University of Pennsylvania Press, 2009), 45.

Woods, Mary N. *Beyond the Architect's Eye: Photographs and the American Built Environment*. Philadelphia: University of Pennsylvania Press, 2009.

2. Basic format for an online book

2. John Dewey, *Democracy and Education* (1916; ILT Digital Classics, 1994), chap. 4, http://www.ilt.columbia.edu/publications/dewey.html.

Dewey, John. *Democracy and Education*. 1916. ILT Digital Classics, 1994. http://www.ilt.columbia.edu/publications/dewey.html.

3. Basic format for an e-book (electronic book)

3. Leo Tolstoy, *War and Peace*, trans. Richard Pevear and Larissa Volokhonsky (New York: Knopf, 2007), Kindle edition, vol. 1, pt. 1, chap. 3.

Tolstoy, Leo. *War and Peace*. Translated by Richard Pevear and Larissa Volokhonsky. New York: Knopf, 2007. Kindle edition.

4. Two or more authors   For a work with two or three authors, give all authors' names in both the note and the bibliography entry. For a work with four or more authors, in the note give the first author's name followed by "et al." (for "and others"); in the bibliography entry, list all authors' names.

4. Chris Stringer and Peter Andrews, *The Complete World of Human Evolution* (London: Thames and Hudson, 2005), 45.

Stringer, Chris, and Peter Andrews. *The Complete World of Human Evolution*. London: Thames and Hudson, 2005.

4. Lynn Hunt et al., *The Making of the West: Peoples and Cultures*, 3rd ed. (Boston: Bedford/St. Martin's, 2009), 541.

Hunt, Lynn, Thomas R. Martin, Barbara H. Rosenwein, R. Po-chia Hsia, and Bonnie G. Smith. *The Making of the West: Peoples and Cultures*. 3rd ed. Boston: Bedford/St. Martin's, 2009.

5. Organization as author

5. Dormont Historical Society, *Images of America: Dormont* (Charleston, SC: Arcadia Publishing, 2008), 24.

Dormont Historical Society. *Images of America: Dormont*. Charleston, SC: Arcadia Publishing, 2008.

6. Unknown author

6. *The Men's League Handbook on Women's Suffrage* (London, 1912), 23.

The Men's League Handbook on Women's Suffrage. London, 1912.

7. Multiple works by the same author   In the bibliography, use three hyphens in place of the author's name in the second and subsequent entries. Arrange the entries alphabetically by title.

Harper, Raymond L. *A History of Chesapeake, Virginia*. Charleston, SC: History Press, 2008.

---. *South Norfolk, Virginia, 1661-2005*. Charleston, SC: History Press, 2005.

Directory to *Chicago*-style notes and bibliography entries

Books (print and online)

1. Basic format for a print book, 701
2. Basic format for an online book, 701
3. Basic format for an e-book (electronic book), 702
4. Two or more authors, 702
5. Organization as author, 702
6. Unknown author, 702
7. Multiple works by the same author, 702
8. Edited work without an author, 704
9. Edited work with an author, 704
10. Translated work, 704
11. Edition other than the first, 704
12. Volume in a multivolume work, 704
13. Work in an anthology, 704
14. Introduction, preface, foreword, or afterword, 705
15. Republished book, 705
16. Work with a title in its title, 705
17. Letter in a published collection, 705
18. Work in a series, 705
19. Encyclopedia or dictionary entry, 705
20. Sacred text, 706
21. Source quoted in another source, 706

Articles in periodicals (print and online)

22. Article in a print journal, 706
23. Article in an online journal, 707
24. Journal article from a database, 707
25. Article in a print magazine, 707

26. Article in an online magazine, 707
27. Magazine article from a database, 708
28. Article in a print newspaper, 708
29. Article in an online newspaper, 708
30. Newspaper article from a database, 708
31. Unsigned newspaper article, 709
32. Book review, 709
33. Letter to the editor, 709

Online sources

34. Web site, 709
35. Short work from a Web site, 710
36. Online posting or e-mail, 710
37. Blog (Weblog) post, 710
38. Podcast, 710
39. Online audio or video, 711

Other sources (including online versions)

40. Government document, 711
41. Unpublished dissertation, 711
42. Personal communication, 712
43. Published or broadcast interview, 712
44. Published proceedings of a conference, 712
45. Video or DVD, 712
46. Sound recording, 712
47. Musical score or composition, 712
48. Work of art, 713
49. Performance, 713

8. Edited work without an author

8. Jack Beatty, ed., *Colossus: How the Corporation Changed America* (New York: Broadway Books, 2001), 127.

Beatty, Jack, ed. *Colossus: How the Corporation Changed America*. New York: Broadway Books, 2001.

9. Edited work with an author

9. Ted Poston, *A First Draft of History,* ed. Kathleen A. Hauke (Athens: University of Georgia Press, 2000), 46.

Poston, Ted. *A First Draft of History*. Edited by Kathleen A. Hauke. Athens: University of Georgia Press, 2000.

10. Translated work

10. Tonino Guerra, *Abandoned Places*, trans. Adria Bernardi (Barcelona: Guernica, 1999), 71.

Guerra, Tonino. *Abandoned Places*. Translated by Adria Bernardi. Barcelona: Guernica, 1999.

11. Edition other than the first

11. Arnoldo DeLeon, *Mexican Americans in Texas: A Brief History*, 3rd ed. (Wheeling, IL: Harlan Davidson, 2009), 34.

DeLeon, Arnoldo. *Mexican Americans in Texas: A Brief History*. 3rd ed. Wheeling, IL: Harlan Davidson, 2009.

12. Volume in a multivolume work

12. Charles Reagan Wilson, ed., *Myth, Manner, and Memory,* vol. 4 of *The New Encyclopedia of Southern Culture* (Chapel Hill: University of North Carolina Press, 2006), 198.

Wilson, Charles Reagan, ed. *Myth, Manner, and Memory*. Vol. 4 of *The New Encyclopedia of Southern Culture*. Chapel Hill: University of North Carolina Press, 2006.

13. Work in an anthology

13. Zora Neale Hurston, "From *Dust Tracks on a Road*," in *The Norton Book of American Autobiography*, ed. Jay Parini (New York: Norton, 1999), 336.

Hurston, Zora Neale. "From *Dust Tracks on a Road*." In *The Norton Book of American Autobiography*, edited by Jay Parini, 333-43. New York: Norton, 1999.

14. Introduction, preface, foreword, or afterword

14. Nelson DeMille, foreword to *Flag: An American Biography*, by Marc Leepson (New York: Thomas Dunne, 2005), xii.

DeMille, Nelson. Foreword to *Flag: An American Biography*, by Marc Leepson, xi-xiv. New York: Thomas Dunne, 2005.

15. Republished book

15. Garry Wills, *Inventing America: Jefferson's Declaration of Independence* (1978; repr., Boston: Houghton Mifflin, 2002), 86.

Wills, Garry. *Inventing America: Jefferson's Declaration of Independence*. 1978. Reprint, Boston: Houghton Mifflin, 2002.

16. Work with a title in its title   Use quotation marks around any title within an italicized title.

16. Gary Schmidgall, ed., *Conserving Walt Whitman's Fame: Selections from Horace Traubel's "Conservator," 1890-1919* (Iowa City: University of Iowa Press, 2006), 165.

Schmidgall, Gary, ed. *Conserving Walt Whitman's Fame: Selections from Horace Traubel's "Conservator," 1890-1919*. Iowa City: University of Iowa Press, 2006.

17. Letter in a published collection   Use the day-month-year form for the date of the letter. If the letter writer's name is part of the book title, begin the note with only the last name but begin the bibliography entry with the full name.

17. Mitford to Esmond Romilly, 29 July 1940, in *Decca: The Letters of Jessica Mitford*, ed. Peter Y. Sussman (New York: Knopf, 2006), 55-56.

Mitford, Jessica. *Decca: The Letters of Jessica Mitford*. Edited by Peter Y. Sussman. New York: Knopf, 2006.

18. Work in a series

18. R. Keith Schoppa, *The Columbia Guide to Modern Chinese History*, Columbia Guides to Asian History (New York: Columbia University Press, 2000), 256-58.

Schoppa, R. Keith. *The Columbia Guide to Modern Chinese History*. Columbia Guides to Asian History. New York: Columbia University Press, 2000.

19. Encyclopedia or dictionary entry

19. *Encyclopaedia Britannica*, 15th ed., s.v. "Monroe Doctrine."

19. Bryan A. Garner, *Garner's Modern American Usage* (Oxford: Oxford University Press, 2003), s.v. "brideprice."

Garner, Bryan A. *Garner's Modern American Usage*. Oxford: Oxford University Press, 2003.

The abbreviation "s.v." is for the Latin *sub verbo* ("under the word").

Well-known reference works such as encyclopedias do not require publication information and are usually not included in the bibliography.

20. Sacred text

20. Matt. 20:4-9 (Revised Standard Version).

20. Qur'an 18:1-3.

Sacred texts are usually not included in the bibliography.

21. Source quoted in another source

21. Ron Grossman and Charles Leroux, "A Local Outpost of Democracy," *Chicago Tribune*, March 5, 1996, quoted in William Julius Wilson and Richard P. Taub, *There Goes the Neighborhood: Racial, Ethnic, and Class Tensions in Four Chicago Neighborhoods and Their Meaning for America* (New York: Knopf, 2006), 18.

Grossman, Ron, and Charles Leroux. "A Local Outpost of Democracy." *Chicago Tribune*, March 5, 1996. Quoted in William Julius Wilson and Richard P. Taub, *There Goes the Neighborhood: Racial, Ethnic, and Class Tensions in Four Chicago Neighborhoods and Their Meaning for America* (New York: Knopf, 2006), 18.

Articles in periodicals (print and online)

22. Article in a print journal   Include the volume and issue numbers and the date; end the bibliography entry with the page range of the article.

22. T. H. Breen, "Will American Consumers Buy a Second American Revolution?," *Journal of American History* 93, no. 2 (2006): 405.

Breen, T. H. "Will American Consumers Buy a Second American Revolution?" *Journal of American History* 93, no. 2 (2006): 404-8.

23. Article in an online journal   Give the DOI if the article has one; if there is no DOI, give the URL for the article. For unpaginated online articles, you may include in your note a locator, such as a numbered paragraph or a heading from the article.

23. Brian Lennon, "New Media Critical Homologies," *Postmodern Culture* 19, no. 2 (2009), http://pmc.iath.virginia.edu/text-only/issue.109 /19.2lennon.txt.

Lennon, Brian. "New Media Critical Homologies." *Postmodern Culture* 19, no. 2 (2009). http://pmc.iath.virginia.edu/text-only/issue.109 /19.2lennon.txt.

24. Journal article from a database   Give whatever identifying information is available in the database listing: a DOI for the article; or the name of the database and the number assigned by the database; or a "stable" or "persistent" URL for the article.

24. Constant Leung, "Language and Content in Bilingual Education," *Linguistics and Education* 16, no. 2 (2005): 239, doi:10.1016 /j.linged.2006.01.004.

Leung, Constant. "Language and Content in Bilingual Education." *Linguistics and Education* 16, no. 2 (2005): 238-52. doi:10.1016 /j.linged.2006.01.004.

25. Article in a print magazine

25. Tom Bissell, "Improvised, Explosive, and Divisive," *Harper's*, January 2006, 42.

Bissell, Tom. "Improvised, Explosive, and Divisive." *Harper's*, January 2006, 41-54.

26. Article in an online magazine   Include the URL for the article.

26. Katharine Mieszkowski, "A Deluge Waiting to Happen," *Salon*, July 3, 2008, http://www.salon.com/news/feature/2008/07/03/floods /index.html.

Mieszkowski, Katharine. "A Deluge Waiting to Happen." *Salon*, July 3, 2008.
http://www.salon.com/news/feature/2008/07/03/floods/index.html.

27. Magazine article from a database Give whatever identifying information is available in the database listing: a DOI for the article; or the name of the database and the number assigned by the database; or a "stable" or "persistent" URL for the article.

27. "Facing Facts in Afghanistan," *National Review*, November 2, 2009, 14, Expanded Academic ASAP (A209905060).

"Facing Facts in Afghanistan." *National Review*, November 2, 2009, 14. Expanded Academic ASAP (A209905060).

28. Article in a print newspaper Page numbers are not necessary; a section letter or number, if available, is sufficient.

28. Randal C. Archibold, "These Neighbors Are Good Ones without a New Fence," *New York Times*, October 22, 2008, sec. A.

Archibold, Randal C. "These Neighbors Are Good Ones without a New Fence." *New York Times*, October 22, 2008, sec. A.

29. Article in an online newspaper Include the URL for the article; if the URL is very long, use the URL for the newspaper's home page. Omit page numbers, even if the source provides them.

29. Doyle McManus, "The Candor War," *Chicago Tribune*, July 29, 2010, http://www.chicagotribune.com/.

McManus, Doyle. "The Candor War." *Chicago Tribune*, July 29, 2010. http://www.chicagotribune.com/.

30. Newspaper article from a database Give whatever identifying information is available in the database listing: a DOI for the article; or the name of the database and the number assigned by the database; or a "stable" or "persistent" URL for the article.

30. Clifford J. Levy, "In Kyrgyzstan, Failure to Act Adds to Crisis," *New York Times*, June 18, 2010, General OneFile (A229196045).

Levy, Clifford J. "In Kyrgyzstan, Failure to Act Adds to Crisis." *New York Times*, June 18, 2010. General OneFile (A229196045).

31. Unsigned newspaper article

31. "Renewable Energy Rules," *Boston Globe*, August 11, 2003, sec. A.

Boston Globe. "Renewable Energy Rules." August 11, 2003, sec. A.

32. Book review

32. Benjamin Wittes, "Remember the Titan," review of *Louis D. Brandeis: A Life*, by Melvin T. Urofsky, *Wilson Quarterly* 33, no. 4 (2009): 100.

Wittes, Benjamin. "Remember the Titan." Review of *Louis D. Brandeis: A Life*, by Melvin T. Urofsky. *Wilson Quarterly* 33, no. 4 (2009): 100-101.

33. Letter to the editor Do not use the letter's title, even if the publication gives one.

33. David Harlan, letter to the editor, *New York Review of Books*, October 9, 2008.

Harlan, David. Letter to the editor. *New York Review of Books*, October 9, 2008.

Online sources

For most Web sites, include an author if a site has one, the title of the site, the sponsor, the date of publication or modified (update) date, and the site's URL. Do not italicize a Web site title unless the site is an online book or periodical. Use quotation marks for the titles of sections or pages in a Web site. If a site does not have a date of publication or modified date, give the date you accessed the site ("accessed January 3, 2010").

34. Web site

34. Chesapeake and Ohio Canal National Historical Park, National Park Service, last modified April 9, 2010, http://www.nps.gov/choh/index.htm.

Chesapeake and Ohio Canal National Historical Park. National Park Service. Last modified April 9, 2010. http://www.nps.gov/choh/index.htm.

35. Short work from a Web site   Place the title of the short work in quotation marks.

35. George P. Landow, "Victorian and Victorianism," Victorian Web, last modified August 2, 2009, http://victorianweb.org/vn/victor4.html.

Landow, George P. "Victorian and Victorianism." Victorian Web. Last modified August 2, 2009. http://victorianweb.org/vn/victor4.html.

36. Online posting or e-mail   If an online posting has been archived, include a URL. E-mails that are not part of an online discussion are treated as personal communications (see item 42). Online postings and e-mails are not included in the bibliography.

36. Susanna J. Sturgis to Copyediting-L discussion list, July 17, 2010, http://listserv.indiana.edu/archives/copyediting-l.html.

37. Blog (Weblog) post   Treat as a short document from a Web site (see item 35). Put the title of the posting in quotation marks, and italicize the name of the blog. Insert "blog" in parentheses after the name if the word *blog* is not part of the name.

37. Miland Brown, "The Flawed Montevideo Convention of 1933," *World History Blog,* May 31, 2008, http://www.worldhistoryblog.com/2008 /05/flawed-montevideo-convention-of-1933.html.

Brown, Miland. "The Flawed Montevideo Convention of 1933." *World History Blog.* May 31, 2008. http://www.worldhistoryblog.com/2008 /05/flawed-montevideo-convention-of-1933.html.

38. Podcast   Treat as a short work from a Web site (see item 35), including the following, if available: the author's (or speaker's) name; the title of the podcast, in quotation marks; an identifying number, if any; the title of the site on which it appears; the sponsor of the site; and the URL. Identify the type of podcast or file format and the date of posting or your date of access before the URL.

38. Paul Tiyambe Zeleza, "Africa's Global Past," Episode 40, Africa Past and Present, African Online Digital Library, podcast audio, April 29, 2010, http://afripod.aodl.org/.

Zeleza, Paul Tiyambe. "Africa's Global Past." Episode 40. Africa Past and Present. African Online Digital Library. Podcast audio. April 29, 2010. http://afripod.aodl.org/.

39. Online audio or video   Cite as a short work from a Web site (see item 35). If the source is a downloadable file, identify the file format or medium before the URL.

39. Richard B. Freeman, "Global Capitalism, Labor Markets, and Inequality," Institute of International Studies, University of California at Berkeley, October 31, 2007, http://www.youtube.com /watch?v=cgNCFsXGUaO.

Freeman, Richard B. "Global Capitalism, Labor Markets, and Inequality." Institute of International Studies, University of California at Berkeley. October 31, 2007. http://www.youtube.com /watch?v=cgNCFsXGUaO.

Other sources (including online versions)

40. Government document

40. U.S. Department of State, *Foreign Relations of the United States: Diplomatic Papers, 1943* (Washington, DC: GPO, 1965), 562.

U.S. Department of State. *Foreign Relations of the United States: Diplomatic Papers, 1943*. Washington, DC: GPO, 1965.

41. Unpublished dissertation

41. Stephanie Lynn Budin, "The Origins of Aphrodite" (PhD diss., University of Pennsylvania, 2000), 301-2, ProQuest (AAT 9976404).

Budin, Stephanie Lynn. "The Origins of Aphrodite." PhD diss., University of Pennsylvania, 2000. ProQuest (AAT 9976404).

42. Personal communication

42. Sara Lehman, e-mail message to author, August 13, 2009.

Personal communications are not included in the bibliography.

43. Published or broadcast interview

43. Robert Downey Jr., interview by Graham Norton, *The Graham Norton Show*, BBC America, December 14, 2009.

Downey, Robert, Jr. Interview by Graham Norton. *The Graham Norton Show*. BBC America, December 14, 2009.

44. Published proceedings of a conference

44. Julie Kimber, Peter Love, and Phillip Deery, eds., *Labour Traditions: Proceedings of the Tenth National Labour History Conference*, University of Melbourne, Carlton, Victoria, Australia, July 4-6, 2007 (Melbourne: Australian Society for the Study of Labour History, 2007), 5.

Kimber, Julie, Peter Love, and Phillip Deery, eds. *Labour Traditions: Proceedings of the Tenth National Labour History Conference*. University of Melbourne, Carlton, Victoria, Australia, July 4-6, 2007. Melbourne: Australian Society for the Study of Labour History, 2007.

45. Video or DVD

45. *The Secret of Roan Inish*, directed by John Sayles (1993; Culver City, CA: Columbia TriStar Home Video, 2000), DVD.

The Secret of Roan Inish. Directed by John Sayles. 1993; Culver City, CA: Columbia TriStar Home Video, 2000. DVD.

46. Sound recording

46. Gustav Holst, *The Planets*, Royal Philharmonic Orchestra, conducted by André Previn, Telarc 80133, compact disc.

Holst, Gustav. *The Planets*. Royal Philharmonic Orchestra. Conducted by André Previn. Telarc 80133, compact disc.

47. Musical score or composition

47. Antonio Vivaldi, *L'Estro armonico*, op. 3, ed. Eleanor Selfridge-Field (Mineola, NY: Dover, 1999).

Vivaldi, Antonio. *L'Estro armonico*, op. 3. Edited by Eleanor Selfridge-Field. Mineola, NY: Dover, 1999.

48. Work of art

48. Aaron Siskind, *Untitled (The Most Crowded Block)*, gelatin silver print, 1939, Kemper Museum of Contemporary Art, Kansas City, MO.

Siskind, Aaron. *Untitled (The Most Crowded Block)*. Gelatin silver print, 1939. Kemper Museum of Contemporary Art, Kansas City, MO.

49. Performance

49. Robert Schenkkan, *The Kentucky Cycle*, directed by Richard Elliott, Willows Theatre, Concord, CA, August 31, 2007.

Schenkkan, Robert. *The Kentucky Cycle*. Directed by Richard Elliott. Willows Theatre, Concord, CA, August 31, 2007.

hackerhandbooks.com/bedhandbook > Research exercises
> *Chicago* > E-ex 57–12 to 57–19

57e *Chicago* manuscript format

The following guidelines for formatting a *Chicago*-style paper and preparing its endnotes and bibliography are based on *The Chicago Manual of Style*, 16th ed. (Chicago: U of Chicago P, 2010). For a sample paper, see 57f.

Formatting the paper

Chicago manuscript guidelines are fairly generic because they were not created with a specific type of writing in mind.

Materials and font   Use good-quality $8\frac{1}{2}''$ × $11''$ white paper. Avoid a font that is unusual or hard to read.

Title page   Include the full title of your paper, your name, the course title, the instructor's name, and the date. See page 718 for a sample title page.

Pagination Using arabic numerals, number the pages in the upper right corner. Do not number the title page but count it in the manuscript numbering; that is, the first page of the text will be numbered 2. Depending on your instructor's preference, you may also use a short title or your last name before the page numbers to help identify pages.

Margins and line spacing Leave margins of at least one inch at the top, bottom, and sides of the page. Double-space the body of the paper, including long quotations that have been set off from the text. (For line spacing in notes and the bibliography, see p. 716.) Left-align the text.

Capitalization and italics In titles of works, capitalize all words except articles (*a*, *an*, *the*), prepositions (*at*, *from*, *between*, and so on), coordinating conjunctions (*and*, *but*, *or*, *nor*, *for*, *so*, *yet*), and *to* and *as*—unless one of these words is first or last in the title or subtitle. Follow these guidelines in your paper even if the title is styled differently in the source.

Lowercase the first word following a colon even if the word begins a complete sentence. When the colon introduces a series of sentences or questions, capitalize all sentences in the series, including the first.

Italicize the titles of books and other long works. Use quotation marks around the titles of periodical articles, short stories, poems, and other short works.

Long quotations You can choose to set off a long quotation of five to ten typed lines by indenting the entire quotation one-half inch from the left margin. (You should always set off quotations of ten or more lines.) Double-space the quotation; do not use quotation marks. (See pp. 720 and 722 for long quotations in the text of a paper; also see p. 695.)

Visuals *Chicago* classifies visuals as tables and illustrations (illustrations, or figures, include drawings, photographs, maps, and charts). Keep visuals as simple as possible.

Label each table with an arabic numeral (Table 1, Table 2, and so on) and provide a clear title that identifies the table's subject. The label and the title should appear on separate lines above the table, flush left. Below the table, give its source in a note like this one:

> *Source:* Edna Bonacich and Richard P. Appelbaum, *Behind the Label* (Berkeley: University of California Press, 2000), 145.

For each figure, place a label and a caption below the figure, flush left. The label and caption need not appear on separate lines. The word "Figure" may be abbreviated to "Fig."

In the text of your paper, discuss the most significant features of each visual. Place visuals as close as possible to the sentences that relate to them unless your instructor prefers that visuals appear in an appendix.

Web addresses (URLs) When a URL must break across lines, do not insert a hyphen or break at a hyphen if the URL contains one. Instead, break the URL after a colon or a double slash or before any other mark of punctuation. If your word processing program automatically turns URLs into links (by underlining them and changing the color), turn off this feature.

Headings *Chicago* does not provide guidelines for the use of headings in student papers. If you would like to insert headings in a long essay or research paper, check first with your instructor. See the sample *Chicago*-style paper on pages 718–26 for typical placement and formatting of headings.

Preparing the endnotes

Begin the endnotes on a new page at the end of the paper. Center the title Notes about one inch from the top of the page, and number the pages consecutively with the rest of the manuscript. See page 724 for an example.

Indenting and numbering Indent the first line of each note one-half inch from the left margin; do not indent additional lines in the note. Begin the note with the arabic numeral that corresponds to the number in the text. Put a period after the number.

Line spacing Single-space each note and double-space between notes (unless your instructor prefers double-spacing throughout).

Preparing the bibliography

Typically, the notes in *Chicago*-style papers are followed by a bibliography, an alphabetically arranged list of all the works cited or consulted. Center the title Bibliography about one inch from the top of the page. Number bibliography pages consecutively with the rest of the paper. See page 726 for a sample bibliography.

Alphabetizing the list Alphabetize the bibliography by the last names of the authors (or editors); when a work has no author or editor, alphabetize it by the first word of the title other than *A*, *An*, or *The*.

If your list includes two or more works by the same author, use three hyphens instead of the author's name in all entries after the first. Arrange the entries alphabetically by title.

Indenting and line spacing Begin each entry at the left margin, and indent any additional lines one-half inch. Single-space each entry and double-space between entries (unless your instructor prefers double-spacing throughout).

57f Sample *Chicago* research paper

Following is a research paper by Ned Bishop, a student in a history class. Bishop was asked to document his paper using *Chicago*-style endnotes and bibliography. In preparing his manuscript, Bishop also followed *Chicago* guidelines.

hackerhandbooks.com/bedhandbook > Model papers > *Chicago* paper: Bishop

Title of paper.

The Massacre at Fort Pillow:

Holding Nathan Bedford Forrest Accountable

Writer's name.

Ned Bishop

Title of course,
instructor's name,
and date.

History 214

Professor Citro

March 22, 2001

Marginal annotations indicate *Chicago*-style formatting and effective writing.

Bishop 2

Although Northern newspapers of the time no doubt exaggerated some of the Confederate atrocities at Fort Pillow, most modern sources agree that a massacre of Union troops took place there on April 12, 1864. It seems clear that Union soldiers, particularly black soldiers, were killed after they had stopped fighting or had surrendered or were being held prisoner. Less clear is the role played by Major General Nathan Bedford Forrest in leading his troops. Although we will never know whether Forrest directly ordered the massacre, evidence suggests that he was responsible for it.

What happened at Fort Pillow?

Fort Pillow, Tennessee, which sat on a bluff overlooking the Mississippi River, had been held by the Union for two years. It was garrisoned by 580 men, 292 of them from United States Colored Heavy and Light Artillery regiments, 285 from the white Thirteenth Tennessee Cavalry. Nathan Bedford Forrest commanded about 1,500 troops.[1]

The Confederates attacked Fort Pillow on April 12, 1864, and had virtually surrounded the fort by the time Forrest arrived on the battlefield. At 3:30 p.m., Forrest demanded the surrender of the Union forces, sending in a message of the sort he had used before: "The conduct of the officers and men garrisoning Fort Pillow has been such as to entitle them to being treated as prisoners of war. . . . Should my demand be refused, I cannot be responsible for the fate of your command."[2] Union Major William Bradford, who had replaced Major Booth, killed earlier by sharpshooters, asked for an hour to consider the demand. Forrest, worried that vessels in the river were bringing in more troops, "shortened the time to twenty minutes."[3] Bradford refused to surrender, and Forrest quickly ordered the attack.

The Confederates charged to the fort, scaled the parapet, and fired on the forces within. Victory came quickly, with the Union forces

Thesis asserts Bishop's main point.

Headings, centered, help readers follow the organization.

Statistics are cited with an endnote.

Quotation is cited with an endnote.

Bishop 3

running toward the river or surrendering. Shelby Foote describes the scene like this:

Some kept going, right on into the river, where a number drowned and the swimmers became targets for marksmen on the bluff. Others, dropping their guns in terror, ran back toward the Confederates with their hands up, and of these some were spared as prisoners, while others were shot down in the act of surrender.[4]

In his own official report, Forrest makes no mention of the massacre. He does make much of the fact that the Union flag was not lowered by the Union forces, saying that if his own men had not taken down the flag, "few, if any, would have survived unhurt another volley."[5] However, as Jack Hurst points out and Forrest must have known, in this twenty-minute battle, "Federals running for their lives had little time to concern themselves with a flag."[6]

The federal congressional report on Fort Pillow, which charged the Confederates with appalling atrocities, was strongly criticized by Southerners. Respected writer Shelby Foote, while agreeing that the report was "largely" fabrication, points out that the "casualty figures . . . indicated strongly that unnecessary killing had occurred."[7] In an important article, John Cimprich and Robert C. Mainfort Jr. argue that the most trustworthy evidence is that written within about ten days of the battle, before word of the congressional hearings circulated and Southerners realized the extent of Northern outrage. The article reprints a group of letters and newspaper sources written before April 22 and thus "untainted by the political overtones the controversy later assumed."[8] Cimprich and Mainfort conclude that these sources "support the case for the occurrence of a massacre" but that Forrest's role remains "clouded" because of inconsistencies in testimony.[9]

Margin notes:

Long quotation is set off from text by indenting. Quotation marks are omitted.

Bishop uses a primary source as well as secondary sources.

Quotation is introduced with a signal phrase.

Bishop draws attention to an article that reprints primary sources.

Bishop 4

Did Forrest order the massacre?

We will never really know whether Forrest directly ordered the massacre, but it seems unlikely. True, Confederate soldier Achilles Clark, who had no reason to lie, wrote to his sisters that "I with several others tried to stop the butchery . . . but Gen. Forrest ordered them [Negro and white Union troops] shot down like dogs[,] and the carnage continued."[10] But it is not clear whether Clark heard Forrest giving the orders or was just reporting hearsay. Many Confederates had been shouting "No quarter! No quarter!" and, as Shelby Foote points out, these shouts were "thought by some to be at Forrest's command."[11] A Union soldier, Jacob Thompson, claimed to have seen Forrest order the killing, but when asked to describe the six-foot-two general, he called him "a little bit of a man."[12]

Perhaps the most convincing evidence that Forrest did not order the massacre is that he tried to stop it once it had begun. Historian Albert Castel quotes several eyewitnesses on both the Union and Confederate sides as saying that Forrest ordered his men to stop firing.[13] In a letter to his wife three days after the battle, Confederate soldier Samuel Caldwell wrote that "if General Forrest had not run between our men & the Yanks with his pistol and sabre drawn not a man would have been spared."[14]

In a respected biography of Nathan Bedford Forrest, Hurst suggests that the temperamental Forrest "may have ragingly ordered a massacre and even intended to carry it out—until he rode inside the fort and viewed the horrifying result" and ordered it stopped.[15] While this is an intriguing interpretation of events, even Hurst would probably admit that it is merely speculation.

Can Forrest be held responsible for the massacre?

Even assuming that Forrest did not order the massacre, he can still be held accountable for it. That is because he created an

Topic sentence states the main idea for this section.

Writer presents a balanced view of the evidence.

Topic sentence for this section reinforces the thesis.

Bishop 5

atmosphere ripe for the possibility of atrocities and did nothing
to ensure that it wouldn't happen. Throughout his career Forrest
repeatedly threatened "no quarter," particularly with respect
to black soldiers, so Confederate troops had good reason to
think that in massacring the enemy they were carrying out his
orders. As Hurst writes, "About all he had to do to produce a
massacre was issue no order against one."[16] Dudley Taylor
Cornish agrees:

> It has been asserted again and again that Forrest did not order
> a massacre. He did not need to. He had sought to terrify the
> Fort Pillow garrison by a threat of no quarter, as he had done
> at Union City and at Paducah in the days just before he turned
> on Pillow. If his men did enter the fort shouting "Give them no
> quarter; kill them; kill them; it is General Forrest's orders," he
> should not have been surprised.[17]

The slaughter at Fort Pillow was no doubt driven in large part
by racial hatred. Numbers alone suggest this: of 295 white troops, 168
were taken prisoner, but of 262 black troops, only 58 were taken into
custody, with the rest either dead or too badly wounded to walk.[18] A
Southern reporter traveling with Forrest makes clear that the
discrimination was deliberate: "Our troops maddened by the
excitement, shot down the ret[r]eating Yankees, and not until they
had attained t[h]e water's edge and turned to beg for mercy, did any
prisoners fall in [t]o our hands—Thus the whites received quarter,
but the negroes were shown no mercy."[19] Union surgeon Dr. Charles
Fitch, who was taken prisoner by Forrest, testified that after he was in
custody he "saw" Confederate soldiers "kill every negro that made his
appearance dressed in Federal uniform."[20]

Fort Pillow is not the only instance of a massacre or threatened
massacre of black soldiers by troops under Forrest's command.

Transition sentence links new material to old.

Bishop 6

Biographer Brian Steel Wills points out that at Brice's Cross Roads in June 1864, "black soldiers suffered inordinately" as Forrest looked the other way and Confederate soldiers deliberately sought out those they termed "the damned negroes."[21] Just a day after Fort Pillow, on April 13, 1864, one of Forrest's generals, Abraham Buford, after consulting with Forrest, demanded that the federal garrison in Columbus, Kentucky, surrender. The demand stated that if an attack became necessary, "no quarter will be shown to the negro troops whatever; the white troops will be treated as prisoners of war."[22]

Nathan Bedford Forrest, a crude man who had made his fortune as a slave trader, was noted for both his violence and his hatred of blacks. In the words of historian James M. McPherson, "Forrest possessed a killer instinct toward . . . blacks in any capacity other than slave."[23] Forrest's battle successes were largely due to his brazen tactics—tactics that Hurst says would not have occurred to the "aristocratic, well-educated Confederate military hierarchy."[24] Some Southerners, in fact, found Forrest's leadership style distasteful. As one Mississippi aristocrat put it, "Forrest may be, and no doubt is, the best cavalry officer in the West, but I object to a tyrrannical [*sic*], hot-headed vulgarian's commanding me."[25]

Because he was so crudely racist, Forrest surely understood the rage that his troops felt toward the very idea of blacks as soldiers. Further, he must have known that his standard threats of "No quarter" would fuel the Confederate soldiers' rage. Although Forrest may have tried to prevent the massacre once it was under way, he can still be held accountable for it. That is because he created the conditions that led to the massacre (especially of black troops) and with full knowledge of those conditions took no steps to prevent what was a nearly inevitable bloodbath.

Ellipsis mark indicates that words have been omitted.

Conclusion supports the writer's central argument.

Notes begin on a new page.

Bishop 7

Notes

First line of each note is indented ½".

1. John Cimprich and Robert C. Mainfort Jr., eds., "Fort Pillow Revisited: New Evidence about an Old Controversy," *Civil War History* 28, no. 4 (1982): 293-94.

Note number is not raised and is followed by a period.

2. Quoted in Brian Steel Wills, *A Battle from the Start: The Life of Nathan Bedford Forrest* (New York: HarperCollins, 1992), 182.

3. Ibid., 183.

4. Shelby Foote, *The Civil War, a Narrative: Red River to Appomattox* (New York: Vintage, 1986), 110.

Authors' names are not inverted.

5. Nathan Bedford Forrest, "Report of Maj. Gen. Nathan B. Forrest, C. S. Army, Commanding Cavalry, of the Capture of Fort Pillow," Shotgun's Home of the American Civil War, accessed March 6, 2001, http://www.civilwarhome.com/forrest.htm.

6. Jack Hurst, *Nathan Bedford Forrest: A Biography* (New York: Knopf, 1993), 174.

Last name and title refer to an earlier note by the same author.

7. Foote, *Civil War*, 111.

8. Cimprich and Mainfort, "Fort Pillow," 295.

9. Ibid., 305.

10. Ibid., 299.

11. Foote, *Civil War,* 110.

12. Quoted in Wills, *Battle from the Start*, 187.

Notes are single-spaced, with double-spacing between notes. (Some instructors may prefer double-spacing throughout.)

13. Albert Castel, "The Fort Pillow Massacre: A Fresh Examination of the Evidence," *Civil War History* 4, no. 1 (1958): 44-45.

14. Cimprich and Mainfort, "Fort Pillow," 300.

15. Hurst, *Nathan Bedford Forrest*, 177.

16. Ibid.

Bishop 8

17. Dudley Taylor Cornish, *The Sable Arm: Black Troops in the Union Army, 1861-1865* (Lawrence: University Press of Kansas, 1987), 175.

18. Foote, *Civil War*, 111.

19. Cimprich and Mainfort, "Fort Pillow," 304.

20. Quoted in Wills, *Battle from the Start*, 189.

21. Ibid., 215.

22. Quoted in Hurst, *Nathan Bedford Forrest*, 177.

23. Quoted in James M. McPherson, *Battle Cry of Freedom: The Civil War Era* (New York: Oxford University Press, 1988), 402.

24. Hurst, *Nathan Bedford Forrest*, 74.

25. Quoted in Foote, *Civil War*, 106.

Bibliography begins on a new page.

Bishop 9

Bibliography

Entries are alphabetized by authors' last names.

Castel, Albert. "The Fort Pillow Massacre: A Fresh Examination of the Evidence." *Civil War History* 4, no. 1 (1958): 37-50.

Cimprich, John, and Robert C. Mainfort Jr., eds. "Fort Pillow Revisited: New Evidence about an Old Controversy." *Civil War History* 28, no. 4 (1982): 293-306.

First line of entry is at left margin; additional lines are indented ½".

Cornish, Dudley Taylor. *The Sable Arm: Black Troops in the Union Army, 1861-1865*. Lawrence: University Press of Kansas, 1987.

Foote, Shelby. *The Civil War, a Narrative: Red River to Appomattox*. New York: Vintage, 1986.

Forrest, Nathan Bedford. "Report of Maj. Gen. Nathan B. Forrest, C. S. Army, Commanding Cavalry, of the Capture of Fort Pillow." Shotgun's Home of the American Civil War. Accessed March 6, 2001. http://www.civilwarhome.com/forrest.htm.

Entries are single-spaced, with double-spacing between entries. (Some instructors may prefer double-spacing throughout.)

Hurst, Jack. *Nathan Bedford Forrest: A Biography*. New York: Knopf, 1993.

McPherson, James M. *Battle Cry of Freedom: The Civil War Era*. New York: Oxford University Press, 1988.

Wills, Brian Steel. *A Battle from the Start: The Life of Nathan Bedford Forrest*. New York: HarperCollins, 1992.

Part X
Document Design

727

The term *document* is broad enough to describe anything you might write in a college class, in the business world, and in everyday life. How you design a document (format it for the printed page or for a computer screen) will affect how readers respond to it.

58 Become familiar with the principles of document design.

Good document design promotes readability, but what *readability* means depends on your purpose and audience and perhaps on other elements of your writing situation, such as your subject, length restrictions, or any other specific requirements (see the checklist on p. 9). All of your design choices—formatting options, headings, and lists—should be made with your writing situation in mind. Likewise, different types of visuals—tables, charts, and images—can support your writing if they are used appropriately.

58a Select appropriate format options.

Similar types of documents share similar design features. Taken together, these features—layout, margins and line spacing, alignment, fonts, and font styles—form an appearance that helps to guide readers.

Layout

Most readers have set ideas about how different kinds of documents should look. Advertisements, for example, have a distinctive appearance, as do newsletters and brochures. Instructors have expectations about how a college paper should look (see 59). Employers too expect documents such as letters, résumés, memos, and e-mail messages to be presented in standard ways (see 60).

Unless you have a compelling reason to stray from convention, it's best to choose a document layout that conforms to your readers' expectations. If you're not sure what readers expect, look at examples of the kind of document you are producing.

Margins, line spacing, and alignment

Margins help control the look of a page. For most academic and business documents, leave a margin of one to one and a half inches on all sides. These margins create a visual frame for the text and provide room for annotations, such as an instructor's comments or an editor's suggestions. Tight margins generally make a page crowded and difficult to read.

Most manuscripts in progress are double-spaced to allow room for editing. Final copy is often double-spaced as well, since single-spaced text is less inviting to read. If you are unsure about margin and spacing requirements for your document, check with your instructor or consult documents similar to the one you are writing.

At times, the advantages of wide margins and double-spaced lines are offset by other considerations. For example, most business and technical documents are single-spaced, with double-spacing between paragraphs, to save paper and promote quick scanning. Keep your purpose and audience in mind as you determine appropriate margins and line spacing for your document.

SINGLE-SPACED, UNFORMATTED

DOUBLE-SPACED, FORMATTED

Word processing programs allow you to align text and visuals on a page in four ways:

| LEFT-ALIGNED | RIGHT-ALIGNED | CENTERED | JUSTIFIED |

Most academic and business documents are left-aligned for easy reading.

Fonts

If you have a choice, select a font that fits your writing situation in an easy-to-read size (usually 10 to 12 points). Although offbeat fonts may seem attractive, they slow readers down and can distract them from your ideas. For example, using Comic Sans, a font with a handwritten, childish feel, can make an essay seem too informal or unpolished, regardless of how well it's written. Fonts that are easy to read and appropriate for college and workplace documents include the following: Arial, Courier, Georgia, Times New Roman, and Verdana. Check with your instructor; he or she may expect or prefer a particular font.

Font styles

Font styles—such as **boldface**, *italics*, and <u>underlining</u>—can be useful for calling attention to parts of a document. On the whole, it is best to use restraint when selecting styles. Applying too many different styles within a document can result in busy-looking pages and may confuse readers.

TIP: Never write a document in all capital or all lowercase letters. Doing so can frustrate or annoy readers. Although some readers have become accustomed to instant messages and e-mails that omit capital letters entirely, their absence makes a piece of writing difficult to read.

58b Use headings to guide readers.

You will have little need for headings in short essays, especially if you use paragraphing and clear topic sentences to guide readers. In more complex documents, however, such as longer essays, research papers, business reports, and Web sites, headings can be a useful visual cue for readers.

Headings help readers see at a glance the organization of a document. If more than one level of heading is used, the headings also indicate the hierarchy of ideas—as they do throughout this book.

Headings serve a number of functions, depending on the needs of different readers. When readers are simply looking up information, headings will help them find it quickly. When readers are scanning, hoping to pick up a document's meaning or message, headings will guide them. Even when readers are committed enough to read every word, headings can help them preview a document before they begin reading.

TIP: While headings can be useful, they cannot substitute for transitions between paragraphs (see 3d). Keep this in mind as you write college essays.

Phrasing headings

Headings should be as brief and as informative as possible. Certain styles of headings—the most common being -*ing* phrases, noun phrases, questions, and imperative sentences—work better for some purposes, audiences, and subjects than others.

Whatever style you choose, use it consistently. Headings on the same level of organization should be written in parallel structure (see 9), as in the following examples from a report, a history textbook, a financial brochure, and a nursing manual, respectively.

-*ING* PHRASES AS HEADINGS
Safeguarding the earth's atmosphere
Charting the path to sustainable energy
Conserving global forests

NOUN PHRASES AS HEADINGS
The antiwar movement
The civil rights movement
The feminist movement

QUESTIONS AS HEADINGS
How do I buy shares?
How do I redeem shares?
How has the fund performed in the past three years?

IMPERATIVE SENTENCES AS HEADINGS
Ask the patient to describe current symptoms.
Take a detailed medical history.
Record the patient's vital signs.

Placing and formatting headings

Headings on the same level of organization should be placed and formatted in a consistent way. If you have more than one level of heading, you might center your first-level headings and make them boldface; then you might make the second-level headings left-aligned and italicized, like this:

First-level heading
Second-level heading

A college paper with headings typically has only one level, and the headings are often centered, as in the sample paper on pages 674–83. Business memos often include headings. Important headings can be highlighted by using white space around them. Less important headings can be downplayed by using less white space or by running them into the text.

58c Use lists to guide readers.

Lists are easy to read or scan when they are displayed, item by item, rather than run into your text. You might choose to display the following kinds of lists:

- steps in a process
- advice or recommendations
- items to be discussed
- criteria for evaluation (as in checklists)
- parts of an object

Lists are usually introduced with an independent clause followed by a colon (*All mammals share the following five characteristics:*). Periods are not used after items in a list unless the items are complete sentences. Lists are most readable when they are presented in parallel grammatical form (see 9).

If you are describing a sequence or a set of steps, number your list with arabic numerals (1, 2, 3) followed by periods. If the order of items is not important, you can use bullets (circles or squares) or dashes to draw readers' eyes to a list.

Although lists can be useful visual cues, don't overdo them. Too many will clutter a document.

58d Add visuals to support your purpose.

Visuals can convey information concisely and powerfully. Charts, graphs, and tables, for example, can simplify complex numerical information. Images—including photographs and diagrams—often express an idea more vividly than words can. With access to the Internet, digital photography, and word processing or desktop publishing software, you can download or create your own visuals to enhance your document. Keep in mind that if you download a visual—or use published information to create your own visual—you must credit your source (see 48).

Choosing appropriate visuals

Use visuals to supplement your writing, not to substitute for it. Always consider how a visual supports your purpose and how your audience might respond to it. A student writing about electronic surveillance in the workplace, for example, used a cartoon to illustrate her point about employees' personal use of the Internet at work (see 54c). Another student, writing about treatments for childhood obesity, created a table to display data she had found in two different sources and discussed in her paper (see 56f).

As you draft and revise a document, choose carefully the visuals that support your main point, and avoid overloading your text with too many images. The chart on pages 736–37 describes eight types of visuals and their purposes.

Placing and labeling visuals

A visual may be placed in the text of a document, near a discussion to which it relates, or it can be put in an appendix, labeled, and referred to in the text.

Placing visuals in the text of a document can be tricky. Usually you will want the visual to appear close to the sentences that relate to it, but page breaks won't always allow this placement. At times you may need to insert the visual at a later point and tell readers where it can be found; sometimes you can make the text flow, or wrap, around the visual. No matter where you place a visual, refer to it in your text. Don't expect visuals to speak for themselves.

Making the most of your handbook

Guidelines for using visuals vary by academic discipline.

▶ English and other humanities: 54a
▶ Social sciences: 56e
▶ History: 57e

Most of the visuals you include in a document will require some sort of label. A label, which is typically placed above or below the visual, should be brief but descriptive. Most commonly, a visual is labeled with the word "Figure" or the abbreviation "Fig.," followed by a number: *Fig. 4.* Sometimes a title might be included to explain how the visual relates to the text: *Fig. 4. Voter turnout by age.*

Using visuals responsibly

Most word processing and spreadsheet software will allow you to produce your own visuals. If you create a chart, a table, or a graph using information from your research, you must cite the source of the information even though the visual is your own. The visual on page 735 credits the source of its data.

VISUAL WITH A SOURCE CREDITED

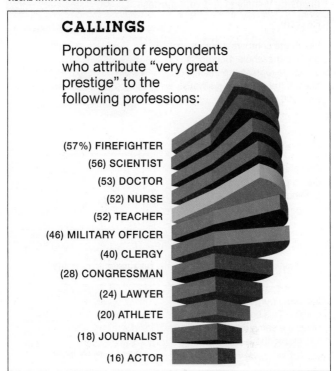

CALLINGS

Proportion of respondents who attribute "very great prestige" to the following professions:

- (57%) FIREFIGHTER
- (56) SCIENTIST
- (53) DOCTOR
- (52) NURSE
- (52) TEACHER
- (46) MILITARY OFFICER
- (40) CLERGY
- (28) CONGRESSMAN
- (24) LAWYER
- (20) ATHLETE
- (18) JOURNALIST
- (16) ACTOR

Source: The New York Times Company, September 21, 2008, from data by the Harris Poll, July 2008.

If you download a photograph from the Web or scan an image from a magazine or book, you must credit the person or organization that created it, just as you would cite any other source you use in a college paper (see 48). Make sure any cropping or other changes you make to the visual do not distort the meaning of the original. If your document is written for publication outside the classroom, you will need to request permission to use any visual you borrow.

Choosing visuals to suit your purpose

Pie chart

Pie charts compare a part or parts to the whole. Segments of the pie represent percentages of the whole (and always total 100 percent).

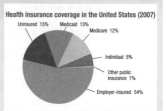

Health insurance coverage in the United States (2007)
Uninsured 15% Medicaid 13% Medicare 12%
Individual 5%
Other public insurance 1%
Employer-insured 54%

Line graph

Line graphs highlight trends over a period of time or compare numerical data.

THE PURSUIT OF PROPERTY
Home ownership rates in the United States
70% 60% 50% 40% 30% 20%
1930 1940 1950 1960 1970 1980 1990 2000

Bar graph

Bar graphs can be used for the same purpose as line graphs. This bar graph displays the same data as in the line graph above.

THE PURSUIT OF PROPERTY
Home ownership rates in the United States
70% 60% 50% 40% 30% 20%
1930 1940 1950 1960 1970 1980 1990 2000

Table

Tables organize complicated numerical information into a digestible format.

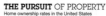

Prices of daily doses of AIDS drugs
($US)

Drug	Brazil	Uganda	Côte d'Ivoire	US
3TC (Lamuvidine)	1.56	3.28	2.95	8.70
ddC (Zalcitabine)	0.24	4.17	3.75	8.80
Didanosine	2.04	5.26	3.48	7.25
Efavirenz	6.96	n/a	6.41	13.13
Indinavir	10.32	12.79	9.07	14.93
Nelfinavir	4.14	4.45	4.39	6.47
Nevirapine	5.04	n/a	n/a	8.48
Saquinavir	8.24	7.37	5.52	6.50
Stavudine	0.56	6.19	4.10	9.07
ZDV/3TC	1.44	7.34	n/a	18.78
Zidovudine	1.08	4.34	2.43	10.12

Source: UNAIDS, 2000

Sources [top to bottom]: Kaiser Foundation; US Census Bureau; US Census Bureau; UNAIDS.

Photograph

Photographs vividly depict people, scenes, or objects discussed in a text.

Diagram

Diagrams, useful in scientific and technical writing, concisely illustrate processes, structures, or interactions.

Flowchart

Flowcharts show structures or steps in a process. (See also p. 227 for another example of a flowchart.)

Map

Maps indicate distances, historical information, or demographics.

Sources [top to bottom]: Fred Zwicky; NIAMS; Arizona Board of Regents; Lynn Hunt et al.

59 Use standard academic formatting.

Instructors have certain expectations about how a college paper should look. If your instructor provides guidelines for formatting an essay, a report, a research paper, or another document, you should follow them. Otherwise, use the manuscript format that is recommended for your academic discipline.

In most English and other humanities classes, you will be asked to use the MLA (Modern Language Association) format (see 54a). In most social science classes, such as psychology and sociology, and in most business and health-related classes, you will be asked to use APA (American Psychological Association) format (see 56e). In history and some other humanities classes, you will be asked to use *Chicago* format (see 57e).

Most composition instructors require MLA format, which is illustrated in the sample on pages 739–40. For more detailed MLA manuscript guidelines and a sample MLA-style research paper, see 54.

60 Use standard business formatting.

This section provides guidelines for preparing business letters, résumés, and memos.

60a Use established conventions for business letters.

In writing a business letter, be direct, clear, and courteous, but do not hesitate to be firm if necessary. State your purpose or request at the beginning of the letter and include only relevant information in the body. By being as direct and concise as possible, you show that you value your reader's time.

For the format of the letter, use established business conventions. The sample business letter on page 741 is typed in what is known as *full block* style. Paragraphs are not indented and are typed single-spaced, with double-spacing between them.

MLA ESSAY FORMAT

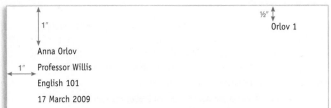

1"

½"
Orlov 1

1"

Anna Orlov

Professor Willis

English 101

17 March 2009

Online Monitoring: Title is centered.

A Threat to Employee Privacy in the Wired Workplace

½" As the Internet has become an integral tool of businesses,

company policies on Internet usage have become as common as

policies regarding vacation days or sexual harassment. A 2005 study by

the American Management Association and ePolicy Institute found that

76% of companies monitor employees' use of the Web, and the number   1"

of companies that block employees' access to certain Web sites has

increased 27% since 2001 (1). Unlike other company rules, however,   Double-spacing is
                                                                        used throughout.
Internet usage policies often include language authorizing companies

to secretly monitor their employees, a practice that raises questions

about rights in the workplace. Although companies often have

legitimate concerns that lead them to monitor employees' Internet

usage—from expensive security breaches to reduced productivity—the

benefits of electronic surveillance are outweighed by its costs to

employees' privacy and autonomy.

While surveillance of employees is not a new phenomenon,

electronic surveillance allows employers to monitor workers with

unprecedented efficiency. In his book *The Naked Employee*, Frederick

Lane describes offline ways in which employers have been permitted

to intrude on employees' privacy for decades, such as drug testing,

background checks, psychological exams, lie detector tests, and in-store

video surveillance. The difference, Lane argues, between these old

methods of data gathering and electronic surveillance involves quantity:

1"

MLA ESSAY FORMAT (*continued*)

Heading is centered.

½″
1″
Orlov 6

Works Cited

Adams, Scott. *Dilbert and the Way of the Weasel*. New York: Harper, 2002. Print.

American Management Association and ePolicy Institute. "2005 Electronic Monitoring and Surveillance Survey." *American Management Association*. Amer. Management Assn., 2005. Web. 15 Feb. 2009.

"Automatically Record Everything They Do Online! Spector Pro 5.0 FAQ's." *Netbus.org*. Netbus.Org, n.d. Web. 17 Feb. 2009.

Flynn, Nancy. "Internet Policies." *ePolicy Institute*. ePolicy Inst., n.d. Web. 15 Feb. 2009.

Frauenheim, Ed. "Stop Reading This Headline and Get Back to Work." *CNET News.com*. CNET Networks, 11 July 2005. Web. 17 Feb. 2009.

Gonsalves, Chris. "Wasting Away on the Web." *eWeek.com*. Ziff Davis Enterprise Holdings, 8 Aug. 2005. Web. 16 Feb. 2009.

Kesan, Jay P. "Cyber-Working or Cyber-Shirking? A First Principles Examination of Electronic Privacy in the Workplace." *Florida Law Review* 54.2 (2002): 289-332. Print.

Double-spacing is used throughout; no extra space between entries.

Lane, Frederick S., III. *The Naked Employee: How Technology Is Compromising Workplace Privacy*. New York: Amer. Management Assn., 2003. Print.

Tam, Pui-Wing, et al. "Snooping E-mail by Software Is Now a Workplace Norm." *Wall Street Journal* 9 Mar. 2005: B1+. Print.

Tynan, Daniel. "Your Boss Is Watching." *PC World*. PC World Communications, 6 Oct. 2004. Web. 17 Feb. 2009.

Verespej, Michael A. "Inappropriate Internet Surfing." *Industry Week*. Penton Media, 7 Feb. 2000. Web. 16 Feb. 2009.

This style is usually preferred when the letter is typed on letterhead stationery, as in the example.

Below the signature, aligned at the left, you may include the abbreviation *Enc.* to indicate that something is enclosed with the letter or the abbreviation *cc* followed by a colon and the name of someone who is receiving a copy of the letter.

BUSINESS LETTER IN FULL BLOCK STYLE

LatinoVoice

March 16, 2009 ⎯⎯⎯ Date

Jonathan Ross
Managing Editor
Latino World Today ⎯⎯⎯ Inside address
2971 East Oak Avenue
Baltimore, MD 21201

Dear Mr. Ross: ⎯⎯⎯ Salutation

Body

Thank you very much for taking the time yesterday to speak to the University of Maryland's Latino Club. A number of students have told me that they enjoyed your presentation and found your job search suggestions to be extremely helpful.

As I mentioned to you when we first scheduled your appearance, the club publishes a monthly newsletter, *Latino Voice*. Our purpose is to share up-to-date information and expert advice with members of the university's Latino population. Considering how much students benefited from your talk, I would like to publish excerpts from it in our newsletter.

I have taken the liberty of transcribing parts of your presentation and organizing them into a question-and-answer format for our readers. When you have a moment, would you mind looking through the enclosed article and letting me know if I may have your permission to print it? I would be happy, of course, to make any changes or corrections that you request. I'm hoping to include this article in our next newsletter, so I would need your response by April 4.

Once again, Mr. Ross, thank you for sharing your experiences with us. You gave an informative and entertaining speech, and I would love to be able to share it with the students who couldn't hear it in person.

Sincerely, ⎯⎯⎯ Close

Jeffrey Richardson

⎯⎯⎯ Signature

Jeffrey Richardson
Associate Editor

Enc.

210 Student Center University of Maryland College Park MD 20742

60b Write effective résumés and cover letters.

An effective résumé gives relevant information in a clear and concise form. You may be asked to produce a traditional résumé, a scannable résumé, or a Web résumé. The cover letter gives a prospective employer a reason to look at your résumé. The trick is to present yourself in a favorable light without including unnecessary details.

Cover letters Always include a cover letter to introduce yourself, state the position you seek, and tell where you learned about it. The letter should also highlight past experiences that qualify you for the position and emphasize what you can do for the employer (not what the job will do for you). End the letter with a suggestion for a meeting, and tell your prospective employer when you will be available.

Traditional résumés Traditional résumés are produced on paper, and they are screened by people, not by computers. Because screeners often face stacks of applications, they may spend very little time looking at each résumé. Therefore, you will need to make your résumé as reader-friendly as possible. Here are a few guidelines:

- Limit your résumé to one page if possible, two pages at the most. (If your résumé is longer than a page, repeat your name at the top of the second page.)

- Organize your information into clear categories—Education, Experience, and so on.

- Present the information in each category in reverse chronological order to highlight your most recent accomplishments.

- Use bulleted lists or some other simple, clear visual device to organize information.

- Use strong, active verbs to state your accomplishments. Use present-tense verbs (*manage*) for current activities and past-tense verbs (*managed*) for past activities.

TRADITIONAL RÉSUMÉ

Jeffrey Richardson
121 Knox Road, #6
College Park, MD 20740
301–555–2651
jrichardson@jrichardson.localhost

OBJECTIVE	To obtain an editorial internship with a magazine
EDUCATION	
Fall 2006–present	University of Maryland
	• BA expected in June 2010
	• Double major: English and Latin American studies
	• GPA: 3.7 (on a 4-point scale)
EXPERIENCE	
Fall 2008–present	Associate editor, *Latino Voice*, newsletter of Latino Club
	• Assign and edit feature articles
	• Coordinate community outreach
Fall 2007–present	Photo editor, *The Diamondback*, college paper
	• Shoot and organize photos for print and online publication
	• Oversee photo staff assignments; evaluate photos
Summer 2008	Intern, *The Globe,* Fairfax, Virginia
	• Wrote stories about local issues and personalities
	• Interviewed political candidates
	• Edited and proofread copy
	• Coedited "The Landscapes of Northern Virginia: A Photoessay"
Summers 2007, 2008	Tutor, Fairfax County ESL Program
	• Tutored Latino students in English as a Second Language
	• Trained new tutors
ACTIVITIES	Photographers' Workshop, Latino Club
PORTFOLIO	Available at http://jrichardson.localhost/jrportfolio.htm
REFERENCES	Available on request

Scannable résumés Scannable résumés might be submitted on paper, by e-mail, or through an online employment service. The résumés are scanned and searched electronically, and a database matches keywords in the job description with keywords in the résumés. A human screener reads the résumés selected by the database.

In general, follow these guidelines when preparing a scannable résumé:

- Include a Keywords section that lists words likely to be searched by a scanner. Use nouns (*manager*), not verbs (*manage* or *managed*).
- Use standard résumé headings (for example, Education, Experience, References).
- Avoid special characters, graphics, or font styles.
- Avoid formatting such as tabs, indents, columns, or tables.

Web résumés Posting your résumé on a Web site is an easy way to provide recent information about your goals and accomplishments. Most guidelines for traditional résumés apply to Web résumés; keep the following guidelines in mind as well.

- Make the opening screen of your Web site simple and concise. Provide links to your résumé and to any other relevant pages, such as an electronic portfolio.
- Consider providing your résumé in HTML format and as a PDF file.
- Include your name, address, phone number, and e-mail address at the top of your résumé page.
- Always list the date that you last updated the résumé.

60c Write clear and concise memos.

Usually brief and to the point, a memo reports information, makes a request, or recommends an action. The format of a memo, which varies from company to company, is designed for easy distribution, quick reading, and efficient filing.

BUSINESS MEMO

COMMONWEALTH PRESS

MEMORANDUM

February 26, 2009

To:	Editorial assistants, Advertising Department
cc:	Stephen Chapman
From:	Helen Brown
Subject:	New database software

The new database software will be installed on your computers
next week. I have scheduled a training program to help you become
familiar with the software and with our new procedures for data entry
and retrieval.

Training program
A member of our IT staff will teach in-house workshops on how to
use the new software. If you try the software before the workshop,
please be prepared to discuss any problems you encounter.

We will keep the training groups small to encourage hands-on
participation and to provide individual attention. The workshops will
take place in the training room on the third floor from 10:00 a.m. to
2:00 p.m.

Lunch will be provided in the cafeteria.

Sign-up
Please sign up by March 1 for one of the following dates by adding
your name in the department's online calendar:

- Wednesday, March 4
- Friday, March 6
- Monday, March 9

If you will not be in the office on any of those dates, please let me
know by March 1.

Most memos display the date, the name of the recipient, the name of the sender, and the subject on separate lines at the top. Many companies have preprinted forms for memos, and most word processing programs have memo templates. Memos are often distributed via e-mail.

The subject line of a memo, on paper or in e-mail, should describe the topic as clearly and concisely as possible, and the introductory paragraph should get right to the point. In addition, the body of the memo should be well organized and easy to skim. To promote skimming, use headings where possible and set off any items that deserve special attention (in a list, for example, or in boldface). A sample memo appears on page 745.

60d Write effective e-mail messages.

In business and academic contexts, you will want to show readers that you value their time. Your e-mail message may be just one of many that your readers have to wade through. Here are some strategies for writing effective e-mails:

- Use a meaningful, concise subject line to help readers sort through messages and set priorities.
- Put the most important part of your message at the beginning so it will be seen without scrolling.
- For long, detailed messages, provide a summary at the beginning.
- Write concisely, and keep paragraphs fairly short.
- Avoid writing in all capital letters or all lowercase letters.
- Use an appropriate tone.
- Before forwarding an e-mail message, check that the original sender has no objections.
- Be sparing with boldface, italics, and special characters; not all e-mail systems handle such elements consistently.
- Proofread for typos and obvious errors that are likely to slow down readers.

Part XI
Grammar Basics

61 Parts of speech

Traditional grammar recognizes eight parts of speech: noun, pronoun, verb, adjective, adverb, preposition, conjunction, and interjection. Many words can function as more than one part of speech. For example, depending on its use in a sentence, the word *paint* can be a noun (*The paint is wet*) or a verb (*Please paint the ceiling next*).

A quick-reference chart of the parts of speech appears on pages 760–62.

61a Nouns

A noun is the name of a person, place, thing, or concept.

> N   N   N
> The *lion* in the *cage* growled at the *zookeeper*.

Nouns sometimes function as adjectives modifying other nouns. Because of their dual roles, nouns used in this manner may be called *noun/adjectives*.

> N/ADJ   N/ADJ
> The *leather* notebook was tucked in the *student's* backpack.

Nouns are classified in a variety of ways. *Proper* nouns are capitalized, but *common* nouns are not (see 45a). For clarity, writers choose between *concrete* and *abstract* nouns (see 18b). The distinction between *count* nouns and *noncount* nouns can be especially helpful to multilingual writers (see 29a). Most nouns have singular and plural forms; *collective* nouns may be either singular or plural, depending on how they are used (see 21f and 22b). *Possessive* nouns require an apostrophe (see 36a).

EXERCISE 61–1 Underline the nouns (and noun/adjectives) in the following sentences. Answers to lettered sentences appear in the back of the book. Example:

The best <u>part</u> of <u>dinner</u> was the <u>chef's</u> newest <u>dessert.</u>

a. The stage was set for a confrontation of biblical proportions.
b. The courage of the mountain climber was an inspiration to the rescuers.
c. The need to arrive before the guest of honor motivated us to navigate the thick fog.
d. The defense attorney made a final appeal to the jury.
e. A national museum dedicated to women artists opened in 1987.

1. Truthfulness is a virtue lacking in many public officials.
2. The Wright Brothers used a wind tunnel to test their airplane designs.
3. The miners' work clothes were clogged with fine black dust.
4. Virginia Woolf wrote that women needed their own income and their own space.
5. The child's language was a charming combination of her father's English and her mother's French.

hackerhandbooks.com/bedhandbook > Grammar exercises > Grammar basics
> E-ex 61–5 and 61–6

61b Pronouns

A pronoun is a word used in place of a noun. Usually the pronoun substitutes for a specific noun, known as its *antecedent*.

When the *battery* wears down, we recharge *it*.

Although most pronouns function as substitutes for nouns, some can function as adjectives modifying nouns. Because they have the form of a pronoun and the function of an adjective, such pronouns may be called *pronoun/adjectives*.

PN / ADJ
This bird was at the same window yesterday morning.

Pronouns are classified as personal, possessive, intensive and reflexive, relative, interrogative, demonstrative, indefinite, and reciprocal.

Personal pronouns   Personal pronouns refer to specific persons or things. They always function as noun equivalents.

Singular: I, me, you, she, her, he, him, it

Plural: we, us, you, they, them

Possessive pronouns Possessive pronouns indicate ownership.

Singular: my, mine, your, yours, her, hers, his, its

Plural: our, ours, your, yours, their, theirs

Some of these possessive pronouns function as adjectives modifying nouns: *my*, *your*, *his*, *her*, *its*, *our*, *their*.

Intensive and reflexive pronouns Intensive pronouns emphasize a noun or another pronoun (The senator *herself* met us at the door). Reflexive pronouns, which have the same form as intensive pronouns, name a receiver of an action identical with the doer of the action (Paula cut *herself*).

Singular: myself, yourself, himself, herself, itself

Plural: ourselves, yourselves, themselves

Relative pronouns Relative pronouns introduce subordinate clauses functioning as adjectives (The writer *who won the award* refused to accept it). In addition to introducing the clause, the relative pronoun, in this case *who*, points back to a noun or pronoun that the clause modifies (*writer*). (See 63e.)

who, whom, whose, which, that

Some textbooks also treat *whichever*, *whoever*, *whomever*, *what*, and *whatever* as relative pronouns. These words introduce noun clauses; they do not point back to a noun or pronoun. (See "Noun clauses" in 63e.)

Interrogative pronouns Interrogative pronouns introduce questions (*Who* is expected to win the election?).

who, whom, whose, which, what

Demonstrative pronouns Demonstrative pronouns identify or point to nouns. Frequently they function as adjectives (*This* chair is my favorite), but they may also function as noun equivalents (*This* is my favorite chair).

> this, that, these, those

Indefinite pronouns Indefinite pronouns refer to nonspecific persons or things. Most are always singular (*everyone*, *each*); some are always plural (*both*, *many*); a few may be singular or plural (see 21e). Most indefinite pronouns function as noun equivalents (*Something* is burning), but some can also function as adjectives (*All* campers must check in at the lodge).

all	anything	everyone	nobody	several
another	both	everything	none	some
any	each	few	no one	somebody
anybody	either	many	nothing	someone
anyone	everybody	neither	one	something

Reciprocal pronouns Reciprocal pronouns refer to individual parts of a plural antecedent (By turns, the penguins fed *one another*).

> each other, one another

NOTE: Pronouns can cause a variety of problems for writers. See pronoun-antecedent agreement (22), pronoun reference (23), distinguishing between pronouns such as *I* and *me* (24), and distinguishing between *who* and *whom* (25).

EXERCISE 61–2 Underline the pronouns (and pronoun/adjectives) in the following sentences. Answers to lettered sentences appear in the back of the book. Example:

> <u>We</u> were intrigued by the video <u>that</u> the fifth graders
>
> produced as <u>their</u> final technology project.

a. The governor's loyalty was his most appealing trait.
b. In the fall, the geese that fly south for the winter pass through our town in huge numbers.
c. Carl Sandburg once said that even he himself did not understand some of his poetry.
d. I appealed my parking ticket, but you did not get one.
e. Angela did not mind gossip as long as no one gossiped about her.

1. The Tigers stood unhappily in front of their dugout while the victorious Jaguars tossed their hats in the air.
2. Nothing fascinated the toddler like something that was not his.
3. We understood that we were expected to submit our dissertations in triplicate.
4. The trick-or-treaters helped themselves to their neighbors' candy.
5. She found herself peering into the mouth of a creepy cave.

hackerhandbooks.com/bedhandbook > Grammar exercises > Grammar basics
> E-ex 61–7 and 61–8

61c Verbs

The verb of a sentence usually expresses action (*jump, think*) or being (*is, become*). It is composed of a main verb possibly preceded by one or more helping verbs.

MV
The horses *exercise* every day.

HV   MV
The task force report *was* not *completed* on schedule.

HV HV   MV
No one *has been defended* with more passion than our pastor.

Notice that words, usually adverbs, can intervene between the helping verb and the main verb (was *not* completed). (See 61e.)

Helping verbs

There are twenty-three helping verbs in English: forms of *have, do,* and *be,* which may also function as main verbs; and nine modals, which function only as helping verbs. *Have, do,* and *be* change form to indicate tense; the nine modals do not.

FORMS OF *HAVE*, *DO*, AND *BE*

have, has, had

do, does, did

be, am, is, are, was, were, being, been

MODALS

can, could, may, might, must, shall, should, will, would

The verb phrase *ought to* is often classified as a modal as well.

Main verbs

The main verb of a sentence is always the kind of word that would change form if put into these test sentences:

BASE FORM	Usually I (*walk*, *ride*).
PAST TENSE	Yesterday I (*walked*, *rode*).
PAST PARTICIPLE	I have (*walked*, *ridden*) many times before.
PRESENT PARTICIPLE	I am (*walking*, *riding*) right now.
-S FORM	Usually he / she / it (*walks*, *rides*).

If a word doesn't change form when slipped into the test sentences, you can be certain that it is not a main verb. For example, the noun *revolution*, though it may seem to suggest an action, can never function as a main verb. Just try to make it behave like one (*Today I revolution . . . Yesterday I revolutioned . . .*) and you'll see why.

When both the past-tense and the past-participle forms of a verb end in *-ed*, the verb is regular (*walked*, *walked*). Otherwise, the verb is irregular (*rode*, *ridden*). (See 27a.)

The verb *be* is highly irregular, having eight forms instead of the usual five: the base form *be*; the present-tense forms *am*, *is*, and *are*; the past-tense forms *was* and *were*; the present participle *being*; and the past participle *been*.

Helping verbs combine with the various forms of main verbs to create tenses. For a survey of tenses, see 27f.

NOTE: Some verbs are followed by words that look like prepositions but are so closely associated with the verb that they are a part of its meaning. These words are known as *particles*. Common verb-particle combinations include *bring up*, *call off*, *drop off*, *give in*, *look up*, *run into*, and *take off*.

> Sharon *packed up* her broken laptop and *sent* it *off* to the repair shop.

TIP: You can find more information about using verbs in other sections of the handbook: active verbs (8), subject-verb agreement (21), standard English verb forms (27), verb tense and mood (27f and 27g), and ESL challenges with verbs (28).

EXERCISE 61–3   Underline the verbs in the following sentences, including helping verbs and particles. If a verb is part of a contraction (such as *is* in *isn't* or *would* in *I'd*), underline only the letters that represent the verb. Answers to lettered sentences appear in the back of the book. Example:

> **The ground under the pine trees <u>wasn't</u> wet from the rain.**

a.   My grandmother always told me a soothing story before bed.
b.   There were fifty apples on the tree before the frost killed them.
c.   Morton brought down the box of letters from the attic.
d.   Stay on the main road and you'll arrive at the base camp before us.
e.   The fish struggled vigorously but was trapped in the net.

1.   Do not bring that issue up again.
2.   Galileo lived the last years of his life under house arrest because of his revolutionary theories about the universe.
3.   Cynthia asked for a raise, but she didn't expect one immediately.
4.   We should plant the roses early this year.
5.   The documentary was engrossing. It humanized World War II.

hackerhandbooks.com/bedhandbook > Grammar exercises > Grammar basics
> E-ex 61–9 and 61–10

61d Adjectives

An adjective is a word used to modify, or describe, a noun or pronoun. An adjective usually answers one of these questions: Which one? What kind of? How many?

ADJ
the *frisky* horse [Which horse?]

ADJ   ADJ
cracked old plates [What kind of plates?]

ADJ
nine months [How many months?]

Adjectives usually precede the words they modify. They may also follow linking verbs, in which case they describe the subject. (See 62b.)

ADJ
The decision was *unpopular.*

The definite article *the* and the indefinite articles *a* and *an* are also classified as adjectives.

ART   ART   ART
A defendant should be judged on *the* evidence provided to *the* jury, not on hearsay.

Some possessive, demonstrative, and indefinite pronouns can function as adjectives: *their, its, this, all* (see 61b). And nouns can function as adjectives when they modify other nouns: *apple pie* (the noun *apple* modifies the noun *pie*; see 61a).

TIP: You can find more details about using adjectives in 26. If you are a multilingual writer, you may also find help with articles and specific uses of adjectives in 29, 30g, and 30h.

61e Adverbs

An adverb is a word used to modify, or qualify, a verb (or verbal), an adjective, or another adverb. It usually answers one of these questions: When? Where? How? Why? Under what conditions? To what degree?

Pull *firmly* on the emergency handle. [Pull how?]

Read the text *first* and *then* work the exercises. [Read when? Work when?]

Adverbs modifying adjectives or other adverbs usually intensify or limit the intensity of the word they modify.

ADV   ADV

Be *extremely* kind, and you will *probably* have many friends.

Adverbs modifying adjectives and other adverbs are not movable. It is not correct to write "Be kind *extremely*" or "*Extremely* be kind."

Adverbs can modify prepositional phrases, subordinate clauses, or whole sentences (independent clauses).

The budget is *barely* on target.

We will try to attend, *especially* if you will be there.

Certainly Joe did not intend to insult you.

The negators *not* and *never* are classified as adverbs. A word such as *cannot* contains the helping verb *can* and the adverb *not*. A contraction such as *can't* contains the helping verb *can* and a contracted form of the adverb *not*.

TIP: You can find more details about using adverbs in 26b–26d. Multilingual writers can find more about the placement of adverbs in 30f.

EXERCISE 61–4 Underline the adjectives and circle the adverbs in the following sentences. If a word is a noun or pronoun functioning as an adjective, underline it and mark it as a noun/adjective or pronoun/adjective. Also treat the articles *a*, *an*, and *the* as adjectives. Answers to lettered sentences appear in the back of the book. Example:

Searching for <u>an</u> <u>available</u> room during <u>the</u> convention

was (not) <u>an</u> <u>easy</u> task.

a. Generalizations lead to weak, unfocused essays.
b. The Spanish language is wonderfully flexible.
c. The wildflowers smelled especially fragrant after the steady rain.
d. I'd rather be slightly hot than bitterly cold.
e. The cat slept soundly in its wicker basket.

1. Success can be elusive to those who object to working hard.
2. After three hours, the discussion had dwindled from a lively sprint to a tedious crawl.
3. She made a fairly earnest attempt at solving the most difficult calculus problems.
4. The black bear sniffed eagerly at the broken honeycomb.
5. The bacteria in the dish grew steadily over twenty-four hours.

hackerhandbooks.com/bedhandbook > Grammar exercises > Grammar basics
> E-ex 61–11 to 61–14

61f Prepositions

A preposition is a word placed before a noun or pronoun to form a phrase modifying another word in the sentence. The prepositional phrase nearly always functions as an adjective or as an adverb.

P   P   P
The road *to* the summit travels *past* craters *from* an extinct volcano.

To the summit functions as an adjective modifying the noun *road*; *past craters* functions as an adverb modifying the verb *travels*; *from an extinct volcano* functions as an adjective modifying the noun *craters*. (For more on prepositional phrases, see 63a.)

English has a limited number of prepositions. The most common are included in the following list.

about	beside	from	outside	toward
above	besides	in	over	under
across	between	inside	past	underneath
after	beyond	into	plus	unlike
against	but	like	regarding	until
along	by	near	respecting	unto
among	concerning	next	round	up
around	considering	of	since	upon
as	despite	off	than	with
at	down	on	through	within
before	during	onto	throughout	without
behind	except	opposite	till	
below	for	out	to	

Some prepositions are more than one word long. *Along with,
as well as, in addition to, next to,* and *rather than* are common
examples.

TIP: Prepositions are used in idioms such as *capable of* and *try to*
(see 18d). For a discussion of specific issues for multilingual
writers, see 31.

61g Conjunctions

Conjunctions join words, phrases, or clauses, and they indicate the relation between the elements joined.

Coordinating conjunctions A coordinating conjunction is
used to connect grammatically equal elements. The coordinating conjunctions are *and, but, or, nor, for, so,* and *yet.*

> The sociologist interviewed children *but* not their parents.
>
> Write clearly, *and* your readers will appreciate your efforts.

In the first sentence, *but* connects two noun phrases; in the
second, *and* connects two independent clauses.

Correlative conjunctions Correlative conjunctions come in
pairs. Like coordinating conjunctions, they connect grammatically equal elements.

> either . . . or　　　　　　whether . . . or
> neither . . . nor　　　　　both . . . and
> not only . . . but also
>
> *Either* the painting was brilliant *or* it was a forgery.

Subordinating conjunctions A subordinating conjunction introduces a subordinate clause and indicates the relation of the
clause to the rest of the sentence. (See 63e.) The most common subordinating conjunctions are *after, although, as, as if,*

because, *before*, *if*, *in order that*, *once*, *since*, *so that*, *than*, *that*, *though*, *unless*, *until*, *when*, *where*, *whether*, and *while*.

> *When* the fundraiser ends, we expect to have raised more than half a million dollars.

Conjunctive adverbs   Conjunctive adverbs connect independent clauses and indicate the relation between the clauses. They can be used with a semicolon to join two independent clauses in one sentence, or they can be used alone with an independent clause. The most common conjunctive adverbs are *finally*, *furthermore*, *however*, *moreover*, *nevertheless*, *similarly*, *then*, *therefore*, and *thus*. (See p. 762 for a longer list.)

> The photographer failed to take a light reading; *therefore*, all the pictures were underexposed.
>
> During the day, the kitten sleeps peacefully. *However*, when night falls, the kitten is wide awake and ready to play.

Conjunctive adverbs can appear at the beginning or in the middle of a clause.

> When night falls, *however*, the kitten is wide awake and ready to play.

TIP: The ability to distinguish between conjunctive adverbs and coordinating conjunctions will help you avoid run-on sentences and make punctuation decisions (see 20, 32a, and 32b). The ability to recognize subordinating conjunctions will help you avoid sentence fragments (see 19).

61h Interjections

An interjection is a word used to express surprise or emotion (*Oh! Hey! Wow!*).

hackerhandbooks.com/bedhandbook > Grammar exercises > Grammar basics
> E-ex 61–15 and 61–16

Parts of speech

- A **noun** names a person, place, thing, or concept.

  Repetition does not transform a *lie* into *truth*.
  (N, N, N)

- A **pronoun** substitutes for a noun.

  Before the attendant let *us* board the small plane, *he* weighed *us* and *our* baggage.
  (PN, PN, PN, PN)

  Personal pronouns: I, me, you, he, him, she, her, it, we, us, they, them

  Possessive pronouns: my, mine, your, yours, her, hers, his, its, our, ours, their, theirs

  Intensive and reflexive pronouns: myself, yourself, himself, herself, itself, ourselves, yourselves, themselves

  Relative pronouns: that, which, who, whom, whose

  Interrogative pronouns: who, whom, whose, which, what

  Demonstrative pronouns: this, that, these, those

  Indefinite pronouns

all	each	many	one
another	either	neither	several
any	everybody	nobody	some
anybody	everyone	none	somebody
anyone	everything	no one	someone
anything	few	nothing	something
both			

  Reciprocal pronouns: each other, one another

- A **helping verb** comes before a main verb.

  Modals: can, could, may, might, must, shall, should, will, would (*also* ought to)

Forms of *be*: be, am, is, are, was, were, being, been

Forms of *have*: have, has, had

Forms of *do*: do, does, did

(The forms of *be*, *have*, and *do* may also function as main verbs.)

- A **main verb** shows action or a state of being.

MV

The novel *opens* with a tense description of a grim murder, but

HV   MV

the author *does* not *maintain* the initial level of suspense.

A main verb will always change form when put into these positions in sentences:

Usually I _____ .   (*walk*, *ride*)
Yesterday I _____ .   (*walked*, *rode*)
I have _____ many times before.   (*walked*, *ridden*)
I am _____ right now.   (*walking*, *riding*)
Usually he _____ .   (*walks*, *rides*)

The highly irregular verb *be* has eight forms: *be*, *am*, *is*, *are*, *was*, *were*, *being*, *been*.

- An **adjective** modifies a noun or pronoun, usually answering one of these questions: Which one? What kind of? How many? The articles *a*, *an*, and *the* are also adjectives.

PN/ADJ N/ADJ ADJ   ADJ   PN/ADJ
Our family's strong ties gave us *welcome* comfort in *our* grief.

- An **adverb** modifies a verb, an adjective, or an adverb, usually answering one of these questions: When? Where? Why? How? Under what conditions? To what degree?

                ADV   ADV
Young people *often* approach history *skeptically.*

- A **preposition** indicates the relationship between the noun or pronoun that follows it and another word in the sentence.

        P   P
A journey *of* a thousand miles begins *with* a single step.

Parts of speech, *continued*

Common prepositions

about	besides	like	since
above	between	near	than
across	beyond	next	through
after	but	next to	throughout
against	by	of	till
along	concerning	off	to
along with	considering	on	toward
among	despite	onto	under
around	down	opposite	underneath
as	during	out	unlike
as well as	except	outside	until
at	for	over	unto
because of	from	past	up
before	in	plus	upon
behind	in addition to	rather than	with
below	inside	regarding	within
beside	into	respecting	without

- A **conjunction** connects words or word groups.

  Coordinating conjunctions: and, but, or, nor, for, so, yet

  Subordinating conjunctions: after, although, as, as if, because, before, even though, if, in order that, once, since, so that, than, that, though, unless, until, when, where, whether, while

  Correlative conjunctions: either . . . or; neither . . . nor; not only . . . but also; both . . . and; whether . . . or

  Conjunctive adverbs: accordingly, also, anyway, besides, certainly, consequently, conversely, finally, furthermore, hence, however, incidentally, indeed, instead, likewise, meanwhile, moreover, nevertheless, next, nonetheless, now, otherwise, similarly, specifically, still, subsequently, then, therefore, thus

- An **interjection** expresses surprise or emotion (*Oh! Wow! Hooray!*).

62 Sentence patterns

Most English sentences flow from subject to verb to any objects or complements. The vast majority of sentences conform to one of these five patterns:

subject / verb / subject complement

subject / verb / direct object

subject / verb / indirect object / direct object

subject / verb / direct object / object complement

subject / verb

Adverbial modifiers (single words, phrases, or clauses) may be added to any of these patterns, and they may appear nearly anywhere—at the beginning, the middle, or the end.

Predicate is the grammatical term given to the verb plus its objects, complements, and adverbial modifiers.

For a quick-reference chart of sentence patterns, see page 769.

62a Subjects

The subject of a sentence names who or what the sentence is about. The *complete subject* is usually composed of a *simple subject*, always a noun or pronoun, plus any words or word groups modifying the simple subject.

The complete subject

To find the complete subject, ask Who? or What?, insert the verb, and finish the question. The answer is the complete subject.

├─────── COMPLETE SUBJECT ───────┤
The devastating effects of famine can last for many years.

Who or what lasts for many years? *The devastating effects of famine.*

COMPLETE SUBJECT
Adventure novels that contain multiple subplots are often made into successful movies.

Who or what are made into movies? *Adventure novels that contain multiple subplots*.

COMPLETE SUBJECT
Within one city neighborhood, income levels can vary greatly.

Who or what can vary greatly? *Income levels*. Notice that *Within one city neighborhood, income levels* is not a sensible answer to the question. *Within one city neighborhood* is a prepositional phrase modifying the verb *can vary*. Since sentences frequently open with such modifiers, it is not safe to assume that the subject must always appear first in a sentence.

The simple subject

To find the simple subject, strip away all modifiers in the complete subject. This includes single-word modifiers such as *the* and *devastating*, phrases such as *of famine*, and subordinate clauses such as *that contain multiple subplots*.

SS
The devastating effects of famine can last for many years.

SS
Adventure novels that contain multiple subplots are often made into successful movies.

SS
Within one city neighborhood, *income levels* can vary greatly.

A sentence may have a compound subject containing two or more simple subjects joined with a coordinating conjunction such as *and*, *but*, or *or*.

SS   SS
Great commitment and a little luck make a successful actor.

Understood subjects

In imperative sentences, which give advice or issue commands, the subject is understood but not actually present in the sentence. The subject of an imperative sentence is understood to be *you*.

[*You*] Put your clothes in the hamper.

Subject after the verb

Although the subject ordinarily comes before the verb (*the planes took off*) occasionally it does not. When a sentence begins with *There is* or *There are* (or *There was* or *There were*), the subject follows the verb. The word *There* is an expletive in such inverted constructions, an empty word serving merely to get the sentence started.

┌─ SS ─┐
There are *eight planes waiting to take off.*

Occasionally a writer will invert a sentence for effect.

┌─ SS ─┐
Joyful is *the child whose school closes for snow.*

Joyful is an adjective, so it cannot be the subject. Turn this sentence around and its structure becomes obvious.

The *child* whose school closes for snow is joyful.

In questions, the subject frequently appears in an unusual position, sandwiched between parts of the verb.

┌──── SS ────┐
Do *Kenyan marathoners* train year-round?

Turn the question into a statement, and the words will appear in their usual order: *Kenyan marathoners do train year-round.* (*Do train* is the verb.)

For more about unusual sentence patterns, see 62c.

TIP: The ability to recognize the subject of a sentence will help you edit for a variety of problems: sentence fragments (19), subject-verb agreement (21), choice of pronouns such as *I* and *me* (24), missing subjects (30b), and repeated subjects (30c).

EXERCISE 62–1 In the following sentences, underline the complete subject and write *SS* above the simple subject(s). If the subject is an understood *you*, insert *you* in parentheses. Answers to lettered sentences appear in the back of the book. Example:

$\overset{SS}{\underline{\text{Parents}}}$ and their $\overset{SS}{\underline{\text{children}}}$ often look alike.

a. The hills and mountains seemed endless, and the snow atop them glistened.
b. In foil fencing, points are scored by hitting an electronic target.
c. Do not stand in the aisles or sit on the stairs.
d. There were hundreds of fireflies in the open field.
e. The evidence against the defendant was staggering.

1. The size of the new building caused an uproar in the town.
2. Eat heartily. You need your strength.
3. In the opinion of the court, siblings must be kept together.
4. All of the books in the old library smelled like mothballs.
5. There were no tour buses at the customs booth.

hackerhandbooks.com/bedhandbook > Grammar exercises > Grammar basics
> E-ex 62–4 and 62–5

62b Verbs, objects, and complements

Section 61c explains how to find the verb of a sentence. A sentence's verb is classified as linking, transitive, or intransitive, depending on the kinds of objects or complements the verb can (or cannot) take.

Linking verbs and subject complements

Linking verbs connect the subject to a subject complement, a word or word group that completes the meaning of the subject by renaming or describing it. They fit into the sentence pattern subject/verb/subject complement.

If the subject complement renames the subject, it is a noun or noun equivalent (sometimes called a *predicate noun*).

$\overbrace{\text{An e-mail requesting personal information}}^{S}$ $\overbrace{\text{may be}}^{V}$ $\overbrace{\text{a scam.}}^{SC}$

If the subject complement describes the subject, it is an adjective or adjective equivalent (sometimes called a *predicate adjective*).

$$\overbrace{\text{Last month's temperatures}}^{\text{S}} \overbrace{\text{were}}^{\text{V}} \overset{\text{SC}}{\text{mild.}}$$

Whenever they appear as main verbs (rather than helping verbs), the forms of *be*—*be, am, is, are, was, were, being, been*—usually function as linking verbs. In the preceding examples, for instance, the main verbs are *be* and *were*.

Verbs such as *appear, become, feel, grow, look, make, seem, smell, sound,* and *taste* are sometimes linking, depending on the sense of the sentence.

Before we knew it, $\overbrace{\text{our toddler's disjointed words}}^{\text{S}}$ $\overbrace{\text{had become}}^{\text{V}}$
$\overset{\text{SC}}{\text{sentences.}}$

As it thickens, $\overbrace{\text{the sauce}}^{\text{S}}$ $\overbrace{\text{will look}}^{\text{V}}$ $\overset{\text{SC}}{\text{unappealing.}}$

When you suspect that a verb such as *becomes* or *looks* is linking, check to see if the word or words following it rename or describe the subject. In the preceding examples, *sentences* renames *words*, and *unappealing* describes *sauce*.

Transitive verbs and direct objects

A transitive verb takes a direct object, a word or word group that names a receiver of the action. It fits into the sentence pattern subject/verb/direct object.

$$\overbrace{\text{The hungry cat}}^{\text{S}} \overset{\text{V}}{\text{clawed}} \overbrace{\text{the bag of dry food.}}^{\text{DO}}$$

The simple direct object is always a noun or pronoun, in this case *bag*. To find it, simply strip away all modifiers.

Transitive verbs usually appear in the active voice, with the subject doing the action and a direct object receiving the action.

Active-voice sentences can be transformed into the passive voice, with the subject receiving the action instead. (See 62c.)

Transitive verbs, indirect objects, and direct objects

The direct object of a transitive verb is sometimes preceded by an indirect object, a noun or pronoun telling to whom or for whom the action of the sentence is done. It fits into the sentence pattern subject/verb/indirect object/direct object.

$$\overset{\text{S}}{\text{You}} \overset{\text{V}}{\text{give}} \overset{\text{IO}}{\text{her}} \overset{\text{DO}}{\text{some yarn}}, \text{and } \overset{\text{S}}{\text{she}} \overset{\text{V}}{\text{will knit}} \overset{\text{IO}}{\text{you}} \overset{\text{DO}}{\text{a scarf}}.$$

The simple indirect object is always a noun or pronoun. To test for an indirect object, insert the word *to* or *for* before the word or word group in question. If the sentence makes sense, the word or word group is an indirect object.

You give [to] *her* some yarn, and she will knit [for] *you* a scarf.

An indirect object may be turned into a prepositional phrase using *to* or *for*: *You give some yarn to her, and she will knit a scarf for you.*

Only certain transitive verbs take indirect objects. Some examples are *ask, bring, find, get, give, hand, lend, make, offer, pay, promise, read, send, show, teach, tell, throw,* and *write.*

Transitive verbs, direct objects, and object complements

The direct object of a transitive verb is sometimes followed by an object complement, a word or word group that renames or describes the object. It fits into the sentence pattern subject/verb/direct object/object complement.

$$\overset{\text{S}}{\text{People}} \text{ often } \overset{\text{V}}{\text{consider}} \overset{\text{DO}}{\text{chivalry}} \overset{\text{OC}}{\text{a thing of the past}}.$$

$$\overset{\text{S}}{\text{The kiln}} \overset{\text{V}}{\text{makes}} \overset{\text{DO}}{\text{clay}} \overset{\text{OC}}{\text{firm and strong}}.$$

When the object complement renames the direct object, it is a noun or pronoun (such as *thing*). When it describes the direct object, it is an adjective (such as *firm* and *strong*).

Sentence patterns

Subject / linking verb / subject complement

    S   V SC
Acting is art. [*Art* renames *Acting*.]

    ——— S ——— V   SC
Good researchers are curious. [*Curious* describes *researchers*.]

Subject / transitive verb / direct object

    ——— S ——— — V — ——— DO ———
An antihistamine may prevent an allergic reaction.

Subject / transitive verb / indirect object / direct object

    ——————— S ——————— V   IO   ——— DO ———
The elevator's rapid ascent gave Irina an attack of vertigo.

Subject / transitive verb / direct object / object complement

    ——— S ——— V — DO — — OC ———
The reviewer called the film a masterpiece. [*Masterpiece* renames *film*.]

    ——————— S ——————— V — DO — OC
The new double-glazed windows made the house warmer. [*Warmer* describes *house*.]

Subject / intransitive verb

    — S —   V
The kettle whistles.

Intransitive verbs

Intransitive verbs take no objects or complements. Their sentence pattern is subject/verb.

    ——— S ———   V
The audience laughed.

    ——— S ———   V
The driver accelerated in the straightaway.

Nothing receives the actions of laughing and accelerating in these sentences, so the verbs are intransitive. In the second sentence, *in the straightaway* is not an object; it is a prepositional phrase modifying *accelerated*.

NOTE: The dictionary will tell you whether a verb is transitive or intransitive. Some verbs can have both functions.

TRANSITIVE   Sandra *flew* her small plane over the canyon.

INTRANSITIVE   A flock of migrating geese *flew* overhead.

In the first example, *flew* has a direct object that receives the action: *her small plane*. In the second example, the verb is followed by an adverb (*overhead*), not by a direct object.

EXERCISE 62–2 Label the subject complements and direct objects in the following sentences, using the labels *SC* and *DO*. If a subject complement or direct object consists of more than one word, bracket and label all of it. Answers to lettered sentences appear in the back of the book. Example:

> ┌───DO───┐
> **The sharp right turn confused most drivers.**

a. Textbooks are expensive.
b. Samurai warriors never fear death.
c. Successful coaches always praise their players' efforts.
d. St. Petersburg was the capital of the Russian Empire for two centuries.
e. The medicine tasted bitter.

1. Solar flares emit UV radiation.
2. The friends' quarrel was damaging their relationship.
3. Feng shui is the practice of achieving harmony between the physical and the spiritual in one's environment.
4. A well-made advertisement captures viewers' attention.
5. The island's climate was neither too hot nor too rainy.

EXERCISE 62–3 Each of the following sentences has either an indirect object followed by a direct object or a direct object followed by an object complement. Label the objects and complements, using the labels *IO*, *DO*, and *OC*. If an object or a complement consists of

more than one word, bracket and label all of it. Answers to lettered
sentences appear in the back of the book. Example:

$$\overbrace{\text{Most people consider their own experience}}^{\text{DO}} \overbrace{\text{normal.}}^{\text{OC}}$$

a. Stress can make adults and children weary.
b. Zita has made community service her priority this year.
c. Consider the work finished.
d. We showed the agent our tickets, and she gave us boarding
    passes.
e. The dining hall offered students healthy meal choices.

1. Send the registrar your scholarship form today.
2. The independent research institute gives its scholars the free-
    dom to work without government or military interference.
3. Computer viruses make networks vulnerable.
4. Give me a book's title, and I can tell you the author.
5. The dire forecast made us extremely cautious about riding out
    the storm at home.

hackerhandbooks.com/bedhandbook > Grammar exercises > Grammar basics
> E-ex 62–6 to 62–9

62c Pattern variations

Although most sentences follow one of the five patterns in
the chart on page 769, variations of these patterns commonly
occur in questions, commands, sentences with delayed subjects, and passive transformations.

Questions and commands

Questions are sometimes patterned in normal word order,
with the subject preceding the verb.

$$\overset{\text{S}}{\text{Who}} \overbrace{\text{will have}}^{\text{V}} \text{the most hits this season?}$$

Just as frequently, however, the pattern of a question is
inverted, with the subject appearing between the helping and
main verb or after the verb.

HV S MV
Will he have the most hits this season?

V ┌───── S ─────┐
Why is the number of hits an important statistic?

In commands, the subject of the sentence is an understood *you*.

S   V
[You] Pay attention to the road.

Sentences with delayed subjects

Writers sometimes choose to delay the subject of a sentence to achieve a special effect such as suspense or humor.

V ┌──── S ────┐
Behind the phony tinsel of Hollywood lies the real tinsel.

The subject of the sentence is also delayed in sentences opening with the expletive *There* or *It*. When used as expletives, the words *There* and *It* have no strict grammatical function; they serve merely to get the sentence started.

V ┌────── S ──────┐
There are thirty thousand spectators in the stadium.

V   ┌──── S ────┐
It is best to avoid trans fats.

The subject in the second example is an infinitive phrase. (See 63b.)

Passive transformations

Transitive verbs, those that can take direct objects, usually appear in the active voice. In the active voice, the subject does the action and a direct object receives the action.

┌───── S ─────┐   V   ┌──── DO ────┐
ACTIVE   The fireworks display dazzled the viewers on the

┌────┐
Esplanade.

Sentences in the active voice may be transformed into the passive voice, with the subject receiving the action instead.

```
                        ┌─────────── S ───────────┐   HV     MV
PASSIVE                  The viewers on the Esplanade were dazzled by the fire-
                         works display.
```

What was once the direct object (*the viewers on the Esplanade*) has become the subject in the passive-voice transformation, and the original subject appears in a prepositional phrase beginning with *by*. The *by* phrase is frequently omitted in passive-voice constructions.

PASSIVE   The viewers on the Esplanade were dazzled.

Verbs in the passive voice can be identified by their form alone. The main verb is always a past participle, such as *dazzled* (see 61c), preceded by a form of *be* (*be, am, is, are, was, were, being, been*): *were dazzled*. Sometimes adverbs intervene (*were usually dazzled*).

TIP: Avoid using the passive voice when the active voice would be more appropriate (see 8a).

63 Subordinate word groups

Subordinate word groups include phrases and clauses. Phrases are subordinate because they lack a subject and a verb; they are classified as prepositional, verbal, appositive, and absolute (see 63a–63d). Subordinate clauses have a subject and a verb, but they begin with a word (such as *although*, *that*, or *when*) that marks them as subordinate (see 63e).

63a Prepositional phrases

A prepositional phrase begins with a preposition such as *at, by, for, from, in, of, on, to,* or *with* (see 61f) and usually ends with a noun or noun equivalent: *on the table, for him, by sleeping late*. The noun or noun equivalent is known as the *object of the preposition*.

Prepositional phrases function either as adjectives modifying nouns or pronouns or as adverbs modifying verbs, adjectives, or other adverbs.

When functioning as an adjective, a prepositional phrase nearly always appears immediately following the noun or pronoun it modifies.

The hut had *walls of mud.*

Adjective phrases usually answer one or both of the questions Which one? and What kind of? If we ask Which walls? or What kind of walls? we get a sensible answer: *walls of mud.*

Adverbial prepositional phrases that modify the verb can appear nearly anywhere in a sentence.

James *walked* his dog *on a leash.*

Sabrina *will in time adjust* to life in Ecuador.

During a mudslide, the terrain *can change* drastically.

If a prepositional phrase is movable, you can be certain that it is adverbial.

In the cave, the explorers found well-preserved prehistoric drawings.

The explorers found well-preserved prehistoric drawings *in the cave*.

Adverbial word groups usually answer one of these questions: When? Where? How? Why? Under what conditions? To what degree?

James walked his dog *how*? *On a leash.*

Sabrina would adjust to life in Ecuador *when*? *In time.*

The terrain can change drastically *under what conditions*? *During a mudslide.*

In questions and subordinate clauses, a preposition may appear after its object.

What are you afraid *of*?

We avoided the bike trail *that* John had warned us *about*.

The object of a preposition might itself be modified by a prepositional phrase.

There are many *paths to the top of the mountain.*

The complete object of *to* is *the top of the mountain*. The prepositional phrase *of the mountain* modifies the noun *top*. And the prepositional phrase *to the top of the mountain* modifies the noun *paths*.

EXERCISE 63–1 Underline the prepositional phrases in the following sentences. Tell whether each phrase is an adjective or an adverb phrase and what it modifies in the sentence. Answers to lettered sentences appear in the back of the book. Example:

Flecks <u>of mica</u> glittered <u>in the new granite floor</u>. (Adjective phrase modifying "Flecks"; adverb phrase modifying "glittered")

a. In northern Italy, some people speak German as their first language.
b. William completed the hike through the thick forest with ease.
c. To my boss's dismay, I was late for work again.
d. The traveling exhibit of Mayan artifacts gave viewers new insight into pre-Columbian culture.
e. In 2002, the euro became the official currency in twelve European countries.

1. The Silk Road was an old trade route between China and other parts of the world.
2. Dough with too much flour yields heavy baked goods.

3. On one side of the barricades were revolutionary students; on the other was a government militia.
4. You can tell with just one whiff whether the milk is fresh.
5. At first, we couldn't decide whether to take the car or the train, but in the end we decided to take the train.

hackerhandbooks.com/bedhandbook > **Grammar exercises** > **Grammar basics**
> E-ex 63–4 to 63–6

63b Verbal phrases

A verbal is a verb form that does not function as the verb of a clause. Verbals include infinitives (the word *to* plus the base form of the verb), present participles (the *-ing* form of the verb), and past participles (the verb form usually ending in *-d*, *-ed*, *-n*, *-en*, or *-t*). (See 27a and 61c.)

INFINITIVE	PRESENT PARTICIPLE	PAST PARTICIPLE
to dream	dreaming	dreamed
to choose	choosing	chosen
to build	building	built
to grow	growing	grown

Instead of functioning as the verb of a clause, a verbal functions as an adjective, a noun, or an adverb.

ADJECTIVE   *Broken* promises cannot be fixed.

NOUN   Constant *complaining* becomes wearisome.

ADVERB   Can you wait *to celebrate*?

Verbals with objects, complements, or modifiers form verbal phrases.

In my family, *singing loudly* is more appreciated than *singing well*.

Governments exist *to protect the rights of minorities*.

The verbal *singing* is modified by the adverbs *loudly* and *well*; the verbal *to protect* is followed by a direct object, *the rights of minorities*.

Like single-word verbals, verbal phrases function as adjectives, nouns, or adverbs. Verbal phrases are ordinarily classified as participial, gerund, and infinitive.

Participial phrases

Participial phrases always function as adjectives. Their verbals are either present participles (such as *dreaming*, *asking*) or past participles (such as *stolen*, *reached*).

Participial phrases frequently appear immediately following the noun or pronoun they modify.

Congress shall make no *law abridging the freedom of speech or of the press*.

Truth kept in the dark will never save the world.

Unlike other adjectival word groups (prepositional phrases, infinitive phrases, adjective clauses), which must always follow the noun or pronoun they modify, participial phrases are often movable. They can precede the word they modify.

Being a weight-bearing joint, the *knee* is among the most frequently injured.

They may also appear at some distance from the word they modify.

Last night we saw a *play* that affected us deeply, *written with profound insight into the lives of immigrants*.

Gerund phrases

Gerund phrases are built around present participles (verb forms that end in *-ing*), and they always function as nouns:

usually as subjects, subject complements, direct objects, or objects of a preposition.

$$\overline{\text{S}}$$
Rationalizing a fear can eliminate it.

$$\overline{\text{SC}}$$
The key to good sauce is browning the mushrooms.

$$\overline{\text{DO}}$$
Lizards usually enjoy sunning themselves.

The American Heart Association has documented the benefits
$$\overline{\text{OBJ OF PREP}}$$
of diet and exercise in reducing the risk of heart attack.

Infinitive phrases

Infinitive phrases, usually constructed around *to* plus the base form of the verb (*to call*, *to drink*), can function as nouns, as adjectives, or as adverbs.

When functioning as a noun, an infinitive phrase may appear in almost any noun slot in a sentence, usually as a subject, subject complement, or direct object.

$$\overline{\text{S}}$$
To live without health insurance is risky.

$$\overline{\text{DO}}$$
The orchestra wanted to make its premier season memorable.

Infinitive phrases functioning as adjectives usually appear immediately following the noun or pronoun they modify.

The Twentieth Amendment gave women the *right to vote*.

The infinitive phrase modifies the noun *right*. Which right? *The right to vote*.

Adverbial infinitive phrases usually qualify the meaning of the verb, telling when, where, how, why, under what conditions, or to what degree an action occurred.

Volunteers *rolled up* their pants *to wade through the flood waters.*

Why did they roll up their pants? *To wade through the flood waters.*

NOTE: In some constructions, the infinitive is unmarked; in other words, the *to* does not appear. (See 28f.)

Graphs and charts can help researchers [*to*] *present complex data.*

EXERCISE 63–2   Underline the verbal phrases in the following sentences. Tell whether each phrase is participial, gerund, or infinitive and how each is used in the sentence. Answers to lettered sentences appear in the back of the book. Example:

Do you want to watch that documentary? (Infinitive phrase used as direct object of "Do want")

a. Updating your software will fix the computer glitch.
b. The challenge in decreasing the town budget is identifying non-essential services.
c. Cathleen tried to help her mother by raking the lawn.
d. Understanding little, I had no hope of passing my biology final.
e. Working with animals gave Steve a sense of satisfaction.

1. Driving through South Carolina, we saw kudzu growing out of control along the roadside.
2. Some people now use a patch to repel mosquitoes.
3. We helped the schoolchildren find their way to the station.
4. Painting requires the ability to keep a steady hand.
5. My father could not see a weed without pulling it out of the ground.

hackerhandbooks.com/bedhandbook > Grammar exercises > Grammar basics
> E-ex 63–7 and 63–8

63c Appositive phrases

Though strictly speaking they are not subordinate word groups, appositive phrases function somewhat as adjectives do, to describe nouns or pronouns. Instead of modifying nouns or pronouns, however, appositive phrases rename them. In form they are nouns or noun equivalents.

Appositives are said to be "in apposition" to the nouns or pronouns they rename.

Bloggers, *conversationalists at heart*, are the online equivalent of radio talk show hosts.

Conversationalists at heart is in apposition to the noun *Bloggers*.

63d Absolute phrases

An absolute phrase modifies a whole clause or sentence, not just one word, and it may appear nearly anywhere in the sentence. It consists of a noun or noun equivalent usually followed by a participial phrase.

Her words reverberating in the hushed arena, the senator urged the crowd to support her former opponent.

The senator urged the crowd to support her former opponent, *her words reverberating in the hushed arena*.

63e Subordinate clauses

Subordinate clauses are patterned like sentences, having subjects and verbs and sometimes objects or complements. But they function within sentences as adjectives, adverbs, or nouns. They cannot stand alone as complete sentences.

A subordinate clause usually begins with a subordinating conjunction or a relative pronoun. The chart on page 783 classifies these words according to the kinds of clauses (adjective, adverb, or noun) they introduce.

Adjective clauses

Like other word groups functioning as adjectives, adjective clauses modify nouns or pronouns. An adjective clause nearly always appears immediately following the noun or pronoun it modifies.

A *flower that is planted in summer* will grow quickly.

The coach chose *players who would benefit from intense drills*.

To test whether a subordinate clause functions as an adjective, ask the adjective questions: Which one? What kind of? The answer should make sense. Which flower? *The flower that is planted in summer.* What kind of players? *Players who would benefit from intense drills.*

Most adjective clauses begin with a relative pronoun (*who, whom, whose, which,* or *that*), which marks them as grammatically subordinate. In addition to introducing the clause, the relative pronoun points back to the noun that the clause modifies.

A *book that goes unread* is a writer's worst nightmare.

Relative pronouns are sometimes "understood."

The things [*that*] *we cherish most* are the things [*that*] *we might lose.*

Occasionally an adjective clause is introduced by a relative adverb, usually *when, where,* or *why.*

The aging actor returned to the *stage where he had made his debut as Hamlet half a century earlier.*

The parts of an adjective clause are often arranged as in sentences (subject/verb/object or complement).

Sometimes it is our closest friends who disappoint us.
                                                        (S V DO)

Frequently, however, the object or complement appears first, violating the normal order of subject/verb/object.

They can be the very friends whom we disappoint.
                                    (DO S V)

TIP: For punctuation of adjective clauses, see 32e and 33e. For advice about avoiding repeated words in adjective clauses, see 30d.

Adverb clauses

Adverb clauses usually modify verbs. In such cases, they may appear nearly anywhere in a sentence—at the beginning, at the end, or in the middle. Like other adverbial word groups, they tell when, where, why, how, under what conditions, or to what degree an action occurred or a situation existed.

When the sun went down, the hikers *prepared* their camp.

Laurabeth *would have made* the basketball team *if she hadn't broken her ankle*.

When did the hikers prepare their camp? *When the sun went down*. Under what conditions would Laurabeth have made the team? *If she hadn't broken her ankle*.

Adverb clauses are usually movable when they modify a verb. In the preceding examples, for instance, the adverb clauses can be moved without affecting the meaning of the sentences.

The hikers prepared their camp *when the sun went down*.

If she hadn't broken her ankle, Laurabeth would have made the basketball team.

When an adverb clause modifies an adjective or an adverb, it is not movable; it must appear next to the word it modifies. In the following examples, the *when* clause modifies the adjective *Uncertain*, and the *than* clause modifies the adverb *better*.

Uncertain *when the baby would be born*, Ray and Leah stayed close to home.

Jackie can dance better *than I can walk*.

Adverb clauses always begin with a subordinating conjunction (see the chart on p. 783 for a list). Subordinating conjunctions introduce clauses and express their relation to the rest of the sentence.

Words that introduce subordinate clauses

Words introducing adverb clauses

Subordinating conjunctions: after, although, as, as if, because, before, even though, if, in order that, since, so that, than, that, though, unless, until, when, where, whether, while

Words introducing adjective clauses

Relative pronouns: that, which, who, whom, whose
Relative adverbs: when, where, why

Words introducing noun clauses

Relative pronouns: that, which, who, whom, whose
Other pronouns: whoever, whomever, what, whatever, whichever
Other subordinating words: how, if, when, whenever, where, wherever, whether, why

Adverb clauses are sometimes elliptical, with some of their words being understood but not appearing in the sentence.

When [it is] renovated, the dorm will hold six hundred students.

Noun clauses

Because they do not function as modifiers, noun clauses are not subordinate in the same sense as adjective and adverb clauses are. They are called subordinate only because they cannot stand alone: They must function within a sentence, always as nouns.

A noun clause functions just like a single-word noun, usually as a subject, subject complement, direct object, or object of a preposition.

Whoever leaves the house last must double-lock the door. [S]

Copernicus argued that the sun is the center of the universe. [DO]

A noun clause begins with a word that marks it as subordinate (see the list on p. 783). The subordinating word may or may not play a significant role in the clause. In the preceding example sentences, *Whoever* is the subject of its clause, but *that* does not perform a function in its clause.

As with adjective clauses, the parts of a noun clause may appear out of their normal order (subject/verb/object).

DO   S   V
New Mexico is where we live.

The parts of a noun clause may also appear in normal order.

S   V   ——DO——
Loyalty is what keeps a friendship strong.

EXERCISE 63–3 Underline the subordinate clauses in the following sentences. Tell whether each clause is an adjective, adverb, or noun clause and how it is used in the sentence. Answers to lettered sentences appear in the back of the book. Example:

Show the committee the latest draft <u>before you print the</u>

<u>final report</u>. *(Adverb clause modifying "Show")*

a. The city's electoral commission adjusted the voting process so that every vote would count.
b. A marketing campaign that targets baby boomers may not appeal to young professionals.
c. After the Tambora volcano erupted in the southern Pacific in 1815, no one realized that it would contribute to the "year without a summer" in Europe and North America.
d. The concept of peak oil implies that at a certain point there will be no more oil to extract from the earth.
e. Details are easily overlooked when you are rushing.

1. What her internship taught her was that she worked well with children with special needs.
2. Whether you like it or not, you cannot choose your family.

3. The meteorologist who underestimated the total snowfall of the first winter storm was right on target about the second storm.
4. If Ramon didn't have to work every afternoon, he would be willing to sign up for the yoga class with Andrea.
5. The book that we saw in the shop in Dublin was not available when we returned home.

hackerhandbooks.com/bedhandbook > Grammar exercises > Grammar basics
> E-ex 63–9 to 63–12

64 Sentence types

Sentences are classified in two ways: according to their structure (simple, compound, complex, and compound-complex) and according to their purpose (declarative, imperative, interrogative, and exclamatory).

64a Sentence structures

Depending on the number and types of clauses they contain, sentences are classified as simple, compound, complex, or compound-complex.

Clauses come in two varieties: independent and subordinate. An independent clause contains a subject and a predicate, and it either stands alone or could stand alone. A subordinate clause also contains a subject and a predicate, but it functions within a sentence as an adjective, an adverb, or a noun; it cannot stand alone. (See 63e.)

Simple sentences

A simple sentence is one independent clause with no subordinate clauses.

INDEPENDENT CLAUSE

Without a passport, Eva could not visit her grandparents in

Hungary.

This sentence contains a subject (*Eva*), a verb with an adverb modifier (*could not visit*), a direct object (*her grandparents in Hungary*), and two prepositional phrases (*Without a passport* and *in Hungary*).

A simple sentence may contain compound elements—a compound subject, verb, or object, for example—but it does not contain more than one full sentence pattern. The following sentence is simple because its two verbs (*comes in* and *goes out*) share a subject (*Spring*).

———————— INDEPENDENT CLAUSE ————————
Spring comes in like a lion and goes out like a lamb.

Compound sentences

A compound sentence is composed of two or more independent clauses with no subordinate clauses. The independent clauses are usually joined with a comma and a coordinating conjunction (*and, but, or, nor, for, so, yet*) or with a semicolon. (See 14a.)

INDEPENDENT — CLAUSE — | INDEPENDENT — CLAUSE —
The car broke down, but a rescue van arrived within minutes.

——— INDEPENDENT CLAUSE ——— | ——— INDEPENDENT CLAUSE———
A shark was spotted near shore; people left immediately.

Complex sentences

A complex sentence is composed of one independent clause with one or more subordinate clauses. (See 63e.)

ADJECTIVE SUBORDINATE — CLAUSE —
The pitcher who won the game is a rookie.

ADVERB SUBORDINATE — CLAUSE —
If you leave late, take a cab home.

SUBORDINATE
CLAUSE

NOUN   What matters most to us is a quick commute.

Compound-complex sentences

A compound-complex sentence contains at least two independent clauses and at least one subordinate clause. The following sentence contains two full sentence patterns that can stand alone.

INDEPENDENT CLAUSE   INDEPENDENT CLAUSE
Tell the doctor how you feel, and she will decide whether

you can go home.

And each independent clause contains a subordinate clause, making the sentence both compound and complex.

INDEPENDENT CLAUSE   INDEPENDENT CLAUSE
SUB CL
Tell the doctor how you feel, and she will decide whether

SUB CL
you can go home.

64b Sentence purposes

Writers use declarative sentences to make statements, imperative sentences to issue requests or commands, interrogative sentences to ask questions, and exclamatory sentences to make exclamations.

DECLARATIVE   The echo sounded in our ears.

IMPERATIVE   Love your neighbor.

INTERROGATIVE   Did the better team win tonight?

EXCLAMATORY   We're here to save you!

EXERCISE 64–1 Identify the following sentences as simple, compound, complex, or compound-complex. Identify the subordinate clauses and classify them according to their function: adjective, adverb, or noun. (See 63e.) Answers to lettered sentences appear in the back of the book. Example:

The deli in Courthouse Square was crowded with lawyers

at lunchtime. (Simple)

a. Fires that are ignited in dry areas spread especially quickly.
b. The early Incas were advanced; they used a calendar and developed a decimal system.
c. Elaine's jacket was too thin to block the wintry air.
d. Before we leave for the station, we always check the Amtrak Web site.
e. Decide when you want to leave, and I will be there to pick you up.

1. The fact is that the network outage could have been avoided.
2. Those who lose a loved one in a tragic accident may find group therapy comforting.
3. The outlets in the garment district are the best places to find Halloween costumes.
4. There were six lunar Apollo missions, but people usually remember Apollo 13 best.
5. Our generator kicks in whenever we lose power.

hackerhandbooks.com/bedhandbook > Grammar exercises > Grammar basics
> E-ex 64–2

Glossary of Usage

This glossary includes words commonly confused (such as *accept* and *except*), words commonly misused (such as *aggravate*), and words that are nonstandard (such as *hisself*). It also lists colloquialisms and jargon. Colloquialisms are casual expressions that may be appropriate in informal speech but are inappropriate in formal writing. Jargon is needlessly technical or pretentious language that is inappropriate in most contexts. If an item is not listed here, consult the index. For irregular verbs (such as *sing, sang, sung*), see 27a. For idiomatic use of prepositions, see 18d.

> **Grammar checkers** can point out commonly confused words and suggest that you check your usage. It is up to you, however, to determine the correct word for your intended meaning.

hackerhandbooks.com/bedhandbook > Language Debates
> Absolute concepts such as *unique*
bad versus *badly*
however at the beginning of a sentence
lie versus *lay*
myself
that versus *which*
who versus *which* or *that*
who versus *whom*
you

a, an Use *an* before a vowel sound, *a* before a consonant sound: *an apple, a peach*. Problems sometimes arise with words beginning with *h* or *u*. If the *h* is silent, the word begins with a vowel sound, so use *an: an hour, an honorable deed*. If the *h* is pronounced, the word begins with a consonant sound, so use *a: a hospital, a historian, a hotel*. Words such as *university* and *union* begin with a consonant sound (a *y* sound), so use *a: a union*. Words such as *uncle* and *umbrella* begin with a vowel sound, so use *an: an underground well*. When an abbreviation or an acronym begins with a vowel sound, use *an: an EKG, an MRI, an AIDS prevention program*.

accept, except *Accept* is a verb meaning "to receive." *Except* is usually a preposition meaning "excluding." *I will accept all the packages except that one. Except* is also a verb meaning "to exclude." *Please except that item from the list.*

adapt, adopt *Adapt* means "to adjust or become accustomed"; it is usually followed by *to*. *Adopt* means "to take as one's own." *Our family adopted a Vietnamese child, who quickly adapted to his new life.*

adverse, averse *Adverse* means "unfavorable." *Averse* means "opposed" or "reluctant"; it is usually followed by *to*. *I am averse to your proposal because it could have an adverse impact on the economy.*

advice, advise *Advice* is a noun, *advise* a verb. *We advise you to follow John's advice.*

affect, effect *Affect* is usually a verb meaning "to influence." *Effect* is usually a noun meaning "result." *The drug did not affect the disease, and it had adverse side effects. Effect* can also be a verb meaning "to bring about." *Only the president can effect such a dramatic change.*

aggravate *Aggravate* means "to make worse or more troublesome." *Overgrazing aggravated the soil erosion.* In formal writing, avoid the use of *aggravate* meaning "to annoy or irritate." *Her babbling annoyed* (not *aggravated*) *me.*

agree to, agree with *Agree to* means "to give consent to." *Agree with* means "to be in accord with" or "to come to an understanding with." *He agrees with me about the need for change, but he won't agree to my plan.*

ain't *Ain't* is nonstandard. Use *am not, are not* (*aren't*), or *is not* (*isn't*). *I am not* (not *ain't*) *going home for spring break.*

all ready, already *All ready* means "completely prepared." *Already* means "previously." *Susan was all ready for the concert, but her friends had already left.*

all right *All right* is written as two words. *Alright* is nonstandard.

all together, altogether *All together* means "everyone or everything in one place." *Altogether* means "entirely." *We were not altogether certain that we could bring the family all together for the reunion.*

allude To *allude* to something is to make an indirect reference to it. Do not use *allude* to mean "to refer directly." *In his lecture, the professor referred* (not *alluded*) *to several pre-Socratic philosophers.*

allusion, illusion An *allusion* is an indirect reference. An *illusion* is a misconception or false impression. *Did you catch my allusion to Shakespeare? Mirrors give the room an illusion of depth.*

a lot *A lot* is two words. Do not write *alot*. *Sam lost a lot of weight.* See also *lots, lots of.*

among, between See *between, among.*

amongst In American English, *among* is preferred.

amoral, immoral *Amoral* means "neither moral nor immoral"; it also means "not caring about moral judgments." *Immoral* means "morally wrong." *Until recently, most business courses were taught from an amoral perspective. Murder is immoral.*

amount, number Use *amount* with quantities that cannot be counted; use *number* with those that can. *This recipe calls for a large amount of sugar. We have a large number of toads in our garden.*

an See *a, an.*

and etc. *Et cetera* (*etc.*) means "and so forth"; *and etc.* is redundant. See also *etc.*

and/or Avoid the awkward construction *and/or* except in technical or legal documents.

angry at, angry with Use *angry with*, not *angry at*, when referring to a person. *The coach was angry with the referee.*

ante-, anti- The prefix *ante-* means "earlier" or "in front of"; the prefix *anti-* means "against" or "opposed to." *William Lloyd Garrison was a leader of the antislavery movement during the antebellum period. Anti-* should be used with a hyphen when it is followed by a capital letter or a word beginning with *i.*

anxious *Anxious* means "worried" or "apprehensive." In formal writing, avoid using *anxious* to mean "eager." *We are eager* (not *anxious*) *to see your new house.*

anybody, anyone *Anybody* and *anyone* are singular. (See 21e and 22a.)

anymore Reserve the adverb *anymore* for negative contexts, where it means "any longer." *Moviegoers are rarely shocked anymore by profanity.* Do not use *anymore* in positive contexts. Use *now* or *nowadays* instead. *Summer jobs for high school students are so scarce nowadays* (not *anymore*) *that more students are turning to volunteer opportunities.*

anyone See *anybody, anyone.*

anyone, any one *Anyone,* an indefinite pronoun, means "any person at all." *Any one,* the pronoun *one* preceded by the adjective *any,* refers to a particular person or thing in a group. *Anyone from the winning team may choose any one of the games on display.*

anyplace In formal writing, use *anywhere.*

anyways, anywheres *Anyways* and *anywheres* are nonstandard. Use *anyway* and *anywhere.*

as Do not use *as* to mean "because" if there is any chance of ambiguity. *We canceled the picnic because* (not *as*) *it began raining. As* here could mean "because" or "when."

as, like See *like, as.*

as to *As to* is jargon for *about. He inquired about* (not *as to*) *the job.*

averse See *adverse, averse.*

awful The adjective *awful* and the adverb *awfully* are not appropriate in formal writing.

awhile, a while *Awhile* is an adverb; it can modify a verb, but it cannot be the object of a preposition such as *for.* The two-word form *a while* is a noun preceded by an article and therefore can be the object of a preposition. *Stay awhile. Stay for a while.*

back up, backup *Back up* is a verb phrase. *Back up the car carefully. Be sure to back up your hard drive. Backup* is a noun meaning "a copy of electronically stored data." *Keep your backup in a safe place. Backup* can also be used as an adjective. *I regularly create backup disks.*

bad, badly *Bad* is an adjective, *badly* an adverb. *They felt bad about ruining the surprise. Her arm hurt badly after she slid into second base.* (See 26c.)

being as, being that *Being as* and *being that* are nonstandard expressions. Write *because* instead. *Because* (not *Being as*) *I slept late, I had to skip breakfast.*

beside, besides *Beside* is a preposition meaning "at the side of" or "next to." *Annie Oakley slept with her gun beside her bed. Besides* is a preposition meaning "except" or "in addition to." *No one besides Terrie can have that ice cream. Besides* is also an adverb meaning "in addition." *I'm not hungry; besides, I don't like ice cream.*

between, among Ordinarily, use *among* with three or more entities, *between* with two. *The prize was divided among several contestants. You have a choice between carrots and beans.*

bring, take Use *bring* when an object is being transported toward you, *take* when it is being moved away. *Please bring me a glass of water. Please take these forms to Mr. Scott.*

burst, bursted; bust, busted *Burst* is an irregular verb meaning "to come open or fly apart suddenly or violently." Its past tense is *burst.* The past-tense form *bursted* is nonstandard. *Bust* and *busted* are slang for *burst* and, along with *bursted,* should not be used in formal writing.

can, may The distinction between *can* and *may* is fading, but some writers still observe it in formal writing. *Can* is traditionally reserved for ability, *may* for permission. *Can you speak French? May I help you?*

capital, capitol *Capital* refers to a city, *capitol* to a building where lawmakers meet. *Capital* also refers to wealth or resources. *The capitol has undergone extensive renovations. The residents of the state capital protested the development plans.*

censor, censure *Censor* means "to remove or suppress material considered objectionable." *Censure* means "to criticize severely." *The administration's policy of censoring books has been censured by the media.*

cite, site *Cite* means "to quote as an authority or example." *Site* is usually a noun meaning "a particular place." *He cited the zoning law in his argument against the proposed site of the gas station.* Locations on the Internet are usually referred to as *sites. The library's Web site improves every week.*

climactic, climatic *Climactic* is derived from *climax,* the point of greatest intensity in a series or progression of events. *Climatic* is derived from *climate* and refers to meteorological conditions. *The climactic period in the dinosaurs' reign was reached just before severe climatic conditions brought on an ice age.*

coarse, course *Coarse* means "crude" or "rough in texture." *The coarse weave of the wall hanging gave it a three-dimensional quality. Course* usually refers to a path, a playing field, or a unit of study; the expression *of course* means "certainly." *I plan to take a course in car repair this summer. Of course, you are welcome to join me.*

compare to, compare with *Compare to* means "to represent as similar." *She compared him to a wild stallion. Compare with* means "to examine similarities and differences." *The study compared the language ability of apes with that of dolphins.*

complement, compliment *Complement* is a verb meaning "to go with or complete" or a noun meaning "something that completes." *Compliment* as a verb means "to flatter"; as a noun, it means "flattering remark." *Her skill at rushing the net complements his skill at volleying. Martha's flower arrangements receive many compliments.*

conscience, conscious *Conscience* is a noun meaning "moral principles." *Conscious* is an adjective meaning "aware or alert." *Let your conscience be your guide. Were you conscious of his love for you?*

continual, continuous *Continual* means "repeated regularly and frequently." *She grew weary of the continual telephone calls. Continuous* means "extended or prolonged without interruption." *The broken siren made a continuous wail.*

could care less *Could care less* is nonstandard. Write *couldn't care less* instead. *He couldn't* (not *could*) *care less about his psychology final.*

could of *Could of* is nonstandard for *could have. We could have* (not *could of*) *taken the train.*

council, counsel A *council* is a deliberative body, and a *councilor* is a member of such a body. *Counsel* usually means "advice" and can also mean "lawyer"; a *counselor* is one who gives advice or guidance. *The councilors met to draft the council's position paper. The pastor offered wise counsel to the troubled teenager.*

criteria *Criteria* is the plural of *criterion,* which means "a standard or rule or test on which a judgment or decision can be based." *The only criterion for the scholarship is ability.*

data *Data* is a plural noun technically meaning "facts or results." But *data* is increasingly being accepted as a singular noun. *The new data suggest* (or *suggests*) *that our theory is correct.* (The singular *datum* is rarely used.)

different from, different than Ordinarily, write *different from. Your sense of style is different from Jim's.* However, *different than* is acceptable to avoid an awkward construction. *Please let me know if your plans are different than* (to avoid *from what*) *they were six weeks ago.*

differ from, differ with *Differ from* means "to be unlike"; *differ with* means "to disagree with." *She differed with me about the wording of the agreement. My approach to the problem differed from hers.*

disinterested, uninterested *Disinterested* means "impartial, objective"; *uninterested* means "not interested." *We sought the advice of a disinterested counselor to help us solve our problem. Mark was uninterested in anyone's opinion but his own.*

don't *Don't* is the contraction for *do not. I don't want any. Don't* should not be used as the contraction for *does not,* which is *doesn't. He doesn't* (not *don't*) *want any.*

due to *Due to* is an adjective phrase and should not be used as a preposition meaning "because of." *The trip was canceled because of* (not *due to*) *lack of interest. Due to* is acceptable as a subject complement and usually follows a form of the verb *be. His success was due to hard work.*

each *Each* is singular. (See 21e and 22a.)

effect See *affect, effect.*

e.g. In formal writing, replace the Latin abbreviation *e.g.* with its English equivalent: *for example* or *for instance.*

either *Either* is singular. (See 21e and 22a.) For *either . . . or* constructions, see 21d and 22d.

elicit, illicit *Elicit* is a verb meaning "to bring out" or "to evoke." *Illicit is an adjective meaning "unlawful." The reporter was unable to elicit any information from the police about illicit drug traffic.*

emigrate from, immigrate to *Emigrate* means "to leave one country or region to settle in another." *In 1903, my great-grandfather emigrated from Russia to escape the religious pogroms. Immigrate* means "to enter another country and reside there." *More than fifty thousand Bosnians immigrated to the United States in the 1990s.*

eminent, imminent *Eminent* means "outstanding" or "distinguished." *We met an eminent professor of Greek history. Imminent* means "about to happen." *The snowstorm is imminent.*

enthused Many people object to the use of *enthused* as an adjective. Use *enthusiastic* instead. *The children were enthusiastic* (not *enthused*) *about going to the circus.*

etc. Avoid ending a list with *etc.* It is more emphatic to end with an example, and in most contexts readers will understand that the list is not exhaustive. When you don't wish to end with an example, *and so on* is more graceful than *etc.* (See also *and etc.*)

eventually, ultimately Often used interchangeably, *eventually* is the better choice to mean "at an unspecified time in the future," and *ultimately* is better to mean "the furthest possible extent or greatest extreme." *He knew that eventually he would complete his degree. The existentialists considered suicide the ultimately rational act.*

everybody, everyone *Everybody* and *everyone* are singular. (See 21e and 22a.)

everyone, every one *Everyone* is an indefinite pronoun. *Every one,* the pronoun *one* preceded by the adjective *every,* means "each individual or thing in a particular group." *Every one* is usually followed by *of. Everyone wanted to go. Every one of the missing books was found.*

except See *accept, except.*

expect Avoid the informal use of *expect* meaning "to believe, think, or suppose." *I think* (not *expect*) *it will rain tonight.*

explicit, implicit *Explicit* means "expressed directly" or "clearly defined"; *implicit* means "implied, unstated." *I gave him explicit instructions not to go swimming. My mother's silence indicated her implicit approval.*

farther, further *Farther* usually describes distances. *Further* usually suggests quantity or degree. *Chicago is farther from Miami than I thought. I would be grateful for further suggestions.*

fewer, less Use *fewer* for items that can be counted; use *less* for items that cannot be counted. *Fewer people are living in the city. Please put less sugar in my tea.*

finalize *Finalize* is jargon meaning "to make final or complete." Use ordinary English instead. *The architect prepared final drawings* (not *finalized the drawings*).

firstly *Firstly* sounds pretentious, and it leads to the ungainly series *firstly, secondly, thirdly,* and so on. Write *first, second, third* instead.

further See *farther, further.*

get *Get* has many colloquial uses. In writing, avoid using *get* to mean the following: "to evoke an emotional response" (*That music always gets to me*); "to annoy" (*After a while his sulking got to me*); "to take revenge on" (*I got back at her by leaving the room*); "to become" (*He got sick*); "to start or begin" (*Let's get going*). Avoid using *have got to* in place of *must. I must* (not *have got to*) *finish this paper tonight.*

good, well *Good* is an adjective, *well* an adverb. (See 26c.) *He hasn't felt good about his game since he sprained his wrist last season. She performed well on the uneven parallel bars.*

graduate Both of the following uses of *graduate* are standard: *My sister was graduated from UCLA last year. My sister graduated from UCLA last year.* It is nonstandard, however, to drop the word *from: My sister graduated UCLA last year.* Though this usage is common in informal English, many readers object to it.

grow Phrases such as *to grow the economy* and *to grow a business* are jargon. Usually the verb *grow* is intransitive (it does not take a direct object). *Our business has grown very quickly.* Use *grow* in a transitive sense, with a direct object, to mean "to cultivate" or "to allow to grow." *We plan to grow tomatoes this year. John is growing a beard.*

hanged, hung *Hanged* is the past-tense and past-participle form of the verb *hang* meaning "to execute." *The prisoner was hanged at dawn. Hung* is the past-tense and past-participle form of the verb *hang* meaning "to fasten or suspend." *The stockings were hung by the chimney with care.*

hardly Avoid expressions such as *can't hardly* and *not hardly,* which are considered double negatives. *I can* (not *can't*) *hardly describe my surprise at getting the job.* (See 26e.)

has got, have got *Got* is unnecessary and awkward in such constructions. It should be dropped. *We have* (not *have got*) *three days to prepare for the opening.*

he At one time *he* was commonly used to mean "he or she." Today such usage is inappropriate. (See 17f and 22a.)

he/she, his/her In formal writing, use *he or she* or *his or her*. For alternatives to these wordy constructions, see 17f and 22a.

hisself *Hisself* is nonstandard. Use *himself*.

hopefully *Hopefully* means "in a hopeful manner." *We looked hopefully to the future.* Some usage experts object to the use of *hopefully* as a sentence adverb, apparently on grounds of clarity. To be safe, avoid using *hopefully* in sentences such as the following: *Hopefully, your son will recover soon.* Instead, indicate who is doing the hoping: *I hope that your son will recover soon.*

however In the past, some writers objected to the conjunctive adverb *however* at the beginning of a sentence, but current experts allow placing the word according to the intended meaning and emphasis. All of the following sentences are correct. *Pam decided, however, to attend Harvard. However, Pam decided to attend Harvard.* (She had been considering other schools.) *Pam, however, decided to attend Harvard.* (Unlike someone else, Pam opted for Harvard.) (See 32f.)

hung See *hanged, hung*.

i.e. In formal writing, replace the Latin abbreviation *i.e.* with its English equivalent: *that is*.

if, whether Use *if* to express a condition and *whether* to express alternatives. *If you go on a trip, whether to Nebraska or Italy, remember to bring traveler's checks.*

illusion See *allusion, illusion*.

immigrate See *emigrate from, immigrate to*.

imminent See *eminent, imminent*.

immoral See *amoral, immoral*.

implement *Implement* is a pretentious way of saying "do," "carry out," or "accomplish." Use ordinary language instead. *We carried out* (not *implemented*) *the director's orders.*

imply, infer *Imply* means "to suggest or state indirectly"; *infer* means "to draw a conclusion." *John implied that he knew all about computers, but the interviewer inferred that John was inexperienced.*

in, into *In* indicates location or condition; *into* indicates movement or a change in condition. *They found the lost letters in a box after moving into the house.*

in regards to *In regards to* confuses two different phrases: *in regard to* and *as regards*. Use one or the other. *In regard to* (or *As regards*) *the contract, ignore the first clause.*

irregardless *Irregardless* is nonstandard. Use *regardless*.

is when, is where These mixed constructions are often incorrectly used in definitions. *A run-off election is a second election held to break a tie* (not *is when a second election is held to break a tie*). (See 11c.)

its, it's *Its* is a possessive pronoun; *it's* is a contraction for *it is*. (See 36c and 36e.) *It's always fun to watch a dog chase its tail.*

kind(s) *Kind* is singular and should be treated as such. Don't write *These kind of chairs are rare.* Write instead *This kind of chair is rare. Kinds* is plural and should be used only when you mean more than one kind. *These kinds of chairs are rare.*

kind of, sort of Avoid using *kind of* or *sort of* to mean "somewhat." *The movie was somewhat* (not *sort of*) *boring.* Do not put *a* after either phrase. *That kind of* (not *kind of a*) *salesclerk annoys me.*

lay, lie See *lie, lay.*

lead, led *Lead* is a metallic element; it is a noun. *Led* is the past tense of the verb *lead*. *He led me to the treasure.*

learn, teach *Learn* means "to gain knowledge"; *teach* means "to impart knowledge." *I must teach* (not *learn*) *my sister to read.*

leave, let *Leave* means "to exit." Avoid using it with the nonstandard meaning "to permit." *Let* (not *Leave*) *me help you with the dishes.*

less See *fewer, less.*

let, leave See *leave, let.*

liable *Liable* means "obligated" or "responsible." Do not use it to mean "likely." *You're likely* (not *liable*) *to trip if you don't tie your shoelaces.*

lie, lay *Lie* is an intransitive verb meaning "to recline or rest on a surface." Its principal parts are *lie, lay, lain. Lay* is a transitive verb meaning "to put or place." Its principal parts are *lay, laid, laid.* (See 27b.)

like, as *Like* is a preposition, not a subordinating conjunction. It can be followed only by a noun or a noun phrase. *As* is a subordinating conjunction that introduces a subordinate clause. In casual speech, you may say *She looks like she hasn't slept* or *You don't know her like I do.* But in formal writing, use *as. She looks as if she hasn't slept. You don't know her as I do.* (See also 61f and 61g.)

loose, lose *Loose* is an adjective meaning "not securely fastened." *Lose* is a verb meaning "to misplace" or "to not win." *Did you lose your only loose pair of work pants?*

lots, lots of *Lots* and *lots of* are informal substitutes for *many, much,* or *a lot.* Avoid using them in formal writing.

mankind Avoid *mankind* whenever possible. It offends many readers because it excludes women. Use *humanity, humans, the human race,* or *humankind* instead. (See 17f.)

may See *can, may.*

maybe, may be *Maybe* is an adverb meaning "possibly." *May be* is a verb phrase. *Maybe the sun will shine tomorrow. Tomorrow may be brighter.*

may of, might of *May of* and *might of* are nonstandard for *may have* and *might have. We might have* (not *might of*) *had too many cookies.*

media, medium *Media* is the plural of *medium. Of all the media that cover the Olympics, television is the medium that best captures the spectacle of the events.*

most *Most* is informal when used to mean "almost" and should be avoided. *Almost* (not *Most*) *everyone went to the parade.*

must of See *may of.*

myself *Myself* is a reflexive or intensive pronoun. Reflexive: *I cut myself.* Intensive: *I will drive you myself.* Do not use *myself* in place of *I* or *me. He gave the flowers to Melinda and me* (not *myself*). (See also 24b.)

neither *Neither* is singular. (See 21e and 22a.) For *neither . . . nor* constructions, see 21d and 22d.

none *None* may be singular or plural. (See 21e.)

nowheres *Nowheres* is nonstandard. Use *nowhere* instead.

number See *amount, number.*

of Use the verb *have,* not the preposition *of,* after the verbs *could, should, would, may, might,* and *must. They must have* (not *must of*) *left early.*

off of *Off* is sufficient. Omit *of. The ball rolled off* (not *off of*) *the table.*

OK, O.K., okay All three spellings are acceptable, but avoid these expressions in formal speech and writing.

parameters *Parameter* is a mathematical term that has become jargon for "fixed limit," "boundary," or "guideline." Use ordinary English instead. *The task force worked within certain guidelines* (not *parameters*).

passed, past *Passed* is the past tense of the verb *pass. Ann passed me another slice of cake. Past* usually means "belonging to a former time" or "beyond a time or place." *Our past president spoke until past midnight. The hotel is just past the next intersection.*

percent, per cent, percentage *Percent* (also spelled *per cent*) is always used with a specific number. *Percentage* is used with a descriptive term such as *large* or *small*, not with a specific number. *The candidate won 80 percent of the primary vote. A large percentage of registered voters turned out for the election.*

phenomena *Phenomena* is the plural of *phenomenon*, which means "an observable occurrence or fact." *Strange phenomena occur at all hours of the night in that house, but last night's phenomenon was the strangest of all.*

plus *Plus* should not be used to join independent clauses. *This raincoat is dirty; moreover* (not *plus*), *it has a hole in it.*

precede, proceed *Precede* means "to come before." *Proceed* means "to go forward." *As we proceeded up the mountain path, we noticed fresh tracks in the mud, evidence that a group of hikers had preceded us.*

principal, principle *Principal* is a noun meaning "the head of a school or an organization" or "a sum of money." It is also an adjective meaning "most important." *Principle* is a noun meaning "a basic truth or law." *The principal expelled her for three principal reasons. We believe in the principle of equal justice for all.*

proceed, precede See *precede, proceed.*

quote, quotation *Quote* is a verb; *quotation* is a noun. Avoid using *quote* as a shortened form of *quotation. Her quotations* (not *quotes*) *from current movies intrigued us.*

raise, rise *Raise* is a transitive verb meaning "to move or cause to move upward." It takes a direct object. *I raised the shades. Rise* is an intransitive verb meaning "to go up." *Heat rises.*

real, really *Real* is an adjective; *really* is an adverb. *Real* is sometimes used informally as an adverb, but avoid this use in formal writing. *She was really* (not *real*) *angry.* (See 26b.)

reason . . . is because Use *that* instead of *because. The reason she's cranky is that* (not *because*) *she didn't sleep last night.* (See 11c.)

reason why The expression *reason why* is redundant. *The reason* (not *The reason why*) *Jones lost the election is clear.*

relation, relationship *Relation* describes a connection between things. *Relationship* describes a connection between people. *There is a relation between poverty and infant mortality. Our business relationship has cooled over the years.*

respectfully, respectively *Respectfully* means "showing or marked by respect." *Respectively* means "each in the order given." *He respectfully submitted his opinion to the judge. John, Tom, and Larry were a butcher, a baker, and a lawyer, respectively.*

sensual, sensuous *Sensual* means "gratifying the physical senses," especially those associated with sexual pleasure. *Sensuous* means "pleasing to the senses," especially those involved in the experience of art, music, and nature. *The sensuous music and balmy air led the dancers to more sensual movements.*

set, sit *Set* is a transitive verb meaning "to put" or "to place." Its past tense is *set. Sit* is an intransitive verb meaning "to be seated." Its past tense is *sat. She set the dough in a warm corner of the kitchen. The cat sat in the doorway.*

shall, will *Shall* was once used in place of the helping verb *will* with *I* or *we: I shall, we shall.* Today, however, *will* is generally accepted even when the subject is *I* or *we.* The word *shall* occurs primarily in polite questions (*Shall I find you a pillow?*) and in legalistic sentences suggesting duty or obligation (*The applicant shall file form A by December 31*).

should of *Should of* is nonstandard for *should have. They should have* (not *should of*) *been home an hour ago.*

since Do not use *since* to mean "because" if there is any chance of ambiguity. *Because* (not *Since*) *we won the game, we have been celebrating with a pitcher of root beer. Since* here could mean "because" or "from the time that."

sit See *set, sit.*

site See *cite, site.*

somebody, someone *Somebody* and *someone* are singular. (See 21e and 22a.)

something *Something* is singular. (See 21e.)

sometime, some time, sometimes *Sometime* is an adverb meaning "at an indefinite or unstated time." *Some time* is the adjective *some* modifying the noun *time* and means "a period of time." *Sometimes* is an adverb meaning "at times, now and then." *I'll see you sometime soon. I haven't lived there for some time. Sometimes I see him at the library.*

suppose to Write *supposed to.*

sure and Write *sure to. We were all taught to be sure to* (not *sure and*) *look both ways before crossing a street.*

take See *bring, take.*

than, then *Than* is a conjunction used in comparisons; *then* is an adverb denoting time. *That pizza is more than I can eat. Tom laughed, and then we recognized him.*

that See *who, which, that.*

that, which Many writers reserve *that* for restrictive clauses, *which* for nonrestrictive clauses. (See 32e.)

theirselves *Theirselves* is nonstandard for *themselves. The crash victims pushed the car out of the way themselves* (not *theirselves*).

them The use of *them* in place of *those* is nonstandard. *Please take those* (not *them*) *flowers to the patient in room 220.*

then, than See *than, then.*

there, their, they're *There* is an adverb specifying place; it is also an expletive (placeholder). Adverb: *Sylvia is lying there unconscious.* Expletive: *There are two plums left. Their* is a possessive pronoun. *Fred and Jane finally washed their car. They're* is a contraction of *they are. They're later than usual today.*

they The use of *they* to indicate possession is nonstandard. Use *their* instead. *Cindy and Sam decided to sell their* (not *they*) *1975 Corvette.*

this kind See *kind(s).*

to, too, two *To* is a preposition; *too* is an adverb; *two* is a number. *Too many of your shots slice to the left, but the last two were just right.*

toward, towards *Toward* and *towards* are generally interchangeable, although *toward* is preferred in American English.

try and *Try and* is nonstandard for *try to. The teacher asked us all to try to* (not *try and*) *write an original haiku.*

ultimately, eventually See *eventually, ultimately.*

unique Avoid expressions such as *most unique, more straight, less perfect, very round.* Either something is unique or it isn't. It is illogical to suggest degrees of uniqueness. (See 26d.)

usage The noun *usage* should not be substituted for *use* when the meaning is "employment of." *The use* (not *usage*) *of insulated shades has cut fuel costs dramatically.*

use to Write *used to.*

utilize *Utilize* means "to make use of." It often sounds pretentious; in most cases, *use* is sufficient. *I used* (not *utilized*) *the laser printer.*

wait for, wait on *Wait for* means "to be in readiness for" or "to await." *Wait on* means "to serve." *We're only waiting for* (not *waiting on*) *Ruth to take us to the museum.*

ways *Ways* is colloquial when used to mean "distance." *The city is a long way* (not *ways*) *from here.*

weather, whether The noun *weather* refers to the state of the atmosphere. *Whether* is a conjunction referring to a choice between alternatives. *We wondered whether the weather would clear.*

well, good See *good, well.*

where Do not use *where* in place of *that. I heard that* (not *where*) *the crime rate is increasing.*

which See *that, which* and *who, which, that.*

while Avoid using *while* to mean "although" or "whereas" if there is any chance of ambiguity. *Although* (not *While*) *Gloria lost money in the slot machine, Tom won it at roulette.* Here *While* could mean either "although" or "at the same time that."

who, which, that Do not use *which* to refer to persons. Use *who* instead. *That,* though generally used to refer to things, may be used to refer to a group or class of people. *The player who* (not *that* or *which*) *made the basket at the buzzer was named MVP. The team that scores the most points in this game will win the tournament.*

who, whom *Who* is used for subjects and subject complements; *whom* is used for objects. (See 25.)

who's, whose *Who's* is a contraction of *who is; whose* is a possessive pronoun. *Who's ready for more popcorn? Whose coat is this?* (See 36c and 36e.)

will See *shall, will.*

would of *Would of* is nonstandard for *would have. She would have* (not *would of*) *had a chance to play if she had arrived on time.*

you In formal writing, avoid *you* in an indefinite sense meaning "anyone." (See 23d.) *Any spectator* (not *You*) *could tell by the way John caught the ball that his throw would be too late.*

your, you're *Your* is a possessive pronoun; *you're* is a contraction of *you are. Is that your new bike? You're in the finals.* (See 36c and 36e.)

Answers to Tutorials and Lettered Exercises

Tutorial 1, page xxviii

1. A verb has to agree with its subject. (21)
2. Avoid sentence fragments. (19)
3. It's important to use apostrophes correctly. (36)
4. If your sentence begins with a long introductory word group, use a comma to separate the word group from the rest of the sentence. (32b)
5. Watch out for dangling modifiers. (12e)

Tutorial 2, page xxviii

1. The index entry *"each"* mentions that the word is singular, so you might not need to look further to realize that the verb should be *has*, not *have*. The first page reference takes you to section 21, which explains in more detail why *has* is correct. The index entry *"has* vs. *have"* also leads you to section 21.
2. The index entry *"lying* vs. *laying"* takes you to section 27b, where you will learn that *lying* (meaning "reclining or resting on a surface") is correct.
3. Look up *"only"* and you will be directed to section 12a, which explains that limiting modifiers such as *only* should be placed before the words they modify. The sentence should read *We looked at only two houses before buying the house of our dreams.*
4. Looking up *"you,* inappropriate use of" leads you to section 23d and the Glossary of Usage, which explain that *you* should not be used to mean "anyone in general." You can revise the sentence by using *a person* or *one* instead of *you*, or you can restructure the sentence completely: *In Saudi Arabia, accepting a gift is considered ill mannered.*
5. The index entries *"I* vs. *me"* and *"me* vs. *I"* take you to section 24, which explains why *her sister and me* is correct.

Tutorial 3, page xxix

1. Section 32c states that, although usage varies, most experts advise using a comma between all items in a series — to prevent possible misreadings or ambiguities. To find this section, you would probably use the menu system.
2. You and the student would consult section 29, on articles. This section is easy to locate in the menu system.
3. In the menu system, you will find "Writing MLA papers" and then section 52, "Integrating sources."
4. You can send your interns to sections 21 and 27c, which you can find in the menu system if you know to look under "Subject-verb agreement" or "Standard English verb forms." If you aren't sure about the grammatical terminology, you can look in the index under "*-s,* as verb ending" or "Verbs, *-s* form of."
5. The index entry "Tenses, verb" contains a subentry "present, in writing about literature." This leads you to discussions about present tense and

804

about how to avoid shifting tenses. The entry "Literature, writing about" contains an entry "shifts in tense, avoiding," which directs you to how and why to avoid shifting tenses.

Tutorial 4, page xxx

1. Changing attitudes toward alcohol have *affected* the beer industry.
2. It is *human* nature to think wisely and act foolishly.
3. Correct
4. Our goal this year is to *increase* our profits by 9 percent.
5. Most sleds are pulled by no *fewer* than two dogs and no more than ten.

Tutorial 5, page xxxi

Alim, H. Samy. "360 Degreez of Black Art Comin at You: Sista Sonia Sanchez and the Dimensions of a Black Arts Continuum." *BMa: The Sonia Sanchez Literary Review* 6.1 (2000): 15-33. Print.

Chang, Jeff. *Can't Stop, Won't Stop: A History of the Hip-Hop Generation*. New York: St. Martin's, 2005. Print.

Davis, Kimberly. "The Roots Redefine Hip-Hop's Past." *Ebony* June 2003: 162-64. *Expanded Academic ASAP*. Web. 13 Apr. 2008.

Randall, Kay. "Studying a Hip Hop Nation." *University of Texas at Austin*. U of Texas at Austin, 9 Oct. 2008. Web. 13 Aug. 2009.

Sugarhill Gang. "Rapper's Delight." *Sugarhill Gang*. DBK Works, 2008. CD.

Exercise 6–1, page 128

a. hasty generalization; b. false analogy; c. biased language;
d. faulty cause-and-effect reasoning; e. *either . . . or* fallacy

Exercise 8–1, page 146

Possible revisions:

a. The Prussians defeated the Saxons in 1745.
b. Ahmed, the producer, manages the entire operation.
c. The travel guides expertly paddled the sea kayaks.
d. Emphatic and active; no change
e. Protesters were shouting on the courthouse steps.

Exercise 9–1, page 150

Possible revisions:

a. Police dogs are used for finding lost children, tracking criminals, and detecting bombs and illegal drugs.
b. Hannah told her rock climbing partner that she bought a new harness and that she wanted to climb Otter Cliffs.
c. It is more difficult to sustain an exercise program than to start one.
d. During basic training, I was told not only what to do but also what to think.
e. Jan wanted to drive to the wine country or at least to Sausalito.

Exercise 10–1, page 155

Possible revisions:

a. A grapefruit or an orange is a good source of vitamin C.
b. The women entering VMI can expect haircuts as short as those of the male cadets.
c. Looking out the family room window, Sarah saw that her favorite tree, which she had climbed as a child, was gone.
d. The graphic designers are interested in and knowledgeable about producing posters for the balloon race.
e. Reefs are home to more species than any other ecosystem in the sea.

Exercise 11–1, page 159

Possible revisions:

a. Using surgical gloves is a precaution now taken by dentists to prevent contact with patients' blood and saliva.
b. A career in medicine, which my brother is pursuing, requires at least ten years of challenging work.
c. The pharaohs had bad teeth because tiny particles of sand found their way into Egyptian bread.
d. Recurring bouts of flu caused the team to forfeit a record number of games.
e. This box contains the key to your future.

Exercise 12–1, page 164

Possible revisions:

a. More research is needed to evaluate effectively the risks posed by volcanoes in the Pacific Northwest.
b. Many students graduate from college with debt totaling more than fifty thousand dollars.
c. It is a myth that humans use only 10 percent of their brains.
d. A coolhunter is a person who can find the next wave of fashion in the unnoticed corners of modern society.
e. Not all geese fly beyond Narragansett for the winter.

Exercise 12–2, page 168

Possible revisions:

a. Though Martha was only sixteen, UCLA accepted her application.
b. To replace the gear mechanism, you can use the attached form to order the part by mail.
c. As I settled in the cockpit, the pounding of the engine was muffled only slightly by my helmet.
d. After studying polymer chemistry, Phuong found computer games less complex.
e. When I was a young man, my mother enrolled me in tap dance classes.

Exercise 13–3, page 175

Possible revisions:

a. An incredibly talented musician, Ray Charles mastered R&B, soul, and gospel styles. He even performed country music well.

b. Environmentalists point out that shrimp farming in Southeast Asia is polluting water and making farmlands useless. They warn that governments must act before it is too late.
c. We observed the samples for five days before we detected any growth. *Or* The samples were observed for five days before any growth was detected.
d. In his famous soliloquy, Hamlet contemplates whether death would be preferable to his difficult life and, if so, whether he is capable of committing suicide.
e. The lawyer told the judge that Miranda Hale was innocent and asked that she be allowed to prove the allegations false. *Or* The lawyer told the judge, "Miranda Hale is innocent. Please allow her to prove the allegations false."

Exercise 13–4, page 175

Possible revisions:

a. Courtroom lawyers have more than a touch of theater in their blood.
b. The interviewer asked if we had brought our proof of citizenship and our passports.
c. Reconnaissance scouts often have to make fast decisions and use sophisticated equipment to keep their teams from being detected.
d. After the animators finish their scenes, the production designer arranges the clips according to the storyboard and makes synchronization notes for the sound editor and the composer.
e. Madame Defarge is a sinister figure in Dickens's *A Tale of Two Cities*. On a symbolic level, she represents fate; like the Greek Fates, she knits the fabric of individual destiny.

Exercise 14–1, page 181

Possible revisions:

a. Williams played for the Boston Red Sox from 1939 to 1960, and he managed the Washington Senators and Texas Rangers for several years after retiring as a player.
b. In 1941, Williams finished the season with a batting average of .406; no player has hit over .400 for a season since then.
c. Although he acknowledged that Joe DiMaggio was a better all-around player, Williams felt that he was a better hitter than DiMaggio.
d. Williams was a stubborn man; for example, he always refused to tip his cap to the crowd after a home run because he claimed that fans were fickle.
e. Williams's relationship with the media was unfriendly at best; he sarcastically called baseball writers the "knights of the keyboard" in his memoir.

Exercise 14–2, page 183

Possible revisions:

a. The X-Men comic books and Japanese woodcuts of kabuki dancers, all part of Marlena's research project on popular culture, covered the tabletop and the chairs.
b. Our waitress, costumed in a kimono, had painted her face white and arranged her hair in a lacquered beehive.

c. Students can apply for a spot in the leadership program, which teaches thinking and communication skills.
d. Shore houses were flooded up to the first floor, beaches were washed away, and Brant's Lighthouse was swallowed by the sea.
e. Laura Thackray, an engineer at Volvo Car Corporation, addressed women's needs by designing a pregnant crash-test dummy.

Exercise 14–3, page 185

Possible revisions:

a. These particles, known as "stealth liposomes," can hide in the body for a long time without detection.
b. Irena, a competitive gymnast majoring in biochemistry, intends to apply her athletic experience and her science degree to a career in sports medicine.
c. Because students, textile workers, and labor unions have loudly protested sweatshop abuses, apparel makers have been forced to examine their labor practices.
d. Developed in a European university, IRC (Internet relay chat) was created as a way for a group of graduate students to talk about projects from their dorm rooms.
e. The cafeteria's new menu, which has an international flavor, includes everything from enchiladas and pizza to pad thai and sauerbraten.

Exercise 14–4, page 188

Possible revisions:

a. Working as an aide for the relief agency, Gina distributed food and medical supplies.
b. Janbir, who spent every Saturday learning tabla drumming, noticed with each hour of practice that his memory for complex patterns was growing stronger.
c. When the rotor hit, it gouged a hole about an eighth of an inch deep in my helmet.
d. My grandfather, who was born eighty years ago in Puerto Rico, raised his daughters the old-fashioned way.
e. By reversing the depressive effect of the drug, the Narcan saved the patient's life.

Exercise 15–1, page 195

Possible revisions:

a. Across the hall from the fossils exhibit are the exhibits for insects and spiders.
b. After growing up desperately poor in Japan, Sayuri becomes a successful geisha.
c. What caused Mount St. Helens to erupt? Researchers believe that a series of earthquakes in the area was a contributing factor.
d. Ice cream typically contains 10 percent milk fat, but premium ice cream may contain up to 16 percent milk fat and has considerably less air in the product.
e. If home values climb, the economy may recover more quickly than expected.

Exercise 16–1, page 202

Possible revisions:

a. Martin Luther King Jr. set a high standard for future leaders.
b. Alice has loved cooking since she could first peek over a kitchen tabletop.
c. Bloom's race for the governorship is futile.
d. A successful graphic designer must have technical knowledge and an eye for color and balance.
e. You will deliver mail to all employees.

Exercise 17–1, page 206

Possible revisions:

a. When I was young, my family was poor.
b. This conference will help me serve my clients better.
c. The meteorologist warned the public about the possible dangers of the coming storm.
d. Government studies show a need for after-school programs.
e. Passengers should try to complete the customs declaration form before leaving the plane.

Exercise 17–4, page 214

Possible revisions:

a. Dr. Geralyn Farmer is the chief surgeon at University Hospital. Dr. Paul Green is her assistant.
b. All applicants want to know how much they will earn.
c. Elementary school teachers should understand the concept of nurturing if they intend to be effective.
d. Obstetricians need to be available to their patients at all hours.
e. If we do not stop polluting our environment, we will perish.

Exercise 18–2, page 219

Possible revisions:

a. We regret this delay; thank you for your patience.
b. Ada's plan is to acquire education and experience to prepare herself for a position as property manager.
c. Tiger Woods, the ultimate competitor, has earned millions of dollars just in endorsements.
d. Many people take for granted that public libraries have up-to-date computer systems.
e. The effect of Gao Xinjian's novels on Chinese exiles is hard to gauge.

Exercise 18–3, page 220

Possible revisions:

a. Queen Anne was so angry with Sarah Churchill that she refused to see her again.
b. Correct
c. The parade moved off the street and onto the beach.
d. The frightened refugees intend to make the dangerous trek across the mountains.
e. What type of wedding are you planning?

Exercise 18–4, page 223

Possible revisions:

a. John stormed into the room like a hurricane.
b. Some people insist that they'll always be available to help, even when they haven't been before.
c. The Cubs easily beat the Mets, who were in trouble early in the game today at Wrigley Field.
d. We worked out the problems in our relationship.
e. My mother accused me of evading her questions when in fact I was just saying the first thing that came to mind.

Exercise 19–1, page 233

Possible revisions:

a. Listening to the CD her sister had sent, Mia was overcome with a mix of emotions: happiness, homesickness, nostalgia.
b. Cortés and his soldiers were astonished when they looked down from the mountains and saw Tenochtitlán, the magnificent capital of the Aztecs.
c. Although my spoken Spanish is not very good, I can read the language with ease.
d. There are several reasons for not eating meat. One reason is that dangerous chemicals are used throughout the various stages of meat production.
e. To learn how to sculpt beauty from everyday life is my intention in studying art and archaeology.

Exercise 20–1, page 241

Possible revisions:

a. The city had one public swimming pool that stayed packed with children all summer long.
b. The building is being renovated, so at times we have no heat, water, or electricity.
c. The view was not what the travel agent had described. Where were the rolling hills and the shimmering rivers?
d. All those gnarled equations looked like toxic insects; maybe I was going to have to rethink my major.
e. City officials had good reason to fear a major earthquake: Most [or most] of the business district was built on landfill.

Exercise 20–2, page 242

Possible revisions:

a. Wind power for the home is a supplementary source of energy that can be combined with electricity, gas, or solar energy.
b. Correct
c. In the Middle Ages, when the streets of London were dangerous places, it was safer to travel by boat along the Thames.
d. "He's not drunk," I said. "He's in a state of diabetic shock."
e. Are you able to endure extreme angle turns, high speeds, frequent jumps, and occasional crashes? Then supermoto racing may be a sport for you.

Exercise 21–2, page 255

a. One of the main reasons for elephant poaching is the profits received from selling the ivory tusks.
b. Correct
c. A number of students in the seminar were aware of the importance of joining the discussion.
d. Batik cloth from Bali, blue and white ceramics from Delft, and a bocce ball from Turin have made Angelie's room the talk of the dorm.
e. Correct

Exercise 22–1, page 261

Possible revisions:

a. Every presidential candidate must appeal to a wide variety of ethnic and social groups to win the election.
b. David lent his motorcycle to someone who allowed a friend to use it.
c. The aerobics teacher motioned for all the students to move their arms in wide, slow circles.
d. Correct
e. Applicants should be bilingual if they want to qualify for this position.

Exercise 23–1, page 266

Possible revisions:

a. Some professors say that engineering students should have hands-on experience with dismantling and reassembling machines.
b. Because she had decorated her living room with posters from chamber music festivals, her date thought that she was interested in classical music. Actually she preferred rock.
c. In my high school, students didn't need to get all A's to be considered a success; they just needed to work to their ability.
d. Marianne told Jenny, "I am worried about your mother's illness." [or "... about my mother's illness."]
e. Though Lewis cried for several minutes after scraping his knee, eventually his crying subsided.

Exercise 24–1, page 273

a. Correct [But the writer could change the end of the sentence: ... *than he is.*]
b. Correct [But the writer could change the end of the sentence: ... *that she was the coach.*]
c. She appreciated his telling the truth in such a difficult situation.
d. The director has asked you and me to draft a proposal for a new recycling plan.
e. Five close friends and I rented a station wagon, packed it with food, and drove two hundred miles to Mardi Gras.

Exercise 25–1, page 279

a. The roundtable featured scholars whom I had never heard of. [*or* ... scholars I had never heard of.]
b. Correct
c. Correct

d. Daniel always gives a holiday donation to whoever needs it.
e. So many singers came to the audition that Natalia had trouble deciding whom to select for the choir.

Exercise 26–1, page 286

Possible revisions:

a. Did you do well on last week's chemistry exam?
b. With the budget deadline approaching, our office has hardly had time to handle routine correspondence.
c. Correct
d. The customer complained that he hadn't been treated nicely.
e. Of all my relatives, Uncle Roberto is the cleverest.

Exercise 27–1, page 293

a. When I get the urge to exercise, I lie down until it passes.
b. Grandmother had driven our new hybrid to the sunrise church service on Savage Mountain, so we were left with the station wagon.
c. A pile of dirty rags was lying at the bottom of the stairs.
d. How did the computer know that the gamer had gone from the room with the blue ogre to the hall where the gold was heaped?
e. Abraham Lincoln took good care of his legal clients; the contracts he drew for the Illinois Central Railroad could never be broken.

Exercise 27–2, page 299

a. The glass sculptures of the Swan Boats were prominent in the brightly lit lobby.
b. Visitors to the glass museum were not supposed to touch the exhibits.
c. Our church has all the latest technology, even a closed-circuit television.
d. Christos didn't know about Marlo's promotion because he never listens. He is [*or* He's] always talking.
e. Correct

Exercise 27–3, page 307

Possible revisions:

a. Correct
b. Watson and Crick discovered the mechanism that controls inheritance in all life: the workings of the DNA molecule.
c. When city planners proposed rezoning the waterfront, did they know that the mayor had promised to curb development in that neighborhood?
d. Correct
e. Correct

Exercise 28–1, page 314

a. In the past, tobacco companies denied any connection between smoking and health problems.
b. There is nothing in the world that TV has not touched on.
c. I want to register for a summer tutoring session.
d. By the end of the year, the state will have tested 139 birds for avian flu.
e. The benefits of eating fruits and vegetables have been promoted by health care providers.

Exercise 28–2, page 315

a. A major league pitcher can throw a baseball more than ninety-five miles per hour.
b. The writing center tutor will help you revise your essay.
c. A reptile must adjust its body temperature to its environment.
d. Correct
e. My uncle, a cartoonist, could sketch a face in less than two minutes.

Exercise 28–3, page 323

Possible revisions:

a. The electrician might have discovered the broken circuit if she had gone through the modules one at a time.
b. If Verena wins a scholarship, she will go to graduate school.
c. Whenever there is a fire in our neighborhood, everybody comes out to watch.
d. Sarah will take the paralegal job unless she gets a better offer.
e. If I lived in Budapest with my cousin Szusza, she would teach me Hungarian cooking.

Exercise 28–4, page 326

a. I enjoy riding my motorcycle.
b. The tutor told Samantha to come to the writing center.
c. The team hopes to work hard and win the championship.
d. Ricardo and his brothers miss surfing during the winter.
e. The babysitter let Roger stay up until midnight.

Exercise 29–1, page 335

a. Doing volunteer work often brings satisfaction.
b. As I looked out the window of the plane, I could see Cape Cod.
c. Melina likes to drink her coffee with lots of cream.
d. Correct
e. I completed my homework assignment quickly. *Or* I completed the homework assignment quickly.

Exercise 30–1, page 341

a. There are some cartons of ice cream in the freezer.
b. I don't use the subway because I am afraid.
c. The prime minister is the most popular leader in my country.
d. We tried to get in touch with the same manager whom we spoke to earlier.
e. Recently there have been a number of earthquakes in Turkey.

Exercise 30–2, page 343

Possible revisions:

a. Although freshwater freezes at 32 degrees Fahrenheit, ocean water freezes at 28 degrees Fahrenheit.
b. Because we switched cable packages, our channel lineup has changed.
c. The competitor confidently mounted his skateboard.
d. My sister performs the *legong*, a Balinese dance, well.
e. Correct

Exercise 30–3, page 345

a. Listening to everyone's complaints all day was irritating.
b. The long flight to Singapore was exhausting.
c. Correct
d. After a great deal of research, the scientist made a fascinating discovery.
e. That blackout was one of the most frightening experiences I've ever had.

Exercise 30–4, page 346

a. an attractive young Vietnamese woman
b. a dedicated Catholic priest
c. her old blue wool sweater
d. Joe's delicious Scandinavian bread
e. many beautiful antique jewelry boxes

Exercise 31–1, page 348

a. Whenever we eat at the Centerville Café, we sit at a small table in the corner of the room.
b. Correct
c. On Thursday, Nancy will attend her first home repair class at the community center.
d. Correct
e. We decided to go to a restaurant because there was no fresh food in the refrigerator.

Exercise 32–1, page 356

a. Alisa brought the injured bird home and fashioned a splint out of Popsicle sticks for its wing.
b. Considered a classic of early animation, *The Adventures of Prince Achmed* used hand-cut silhouettes against colored backgrounds.
c. If you complete the enclosed evaluation form and return it within two weeks, you will receive a free breakfast during your next stay.
d. Correct
e. Roger had always wanted a handmade violin, but he couldn't afford one.

Exercise 32–2, page 357

a. J. R. R. Tolkien finished writing his draft of *The Lord of the Rings* trilogy in 1949, but the first book in the series wasn't published until 1954.
b. In the first two minutes of its ascent, the space shuttle had broken the sound barrier and reached a height of over twenty-five miles.
c. German shepherds can be gentle guide dogs, or they can be fierce attack dogs.
d. Some former professional cyclists claim that the use of performance-enhancing drugs is widespread in cycling, and they argue that no rider can be competitive without doping.
e. As an intern, I learned most aspects of the broadcasting industry, but I never learned about fundraising.

Exercise 32–3, page 360

a. The cold, impersonal atmosphere of the university was unbearable.

b. An ambulance threaded its way through police cars, fire trucks, and irate citizens.
c. Correct
d. After two broken arms, three cracked ribs, and one concussion, Ken quit the varsity football team.
e. Correct

Exercise 32–4, page 361

a. NASA's rovers on Mars are equipped with special cameras that can take close-up, high-resolution pictures of the terrain.
b. Correct
c. Correct
d. Love, vengeance, greed, and betrayal are common themes in Western literature.
e. Many experts believe that shark attacks on surfers are a result of the sharks' mistaking surfboards for small injured seals.

Exercise 32–5, page 365

a. Choreographer Alvin Ailey's best-known work, *Revelations*, is more than just a crowd-pleaser.
b. Correct
c. Correct
d. A member of an organization that provides job training for teens was also appointed to the education commission.
e. Brian Eno, who began his career as a rock musician, turned to meditative compositions in the late seventies.

Exercise 32–6, page 371

a. Cricket, which originated in England, is also popular in Australia, South Africa, and India.
b. At the sound of the starting pistol, the horses surged forward toward the first obstacle, a sharp incline three feet high.
c. After seeing an exhibition of Western art, Gerhard Richter escaped from East Berlin and smuggled out many of his notebooks.
d. Corrie's new wet suit has an intricate blue pattern.
e. The cookies will keep for two weeks in sturdy, airtight containers.

Exercise 32–7, page 371

a. On January 15, 2008, our office moved to 29 Commonwealth Avenue, Mechanicsville, VA 23111.
b. Correct
c. Ms. Carlson, you are a valued customer whose satisfaction is very important to us.
d. Mr. Mundy was born on July 22, 1939, in Arkansas, where his family had lived for four generations.
e. Correct

Exercise 33–1, page 377

a. Correct
b. Tricia's first artwork was a bright blue clay dolphin.

c. Some modern musicians (trumpeter John Hassell is an example) blend several cultural traditions into a unique sound.
d. Myra liked hot, spicy foods such as chili, kung pao chicken, and buffalo wings.
e. On the display screen was a soothing pattern of light and shadow.

Exercise 34–1, page 382

a. Do not ask me to be kind; just ask me to act as though I were.
b. When men talk about defense, they always claim to be protecting women and children, but they never ask the women and children what they think.
c. When I get a little money, I buy books; if any is left, I buy food and clothes.
d. Correct
e. Wit has truth in it; wisecracking is simply calisthenics with words.

Exercise 34–2, page 383

a. Strong black coffee will not sober you up; the truth is that time is the only way to get alcohol out of your system.
b. Margaret was not surprised to see hail and vivid lightning; conditions had been right for violent weather all day.
c. There is often a fine line between right and wrong, good and bad, truth and deception.
d. Correct
e. Severe, unremitting pain is a ravaging force, especially when the patient tries to hide it from others.

Exercise 35–1, page 386

a. Correct [Either *It* or *it* is correct.]
b. If we have come to fight, we are far too few; if we have come to die, we are far too many.
c. The travel package includes a round-trip ticket to Athens, a cruise through the Cyclades, and all hotel accommodations.
d. The news article portrays the land use proposal as reckless, although 62 percent of the town's residents support it.
e. Psychologists Kindlon and Thompson (2000) offer parents a simple starting point for raising male children: "Teach boys that there are many ways to be a man" (p. 256).

Exercise 36–1, page 391

a. Correct
b. The innovative shoe fastener was inspired by the designer's young son.
c. Each day's menu features a different European country's dish.
d. Sue worked overtime to increase her family's earnings.
e. Ms. Jacobs is unwilling to listen to students' complaints about computer failures.

Exercise 37–1, page 398

a. As for the advertisement "Sailors have more fun," if you consider chipping paint and swabbing decks fun, then you will have plenty of it.

b. Correct
c. After winning the lottery, Juanita said that she would give half the money to charity.
d. After the movie, Vicki said, "The reviewer called this flick 'trash of the first order.' I guess you can't believe everything you read."
e. Correct

Exercise 39–1, page 407

a. A client has left his or her [*or* a] cell phone in our conference room.
b. The films we made of Kilauea on our trip to Hawaii Volcanoes National Park illustrate a typical spatter cone eruption.
c. Correct
d. Correct
e. Of three engineering fields—chemical, mechanical, and materials—Keegan chose materials engineering for its application to toy manufacturing.

Exercise 40–1, page 412

a. Correct
b. Some combat soldiers are trained by government diplomats to be sensitive to issues of culture, history, and religion.
c. Correct
d. How many pounds have you lost since you began running four miles a day?
e. Denzil spent all night studying for his psychology exam.

Exercise 41–1, page 415

a. The carpenters located three maple timbers, twenty-one sheets of cherry, and ten oblongs of polished ebony for the theater set.
b. Correct
c. Correct
d. Eight students in the class had been labeled "learning disabled."
e. The Vietnam Veterans Memorial in Washington, DC, had 58,132 names inscribed on it when it was dedicated in 1982.

Exercise 42–1, page 418

a. Howard Hughes commissioned the *Spruce Goose*, a beautifully built but thoroughly impractical wooden aircraft.
b. The old man screamed his anger, shouting to all of us, "I will not leave my money to you worthless layabouts!"
c. I learned the Latin term *ad infinitum* from an old nursery rhyme about fleas: "Great fleas have little fleas upon their back to bite 'em, / Little fleas have lesser fleas and so on *ad infinitum*."
d. Correct
e. Neve Campbell's lifelong interest in ballet inspired her involvement in the film *The Company*, which portrays a season with the Joffrey Ballet.

Exercise 44–1, page 431

a. Correct
b. The swiftly moving tugboat pulled alongside the barge and directed it away from the oil spill in the harbor.
c. Correct

d.   Your dog is well known in our neighborhood.
e.   Roadblocks were set up along all the major highways leading out of the city.

Exercise 45–1, page 436

a.   Assistant Dean Shirin Ahmadi recommended offering more world language courses.
b.   Correct
c.   Kalindi has an ambitious semester, studying differential calculus, classical Hebrew, brochure design, and Greek literature.
d.   Lydia's aunt and uncle make modular houses as beautiful as modernist works of art.
e.   We amused ourselves on the long flight by discussing how spring in Kyoto stacks up against summer in London.

Exercise 61–1, page 748

a. stage, confrontation, proportions; b. courage, mountain (noun/adjective), climber, inspiration, rescuers; c. need, guest, honor, fog; d. defense (noun/adjective), attorney, appeal, jury; e. museum, women (noun/adjective), artists, 1987

Exercise 61–2, page 751

a. his; b. that, our (pronoun/adjective); c. that, he, himself, some, his (pronoun/adjective); d. I, my (pronoun/adjective), you, one; e. no one, her

Exercise 61–3, page 754

a. told; b. were, killed; c. brought down; d. Stay, 'll [will] arrive; e. struggled, was trapped

Exercise 61–4, page 756

a. Adjectives: weak, unfocused; b. Adjectives: The (article), Spanish, flexible; adverb: wonderfully; c. Adjectives: The (article), fragrant, the (article) steady; adverb: especially; d. Adjectives: hot, cold; adverbs: rather, slightly, bitterly; e. Adjectives: The (article), its (pronoun/adjective), wicker (noun/adjective); adverb: soundly

Exercise 62–1, page 766

a. Complete subjects: The hills and mountains, the snow atop them, simple subjects: hills, mountains, snow; b. Complete subject: points; simple subject: points; c. Complete subject: (You); d. Complete subject: hundreds of fireflies; simple subject: hundreds; e. Complete subject: The evidence against the defendant; simple subject: evidence

Exercise 62–2, page 770

a. Subject complement: expensive; b. Direct object: death; c. Direct object: their players' efforts; d. Subject complement: the capital of the Russian Empire; e. Subject complement: bitter

Exercise 62–3, page 770

a. Direct objects: adults and children; object complement: weary; b. Direct object: community service; object complement: her priority; c. Direct object: the work; object complement: finished; d. Indirect objects: agent, us; direct objects: our tickets, boarding passes; e. Indirect object: students; direct object: healthy meal choices

Exercise 63–1, page 775

a. In northern Italy, as their first language (adverb phrases modifying *speak*); b. through the thick forest (adjective phrase modifying *hike*); with ease (adverb phrase modifying *completed*); c. To my boss's dismay (adverb phrase modifying *was*); for work (adverb phrase modifying *late*); d. of Mayan artifacts (adjective phrase modifying *exhibit*); into pre-Columbian culture (adjective phrase modifying *insight*); e. In 2002, in twelve European countries (adverb phrases modifying *became*)

Exercise 63–2, page 779

a. Updating your software (gerund phrase used as subject); b. decreasing the town budget (gerund phrase used as object of the preposition *in*); identifying nonessential services (gerund phrase used as subject complement); c. to help her mother by raking the lawn (infinitive phrase used as direct object); raking the lawn (gerund phrase used as object of the preposition *by*); d. Understanding little (participial phrase modifying *I*); passing my biology final (gerund phrase used as object of the preposition *of*); e. Working with animals (gerund phrase used as subject)

Exercise 63–3, page 784

a. so that every vote would count (adverb clause modifying *adjusted*); b. that targets baby boomers (adjective clause modifying *campaign*); c. After the Tambora volcano erupted in the southern Pacific in 1815 (adverb clause modifying *realized*); that it would contribute to the "year without a summer" in Europe and North America (noun clause used as direct object of *realized*); d. that at a certain point there will be no more oil to extract from the earth (noun clause used as direct object of *implies*); e. when you are rushing (adverb clause modifying *are overlooked*)

Exercise 64–1, page 787

a. Complex; that are ignited in dry areas (adjective clause); b. Compound; c. Simple; d. Complex; Before we leave for the station (adverb clause); e. Compound-complex; when you want to leave (noun clause)

Index

ESL Menu

A List of Charts

Revision Symbols
Boldface numbers refer to sections of the handbook.

abbr	abbreviation	40	p	punctuation	
adj	misuse of adjective	26	⌃	comma	32
add	add needed word	10	no ,	no comma	33
adv	misuse of adverb	26	;	semicolon	34
agr	agreement	21, 22	:	colon	35
appr	inappropriate language	17	⌣	apostrophe	36
art	article (*a, an, the*)	29	" "	quotation marks	37
awk	awkward		. ?	period, question mark	38
cap	capital letter	45	!	exclamation point	38
case	pronoun case	24, 25	— ( )	dash, parentheses	39
cliché	cliché	18e	[ ] …	brackets, ellipsis mark	39
coh	coherence	3d	/	slash	39
coord	coordination	14	¶	new paragraph	3e
cs	comma splice	20	pass	ineffective passive	8
dev	inadequate development	3b	ph agr	pronoun agreement	22
			proof	proofreading problem	2b
dm	dangling modifier	12e	ref	pronoun reference	23
-ed	*-ed* ending	27d	run-on	run-on sentence	20
emph	emphasis	14	-s	*-s* ending	27c, 21
ESL	English as a second language	28–31	sexist	sexist language	17f, 22a
			shift	distracting shift	13
exact	inexact language	18	sl	slang	17d
frag	sentence fragment	19	sp	misspelled word	43
fs	fused sentence	20	sub	subordination	14
gl/us	see Glossary of Usage		sv agr	subject-verb agreement	21, 27c
hyph	hyphen	44			
idiom	idioms	18d	t	verb tense	27f, 28a
inc	incomplete construction	10	trans	transition needed	3d
			usage	see Glossary of Usage	
irreg	irregular verb	27a	v	voice	8a, 28c
ital	italics	42	var	lack of variety in sentence structure	14, 15
jarg	jargon	17a			
lc	lowercase	45	vb	verb problem	27, 28
mix	mixed construction	11	w	wordy	16
mm	misplaced modifier	12a–d	//	parallelism	9
mood	mood of verb	27g	⌃	insert	
nonst	nonstandard usage	17d, 27	#	insert space	
num	use of numbers	41	⌒	close up space	
om	omitted word	10, 29, 30a–b			

A List of Grammatical Terms

Boldface numbers refer to sections of the handbook.

Writing the One-Draft Essay

Writing in class and writing outside of class are two completely different activities. When writing outside of class, you have plenty of time to think, experiment, and plan, but in class, time is usually limited, so it is important to use every minute effectively

First, take time to think about the topic. Don't write about the first thing that pops into your head because that is probably the first thing that popped into many other students' heads. Take a few minutes to play with the topic, let your mind wander off on interesting tangents, and see where you end up

When you are happy with your topic, start planning. Before you start your draft, have the entire essay planned—use an outline that shows the main topic, the subtopics, and the supporting details. It is important to know where you are going with your essay and how you are going to get there. Briefly look over the outline and make sure that it is complete and that your thoughts are organized effectively.

Next, start your draft. With your outline complete, you know what you are going to say and when you are going to say it, so all you have to do now is think about how you are going to say it. Work on wording your ideas clearly and directly. Write legibly and double space your text—this will make it easier to make corrections later, and will also mean that you won't have to waste time recopying your essay.

Make sure you start off with a good introduction. Avoid the two sentence introduction where the first sentence is general information and the second sentence is your thesis. Try to find an interesting way to lead into your thesis, and also provide background information if it is needed. Focus the introduction on a tight,

1

controlling thesis statement that leads the reader into the body of your essay.

In the body, start each paragraph with a topic sentence, and then provide plenty of concrete details—do not generalize. Specific, concrete details show the reader that you know what you are talking about. Try to build paragraphs that fully develop the subtopic. Then, end the paragraph with a concluding statement.

For your conclusion, start with a solid concluding statement that either restates the thesis or summarizes the content of your essay. Then spend the rest of the conclusion discussing topics that are related to or influenced by the content of the paper. Make sure that you leave the reader with something profound to thing about.

With the draft finished, take a short mental break, and then proofread. You should proofread twice, once word by word and once sentence by sentence. You carefully planned your essay, then expressed your ideas clearly as you drafted, so it should be organized, developed, and well-worded—now, all you have to do is find the little mistakes.

As you read word by word, point at each, individual word and either say the word out loud or move your lips—make sure that this is the word that you intended to write. Check spelling, usage, pronoun reference, and subject-verb agreement. Look for missing or doubled words. Then, when you read sentence by sentence, make sure your sentences are clear and complete—also look for run-ons and comma splices. Make sure that point of view and tense remain consistent throughout.

By breaking the process down into three simple steps, it is easier to write a complete, coherent, and correct essay in one sitting. These skills will also assist you in writing outside of class with your other writing assignments. Writing in class will not be as much fun or allow you to be as creative, but it can be as rewarding as writing outside of class.

Sample Introductions

Does the introduction:

- Interest the reader?
- Provide necessary background information?
- Focus on a tight controlling thesis statement?

Introduction 1

A time I would like to return to is the time when the movie *Gangs of New York* was filmed. 1863 was the year the film took place in, and I love the old fashioned clothes and just their way of living.

Introduction 2

"Get off the grass!" I yelled as a third grader tried to cut through the grass where my patrol area was. As I paced up and down the hall next to the school store, I wore my safety patrol belt with pride. When I wore that safety patrol belt, I felt like I was the king of the world—well I guess in my case it would have been the queen, but nonetheless, I had power which I had never had before. If many of us had the options to go back in time to a period in our lives, I'm sure we would take it. If I had a chance, I would definitely go back to the time when I was in the fifth grade as a safety patrol. In the fifth grade as a safety patrol, I was finally gaining responsibilities, I got to go on special field trips, and I had many privileges. If given the chance to go back to when I was a safety patrol, I would have to say, "yes!"

4 Palm Beach State College

Introduction 3

The problem with math is that numbers can be so intimidating. There are different formulas that you need to understand. Some algebraic signs look Greek and make you wonder, "Who thought up these signs?" and "How did Albert Einstein understand them himself?"

Introduction 4

"Happy endings are just stories that haven't finished yet," states Angelina Jolie when playing the character of Mrs. Smith in the movie *Mr. and Mrs. Smith*. Jolie is an American actress, model, student, and goodwill ambassador. I admire her work because she helps refugees, influences others, and is incredibly talented.

Introduction 5

Celebrities aren't exactly the best role models for children. Recently, there have been a lot of celebrities involved in scandalous stories. There are the sex scandals and sex tapes, there are the drug problems, and then there are those scandals that involve celebrities being careless and selfish. These are not the type of people that children should be trying to act like. There are always some exceptions and not all celebrities are bad. Cameron Diaz is one of those exceptions. She is involved directly with children, she is generous and caring towards the environment, and she is always portrayed as a happy person.

Introduction 6

Over 80% of Americans would rather die than to talk to a large crowd of people. However you don't have to kill yourself over stage fright because there are many ways to overcome your fear.

Introduction 7

I learned a lot during my trip to Costa Rica. It was my senior trip and my whole class was going. Not only did we go to have fun, but we also went for a mission trip. We were all so excited to go that we could not wait. My class was so loud on the plane because we could not wait any longer.

Introduction 8

My grandfather used to tell me about the good old days when he was a spunky, little kid and had all kinds of adventures with his friends. He would always end those stories by telling me how lucky I was that I was still a kid. Personally, I hated being a kid at the time and considered the old man lucky to have gotten those pesky years of childhood over with. Now that I am way past adolescence, I often look back at my childhood and my grandfather's sage advice and say to myself, "Gee, the old man was right."

Sample Conclusions

Does the conclusion:

- Summarize or restate the thesis?
- Leave the reader with something to think about?

Conclusion 1

Any field of study or career in the modern world will increasingly require some level of familiarity with computers. First, users would want to gain access to a computer, then find an interesting use for it, and once they feel comfortable with the basic uses for a computer, they can move on to more advanced instructions. Following these three main steps should allow even the most computer illiterate users to lose their fear of computers.

Conclusion 2

Behind all the fame, drama, and huge salary hides a real, genuine person. Angelina Jolie is incredibly talented as an actress and model. She encourages and inspires others to work hard by example. Jolie also helps the less fortunate as a goodwill ambassador.

Conclusion 3

The experiences that we face in life could be viewed as changes for the better or worse depending on how we choose to view them. These changes have the effect of altering our perception of situations that we encounter in our daily lives and also alter the way we feel about life itself. Although my personal experience has contributed to my great amount of daily pain and my automatic and immediate fear of heights, it has also modified my view on life and the curves that are presented to us daily. These are the events that make life as interesting and intriguing as it is. Many of these situations can improve our vision of life and the way we feel and act toward each other.

Conclusion 4

My childhood was beautiful, and I honestly can not complain; it was peaceful, and in my eyes, I could not have asked for more. I would definitely love to return to being a child and having the ability to be so naïve and not know so much about all the bad things that occur in this world. I know that these are things that have made me who I am, and I work harder because of them; however, I never had the ability to fully enjoy my complete youth. Those are the times I will never get back, and I will never be that person again. If I had a second chance to return to whatever time I desired, I would jump at the opportunity to be a child. There are few things more wonderful than being a child, and if I was given a second chance at being a child, I would not grow up so quickly the second time.

Conclusion 5

A lot of people have a misconception about how the Big Apple is the greatest city in the world and how much they love it. In all actuality, New York City is very loud, crowded, and disgusting.

Conclusion 6

Although most students at the end of high school don't know what they want to do with their lives, most of them experience the same situation in life. The decision students make early on in their college years will have a huge impact on the outcome of life and possibly the quality of life, as well. They could end up attending longer than expected, wasting valuable time, money, and energy. Also, living with a small income for the years they are enrolled will be very hard on them. These are some of the reasons I would like to return to the time when I just graduated from high school. If I would have made up my mind on what I wanted to study or used the resources available to me, such as academic advisors, I most likely would not have experienced any of this.

Conclusion 7

In conclusion, this is the house that has the most misconceptions. But I still come back for more.

Conclusion 8

Overcoming procrastination is not easy, but is not impossible. I overcame this problem by planning ahead, self-realizing, and avoiding temptation. I am now safe.

Sample Essays

The following sample essays contain errors on the word, sentence, and paragraph levels. Work with your instructor to identify errors and to consider how these essays can be further improved.

Last Name 1

Student's Name

Professor's Name

Class

Date

A time I would like to return to

Have you ever been somewhere who you wish you could return to? I have! This place I would like to return to is my favorite place ever. It's in the mountains up in north Carolina. It's where I go to ever summer. It's a camp ground called Davison river. It is absolutely the funniest most relaxing place I have ever been in my whole life.

Sometimes we either go in a camper or just put tents up, either way it is fun. It's a huge camp ground, and I have never seen one similar. You can either camp on a site on the river or you don't have to. But any who you can either rent inter tubes or by your own and what you do is go on the river trail and you just get in the water and go down stream in the inner tube. They also have a swim hole where you can swim for fun, or jump off this big rock or just sort of watch other people play in the water. They also have nice looking smooth rocks up there. Up there in North Carolina not far from the camp sites is a place called sliding rock. It is an enormous rock that a ton of people go to where water runs down and when u slide off the rock at the end you land in this pool of ice cold water. It is so fun. Also back at the camp site there is a running train, places just to walk around and look at stuff and also at night ever site has a fire place and we usually run a fire and cook s'mores or hotdogs or something fun. Also when I was younger me and my sibling would go at night and catch fire flies. And we use to bring our bikes but any ways it's so fun. I will never not want to return.

Last Name 1

Student's Name

Professor's Name

Class

Date

The Person I Admired When Growing Up

When growing up, children idolize many different people they encounter. I think in some aspect, I was aware of that as a kid. A cashier I once saw in a grocery store wore makeup. That was the first time I wanted to start wearing makeup. I remember seeing random people on the street and liking or disliking their tastes or actions. Children watch a lot of these things and can remember many of them as well. But through all the things that children see growing up, their actions are made to impress or attract someone close to them. Getting a family member or friend's attention can mean the world to a child. Although, I do remember admiring people in my life, none of their influences can compare to my cousin, Angela.

I was born in Ohio where I have a large family. Shortly after kindergarten, my parents moved my brother and me to Florida. Although I missed Ohio and my family very much, I missed Angela more then anything. Up until I moved, my cousin and I were inseparable. My parents would take us up to visit family in the summer time and at Christmas which I always looked forward to. Angela and I would spend the entire time together. When we had to leave again, we wrote each other goodbye letters and put them in each others pillow cases. As you can see, we were closely attached. Angela is six years older then I am which makes her like my big sister. When growing up, I thought she was the prettiest girl I new. I loved her style, her talents, and her taste. She was so cool. I used to follow her everywhere, did the same thing she did, bought the same thing she bought, and even started liking the same things as she liked. Although I admired her greatly, she was not perfect.

When I started entering middle school, she was going through high school. I would here things from my family that she was sick and doing all these bad things. To make a long story short, she always had a ruff childhood that I never understood till now. She began running away from home, using a lot of drugs, and ending up in the hospital continuously. When we went to visit the family, I would ask her why she did all this. I used to tell her that I loved her and she was my favorite person. Eventually she explained to me what was wrong. She was manic depressive,

Last Name 3

bulimic, and anorexic. I was very scared for her, but she worked it out and made it through high school.

Although I will never understand how she felt at that time in her life, I always will admire her courage and strength. When I started to experience high school as well as other bumps in the road, I would think of Angela, my guardian angel. I still think she is the most beautiful girl I know, the funniest, and greatest person to be with. Although we are so far away from each other, she is such a simple thing for me to admire and I am so proud of her.

Last Name 1

Student's Name

Professor's Name

Class

Date

A Life Changing Event

People may think just because I am twenty years old that nothing could have happened in my life. There are many things that I have been through, but I will only talk about the most important one. On May 17, 2004 my mom passed away from a deadly type of skin cancer called Melanoma. That day changed my life forever.

I was in Europe on my senior class trip when I received the news. I had to call my dad on the first day that I was there. I was emotionally damaged and had no idea what I was going to do with myself. My mom was my best friend, how could I live without her? That night I barely slept and the next day was even harder when all my classmates were told. My teachers and fellow classmates were very supportive and tried to help the best that they could. I knew that it was a very hard place to be because there aren't many people who lose their mom at eighteen. I did the best that I could to make everyone feel okay talking to me

Last Name 2

and never once brought it up. I talked to the ones close to me and shed many tears but I felt that I was just getting closer to my friends rather than farther apart.

Throughout the entire trip I wished that I was home with my family. I couldn't call home because I would just start crying so it didn't work out to well. The best thing for me to do was to finish out my trip because that is what my mom wanted me to do. Two teachers sat with me and talked and told me to let it out, but it was hard for me because I was not open about it ever. I liked keeping things inside and never expressing my true feelings. I hate letting people see me cry when they know that I am hurting, it makes me think that they just feel sorry for me and that's not what I wanted to happen.

My mother passing away has helped shaped me into becoming a person who can share their feelings and not close up and be afraid. Before anything had happened people tried to talk to me about it and I would say nothing because I thought that I could handle it myself. Also she has helped me in realizing that no one is promised tomorrow so we need to live each day to the fullest. That is an overused quote but it really helps me day to on your mind and what you are feeling. I got to say goodbye before I left for my trip, but I never got to say goodbye before she left me forever. It has been hard but I think that I have done well with the things that God has left me to deal with.

Words cannot express how much I miss my mother. Everyday I think about her and wish she was coming home today. She has helped me in ways that no one else could have and all I can do is thank her daily. The things that I have listed mean a lot to me today, and I am glad that I can grow from this experience instead of being trapped like I was.

Last Name 1

Student's Name

Professor's Name

Class

Date

Algebra Test

Many people have problems or limitations that can be overcome. One problem that people can overcome is passing a class. The class is algebra. Algebra at times can cause a problem to understand what is being teach. At a point or any people can overcome the subject at all points.

The first point is realizing you are not understanding the subject at all. For example, you are in class the teacher teaches you one lesson in class. Once, it's time to take a test you do the best you can and hand in the test. So, you get your test back and you see that you earned a F on the test. Eventually, you decided you want to do better than that.

The second point is you are asking for help. For example, you are in class and the teacher is going over the homework. You decided that you didn't understand it and ask her to help you

Last Name 2

with the problems you couldn't do. Also, you ask your fellow classmates on the homework or class work ahead of time.

The next point that you can do on your own is studying. For example, you can study everyday instead study the day of the the test. In addition, you can practice problems over and over again until you get it.

My conclusion is that once you have a problem find a way you can overcome it. By even taking it step by step in a process or do it the way you feel comfortable with. In fact, I know that you can overcome a problem by putting your mind to it.

Last Name 1

Student's Name

Professor's Name

Class

Date

Pillar of Strength

She was a pillar of a woman. She grew up poor in a small town in Colombia in the 1920s and was married off at fourteen. Her matriarchal and wifely sense of duty and responsibility was never at issue and although there is reason to doubt whether she ever really loved this man, she lent no shred of evidence with her reticence about the matter. Even after my grandfather's death and until the day she passed, she never looked at another man—maintaining marriage was until both deaths do you part. She gave birth to eleven children, her youngest daughter being my mother, and at first chance, moved her five youngest children stateside in hopes of a better life for her whole family. When her oldest daughter, my aunt Ruby, drowned trying to save a little boy from the same fate at a family picnic, she held everyone together and urged everyone to push on to greatness. She never gave up on anything or anyone. Her hope and faith in all of us, regardless of our actions, illuminated the darkest times in my life.

When I was an elementary aged child, she took care of me until my mom got back from drug deals. There was many things I could count on from her, two were chicken noodle soup and orange kool-aid. As an adult I realize now the importance of routine and consistency for a child to grow up secure. Try as hard as I might, she was the only one that, through her little things like having the same after school television show on for me and having the pull out bed ready for my after school nap created a sense of security and stability early on in my development that would carry me through my rocky life.

I grew up hard and fast when I turned twelve years old. Within six months I went from a millionaire drug dealer's daughter to almost being placed in foster care. My mother had been arrested and was in jail for what would prove to be many years. My father, whom I barely knew, died four months later from complications with Diabetes. My time between these two major events was spent being bounced around from family friends and relatives who opted out of caring for me for one reason or another. I suppose my immature coping and understanding skills, my mood swings, outbursts, and cries for attention through criminal behavior to a point where family and friends could take me no longer. One person rescued me from becoming a ward of the state, my grandmother.

At her insistence, my family set me up in my own apartment for the duration of my high school education. Left to my own devices and having no one to act up for, I straightened out slowly but surely, grew up emotionally and graduated with honors. I excelled at most everything I chose to do. I even secured a full academic or athletic scholarship from Nova Southeastern University. I didn't see that for myself when I was stealing jewelry from family and leaving it out conspicuously on my night stand for people to find. But the entire time she saw my drive, my intelligence, and personal strength reflected from her own. She never saw me as a little punk and thief like everyone else was beginning to assume. She constantly checked on me and expected me to come by whereupon she would fill grocery bags from her own cupboard to make sure I ate right.

She wasn't a pushy person in her fight for my life. She somehow trusted me and my decision making. She let me make mistakes. Unlike my mother, she would be disappointed sometimes, but she never screamed at me, beat me, or denigrated me in any way. When I dropped out of college, she was still there and supportive. She was there without judgments when I lost my baby at nineteen. She embraced every loser boyfriend I brought home the same way. She only supported and looked past the ephemeral stupidity. She believed in me when I didn't and I hold that as the biggest treasure of my life. Her memory, strength, and hope for me stand behind my present and future life choices.

So when asked whom I admire, hands down Esther Ramirez. Her immutable values, morals, strength, sense of responsibility, and almost ethereal sense of hope and faith in the family is what I look to measure up to as an adult. No one has or ever will for that matter, affect me so strongly and benevolently as my grandmother. She is and was the miracle of my life.

22 Palm Beach State College

Student's Name

Professor's Name

Class

Date

Gelsey Kirkland

When I was three years old I began taking dance lessons. My mother enrolled me in a ballet class and a tap class at a local dance studio called Marilyn's School of Dance. Not surprisingly, the level of difficulty in the steps and positions that we learned were fairly low, as three and four year olds tend to be still developing their coordination skills and consequently are a bit wobbly on their feet. In fact, the home video of our recital is so comical that I still watch it to this day when I really need some humor in my life. Regardless, I was hooked; I caught the dance bug in a big way. For the next ten years of my life I was obsessed with all things dance and my heroes tended to be those who were famous in the dance world.

I remember reading a book about a young ballerina who was famous in the early nineteen eighties named Gelsey Kirkland. It was one of those biographies that was made even more exciting by the vivid descriptions of drug addiction, sexual

Last Name 2

promiscuity, and suffering by the protagonist. The title was the uplifting "Dancing On My Grave," and I believe that it was my grandmother who gave it to me to read, although I don't think that she actually knew what it was about, rather that she saw the ballet slipper on the cover and thought of me.

I must have been around eight or nine when I read this, and I remember instantly falling in love with Ms. Kirkland. I wanted to meet her, to be her, to have lived her life and danced with Mikhail Baryshnikov like she had. In hindsight, I recall that her stories of chemical dependency and abusive relationships titillated me as well. Rather than reading her book and viewing these parts as a warning against the darker side of fame, my desire to immerse myself in the world of the arts took a twist to include the seedy underbelly that is always present where money, adulation, and success converge. In looking back, I am a bit surprised to realize that this was the first instance that I can recall where someone's emotional baggage and hardships not only made them a hero for me, but made me want to emulate their actions, specifically the self-destructive impulses that they eventually overcome and write about for their adoring public to forgive. I cared less about the quality of life and lessons learned

Last Name 3

now that she had survived her past, and more about figuring out how I could get a piece of the exciting but sleazy life that she used to live.

Initially after reading Miss Kirkland's book, I looked for as much information as I could find on her. I believe I even used her book as a topic for a school book report, much to the horror of my teachers. However, a sober and contrite woman who had to leave the world of dance for her own salvation was much less exciting to me than the young woman that she had described in her biography who was profoundly unhappy, yet danced with the New York City ballet in between snorting coke, throwing up, and engaging in high risk sex.

Eventually, as happens in so many teenage girls' lives, the hobbies and heroes of younger years fall by the wayside to make room for the rock gods and goddesses of our teens, and I all but forgot about Miss Kirkland. In fact, until I was challenged to recall a figure that I admired as a youngster, I can honestly say that I haven't thought of this ex-ballerina or her story in years. I think that who Gelsey Kirkland was is less important when looking back on her effect on me, than what she symbolized for me, and also how my experience in reading about her life imprinted a new set

Last Name 4

of desires on me which would continue to be reflected in those

that I would seek to admire and emulate for the next fifteen years.

Last Name 1

Student's Name

Professor's Name

Class

Date

Having Your Wisdom Teeth Pulled:

It May Hurt like Heck, But You'll Be Grateful

Out of all the surgeries you can have on yourself, not counting corrective or cosmetic, oral surgeries are probably one of the most painful. A well-known procedure, like pulling wisdom teeth, is a pretty hurtful one. It will not only change your mouth, but your life, as well.

Ever since I had braces, my mouth had always known pain. From the tightening and replacing of extra tight rubber bands, to the pricking of exposed wires leaving scratches and gashes on the inside of my mouth, my mouth was a throbbing, metallic mess. But all that work would be made to look like child's play once my orthodontist told me that I needed my wisdom teeth pulled, and soon. By this time I already felt those four little nuisances poking through my gums, so I knew they were there. When my dad explained to me how he never had his taken out, I was a little surprised. He also told me about how his wisdom teeth

Last Name 2

grew perpendicular to his teeth, not growing upright normally.
Since my dad was a little gray-haired and all, I thought that maybe
I didn't have to go through with that procedure at all. But my father
explained to me that he couldn't get his taken out without
paralyzing his face, and that I needed mine to be taken out before
they grew completely, or all of the work that I had done would
have been for nothing. I was crushed. I pretty much knew from
watching TV shows that oral surgeries were no picnic. Now I learn
that I actually have to have this thing done? I was crushed.

When I got to the dental surgeon's office I was a wreck. It
had been a couple of weeks since my orthodontist had advised
me to get this surgery done, so by then my wisdom teeth were
actually causing me some pain. The doctor gave me the choice of
either Novocain, or sedation. My previous bad experiences with
Novocain made me cry out for sedation. After the procedure was
done, the real pain began. I had both sides of my face swollen
and my mouth constantly bleeding. After taking penicillin and
painkillers for a couple of days, my pain subsided.

Now that my wisdom teeth are gone, my mouth still hurts,
with braces shifting to the new space. But I'm glad I didn't wait like
my dad who still experiences that pain every once in a while. In

the future, I'd say it was worth it, and it changed my life for the better, but since I'm still in pain, I'd say I'm grateful for having it done.

Last Name 1

Student's Name

Professor's Name

Class

Date

Misconceptions about New York and Florida

The Big Apple, New York, also known as the city of opportunities, and the sunshine state, Florida, the citrus state, are both not only at opposite ends in the United States but opposites completely. As a native New Yorker, I myself have experienced living in both places. I was born and raised in Brooklyn, New York, and now have been finishing off my schooling years in West Palm Beach, Florida.

Living in New York I had many high thoughts of Florida, and now living in Florida I have realized that just as I had misconceptions of Florida, there are many Floridians that have misconceptions about New Yorkers and New York overall. Living in New York and in the fast "gotta go, gotta go" state of mind, I always wondered what it was like in Florida. Summer all year round, palm trees everywhere, pools, beaches and just the sunny hot weather which was the most that I thought about, being that I was stuck in cold freezing New York. I visited West Palm Beach,

Florida for the first time in the summer of 1998. I'll never forget it. I was so excited and overwhelmed that I was going to Florida. And of course right away Disney World came into mind, along with the beaches and pool.

My family and I finally arrived in Florida. It was nothing like I pictured. The streets were so clean! Unlike New York, where there's homeless people and dirty polluted streets everywhere, West Palm Beach was beautiful clean. One of the most amusing things I found were that it had palm trees everywhere, not seen in New York at all. I was so excited about being in Florida, I could barely sleep, it was beautiful and I just wanted to stay here forever.

Well then, I got what I wished for. Exactly that, my parents bought a house here in Florida about two years later, and I pretty much had two weeks to get my things together and go. Leaving my friends that I knew since my childhood, and the newly built high school I started attending with all my friends, all gone down the drain. I was so overwhelmed I didn't know what to feel. Yes I wanted to move to beautiful Florida, but had never moved period.

Last Name 3

The many things I thought I would do if I lived in Florida didn't really happen. Going to Disney every weekend was something that didn't happen, silly but yes a thought that many non-Florida residents have. Going to the beach', I live about 10 minutes from the beach and I can honestly say I only visit the beach when I have family members coming down from up north that want to visit the beach. Since its something that I only had in the summer, and barely went to my entire life, I'm not really used to having a beach and not appreciative enough of it.

Life in Florida was a little to calm and quiet for me, and having classmates wanting to imitate my New York accent that I never knew existed made me miss my old home more and more everyday. Something I also learned about Floridians was that just as bad as they wanted to move to New York, and "talk the talk," New Yorkers wanted to move to Florida because they, along with me, thought that you're rich if you live in Florida, which is not true at all. Living in a house is cheaper and more affordable in Florida, but I've noticed that clothing and businesses are cheaper in New York.

In conclusion, it's true when people say "don't judge a book by its cover," because when you open it, it's a whole

Last Name 4

different story. The Big Apple is to me home and all I had ever seen my entire life until I moved to the Sunshine State, which yes has brought me many great opportunities, but didn't live up to be as I dreamt it up to be. In the end you will never know what's real about a place until you go see it and make decisions as to if your misconceptions are true, but then again, it's a different picture when you see it in person.

Acknowledgments

We would like to thank the following students for letting us use their work: Nicole Stewart, Jennifer James, Arianna Gaspar, Stephen Navarro, Meagan Riggsbee, Veronica Velez, Johnny Rodriguez, Peter Sakellarios, Jeff Thomsen, Joshua Leith, Maurice Saddler, Christi Hill, Dislande Erstime, Jerry Charles, Christina Colletti, Kyrsti Rouse, Emily Brito, Abbie Chaney, Keshia Nicolas, Juan Pino, and Katherine Simmons.

Detailed Menu